Stadium Games

Stadium Games

Fifty Years of Big League Greed and Bush League Boondoggles

Jay Weiner

University of Minnesota Press
Minneapolis • London

Published by the University of Minnesota Press
111 Third Avenue South, Suite 290
Minneapolis, MN 55401-2520
http://www.upress.umn.edu

Library of Congress Cataloging-in-Publication Data
Weiner, Jay, 1954–
    Stadium games : fifty years of big league greed and bush league
boondoggles / Jay Weiner.
        p. cm.
Includes bibliographical references.
    ISBN 0-8166-3434-3 (HC : alk. paper) — ISBN 0-8166-3435-1 (PB : alk.
paper)
    1. Professional sports—Economic aspects—Minnesota—Minneapolis. 2.
Stadiums—Economic aspects—Minnesota—Minneapolis. 3. Sports
franchises—Economic aspects—Minnesota—Minneapolis.   I. Title.
    GV716 .W43 2000
    796′.06′8776579—dc21
                                                                99-050612

Printed in the United States of America on acid-free paper

The University of Minnesota is an equal-opportunity educator and employer.

11 10 09 08 07 06 05 04 03 02 01 00   10 9 8 7 6 5 4 3 2 1

For my family

Contents

Acknowledgments

This is a cocktail of interpretive journalism and history. In gathering some of the information, I had to assure some sources that I would protect their identity. I always sought people to be "on the record." I am cognizant of, and comfortable with, the motivations and agendas of all the people I interviewed. I conducted face-to-face interviews in preparation for the book with more than eighty people. This doesn't include the countless and brief phone interviews and e-mail exchanges I conducted, the hours on the World Wide Web gathering and confirming facts, or the five years of duty I performed as a reporter for the *Star Tribune*, the Minneapolis–St. Paul newspaper. Any errors herein, of course, are mine. Please alert me to them at *JayWeiner@aol.com*. The final chapter of Minnesota sports hasn't been written.

Special thanks are owed to many colleagues at the *Star Tribune*, where I've worked for—gulp—twenty years. Hats off to editor Tim McGuire and managing editor Pam Fine for granting me my leave of absence so that I could devote a year to this book and my family. Applause to Robert Whereatt, the state capitol dean, a real newspaper hero and inspiration, and to Dennis McGrath, the state politics editor, who wisely and evenhandedly guided our stadium coverage in 1997. Cheers to Bob Jansen, Roberta Hovde, Sandy Date, and Linda Scheimann of the *Star Tribune* library for their assistance.

The History Center of the Minnesota Historical Society is one of the state's jewels. Without the well-organized and easily retrievable files at the center's library, I couldn't have studied and understood much of the early history of big-league sports and facilities construction in Minnesota.

Also, special thanks to two reporters who shared their notes: Steve Berg, the former national correspondent for the *Star Tribune*, and now an editorial writer, who helped on Don Beaver background material; and Stew Thornley, the expert on the Minneapolis Millers minor-league team and baseball in the Twin Cities in the 1950s. Special I-couldn't-have-done-it-without-yous to two colleagues who became friends during coverage of the stadium story: Justin Catanoso, editor of the *Business Journal of the Greater Triad Area in North Carolina*, who covered the alleged Twins sale and subsequent Greensboro–Winston-Salem referendum when he was the ace business reporter for the *Greensboro News and Record*; and Patrick Sweeney of the *St. Paul Pioneer Press*, who was my "competition" during the stadium story, and far too often the victor.

Thanks, too, to Todd Orjala of the University of Minnesota Press for all of his help and guidance.

Finally, thanks to my Philadelphia family, Hilda and Ed Weiner, and my late father, Sam, who provided me with a great foundation and unconditional support. And of course, to my St. Paul family—Ann, Henry, and Nate—for all their aid, comfort, and love.

St. Paul, January 2000

A Time Line of Minnesota Stadiums

1952   Charles Johnson, Norm McGrew, and Jerry Moore decide the Twin Cities need a major-league baseball stadium.

1956   Met Stadium opens in Bloomington.

1957   New York Giants, seemingly bound for Minneapolis, move to San Francisco instead.

1959   Continental League threatens major leagues and plans to place franchise at Met Stadium.

1960   NFL awards Vikings to Twin Cities and Washington Senators owner Calvin Griffith moves his team to Met Stadium.

1965   Twins play in World Series, and Jerry Moore says Met Stadium is too small. Vikings add bleachers to increase the stadium's capacity for football.

1967   Metropolitan Sports Center, a new indoor hockey arena, is built privately and then turned over to Metropolitan Sports Area Commission. Minnesota North Stars, an expansion NHL team, begin play there.

1969   Feasibility study is ordered to determine future of Met Stadium and possible new stadium.

1970   A downtown domed stadium for football is considered even as refurbishing Met Stadium for baseball is pondered by Metropolitan Sports Area Commission.

1973   To compete with Met Center and to keep St. Paul in the mix, city fathers build St. Paul Civic Center.

1973–79 State legislature and various city councils debate about new stadiums or fixing Met Stadium. Bill passed and leases signed for Vikings and Twins to move into downtown Minneapolis dome. Twins get escape clause in lease.

1982–84 Twins suffer instant on-field and off-field failure. Reports have team moving to Florida. Griffith sells to little-known Twin Cities banker named Carl Pohlad.

1988 A year after Twins win World Series, Pohlad gets lease improvement that runs for ten years. Pohlad retains escape clause first won by Griffith in 1979. Clock begins to tick for next Twins stadium debate.

1988 New downtown Minneapolis arena is planned to house new NBA expansion Minnesota Timberwolves. Team owners Marv Wolfenson and Harvey Ratner vow to construct the arena privately, and do.

1993 After years of seeking to gain land concessions from Metropolitan Sports Facilities Commission and after sexual harassment revelations, North Stars owner Norm Green moves hockey team to Dallas.

1994 Met Center blown up . . . literally.

1994 After debt burden becomes too high, Wolfenson and Ratner, facing bankruptcy, attempt to sell Wolves out of town; it leads to buyout of their arena by the city of Minneapolis and sale of team.

1995 Twins officials declare Metrodome economically obsolete and begin to seek new baseball stadium. Vikings owners get in line, not wanting Twins to get something the football team won't.

1995 Attempts to bring new NHL team to city-owned Target Center fail when it becomes clear that the five-year-old arena can't produce enough revenues to support NHL and NBA teams.

1996–97 Attempts to win public funding for a Twins stadium fail in legislature. Vikings bang the drum for their own new stadium.

1998 St. Paul mayor Norm Coleman, brilliantly staying below the radar and winning the support of his city council and legislative delegation, gets approval of $130 million in public funds for a new arena to house an NHL expansion team.

1998 Vikings are sold by Minnesota ownership group, and new owner, Texan Red McCombs, increases pressure for public to build a new stadium.

1999 Mayor Coleman, eager to rehabilitate his political career, vows to build Twins a new ballpark in St. Paul and sets November referendum. Minneapolis and Hennepin County officials scramble to create their own plan. Sports Facilities Commission offers plans to renovate the Dome for one team, assuming the other will get a new stadium. Both teams reject refurbishing concept. McCombs threatens to move Vikings.

1999 McCombs kicks off campaign for new stadium.

1999 St. Paul voters reject sales tax increase to fund Twins ballpark.

2000 Legislature convenes with no apparent political will to play another stadium game.

Introduction

The legislature finds that the population in the metropolitan area has a
need for sports facilities. . . . It is therefore necessary for the public health,
safety and general welfare to establish a procedure for the acquisition and
betterment of sports facilities.

—Laws of Minnesota, 1977, chapter 89, section 2

The beginning of the end for a Twins ballpark was born in the office of
Arne Carlson, the governor of Minnesota. It was January 7, 1997. Major-
league sports in Minnesota already teetered on the brink of alienating just
about everybody, including their most passionate fans. The governor and
his top aide pushed the populace over the edge. A stadium war was about
to break out all over.

St. Paul Pioneer Press reporter Patrick Sweeney, as polite a gentleman as you'll ever meet, instigated it all. Sweeney lit the match that set the
prairie fire. Ostensibly, he wanted to talk about hockey. Or at least that's
what he told Carlson. It made sense. There were fifteen inches of snow on
the ground. The temperature was minus six degrees. The clock showed
9:10 A.M.

Within minutes of Sweeney's arrival for an interview, Carlson
would enable the biggest mistake in the history of professional sports in
Minnesota. It wasn't a missed ground ball, a dropped pass in the flat, a
stupid slashing penalty, or a last-second personal foul. It was a felony of
the mouth. Following orders, Morrie Anderson, Carlson's chief of staff,
uttered the words that would poison the well for Minnesota stadium construction perhaps forever. With Anderson's revelation to Sweeney of a
stadium finance deal that was neither complete nor comprehensible, the
governor's top lieutenant precipitated the most damaging figurative train
wreck in the state's forty-five-year-long major-league sports experience.

A day later—the fateful January 8, 1997—a painfully botched news conference was held. It was filled with half-truths, omissions, and empty smiles. The Twins and the governor's lead negotiator, a country lawyer named Henry Savelkoul, told only part of a complex story. With this meandering presentation to the Twin Cities' media, the credibility of Twins owner Carl Pohlad, Carlson, and the deal they had crafted swirled down the drain of public scrutiny. Were they fools? Or were they knaves? Were they unprepared? Or were they purposely deceitful?

Sweeney didn't know such fundamental questions would result from his simple interview. He didn't know such history was on tap. The diligent reporter for the *Pioneer Press* was simply doing his job, covering the never-ending story of Minnesota's professional sports stadiums and arenas. Carlson was the powerful, if erratic, governor of Minnesota, with his fingers and words in everything, including, very often, sports. A habitual wearer of a gold University of Minnesota cardigan with a giant maroon *M*, Carlson had become known as Minnesota's number one sports fan. His sport of choice was college basketball, but he was a boorish supporter of all things jockish. He was also a fan of St. Paul mayor Norm Coleman. Carlson wanted to set up Coleman to be the next governor, in 1998.

Mostly for political reasons—certainly not because Minnesota needed another arena or even another team—Carlson was joined at the hip with Coleman in attempting to lure a National Hockey League franchise back to the Twin Cities, specifically to downtown St. Paul. Minnesota was supposed to be the center of the hockey universe in the United States. Downtown St. Paul needed something, anything, to give it a bit of nighttime pizzazz. The Minnesota North Stars, the state's NHL team for twenty-six years, jettisoned the state and its fans in 1993. It happened for a variety of reasons, good and bad, that were, in the end, nobody's fault but the team's unpredictable owner, Norman Green. His departure was the first crack in Minnesota's relationship with professional sports, a small sliver of a disconnect that would develop into a cultural schism.

The Stars move happened on Carlson's watch. It's something he never wanted to oversee again, a major-league team leaving town. Carlson wanted a new NHL team to replace the dearly departed Stars while he was in office. A refurbished St. Paul Civic Center with some state subsidies was Carlson's dream as he and Sweeney began their conversation. It would help the capital city. It would boost Coleman's profile. Carlson desired something else, something bigger, something for his legacy. He wanted a baseball stadium for the Minnesota Twins, the team that first put Minnesota on the big-league map in 1961. The Minnesota legislature was convening that day, and whereas a fixed-up arena for a new NHL team would be nice, a spanking new ballpark for the decreasingly popular Twins would be a home run. It would push Minnesota up the stadium ladder, matching the new edifices in Baltimore, Denver, Cleveland, and soon nearby Milwaukee.

There sat the silver-haired Sweeney. He'd set up the interview in Carlson's capitol office explaining that he wanted to quiz the governor about how any hockey arena finance plan would affect the city of St. Paul. But Sweeney knew that baseball was the more significant sports issue sitting on Carlson's oak desk. For two years, Twins' owner Pohlad, the state's second richest man, had sought a new ballpark for his lowly team. For the previous six months, the issue of public funding for the stadium— framed as a subsidy to billionaire Pohlad—rattled around every political campaign, radio talk show, editorial page, and sports bar. With the House and Senate set to meet in two hours, rumbles were everywhere that a new, innovative Twins proposal was about to be unveiled. Pohlad had been in negotiations with state officials, appointed by Carlson, since the spring of 1996, hammering out what he hoped would be a plan to stop his bleeding; the team had been suffering massive operating losses—approaching $10 million in some years—in the Metrodome, another stadium built with public financing twenty years earlier.

For sure, Carlson and Pohlad wanted any stadium plan to be creative, innovative, eye-popping. Privately, lobbyists hired by the Twins to sell the forthcoming deal to the legislature and the public had urged Pohlad to put in "real money" to any stadium proposal. Lots of it, big checks like the kind you see golfers get at the end of a victorious tournament. Pohlad's cold cash could generate tons of momentum for an even more sizable public piece of financing, the lobbyists believed. Meanwhile, Carlson and his minions were hot for the idea of "public ownership" in the team. It intrigued Pohlad, too, an eighty-three-year-old man in search of a cuddlier legacy than seemed destined for him. Anything that looked or felt like the unique Green Bay Packers model of community ownership would be appealing, they thought. The new paradigm was in a box and about to be unwrapped. Perhaps even that hockey arena that Sweeney sought to ask about and the ballpark, which was priority number one, would be married during this legislative session.

Pohlad, his three sons, and their financial, public relations, and baseball advisers had been trying to hammer out a deal with Savelkoul, a former Republican legislator and prosperous attorney from tiny Albert Lea, Minnesota, one hundred miles south of the capital. Also deeply involved in the talks was Anderson, Carlson's chief of staff and a number cruncher so extreme that having a conversation with him was like talking to an IRS statute come to life. Anderson's sentences were constantly filled with phrases like "time value of money," "revenue streams," "net present value," and "above the line or below the line."

If Anderson was incomprehensible, then Savelkoul was secretive. Cordial, but secretive. He was so secretive that even key members of the agency he headed, the Metropolitan Sports Facilities Commission, knew virtually nothing about the deal he was negotiating. The commission was a collection of mostly Democratic-Farmer-Labor Party loyalists appointed by the Minneapolis City Council. The commission legally owned and operated the Metrodome, the home stadium for the Twins and the National Football League Minnesota Vikings. Savelkoul didn't have much in common with his urban fellow commissioners. In fact, he trusted them about as far as he could throw them, and at five feet seven, he couldn't throw them far at all. His intentional withdrawal from them was troublesome, even self-defeating. After all, the six other commissioners with ties to the city council, like it or not, were going to have to support and lobby for any Twins plan. But Savelkoul told them nothing. Personally, Savelkoul loathed some of his commission's members, especially a barrel-chested, often pompous, starch-shirted businessman named Paul

Rexford Thatcher. Thatcher, a diehard Democrat, lunched frequently at the tony Minneapolis Club and wouldn't have set foot in hayseed Albert Lea with his shiny loafers if his life depended on it. Savelkoul's pleasant, quiet existence on South Newton Avenue in Albert Lea was a million miles from Thatcher's downtown Minneapolis high-rise condominium.

Savelkoul hated consulting with Thatcher, who was an expert on the Dome's finances, or any of the other commissioners on matters as important as a potentially innovative Twins deal. Savelkoul wouldn't even inform Loanne Thrane, the commission's lone Republican and a respected Republican Party strategist. Savelkoul was Carlson's man, and merely the commission's figurehead. If he wore two hats—Sports Facilities Commission chairman and governor's negotiator—only one mattered; Savelkoul told anyone who would listen that he had one constituent, "Arne."

Pohlad and his advisers were opposed to the light of public disclosure. Although any stadium plan was sure to require hundreds of millions of dollars of government aid, the Pohlads viewed the stadium negotiations as a business deal. Savelkoul and Anderson allowed them to believe that. They endeared themselves to the Pohlads early in the negotiation by expressly stating that the stadium proposal should be considered a business arrangement, not a political deal. This tickled the Pohlads. The talks to develop a stadium plan were mostly held in the offices of the Twins chief financial consultant Bob Starkey, an accountant with the Arthur Andersen firm. Sometimes the meetings moved to Pohlad's thirty-eighth-floor conference room in the gleaming Dain Bosworth Tower on Sixth Street in Minneapolis. As 1997 approached and the talks were on-again, off-again, Anderson's small capitol office, the governor's ornate reception room, or a capitol basement conference room were used. Even though Savelkoul and Anderson were supposed to be doing "the people's work," the stadium deal was top secret, hush-hush, private. Too private.

What we had here, before Anderson revealed it all to Sweeney, was a group of white men, in nifty suits, who were putting together a $300 to $400 million public-private partnership with no input from the public. They were falling in love. Not with each other, necessarily, but with a deal, with terms and conditions that only they understood. They were isolated. They were convinced they were devising the most thoughtful stadium plan in history, and in some ways, they were. Had they talked with anyone else, they may have been on a marvelous, innovative track. They may have been headed for true victory for the people of Minnesota. But they were victims of a sort of Stockholm syndrome. That's the effect that kidnap victims experience. If you're with your captors long enough, you begin to identify with them. Savelkoul and Anderson became captives of the Pohlad mystique, seduced by the intricacies of any deal that a billionaire could devise. Pohlad and his aides became captives of Savelkoul's and Anderson's hubris that their deal could get done even if the public knew little about its forthcoming details, even if no outreach had been conducted among a populace that seemed fed up with pro sports, even if legislative leaders had been kept in the dark.

Then Sweeney, forty-eight, dogged and serious, a burrower of facts, visited Carlson. Ushered into the governor's office and soon chatting with Carlson, Sweeney noticed that Anderson had wandered in, too. Putting hockey aside, Sweeney asked, "How's baseball goin'?" Anderson, having told Twins officials he would keep the details of a Twins stadium deal confidential until all sides were ready to roll out the plan, remained mum. The deal wasn't truly done. Close, but not close enough for public disclosure. Principles had been established. Numbers were being nailed down. Leaks had been occurring in the gossip column of Sweeney's colleague, sportswriter Charley Walters, and they were tossing out all sorts of dollar amounts.[1] Anderson and Carlson suspected that the incorrect information—that generally made the Twins look good—was coming from the team's marketing consultant Pat Forciea, but they weren't sure.

Anderson was reluctant to provide Sweeney with details. But Carlson, who had a remarkably bad sense of timing throughout the Twins stadium debate, said to Anderson, "Yeah, how's baseball goin'?" Anderson took that as a signal that his boss, the governor, was curious and open to sharing the information with Sweeney. After months of closed doors and secret meetings, after weeks of trying to keep the details away from the state's taxpayers, Anderson told Sweeney the deal, or at least the deal as Anderson knew it and understood it at that moment.

Pro sports in Minnesota would literally never be the same. Anderson's revelation, published in the next day's newspaper, was a fatal error. It triggered that misspoken and misbegotten January 8 news conference. It cut off Pohlad at his knees. It emboldened critics, helping to create a grassroots movement opposed to pro sports taxation. It froze legislators in their places, hardening any chance to gain much-needed votes. It led to two defeats in the legislature, including one during a special session convened specifically to address the Twins' future. It was a session doomed from its opening gavel. In the end, Anderson's disclosure created the necessity for a plot that was hatched in the same office where he had fed Sweeney the damaging information. It was the office of the governor of Minnesota. The plot was to threaten the people of Minnesota with a charade.

The events of January 7 and January 8, 1997, rendered any Twins' stadium hopes dead for three years after, and perhaps even more to come. Those days served, too, as a final straw on a larger process: the breakdown in the relationship between pro sports and Minnesota's public. It followed the 1993 departure by the North Stars, a keenly felt reduction in the state's cultural assets. It followed the controversial and gut-wrenching public buyout of the privately built—and nearly bankrupt—Target Center arena. It came on the heels of the 1994 lockout of baseball's players by the sport's owners. It mingled with a series of off-field escapades, from the National Basketball Association Timberwolves wunderkind J. R. Rider kicking a sports bar manager at the Mall of America to National Football League Vikings quarterback Warren Moon being charged with, then acquitted of, domestically abusing his wife. The Twins stadium war was the cherry on the top of a mushy cake of sports goo.

In January 1999, the Minnesota Vikings seemed bound for the Super Bowl. The entire state was wearing purple and rooting for its team. The outlandish salaries paid to the players, the ridiculous arrival of a new billionaire owner from Texas telling us what to do with our stadium situation, the amount of mind-numbing media coverage—we all dealt with it. That's because in a time when we Minnesotans were so detached, when people from Stillwater to Maple Grove seemed to communicate only with turn signals on the freeway, this team of men in pads and helmets gave us a common cause to cheer. It is clichéd and corny, but true: from the mostly African American neighborhoods of central St. Paul to the Volvo-laced culs-de-sac of lakeside Minnetonka, we were all connected by this silly thing called a sports team with the name "Minnesota" attached to it. It was our team.

The Vikings lost to Atlanta. They never made it to the Super Bowl. Whew, that was good. Because the new Vikings ownership, in place just weeks before the 1998 season began, attempted to leverage the team's winning streak into an instant and irrational call for the construction of a new football stadium. They had a frenzy on their hands, and they exploited it. The new owner was a swaggering Texas car salesman named Red McCombs. He barged into town, giving new life and personality to a Twin Cities sports community that had been drowning in its tears because of bad teams and bad vibes about pro sports. He almost single-handedly whipped the fans—the taxpayers—into a stadium-building mode. Stadiums can't be built on emotion. They shouldn't be kiboshed by emotion either.

The rational, fundamental question is this: "What is it worth to retain the legitimate feeling, the special experience, and the unmatched community-building that a successful Vikings or Timberwolves or Twins season provides us?"

The goal of this book is to help the Twin Cities—and other middle-size major-league marketplaces—take back pro sports. I offer solutions—however idealistic—to our pro sports quagmire, in an attempt to begin a new kind of conversation about what a stadium and teams can mean to a community. I believe we should build a new baseball stadium in the Twin Cities, but it should be our ballpark. I believe that it should be as public as possible and that it should be used 365 days a year, not just for eighty-one Twins home games. I also believe we should refurbish the Metrodome, one of the nation's most publicly friendly and financially successful stadiums, so that a National Football League team will play there. After all, at its foundation, the Dome was built with football in mind.

Some believe that by simply saying, "Hell, no," we can lead the nation, its taxpayers, and its sports fans into a revolutionary new dawn and avoid the experiences of Nashville, St. Louis, Seattle, and other cities that have given away their souls and public treasuries to lure pro sports teams. I believe that by coming up with our own socially responsible solutions, we can help the rest of the nation even more.

First let's return to a certain unique yesteryear, when ballplayers were paid $13,300 per season and when this region was collectively fresh faced.[2] It was 1952. The Twin Cities were prairie towns seeking to compete with Milwaukee and Kansas City. The political and economic foundations for Minnesota's first major-league stadium were laid by a community—workers, captains of industry, and politicians—that wanted pro sports, that felt a team and a ballpark would gather them together, not tear them apart. Major-league sports would put Minnesota on the map. Getting teams was the cause; major-league sports would allow this overlooked section of the nation to, literally, play with the big boys. The symbol of arrival on the national scene was an Erector set of a stadium, plopped in the middle of a rural-suburban nowhere. It was known as Met Stadium. It helped to define a Twin Cities of another era.

CHAPTER 1

If You Build It

Minnesota's Quest to Become Major League

During the first week of July in 1952, Adlai Stevenson was lining up votes for the Democratic presidential nomination. Men's suits cost $29.95 at the stylish Young Quinlan store in downtown Minneapolis. Hubert H. Humphrey called for no retreat on civil rights in a speech to the National Association for the Advancement of Colored People. Northwestern National Bank introduced a revolutionary process: drive-in banking at its flagship branch. Set to speak at the Republican convention that would eventually tab World War II hero Dwight D. Eisenhower as its candidate was Wisconsin Senator Joseph McCarthy, the crazed anti-Communist.

Despite the crackling energy of that historic period, three men lunching at the Minneapolis Athletic Club preferred to discuss more mundane topics. All around them, suburbia was growing, the baby boom was underway, and the American political landscape was in turmoil. But Charles O. Johnson, Gerald Moore, and Norman McGrew were talking sports. For the long-term civic imagery of the growing metropolitan area of Minneapolis and St. Paul—and for regional self-esteem—their chat was profound and far-reaching. On that summer's day, they quietly set the course for stadium construction in Minnesota, then and now.

They had no idea what lay ahead of them, of how they, and their community, would be exploited by baseball team owners and the major leagues, of how they would have to change course and put up a good fight, and how, almost as if by coincidence or luck, they would land two major-league sports teams within a ten-month span. They also didn't know they'd have to wait for all that for more than seven years. A stadium—paid for largely by users and devoted fans—would eventually get them where they wanted to go.

Mature men, the three believed that this major-league thing would arrive sooner, rather than later. They truly thought it was easier to do than it turned out to be. In the end, it was hard. Charlie Johnson, Jerry Moore, and Norm McGrew were Minnesota's major-league sports founding fathers. They would acquire a posse of aides, patrons, ideologues, and soldiers. But make no mistake, everything that follows flows from them and that lunch on that warm July day.[1]

Three Common Men

In 1952 Minneapolis–St. Paul was a seeker of teams, naively eager to join a very exclusive club of "major-league" cities. In 1952 "major league" meant only baseball. The National Football League, or NFL, was in its development stages. The National Basketball Association, or NBA, could barely outdraw the circus for attention. The National Hockey League, or NHL, was a rumor in all but six cities. But fast-forward to the 1990s, wade through the ebbs and flows of sports history, and the Twin Cities would become the hunted. By 1993, Minnesota's NHL team, the North Stars, would move to Dallas, just a year before Minnesota's NBA team, the Timberwolves, would threaten to move to Nashville or New Orleans. By 1997, the Major League Baseball Twins were going through the motions of seemingly moving to Charlotte or Greensboro, North Carolina, among the next generation of eager cities on the prowl. And the Vikings, the NFL team? Their ownership, old and new, was harrumphing that if it didn't get a new or improved stadium, well, it had options, too, and there were always greener pastures to at least gaze at and threaten with. A half century of geographic change, attitudinal shifts, and sports economics explosion had reshaped Minnesota's relationship to pro sports. The romance was gone. But the modus operandi and the necessities are enduring. Cities seek teams. Owners leverage that desire. Leagues keep the teams scarce. Sports facilities—generally funded by the public—tip the balance as to which region gets and keeps teams.

But we get ahead of ourselves. For in Johnson, Moore, and McGrew, we see the true construction workers of a foundation for Minnesota's relationship between "the public" and major-league sports. They poured the cement, but they had no ability to steer its unpredictable long-term course. They couldn't have predicted that their dream in 1952 would turn into the most emotional public-policy debate in the state's history forty-five years later, or that their dream would have lost most of its magic by the end of the century. It is as if our collective status can't be rolled into one shining symbol anymore. Then, as Stevenson and Eisenhower were poised to slug it out for the presidency, the symbol, the icon, was clear, even convincing. Get "major-league" sports status, and Minneapolis–St. Paul would become a major-league city, in every way. The Twin Cities would become what the academics have come to call "high-order urban centers," where corporate headquarters, professional services, elite arts organizations, and pro sports thrive. "Those activities combine with their skylines to make the high-order cities the main symbols of metropolitan America," is how University of Minnesota geographer John R. Borchert put it.[2]

That was the belief and reality in 1952. Major-league sports—particularly baseball—would symbolize the Twin Cities' arrival on the national scene. From 1903, when the American and National Leagues began relating as partners in a court-approved monopoly until the afternoon when Johnson, Moore, and McGrew gathered for lunch, there had been only sixteen major-league teams in ten cities. Those ten—New York, Chicago, Philadelphia, Pittsburgh, Cincinnati, St. Louis, Cleveland, Detroit, Boston, and Washington, D.C.—were de facto "major-league" cities because they had major-league teams, and only they. And in 1952 those big-league cities represented ten of the fifteen largest cities in the United States. The five without teams? Los Angeles, San Francisco, Baltimore, Minneapolis–St. Paul, and Buffalo, New York.[3]

But in this post–World War II moment, places like the Twin Cities, Dallas–Fort Worth, Houston, and Denver were turning into—or had already become—legitimate metropolises. With air travel and personal ownership of automobiles proliferating, it was only a matter of time before major-league sports teams would move to greener (as in dollars) pastures or leagues would expand into new markets. There had been discussions by established owners of adding teams, but there was also protection in mind. Baseball's owners didn't want to share their pie. After all, it was protected by U.S. Supreme Court decisions that said that "the business of baseball" was exempt from the nation's antitrust laws. Thus baseball was a protected cartel and could do whatever it darn well pleased. It had complete control over the movement of its players. It had control over the system of minor leagues. It could add teams only when it wanted. It could relocate teams only when it wanted. It could keep teams in place even over the objections of impatient, wanderlusting individual owners. And in 1952, no major-league team had moved for forty-nine years.

These three fellows weren't the heaviest of hitters of the Twin Cities. They had their own significant spheres of influence, but they weren't captains of industry. They were worker bees. Moore was a sales manager of a storage and moving company. A seeker of influence, he rose to the position of president of the Minneapolis Chamber of Commerce and eventually became the head of the then-influential Minneapolis Downtown Council. He was a sociable salesman, singular in his ability to drink Scotch with one prospective baseball owner named Horace Stoneham of the New York Giants and successfully able to charm another prospect named Calvin Griffith, who owned the Washington Senators.

McGrew was a hired hand of the Minneapolis Chamber of Commerce, a tireless behind-the-scenes coordinator of details and a marketer before the term "sports marketing" was part of the industry vocabulary. Charles O. "Charlie" Johnson was an opinionated, hard-drinking sports editor and columnist of the *Minneapolis Star* and *Tribune*. He wrote five well-read columns a week for the afternoon *Star* and a sixth column on Sundays in the widely circulated *Tribune*. He oversaw the production and content of both newspapers before sports talk radio and fair-haired television anchormen. He was an old-fashioned sports columnist, the kind who knew no ethical boundaries, the sort who was a player as well as a chronicler. Johnson was the not so secret agent of John Cowles Sr., the owner of the state's and region's most powerful newspaper. It is a newspaper that throughout the state's history of major-league sports—and sports facilities—has made its mark and flexed its muscles, for better and for worse.

Johnson, on the phone with contacts nationwide, had superb inside intelligence. With him at the vortex, with Moore reaching out, and with McGrew organizing support on the ground, the Twin Cities were ahead of the curve. Their timing was impeccable.

Building a Dream

"At that first lunch, we agreed to build a stadium."

That's how McGrew remembered it during the summer of 1998. Seventy-eight years old, he was still organizing and planning, now for the local semisecret sports booster group known as "the Dunkers," a sort of blood-oath civic klatch that meets for breakfast frequently, often at that same Minneapolis Athletic Club, sometimes hosting national sports figures. Recently women were admitted to the group. Only one journalist, Charlie Johnson's protégé, Sid Hartman, a throwback sports columnist cum booster, has ever been allowed to belong to the Dunkers.

That seemingly casual decision in 1952 to build a stadium developed out of a more fundamental sentiment that had been developing in the Twin Cities ever since 1945. That's when McGrew, age twenty-five, fresh home from World War II, started a forty-year career with the Minneapolis Chamber of Commerce. He was given two initial major responsibilities: to enhance the Twin Cities airport and make sure that Northwest Orient Airlines stayed in town, and to lure big-league sports to the Twin Cities. Think of that: a world-class airport and major-league sports were the priorities of the Chamber of Commerce. By 1948, there was talk of an NFL team moving to the Twin Cities. But not until 1952, when Johnson, especially, began to understand that major-league baseball teams would soon begin to relocate, did the stadium idea seriously begin to bloom.

There was precedent. Just 340 miles away to the east, Milwaukee, Wisconsin, officials had taken a giant risk. Those in the know in the Twin Cities watched with a certain amount of envy. Without a team in site, the Milwaukee leaders decided in 1947 to build what would become a major-league baseball stadium. Milwaukee, the nation's sixteenth largest urban area in the early 1950s, seemed an odd spot to imagine a big-league team, what with larger cities such as Los Angeles, San Francisco, Baltimore, and the Twin Cities still wanting teams. Besides, Chicago was so close, and Milwaukee didn't seem to have the percolating economic energy of the emerging western cities of, say, Dallas–Fort Worth, Houston, or Denver. But there was tradition and a memory. Way back in 1901, Milwaukee was home to one of the original American League teams. A year later, those original Brewers moved to Baltimore to become the Orioles, and the major leagues never looked back to the Germanic city that made beer famous. For nearly four decades, Milwaukee had the taste to recapture a big-league team. As Johnson, Moore, and McGrew began to plot, Milwaukee had a Triple-A American Association team in hand, just like Minneapolis had the Class AAA Millers and St. Paul had the Triple-A Saints. But Milwaukee was already building, already preparing.

Soon after that brainstorming lunch, Johnson, Moore, and McGrew began to spread the word of their intentions, and things began to happen. The Chamber of Commerce board officially directed Moore to look into acquiring a big-league team. Moore decided that Johnson should travel to New York to meet with baseball commissioner Ford Frick to discuss whether baseball had plans to expand. Frick discouraged Johnson, but a committee of mostly Minneapolis businessmen was named to begin to put together a plan for a major-league effort. By March 1953, the Twin Cities boosters held their first meeting.[4] Weeks afterward, a remarkable event occurred that would jump-start serious stadium efforts in the Twin Cities: the National League Boston Braves, struggling financially, up and moved to Milwaukee. For the first time in nearly a half century, major-league baseball had allowed a franchise to relocate. The landscape instantly changed.

Why? Because Lou Perini, the owner of the Braves, said his team was failing in the two-team town of Boston, where the Red Sox had the upper hand. Conveniently, the minor-league Milwaukee Brewers were the Class AAA affiliate of the Braves. A relationship was in place. More important, that sparkling new, publicly paid-for $6.6 million Milwaukee

County Stadium stood ready to play in. There was a fresh market. It was the first major-league franchise move since Theodore Roosevelt was president. And other owners took notice, some with glee.

"Loooouuuuuu, that's why you're so brave and brilliant," Brooklyn Dodgers owner Walter O'Malley told Perini in supporting the sudden move. "That is why you're a pioneer."[5]

Later that year, the American League St. Louis Browns, the second-fiddle team to the Cardinals in a two-team city, moved to Baltimore to become the Orioles for the 1954 season. (The earlier Orioles, once in Milwaukee, moved in 1903 to New York to become the Yankees.) Why Baltimore again? That city in the shadows of Washington, D.C., had a city-built stadium waiting for any team ready to come. And by the fall of 1954, the Philadelphia Athletics were announcing their move to Kansas City. Why? City officials paid to refurbish the aging Muelbach Stadium there, renaming it Municipal Stadium. In the cases of the As and Browns, the Twin Cities baseball committee had been contacted by the teams' owners. But there was no adequate place to play in the Twin Cities with two minor-league teams, the Millers and Saints, laboring in two aging minor-league ballparks in the hearts of each of their cities, both too small and not prepared to take on the new car-dependent culture of a growing metropolis with emerging suburbs. It was becoming increasingly clear that if they built it, a major-league team would come to a new stadium in Minnesota. The question was how to build it and where to build it. Then, no problem, there'd be a team. Any day now—or so it seemed in 1953.

Sibling Rivalry

Three years earlier, in 1950, the U.S. government released its first comprehensive metropolitan-area focused census. "All of a sudden, this place shows up on the screen of all sorts of national advertisers and business firms," said John Borchert, a geographer and expert on the history and development of the Twin Cities. "We were the new guy on the block." From the outside looking in, Minneapolis–St. Paul had gone overlooked by the buyers and sellers in New York and Chicago. But with two cities with combined populations of more than 800,000 and some "streetcar suburbs" of about 300,000 residents already in place, the Twin Cities were a metropolis with more than 1 million people. The newfangled census rankings exposed the area's growth and newfound size to the rest of the nation.

From the inside looking out, however, we were more than Twin Cities. We were dueling cities. We were negatively schizophrenic. We were siblings in heated, unending, illogical rivalry. At the time of that explosive new census, a rider on public transportation still had to pay twice—once when he or she got on the streetcar in St. Paul and then again if and when it crossed into Minneapolis. There was an extra charge on intercity phone calls. "Comparatively few functions are developed in either city to serve both," Richard Hartshorne wrote in his 1932 article "The Twin City District," the first thorough critique of the bifurcated metro area.[6] For sure, there were two minor-league baseball teams, one for each city; there were distinct downtowns, city-specific newspapers that rarely covered the goings-on in the other city, separate chambers of commerce, and a sense that St. Paul, the older, eastern city, was falling behind the booming western prairie town that would become sprawling Minneapolis and its upscale suburbs. "Even the two city planning boards have no mutual relations," Hartshorne wrote.

What developed to link the cities was a sort of demilitarized zone of commerce that we have come to know to this day as the Midway District, tucked on the western edge of St. Paul, actually closer to downtown Minneapolis than to the riverfront of central St. Paul. The Midway District developed to link the major railroads that delivered goods to both Minneapolis and St. Paul. This middle zone of rail and truck transferring was needed because two distinctly separate cores developed in the first half of the nineteenth century, with St. Paul settled around 1840 and Minneapolis a decade later. Until about 1870, St. Paul was the regional capital. But as the lumber, flour, and grain trade intensified, Minneapolis began to gain the upper hand, with the farmers to the west nearer to the City of Lakes than to St. Paul. Still, into the mid-1930s, as Hartshorne described it, the Twin Cities were "a double center of separated cores," even if by 1900 the status of Minneapolis had pushed it clearly ahead of St. Paul.

The Midway District remained a key industrial zone, but as World War II ended and the prosperous 1950s blanketed the Twin Cities, the region's "population center of gravity" saw a swing to the west .[7] As those southern and western suburbs grew, the idea of a stadium for major-league sports was born. With more and more financial power in the hands of Minneapolis capitalists and with a more vigorous corporate spirit driving the Minneapolis vision, pro sports seemed to be destined for the Minneapolis side of the metropolitan area.

Of course, St. Paul advocates objected. And the Midway District would become a place where St. Paul boosters believed that a major-league team should play. They believed that team should be St. Paul's team. A site just north and west of the Midway on the University of Minnesota's St. Paul campus had early appeal to boosters on both sides of the river, but the university regents rejected the idea. Another potential St. Paul site was on West Seventh Street, near downtown. In the end, Minneapolis's collective mind-set, which thought regionally, won out over St. Paul's dogged, but regressive, parochialism. "The St. Paul people had a hard time thinking of anything in a metropolitan sense for fear it would benefit Minneapolis and disadvantage them," said Borchert.[8]

Led by Walter Seeger, who owned a St. Paul refrigeration company, St. Paul boosters got a $2 million stadium referendum passed in November 1953 to build a stadium in the Midway District. It would be the beginning of what the St. Paulites thought was a serious effort to become the site for a major-league team. But even though the Midway was in the core of the cities, even though it was accessible by public transportation, the effort was futile. Minneapolitans already had their eyes on land near Wold Chamberlain Field, the Twin Cities airport. Home building had been ruled out on the site south of the airport; because of airport noise and anticipated congestion, neither Federal Housing Administration nor GI Bill loans were being made available for homes in what would become the stadium zone.

Baseball's owners weren't interested in the intercity squabbling or the site selection process. They cared more about the movers and shakers, about sure-thing ballparks and guaranteed dollars. It has been forever thus. Charlie Johnson, with the aid of his boss, Cowles, and with connections to the Chamber of Commerce, was the man in the middle. He was attached to Minneapolis, the larger of the spatting siblings. By the end of 1953, with teams moving, the Twin Cities became a possible landing spot. The first owner came calling within a year, although he had been toying with the idea of moving to Minneapolis–St. Paul for three years already. He would seduce. He would come close to committing. But Horace Stoneham would soon break the boosters' hearts. The ensuing disappointment would galvanize their effort.

Teasing the Locals

Even before Johnson, Moore, and McGrew met to get the ball rolling on a Minneapolis stadium effort, Stoneham, the owner of the New York Giants, began to consider his options. His team's legendary Polo Grounds lease was soon to expire, and the ballpark was frayed at the edges. The New York market, with its three big-league teams, was getting stretched. Attendance was down, barely recovering from the steep decline during World War II. New York City crime was up, and fans were nervous about attending games. Stoneham seemed to have an out. He already owned the Minneapolis Millers, controlled the Minneapolis territory, and saw the growth potential. He also knew that his Millers would soon need a new stadium because Nicollet Park, at Nicollet and Thirty-first Street, was teetering toward extinction, and the city had redevelopment plans.

Documents buried in the file drawers of the Hennepin County clerk reveal that on May 1, 1951, Stoneham purchased forty acres of land that was "all that part of Government Lot Five (5), Section Four (4), Township One Hundred Seventeen (117) North, Range Twenty-One (21) West, lying South of the new Wayzata Boulevard (also known as State Highway No. 12)." It is land that today houses a strip mall and the DoubleTree Suites hotel, on the western edge of Minneapolis and at the entry to St. Louis Park, on the south side of what is now Highway 394. It's where the Cooper Theater once stood. Not a bad spot, really, for a ballpark, just a short drive from downtown Minneapolis and smack-dab in the middle of a suburban swath. Whether it was Stoneham's idea simply to move the

Millers there or move the Giants there is unclear. Whether he would build the stadium on his own or seek some sort of public funding as was developing in other cities is also unknown. But by 1954, with the Braves, Browns, and As on the move, Stoneham flatly stated that he was going to move the Giants to Minnesota. Where? When? Like all good sports team owners, he kept his options open.

The most memorable declaration of Stoneham's intentions came on the night of January 25, 1954. Stoneham was in Minneapolis for an annual baseball banquet at the old Radisson Hotel.[9] George Brophy, who was then the Millers general manager, remembered that Stoneham was detailed in his intentions on that night, the same night that Bill Rigney was named the Millers manager. Late into the night, Stoneham, Brophy, and a gang of other Millers employees tipped more than a few alcoholic beverages in Stoneham's suite. "Every time I wanted to leave, he'd just say, 'Sitsy,'" Brophy reported.[10] "Sitsy" meant sit down and have another drink. During that hazy evening, Stoneham told Brophy that he had plans to move the Giants to Minneapolis, probably to the new stadium that would somehow be built on his land on Highway 12. The Giants' relocation would be part of a move to send the Cincinnati Reds to New York in exchange for the Giants move to the Twin Cities. Cincinnati was then the smallest market in the big-leagues. Brophy, an inveterate gabber, spread the news. Stoneham, lubricated by Scotch, had raised everyone's hopes.

Bloomington

Stoneham may have had his acres to the west of downtown Minneapolis, but leaders of a stadium search committee identified farmland to the south of both downtown Minneapolis and St. Paul that could handle not only a new stadium but that new phenomenon called parking lots. The automobile was becoming king. Freeways were on the drawing board. In the minds of search committee members such as Lyman Wakefield, then with First National Bank of Minneapolis and the Minneapolis Chamber of Commerce, the southern site in the village of Bloomington had pacifist overtones: it was equidistant from downtown Minneapolis and downtown

St. Paul, about nine miles from each loop. As time passed, Stoneham's St. Louis Park site was seen as being simply "too Minneapolis" and would have been a direct slap at St. Paul. One more thing: the 164 acres of Bloomington land that would contain the ballpark, parking lots, and room for other family recreational activity was relatively cheap.

As 1953 rolled into 1954, there was an increasing sense of urgency. Before the St. Louis Browns jumped to Baltimore at the end of the 1953 season, the Minnesota baseball boosters were questioned about their desires for that struggling franchise. Parade Stadium, just west of downtown Minneapolis, was considered as a temporary playing field, but it was inadequate. As the Philadelphia As hopscotched to Kansas City in 1954, the Twin Cities again were considered as a relocation spot. There wasn't a ballpark. Minnesota had to get its act together.

By August 13, 1954, a new agency called the Metropolitan Sports Area Commission was formed, backed by the city of Minneapolis and Bloomington. (Later, another inner-ring suburb, Richfield, would be added to the commission's makeup because Bloomington's water supply wasn't adequate and Richfield's proximity to the Minneapolis sewer system allowed Richfield to play the role of community plumber. Without the Richfield link between Minneapolis and Bloomington, all the toilets wouldn't have flushed in the new stadium.) In days when business and public officials were not wise to the ethics of the 1990s, Jerry Moore, the baseball booster and former head of the Chamber, was named chairman of the Sports Area Commission, too. Wearing a bundle of hats didn't seem to bother anyone.

About the same time, a fraternal organization called the Minute Men was formed. It was created to help the commission put up for sale $4.5 million worth of bonds that were to pay for a new stadium. The bonds were to be paid back with the revenues from the stadium. Even though the land that was identified as the potential stadium site was in Bloomington, the city of Minneapolis aided in issuing the bonds. Minneapolis specifically refused to allow the bonds to be of a general-obligation nature; that is, if the stadium project failed, Minneapolis taxpayers wouldn't have been on the hook for the debt. The idea was this: the revenues generated by fans—via team rent, stadium concessions, and parking—would help to pay off the bond buyers.

There were two classes of bonds, creatively named "A" and "B." Two million dollars worth of the B bonds were literally called "civic" bonds in the prospectus and were to be sold to Minnesota-based firms and individuals. They could be sold in denominations of as little as $500. They were marketed as civic contributions and not investment instruments. We can be sure of this because the return on a bond buyer's investment was to be a grand total of 2 percent. Once those B bonds were sold, then a series of A bonds, at $1,000 apiece, were to be offered to investment houses; the promised interest rate of return on these higher-paying tax-exempt bonds was 4 percent. Ostensibly, the bond brokers would have gained confidence in buying the remaining $2.5 million in stadium revenue bonds on the strength of the local civic commitment of citizens and businesses. No matter what, no principal or interest would be paid to any bond buyers unless and until the operating costs of the proposed stadium were first paid for. (And before Minnesota's major-league teams arrived, the stadium didn't support itself, with bond buyers forgoing interest.)

The prospectus document developed to help sell the bonds is a gem.[11] Much of it is believed to have been written and conceived by a Minneapolis lawyer named Hugh Barber, who was the legal and ethical brains behind much of the new stadium's finance plan. With the graphic bells and high-tech whistles that often accompany stadium presentations and marketing efforts today, this 1954 version is so sweetly stripped down that it would have been impossible to refuse laying down $500 for the community. Besides, this new "stadium area" wasn't just for pro sports. The prospectus describes an adjacent "recreational center," with picnic areas, shuffleboard courts, badminton, a golf driving range, and tennis and croquet courts. It was going to be a community gathering place, another venue for Twin Citians to spend a day at the beach.

The stadium construction notion was framed such that the five hundred bucks were a community contribution as much as a sports investment. The stadium, of course, was to belong to no particular team because there was no particular team set to play in it. There was no wealthy owner to resent for his subsidies because there was no wealthy owner on the scene to grab a subsidy. Indeed, at this point in Minnesota sports history, a wealthy owner was to be a welcome new member of the community. For all anyone knew, they were building the ballpark for the New York Giants, who would become "ours" when we had "our stadium." Imagine that? At its core, this ballpark, which didn't yet have a name, was being built for "us." The stadium was a vehicle to make this place "big league" and to be mentioned in the same breath with other important metropolises. That is, the stadium was considered to be a completely public place, built for the good of the metropolitan area. And save for some extremists in St. Paul who believed any team and ballpark should be located there, there was general agreement that the ballpark should be in the near—and about to explode—southern suburbs. What would become Metropolitan Stadium served to sanctify the legitimacy of the suburbs as a place to do business, especially with the airport as a synergistic neighbor. But at that time, there was never the anticipation that the suburbs would eventually gobble up and overwhelm the two core cities.

The fifteen-page prospectus, which looked more like a souvenir game program than a financial document, had a simple cover of a right-handed pitcher, in a classic baggy flannel uniform, following through on a pitch—presumably to the potential investor. Beneath the player were the simple words "A Prospectus Of A METROPOLITAN SPORTS AREA For the Twin Cities." Included was a series of thirteen questions and answers. A handful are especially poignant. Question 4, for instance, asked what a bond buyer would receive besides the guaranteed 2 percent interest rate. "He will get a priority on the purchase of tickets" was the answer. This is, without question, the most elemental form of the modern-day "private-seat license." Today new stadiums are financed by asking potential season ticket holders for a substantial up-front investment—say $1,500 to $3,000—to aid in building a new ballpark. In exchange, the "seat license" buyer "owns" his or her seat—presumably a good one—and then pays the freight of continuing season tickets. This was the concept devised by Barber and others back in 1954.

Question 12 was wonderfully optimistic: "When will the $4½ million be spent?" The answer: "A major league baseball commitment is expected in 1955 when the stadium is partially built. If so, then it's 'full steam ahead' to finish the stadium. If not, then about 20,000 seats, for example, are to be completed at the cost of around $2 or $2½ million for minor league baseball and other activities. The stadium will then be finished when a major league franchise comes to Minnesota."

Finally, there's question 13: "Will Minnesota get major league baseball by 1956 when the stadium is finished?" Answer: "Based on numerous contacts with major league officials, the committee is convinced we will. It's reasonable to understand why a major league franchise owner won't commit himself now when he knows he must play the 1955 season in his present location."

The exuberance of the baseball committee and the new public agency was charming. But it was irrational. First, to land a big-league team, the stadium wasn't enough. Polite Minneapolis was going to have to take on the lords of baseball before a team would settle in the prairies. Building a ballpark sets the stage; political pressure and the natural physics of sports economics get—and keep—teams.

Second, the proposed $4.5 million was about half of what was eventually spent for Met Stadium. Because revenues from the ballpark didn't originally support its bond debt service, the city of Minneapolis eventually had to stick its financial neck out to refinance the stadium's debt. By 1960, most of the Met's debt load—some of it needed to expand Met Stadium from 20,000 to 40,000 seats—was on the property owners of Minneapolis. The lesson there: initial cost estimates usually fall short.

Third, although the ballpark was located in the new suburbs and supposedly placed there to be in proximity to St. Paul, it was the citizens and city council of Minneapolis who would end up taking the risk on pro sports. A precedent was set: when in doubt, major-league sports stadium financing has generally looked to Minneapolis for aid.

Principles

Hugh Barber is the unsung hero of Minnesota stadium history. Johnson, Moore, and McGrew, auto dealer and Chamber of Commerce activist Bill Boyer, newspaper publisher John Cowles Sr., Donald and Kenneth Dayton, of the department store, and young businessmen Wheelock Whitney and Gordon Ritz were in the middle of the struggle, and often in the middle of the press clippings. But Barber was the brains and the soul of the deal. He brought values to the discussion with his principles of what a stadium was to be all about.

Known as a quiet man in the offices of what was then called Dorsey, Coleman, Barker, Scott and Barber—known today as Dorsey & Whitney, Minneapolis's largest law firm—Barber was the head of the firm's municipal bond department. It was a legal category that wasn't so lucrative in the 1950s, certainly not in the Midwestern hinterlands. The nation's top bond attorneys were in New York, or maybe Chicago. The revenue bond concept—having an enterprise pay for itself via the revenues it generated—was in its infancy, said Tim Brown, a former colleague of Barber's and, coincidentally, Barber's son-in-law. "The revenue bond hadn't been done for a private enterprise before," Brown explained. "Hugh had a different view."

Barber's view was that a stadium served a public purpose. Thus, tax-exempt revenue bonds to fund a ballpark were for the public good, not for the private benefit of the tenants of the ballpark. Brown remembers Yale-educated Barber having repeated arguments with some local business leaders. "Hugh used to try to convince them that this was truly a public purpose," Brown recalled. "But there were many people who felt it wasn't proper. Most people were saying, 'I run my own business. Who's going to be the deep pockets if this team fails?'"[12]

Barber, in his mid-sixties during the period of trying to get a big-league team, tried to convince his high-level associates that the New York Giants were a sure thing to be moving to the Twin Cities and that a proposed stadium was a safe bet. Barber visited New York and later Washington as the Senators seemed to be on the line to move to Minnesota. And Brown said, "He'd come back jubilant, thinking he had a deal. Then, days later, I'd see him with his head in his hands." Either Stoneham or Senators owner Calvin Griffith became less certain of their intentions or reneged on verbal promises.

No matter, Barber's concepts in the 1950s were elegant in their simplicity. He believed that the public needed to be protected from the idiosyncrasies of major-league sports even as that same public needed to build a facility that would attract a big-league team. In a sense, the stadium in Barber's vision was a totally public space, existing for the pleasure of the community. The teams were to be users and tenants of "our" building.

Perhaps we can understand his thinking best in an August 19, 1957, memo that he wrote to the members of the Sports Area Commission, apparently to guide them in negotiations with, he thought, the New York Giants. In it, he detailed some notions that have carried through to today. For instance, a contract between the community and a team shouldn't be called "a lease" but rather be called "a playing agreement." He believed that this would "fortify the tax-exempt status of the properties."

He emphasized that the Sports Area Commission "is an official public body which acts as a representative" of the public, especially the municipalities that appointed members to it. He was exacting in defining which part of the new Metropolitan Stadium could and should be used by a team owner and those areas from which "the Club Owner is completely excluded." He emphasized "the need to use the Sports Area for events other than baseball, thus maintaining the public ownership and public use concept."[13]

Barber also believed that the public should be a partner with the club owner. Unlike the economic paradigm of the late 1990s, in which teams control virtually all the revenues of a stadium, the 1950s view was that the public—which owned the stadium—should be in the driver's seat. For instance, Barber proposed a ticket tax, a user fee. He proposed that the Sports Area Commission share in team concessions revenues. He proposed that parking income should be controlled by the commission. More presciently, he believed that television revenues should be split between the public and the team, an idea whose time still hasn't come. In 1957, Barber, as if gazing into a crystal ball, wrote: "The Commission should be allowed a suitable share of income from any pay-as-you-view television if that comes into use, the Commission's share being designed to offset its resulting losses from lowered attendance." How brilliant. To protect the public's investment in the stadium, Barber wanted the stadium commission to be protected against the rise of television, and he also wanted the commission to benefit from its rise.

Beyond conceptually divvying up the cash, he wanted to make one thing perfectly clear: "The Commission's net income from baseball cannot be less than 36 cents net per patron, including the 13 cents anticipated from parking. Less than this will not service the bonds." That's thirteen pennies from parking. In the ongoing stadium discussion of 1999 and 2000, the Vikings football team has talked about how some NFL teams expect $13 per car, as in dollars, not cents.

Barber's memo, with the public's protection always in mind, was delivered to the commission on an odd day. Stoneham, who had offhandedly promised that he would move his team to Minneapolis, announced on August 18, 1957, a day before Barber's memo is dated, that he was moving to San Francisco. Stoneham uttered the classically snide owner's relocation statement: "We're sorry to disappoint the kids of New York, but we didn't see many of their parents out there at the Polo Grounds in recent years."[14] Still, the beauty of Barber's principles is that they applied to any potential tenant.

Barber set the foundation for the relationship between public agencies, the taxpayers, the teams, and the facility. He sought to take from the teams what was necessary to pay for the stadium, the public's stadium. The philosophy behind the relationship—embodied in that "playing agreement" between "the public" and a team—is at the heart of a community's ability to devise strategies to lure and retain franchises to this day.

Our Stadium

If Hugh Barber was the theorist, then Gunnar Rovick was the leading practitioner. He was the chief salesman for Metropolitan Stadium bonds. He was a key member of the Minute Men, a group of 160 men—all white, Rovick remembers—who were formed to sell the bonds for the Bloomington ballpark. He was the top cheerleader in an effort that if undertaken today could only be described as "community ownership." While Barber intellectually and legally framed the debate, the grassroots community got on board to raise the necessary money to build the stadium.

Let's try to put this in a modern context. During stadium debates in Minnesota that would follow Barber, McGrew, Johnson, Moore, and Rovick in the 1970s (over the Metrodome) and in the 1990s (over a potential new Twins ballpark), critics looked toward the idea of "community ownership" of the local baseball team. There was consistent aversion to public funding for the facilities. The idea was that a stadium is a depreciating asset while teams are appreciating assets.

The attitude in 1954 was different. It was so because there was a social cause, a collective community understanding that the stadium would be a vehicle for other things: for national recognition, for metropolitan imagery, for getting a place on the major-league map. "There was no benefit to buy a bond," said Rovick. "It was all civic pride."[15]

Rovick was an advertising salesman for the *Star* and the *Tribune*, a man with a direct link to John Cowles Sr. only because of his middle-level administrative position at the newspaper. Rovick knew a lot of folks in town and, as an ad man for the largest newspaper, could put a bit of pressure on customers to buy $500 bonds for the new stadium effort.

The Minute Men divided themselves into sales "teams," giving themselves the names of the existing major-league squads. Rovick, for instance, was on the "Cleveland Indians" sales team, wearing an Indians hat whenever he went calling to sell bonds. The financial instruments yielded that paltry 2 percent interest, and as it turned out, for the first few years of the new stadium, when there was no big-league team there, the interest wasn't even paid. There was also the attached promise that bond buyers would get priority seating at games of the major-league team that was sure to come as a result of the new stadium's existence. But that never happened, either. "That was the big lie," said Rovick with a chuckle. "I was putting the arm on everybody to buy the bonds and saying, 'You're going to get priority seating, too.' When you're selling something like that, once in a while you fabricate."

One thing was genuine: the basic commitment by Minnesotans to bring major-league sports to the state. For instance, Rovick said, he'd go into a restaurant or a bar and sell bonds to groups of employees who would pool their money for one $500 bond. (By the way, that's about

$3,000 in 1999 dollars.) "We were selling $500 bonds to waitresses, bartenders, to people who couldn't really afford it, but they felt civically and economically that it couldn't do anything but enhance the image of Minneapolis. They knew we had to get a stadium built first." It was a social movement.

An examination of the list of bond buyers—a total of 2,600—supports Rovick's recollections. Unions bought bonds. Jo and Ann's Café bought a bond. Hansford Pontiac Co. bought a bond. Fisher Nut Co. bought a bond. Danny's Bar, Mazey Florists, St. Anthony Pharmacy, Sirmai's Budapest Tavern, and hundreds of folks named Schrandt and Pikovsky, Nystrom and Miskowiec, Lundeen and Lifson. Putting their money where their mouth was, Hugh Barber and Charles Johnson were also listed as bond buyers.[16]

The attitudes of fans and nonfans alike toward pro sports have changed drastically from 1952 to 2000. The dynamics of players' salaries, owners' wealth, and demands on citizens to subsidize stadiums that cost $350 million, not $4.5 millon, have altered the relationships between athletes, leagues, teams, and consumers. But let's not forget that the first phase of the first major-league stadium in Minnesota was built primarily with cash from the pockets of ordinary citizens. The waitresses and bartenders, the auto dealers and flower shops, were willing to pay to acquire a vehicle for civic identity. What a concept.

Selling the Game

As they sold the idea, they also sold the dream. The Minneapolis baseball committee hired Market Facts, Inc., of Chicago to develop a database to show prospective stadium bond buyers that Minneapolis–St. Paul was just as fit to support a major-league baseball team as Milwaukee and Baltimore, which had just landed their big-league teams. There is almost a defiance in the prose of the prospectus that shouts, "Damn it, if Milwaukee can get a team, well, then, we should get ours, too!"

For one, the Millers and Saints together consistently outdrew the minor-league Brewers almost two to one. Second, the Twin Cities' so-called "trading area," stretching into North and South Dakota, Iowa, and western Wisconsin, comprised nearly twice as many people as Milwaukee's. There was a keeping-up-with-the-Joneses attitude in the prospectus, with a section noting that Milwaukee, Baltimore, and Kansas City got their teams by building new facilities. "No one will make a definite commitment until the Twin Cities have stadium facilities available," the prospectus read.

Tone aside, the fundamental information that Market Facts gathered in late 1953 and synthesized can actually apply to the Twin Cities sports market today. For one, the company concluded that the Twin Cities is a better baseball market than Milwaukee and could surely match the first-year success of the Braves, who drew 1.8 million fans. More succinctly, the marketing company concluded that baseball attendance can be predicted based on five key facts: the so-called natural trading area, that is, the health of the regional economy; team standing, or how much it wins; the closeness of the league's pennant race, or how balanced the competition in a league is; spectacular or colorful players on a team, that is, stars; and skillful promotion, that is, the creative marketing of the franchise; "and other variables." Do not pinch yourself. Clearly these criteria apply to any major-league team no matter when, no matter where. And they apply today as the current major-league team, the Twins, languishes in a competitive public relations morass.

During the latter years of the 1990s, the Twins' fundamentals ran counter to the vision of that Chicago marketing firm's guidelines, save for one: the health of the so-called trading area remained strong. Otherwise, the team's standing was inevitably low; there was faint hope that the team could compete in the standings; there were no stars; there was limited promotion or marketing; and as for the "other variables," the owner was mistrusted and the stadium in which the team played, the Metrodome, was generally trashed as a poor venue.

But back in 1954 those guidelines buoyed boosters of major-league baseball, who believed the Twin Cities would support a team, and likely an existing team, not an expansion team. If such variables existed and if a stadium was in place, Minnesota's big-league team would succeed, the study suggested. It might do well for current and future baseball team owners in the Twin Cities to dust off that pioneering market research today and restudy it.

St. Paul Won't Give Up

As the Minneapolis civic steamroller seemed to push inexorably toward a team, St. Paul refused to concede. On the strength of the $2 million approval from city voters in 1953, Walter G. Seeger continued to advocate a Midway-area stadium, at the southeast corner of Snelling Avenue and what is now Energy Park Drive. Seeger, who led a committee appointed by St. Paul mayor Joseph E. Dillon, believed that St. Paul should be the major-league city, not Minneapolis or its suburbs. And on July 1, 1954, a few months before Rovick and the Minute Men kicked off their campaign—but on the very day that it was reported that Minneapolis would issue the revenue bonds to finance the Bloomington ballpark—Dillon declared that "under no circumstances" would his city support the suburban stadium idea.

A year passed, but the sibling spatting did not. On August 10, 1955, just six weeks after ground was broken in Bloomington for what was to become Metropolitan Stadium, the St. Paul committee produced a glossy, seventeen-by-eleven-inch brochure heralding the construction of the new Midway Stadium. More than a boring, numbers-filled prospectus—as was the offer for Met Stadium bonds—this was a relatively lavish marketing tool. Whereas the Minneapolis prospectus was an obviously low-key sales effort, the Seeger pamphlet had life and vision, with colorful maps showing just how close the Midway area was to both downtowns and how vibrant a stadium this twelve-thousand-seat beginning could become. On its green-and-white cover was a drawing of a batter following through with his right-handed swing. To his left was a drawing of the Minneapolis downtown, with the Foshay Tower dominating. On the right, equidistant from the player, was downtown St. Paul, with the First National Bank of St. Paul building controlling the upper atmosphere. The player was standing smack-dab in the middle of the two cities, with no acknowledgment that there was any Twin Cities development anywhere outside of the cities' limits. "Midway Stadium, a modern sports center in the heart of the Twin Cities," read the brochure's cover. "The finest municipal stadium in America and an invitation to Major League Baseball."[17]

The stadium was to be sited on ninety-three acres, amid the railroad tracks of the Midway, with four off-street parking lots that could accommodate as many as 9,300 automobiles. "From the standpoint of encouraging attendance at major league baseball games by making a stadium convenient to the largest population, the corporate cities of Saint Paul and Minneapolis must be considered as one highly populated metropolitan area," the brochure said. Using the courthouses in both cities, the claim was that Midway would be just 4.5 miles away from each downtown. It was pitched as especially convenient for visitors who arrive by train or bus at downtown depots. "For people dependent upon public transportation it's important that the stadium be easily reached by regular bus lines." With no mention of the potential Bloomington stadium in their brochure, the St. Paulites wrote, "Vision ... added to present action ... places Saint Paul in an ideal position to work with others in developing Major League Baseball for the Twin Cities and area."

As for funding, the attitude and concept were clear. This ballpark was to be built to make this city as good as every other city. "By not asking for private capital or contributions to build a stadium, Saint Paul is right in line with the thinking that it is best to have stadiums owned by municipalities—as are the stadiums in Milwaukee, Kansas City, Baltimore, Cleveland and other cities."

Apparently, St. Paul's mayor, the Chamber of Commerce, and the unions had agreed to support methods to finance expansion of Midway if a big-league team were to move there. But it was all a pipe dream. A building may have been on tap, but St. Paul had developed no solid relationships with big-league owners.

"Minneapolis and St. Paul hated each other in those days," said Gunnar Rovick, who led Minneapolis's bond effort. "Everyone was trying to outdo the other. We knew they were building their own stadium. But it was kind of ha-ha-ha. We knew it was a little dinky stadium."

The rivalry that had begun one hundred years earlier would be solidified—not reduced—by the location of the new cultural asset known as major-league sports. As time wore on, the rivalry would rear its ugly head again. In the 1960s, when an arena was built in Bloomington near Metropolitan Stadium, St. Paul couldn't stand it and built its own arena. In the 1970s, when a new stadium was proposed to replace the twenty-year-old Met Stadium, St. Paul forces tried to block Minneapolis's aspirations to bring the sports teams into downtown Minneapolis. And in the 1990s, St. Paul, attempting to assert itself once more, built an unnecessary new hockey arena to compete with Minneapolis's Target Center. In 1999, St. Paul mayor Norm Coleman sought to lure the Twins from Minneapolis. His tactic was to bash the bigger city to the west. To this day, our two distinct cities continue to engage in a bifurcated sports facilities policy that disserves the public.

Getting the Team

By April 1955, the Minute Men had sold $2.2 million in bonds to individuals and businesses in the Twin Cities. As it turned out, various investment firms reneged on an earlier agreement and sold only $1 million worth of so-called Series A bonds. Within a month, 164 acres of land in Bloomington were purchased for $478,899, or $2,900 per acre. (Eventually, that same area of land was sold in two parcels—in 1984 and 1998—for a total of $40 million, or about $244,000 per acre.) With the first of the bonds sold, the heavy lifting began. The stadium had to be built, and the major-league team that would justify the construction had to be acquired.

Once dirt was turned for what would become Metropolitan Stadium, or the Met, the Twin Cities became the sitting ducks for any and all team owners who wanted to make nice-nice, but not a real commitment. (Minnesota in the fifties was what Tampa–St. Petersburg was in the eighties and what Charlotte is in the nineties: "option cities" for owners to use as leverage against their hometown political and business leaders and fans.) New York's Stoneham, with his familiarity with the Twin Cities, was the biggest philanderer of them all. Barely a month after Met Stadium opened in 1956, with the Triple-A Millers now using it as their home field, Stoneham declared publicly for the first time—but more than two years after his drunken exchange with George Brophy—that "he was considering moving the New York Giants to Minneapolis."[18] Stoneham's comments came a month after St. Paul's boosters broke ground on their own stadium, and guess who was there to oversee the ceremony? A fellow named Walter O'Malley, owner of the Brooklyn Dodgers; the Saints were the Dodgers' Class AAA team. Indeed, through the strange machinations to come, it would be O'Malley, as much as Stoneham, who would play a central role in a major-league baseball team coming to the Twin Cities.

Local newspapers reflected an air of confidence that it was only a matter of time before Stoneham made the move. Minneapolis business-man Robert Dayton, who would later be a central figure in the efforts to get a new stadium built in the 1990s, remembers his father, Donald, the chief executive officer of Dayton's department store, coming home one night after lengthy discussions with Stoneham and telling his little boy that the deal was so close they were "negotiating the price of the pop-corn."[19] Later, Stoneham admitted the Twin Cities was his first choice. "I had intended to move the Giants out of New York even before I knew Mr. O'Malley was intending to move.... I had intended to go to Min-neapolis," he said.[20]

But by the fall of 1956, at the end of Met Stadium's first season, O'Malley had visions of moving his team to Los Angeles and of bringing Stoneham's Giants to California with the Dodgers. Curiously, almost laughably, a man named Calvin Griffith was in the middle of it all, too. During the 1956 World Series, Los Angeles officials made initial over-tures to Griffith, whose Washington Senators team was always financially struggling, to move his franchise to the West Coast. "Los Angeles Sena-tors. Sounds pretty good to me," is what Griffith reportedly said. But O'Malley intervened and told Los Angeles leaders to consider him, not Griffith.[21] The rest, as they say, is history. And painful history, at that, for Twin Cities boosters, who would learn that major-league owners are difficult to predict. After all, just months later, Griffith vowed never to move the Senators from Washington. "This is my home," he said of Washington, D.C. "I intend that it shall remain my home for the rest of my life ... Forever."[22]

By spring training in 1957, the Dodgers' O'Malley and the Giants' Stoneham were in an emerging conspiracy, hatched by O'Malley, who didn't want to go to California alone and hoped to leverage the emerging Los Angeles and San Francisco television markets—perhaps even pay TV—and the craving for teams. What followed was the setting of the market rate for attracting a team, which raised the bar for the Twin Cities, and a flurry of activity that reflected the white-hot change going on in pro sports during this period. It was as if major-league sports, so small, so simple for so long, was in an incubator, growing and maturing. And Minnesota, which felt it had responded by merely building a stadium, now had to respond in different ways. By the spring of 1957, the Twin Cities were scrambling for credibility. Having a ballpark wasn't enough.

A negative economic indicator darkened the Minnesota sports scene. The National Basketball Association Lakers were facing bankruptcy. A series of fund-raising appeals were published in the newspapers to raise $200,000 to keep the team in Minneapolis. How could a city support major-league baseball if it couldn't support a relatively minor NBA team? Again, *Star* and *Tribune* sports editor Charles Johnson was in the middle of the effort, cochairing the committee that was formed for the task.

As Johnson juggled keeping and attracting teams, Stoneham was playing games. Even as he and O'Malley were forming a pact, he was still leading the Twin Cities on. The minutes from the Sports Area Commission would be comical if Stoneham hadn't been so deceptive, or so unable to deliver bad news. Stoneham wasn't known to be sinister, but just someone who was eager to get along with anybody willing to down a Scotch or two with him, as Moore was highy qualified to do.

"Chairman Moore called upon Co-Chairman Boyer to report on his April 28, 1957, meeting together with Donald Dayton and Horace C. Stoneham in New York. Mr. Boyer stated that Mr. Stoneham was most receptive and expressed deep interest in moving his Club to the Metropolitan Stadium. Terms were discussed in considerable detail with both sides presenting comprehensively what was needed to consummate a satisfactory transaction. Mr. Boyer stated a strenuous effort was made in their presentation with an effort to secure an immediate affirmative commitment from Mr. Stoneham. Mr. Stoneham stated he would contact the negotiators at a later date."[23]

He never did. He just moved to San Francisco. What's so comical is that Boyer's report was made at the Sports Area Commission meeting of June 6, 1957, a full eleven days after Stoneham made it known he had plans to move to San Francisco. (As an aside and as an example of the creative measures used at the time to lure and retain teams, on the same day, a plan was floated in New York to convince Stoneham not to move. The idea was to sell the Giants to the public, via stock, and then build a new publicly funded stadium. Obviously, it never got off the ground. The concept is still, today, ahead of its time.)[24]

On May 27, 1957, United Press, then a dominant news service, reported that the Dodgers on that day would announce their move to Los Angeles, with the Giants heading to San Francisco and the Cincinnati Reds to New York. (Shades of the Stoneham revelation to Brophy three years earlier!) Johnson, the sports editor cum civic booster, expressed intense skepticism at the report in a story displayed next to it in that afternoon's *Star*. Under the headline "Shifts Now Just Don't Make Sense," Johnson wrote, "Today's reports sound too fantastic to merit much serious consideration in any quarter."[25] Clearly he and his cohorts had been blindsided by Stoneham. A day later, two things occurred: the Cincinnati Chamber of Commerce set up a committee to look into a new stadium to replace aging Crosley Field, and Johnson wrote that a "wild-eyed fairy tale concocted by a New York newspaperman" was all that the Dodgers-Giants move story was about. By now, Johnson was out of touch with what was true.[26]

By May 29, in a front-page story, Johnson had come to grips with the reality of it all, but he still called the entire Dodgers-Giants move announcement "a poker game" and angrily blamed O'Malley for corrupting Stoneham.[27] Meanwhile Johnson's usually more circumspect colleague Dick Cullum wrote that the dramatic relocation talk was all a ploy and that, in the long run, Stoneham would still bring the Giants to Minneapolis. "Perhaps yesterday's meetings changed the odds slightly, but it remains a good betting proposition that Uncle Horace will make the right guess" and move to the Twin Cities rather than San Francisco, Cullum wrote, where the "unfavorable summer weather" made the Bay Area "not a well-chosen place."[28]

But a day later, Johnson was steaming mad. Remember, this is the fellow who had been, and would continue to be, the best-known member of the Twin Cities delegation attempting to lure a team to Met Stadium, a man who put his reputation on the line to get the stadium built and had been implying, if not promising, that if they built the stadium, a team would come posthaste. "Professional baseball is staggering around in confusion and bewilderment right now with no one leader to carry the ball," Johnson wrote. "Only once before in the history of the game has this sport found itself in such a bad way. That was after the famous Black Sox scandal in 1919," he said, referring to the World Series fix by Chicago White Sox players. Johnson railed on that the owners had stripped commissioner Ford Frick of any power. "Every club owner runs wild. More important, there is no direction nor leadership in any phase of the sport." In a final lashing, he wrote, "Baseball is suffering plenty all over the country because of Walter O'Malley's activities."

By August, the deed was done. The Giants board of directors decided to move to San Francisco, and Stoneham, who had at one point been talking popcorn prices in Minneapolis, was opining, "As far as I'm concerned, next to New York, San Francisco is the only city in the United States." And no wonder. As part of his deal, the city of San Francisco agreed to build a 40,000- to 45,000-seat ballpark. All the concessions money would go to the team. Rent would be capped at 5 percent of net receipts, considered a great deal. The team would operate the stadium for all other events. The only innovative public-protection clause was that the lease was to run for thirty-five years; in the cases of Milwaukee, Kansas City, and Baltimore, when teams moved a few years earlier, three-year leases were the standard. Now Johnson, knowing how good an arrangement Stoneham received, began to criticize San Francisco for its irresponsible subsidy. "We'll have to agree with Stoneham when he told Minneapolis a short time back the San Francisco offer was too fabulous to ask any rival bidder to consider.... Throw in a minimum of $1,000,000 guaranteed by pay-TV people, or someone, to the Giants and baseball has put over one of the greatest 'steals' in the history of the sport."[29]

Still, for all his bitterness, Johnson possessed a strain of common sense that was distinctly Minnesotan. Hugh Barber must have gotten to him. Because on August 21, 1957, in his final statement about the Giants move, Johnson wrote: "We have contended for years that when any city has to subsidize baseball teams to the point where unreasonable demands are placed on the public, the sport suffers as much as the donors."[30] The booster journalist was coming of age. He was realizing that it was going to be harder to get a team than he had imagined. But he and his gang of boosters wouldn't quit.

Months after the Giants' move, there was another brief encounter, this time with the Cleveland Indians, whose ownership group included I. A. O'Shaughnessy, of St. Paul. Because of connections to *Minneapolis Tribune* columnist Sid Hartman, Johnson's protégé, negotiations began to bring the Indians to the new Bloomington stadium. To sweeten the talks, *Star* and *Tribune* owner John Cowles Sr. ordered that an especially favorable article on O'Shaughnessy be rushed into print in the newspaper's Sunday magazine to butter up the Cleveland owner.[31] Legal realities tied to the Indians' lease in Cleveland blocked any serious move discussions.

Minnesota was beginning to look foolish. Every team was using the Twin Cities as leverage in its home city or with other fresh-faced new markets competing with the Twin Cities. The last man to engage in such a strategy was Calvin Griffith, owner of the perennially last-place and money-losing Washington Senators, who was wooed by Los Angeles and lost out to O'Malley. Griffith inherited the Senators from his uncle, Clark Griffith, in 1955. Minnesota, punched by Stoneham and jabbed by Cleveland, picked itself up, dusted itself off, and started all over again.

Rovick, the Minute Men bond salesman, actually remembers how Griffith was introduced into the Minnesota effort. One day, Rovick's boss was out of town, so as the assistant classified ad manager of the *Star* and the *Tribune*, Rovick attended the weekly managers' meeting. There sat John Cowles Sr., the owner of the paper, and Joyce Swan, the publisher, both pro sports proponents. Sometime in 1957, Cowles sent Johnson to

Washington to meet with Griffith, who had been making noise about wanting to move his Senators. Johnson previously met with Griffith and his uncle Clark, just before the elder died.

As Rovick recalls, "John Senior said, 'Charlie, tell me about this man Griffith. Give me some background.'"

Johnson replied curtly: "John, the only thing I can tell you is he's a nice, dumb man."

As intellectually challenged as Johnson might have thought Griffith to be, the Senators' owner sure held his own with the Minnesotans. Indeed, he would toy with Minneapolis officials and, for that matter, with his fellow American League owners for two more years. He would let Moore come to Washington and watch games with him behind the Senators' dugout, but Griffith never let on to Washingtonians that he planned to move.

"Jerry Moore used to come to Washington, seemed four or five times a year," Griffith remembered. "I used to introduce him as Mr. Black or Mr. Brown or Mr. White. I didn't want to identify him as Jerry Moore from Minnesota."

But Griffith had plans. And others had plans for him. In December 1957, with the Giants moving west, the Boston Red Sox took over the Minneapolis Millers. Sports Area Commission lawyer Peter Dorsey negotiated with Red Sox general manager Joe Cronin over the details of the Met Stadium lease, an exercise that should have been easy enough. Curiously, though, Cronin had a request: he wanted to include a major-league option in the lease for the Red Sox. "At the time, I didn't know why he'd want that," Dorsey remembered more than forty years later in his downtown Minneapolis office. "The Red Sox sure weren't going anywhere." But soon afterward Griffith contacted Dorsey. Cronin was his brother-in-law and, it seemed, was reserving the Met for the Senators, not for the Red Sox.

By July 7, 1958, Griffith even asked his fellow American League owners to allow him to move, but they told him to keep mum, for gosh sakes; the U.S. Senate was conducting hearings into baseball's antitrust exemption, and now was not the time to be relocating a team from the nation's capital. Two days later, Griffith testified—presumably honestly—before the committee and vowed that he'd never leave the capital, saying he'd stay as long "as is humanly possible."[32]

South Dakota senator Karl Mundt was especially outspoken, saying that owners had better "respect the public in considering shifts of franchises." Mundt's concern for the fans triggered a frontal assault in the *Minneapolis Tribune* by Dick Cullum. Mundt should be more sympathetic to the Twin Cities' needs, given his state's proximity, Cullum suggested. "Who is to decide when an owner is free of his obligation to a given public? And why is one public more entitled to respect than another? Why are the Washington public and the Cleveland public, which have major league baseball but do not want it much, more entitled to respect than the Minneapolis public and the Houston public, which do not have it but want it? . . . We think we have a pretty respectable public in Minneapolis." All this reads like the words of a poor little defenseless Minnesotan. They resonated even at the end of the 1990s, when the Twin Cities were a region trying to keep teams, not lure them from elsewhere.

Two weeks after telling real senators he'd never move his baseball Senators and after Cullum's diatribe, Griffith made his first visit to Minnesota. His team faced the Philadelphia Phillies in an exhibition game at Met Stadium promoted by the usual suspects—Jerry Moore, Norm McGrew, Charlie Johnson, the Minute Men, and stadium manager Chet Roan. For two straight days, Johnson sucked up big-time to Griffith. He defended Griffith against the slings and arrows of the Washington, D.C., press corps. He defended Griffith as only doing what others—such as O'Malley and Stoneham—had done. Johnson wrote: "We welcome Calvin Griffith and his family to Minnesota today. They can rest assured that out here in the Upper Midwest they'll find people who are a little more fair minded in the treatment of fellow humans than in some other places in the nation."[33]

The push was on. The boosters could taste it. Griffith was the one. A major-league team for Minnesota was just around the corner.

CHAPTER 2

Something to Cheer For

The Met Welcomes the Vikings and the Twins

There was more work to do on the stadium. The general public—not just its civic-minded members—would have to pay this time. With no team on the foreseeable horizon, and with professional football beginning to add teams, a decision was made to expand Met Stadium beyond its 20,000 seats to about 40,000. That initial bond issuance of $4.5 million just wasn't enough. Jerry Moore of the Chamber of Commerce, also with the Downtown Council, and also chairman of the Metropolitan Sports Area Commission, went calling on the Minneapolis City Council. He needed more dough to fix the stadium. Now it was 1958. Moore and Metropolitan Stadium's manager Chet Roan were intensifying their relationship with Griffith. Again, they thought they had an owner poised to move to the Twin Cities, perhaps as soon as the 1959 season.

But first Moore needed that stadium expansion. Only the city of Minneapolis could raise the necessary funds to pay for it. And it was a lot. Moore and the other boosters wanted the city to stick its neck out for a total of $9 million. That total would include buying out the 2,600 people and businesses who had purchased the original "civic bonds" for the initial construction of the Met. But $5.75 million of the new bonds that Moore was seeking wouldn't be revenue bonds that were backed by the cash flowing into the stadium. These would be good, old-fashioned general-obligation bonds; that is, bonds that, if they failed, would be guaranteed by the city of Minneapolis's taxpayers via their property taxes.

Thus, in August 1958, the first true pro sports subsidy by the government came into play. It wasn't pretty. A particularly ugly side of it emerged from the newsroom of the *Minneapolis Tribune*, owned by John Cowles Sr., who was backing the baseball push. Also, remember that Charlie Johnson, who supervised the sports sections of both the morning *Tribune* and afternoon *Star*, was an integral member of the inner circle and the mentor of the *Tribune*'s increasingly influential number two columnist, Sid Hartman.

At the Board of Estimate and Taxation's August 27, 1958, meeting, city council member Byron Nelson, a stalking horse for the boosters, said that if the stadium was expanded and the general-obligation bonds issued, then it was "a dead cinch" that the Senators would immediately move to Met Stadium. In fact, the Senators board of directors was set to meet the next day. Minneapolis mayor P. Kenneth Peterson claimed that approval of the bond deal and the relocation of the Senators were "to be as simultaneous as possible."

But the fact was that some key investors in the stadium, including leading Twin Cities businesses, weren't willing to risk more money for the Met's expansion. The projections suggested that the revenues into the stadium could support the new bond debt—assuming a big-league team was playing in the stadium—but who knew? Moore, Johnson, and the other baseball committee members figured it was time for the city's property tax payers to take the risk. The law allowed it, but the circumstances were mind-boggling: the boosters were expanding a stadium in Bloomington using the full faith and credit of the city of Minneapolis as backing. Woe betide anyone who would suggest such an arrangement today.

Here's where it gets ugly. Frank Wright, the city hall reporter for the *Tribune*, wrote a long and detailed story about the tax implications of the stadium expansion plan and how city taxpayers could be on the hook. And when the early edition of the *Tribune*, called the "Blue Streak," hit the streets about 7 P.M.—and was placed on trains to get to North and South Dakota by the next morning—its readers learned of the tax liabilities that city residents might face.

Hartman, who has worked sixteen hours a day his entire life and was in the office, saw the "Blue Streak" story and, according to Wright, panicked. Hartman called the executive editor, Bill Steven, the man in charge of both papers at the time, and said the story had to be killed. Hartman's reasoning: if the public ever found out they might be liable for millions in taxes for the ballpark, they would rise in anger, descend on the council, kill the deal, and end chances for major-league baseball forever and ever. Steven bought the argument. He ordered the news desk to cleanse the story in later editions of every reference to the prospect that taxpayers might have to pay for the stadium. The news desk followed his order.

Orwellian though it may be, the "Blue Streak" editions—because they were essentially rough drafts of the next day's newspaper—weren't retained in the *Star* and the *Tribune*'s microfilm archives. All that remains is the final-edition story, which did run on page 1 of the August 28, 1958, *Tribune*. And in Wright's twenty-one-paragraph story—at least the one for history—it isn't until the nineteenth paragraph that there's even a mention that the city would guarantee $5.75 million of the debt. (By the way, $5.75 million in 1958 would be worth $32.1 million in 1999, a substantial amount of municipal debt.)

An editor inserted in the next-to-last paragraph—on the so-called "jump," or continuation, page, buried next to a children's shoe store advertisement—that should the stadium revenues be insufficient to cover bond debt service, "property taxes would be used to pay the balance. City officials and baseball backers regard that as a highly remote possibility."

Wright woke up the next morning, saw how his story had been butchered, and went ballistic. "You can imagine the furor in the newsroom the next morning," he said in an interview. "The managing editor, news editor, city editor, my assistant city editor, and I, none of whom had been consulted by Steven, descended on him. It was a testy session, to say the least. Two things came out of it. One, at one point the executive editor said something that still rings in my ears: 'Sometimes you have to decide whether you want a news story or a major-league baseball team.' And, two, in the end, he acquiesced in our insistence that we had to cover the story fully." Wright, who went on to become the *Tribune*'s managing editor during the years the Metrodome was being built, added, "Thereafter,

I had no problems in covering the story fully, including the inclusion of the tax backup. The public did not rise up. The deal went through."

In the days between the Board of Estimate and Taxation's initial vote and the city council's final approval, the pressure intensified. *Tribune* columnist Dick Cullum wrote that he understood that many Minnesotans didn't want to contribute to a stadium that would be inhabited by the generally awful Senators, "first in war, first in peace and last in the American League," as the slogan went. But, Cullum went on, "Other cities are planning stadiums. We are in a period when a new wave of civic building is starting, both stadiums and arenas. Many cities have approved or are about to vote on huge bond issues for these purposes.... Some say, 'Let's be choosey.' A better idea might be to take advantage of our favorable position while we still have it. Get the team here; then, by strong support, help it gain strength and move up in the race."[1]

Meanwhile, Griffith was playing all his cards. The matter turned political and presidential. As the city council was deliberating, Peter Dorsey, the lawyer for the Sports Area Commission, was sending a proposed Met Stadium lease agreement to Griffith. In two weeks, the American League was set to meet, ostensibly to discuss Griffith's plans. With his team struggling at the gate in Washington—they hadn't attracted 500,000 fans per season for four straight seasons—and his entire net worth tied up in the team, he was seeking relief somewhere, anywhere. But as in most sports business decisions, Griffith's wasn't being made in a vacuum. The Senators were the team in the nation's capital, and on the day Dorsey was mailing his proposed contract to Griffith, President Dwight Eisenhower urged the team to stay. But he added, "I think they should have a little better club." He also noted that since he didn't have to pay to get into games, he couldn't financially aid the team.[2] More impressive, members of Congress again made noises that the departure of a team from Washington, D.C.—the movement of the national pastime from the nation's capital—could mean an inquiry into baseball's antitrust exemption, which dated back to 1922. That exemption allowed baseball's owners to limit the movement of players and franchises. The owners, by use of the "reserve clause" in player contracts, could control how long they kept players on their rosters. This was obviously before "free agency." And with the Supreme Court's continuous permission, owners could ban teams from moving from one city to another or, on the other hand, vote as a group to allow teams to move.

What annoyed some members of Congress was that Griffith and the Minnesotans were conducting business while Congress wasn't in session. The most outspoken pol was Representative Emanuel Celler of New York, who happened to be the chairman of the House Antitrust Subcommittee. He was still stinging from the Dodgers and Giants moves to California.

With all that going on, the Minneapolis City Council went on to pass the resolution to sell the bonds and make most of them general-obligation in nature. But they placed a sunset date on the sale. If there was no major-league team in hand by January 1, 1959, just four months down the road, the bonds wouldn't be issued, and the ballpark's expansion wouldn't take place. There was wisdom in that.

A week later, with Minneapolis baseball backers assembled at Chicago's Edgewater Beach Hotel for the American League owners' meetings, Griffith announced he wasn't going to move to Minnesota, that he believed his roots were still in Washington. While he felt his situation at Griffith Stadium meant he'd have to move by 1961, he was going to stay put despite a promise on the Minnesotans part that they would guarantee him 750,000 fans in attendance for at least his first three seasons at Met Stadium. Some minor shareholders in the Senators also sued Griffith over the potential move. And the powerful Yankees seemed to be opposed to the relocation.

Still, Griffith's decision to stay put signaled erraticism, not logic. In the first indication that they were fed up with the entire process and no longer willing to simply suck up to baseball, the Minneapolis booster group struck back: it formally withdrew any proposals it had made to the Senators owner. The boosters made their announcement via a press release that was written by Johnson and first reported by Hartman, Johnson's employee.[3] The next day, Johnson, in his own column, reported that American League officials promised Minnesota the next team available.[4]

Johnson may have wanted to keep the process going, but some Minnesotans were growing tired. The threats and the potential moves were making the community weary, much the same way that stadium threats and alleged relocations angered and created cynicism nearly forty years later during the most recent stadium debate.

"I am as interested as anyone in seeing a major league team in Metropolitan Stadium, but my point is that I wouldn't want Minneapolis classified as a 'sucker,'" wrote W. F. Gilbert of Minneapolis to the *Star* in a feedback letter printed in the "People's Column." "I think we should do a job of 'selling' a team on the advantages of locating in Minneapolis, but not discolor the picture to the extent that the incoming organization loses sight of the fact it must do a job of selling, also.... I hope it never reaches a point here where it becomes our 'civic duty' to support the baseball team because we got down on bended knees and begged them to come."[5]

The Good Fight

The Twin Cities became "a joke." That's how Wheelock Whitney viewed it. Met Stadium, built to attract a team, had been used to gain leverage for teams elsewhere, and the same old minor-league Millers were the home team. Met Stadium was to the 1950s what Tampa–St. Petersburg's domed stadium was to big-league teams in the 1980s: an option that owners used, for ten years, to increase their demands in their home city. "We were being used, that's all," Whitney remembers. For all the team movement from 1953 to 1957, there still had been no expansion, no *new* teams. As swiftly as teams were abandoning multifranchise cities—such as Boston, St. Louis, Philadelphia, and New York—no city with one franchise had seen a team move. There was a shakeout going on, but the owners refused to share their product.

In 1958, Whitney was thirty-two years old, a stockbroker for the J. M. Dain Company, a young man of considerable means who grew up in St. Cloud, attended the Phillips Academy in Andover, Massachusetts, and later Yale University. Beneath his riches, he was—and remains—a wild-eyed sports fan. Barely a rebel, and soon to become a top Twin Cities financial guru, Whitney would begin the first real battle for major-league sports in Minnesota. It is worth noting that before this moment, the powers that be were cozying up to Stoneham or the Cleveland Indians owners or even Griffith or, in the case of football, the American and National Football Leagues' owners. And it might be viewed as a lesson for all stadium debates that making nice with teams and leagues isn't the best way to go. Instead, Whitney joined a group of renegades who were committed to taking on major-league baseball and were even threatening to challenge its precious federal antitrust exemption if it meant new cities could get new teams.

America was growing. And the new regional centers were emerging, be they Minneapolis–St. Paul, Houston, or Denver. These communities wanted teams, too. But baseball's owners, slow on the uptake, didn't want to share any of their monopolistic pie. No one knew that better than Branch Rickey, the fabled baseball executive credited with forming the first "farm system" when he was with the St. Louis Cardinals and then breaking the color barrier when he signed Jackie Robinson for the Brooklyn Dodgers in 1947. Rickey believed that baseball would only truly stand up to its "national pastime" mythology if the game was played in the new cities of the middle part of the country and Canada. "To Rickey, baseball remained a civil religion which acted out public functions organized religion was unable to perform," is how one biographer stated it.[6] Rickey thus began to make plans to begin a third league, dubbed the Continental League, which would include new metropolises and challenge the established big leagues. He was aided in his cause by New York lawyer William Shea, who was outraged that the Dodgers and Giants departed, leaving the nation's biggest city without a National League team. They were men on a mission: Rickey believed that baseball was missing a chance to spread its inherent greatness; Shea believed that New York had been abandoned by a sport that had no soul. Together, they began to organize wealthy potential owners in cities across the country that longed to be major league. Not so coincidentally, Rickey and Shea's campaign was under way at the same time a new professional football league was beginning to build. It was called the American Football League. The energy and notion of new leagues challenging established leagues created a different dynamic for cities to fight for their own status as "major league." If the "major leagues" weren't going to expand—if the established cities weren't going to enlarge the tent—then developing cities and their boosters were going to use their own brushes to paint themselves with the "major-league" label. They were going to turn the tables on the owners and leagues that arrogantly believed they could parcel out civic imagery on their own.

By November 1958, New York mayor Robert Wagner announced that a third baseball league was about to form. Whitney, who was somewhat of a young whippersnapper, read of the fledgling effort. He immediately visited Donald Dayton, who then ran the department store in downtown Minneapolis. Dayton, the man who had discussed popcorn with Stoneham, directed Whitney to Joyce Swan, the publisher of the *Star* and the *Tribune*.

"I said to Swan, 'What do you think?'" Whitney remembers. "And Joyce said, 'I think you ought to go down there and meet Branch Rickey and find out exactly what he's up to. Then, come back and report to Don and me.'"[7]

A sports novice, Whitney picked up the telephone and called Rickey. Rickey, the so-called Mahatma, the most sage executive in all of pro sports, answered from his Manhattan hotel suite. "I told him I was representing the Dayton's store and the newspaper," Whitney remembers. "Mr. Rickey was very warm and welcoming and suggested that I come down to New York."

Rickey, who had forced racial integration onto baseball, was about to take on the game's lords once more. Whitney, the rich kid from Stearns County, was going to go along for the ride, bringing the Twin Cities with him as he challenged the nation's pastime. What developed was a marvelous relationship between a young man whose father had died in 1957 and who may have been in search of a substitute parent figure, and a wise legend who wanted to pass on world of knowledge to a thoughtful go-getter with promise. For Whitney, the personal connection was enduring. For the Twin Cities campaign, the new link to the Continental League meant a midcourse correction in its campaign for a team than can only be described as dramatic and daring. No longer would Minneapolis just wait to get a team. Now Minneapolis was going to link up with other middle-sized markets to force baseball to expand, to push the owners, to rattle the cages of Congress. The coddling was over.

When Whitney met Rickey in the late winter or early spring of 1959, the message from the bushy eyebrowed expert was clear. "I came back and I told Joyce and Donald that Mr. Rickey is convinced moving franchises is over," Whitney remembers. "He told me, 'You're being used. Stop it!' He said the only way new cities are going to get baseball is if there's expansion. And the present major leagues aren't interested in expansion. The only way we'll get expansion is if we force them. And, he said, their only vulnerability is their exemption with Congress, the antitrust exemption. If we can threaten that, we may get some movement. But we've got to be prepared to be in a real fight. He wanted us. He said, 'Join us, Wheelock. It will be a great adventure.'"

When Whitney told Swan and Dayton of Rickey's words, they decided that it was the path to take. "They said, 'Wheelock, do it. Keep us informed at home, but we've got nowhere in our present course. We've been flirting and it hasn't worked.'" So by the spring of 1959, after nearly seven years of kowtowing to baseball and getting nothing but cold shoulders, the strategy changed. The Twin Cities joined a group of insurgents.

They weren't exactly 1950s Communists. Rickey assembled a powerhouse of capitalist rebels to challenge the game. For Houston, his potential owner was Judge Roy Hofheinz, the man who would eventually build the Astrodome stadium. For Denver, it was veteran baseball executive Bob Howsam. For New York, it was lawyer William Shea and a man named Herb Walker, the uncle of future president George Bush. Representing Dallas–Forth Worth was Eamonn Carter, owner of the Fort Worth newspaper. And hoping for a franchise in Toronto was a Canadian businessman named Jack Kent Cooke, who would go on to own the Los Angeles Kings hockey team and the Washington Redskins football team. This was no group of slouches. Still, said Whitney, "People were making fun of us. They were saying, 'You don't have a chance.'"

By July 28, 1959, Whitney had gathered an impressive group of

Twin Cities investors to back his Continental League bid. Among his partners for the $3 million venture were: Morris Chalfen, president of Holiday on Ice; Bob Short, owner of the Lakers NBA team; George S. Pillsbury of the Pillsbury Company; the St. Paul–based Hamm Brewing Company; the Dayton Company; the Star and Tribune Company; and Henry T. McKnight of the St. Paul–based S. T. McKnight Company. The stature of such a group lent credibility to Whitney's efforts. It also offered a prospect of bringing Minneapolis and St. Paul together in a sporting effort. No longer were they competing to lure a team to one of their cities. Now, as a community, the Twin Cities were in a war with major-league baseball. Apparently everyone wanted to join. Although some fans in St. Paul began to circulate a petition claiming that they wouldn't support any team unless half of its games were played in St. Paul, the St. Paul media began to show that it was ready to bury the hatchet between the two cities.

The *St. Paul Dispatch*'s Reidar Lund wrote: "One thing certain is that if we get a club, one way or the other, it will play in Metropolitan stadium and we, in St. Paul, might as well own up to that now. Perhaps it is time we knock the chips from our shoulders and get together on baseball. It is better to have a team playing major league baseball in Metropolitan stadium than not to have a team at all."[8]

Days later, a virtually teary-eyed Charles Johnson wrote in the *Tribune*, responding directly to Lund: "We support this new spirit of cooperation.... A new era is at hand. Maybe out of sports we can make Minneapolis and St. Paul the biggest single community in the United States."[9] It was as if the Palestinians and Israelis had signed the ultimate peace treaty. It showed the significance that this baseball effort carried. It was not the mere acquisition of a sports team. It was the arrival of an asset that could bring the historic rival cities closer and transform them into a vibrant new American metropolis.

Rickey was fighting on all fronts. Later that month, he and Shea sent a letter to the Senate antitrust committee, urging it to lift baseball's exemption as it applied to the control of players and the awarding of franchises. This was the very heart and soul of major-league baseball owners' control of their industry. The words resonate loudly to this day. "The present major-league franchise owners apparently have a total lack of loyalty to the communities which support their enterprises. The major league owner today refers to the 'national pastime' with great reverance. And, when it suits him, he behaves as if he were operating a quasi-public trust. But let a better 'deal' be offered in another city and he reverts instantaneously to the hundred percent businessman whose only guide is the earnings statement. The men who would hold franchises in the Continental League are local, civic-minded, financially sound baseball fans of excellent reputation. They pray for legislation which will permit them to exercise their franchises."[10]

As the Continental League effort slowly picked up steam, Griffith's situation in Washington became dire. He resumed discussions with Moore and lawyer Dorsey, even though the Minnesotans had vowed less than a year earlier to stop negotiating with him. In Washington and New York, Griffith was getting blasted, and so were the Twin Cities. Minnesotans might have wanted to be viewed as eager kids seeking their first teddy bear, but in truth, the Twin Cities were aggressively trying to steal a team from a traditional baseball center and from the nation's capital. In some ways, while Griffith might have been viewed as a heavy for wanting to leave Washington behind, Twin Cities officials were being viewed as kidnappers.

In an August 1959 column in the *Washington Post*, columnist Shirley Povich called Minneapolis "the shameless hussy ... making goo-goo eyes at Calvin Griffith again after being jilted last year. And Griffith is not only responsive. He's in a flutter and a swivet and the blood is running hot for domicile with Minnie. ... They would prefer a no-Cal ball club but their tolerance is great, like any city hankering to get into the majors after vexing, through all of its municipal history, at the label of bush. ... Washington's only hope is that other American League club owners will take a hard look at Griffith's proposal and even a harder look at Griffith and belt him down again. This would not be cruel. They would only be recommitting him to the simple life with Chrysler Imperials, his mansion house and his debt-free ball club, which Washington's tender fans have provided for two generations of Griffiths. And Minneapolis, a nice if small town, would be escaping a fate it doesn't deserve."[11]

Still, Griffith was ready now, or seemed to be. He was sending Senators' business manager Ossie Bluege to Minneapolis for secret talks. On September 4 and 8, 1959, Bluege met with Moore, *Star* and *Tribune* publisher Swan, auto salesman and civic activist Bill Boyer, and Dorsey to nail details of a lease.[12]

But six weeks later, American League owners again denied Griffith's request to move to the Twin Cities. Congress was still looking over their shoulders, wary of losing the capital's home team. In some ways, Moore and his pals were undercutting Whitney and the Continental League effort. The Twin Cities' attempt to get the Senators angered Shea, who was now seeking all-out loyalty to his new-league cause. "If [the Twin Cities] continue to act as dupes and be suckered into these things, they could wind up without any team in any league," Shea warned.[13]

There, Shea had revealed himself. As much as he and Rickey were promoting a new league, the ultimate goal was to get teams in the "real" big leagues. Rickey's plan all along was to gain leverage, then hammer the American and National Leagues into expansion.

Special Relationship

The richest part of this Continental League moment in Minnesota sports history is the father-son relationship that developed between Whitney and Rickey. It may serve as a bit of a digression here, but it reveals how closely linked that original bid for a Twin Cities team was to Rickey's affection for Whitney and his desire to see Whitney succeed. Without that personal relationship, Whitney wouldn't have been drawn to Rickey, wouldn't have been so loyal, and, in retrospect, wouldn't have been able to draw the rest of the Twin Cities powerful business and media community with him. Throughout the winter of 1960, Whitney traveled around the country with Rickey to all of the potential Continental League cities, from Toronto to Dallas, from Houston to Denver. The various visits were calculated and planned by Rickey. There he met with key newspaper editors, leading politicians, and top business leaders. Whitney latched onto Rickey. "I used to stand beside him in receiving lines and introduce him," Whitney said forty years later, still the little boy in his voice. "I don't know how you say you're somebody's disciple, but I was ready to serve Branch Rickey. I revered him."

The fervor and commitment of Whitney and some other Minnesotans to Rickey's cause is palpable in some of the correspondence that Whitney retained. One is a letter to Whitney from another young Twin Cities businessman named Gordon Ritz. (Both would go on to bring the National Hockey League to the Twin Cities in the 1960s.) Ritz was then an advertising salesman for *Time* magazine in Minneapolis. On November 13, 1959, he attended a Continental League meeting in New York, standing in for Whitney. At that twelve-hour session, Ritz wrote, Rickey declared that the American League was "conducting a skillful delaying operation" by making "willy-nilly offerings of possible new American League franchises to any and all cities that seem to show an interest in supporting a Continental League team. . . . The aim of the American League is to harass the Continental League up through next spring. It is the hope of the American League that the next session of Congress will validate the reserve clause and thus make the formation of the Continental League extremely difficult, if not impossible." (If the reserve clause had been eliminated by Congress from baseball's antitrust exemption, it would have allowed the Continental League to raid the existing major leagues for players.)

Ritz wrote of a plan, detailed by Rickey, for Chicago White Sox owners Bill Veeck and Hank Greenberg to sell their share of that team, watch as Griffith moved to Minnesota, and then swoop in and take over the Washington, D.C., market. But, wrote Ritz, "Although Veeck and Greenberg should not be underestimated as fighters, I find it hard to believe that they can buck the majority of the other owners, who are solidly against expansion." Those sorts of sparring words peppered Ritz's letter to Whitney. It was practically evangelistic. There was true youthful fervor.

"The only way we, or other cities, are to get major league ball is to be strong, to be determined, and to fight. I believe that everybody at the meeting Friday realizes that toughness and determination are our only ways to get major league ball. Mr. Rickey announced that he has never liked to fail in anything he has undertaken. You need to talk to Bill Shea only for five minutes to realize that he also is a very poor loser. These men are determined to make the Continental League go, and I believe that if we follow their leadership with confidence, it will go. If we don't follow the lead of these two men, my personal opinion at this time is that we will never see major league baseball in the Twin Cities, Ritz wrote."[14]

Locally, the Continental League dog and pony show arrived on Thursday, January 7, 1960. It kicked off what would be the most historic year in Twin Cities sports history. Meeting first at the Minnesota Club in St. Paul and then the Minneapolis Club in Minneapolis, Rickey, Shea, and representatives from the other Continental League cities wooed Twin Cities business leaders. The newspapers went gaga over the idea that a putative major league was truly interested in the Twin Cities. Reading the columns of Johnson and Cullum was like listening to Sally Field win the Academy Award and screaming, "You like me! You like me!"

Wrote Johnson, after being seduced by Rickey: "The American and National leagues should know quite emphatically, too, that this area is a little tired of the treatment it has received from the established leagues. . . . The majors had that chance [for expansion] in December by announcing expansion of their present circuits. They didn't. It is quite apparent that they never will. The National has always unalterably opposed such a move. The American never was quite sure until its December vote. . . . There were some reports that Calvin Griffith and Washington had agreed to permit the transfer of that franchise to the Twin Cities in 1961. Such action never was made official and now must be characterized as so much talk from a smoke-filled room."[15]

Shea pushed the idea of local ownership—and not the relocation of a major-league team—as critical to the success of any team. "A baseball team should be owned by the people of the city," he said. "When owners come from outside they are interested in only one thing—money."[16]

Rickey, Shea, and Whitney spouted such rhetoric everywhere they went. They were creating more than reams of newspaper copy. They were feeding into a national atmosphere for pro sports expansion that transcended baseball. Indeed, the first full meeting of the new American

Football League was held in Minneapolis on November 22, 1959, when a local bar owner and sports promoter named Max Winter was still planning to join the start-up league because the established NFL didn't want to expand. The same forces that were pressuring baseball were pressuring football. But football was moving very quickly. Four days after the Continental League entourage was in Minneapolis, Winter linked up with Ole Haugsrud, who had operated pro football teams in Duluth, and Northwest Publications, who owned and operated the *St. Paul Dispatch* and *Pioneer Press*, to seek an NFL franchise. Barely three weeks later, on January 28, 1960, the NFL awarded a franchise to the Twin Cities, with play beginning in the 1961 season at Met Stadium. Minneapolis–St. Paul became "major-league," first in football. Minneapolis interests had been trying to get a pro football team since 1948, but not with the fervor for a baseball team. Football was second banana then in the major-league pecking order, and the University of Minnesota football team satisfied the autumn sports desires. The Minnesota NFL franchise came after Winter literally sat in the lobby of a Miami Beach hotel for ten days, refusing to take no for an answer. The NFL's expansion gave the baseball efforts a shot in the arm. It was a nod that the Twin Cities were legitimate.

The pro sports dynamic was shifting. As soon as the NFL awarded a franchise, Jerry Moore, head of the Sports Area Commission, became concerned about the size and capabilities of Met Stadium. He resumed his push for city-backed funding for the expansion of Met Stadium and eventually got the city council to approve $8.5 million in bonds. Meanwhile, in March, two months after the high of getting a major-league football team, the struggling Lakers basketball team played its final game and moved to Los Angeles. Still, there was the baseball goal.

It would have to wait six more months, when Griffith finally announced he would move his Senators. But before then, Rickey, Whitney, et al. would have to win a showdown with the lords of baseball in theatrical fashion. In July 1960, Rickey got word from Los Angeles Dodgers owner Walter O'Malley and New York Yankees owner Del Webb that both existing big leagues wanted to talk. Each man headed the expansion committee in his respective league. A month later, on August 2, 1960, in the $400-a-day Imperial Suite on the twenty-seventh floor of the Conrad Hilton Hotel, baseball's leaders finally gave in. It started in the morning when, behind Rickey, the Continental troops marched into the suite and began to tell their story. "It was amazing to me that Walter O'Malley called him 'Mr. Rickey,'" Whitney said. "What deference."

Much of that formal deference was dipped in bitterness. Nine years earlier, when Rickey had been the Dodgers' president and a partner in the team, O'Malley had fired him. Rickey owned 25 percent of the team. But under the terms of their partnership deal, O'Malley had to match any bid for Rickey's shares. Rickey engaged in a creative, profitable exercise. He got a friend, New York real estate tycoon William Zeckendorf, to bid $1,050,000 for his 25 percent, for which O'Malley had offered $346,667, or what Rickey had paid in 1943. O'Malley now had to match Zeckendorf's offer to keep a controlling interest in the Dodgers. As legendary sports columnist Red Smith said: "Zeckendorf got $50,000 for this trouble, while Rickey got his million and O'Malley's enduring hostility."[17] What's more, anyone who mentioned Rickey's name in the Dodgers' offices was thenceforth fined one dollar.[18]

With that sort of personal history crackling in the room, Rickey, without a written note to guide his presentation, was "so eloquent, so forceful, so persuasive as to why baseball, if it was going to be the American pastime, had to include cities that were ready," Whitney said. "He had them under a spell." Each Continental city made a five-minute pitch for expansion, or else the proposed league would compete with the existing majors. O'Malley, Webb, and a handful of other owners listened. The men broke for lunch. Two hours later, they returned to the hotel's top floor. Whitney remembered: "We were nervous. They had the cards. It was their league."

But the time had come. O'Malley announced that he and Webb were prepared to recommend that baseball expand, in 1961 and 1962. There were conditions. The Continental League had to disband. And Continental League cities wouldn't necessarily receive expansion teams. "At that moment, I was conscious of the fact that this was history in the making," Whitney said. Even as the Continental conspirators were about to explode with glee, Rickey calmly told O'Malley he needed to recess to ponder the offer. "We got alone, and I tell you, people were acting like kids," Whitney said. "We were slapping each other on the back. We were hugging. And that was even before men hugged."

Rickey interrupted the celebration to speak. He praised his followers for their guts and solidarity. He took no credit. Whitney was moved. "I was by far the youngest person in this group," Whitney said. "I really wanted to say something." He raised his hand. "I would like to say a word to you, Mr. Rickey," Whitney said. "Not of congratulations, but to tell you I'm going to miss you. I think that everyone here will miss you. You've been our leader. You're eighty years old. I don't know where you're headed. But I know what we've been doing the last couple of years. Not having that contact is something I'm going to miss." Whitney, remembering the moment four decades later, had to pause. "It brings tears to my eyes," he said. "I didn't realize at the time the impression that made on him."

But it did. First, Rickey told O'Malley and Webb that the Continental League would go away in exchange for expansion. Then, that night, flying from Chicago back to New York, Rickey took care of some other serious business. He handwrote a six-page letter to Whitney on a yellow legal pad. Although the missive was scrawled from apparent turbulence on his flight, Rickey composed a wonderful treatise to Whitney, providing advice and looking into his crystal ball. In a sports world focused on finances and civic cockiness, Rickey's letter is a virtual aria of personal commitment to making the enterprise ethical and successful. And it is so warmly written that Rickey's affection for Whitney—and the strong feelings that developed out of the Continental League battle— can't go unnoticed.

Dear Wheelock—

It is probable, in my judgement, that Minneapolis will be one of the first four cities to be included in the present expansion program. There is glamour, almost romance in the prospective adventure—and it is just that. Not at any future time do I wish you experience the remotest sense of regret and I write you about a matter of great importance, as I see it, in order to remove, as best we can, the hazard of, first, money loss, and, second, disappointment.

You will not misunderstand my motive in writing you as freely as I intend to do. You have inherited, surely, some very great strong points of character. No one of your age, it seems to me, can acquire by his own efforts so many genuine and uniquely fine qualities—as you most certainly have loyalty, sincerity and good sense—candor under pressure—I can not name them all, but [in] our brief but intensive acquaintance I came to know so many. It is because of my interest in you and your fine colleagues that I take a position of offering unasked-for counsel.

If, indeed, you are to be in either major league in 1961, then you must act immediately on player production. That is the point of my letter to you. And further, if you are included as one of the first four for opening in 1962—indeed the demand for quick action on your point is not much less urgent.

Your people must not trust to the "help" that may be promised or indeed provided as coming from the majors. That will be the "crumbs from the table." You will be confronted with a vicious competition, surely unlike anything you have ever imagined. I shudder, really, when I think of what surely is in front of the 9th and 10th clubs in either major league because and chiefly because of player weakness on the field.

... Immediately, move in several preparatory directions.

1. General manager. That means executive ability in the field of baseball experience. Personal connections or business influence must have nothing to do with your selection. There are very few available men qualified for the job. Get the best. If you are fortunate enough to get the right man, don't debate the price. Get him.

2. Employ as soon as you can a player production department.... You must have a man of minor and major league acquaintance—to head up your production of players.... You must be represented as actively as possible in the very early negotiations on player assignments with the major leagues knowing full well that what you get will be limited to what "they" can "let go." That can mean, at best, only doubtful standing in the second

division. 3 years of that experience can and may mean very substantial money loss before the opening of your 4th year.

My reason for distress in operation of a 9th or 10th club is due to the almost unavoidable disparity in comparative player strength on the field. You want to avoid somehow the probability of winning 40 of the 154 games, even in your first year. The newness of the attractions will sustain you for a time, probably so! But the fantasy wears out rapidly with a discreditable club ...

You were very thoughtful in your personal remarks to me. I am a bit uncomfortable to feel that anyone anywhere feels that I am the object for some sort of sympathy as consolation (although it may and really is an understandable feeling).

About me? I mean to have another fling. St. Louis was good to me. So was Brooklyn and Pittsburgh is coming through! I have plans—I will keep busy. I intend to bring another club to World Series status. In the meantime, we must "settle up" with the majors. We are not out of the woods as yet ...

Sincerely, Branch Rickey ... [P.S.] A bad pen, a rough ride and an illegible hand conspire to give you a problem, I know, in translation. BR.[19]

Such poetry wouldn't ever grace the Twin Cities pro sports land-scape again. Rickey was eloquent, loving, and right. They weren't out of the woods yet.

Movement

By the fall of 1960, baseball decided expansion was ripe. The deal with the Continental League was in place. In mid-October, the National League expanded to New York and Houston. Griffith said then he had no deal in hand for a Twin Cities move, and a week before he actually moved the Senators to Minnesota, he told a Washington newspaper reporter, "I have not talked to anyone about moving. . . . I think I have a good thing here in Washington."[20] He claimed in an interview that he was unaware of how serious the American League owners were about expanding until he arrived at meetings in New York on October 25, 1960.

"I was a surprised person," Griffith said, sitting in his sparsely furnished Edina condominium in the summer of 1998. "I said to myself, 'Jesus Christ, Calvin, you've really got to make up your goddamn mind now, or get the hell out of baseball.'" His fear? New owners would grab new, enthusiastic cities and flourish while he languished in Washington. But he and others also knew that leaving the nation's capital would cause a stir. He promised to help put together a new ownership group for a new Senators team, which was to be instantly formed to replace Griffith's team, which would head to Minnesota.

That night Griffith told the Minneapolis delegation monitoring the meetings that if he got the votes, he was going to move. But there was one more thing. Griffith huddled with Moore, Johnson, and Whitney, who was making sure the Continental League promises were honored. "Calvin said he needed some financial help to move. We said, that's fine. He said, 'I haven't got the money to pay off the indemnity for the territorial rights.'"

The Millers and Saints of the American Association were going to have to be compensated for their turf being conquered. The Red Sox controlled the Millers, and the Dodgers the Saints. They'd want compensation. Whitney remembers saying he'd help, sure, no problem.

"I'll need $250,000," Griffith said. The three Minnesotans winced. "I took a very deep breath," Whitney recalls. "And then I said, 'Take my word for it. I'll see to it that we can cover it.'"

The next day, Joe Cronin, the American League president and Griffith's brother-in-law, gathered the votes. At 2:15 P.M., Minneapolis time, on the third floor of the Savoy-Hilton Hotel in Manhattan, the Washington Senators were officially moved to Minneapolis–St. Paul, and a tenth AL franchise was added in Los Angeles. Not surprisingly, Charlie Johnson wrote the story in the *Tribune* the next day. To the victor go the spoils. But not to Rickey, the mastermind of expanding the game. In his view, the game had barely been distributed nationally via expansion, with New York and L.A. getting two of the teams and Washington, D.C., getting a replacement for the Senators. Thus, of the emerging Continental League cities, only Minneapolis–St. Paul and Houston got their prize.

Rickey called the expansion selections a "breach of good faith" on the part of baseball owners.[21] Minnesotans didn't really care.

For all of Barber's principles, Griffith struck a very favorable deal for his team. Yes, the projected revenues to the Sports Area Commission would go on to nicely pay the debt service. But in the end, Griffith's lease agreement with the Sports Area Commission was nothing revolutionary. It was a tad better for the Twin Cities public than San Francisco's deal with Stoneham, struck three years earlier. The Sports Area Commission got 7 percent of the Twins' net ticket receipts as rent versus the 5 percent that San Francisco got from the Giants. (But there would be no rent required for the new Twins if the team didn't draw 750,000 fans per season, or more than twice as many as the Senators drew at Griffith Stadium in 1960.)

But Griffith signed on for only fifteen years, whereas Stoneham signed an unusually long thirty-five-year arrangement, which the Giants kept. After fifteen years, Griffith and Max Winter's NFL Vikings, who also signed a fifteen-year lease, began asking for a new stadium that became the Metrodome.

Griffith got 90 percent of concessions revenues at Met Stadium, compared to Stoneham's 100 percent.[22] But in a move that would irk the Vikings and come back to bite Griffith in future stadium negotiations, the Twins won the right to control the concessions at all Met Stadium events, including Vikings games. So when the Vikings would go on to be more successful at putting fans in seats at Met Stadium, Griffith still profited from football fans' purchases of hot dogs and pop. The Vikings would remember that and jab back at Griffith years later. Griffith, who said he had just $25,000 in the Senators' bank account at the time of the move, said relocating meant keeping his family in the game and "with food on the table."[23] Peter Dorsey, who negotiated the Met Stadium lease for the Sports Area Commission, remembered Griffith's insistence on high concessions percentages and that they be calculated on a gross basis, not a net basis. "He told me the concession deals carried his family through the Depression years with the Senators," Dorsey said. "He never forgot that."

Another key element to the move was broadcasting dollars. In the 1950s, radio and television rights fees were a booming revenue stream for baseball owners. Moving into virgin major-league territory—with a wide expanse of radio stations in a potential network of stations—was attractive to Griffith. The growth of this electronic revenue was dramatic. In 1950 all major-league teams took in $3.4 million from radio and television.[24] Upon his move to Minnesota ten years later, Griffith won a $600,000-a-year broadcast deal for the Twins, more than twice his radio and TV deal in Washington, D.C.[25]

Beginning in 1961, their first season at Met Stadium, and for nine more, the new Twins drew more than one million fans per season—a key benchmark then—and led the American League in two of their first five seasons in their new place.

The Community Again

The final stroke in Griffith's relocation came more than two years after the announcement of the move. It showed how unified and mobilized the local business community was when it came to pro sports. Remember, Whitney had promised Griffith that the business community would help him pay off the Dodgers and Red Sox for their territorial rights that covered the Saints and Millers. Off the top of his head and by the seat of his pants, Whitney vowed to Griffith that the Twin Cities would aid him on those indemnity payments. Finally, on November 13, 1962, Griffith accepted $225,000 worth of Met Stadium bonds to help him in paying off his debts on the territorial rights. Essentially, Whitney recruited twenty-six investors in the stadium and got them to turn their ballpark bonds over to Griffith. He received the principal *and* interest from those bonds. The largest contributors were the *Star* and *Tribune* ($30,000), Dayton's ($25,000), Northwestern National Bank ($25,000), Northern States Power ($25,000), IDS ($15,000), First National Bank of Minneapolis ($15,000), the Radisson Hotel Company ($10,000), the Coca Cola Bottling Company ($10,000), and the S. T. McKnight Company ($10,000).[26]

"Dear Wheelock," Griffith wrote to Whitney on the day the bond swap was completed, "As you well know, perhaps the deciding factor in our decision to move from Washington, D.C., to Minnesota, was the generous offer of a group of interested and responsible citizens to share in the cost of our indemnities. The amount we would have to pay for the American Association and the individual franchises in St. Paul and Minneapolis was undetermined, but the asking prices were so high that without some outside help it is very doubtful that we would have wanted to undertake this liability on our own. Our decision to move here has been a good one, both for us and we hope for the business community. We are extremely happy here *and fully intend to make this our permanent home"* (italics mine).

Gee, that was good news. The community had just committed $8.5 million to a stadium and another $225,000 to pay off the Saints and Millers. Yet Griffith seemed to be not quite ready to truly consider Minnesota his home. He "fully intended" to stay, but intentions can change. By the time his lease was up, Griffith wasn't so certain. Another stadium debate would ensue by the mid-1970s.

Lessons

The greatest lesson from the arrival of the Twins in Minnesota is this: in the end, the promoters of the effort to bring a team here weren't joined at the hip with the owners of the teams. They conducted a multifront approach, beating up on the powers that be with the Continental League, negotiating with an eager distant owner with the other hammer, but finally negotiating a decent lease.

For sure, the closer government and sports boosters get to their team's owners and the owners' wish lists, the more difficult it is to strike a deal that is good for the public or, even more important, that the public trusts. This was eminently clear in the Twins efforts, in partnership with Governor Arne Carlson, to get a stadium between 1995 and 1998. It applied, too, to the 1999 attempt by Mayor Norm Coleman to get a ballpark in St. Paul. Coleman, eager to rejuvenate a sagging political career, danced too closely with Twins owner Carl Pohlad.

Another lesson to be learned from the arrival of the Vikings and the

Twins is that there needs to be a cause over and above sports to bring the community—or at least its power brokers—together. Throughout the fifties, the cause was "Put the Twin Cities on the map! Don't let Milwaukee and Kansas City get ahead of us! We are important, too!" Getting baseball was but a vehicle for acquiring a big-league mind-set and image. It wasn't just about sports. It was sometimes barely about sports. It was about something that non–sports fans could grasp: status and self-esteem.

Although the Twin Cities pro sports era had just begun, a larger era was ending. When major-league sports arrived in Minnesota, the industry was in a significant transition. Minnesota was at the front end of a new age. Baseball historian David Q. Voigt notes that with the rise and fall of the Continental League and baseball's owners forced expansion, "there was no effective nostrum against charges that baseball was becoming a commercialized entertainment. Truthfully, it always had been, but owners still wallowed in the myth that theirs was a sporting venture. Oddly enough, that dying myth now exposed owners as carpetbaggers who might coldly abandon traditional sites for siren dollars.... As the 1950s passed, so did baseball's old order.... The decade ended amidst confusion as to where the game was heading."[27]

The 1960s began in Minnesota with the pro sports sun rising brightly. But once we got on the pro sports path, it became a treadmill, at least as far as sports facilities are concerned. By 1965, the Vikings were already making "improvements" at Met Stadium to increase its capacity for football. Some would say those changes destroyed the character of the stadium just four years after the arrival of the Twins. By 1969, there was a call for a new stadium. Already the economics of pro sports were changing. The pattern had been set. Teams would need and want more. The public would be asked to help. In the beginning, the cities needed the teams for national identity. The teams recognized that they had the leverage. Being on the map was exciting. Getting pushed off the map could be devastating. The Twin Cities were major league, and memories and gatherings were soon to fill our local history. Although the grassroots drive that built Met Stadium was never to return, at least we were on the national business and recognition radar. The community had an outlet for its increasingly busy, suburban, freeway-filled frustrations. It owned a unifying force: big-league sports.

"You can't get mad at the Guthrie Theater or the Minnesota Orchestra or the Science Museum," Whitney said, with this froggy voice and his heartfelt emotions. "But, boy, can you get mad at the Vikings or the Twins or their ownership. I'm sorry, but I don't wave a handkerchief and scream my head off at the symphony like I do at Vikings' games. Major-league sports is great for the soul of the community. We need something to cheer for."

CHAPTER 3

Where the Sun Don't Shine

Calvin and Max Move under the Teflon Sky

No sooner did Minnesota calm down from celebrating the arrival of major-league baseball and football than the baby steps to the state's first great stadium game were about to be taken. As fast as you could say, "Cash," the Vikings claimed by 1964 that they needed more seats at the Met to satisfy the demand of the local market and of the growing National Football League, which wanted increasingly larger stadium capacities. In a league, more than any other league, in which teams equitably shared revenues, the visiting team took home 40 percent of the gate receipts from a Vikings home game. The Vikings' NFL partners wanted their fair share when they traveled into the frozen tundra for their Sunday pigskin battles just as the Vikings pocketed cash on their road trips to larger, warmer-weather facilities.

As new as Met Stadium seemed to be, it quickly fell behind the edifices coming on-line around the country that were expressly "multi-purpose"; that is, designed for the use of both major-league baseball and NFL teams. The advent of artificial turf, or plastic grass, meant quick transitions from a September or October baseball game to an early-fall NFL contest. So did the efficient setup and takedown of easily moved sections of seats. Met Stadium was getting old. It was nine years old.

Met Stadium, too, was built to lure a major-league baseball team and jury-rigged to accommodate football. This aesthetic and practical imbalance in favor of baseball laid the foundation for the future aesthetic and practical imbalance that tilted toward football in the region's next stadium, the Metrodome. There was a certain tit for tat. If baseball dominated the design and the Twins the economics of Met Stadium, then the football Vikings somehow deserved to drive the design and economics of the next stadium. By 1965 the idea of a new sports facility was already being discussed. Clearly, it was envisioned as a football facility, with baseball the bastard-child second tenant. Thus began a continuous process of stadiums aging and stadiums being planned. Simply put, those stadiums not busy being born were busy dying.

In the mid-sixties, much was percolating on the major-league sports front and in the aging cities of the East Coast and industrial Midwest. Pro sports leagues expanded, and teams began to relocate once more, as they had in the flurry of the mid- and late 1950s when pro sports found its way to the Twin Cities. The Milwaukee Braves—whose move from Boston had triggered the first wave of relocations in the fifties—moved to Atlanta in 1966. The Kansas City Athletics moved to Oakland, California, in 1968. The Houston Astrodome, the covered and first artificially turfed stadium, opened in 1965. The declining great cities of Philadelphia, Pittsburgh, Cincinnati, and St. Louis worried about their futures. Leaders saw downtown or near-downtown sports facilities as possible catalysts for economic and civic-pride redevelopment. At the very least, the stadiums served as beachheads for the inner cities, as spiritual symbols that the business and political leaders of those communities weren't abandoning the core and increasingly black central business districts and neighborhoods for the blossoming suburbs. They constructed new stadiums to accommodate their teams and to make sure they didn't relocate to who-knows-where—but certainly not the suburbs.

The Twin Cities excitedly embraced a Met Stadium that was an Erector set of a Class AAA facility. But other cities soon after built steep, doughnutlike stadiums for their football teams, with their cotenant baseball teams accepting configurations that moved their fans farther from a game that demands intimacy. The beautiful asymmetry of baseball was getting jammed into circles built for football. Gone were the classic urban ballparks that nostalgists today long for: Shibe Park/Connie Mack

1962 Los Angeles / Dodgers Stadium	1970 Pittsburgh / Three Rivers Stadium
1964 New York / Shea Stadium	1970 Cincinnati / Riverfront Stadium
1965 Atlanta / Fulton County Stadium	1971 Philadelphia / Veterans Stadium
1966 Anaheim / Anaheim Stadium	1972 Kansas City / Royals and
1966 St. Louis / Busch Stadium	Arrowhead Stadiums
1966 Oakland / Oakland Coliseum	1976 Montreal / Olympic Stadium
1967 San Diego / Jack Murphy Stadium	1982 Twin Cities / Metrodome

Figure 1. Major-league baseball stadiums ... the first wave. From 1962 to 1976, thirteen major-league stadiums were built and opened, creating the first wave of stadium construction. Most were multipurpose facilities. They outdid the already outmoded Met Stadium, built just six years before the start of this construction boom. Then the Metrodome pulled up the rear, the last multipurpose stadium, a Johnny-come-lately.

Stadium in Philadelphia, Forbes Field in Pittsburgh, Crosley Field in Cincinnati, and the original Busch Stadium in St. Louis. All the idiosyncrasies of cozy fields laid out to fit the oddly shaped blocks of city neighborhoods were abandoned for the cookie-cutter monster spaceshiplike ballparks, often surrounded by acres of parking lots. No matter how ugly or how uncreative, an infrastructure minirevolution swept the sports world. The Twin Cities were quickly left behind.

Minnesota's 1950s stadium, built to join the elite club of major-league cities, was rendered antiquated within ten years. It was the first time—but not the last—that Minnesota dropped behind the curve of stadium construction. It would happen in the next generation, when the Metrodome was built to catch up to the other multipurpose doughnuts, only to be the final one built and to help the Twins and Vikings too little and too late. This rotten timing would happen in the third generation, too. As Minnesota cautiously debated its stadium policy into the year 2000, just about every other major-league community had gone forward into new settings or was farther along in its planning. The Twin Cities have never led. They've always trailed.

Between 1962 and 1976, major-league baseball and football teams moved into new facilities in Anaheim, Atlanta, Cincinnati, Houston, Kansas City, Los Angeles, Montreal, New York, Oakland, Philadelphia,

Pittsburgh, St. Louis, and San Diego.[1] They were all significantly more "modern" than the Met, built larger—with the NFL's needs in mind—with the vision that baseball would flourish unfettered, ready consistently to attract fifty thousand people to a game. In the one foresighted case, Kansas City built separate baseball and football stadiums, maintaining the integrity of baseball with a lovely ballpark and anticipating the requirements of the NFL with a 79,000-seat football coliseum.

Met Stadium was built in 1956 with barely 18,200 seats. When the Twins arrived, there were 24,000 seats for major-league baseball. It kept growing, with 30,637 seats for the Twins opening season of 1961 and then up to 45,919 in 1975. But there were never any permanent decked seats down the left field line. In fact, in the end, the Met had only 24,000 permanent seats through its life span, with the others makeshift bleacher type-seating. The Twins always felt there were limited quality seats for their fans.

In 1965 the Twins won the American League pennant and lost to the Dodgers in the World Series in seven games. Jerry Moore, still the head of the Sports Area Commission, tried then to get the city of Minneapolis to expand the Met to make it more modern. That notion was rejected by city officials, who were becoming increasingly impatient with supporting a Bloomington asset with Minneapolis tax dollars. Also in 1965, the Vikings, using their own $600,000, built football bleachers on the east side of the stadium to increase their game seating capacity. The Sports Area Commission adjusted the Vikings' lease to aid the club with its bleacher investment.

Met Stadium's architectural integrity, as flimsy as it was, was destroyed by the Vikings' addition. A willy-nilly policy was set: additional capacity for the Vikings superseded any major improvements for the Twins. Much of that decision making was tied to the economics of the stadium: the Twins controlled concessions revenues in the stadium, even the hot dogs, popcorn, and pop sold at Vikings games. The Sports Area Commission made its money from parking revenues. The Vikings had to sell tickets and more tickets to make their money. The football team captured no other stadium revenue streams in that period. Met Stadium had been ceded to the Twins when Griffith arrived—a fact the Vikings didn't forget when discussions about a new stadium began.

By 1970, the Metropolitan Sports Area Commission decided to investigate whether a new stadium was needed for either or both the Twins and Vikings. The teams both operated under fifteen-year leases. Nine years had passed since their historic arrivals, with six more to go until they could make their first relocation threats. Forward-looking members of the commission determined that it was time to reevaluate the health of the teams and the cheaply built Met. It wasn't just that cities nationwide were surpassing the facilities in Minnesota. The finance plan to pay off Met Stadium had always been skimpy and shortsighted. There was virtually no funding set aside for capital improvements. Some of the wood seats were replaced along the way, but not many. Most repairs took the form of "a lot of painting," said Dennis Alfton, the longtime operations director at the Met and the Metrodome. Obsolescence was inevitable. With the burgeoning success and popularity of the Vikings, pressure was mounting. Met Stadium had fewer than 48,000 seats for a Sunday football game, the smallest capacity in the NFL. The team, which had cost all of $600,000 to buy a decade earlier, still turned annual profits of about $500,000 a year, but it lagged behind the rest of the flourishing football league.

Meanwhile, Twins owner Calvin Griffith faced the changing—nay, exploding—economics of baseball. (Baseball's economics *always* seem to be changing and exploding, and never for the better of the smaller-sized markets.) After leading the American League in attendance in two of their first five seasons, the novelty of major-league baseball wore off for Minnesota's fans. Note, too, that league-leading attendance in 1965, when the Twins won the AL pennant and lost to the Dodgers in seven games, was a grand total of 1,463,258. In today's environment, that would be reason for a big-league team to consider relocation. By 1971, ten years after moving to Minnesota, Twins attendance fell below one million fans for the first time since Griffith moved the club from Washington, D.C.

On the national front, attendance wasn't the most pressing issue; players' rights were. The Major League Baseball Players Association, the union, grew in strength and anger under a former United Steelworkers of America economist named Marvin Miller. By 1969, the finest center fielder in baseball, Curt Flood of the St. Louis Cardinals, declared that he was refusing a trade to the Philadelphia Phillies. More important, with Miller's backing, Flood challenged the decades-old "reserve clause" in the standard players' contract. That clause tied a player to his team forever, unless he was traded to another team, just like the playing card with his face on it was being arbitrarily transferred from the collection of one little boy to the collection of another. Flood and the union were taking on baseball's sacred antitrust exemption, the one that also allowed owners to control the minor leagues and to determine where big-league teams could be located and how many big-league teams could exist. Baseball's antitrust exemption remained unique among all the pro sports. It was the game's shield. In exchange for a certain public trust ceded to the owners, they were legally exempt from the nation's antitrust laws and free market system. They were allowed to be a monopoly. But they were supposed to be good citizens in return. As owners continuously revealed themselves as cutthroat businessmen, not huggable neighbors, the players fought back. To threaten the game's antitrust protection was to make owners such as Calvin Griffith shiver in their boots. Over time, even with a U.S. Supreme Court decision upholding the reserve clause, arbitrators' rulings and player strikes weakened the owners' hold on players. Free agency, and the meteoric rise in player salaries that accompanied it, was just around the corner. Griffith's mom-and-pop operation was in trouble. That dark cloud hanging over Griffith's future wasn't being seeded only by the players. By 1973, a man named George Steinbrenner, owner of a ship-building fortune from Ohio, bought the New York Yankees. The face of ownership was changing, too. Calvin Griffith and his family could run for only so long. They'd fled Washington for greener pastures in Minnesota to keep their baseball tradition alive. But the walls were caving in on Griffith as his Minnesota lease raced toward its 1975 expiration. Owners and players were getting richer and richer. Griffith couldn't keep up with his 1970s competitors at the 1950s Met using 1930s strategies.

The Sports Area Commission's study looking into options to Met

Stadium was recommended by none other than Moore, the man who brought us Met Stadium. Seventeen years after agreeing with Charlie Johnson and Norm McGrew that a stadium was needed to attract major-league baseball, Moore was beginning to recognize an updated fact: to keep big-league sports—especially football—a new stadium was a necessity. Already there were early, unofficial discussions about a downtown Minneapolis facility. It would keep with the trend in other cities of new urban settings for these new multipurpose eyesores. Vikings owner Max Winter, a patriot of downtown Minneapolis, was instantly a fan of the urban core location. Winter was certainly a fan of a stadium that would increase his capacity by nearly 35 percent. A domed stadium also interested Winter. But in a day and age when sports teams were thoughtful citizens and not gluttons, Vikings president Jim Finks told the commission's study group that while having their own single-purpose football stadium would be "very desirable ... considering the economics and practicality, a dual football-baseball facility is the most reasonable and perfectly acceptable."[2] (How about that for the good old days?)

The Vikings were also concerned about having too many seats to sell. "If there are fewer seats available than could be sold," Finks told the commission, "the sale of season tickets is kept up and attendance is better." Scarcity, not an inventory too large to sell, was what Finks was after. Finks believed that artificial turf, the addition of team offices at Met Stadium, more seats, and an on-site ticket office in Bloomington would help make the facility "viable . . . for the next fifteen or twenty years." This was 1970.

As the Vikings laid the groundwork for a substantial facilities improvement, the Twins grew impatient with Met Stadium. Billy Robertson, Calvin Griffith's half brother and one of the team's administrators, told the commission's study group that the baseball team would be open to a domed facility. Proving that he was a man before his time—something that no Griffith family member has ever been accused of—Robertson opined that if the stadium's roof was "moveable or retractable," then the team would embrace it. "He thought the attendance might increase 150 to 200 thousand during baseball season if the field and stands were protected," the study report concluded. "The weather forecast can affect attendance and if people knew the game would still go on in bad weather they would be more apt to attend. Most people want the outdoor atmosphere they have at a sports event and would probably not want a permanent enclosure which could never be moved or opened. In Mr. Robertson's opinion a permanently enclosed stadium would hurt the game." Key principles and contradictions were being established: the teams seemed resigned to sharing one stadium; a retractable roof would be preferred; the Twins liked Bloomington and were, generally speaking, confused about what was best for their future; Winter, a Minneapolitan, felt strongly about being in the heart of the city he loved.

With Minneapolis types dominating the commission—remember, the Minneapolis taxpayers were the backstop if the Met bonds defaulted—city officials weighed the alternatives. Was it worth it to pour more money into a stadium in Bloomington, with the suburb competing with downtown for the entertainment dollar? Or was it time to emulate other cities such as St. Louis, Philadelphia, Pittsburgh, and Cincinnati, the ones with downtown stadiums? Potential sites were mentioned, including one that became a focus during the stadium game of 1997, the so-called "Mississippi riverfront location," just to the east of the modern-day Hyatt Whitney Hotel, north of Washington Avenue, south of the river and west of Interstate 35-West. Another early consideration for a site was to the west of Hennepin Avenue, behind where the new U.S. Federal Reserve Bank stands. A third site, which became the first legitimate proposal, sat near the Target Center's location. It was a circular, domed stadium with parking ramps as a doughnut to the sports facility's hole. Finally, placing the stadium on the University of Minnesota campus, near where the present-day Mariucci Arena sits, was also considered an option. That "U" site would likely have been a football-only facility shared by the Vikings and Minnesota Gophers. (This concept of the pro and college teams sharing one stadium was revived briefly in 1999 by Vikings owner Red McCombs in his initial push for a new stadium to support his $250 million purchase of the team in 1998.)

Bloomington had plans, too. It was prepared to place a dome, or cover, on the existing Metropolitan Stadium. It had ideas to spruce up the place. Eventually, the idea of a new football stadium, located between the Met and the new Met Sports Center arena, built in 1966 for the arrival of major-league professional ice hockey, would develop. Under that scenario, Met Stadium could be improved for the Twins. The idea of a spiffed-up Met next door to an open-air football and soccer stadium became the vision of Winter's top aide. His name was Mike Lynn. Lynn grew up in New Jersey but was hired by Winter from Memphis in 1974, where he had tried for seven years to get an NFL expansion franchise. Lynn had run a chain of movie theaters and a department store, but he had no football background. Like Winter, Lynn was a good, old-fashioned operator. He worked all the angles. He pushed the envelope. He looked out for himself. Before long, Lynn concluded that a downtown stadium with a roof on it was not in the Vikings' best interest. Lynn favored a Bloomington football facility with no roof, next to the improved Met Stadium.

Imagine today a metropolitan sports area consisting of three facilities housing all of the region's major-league teams, in one place, with adequate surrounding parking. It would have been a concept ahead of its time. Only Kansas City, in 1973, built two stadiums, one for football and one for baseball. There are no cries for new stadiums today in that city. Each team has its own stadium, needing to share revenues with no one other than the public agency that operates it. Imagine how the landscape of the metro area would be different if Bloomington had retained pro sports by creating that new open-air Vikings facility.

How would things be different? There'd be no world-famous shopping mall, the Mall of America, on the site of the former Met Stadium. The tax base of Bloomington would suffer. There'd be no Teflon-covered sports facility in downtown Minneapolis. Met Center, the hockey arena, might still be standing, theoretically enlarged and modernized. Perhaps it would be home still to the North Stars, who moved in 1993, and even shared by an NBA team. Maybe the course of stadium history in Minnesota would have been changed. Imagine.

Why Downtown?

If the construction of Met Stadium in the 1950s was a signal that the suburbs were emerging as a legitimate location for regional assets, then the push for a downtown stadium in the 1970s was an indication that the urbanists planned to fight back. Minneapolis–St. Paul wasn't in decline. In fact, it was one of the urban gems of the nation. But the images nationally of the plight of cities were stark. Cleveland's Cuyahoga River was burning with pollution. Detroit, home of the prosperous U.S. auto industry, was a war zone. White flight altered the complexion of many urban areas; in the Twin Cities, where minorities were like hard-to-find beans in vanilla ice cream, such racial relocation wasn't an issue yet. Cities experienced economic slippage. There was fear that Minneapolis was getting frayed at the edges. Could the Twin Cities, always late to trends, be the next troubled urban core? Even more, could the dynamic of the Twin Cities, always testy because of the two competing downtowns of Minneapolis and St. Paul, become even more complex if the suburbs continued to flourish and eventually dominate?

John Cowles Jr. was the chairman of the Minneapolis Star and Tribune Company, owner of the region's most powerful media outlet and opinion maker. He was also the leader of the downtown stadium effort. His impetus to bring sports into the urban core was triggered by more local issues than global ones. "It was less the specter of a dying downtown than the specter of a third fried egg in our over-easy omelet," Cowles said. Not only were cities in transition, but so were newspapers. With the rise of the suburbs and the increase in traffic, the fate of the afternoon newspaper, the *Star*, was in the balance. Plus, a chain of Twin Cities suburban newspapers was beginning to eat into the circulation and advertising dollars of the monopoly big-city newspapers, the *Star*, the *Tribune*, and the *St. Paul Pioneer Press* and *Dispatch*. There was self-interest in maintaining population and strength in the urban core for Cowles. So, too, for Ken Dayton, chairman of Dayton Hudson Corporation, owners of the region's landmark Dayton's department stores. He was a compatriot of Cowles as the new stadium effort picked up steam. "Anything that you have one of should be downtown," Dayton said. The Twin Cities had one major-league stadium, and it wasn't downtown. That was going to change.

An extremely fit, youthful, and blunt man at age seventy in 1998, Cowles explained that in his view, the Twin Cities metro area has long been like "a skillet with a couple of fried eggs in it, with the eggs being the two downtowns. And Bloomington was showing signs of alarming vigor" as the mid-seventies approached. Bloomington was lifting itself up from the status of mere hash browns to a main course. Cowles and his other downtown business pals didn't like it, felt threatened by it, aimed to stop it.

Bloomington had the airport. The commercial and financial development of the properties lining Interstate 494—"the Strip"—caused concern. Met Center, home to the Minnesota North Stars of the NHL, stood there gleaming, more attractive than any convention center or large facility in Minneapolis. "Even though it lacked skyscrapers at the time, it was alarming for a metropolitan area of our size," said Cowles of Bloomington's rise. "It was a prospect of the further decentralizing of the metro area and the scattering of its assets. If you agree in the theory of critical mass, you have to have as many of the important elements as compactly as possible for pedestrian convenience downtown."

The statistics of economic sprawl during the period in which major-league sports first came to the Twin Cities and the time the Metrodome was built supported Cowles's fears. Of the one million jobs in the metro area in the early 1980s, more than half were in the outer-ring suburbs. Metro area sales rose from $1.3 billion, when Met Stadium was just opened, to $7.3 billion in 1977 when the Dome legislation was passed. In the same period, the downtown share of the total retail sales had fallen to 5 percent in Minneapolis and 1 percent in St. Paul, while the major suburban shopping malls captured 12 percent. [3]

Prudential Insurance moved its offices into the suburbs in 1954; General Mills followed in 1958, and 3M left the core of St. Paul in 1962. Cargill shifted from downtown in 1977. Malls and highways sprang up all over. While the metro area was growing, population in the cities of Minneapolis and St. Paul was in steady decline. When Met Stadium was built, about 83 percent of Twin Citians lived in either of the cities. By 1970, the metro area's population had increased by 50 percent, but city-dwelling had decreased by 12 percent. By 1980, when the debate about a new stadium had ended, the Twin Cities metro area had a population of 2 million, but only 641,000 people lived in Minneapolis and St. Paul.[4] The Vikings' or Twins' leaving the region would be a symbol of decline.

Wearing two hats—that of urban affairs policy wonk and challenged newspaper and business owner—Cowles took the lead in the stadium matter at the request of a small core of other key civic leaders, such as DeWalt H. (Pete) Ankeny, president of First National Bank of Minneapolis; John Morrison, chairman and CEO of Northwestern National Bank; Arley R. Bjella, chairman and CEO of the Lutheran Brotherhood financial services and insurance company; Curt Carlson, president of Carlson Companies, the hospitality conglomerate; and William G. Phillips, chairman of International Multifoods.

The stadium matter was, for Cowles, in his mid-forties and carrying on his family's respected publishing tradition, a happy confluence of self-interest and civic-mindedness. Call it enlightened self-interest. His attitude that the downtown core had to improve its image and profile in the eyes of the populace was shared by other key downtown business leaders, union leaders, and, of course, members of the Minneapolis City Council and Hennepin County Board. They decided that the way to go was to steal the major-league sports teams from the suburbs to the city. It was as simple as that. Cowles winces at the word "steal." "I'd prefer not to use the word 'stealing,'" he said. "But we were certainly trying to move what clearly would have been a bigger and better version of Met Stadium from Bloomington to a downtown location."

If it wasn't stealing, it was hijacking. It was exercising significant political and economic power. It was also wooing Vikings owner Max Winter, who always wanted to be considered a big hitter but who, in the end, was just a little Jewish guy from North Minneapolis who owned the football team. Winter had been the general manager of the old Minneapolis Lakers. His father had sold apples in downtown Minneapolis office buildings to bring Max and his mother from Austria in 1913 before the outbreak of World War I. From patching tires in International Falls to make extra money to developing real estate, staging auto shows, promoting women's golf, and owning a fabled Minneapolis nightclub called the 620 Club, Winter had done all right for himself. But he wasn't a corporate titan.

Now the highfalutin rulers of the Twin Cities embraced Winter, worked with him, made him feel he was one of them . . . as long as he felt strongly that the downtown domed stadium idea was the right one. They would take care of him, if he would stay firm on his desire to move his popular football team downtown. "Max wanted to be at their level," said Mike Lynn. "They played on his ego to be a part of their gang." "Who doesn't want to be wanted?" asked Harvey Mackay, the envelope magnate and Dome troubadour who was among those who cozied up to Winter. And once Winter committed to downtown, he forfeited any leverage, any options. That's why, eventually, the Vikings would sign a lease that has trapped them to this day.

It wasn't exactly like the Twin Cities ripping the Senators out of Washington a decade or so earlier. The team wouldn't leave the general marketplace. But within the confines of the Twin Cities metro area, a shift was desired. The suburbs simply couldn't get whatever they wanted. The future of downtown was at stake, or so it seemed, if you carefully read the documents of the Greater Minneapolis Chamber of Commerce. The stadium was a sort of last stand. And although critics have long yelled about the lack of development around the Dome, there was never any illusion that a downtown stadium would somehow bring an influx of bars, restaurants, and hotels to the area of the sports facility. There was no expectation of direct economic impact on the area around the Dome. The stadium was envisioned as a confidence booster, not an entertainment destination. City planners didn't want another entertainment district to the east competing with bars and restaurants to the west.

Cowles, Dayton, Ankeny, Morrison, and especially city planners didn't want the entertainment district to wander as far east in the central business district as the ballpark would. Hennepin Avenue, to its west, was to be the entertainment zone. Nicollet Avenue was to highlight retail.

Marquette Avenue was to be Minneapolis's Wall Street. The next avenues over were to house city and county government. Besides, if you go to the Dome today, walk into the Twins' second-floor offices, and gaze out their windows, you see the trap that any Dome-related development faced. To the south is Hennepin County Medical Center. To the west is the Juvenile Justice Center jail and the *Star Tribune* newspaper offices. To the north, some warehouses sit. Where was the development going to occur, anyway? One bar, Hubert's, decided to try. "Somehow they snuck through," Cowles said, of the lone hospitality establishment that sprang up around the new stadium.

More than sell more beers or sandwiches in its vicinity, what the stadium was intended to do was to reside as a symbol. It was for the workers and the chairmen, the middle managers and the secretaries, the lawyers and the accountants, to gaze out of their skyscrapers and see a unique sporting palace within the downtown area. It was to trigger in those citizens a feeling that their state's most important city was alive and well. It was to tell them that the suburbs were not for special things; downtown Minneapolis was the zone for self-esteem, and a stadium showed that the central business district had pizzazz.

"Our interest was in the overall downtown thing and not whether there'd be a couple restaurants here or there," said Charles "Chuck" Krusell, the Chamber's vice president during the Dome debate. "You got to remember, on our board we had big companies. They wouldn't be too interested in whether there was a restaurant nearby or not. The proximity of entertainment to the stadium was something we didn't even consider when we picked a site. The question was whether we could get the land and whether it was relatively cheap."

"Do you think if the Twins and Vikings had left that Minneapolis would have built as many office buildings and hotels as it did in the last twenty years?" Cowles asked. "I don't connect the dots to the neighborhood around the stadium. I connect them to the central business district."

Mackay is the one who says he counted how many times announcers said the word "Minneapolis" or "Minnesota" during a *Monday Night*

Football telecast: "274," he said. "When I walk into my office every morning, NBC, CBS, ABC, and CNN aren't there watching us make envelopes. They come for these teams. And all roads lead to downtown. If the image is going the other way, that's not good, and perception was everything."

With that in mind, the Greater Minneapolis Chamber of Commerce claimed in 1988 that in the ten years after downtown Minneapolis was awarded the Dome, more than $3 billion worth of hotel, office, retail, and housing developments happened in and around downtown.

"I know, you can't attribute all that to the Dome," said Krusell, Cowles's right-hand stadium man and the behind-the-scenes guy who made it all happen. "But what if no stadium were built? If nothing happened would other stuff have happened? We can say it all happened, can't we?" There was a knowing twinkle in Krusell's eyes, as if he were seriously pulling everyone's leg. But he needed data to justify all the work they'd done. The decade-long process of building the Dome wasn't just about putting up another stadium. It wasn't just about getting more money for their friends, the team owners. Fact is, Max Winter and Calvin Griffith weren't substantial members of the Minneapolis brotherhood. This was about a cause to keep downtown—the core—as healthy as possible.

The Public Interest

Met Stadium, the first Twin Cities major-league stadium, was conceived and built during the prosperous and calm days of the Eisenhower administration. The region had dreams of growing up. The late 1950s evoke images of *Father Knows Best*, of *American Bandstand*, and of a time when America was hitting its post–World War II stride. This second cycle of stadium discussion, as the sixties turned into the seventies, came with a new set of circumstances. The Vietnam War was under way. Authority was being challenged from every direction. Citizens learned how to speak out against war, against racial injustice, and, soon, against a male-dominated culture. The notion of "the public's interest" was always in mind, even if private interests continued to prevail.

Plus, Minnesota was becoming filled with, and jaded by, professional sports. The accessible warmth and stability of the early Twins and Vikings seasons, when players lived among the populace, was being shattered by expanding leagues, the creeping increase in players' salaries, and a facilities glut. Even as discussion commenced on a new stadium for baseball and football, Bloomington saw the construction in 1966 of a new arena to house the new National Hockey League franchise known as the Minnesota North Stars. In St. Paul, where fear was deep, a Civic Center was under construction to compete with Bloomington; a new, upstart professional hockey league faced off for fans against the NHL North Stars by 1973. Meanwhile the University of Minnesota was in a continuous quandary about whether its on-campus Memorial Stadium was adequate.

In her 1982 book *Uncovering the Dome*, Amy Klobuchar, then a Yale University senior who went on to become Hennepin County attorney fifteen years later, detailed the key issues in the ten-year process to get the new major-league stadium built in the Twin Cities.[5] She wrote how the battle was, as always, about the location of such a unique facility, but also about Minnesotans' once strongly held trust in the political process, and how that was shattered by leaders who didn't listen. The fight, too, was over bringing baseball indoors in a culture where the outdoors in the summer is the only place to be. Finally, the public and some political leaders wondered why taxpayers' dollars should be put at risk or in use to aid professional sports in the face of other social needs. "If the jocks want a stadium, then the jocks can pay for it," was said as often between 1971 and 1977 as it has been since 1994, when talk of yet another Twins stadium began anew in the Twin Cities.[6]

The stadium war of the 1970s centered on Minnesotans' sensibilities and their values, on and off the playing field. Should the sun be shining when our games are played? Should the cold weather be factored out of our lives? Should the core city be strengthened by our sports facilities? Should the safe, convenient suburb, with its parking lots and ease, be abandoned? Should the taxpayer's opinion be taken seriously when major community infrastructural decisions are made?

There was, then, not much discussion about what made a metropolitan area great. The Twin Cities knew how to do great things and seemed committed to it. Minneapolis–St. Paul wanted what other big cities had. There was no malaise in the Twin Cities in the 1970s. Unlike the late 1990s, when people always seem to find ways not to do great things, the atmosphere of the seventies wasn't a matter of *whether* we were going to build things to keep us special. It was a matter of *how* and *where*. The nationally known Guthrie Theater settled in Minneapolis in 1963. John Cowles Jr. was a driving force for it, too. Nicollet Mall made downtown special in 1967. The Walker Art Center signaled the region's fine arts strength in 1971. Orchestra Hall showed we wanted to be part of the symphonic major leagues in 1974. These were times when the Twin Cities were a model for the rest of the country. We spoiled ourselves then and came to believe we would always be special.

Thus there were conflicting interests shooting in from everywhere. City versus suburb. A culture of protest and authority-challenging versus a spirit of can-doism. An elite group seeking to build a covered sports stadium versus an ecological aesthetic that argued for sunshine and nature, not artificiality. It took six years to get a stadium bill passed in the legislature, to get politicians to approve the sale of $55 million in bonds to fund the construction. That dollar amount was barely enough to build what would become the spartan Metrodome. Private dollars were necessary to complete the project, which today remains colorless and antiseptic. It took another year for the inevitable political decision that the stadium should be in downtown Minneapolis, after years of lobbying and years of the *Star* and the *Tribune*, Cowles's personal soapbox, arguing for such an eventuality in its editorial pages.

Klobuchar's book and an unpublished chronology of the Dome debate discovered in the files of former Chamber of Commerce vice president Krusell provide a picture that is shockingly familiar to anyone who has followed the Minnesota stadium war of the nineties.[7] The opponents—antitax Republicans and socially conscious neighborhood-based progressives—fit a similar profile twenty-five years removed from each other. Some of the opponents, most notably Julian Empson, who led the

Save the Met protest group, the most prominent anti-Dome group, lived long enough to oppose a new nineties Twins ballpark, too, for some of the same reasons. The legislature acted in similar ways back then and into the present tense, seemingly killing a stadium bill a thousand times before finally saying yes. The citizenry seemed eager to seek a solution to keep the teams, but news of the day or backlashes pushed and pulled public opinion to and fro.

A major player in the seventies that was missing in the 1990s was the business community. In the run-up to the Dome's political passage and financial creation, a cabal of Minneapolis's major business leaders determined that they would bring the Dome downtown, by hook or by crook. They didn't jump in at the very beginning. They jumped in when the political process turned a tad bit haywire. But when the business leaders decided to get involved, their involvement was deep and unswerving. They seriously put their money where their mouths were. Their throwing hundreds of thousands of dollars down the civic toilet with a snowball's chance in hell of getting any rates of return is legendary.

The effort to back a specific stadium site with a ton of private dollars didn't happen overnight. Three years after the first feasibility study to examine if Met Stadium could be refurbished, the downtown stadium idea suffered its first defeat. A citizen-led referendum to limit city funding for a stadium passed by a wide margin on June 12, 1973. It restricted the city's Board of Estimate and Taxation from allowing $15 million or more to be spend on a stadium. Opponents believed that would stop stadium advocates in their tracks. But city officials soon learned that bonds and taxes could be imposed by other city agencies, such as the Minneapolis Community Development Agency, thus circumventing the letter and spirit of the voters' decision. (In 1997 a similar referendum passed in Minneapolis, again to halt the next Twins stadium effort. This time, sports facilities opponents made sure their language was far more all-encompassing.)

Like all issues that powerful people want to see come to fruition, this stadium matter was revived soon after the referendum passed. Chamber vice president Krusell was the worker bee for the power elite who forged what would become the Dome plan. Krusell was an expert on affordable housing and urban renewal. It was he who (besides members of the Sports Area Commission) first realized that the Met Stadium leases for both the Twins and the Vikings would expire after their respective 1975 seasons. In 1974, a go-getter named Harvey Mackay was named chairman of the Chamber's task force. He would eventually take a one-year leave from his company to wander the state and the boardrooms of the Twin Cities' corporations, personally selling the significance of a new stadium and its importance to downtown Minneapolis. Mackay also conceived an enduring slogan that Hubert Humphrey made famous: Minnesota without pro sports would be "a cold Omaha."

The same year, Lynn became the general manager of the Vikings and Max Winter's stadium liaison. Lynn was wily. He issued veiled threats that the Vikings would move without a new stadium. He had great power over Winter, or tried to. He was at the heart of designing what would become the Vikings' and Twins' new stadium, with the Vikings' priorities always satisfied. Lynn came out smelling sweet. In between, the odor he left behind was not always so pleasant. Meanwhile Twins owner Calvin Griffith was trying to make certain he wasn't left in the dust as Winter was wooed. With the Twin Cities' most powerful and egotistical men all engaged, the edifice complex was everywhere, and the testosterone was pushed into high gear.

Through four years of fighting in the legislature, a bill finally passed in 1977 to construct a facility that required no more than $55 million of public financing.[8] The bill, conceived mostly by Governor Rudy Perpich, was "site neutral" and required that a new agency, to be called the Metropolitan Sports Facilities Commission, would determine within a year the location for the dual-purpose facility. A requirement was that the local unit of government or local stadium backers had to supply the land on which any stadium would be built. Among the legislators who voted yes were two young Republicans, one from Albert Lea, the other from Minneapolis. The rural fellow was named Henry Savelkoul, an ardent Republican and a true conservative; the city guy—a native New Yorker—was Arne Carlson, a former Democrat. Savelkoul was the minority leader of the House, and Carlson was his assistant minority leader. Little did they know that their 1977 stadium vote was small potatoes compared to a stadium game they would play—and lose—twenty years later.

Save the Met

Blame Julian Empson. Absolutely blame the former Met Stadium beer vendor, the kid who grew up in suburban Philadelphia learning to love baseball with his mother. Blame him for never giving up over twenty years, for having thoughtful populist solutions for two decades. Embrace him for being marginalized and treated as if he were a nine year old for twenty years, too. Blame him for creating this whole mess we find ourselves in in the year 2000, and understand he framed a large part of the stadium debate as far back as 1978. As the new damned downtown dome was being discussed, Empson and his cronies yelled and kicked and screamed.

Outdoor baseball, they said, was a necessity. Public ownership of the Twins, they said, was a way to keep the team in Minnesota. Tax dollars for stadiums was obscene, they said. "Build Homes, Not Domes," read their bumper stickers. Empson was one of the leaders—and today is one of the lasting survivors—of the first wave of what I call the "Green fans." Lovers of baseball, committed to the traditions of the game—all grass, no designated hitters, small, noncorporate stadiums—they were thorns in the side of the domed-stadium supporters. They were baseball ecologists. It was the post–Vietnam War period. Protesting, taking to the streets, was a common thing. It was natural for a group called "Save the Met" to emerge, a virtual movement that was an outgrowth of an active, neighborhood-based, grassroots political community, centered on the West Bank of the University of Minnesota campus, just a long fly ball away from the new stadium site. But Save the Met was a coalition, too, of the West Bank rabble-rousers and some fans who, frankly, believed that the Metrodome was, in Empson's words, "going to be a piece of shit. If I take any credit at all, it's for making sure that place turned into a piece of shit. I really hate that place."

As fervent as Empson and his band of antidome agitators were, that's how firm the corporate leaders and their hired hands were on their mission to bring sports downtown under the Teflon sky. It was another time in major-league baseball history, in Twin Cities history. The critic was still considered a loony. The critic was barely listened to. These "Greens" were treated with condescension by the Establishment and the media. "We were cute, but we didn't say anything," Empson remembered. But in my view, as the power elite attempted to kidnap pro sports from the suburbs, the revolutionary sports activists sabotaged baseball and the new Dome forever. Empson helped to ideologically and spiritually condemn the Metrodome before it even opened. He and his friends tainted the place even when it was brand-new. For Empson and his fellow travelers, the new fluffy pillow being built in downtown Minneapolis was an obscenity to the game and a fan's sensibilities. It was a symbol, as far back as 1978, that baseball was becoming an ugly business, not a cuddly member of the family, not a field for memories. By pointing out to the populace—even before the first spade of dirt was turned—that this new structure would transform and irreparably harm the Twin Cities' relationship to baseball, Empson became the Antichrist to the big cigar smokers. He represented the little guy. As John Cowles remembered, "He had such a thing about grass," and he meant the infield sort.

I say to "blame" him because, as in all of Minnesota's various stadium games, the average person gets ground down. In this Dome campaign, the monstrous monolith of big business and Minneapolis government and its single-mindedness to get the stadium built couldn't be stopped. But Empson and his Save the Met gang did the next best thing, as far as they were concerned. For all time, they injured the image and spirit of the Dome. In some ways, the Dome never recovered from the disrepute the Save the Met gang heaped on it.

In 1978 and 1979, the construction of the Dome was a symbol of pro sports' slide toward corporatization. The Save the Met group told everyone who would listen that this new indoor stadium would be a terrible place to watch a game; it was a mere TV studio. They said a modern dual-purpose stadium would have awful sight lines for baseball. They suggested staying down in Bloomington and playing in a cheaper, refurbished Met Stadium. Empson was the theatrical fool never letting anyone forget that moving into the Dome was leaving behind an era in Minnesota sports that could be lost forever.

As with any zealot, Empson brought a personal motivation. When he was a mere four months old, his father, Juliano Loscalzo, died of cancer. Little Julian grew up with the Empson name after his mother married a fellow named Sam Empson. Sam wasn't a fan, but his mother, Fran Hudzy, was. As Julian grew, it was baseball that always brought him and his mother close. A diehard Phillies fan, a boy who grew up in the wooden seats of Connie Mack Stadium, he and his mom could always find a way to talk about Johnny Callison and Richie Allen.

When he moved to Minnesota in the mid-1970s to work with kids on the Mille Lacs Indian Reservation, he began to sell beer at Met Stadium. It was a ballpark that was more of an Erector set than the brick of Connie Mack, but it was good enough. So when the talk began that the Twins would move indoors, and while many Minnesotans gasped, Empson fought back. He lobbied against such a gloomy place at the legislature. Twenty years later, he regrets not having pushed more forcefully for the Vikings to get their own new stadium in Bloomington, with a recycled Met Stadium as the Twins' home. But he is proud of one thing: on March 15, 1979, a full eighteen years before the ownership of the Twins and the governor of Minnesota endorsed the idea, Empson, then age twenty-eight, and Representative John Clawson, a Democrat from Center City, announced a plan for the state of Minnesota to buy both the Twins and the Vikings. Under the plan, the Vikings were to be purchased for about $30 million, and the Twins for $11 million. Met Stadium would have been renovated for another $20 million; that would have included an adjacent practice field for the Vikings with an inflatable dome over it. The total cost of $61 million was just $6 million more than it cost to build the Dome. Bonds for the purchases would have been paid off the same way the Dome's bonds were eventually retired; through ticket taxes and other user fees. It would have been the first time in U.S. history that a government purchased teams.

While socialism was strong in other nations in the late seventies, it wasn't in Minnesota. The efforts to retain the Met and buy the teams were laughed at. So Empson demonstrated with his friends against the construction and did anything they could to remind Minnesotans of their basic instinct; as polls showed, most people didn't want to go inside for baseball. As the Dome was being built, he coincidentally got a job as the community organizer for the Elliott Park neighborhood association in Minneapolis. That's the neighborhood adjacent to the Dome. From his office, every day, Empson would watch the girders go up, and his childhood memories of outdoor baseball be obliterated. "It was my hell," he said of the Dome's construction.

To flash ahead from this Dome construction period to the 1997 debate, Empson was a visionary. Actually, he says, he was "co-opted." At the heart of the 1997 effort by Twins owner Carl Pohlad to get a new stadium were two themes: outdoor baseball and public ownership of the team. As it turned out, the public ownership model that Pohlad and Governor Arne Carlson devised was not as straightforward as Empson's and Clawson's. And as time wore on, the economics of baseball changed so much that just going outdoors wasn't enough to make Empson love the game as much as he had in the seventies. But he remained a warrior for pure baseball then and now. The power of the Save the Met organization was profound. In its twenty or so members, just about all Minnesotans saw themselves. Save the Met types wouldn't even set foot in the Dome. But then something happened.

Empson was friends with Minneapolis City Council member Brian Coyle, who was also a Save the Met activist. In July 1985, with Coyle's clout, they were able to crash the official party held at the Pillsbury Center for the All-Star Game, which was being played at the Dome. This was a special moment for Empson. "I never got past the seafood and cocktail bars," he said. As Empson stuffed himself with the goodies of major-league baseball, who should approach him but Harvey Mackay, the Dome's lobbying ringleader. What a scene that must have been: Empson and Mackay, eating shrimp together.

"So where are you sitting tomorrow night?" Mackay asked.

"What do you mean?" Empson said. "I don't have tickets. I hate that place to begin with, but the thought of sitting in the nosebleed seats makes me want to throw up. I'll watch it from home."

"Give me your name and number," Mackay said.

The next morning, after all the free refreshments, Empson was frankly in no condition to attend a baseball game, let alone get out of bed. "I was trying not to hurt myself," said Empson. The phone rang. Loudly. It was the voice of one of Mackay's always pleasant secretaries. "Harvey has a couple of tickets for you. How would you like to get them? We can courier them over to you, if you'd like."

Empson replied, "Yes, would you please."

"I figured the world would be safer that way. And the son of a bitch sends me over tickets, third row, right near the bullpen," Empson said.

Empson began to warm, ever so slightly, to the Dome. Two years later, Mackay did Empson the same favor. He got the Dome hater tickets for the 1987 World Series, the event that truly sanctified the Dome. Suddenly, all the aversion, all the emotional distance, was reduced, if only for four games, when the Twins won the World Series by harnessing their Dome-field advantage.

Eleven years later, Empson, age forty-seven, a lobbyist for citizen transportation groups, sat in a St. Paul bistro. He wore a "Save the Met" T-shirt—"Extra large now," he volunteered—and needed bifocals to read the menu. Now he was known as Julian Empson Loscalzo, having taken back the surname of his birth father. And he was still singing a certain tune: if baseball in the twenty-first century wants to win fans back, it must allow citizens to own their hometown team via stock sales. If the game wants to reconnect with people, he said, it has to rearrange its economics. Empson Loscalzo had said the same things over and over again for two decades.

"There are still some of us who cherish the game," he said. "Maybe it's worth protecting." He's not opposed to some public funding for a ballpark, but first he wants the public to own the team. Mostly, he wants to be outdoors, sipping a beer, smoking a cigar (yes, Empson is a cigar smoker), watching a major-league baseball game in Minnesota. The St. Paul Saints, the outdoor independent minor-league team that captured the imagination of purist fans in the mid-nineties, were an option. But not a serious option, Empson said. Still, from the moment he chanted, "Save the Met!" at the Dome construction site to his 1998 guerrilla campaign to be baseball commissioner, Empson remembered an especially tender moment.

"It was the first game of the Saints," he said of the June 1995 debut. "Some guy I didn't know from anywhere walked up to me and said, 'You know, if it wasn't for you, we would have never have had this.'" But it was just a little field in the middle of St. Paul. The Met was gone. Empson's biggest defeat could never go away.

"I live," he said in 1998, "a tormented life."

The Business Community

D. J. Leary, a veteran public relations and governmental affairs consultant in Minnesota, tells many stories. For the past thirty-five years, Leary has had his finger in just about every major issue in state politics. No story better describes the underpinnings of the changing attitudes toward pro sports' role in the Twin Cities—and the power of the local business community—than Leary's anecdote about a generic "Mr. Pillsbury." The story occurred around the time of the construction of the Dome. It applied to that period of time when such nationally recognized cultural institutions now taken for granted by the local populace—the Guthrie, the Walker, Orchestra Hall, Nicollet Mall—were also being built by the Twin Cities' captains of industry. Those elites—the "big cigars," as they have come to be known—were driving forces behind sports facilities construction in the Twin Cities in the sixties and seventies, too. There were varying sets of cigar smokers, but Met Center arena, built in 1966 with private money to house a new National Hockey League team, was certainly an example of eight rich guys with civic pride bringing a cultural amenity to the region. And in St. Paul, with public dollars, movers and shakers helped construct the St. Paul Civic Center in 1973, which eventually played host to the short-lived World Hockey Association.

Such energy from the corporate community differentiates that period from today. Almost fifty years since the arrival of major-league sports, but barely twenty years after the opening of the Metrodome in 1982, major-league professional sports' support in the Twin Cities "business community" critically waned. Younger professional managers, many without long-term ties to the community, don't involve themselves with the day-to-day needs of the community like the business leaders did in "the old days." Corporations are more keyed to their quarterly earnings and the demands of their shareholders than to the specific requirements of civic construction. Companies are no longer just "Minnesota based." Pillsbury, for instance, is owned by a European conglomerate. The *Star Tribune* is owned by a Sacramento, California, company. Both of the top banks no longer bear names even affiliated with Minnesota: U.S. Bank and Wells Fargo. "The traditional pillars aren't here and weren't there," former governor Arne Carlson said of the stadium debate of the latter 1990s. "The leadership of Minnesota is changing, and it's having a dramatic impact on politics. Where's labor? The unions used to be there, too."

The surveys of Minnesota business leaders about professional sports and their commitment to keeping teams in the Twin Cities show, at best, ennui, at worst, contempt. In a stunning survey of four hundred leading Twin Cities business executives conducted by *Twin Cities Business Monthly* in 1996, more than 80 percent of business executives said no public money should be used to build a Twins stadium. They placed a Twins stadium dead last in the order of importance of issues facing the 1997 legislature.[9] The Greater Minneapolis Chamber of Commerce, the same organization—in title anyway—that helped drive through the Metrodome legislation, meekly offered "conditional support" for a potential Twins stadium before the 1997 session. Its backing was contingent on the legislature also approving a "regional infrastructure tax" to help fund the Minneapolis Convention Center. The stadium was an afterthought for the organization that was the backbone of the Dome movement.

Veteran corporate stalwarts such as Ken Dayton said the culture of the modern corporation is to link all of its "good work" to advertising, that the day of the straight-ahead corporate contribution for a civic good has come to an end. But Duane Benson, who heads the Minnesota Business Partnership, a sort of upper-level chamber of commerce for the state's biggest companies, disagreed with Dayton. Benson, a former legislator and former NFL player, contended that Minnesota's CEOs "are more deeply involved in this community than ever. But they have accents. They're from different places. They're just as committed. It's just a different kind of commitment." Large national corporations have cookie-cutter approaches to charity and giving; if they can sponsor an early-childhood reading program in Minneapolis, San Antonio, Charlotte, and Boston, it's easier to superimpose such giving. To pick and choose big, controversial, highly political local causes for their money is time-consuming and troublesome to the increasingly aware shareholder. Besides, Benson said, in a highly taxed state, Minnesota CEOs are opposed these days to taxes for things such as stadiums. Furthermore, with historically low unemployment, corporate heads need not worry about funding facilities that serve as diversionary bread and circuses.

In the 1970s, the stadium campaign was a shining, and aggressive, example of the business community's clout, its commitment to the downtown central business districts and to the cultural amenities that made the Twin Cities special. The Dome's birth was another feather in the quality-of-life cap that included the theaters, the orchestra, and the art museums. The Dome effort was also an act of civic affection.

But back to Leary's story, which may be apocryphal, but it serves its purpose. "There was a member of the Pillsbury family some years ago," Leary said, "And he had a big decision to make. Seems there was this young guy, a squeaky-clean MBA who just started with the company. In a staff meeting, he said to Mr. Pillsbury, 'Sir, I have serious doubts that Minnesota is the best place for this company to be located. With all the changes in our business, I'd like to analyze that for you and determine exactly where our business would best flourish.' Mr. Pillsbury heard the young man out and said, 'Son, that's a very good idea. Please do.'

"Well, the guy went ahead and performed his analysis. Lo and behold, he reported that Minneapolis–St. Paul was clearly the absolutely worst place in the world for the Pillsbury Company. He delivered the report to Mr. Pillsbury. A week went by. A month went by. Three months went by. No action, nothing. Finally, at some company gathering, the ambitious MBA found Mr. Pillsbury and questioned him. 'Mr. Pillsbury, I submitted that report that we talked about months ago. It showed beyond a reasonable doubt that this company shouldn't be based here in Minnesota.'

"'Oh, yes, quite a fine report,' Mr. Pillsbury replied. 'An excellent report.'

"'But, sir? Was there something wrong?'

"'You left out one very important fact,' Pillsbury told the genius.

"'What's that, sir?' the MBA said.

"'Son,' Pillsbury replied, 'I like it here.'"

And Leary laughed and laughed at that punch line. The story told of a time when Minnesota's companies were controlled by people whose names they bore, when playing to Wall Street wasn't the top priority, and when civic good was expected. When these gentlemen liked it here, they delivered, even if it meant overriding the wishes of the populace. It wasn't a pure democracy, even if, in the end, the people's elected officials voted "yes" for a stadium. It was, to a certain extent, an aristocracy, perhaps a benevolent dictatorship. After all, there wasn't one popular opinion poll that showed Minnesota's citizens in favor of a downtown domed stadium. But the business leadership had a vision and stuck with it. It had a love for this particular place and was determined to keep it special.

Urban planning wonks were for a downtown facility. The Metropolitan Council, the agency charged with setting planning policy for the region, weighed in in March of 1978 with a staff opinion that urged construction of the new stadium in downtown Minneapolis. Citing "Development Framework Policy 8," which called for "reinforcing development in the Metro Centers," the Met Council staff noted that bringing "regional cultural and entertainment facilities" into downtown Minneapolis and St. Paul could be a catalyst for other beneficial downtown needs: housing, mass transit, jobs, and riverfront development. "The Metro Centers are this region's major source of identity and are the focal points for regional scale development and activities that serve the metro area as a whole and the Upper Midwest, including retail trade, government, medical services, finance, office space, entertainment and the arts."[10]

But Minnesotans shunned such precursory New Urbanism. The *Minneapolis Tribune*'s respected Minnesota Poll from January 28, 1973, through November 26, 1978, didn't once show more than 30 percent of those surveyed ever favoring a downtown multipurpose dome. Often citing poor parking or fears of getting lost, the growing number of suburbanites in the Twin Cities worried about heading into the wilds of downtown. Even though studies showed that it would be quicker to leave a Vikings game from dispersed downtown parking locations than from the massive, gridlocked parking lots around Met Stadium, people still consistently favored an open-air football-soccer stadium in Bloomington that would sit next to a remodeled Met Stadium for baseball. This was a period in which the Minnesota Kicks soccer team was experiencing its halcyon days of youthful support, a spurt of a fad that lasted about as long as the hula hoop and Tickle Me Elmo dolls.

Once, just days before the newly formed Sports Facilities Commission was set to choose where the new stadium should be located, a Minnesota Poll showed that 49 percent of those citizens who favored a new stadium also favored the Minneapolis dome. But only 42 percent of the entire sample supported construction of a stadium at all, even if it was paid for just with user fees and a 2 percent metro area liquor tax. Of the 38 percent of those surveyed who said they supported any kind of stadium, 49 percent of them leaned toward the downtown Dome.[11]

This widely held antidowntown, anti-Dome sentiment was not lost on Vikings general manager Lynn. By 1976, he had come to the conclusion that a domed facility, no matter where, was not in the best interests of the Vikings. He was Winter's hatchet man, keeping open options to feign possible relocation to Phoenix, Memphis, or Los Angeles. There had to be threats. "My job was not to look out for the best interests of Minneapolis," Lynn said. "It was to look out for the best interests of the Minnesota Vikings." He believed that a multipurpose stadium wasn't good for the football team, either. Lynn understood the ever-stressed economics of sports and figured that each team would thrive with its own facility. Besides, these were the early years of "luxury suites," the skyboxes for corporate types. In his view, there was limited need for enclosed fancy suites in a domed stadium in which *everyone* would be enclosed. In an outdoor stadium, Vikings' traditions could continue: opposing teams would shudder at the thought of having to play in subzero temperatures; fans could enjoy pregame tailgating in the expansive parking lots; and maximizing profits could occur. Lynn thought he could sell more than two hundred heated suites in an otherwise outdoor stadium. Corporations would want to keep their clients warm. The Metrodome eventually was built with 115 suites, but the Vikings historically struggled to sell them out. The suites were a focus for Lynn, not just because they meant large chunks of cash for his team but because under NFL rules, revenue from the suites didn't have to be shared with the visiting team. The Vikings saw the suites as the revenue stream of choice. "We weren't going to support anything without us getting the suites," Lynn said. What's more, Lynn had sneakily acquired 10 percent of all suite revenues for himself. It occurred in a roundabout way, but in a typical Mike Lynn sort of way.

In late 1977, after the new stadium legislation passed but before its location was determined, Lynn, behind Max Winter's back, began to make headway with some legislative leaders who wanted to block Minneapolis's stadium effort. Among them was the powerful St. Paul senator Nick Coleman. Lynn still had his heart set on an open-air stadium in Bloomington. All the polls showed that the Vikings were far more popular than the Twins, that citizens thought the Vikings' departure to another city would be a greater loss than a Twins' move would be. Lynn, despite knowing Winter's wishes, lobbied hard to locate the new stadium in Bloomington. "Besides," Lynn remembered, "Max was in Hawaii." Winter spent about six months a year at his Honolulu home, allowing Lynn to run the Vikings' stadium campaign. Winter was soon to learn of Lynn's attempted betrayal.

"I'll never forget this day," Lynn remembered twenty-one years later. "John Cowles called me up. He said, 'I know what you're doing. I know what you're up to. And I just wanted to let you know, I'm at the airport. The plane is leaving for Hawaii in five minutes. And I'm on it, and I'm going to see Max.' And then John hung the phone up."

Cowles can't remember how he got wind that Lynn was up to this particular no good, but Cowles generally suspected Lynn was, on general principles, up to no good. "Mike is very smart and shrewd and a helluva wheeler-dealer," Cowles said. "He's also not very trustworthy."

Cowles called Lynn with a purpose: to alert him so that Lynn would have enough to time to stew, react, call Winter in Hawaii, try to explain himself, and, more important, prepare Winter for Cowles's visit. "I wanted whatever response Max was going to give me to be a considered response," Cowles said. "I didn't want to get there and have Max say, 'Well, let me think about this for forty-eight hours, John.' I had no intention of sitting on Waikiki while Max thought about it."

No, Cowles's intention was this: find out for sure that Winter was committed to a downtown Dome, that there were no hidden shenanigans, and that Lynn was going to be put in his place rather than allowed to sabotage the downtown concept. "I wanted a blood oath from Max that he was serious about proceeding with us," Cowles said. Winter, of course, wanted his relationship with Cowles and his elite buddies to be healthy. Then in his early sixties and eager to leave a legacy beyond being just a sports team owner, Winter wanted to have an honorable final chapter with the city's upper echelon. But at the same time, Winter had no desire to dump Lynn and start looking for a new general manager. "He didn't want to fire Mike right then," Cowles remembered. "I wish he had."

Lynn was frantic. He knew he was playing with the big boys. "In those days it didn't matter what the politicians wanted or what the public wanted," Lynn said. "What the power brokers in downtown Minneapolis wanted is what got done." As soon as Cowles hung up, Lynn scrambled to embark on his own flight to Honolulu to explain himself to Winter. "I tried to catch up to John," Lynn said. "I had to fly to L.A. or San Francisco to make a connection to Hawaii. I got there four or five hours later. Of course, he had his meeting with Max, got back on the plane and flew right back to Minneapolis. And there I was with Max." In Hawaii, a long way from home. "Max was mad ... I was given the ultimatum by Max that I had to stop tinkering with the plan and go all out for the domed stadium." His tail between his legs, Lynn listened, accepted the fact that he'd been nabbed red-handed, and agreed to follow Max's wishes. As he humbled himself, Lynn's ears pricked up. Winter had a consolation prize for him. "Listen, if we get this stadium and we get control of the private suites, you can have 25 percent of the private suite money as a reward for doing it," Winter told Lynn. "How's that?"

Winter, who wanted peace for all time, provided Lynn with a huge incentive to do something Lynn really didn't want to do, that is, publicly push for a downtown Dome. Lynn had his price for his silence. He saw dollar signs on the horizon. It was worth the trip to Hawaii. Eventually, Winter's promise of 25 percent was reduced to 10 percent, but the gift was substantial nonetheless. When the downtown site was approved by the Sports Facilities Commission the next year and the Vikings negotiated a lease, Lynn made sure that the Vikings controlled all of the suite revenues. That wasn't that difficult. The commission didn't have enough money in its $55 million bonding allocation to build the suites, anyway. It asked for private money, and the Vikings agreed to build the suites for $5.5 million. In exchange, the Vikings could control the rental and concession revenues from the suites for all Dome events, even Twins games. With deposits of $50,000 required from potential suite renters, the Vikings got most of their investment back in the first year.

And, of course, as part of Winter's private deal with Lynn, 10 percent of the "adjusted gross income" of those suite rentals traveled directly into Lynn's pocket and continues to do so. "This agreement calls for such payments to continue as long as the Vikings suite lease with the Metropolitan Sports Facilities Commission remains in effect, including options and renewals," an official Vikings financial statement noted in 1997. Between, for instance, 1992 and 1996, Lynn received $1,153,000 from the Vikings, even though he no longer worked for them. That phone call out of the blue from Cowles was a godsend for Lynn.

Power Breakfast

On December 1, 1978, the Sports Facilities Commission was required to determine a site for the new stadium. The bill to authorize the issuance of Metropolitan Council–backed bonds was approved a year earlier by the legislature. The host community of any selected stadium site had to supply the land. Minneapolis city fathers focused on an area of abandoned Rock Island railroad repair sheds on the far east end of downtown, nearly a mile's walk from the heart of Nicollet Mall. This area, devoid of economic activity, home to some poor people, adjacent to Hennepin County

General Hospital and the Minneapolis Star and Tribune Company head-quarters, was unused and had no other prospects. Much of the land was already owned by the Minneapolis Housing and Redevelopment Authority, which would soon become known as the Minneapolis Community Development Agency, or MCDA.

Chuck Krusell, skilled in financing urban renewal housing, came up with an idea to attract corporate funds to acquire the land and then to provide it free to the city of Minneapolis. But Krusell and Cowles also learned that in trying to pool corporate dollars for the land, they simply couldn't ask for charitable contributions from some of the city's firms. By the time Cowles and Krusell came calling, most had already committed their charitable donations for 1978. Krusell had an option for them. He established, essentially, a shell corporation called the the Industry Square Development Company. It would own development rights for the area for fifteen years. It would sell stock. There was virtually no chance that any of the stock would deliver dividends or that its value would appreciate. The Industry Square project encompassed land that ran all along Washington Avenue, including the Milwaukee Depot. It included land on the Mississippi River that began to be privately developed in the late 1990s. But mostly, the corporation was set up to pool heavy-hitting corporate dollars. As expected, if the companies' investments failed, they could be written off as losses, turned into tax benefits and barely felt. They needed $15 million to buy and clear the land. In 1999 dollars, taking inflation into account, that would be worth $37.5 million.

A group of the city's elite gathered for a breakfast meeting at the ivy-covered Minneapolis Club sometime during the summer of 1978. There sat Cowles, Ken Dayton, hotel and premium-stamp magnate Curt Carlson, and the chairmen of Pillsbury, First National Bank of Minneapolis, Northwestern National Bank, Honeywell, the Lutheran Brotherhood, and a few others.

Cowles began the meeting by explaining the situation. The Sports Facilities Commission later that year was going to select a site. For Minneapolis to be picked, the city had to provide the site and pay the costs of preparing it. He and Krusell had devised a way for Minneapolis companies to invest in the Industry Square Development Company or, if they preferred, to make tax-deductible contributions to either the MCDA or the Sports Facilities Commission.

With no flair for drama, with no drumrolls, Cowles said, "And I'll start by putting in two and a half million dollars." There were no reports of any coffee or orange juice being spit across the table and onto the Minneapolis Club's polished oak walls, but there must have been a healthy handful of gulps, even from the city's top executives. The bidding was obviously starting high. Cowles didn't want this meeting to last very long.

Krusell loved Cowles's psychology. "You run a company, and you've been called to a stadium meeting," he said. "You know you're going to be asked for money, and maybe you say, 'I'd be willing to put in $100,000, or whatever.' Then, the leader starts out, tells you we need $15 million and he's putting in two-and-a-half. It kind of changes your frame of mind. Maybe your one hundred thousand becomes five hundred thousand." By the end of that breakfast, Cowles had raised $8.5 million of the $15 million he needed. The remaining $7 million would come soon after.

Talk about golden moments. The financial powers that be still believed that pro sports were significant civic image builders. It was also a time in which the owners of the teams could be viewed as midrange entrepreneurs, not as equals to the business leaders. Once the transition occurred in pro sports to the superrich owning teams and to the teams being managed poorly, the Twin Cities business community checked out of the pro sports booster club. As long as Cowles, Dayton, and their cronies felt they were in the driver's seat, there was consensus within the business community that it should be at the table to keep the Twin Cities in the major-league game and to aid the team owners, who were barely members of the community's inner circle. Winter and Griffith were, all things considered, small-time operators of high-profile assets. Besides, Met Stadium was already twenty years old. It seemed aged. Its obsolescence could be understood in a culture where old homes are treasured, not discarded. But when the likes of billionaire banker Carl Pohlad bought the Twins in 1984 or ten of the richest Minnesotans bought the Vikings in 1988, then the relationships changed. Then that other factor came into play: local companies began to be managed by outside professionals, not by the families. The changing culture of Minnesota's large corporations turned away from edifice building and turned toward their shareholders.

Much later, by 1993, Sid Hartman, the venerable columnist for the *Minneapolis Star Tribune* and longtime mouthpiece for the owners, wrote a column bemoaning the loss of corporate support for pro sports. The headline read: "Bigwigs Don't Care Enough about Teams."[12] Pro sports were no longer on the radar for the nouveau CEO. On this score, Hartman was correct; unless "these geniuses"—that is, the younger, less-attached-to-the-community CEOs—realize that pro sports are a critical cultural component in a major metropolitan area, the future of major-league sports in the Twin Cities is dim. As much as a public-policy decision must be made about allocating some public resources for pro sports, there must be a commitment on the part of the Twin Cities' large corporations; no facilities can be built or maintained without significant investment via luxury suites, season tickets, and in-stadium advertising. Whether the Twin Cities business community of the new millennium is up to the challenge is questionable. If and when a new Twins ballpark proposal faces the public, if and when a Vikings stadium proposal faces the public, when the new St. Paul–based NHL team faces its first financial difficulties (which will be soon), when the Timberwolves declare that Target Center needs renovations, will the "bigwigs" take a stand? Fact is, the equivalent $37 million that Cowles raised at one breakfast won't come close to what the local teams need today. If the owners of Minnesota's four major-league teams have their way, if the Twins and Vikings were ever to get their own stadiums, there would be a total of about three hundred luxury suites in this market. At an average price of, say, $80,000, that would mean local companies would have to invest $24 million *every year* in local sports facilities private boxes. That number doesn't include the 110,000 season tickets that the four teams will want: 60,000 for the Vikings, 20,000 for the Twins, 15,000 for the NHL Wild, and 15,000 for the Timberwolves. The Wild and the Timberwolves will have average ticket prices approaching $50 for forty-one home games. Nor does it include the costs of supporting University of Minnesota sports, including new suitelike lofts at Williams Arena for men's basketball.

Yikes. Will the Twin Cities "bigwigs" of the twenty-first century take that big a stand?

The Twins and Escapism

Cowles didn't have to jet to a tropical island to work things out with Twins owner Calvin Griffith. Griffith was in line. Griffith was even desperate. His team wasn't succeeding. He figured that his move from Washington in the 1960s had jump-started his franchise; perhaps a move indoors to a dome in downtown Minneapolis could give him another boost. "Something has to be done to help us solve our problems with the weather,"[13] he said, as if a new stadium or a public subsidy could seed the clouds and bring only sunshine. What he meant, of course, was that in the chilly late spring and the cool early autumn weeks of a Minnesota baseball season, the frost and wet of Minnesota hurt attendance. For a team that marketed itself as a regional asset, the ability to assure fans from the hinterlands that games would be played, no matter what the weather, could be an advantage. At different points along the way, Griffith seemed to be eager to move into a dome, and then reluctant. He knew that Met Stadium was in need of repair, and there were no funds for renovations. He knew that a new stadium could add new spirit to his franchise. But he worried, too. "Hell, they're hemmed up all winter long in the house," he said in 1998. "They want some fresh air once the summer comes." In his heart, Griffith was never convinced that the Dome was right for him.

Worried but with no other options, Griffith entered into stadium discussions under the impression that the Vikings and Twins would be treated equally by the Sports Facilities Commission as planning ensued. It was a total illusion, and Lynn knew it. "We were the lead dog," Lynn said. "It was the first football stadium built to be convertible to baseball, and not the other way around. We wanted that. We wanted to reverse the trend around the country." Football was king.

Sports Facilities Commission chairman Dan Brutger denied that the Twins were outcasts as his agency planned for the new stadium. All he was doing, Brutger said, was "following the law," which dictated that football, professional soccer, and baseball be accommodated by the new edifice. Football and soccer, of course, are square sports. Baseball is not. Soccer seemed to be an up-and-coming phenomenon, even if in a 1999 interview Brutger said he believed the professional soccer fad was on its way out as the Dome was being conceived. Still, as Brutger and his designers carried on, Calvin Griffith and his son Clark, who negotiated much of the Twins' stadium matters, came to understand that baseball was headed for stepchild status. As the budget got tighter, the Twins kept falling by the wayside. There was no air-conditioning installed; that wasn't a problem for the Vikings, but it sure was for the Twins. The baseball field was stuck in a corner of the stadium, making sight lines horrendous. Some key seats were stationary; a fan sitting down the third base line had a tremendous view of the football field as it was laid out across the width of the stadium. But when the Dome was transformed into a baseball configuration, that same fan, now in the stadium for a Twins game and sitting just beyond third base, was stuck looking directly at the left fielder. To see the action at home plate or in the infield meant turning one's body or one's neck all game long, precipitating a certain postgame visit to one's chiropractor or orthopedist. Only about eight thousand seats were available in the stadium's lower deck between first and third base, prime baseball season ticket areas.

When the Twins learned that all the suite revenues would be directed to the Vikings, that was the final straw. "They lied to us that positively no one was going to benefit over the other," Calvin Griffith remembered. "Then I read in the paper that all the suites are going to the Vikings. I don't know what happened. All I found out was that Lynn got a pretty goddamn good deal." Brutger said the Vikings' control of the suites was a function of the team being able to afford to build them. Lynn said Winter simply wouldn't have signed a lease without the football team's control of the suites. Frankly, Lynn didn't care about fairness. The Twins hadn't been fair to the Vikings during the years in Met Stadium when the Griffiths pocketed all the concession dollars from football games. Brutger noted that the Twins received a significantly higher portion of the Dome's concession revenues than did the Vikings, and that came with the commission's blessings. Brutger's top aide, Don Poss, who was a budget hawk, looked at the Twins' financial projections before the stadium opened and understood that Griffith needed more revenue if he was going to be able to compete. But the concessions take at the Dome for the Twins was going to be minuscule compared to their control of food at the Met. In Bloomington, the Twins controlled it all, even Vikings games. In downtown Minneapolis, their 100 percent take was reduced to 30 percent. Plus Griffith had no cash to invest in construction. In fact, the same men who had brought Minneapolis the $8.5 million power breakfast raised another $1 million to pay for Griffith's offices in the new Dome; the baseball operator simply didn't have it himself.

Whatever the details, whatever the disagreements, whatever the versions of history, by 1979, when lease discussions heated up, one thing was clear to Calvin and Clark Griffith and to Brutger. Before it opened, the new Dome could turn into a black hole for the Twins. Such a conclusion meant a controversial adjustment was going to have to be made to the hard-fought 1977 legislation that authorized the $55 million in bonds to build the dome.

The law that allowed the construction of the Metrodome required that all teams sign thirty-year leases, ensuring that the teams would be in the facility for the life of the bonds to be issued. But Calvin Griffith and Clark Griffith, both uncertain about their potential for success in the Dome, refused to sign on for that long. Calvin simply wouldn't tie his own hands. Clark Griffith, whose experience with the Dome lease piqued his interest in becoming a lawyer, remembers how the clock was ticking toward the required time when a lease had to be signed. Clark Griffith remembers the origins of the clause. He remembers meeting with Brutger in Calvin's Met Stadium offices, with the giant fish on the wall behind Calvin. Almost simultaneously, Brutger and Clark raised the concept of a "renegotiation clause" in the thirty-year lease. "It was as if we both thought about it at the same time," said Griffith, of discussions with Brutger. It came to be called the Twins' "escape clause," but in Clark Griffith's view, it was intended more as a "reopener" of the lease in the event the new domed stadium hurt the Twins rather than helped them in their attendance and their financial bottom line. "They weren't building a baseball stadium for us," Clark Griffith recalled. "We were just one of the tenants."

Escape, reopener, renegotiation clause—however the participants defined it then, it provided an opportunity for the Twins to gain leverage with the public, no matter who owned the team and what decade the public happened to be on the spot. The escape clause was to Calvin Griffith what the Minnesota gambling compacts are to the state's Indian tribes: the first real economic victory for either in hundreds of years. Griffith may always have been on the operational ropes financially because of the changing economics of the baseball industry and his inability to adequately market his team. But he wasn't as dumb as he looked. With the help of one of Minneapolis's top lawyers, Peter Dorsey, Griffith understood the value of the escape clause. It gave him potential freedom. It added value to his franchise; anytime a team can up and leave a community, the team has power and the ability to offer itself up for the highest bid to other cities in search of teams. The team has leverage, every businessman's friend.

"We would not be locked into thirty years in a bad situation," said Clark Griffith. He suggested simple thresholds for bolting: failing to reach league-wide attendance averages or losing money over a three-year period would suggest financial duress. "I said to Brutger, 'If this building is as good as you say it is, you won't have any problem with this [escape clause] language.'"

Dorsey pegged the "insurance clause," as he called it, as "what it would cost to keep the team from going bankrupt. We felt we had to have a certain level of attendance to make it work."

The 1977 legislature's decision to approve a stadium—but only with thirty-year guarantees—was amended by the 1979 legislature. The original language of the bill said that bonds may be issued and construction may commence only when agreements are signed "for a period of not more than 30 years nor less than the term of the longest term bond." Two years later, the altered state law added this sentence: "The agreements may contain provisions negotiated between the organizations and the commission which provide for termination upon conditions related and limited to the bankruptcy, insolvency or financial capability of the organization." Griffith held the key to his future financial health.

On August 10, 1979, the deal was struck: If the Twins didn't sell 1.4 millon tickets per year or the American League average—whichever was less—for three consecutive seasons, then they could escape the thirty-year lease. In 1978, AL teams averaged about 1.47 million tickets per team. There was another out: if, for three straight seasons, the team had "a cumulative net operating loss," then it could terminate the lease deal. There, in the Met Stadium boardroom, when the average annual big-league salary was $143,000 and when a man named Carl Pohlad was an unknown Minneapolis banker, the deal needed to sell the bonds to build the Dome was sealed. It was hammered out by a negotiated loophole. Brutger believed he represented the public reasonably. Others believe that act of permitting the escape language in the lease was more or less criminal.

"That was not a misdemeanor," said Dome booster Harvey Mackay, who worked long and hard for the stadium and then worked longer and harder to save the Twins five years later. "That was a felony. The only reason I took the job [of lobbying for the Dome] was I wouldn't have to think about it for another thirty years. I went out and made a hundred speeches that he's going to sign a thirty-year lease. That was chicanery. The Twins were allowed to sign what amounted to ten three-year leases. I still can't get over it."

With that escape clause in place, before the new downtown stadium was even built, the seeds were sown for the debate about the *next* stadium war, fifteen years down the road. Given the circumstances, it was only a matter of time before Griffith found his escape hatch and walked through. Once the terms of the escape clause were met, all hell could break loose, and it consistently has.

One other legal change made the final dealings of the Dome battle disconcerting. Once the Sports Facilities Commission decided in late 1978 that Minneapolis would be the site of the new stadium, the rest of the metro area revolted. The original stadium law called for a 2 percent metropolitan-area-wide liquor tax to back up the bonds that were to be issued by the Metropolitan Council. But once Minneapolis got its stadium, the suburbs and St. Paul pulled out of the taxing district. They placed the burden of supporting any stadium shortfalls on the backs of Minneapolis taxpayers once more. For the second straight stadium game, Minneapolis, and no other community, carried the load. Minneapolis financed Met Stadium. Now it was going to be on the hook for the Dome, too. A pattern was developing.

When crunch time approached for dirt to be turned and the thing to get built, one of Brutger's and Poss's underlings during the Dome's development emerged to nail down the final points of the escape clause amendment. His name was Jerry Bell. He was a former parks employee in North St. Paul, West St. Paul, and Apple Valley, and a former Metropolitan Council staffer. He was no powerful financial analyst, lawyer, or lobbyist. He literally used to mow the grass at playgrounds. But Bell was on his way up. He would, before long, become the lead dog at the Sports Facilities Commission. He would also become an important player in the future of the Twins. From the other side of the table, he would seek the baseball team's next stadium, sooner than anyone could ever have imagined.

The Public Publisher

An unfortunate sidelight of Cowles's involvement in the stadium effort was the damage to his newspaper's credibility and the uncomfortable position in which it put his staff. A publisher's connection to any community action is always problematic. Business leaders and community activists can't, won't, and shouldn't be expected to delineate between the publisher's support for a project and the news stories his newspaper writes about that project. With Cowles out in front on the stadium matter and with his company apparently benefiting because of its commitment to selling a sports section and its ownership of parking areas around the Dome, critics attacked the *Star* and the *Tribune*. Some of the critics were within the newspaper.

On March 1, 1979, after the ballpark was awarded to Minneapolis, but before ground was broken, forty-five *Tribune* reporters and editors (including a twenty-four-year-old me) paid for and signed an advertisement that blasted and embarrassed the publisher of the newspapers. In part, the advertisement read: "AS JOURNALISTS ... our responsibility is to be dispassionate and fair in covering public issues. Our role is to report, not participate in, these issues. Because we work for the Minneapolis Tribune, we recognize some people may question our fidelity to that principle when John Cowles Jr., chairman of the board of the Minneapolis Star and Tribune Co., is a leading advocate in the debate over whether and where a sports stadium should be built. We bought this advertisement to assure readers that our professional principles have not been undermined by Cowles' involvement in the stadium issue. We neither advocate nor oppose building a stadium, domed or undomed, at any location. Furthermore, neither Cowles nor any other company executive has tried to influence the *Tribune*'s coverage of the issue. But to prevent even an appearance of such a conflict of interest, we believe management should avoid a leadership role in sensitive political and economic issues."

Of course, by placing the ad and making our statement, we got involved and became bit players in the Dome debate. To his credit, Cowles allowed the ad to run. The inmates, for a day, were allowed a little bit of control of the asylum. The anger associated with the episode was part of a long-standing undercurrent between management and union activists at the newspaper. It carried over into a twenty-seven-day strike in 1980. Sophisticated readers can't help but remember the newspaper's stance in the seventies. Those readers remain leery of the *Star Tribune*'s news columns and editorials about sports facilities matters. Readers wonder how they can trust the accuracy and context of the newspaper's stories if the owner of the daily rag is in the trenches every day selling the idea to legislators.

The paper seems not to be able to help itself, from Sid Hartman sitting on that Minneapolis tax story in 1958 to Cowles in the seventies to the relentless pro-stadium editorials in the late 1990s. Although distressing, it made sense. The synergies between daily newspapers in large metropolitan areas and sports teams are natural and increasing daily. Newspapers don't have to pay for the right to write about teams in the way that TV or radio stations pay rights fees to exclusively broadcast games. But newspapers sponsor teams with in-stadium advertising, with billboards that promote sports section coverage of teams, with the daily coverage that serves, more often than not, as free advertising. Sports sections preview and review games—every game—at no cost to the teams. Newspapers don't review every single Guthrie Theater performance or preview every single St. Paul Chamber Orchestra concert. They promote sports out of all sense of proportionality because so much of the readership base and advertisers' targets turn to the sports section.

The *Star Tribune* has been the official sponsor of the NBA Timberwolves. The *Star Tribune* was a major sponsor of the 1998 World Figure Skating Championships in Minneapolis. It should be noted that in some markets, such as Denver, one of the newspapers, the *Rocky Mountain News*, actually owns shares in the Colorado Rockies baseball team. Critics suggest that preserving the sports teams in communities is an act of self-interest for all of the downtown business leaders. For the newspaper owner, the self-interest appeared even more stark. Downtown retailers sell more products if a downtown core is more stable, and downtown banks lend more money when the central business district thrives. Big-city newspapers with large sports section infrastructures need pro sports. There is an organic conflict of interest that we all must live with and navigate.

Thankfully, fortunately, honestly, in retrospect, Cowles's effort to build the Dome was more than self-interest. There was for him and the others of his elite crew a higher purpose. They were lampooned and harpooned for being the "cigar smokers" or "the Brotherhood." It was as if they were up to no good. In my view, they were up to much good. Those who challenged Cowles's right to be active misunderstood his role and that of other publishers. They are business leaders, not journalists. It's the job of reporters to cover their boss as if he were the CEO of another company. It's the job of reporters to hold their boss to the fire, if need be. It's the job of reporters to use their boss as a source, if possible. But reporters should be reporting, writing stories, forming their own opinions, offering their own analysis. Taking out advertisements to show up Cowles was a juvenile, misdirected act. Similarly, any publisher who attempts to influence news coverage because of his personal political agenda does so at much peril. In stadium games, shots get fired from all directions because emotions take over from reason.

Transition

Lo and behold, after barely two years in the Metrodome, Calvin Griffith said things just weren't working out. Just like that, the escape clause was about to launch the Twins into the open market. Varying degrees of seriousness were attached to reports that Griffith would sell the team to investors in Tampa–St. Petersburg and that the Twins would move to Florida after the 1984 season. The escape clause would get some early and good use.

For baseball, the Dome was a disaster. Attendance fell well short of one million fans in each of the first two seasons. With no air-conditioning during the 1982 season, watching some games in July and August was like taking an unintended sauna. The air-conditioning was added for the second season. The Twins were absolutely wretched on the field, finishing thirty-three games and twenty-nine games out of first place in those seasons. By the summer of 1983, it was clear that the Twins weren't going to average 1.4 million fans per game over the three-year period unless they attracted about 2.4 million fans in 1984. That was extremely unlikely. Documents later revealed that Griffith suffered a $1.8 million operating loss in 1983, was headed for a $500,000 operating loss in 1984, and owed players deferred compensation of $3.6 million.[14] He faced steep revenue needs in the coming years. He didn't have the resources. Plus, Griffith hated to go to banks to borrow money. "I'll be goddamed if I'm going to borrow money to pay for players," he said in 1998, recounting his business philosophy.

During the summer and early fall, a group of Tampa-area business leaders was poised to buy the 42 percent of the Twins owned by minority shareholder Gabe Murphy of Washington, D.C. They made overtures to Griffith. (Eventually Murphy sold his Twins shares to the Tampa group, but the deal was rejected by the other American League owners.) Griffith, who swore that he held no serious thoughts of moving the Twins, seemed, however, to have wanderlust. Employing the same modus operandi that he had twenty-five years earlier when he was still in Washington, he denied that he was dickering with the Tampa group but acknowledged that he was consulting them on their stadium construction plans.

By October, a core of the same well-heeled corporate types who had helped build the Dome coalesced to form yet another task force to study how to beef up the Twins' image in the community and preserve the team. The effort had as its ultimate goal finding a new local owner for the Twins. In the interim, the notion of a ticket buyout was born; the idea was to get the corporate community to buy enough tickets to close the escape hatch in the Twins lease. That effort to sell tickets—and paper the Dome house—was spearheaded by Mackay, who had worked so hard just five years earlier to get the Dome built. He was joined in the inner circle of this "Save the Twins" effort by Ankeny of First National Bank, by Curt Carlson, the ubiquitous business leader, and by a new name on the sports and community radar: Carl Pohlad. He was a banker. He had control of a large Pepsi bottling company. He was an investor and deal maker. He was nearly seventy years old. To the average man or woman on the Twin Cities street, Pohlad was just another mumbly rich guy. To some business insiders, he was notorious. Pohlad was in an acquisitive mood.

Marketing

A remarkable document was produced by the task force's marketing subcommittee. Authored by a local consultant named Dick Pomerantz, this report served as a blueprint for how to revive the Twins' status in the community. It never questioned the negative impact of the Metrodome on the team, even though attendance indicated that the stadium alone produced none of the typical attendance spiking that new sports facilities create just because of their newness. Mostly, the report challenged

Griffith—and presumably a future owner—to better market the team and repair the broken relationship between the team and the community. It was part of a body of literature and data that, frankly, confirms that the Twin Cities, for the past twenty years, has been a struggling, even bad, baseball market. Save for the first five years in Twins history and then the period from 1987 to 1993, when the team drew a creditable 2.3 million fans per season, Minneapolis–St. Paul has not been a reliable baseball town. The 218-page report, written in 1984, could well have analyzed the Twins' position in the year 2000 as well.

- "The deteriorating relationship between the Minnesota Twins baseball franchise and the community at large, and the business community in particular, has been allowed to proceed unabated far too long."
- "The concept of poorly promoting a team, ineffectively merchandising the product, of staying with the philosophy of 'hey baseball is a great game we sell at a good price so why shouldn't people come out to the game' is no longer operable nor viable in today's competitive environment."
- "The community [should] be prepared to take whatever action necessary ... if the franchise decided to move without allowing for a viable local matching offer."[15]

These conclusions justified the Mackay-led ticket buyout. Mackay, the business community's Pied Piper, scurried around town to gather the cash to buy the tickets for each game that would push Twins attendance over 2.4 million for the 1984 season. The exercise infuriated Calvin Griffith and embarrassed him. He called it a "farce." He thought the "escape clause" could trigger some economic relief via a new lease. But the handwriting was on the wall. If the Twins were going to be competitive, a new lease might help. But the franchise mostly needed a new owner with more resources. The situation demanded a new personality to change the economic and political dynamic.

The Twins had completed two full seasons in the gleaming new Dome, and not only was it already not enough, but that so-called renegotiating clause was about to trip an alarm. The Twin Cities' citizens, businesses, and political institutions had just authorized the sale of $55 million in low-interest publicly backed bonds. Another $23 million had been contributed by local companies to buy the land, move the juvenile jail for Hennepin County, build the Twins offices, and insure that tickets would be bought so that Vikings football games wouldn't be blacked out for local TV viewers. The region engaged in a decade-long, painful, divisive debate over building the Dome. And instantly the Twins were seemingly headed out of town. It was outrageous. The community had been promised a thirty-year solution in 1977. By 1984, Griffith held the key to his departure.

First, glamour approached. Donald Trump, the New York real estate tycoon, telephoned, and lawyer Peter Dorsey swiftly flew to New York to meet him. At the tower bearing his name, Trump greeted Dorsey.

"You know I got something a lot of people don't have," Trump told Dorsey. "And I don't have something that a lot of people do have."

Dorsey scratched his head and inquired, "Well, what is it you have that a lot of people don't have?"

Trump said: "I've got a helluva lot of money."

"OK," Dorsey said. "What is it you don't have?"

"I don't have a board of directors, and I don't have any shareholders," Trump told Dorsey. "So I'll offer $27 million for the team."

Dorsey replied: "I'll take it back to my client, but I'll tell you now that's not enough."

"Not enough?" Trump responded. "OK, I'll offer twenty-eight." (What's a million among acquaintances?)

Nothing ever developed from it. Trump's connections to gambling hurt his chances to get into baseball. He had designs of moving the Twins to New Jersey, too.

About that time, there was another bid for the team. It came from two men who would later be in the middle of their own professional sports controversy. They were named Marv Wolfenson and Harvey Ratner, two Minneapolis health club and real estate owners who loved their town, loved sports, and were ready to give back to the community. Their front man was Harold Greenwood, president of Midwest Federal Savings and Loan Association, long a sponsor of the Twins broadcasts.

One day in late May 1984, Greenwood visited Griffith in his Metrodome office. Greenwood reportedly made a simple offer: $27 million in cash to Calvin and his sister, Thelma, for the 52 percent of the team they owned. In the room with Griffith were his son, Clark, his brothers Jimmy and Billy Robertson, and his nephew, Bruce Haynes. It was a clean, simple offer that, after capital gains and income taxes, could have meant significant chunks of cool cash in the pockets of Calvin, Thelma, and their families. Marv and Harv would have allowed Calvin to continue to operate the team for them. "Gentlemen, there's your deal," Clark Griffith said to the others in the room. There was nothing like cash to put smiles on a seller's face. But there was silence.

"They all looked at me like I was insane," Clark Griffith said. Calvin Griffith and the Hayneses turned down the Wolfenson-Ratner offer. For some, Calvin Griffith's refusal to sell to Wolfenson and Ratner was tainted with anti-Semitism. There was a belief that he shunned them because they were Jewish. But Griffith had another prospect on the line, someone with whom he'd been negotiating for months. It was this fellow Pohlad. They'd met through their mutual involvement with the Boys and Girls Clubs of Minneapolis. Pohlad had been shopping for a sports team for a couple years. Now he seemed to want the Twins, too. He had presented a deal to Griffith weeks before the Wolfenson-Ratner bid.

Typically, Pohlad's offer was more complicated. It seemed to confuse Calvin. Pohlad offered $24 million for Calvin's 52 percent, but it would be paid over time. Pohlad paid Griffith and his sister $10 million up front, but the rest was paid out annually, with an interest rate of about 9.5 percent. By most analyses—including Pohlad's—Griffith should have taken Wolfenson's and Ratner's offer. An all-cash deal in 1984 was more valuable than money paid out over time.

"I thought it cost [Pohlad] more because of the interest," Calvin Griffith said in 1998 after thirteen years of payments. "Wolfenson and Ratner, they offered me a helluva deal. But Carl was the one who called me up first. I'm not going to get into a goddamn bidding war with people. After I sold the ball club I learned [Wolfenson and Ratner] gave me a better offer. I was too stubborn. Pohlad was the richest guy in the goddamn state. I figured he had the money to run the ball club."

The annuity concept may have worked on the Griffiths, but it didn't with Murphy, the minority stockholder. As Pohlad was completing the deal, he had to unwind Murphy's sale to the Tampa group, and satisfy Murphy. As he did with Griffith, Pohlad tried to obtain Murphy's 42 percent of the team via a series of payments, not up-front cash. Murphy met with a thirty-something lawyer for Pohlad. The youthful attorney offered a five-year note to buy the team, not a simple certified check. Murphy, then in his seventies, was stunned by the terms of the deal.

"Young man," he said firmly, "you go tell Mr. Pohlad that at my age I do not even buy green bananas." Murphy got his cash. Pohlad got his team, 100 percent of it.

Lessons

If there is a bottom line to the entire Dome episode, it must include a series of recognitions that are all sobering.

1. Met Stadium became the first ballpark built in baseball's so-called modern era—after World War II—to be knocked down. It was used for only twenty-six years.
2. As much as the big money guys wanted to bring fans downtown to see that the core city was doing just fine, they allowed a suburban-like spaceship—with nothing urban about it—to be plopped on the edge of the central business district. Perhaps the Dome's construction showed there was still power and political will in Minneapolis. It didn't show any respect for the integrity of the city's architecture or organic ingredients of the sports the Dome was meant to preserve. The chirps and thwacks, the sunburn and sweet smell of grass, were eliminated from the baseball experience. The chill in the air and the mitten-muffled applause of an Arctic audience on a crisp Sunday afternoon were lost from the

football experience. Some may have preferred it this way; sports became convenient, like watching games in one's living room. But as much as the Dome may have signified the continued strength of downtown, it precipitated the decline in the relationship between fans and their games. As Peter Richmond wrote in his thoughtful book *Ballpark*, about Chicago's "new" Comiskey Park, built in 1981, it was "designed so that visitors by car will be able to drive in from the suburbs, park, cross the bridges, and never have to set foot in South Side Chicago at all . . . no interaction at all with the surrounding neighborhood; no relation to the city; no view of anything. The antithesis of how the game began. The epitome of the modern profit machine."[16] Yes, those secretaries and CPAs may have been able to look out their windows, look at the symbolic Dome, and see that downtown still thrived. But no one in the Dome could see the towers of downtown ten blocks away. The Dome was an isolator from, not an integrator to, the city.

3. Cowles's vision to block "a third downtown" was pureed into chopped liver by the sale of the Met Stadium land in 1984. Soon after, a development known as the Mall of America was built, creating the largest and most successful shopping mall in the history of the consumption universe. The mall became the largest tourist attraction in Minnesota, nay, in the United States. While it provided some synergies with downtown Minneapolis and St. Paul hotels and the two cities' convention facilities, the mall established, more or less, the third downtown that Cowles and his cohorts had so desperately sought to block. When the state of Minnesota approved state funding for the mall, Bloomington legislators celebrated. They had retaliated for Minneapolis's heist of major-league football and baseball. Before long, Bloomington would lose its final major-league franchise, the NHL North Stars, and its final sports facility, Met Center.

4. As happy as Minnesotans may have been that the Griffith era was over, one dirty little treasure remained that Pohlad wouldn't ever relinquish: the escape clause. Call it insurance, call it a reopener.

It was money in the bank. For someone who claimed to know very little about sports, Pohlad sure understood the role that a lease plays in the financial stability of a team. For as long as he held the Twins, he understood that. It was, of course, the clause that gave Griffith the power to threaten, then unload, his team and family legacy after just three seasons in the new stadium. For Pohlad, a man who embraced leverage, adored options, and exploited opportunities for a living—and as part of his financial game—the escape clause was his biggest chit. He used it to improve his lease once, twice, three times. It was his biggest hammer in a relationship with the Minnesota public that, from 1984 on, would ride an incredibly bell-shaped wave.

If anyone ever asks what ignited the 1990s Minnesota stadium debate, do this. Go to Fifth Street and Chicago Avenue in Minneapolis. Point to the Teflon-covered bubble that sits so unattractively there. Point to it and answer succinctly: "The Dome."

CHAPTER 4

"I'm Only Human"
Understanding Carl Pohlad

For Pohlad, entering the baseball hierarchy was one thing, a regal thing. But exiting gracefully was another. To understand exactly what he got himself into in 1984, we must depart from this chronology and fast-forward. We must jump ahead fourteen years, if only to bring some perspective to the blocks that built Minnesota's late-1990s attitudes toward professional sports. Fly ahead from that August day in 1984 when, on the field of the Metrodome, Calvin Griffith cried, knowing he was selling his family's special history with the franchise, and when Carl Pohlad threw out the first major-league pitch of his career, wearing his number 84 Twins jersey.

It was a day filled with excitement and hope. It was the day the Twins were "saved." For the moment, though, fast-forward to 1998; skip over the explosive events of 1994, 1995, 1996, and 1997. Know that the major stadium war of Minnesota's ongoing sports facilities saga was over and the scene was no longer green and bright, with a cheering crowd applauding a necessary transition.

The scene was black-and-white. The texture was soft, even sad. Carl Pohlad stood in front of the huge picture windows of his thirty-eighth-floor conference room. A warm winter's day was coming to its mid afternoon close. At eighty-three years old, thin and surprisingly frail, he stood to reduce the pain in his back and his hip, both surgically repaired. For a man who loved to be on the go, sitting still literally hurt.

He intermittently paced, in a shuffling sort of way, painting a picture that could only attract human sympathy.

Fast-forward fourteen years since he bought the team that catapulted him to a stardom that all his banks in Iowa could never deliver. They were fourteen years that turned this ultimate outsider, this rugged individualist, this alleged dirty dealer, from a savior to a genius to a two-time champion ... to the devil. Carl Robert Pohlad once told a friend, "Money is my god," but he claimed he got into baseball as a community service. The first time I met and interviewed Carl Pohlad, soon after he bought the Twins, he told me that making a business deal was "like a drug." I remember thinking he was possessed or obsessed. For the years he'd owned the Twins, the man who claimed he didn't want attention gradually became the focus of an entire metropolitan region, once in glory, later in ignominy. He seemed to be wearing conservative business suits. Nonetheless, the public saw a skull and crossbones tattooed all over him.

Fast-forward fourteen years. It is 1998. Long gone was Calvin Griffith, who used to work in an office at Met Stadium, with a large fish on his wall and baseball memorabilia all over. Now the owner had only a few baseball mementos, a photo of himself and Twins World Series stars Kent Hrbek and Tom Brunansky on a wall down the hallway and a Louisville Slugger bat the length of Kirby Puckett in a conference room. With Griffith, a visitor walked through the corridors of a stadium, past the hot dog stands and forklift trucks. His was the business of baseball. With Pohlad, the environment was elite, like a four-star hotel, with one reception area for his companies, with the fine carpeting, the business journals, and the mints at your touch and smell. Then, when "Mr. Pohlad is ready to see you," there was another short walk, down a narrow hallway to yet another private reception area for Pohlad, with a concierge-secretary just for him, an older, officious woman who, no doubt, had worked for him for thirty years but who still, in the presence of a visitor, referred to him as "Mr. Pohlad."

We're flashing ahead now to understand the man who was at the center of the most contentious stadium battle in the history of the state and, perhaps, the nation. Five years of trying—and failing—to gain a new stadium for the Minnesota Twins had passed. The four-year period from 1994 to 1999 completely wiped out the goodwill that Pohlad was handed in 1984 and that continued through a remarkable seven years of affection for the franchise. There was nothing like 1987, when his Twins, youthful and appealing, accessible and ours, won a World Series that no one expected them to, when the Twin Cities and Minnesota were one big happy family. That's also when the Metrodome—that allegedly cold, antiseptic blob of a scar on the Minneapolis landscape—became our acceptable sporting temple. It had memories now. It had context. It was still a rotten place to watch a baseball game, but it was *our* rotten place, and the games and the memories were great. Then, four years later, there was nothing like winning the World Series again, with a hometown pitcher named Jack Morris heroically throwing the decisive game in what was called perhaps the greatest, most exciting World Series of all time.

Retrieve those snapshots, those special photos for the community album, the one you take out when measuring the collective bonds of Twin Citians. Put them into the emotional bank that any Twins fan or Minnesotan has set aside for the team, for the sport, for the Dome, even for Pohlad. Try to remember the fun.

Then, fast-forward and look at Pohlad on this December 1998 day, fourteen years after the Twin Cities community first got to meet him, although businessmen far and wide had known and disliked him for years. No matter what his history, no matter what his "crimes against humanity," no matter how he might have been misunderstood or how much he thought he deserved, on this day in 1998, as we watched him shuffle helplessly in his conference room, he was a pathetic figure. For the other thirty thousand days of his life, I don't know. He was probably a mean son of a bitch on many of those. History suggests that. But now the outlines of the man were framed by the skyline of the city he had virtually owned just seven years earlier. Now, as 1998 turned into 1999, Pohlad stood in a dark corner of his place of business, gazing across the Mississippi River for which he once had great plans.

He stood stymied. He stood defeated. He wasn't mad anymore, he said. And even if he were, he didn't know who to get even with. "What would you do?" he asked, and he seemed sincerely curious, truly interested in hearing a solution to a problem for which he had no fix. He had stooped so low as to ask a sportswriter, "What would you do?" His voice, as usual, was a bit raspy. His words, typically, were a bit slurred or swallowed. This was a man who had always stood over his opponents like a cocky, victorious boxer. He was used to beating them up and profiting, used to keeping them guessing until the final moment, only to change the deal, or switch direction, or drag them into court.

Now his Minnesota Twins were bleeding red ink, the same type that forced a much poorer Calvin Griffith into pleasant retirement and historic rehabilitation. Pohlad's vision, begun in 1994, of a new Twins stadium on the Minneapolis riverfront, had been eliminated by mistakes—honest and dishonest—and by ardent public opposition to subsidizing him, the second richest man in Minnesota. Now, the man who was known for getting what he wanted at the bargaining table looked as if he was the one who had been punched, knocked back on his heels, even KO'd.

Fourteen years after making sure that he preserved his escape clause at the Dome, Pohlad couldn't bring himself to walk through that door. He had exploited the escape clause for fourteen years, received millions of dollars of rental concessions from the Metropolitan Sports Facilities Commission because of the existence of the clause. But when push came to shove, after all the threats and all the charades that all team owners deploy to seek what they want, Pohlad remained the owner of a struggling baseball team that played in the Metrodome. The more things changed, the more they stayed the same. Carl Pohlad was no Calvin Griffith, but like Griffith before him, Pohlad stood baffled, dazed and confused, with a baseball team on his hands that faced an economic dilemma. Pohlad felt trapped. And no one was throwing him a rope. He was contemptuously and widely disliked. "He's poison," one pro-stadium legislator said weeks before I witnessed a shaken Pohlad, a man with all the riches he could own and none of the happiness anyone would want.

Since the time he bought the Twins from Griffith, a deepening class warfare mentality developed between sports fans and sports owners and athletes in Minnesota. Frustration and anger was directed at Griffith, and it was mostly because he was so cheap, and we all knew it. He was the mom-and-pop baseball operator who we had to kick around. Pohlad, though, was perceived as cheaper because he had so much more money to throw around. He was a *billionaire banker*. It was so convenient to call him that—"billionaire banker Carl Pohlad"—so alliterative. He was a legitimate titan. Pohlad's wealth in constant dollars moved up from about $400 million in the mid-eighties to nearly $2 billion by 1999. The baseball team, which had fallen on hard times when he bought it because Griffith couldn't afford to pay the salaries that attracted and kept good players, won two World Series in 1987 and 1991, an amazing achievement. But by 1996, the downhill slide began again. Pohlad was losing money. The Metrodome didn't generate the revenues of new stadiums. The Twins farm system was in disarray. Baseball's economic structure had failed to keep up with the modern configurations of pro football and pro basketball, whose owners decided to share as much revenues as their own personal greed would allow. Baseball's owners remained selfish islands within their own world. Pohlad seemed perfect for the part—except he was on the short end of his league's stick. His market couldn't generate the media rights that a New York or Boston or Atlanta could. And those big markets wouldn't share. If making deals was a drug, then losing money was going cold turkey for Carl Pohlad. It gave him the cold sweats and shivers.

Fast-forward fourteen years to a beaten man. He gutted his team, its payroll, and the hopes of its fans. He gave up. He wasn't going to lose any more money, borrow more money to cover the losses and see his investment in a dead franchise grow. He allowed his team to be turned into a "studio ball" phenomenon, existing on paper so that other teams could fill out their schedule and satisfy the needs of their television contracts to play 162 major-league games. But the Twins were barely major-league. Attending a Twins game was like visiting a dying mall. Some of the storefronts were still open, but the traffic in the concourses and walkways was sparse. The in-mall kiosks were shut down. The sounds of the air-conditioning dominated the atmosphere. Only loyal shoppers were present. The other potential customers had gone elsewhere. The Metro-dome felt as if it were boarded up, as if "clearance sale" signs should have been posted on the plywood-covered showcase windows.

Fast-forward fourteen years and see him standing there, his jacket off, his tie just right, a shadow of his former self. "Nothing is under my control," he said softly, his mind racing to find that proper exit. "No, I've never been in a spot like this before. This is the only time."

A tragic figure? Can a baseball owner carry such a title? Becoming a tragic figure suggests that nobility was once also a character trait, and that somehow that mantle was shattered so that now the prince or the general was selling pencils on the corner. Tragic? No. Hated within his own land? Yes.

"I don't know if you'd call me evil," Pohlad said. He'd walked slowly from the window, still standing, holding onto a conference table chair to steady himself. "I'm just a guy who won't spend the money for the stadium and who wants to move baseball out of here and should pay for it himself. It's what I'm supposed to do at great financial risk to my family and their families. I've been put into an impossible situation."

What a difference fourteen years made. This somber session with Pohlad was so starkly different from my first encounter with him, soon after he'd bought the Twins. *Star Tribune* colleague Doug Grow, then a sports columnist, accompanied me. That was in Pohlad's former office on the skyway level of the IDS Building. Like he did in 1998, he escorted us into a conference room, away from the personal mementos and phones of his private office. He was running Marquette Banks then, and he was a chipper seventy years old, more than spry, seemingly stylish, with his hair a bit long over the ears accompanied by bushy sideburns, and an air of total confidence around him. He seemed the part of a Hollywood pro-ducer, not a Minnesota banker with roots in Iowa.

He was already his typically mumbly self. He had the trait of smil-ing a bit as he spoke, as if telling himself a joke. In the first moments of a conversation with Carl Pohlad, it is easy for a listener to wonder, "How the hell did *this* guy get so rich?" In the first moments, you figure he must have won the lottery after buying his ticket at a Hudson, Wisconsin,

SuperAmerica. But soon, to make another point, the smile wiped off. The glare was put into place. The man was seriously focused. In 1985, in that first meeting, he literally leaned over the conference table and banged it to make a point.

"The Twins are not a toy for me," he said, his voice rising, his fist hitting the table. "I am working my ass off to keep up this momentum to sell tickets. I'm on that telephone every time I have a spare minute selling season tickets.... Now, normally, I don't get this involved in a business, but I've found out, much to my chagrin, this is an image business.... I don't want to be the personality forever, but I have to be right now because, boy, we have to sell those tickets."[1]

I remember stealing a glance at Grow as we simultaneously raised our eyebrows as if to say, "This fellow can be nasty," while looking for the exit, two scared sportswriters with a ruthless gazillionaire who was determined to make his new company work. He seemed unpredictable. He was engaging. He loved money. He told a story that stuck with me.

I asked Pohlad what he did besides work. Anyone who knew him in the mid-eighties said all he did was work. (Actually, at age eighty-four in 1999, he still went to the office every day.) His answer was perfect. It was rambling. I can see today that toothy, crooked grin on his long face as he spoke. I can see his transition from teddy bear to grizzly bear as he concluded his anecdote.

"Well, now, when you say work, I was in California last month and I spent forty-five minutes to an hour talking with [former ITT chairman] Harold Geneen. We got talking about this business of working," Pohlad said. "It isn't money. It's a way of life. It's a disease.... He says he stays active. He said, 'I'm in deals. I don't care if they're big deals or little deals. Just so I'm active.' ... I dread the thought of going to Florida or Arizona because all I see is a bunch of old guys with the *Wall Street Journal* under one arm and the mail in the other and they don't have anything else to do the rest of the day. This is just my way of life."

"The Depression is something that you cannot take out of my dad's generation," Bob Pohlad, Carl's second oldest son, said. "It permeates everything ... that my dad is made up of.... My dad started with nothing, worked very hard and has been tremendously successful. . . . But my dad, I think, truly believes that if he doesn't work hard, he's gonna be back on a line—a food line or a bread line—looking for his next meal."[2] In another interview, more defensive, Bob Pohlad said, "Most of the people who want to not like my dad because he's got a lot of money are better off than he was when he started."

Work, work, work may have made Carl a dull boy, but not a dumb one, not a poor one. Work, work, work made him an outsider in the Twin Cities business community, a man without a nation. "He believes he's an outsider because he doesn't cater to what people think he needs to," said his colleague Irwin Jacobs, a 1980s corporate raider.

"For years Carl was so far from the establishment that it wasn't even funny," a banker once said. "Most of the establishment—they'd kind of snicker at him. 'What the hell is Pohlad doing now?' they'd ask. Little did they know that the fox was in the hen house."[3]

He walked a line. He wanted to be an outsider. Yet he longed for affection and attention. He denied that he sought such public approval. Yet he acquired a business that is a cultural institution that requires a steward, not an owner; he bought the local baseball team. He put himself in the middle of the spotlight. It once was good. It turned out bad.

Humble Beginnings

Carl Robert Pohlad was born August 23, 1915, in Valley Junction, Iowa, just west of Des Moines, one of eight children. His father, Mike, worked as a railroad brakeman. His mother, Mary, 105 years old in 1999, worked as a maid and laundress for the wealthy families who lived up on "the hill." The Pohlads lived in "the valley." The symbolism is barely poetic. If you were in the valley, you wanted to get up to the hill. Pohlad never forgot the difference and the distance.

The hardworking family ethic that carried Carl, his brother, and six sisters through the Great Depression inspired him to make money and do business any way he could. His first full-time job was working for a banker collecting delinquent loans from struggling farmers. He was an outstanding high school football player, good enough to win a scholarship to Gonzaga University in Spokane, Washington. But he also made money as a boxer. He didn't graduate from Gonzaga, preferring to return to Iowa to make money.

There, he hooked up with his brother-in-law and entered the banking business in Dubuque. World War II dragged him to Europe, where he operated a loan business among soldiers. Returning home after some war injuries—he reportedly earned three Purple Hearts and two Bronze Stars—Pohlad and brother-in-law Russell Stotesbury operated a business that helped banks better manage their business. In one instance, Pohlad consulted with Marquette National Bank in Minneapolis. As the expression goes, he liked the bank so much he gained control of it with Stotesbury. In 1949, Pohlad and his wife, Eloise O'Rourke, relocated to Edina.

The first mention of Carl Pohlad in the public eye came on May 16, 1951, when the *Minneapolis Tribune* noted in a very brief notice that he had been elected director of Marquette National Bank and president of Chicago–Lake State Bank.

In 1955 Stotesbury died, and Pohlad, not yet forty years old, became president of Marquette National Bank. "His first job in a bank was sweeping floors," the *Minneapolis Tribune* reported.[4] He seemed to be virtually hyperactive and superambitious. By the time he took over at Marquette, he was also treasurer of the Independent Bankers Association of America, director of the Bank Share Owners Advisory League, chairman of the Minnesota Bankers Association's pension committee, and a member of the senior advisory committee of the Minneapolis chapter of the American Institute of Banking. The man was everywhere, and he wanted to be other places as well. He was also an avid golfer.

An examination of his rise to wealth and power is easy because that rise seems so simple: he operated banks, he lent money, he became partners with some of his customers, he turned deals, he bought banks, he pocketed profits, he made more deals. He guaranteed the first loans that a twenty-six-year-old go-getter named Harvey Mackay needed to start his envelope company. He met another youngster named Irwin Jacobs, liked his first impression, and turned that relationship into some of his finest profiteering. Some were high profile. Even in the days when business deals mostly weren't scrutinized by the news media, Pohlad's often crossed over to become community events as well as moneymakers for him.

The first inkling of that came in 1960 when he led a consortium of partners in buying the landmark Radisson Hotel in downtown Minneapolis.[5] His partners included a man named Curtis Carlson, who was cashing in on his own niche business of Gold Bond Stamps, and H. P. Skoglund, president of North American Life and Casualty, who had recently become one of the founding partners of the new Minnesota Vikings football team. Pohlad's penchant for attaching himself to show business celebrities was also evident. The other partner in the deal was nationally known bandleader Guy Lombardo, famous to most of us for being *the* musician who annually guided Americans through New Year's Eve into the next year.

The purchase wasn't just a straight business deal. There was an apparent community preservation concept to it. The Kahler Corporation of Rochester, Minnesota, a growing hotel concern, had previously bid for the hotel. Pohlad and his partners believed the Radisson should remain under local control. It was the first evidence that Pohlad had a knack for rescuing local institutions and reviving them. Or at least for being a crossover businessman; his interests seemed to affect the public interest as well. He bought the local bus company. He bought the Farmers and Mechanics Savings Bank in 1982, another noble local landmark.

Comically, his first involvement with major-league baseball came just two months after Calvin Griffith decided to move the Senators to Minnesota. A short story appeared in the *Minneapolis Star* touting the economic impact of the baseball team's move. Seems that Bob Allison, the Senators' star outfielder, had moved to the Twin Cities and opened a bank account at Pohlad's Marquette National Bank. Pohlad was quoted as saying that eighteen Twins baseball families were expected to move to Minnesota soon, and that meant personal income totaling more than $200,000. "In terms of equipment, club facilities, player and managerial salaries, plus gate receipts, our new American League baseball franchise can represent a financial gain to the Twin Cities in excess of $10 million a year," Pohlad said.[6]

Throughout the sixties and seventies, he bought holding companies in Michigan and airlines in Texas. He headed up the financing for Hubert Humphrey's U.S. Senate campaign. He entered into relationships that revealed his penchant for risk taking. Maybe, it could be argued, he was no hypocrite. Wherever there was a deal, Pohlad went. If many business deals have ethical issues attached to them, Pohlad certainly wasn't politically correct. His tendency to push the envelope with how he dealt and with whom he dealt was painstakingly detailed in a mammoth and informative article published in the *Star Tribune* at the height of Pohlad's 1997 request for a publicly funded stadium. The article, which covered two full pages of the April 20, 1997, Sunday edition, had a deleterious effect on Pohlad's already tarnished image. While he and his backers insisted there was nothing new or criminal detailed in the article, it was the constancy of his questionable associations and acts, not the newness, that impressed legislators who had only heard Pohlad stories, not read of them.

His first known entrée into a disreputable deal was his affiliation in 1959 with the Twin Cities Bus Line. As a leader of an investment group that took over the bus line, Pohlad asked state regulators for a rate increase even though the transit company was turning a profit. With those profits, Pohlad and his partners invested in Trans-Texas Airways, his first of many airline ventures.

In the opinion of Steven Dornfeld, a respected editorial writer of the *St. Paul Pioneer Press*, Pohlad's history with the bus company was a precursor to his Twins experience. By the time Pohlad and his partners unloaded the bus company, labor relations had reached a warlike state; the government paid bus line investors $7.9 million for a destroyed asset, and taxpayers, too, had to cover the costs of $10 million in unfunded pension liabilities.[7] The bottom line on the Twin Cities Bus Line episode was that transit regulators believed Pohlad and his partners ignored the bus line while taking public profits—albeit legally—to invest in other endeavors. Looking back, it's an example of Pohlad tinkering with public cash for his own good. This didn't bode well for the public as it tried to be his partner in the stadium effort.

That bus line incident led to Pohlad's relationship with the Tropicana Hotel in Las Vegas, which eventually fell into the hands of mobsters. It also led to his association with the notorious union-busting airline executive Frank Lorenzo. A series of bankruptcy filings by a handful of airlines, such as Continental and Eastern, followed. Pohlad had large stakes in both airlines, which meant lots of time with lawyers all the way through 1990 as shareholders claimed Lorenzo, Pohlad, and others had misrepresented the financial strength of the airline even as it was headed toward bankruptcy. This was only the first time such a shareholders' lawsuit would be served on Pohlad for allegedly providing misleading information.

In 1963 he pleaded no contest to charges that he had conspired with ten other banks to fix interest rates. More recently, when he sold his Marquette Bank shares to the larger First Bank System, he was accused of negotiating a higher price for his shares than for those of minority shareholders. Pohlad denied all that, but First Bank settled with the disgruntled shareholders. In the deal, Pohlad acquired $150 millon of First Bank stock in 1992; by 1998, it was estimated to be worth $400 million. The appreciation of that stock alone could have paid for the stadium he sought in 1997. Legend has it that minutes before he closed the deal on this transaction, he attempted, typically, to extract one more detail from his buyers: the official Marquette Banks silverware and china. He had to get every last piece of that. You couldn't keep anything out of Carl Pohlad's grasp.

Such an anecdote dovetails with one from a former Twins employee who once received a short training lesson on negotiations from Pohlad. Just before the staff person was to enter into negotiations with a local company for a major marketing arrangement with the team, Pohlad called him over to his Dain Bosworth Tower office. Avuncular in his tone, sincerely eager to guide the employee, Pohlad said, "Never tell them what you want until the last minute. Wait until the final moment to disclose your hand." It was a style that was Pohlad's trademark. It was a style that would smash trust in many of his deals.

Another Pohlad-controlled firm, MEI Diversified, became tangled in a lawsuit from shareholders who claimed they had been deceived about the strength of the company before it, too, filed for bankruptcy, and the plaintiffs settled for far less than they invested. MEI, which once included the region's lucrative Pepsi bottling franchise, morphed into owning a hospital supply company and a hair salon chain. Investors were out millions amid allegations of accounting irregularities and ambitious claims by Pohlad that MEI was going to be a winning investment. That it wasn't became another black mark on Pohlad's business record. That anyone lost money was deeply understood by Pohlad. In a deposition taken in that lawsuit, Pohlad was asked, "What is a large sum of money to you?" He answered: "One dollar."[8]

By those standards, he did well in his short-lived ownership stake in the Vikings. He and Jacobs bought 51 percent of the team's stock in 1986 for $25 million. But Mike Lynn, always seeking ways to benefit himself, got himself in a position to control the voting shares of stock. An ugly lawsuit ensued, but not before Jacobs and Pohlad sold out for $50 million, doubling their investment in just six years.

McEnroe and Ison showed a pattern of on-the-edge Pohlad deals, a pattern that people within the Twin Cities business community had long muttered about. "Shady dealing" might be too forceful a description. But Pohlad clearly skirted the boundaries of appropriate business relationships and linked up with questionable or at least maverick characters such as Lorenzo and Jacobs.

Known in headlines as "City Man" or "Local Banker" or "Cities Bus Firm Owner" before taking on the better-known moniker of "Twins Owner," Pohlad was never known as "City Philanthropist." For some of Minneapolis's major community projects, such as the building of a new Orchestra Hall in downtown Minneapolis and the Walker Art Center in the 1970s, Pohlad's name can't be found on a list of the area's top civic givers.[9] His bank would always give, but he, individually, wasn't known as the most generous of community activists.

"He was invisible," said John Cowles Jr. "I'd go calling on him, and I'd always seem to get a nice, 'We'll take a look at it.' I thought Carl had a blind spot. Looking back, if he'd given a little then, he'd have gotten a lot back," Cowles said, meaning that a generous Pohlad might have found more support among his ruling-class buddies during his stadium push than he got. "He wasn't a good citizen," said Cowles. "He built no base of natural allies. I think Carl gave everybody the impression he really wasn't interested in anybody but Carl."

The Daytons. The Cowleses. The Pillsburys. "They are the long-standing Minnesota families we hope to be," Bob Pohlad said. "My dad was never a part of that group. He didn't have the money. He's been a success, but not for as long as those families."

Still, by 1979, when Pohlad was as rich as anyone in town, Cowles went knocking for contributions to the Dome construction effort. He found Pohlad unwilling to kick in the sort of big bucks that other large banks were. His Marquette Bank gave $50,000. Cowles believes that Pohlad gave to get a priority on a Vikings luxury suite, which came with large Dome donations. But First Bank of Minneapolis and Northwestern National Bank of Minneapolis each donated $927,000 to the Dome cause. Midwest Federal Savings and Loan gave $300,000. When the Dome's bonds were issued, First Bank of Minneapolis and First Bank of St. Paul agreed to each buy $15 million in bonds, with Northwestern National Bank buying $20 million of the issuance. St. Paul Companies picked up the remaining $5 million.[10]

For years, Charles Krusell, the Greater Minneapolis Chamber of Commerce's top staff member, recommended that Pohlad be nominated to be an officer of the Chamber. Repeatedly, Krusell said, business leaders on the Chamber's key committees would change the subject or simply raise other people's names. "No one really wanted him to head the Chamber," Krusell said. Although many pledged 5 percent of their annual pretax profits, Chamber records show that Pohlad's companies never did. Only after buying the Twins did Pohlad win over enough of the hearts of his cohorts and become Chamber chairperson in 1986. "It's called dig your well before you're thirsty," said Harvey Mackay.

"I think the truth is that we do reap what we sow," said Paul Thatcher, the Twin Cities businessman and longtime Sports Facilities Commission finance committee chairman. "Carl, fairly or not, does not enjoy a good reputation in this community. That's the truth. Either it's unfair, and it may be, or the chickens came home to roost."

Such an analysis from men with some wealth—but not as great as his—suggests that Pohlad's baggage runs deep among the Twin Cities' power elite. Pohlad seems to know that his popularity isn't high. "If they say those things, that's fine," he said, resigned to his profile. "I can't stop anybody from thinking what they want to think. Supposedly, I have a lot of money. Supposedly I was supposed to pay for [the stadium] myself. That's what I've heard."

His reaction was Pohladian. It wasn't philosophical. It wasn't deep. Unable to reflect on it all, unable to confront the bad feelings that have long been directed at him, he reverted to what he cared about the most: money. Not to personal relationships. Not to honor or grace. That was too bad. Because Pohlad had much to give. The Sharing and Caring homeless shelter in downtown Minneapolis has been one of his favorite charities, with him contributing hundreds of thousands of dollars. He was active in the early stages of the Sister Kenny Institute, the Minneapolis-based organization that aids victims of spinal cord injuries. In November 1998, in a move that cynics viewed as an attempt to rehabilitate his image, Pohlad hired a charitable fund-raiser to help him distribute more of his wealth. He announced he would be giving $5 million a year beginning in 1999 for the next three years. In a press release that garnered very little coverage in the Twin Cities media, Pohlad announced a consolidation and planned increase of all his charitable giving.[11] It was as if he was seeking an avenue to solidify his legacy. His pal Curt Carlson, developer of the Radisson Hotels, TGIF restaurant chain, and Carlson-Wagonlit travel agencies, left much to be remembered, most notably the gleaming Carlson School of Management on the University of Minnesota campus. Pohlad's friend and sometimes rival Glen Taylor, owner of the Minnesota Timberwolves basketball team, donated $8 million to his alma mater, Minnesota State University at Mankato. Pohlad had no monument to himself. It might have been a new ballpark, but he wasn't willing to give enough. Even those who were his beneficiaries understood that. Mary Jo Copeland, the founder of the Sharing and Caring Hands center, loves

Carl Pohlad. But she said, "He doesn't like people who give him a lot of baloney. He's a businessman. You have to be ready to understand he's not going to give that much."

Among his most long-standing charitable commitments was the Boys and Girls Clubs of Minneapolis. There he met another Minnesota transplant named Calvin Griffith, who had moved to the Twin Cities in 1961 after transferring his Washington Senators to the newly built Metropolitan Stadium in Bloomington. There, they first discussed the idea that, if and when Griffith wanted to sell the team, Pohlad would be interested in buying. Such a casual possible happenstance lasted for at least ten years, according to Griffith. Then the deal was done, and Pohlad, claiming a certain ignorance, took over the team in the late summer of 1984.

"Just don't ask me why I got into baseball," Pohlad said in 1985. "I don't even know myself."[12]

Well, for one, he got a good deal, as always. Baseball franchise values were rising, and Pohlad bought the Twins for about $36 million. Today, even in the underperforming Dome, the team is worth $95 to $110 million. In a new stadium—if he could ever get the public to pay for it— the Twins would carry a price tag of more than $150 million. The other reason he bought the Twins? Fame and acceptance.

In 1982, when he scooped up the Farmers and Mechanics Savings Bank and merged it with his Marquette Banks, Pohlad performed self-effacingly well. He claimed then, through all the highly positive publicity, "I don't seek publicity. Some people enjoy it, and that's all right. It's just not my style. I don't consider my life very exciting or newsworthy. I haven't done anything, particularly."[13] Those are the words, it seems, of a man longing to be recognized for his achievements.

Why else seek to buy the Philadelphia Eagles football team in 1983? That was when Pohlad was simply known in headlines as "city banker," just an anonymous rich guy. Even the *Minneapolis Star and Tribune*, his hometown newspaper, referred to him as "a Minneapolis banker."[14] A Minneapolis banker? Is that all? he must have asked. No, Pohlad was approaching sixty-eight years of age. He'd made his money, although he would make more. Now it was time to join the most exclusive of clubs;

sports team ownership. He would later attempt to buy Churchill Downs, site of the fabled Kentucky Derby racetrack, another nice, simple, and quiet investment.

For all his talk of not understanding the game of baseball and not wanting the attention attached to it, he understood, of course, business. He was no fool when it came to realizing the importance of stadium revenues. As far back as the moment he bought the team, he comprehended that. The hits just kept on coming for attempting to squeeze more and more dollars out of the Dome. In some ways, ever since he bought the Twins, Pohlad tried to get a new stadium. As early as 1985, barely a year after he pocketed the Twins, he tried to gain control of the Vikings and buy the Dome, too, with Jacobs as a partner.

From the moment he was negotiating the Twins purchase agreement, however, he sought changes in the Dome lease. Griffith, adding value to his franchise, was able to get the lease changes passed as he simultaneously sold the team, but Pohlad was the beneficiary. The first change in his favor was a 25 percent jump in capturing concessions revenues from the Sports Facilities Commission. He also gained rent breaks. Under Griffith, no rent was required for the first 1 million fans; Pohlad pushed that to 1.2 million fans. Pohlad also vigilantly retained the existing escape clause as part of his four-year rental deal. Again, that four-year term was considered an "amendment" to the provisions of the larger thirty-year deal.

That Pohlad kept the escape clause—and insisted on it as part of his purchase—wasn't lost on critics, including AFL-CIO president David Roe, who thought the commission should demand a longer lease, and Minneapolis city councilman Brian Coyle, a longtime Dome opponent. "The stadium is like a black hole that keeps sucking up more public subsidies," Coyle said.[15]

Why, people asked, did the Twin Cities go through all that angst about Griffith leaving town if Pohlad simply bought the same option? Bell, the executive director of the Sports Facilities Commission, acknowledged that Pohlad retained the same escape rights as Griffith. "But I believe with less risk. I'm convinced Carl Pohlad wants to keep the team here," Bell said, assuming, too, that Pohlad had plans to invest in the team and players.[16]

During that four-year period, including the 1985 through 1988 seasons, the lease improvements that Pohlad won from the commission as part of the sale added up to more than $4 million as he paid less rent and pocketed more concessions revenues.[17] But the real battle—and the real windfall—came after the 1988 season, the most successful in Twins history. Pohlad claimed that the finances of the team allowed him to exercise his escape. This may be difficult to believe because the team attracted a major-league-leading 3,030,672 fans in 1988. But under the language of the escape clause, if the team suffered "cumulative net operating losses" during a three-season span, it could trigger the escape. Between 1985 and 1987, Pohlad's first three years of ownership, he claimed that the team had suffered those losses.

His spokesman on the matter was none other than Jerry Bell, the former executive director of the Sports Facilities Commission, who was named Twins president in January 1987. Bell's hiring, suspicious but legal, indicated Pohlad's deep interest in better managing the Twins' relationship to the commission and the Dome. It also prepared the team to seek significant lease concessions in 1988. It further previewed for the public just how Pohlad would calculate his "losses" once he asked for a new stadium seven years down the road.

In August 1987, Bell said that even though the Twins were on their way to a World Series victory and their first two-million-fan season, the team would "lose money" that season.[18] That statement began an eighteen-month series of negotiations with the Sports Facilities Commission because no one believed the Twins had "lost money." The team, following the lease's guidelines, gave the commission one year's notice after the 1987 season that it would exercise its escape clause without a new lease in place for the 1989 season. Thus began, for the second time in three years, a fight over the Twins' lease and the team's desire to stay in the Dome and, presumably, in Minnesota. There weren't threats to move—not as the team had just won a World Series and was soon to attract that record of 3 million fans—but another wrinkle in the stadium game ensued. Creative accounting became the central issue.

Pohlad claimed by April of 1988 that the team had suffered $23 million in losses during his first three seasons of ownership. In so doing, he believed he was able to exercise the escape clause, even though almost all of those losses were linked to complex depreciation of players' salaries and to interest expenses on money that Pohlad had borrowed. He also included his ongoing sale payments to Griffith as expenses against the revenues of the Twins.

During this period, Pohlad was able to depreciate his players' salaries like any factory owner could depreciate machinery in a plant. Depreciation reflects the theoretical expense for the eventual replacement of the machinery. With a purchase price of $36 million, the Twins players could be valued at up to 50 percent of the purchase price, or $18 million. Amortizing that amount over a five- to seven-year period, Pohlad could reduce his income by up to $3.6 million a year. He also depreciated the value of the franchise.

However he tap-danced to his bottom line, he asserted a $23 million "loss" over the three-year period, even though, on the day-to-day cash flow operations, it appeared as if the Twins took in at least $3 million a year more than they paid out in at least one year, 1987. Pohlad's modus operandi from other business dealings was confirmed: push the envelope. His point of view on the economics of the team and baseball then would be instructive about how he would handle Twins finances in the future.

"When you buy a business, you expect to get a return on your capital," he said. "With a baseball team you have players. They're like a machine, and you have to depreciate them because their longevity is limited. If you didn't depreciate the players, you would soon run out of cash."[19] He also said he'd borrowed $13 million for operating capital and had interest to pay on that.

Looking ahead to 1997, the pattern was becoming clear. Whenever Pohlad said he'd lost money, it had to be weighed against how much he'd borrowed, how much of his losses were paper losses and how much his skilled accountants made his books turn out the way he needed them to. Although the Sports Facilities Commission challenged his numbers, when the 1988 negotiations ended, Pohlad won a new ten-year lease with major improvements for his team. The key improvements: no rent at all,

45 percent of concessions revenues after 1 million in attendance, and the right to sell advertising in parts of the Dome.

The other change involved the escape clause. Instead of needing to fall below a benchmark of 1.4 million fans to trigger their escape from the Dome, the Twins, under terms of the new deal, had to achieve 80 percent of the American League average. In 1988, the AL average was 2 million fans per team; that meant the Twins had to draw an annual average of 1.6 million fans from 1995 to 1997, or the seventh, eighth, and ninth years of the lease. The change actually gave the team a deeper cushion from which to escape.

The logic in the change was that the original 1.4 million fan threshold was keyed to the AL average when Griffith negotiated his first escape clause from the Dome in 1979. However, Major League Baseball attendance grew significantly between 1979 and 1989. Knowing that, the Twins sought to raise the level of the escape hatch. By agreeing to 80 percent of the AL average, it appeared as if Pohlad was giving something up. Wrong. In reality, in real numbers relative to the rest of the American League, the Twins, under the new lease, could escape more easily; even if they drew more fans, they could get out of their lease. The other escape trigger also lived on: regardless of attendance, if the team suffered "cumulative net operating losses" from 1995 to 1997, Pohlad could up and move the team out of the Dome. Thus was sown the stadium game that would begin in 1993. In his hand remained the critical option: the escape. In his hand, too, was the best possible lease he could achieve: no rent.

Only one member of the Sports Facilities Commission had the foresight to see what the new lease meant. The always particular Paul Thatcher voted no, labeling it "a total disregard of the public interest." Thatcher, known for his hyperbole and theatrical outrage, predicted that the changes would give the Twins a $25 million break over the course of the extension.[20] Looking back, you can see that Thatcher wasn't very far off. If you compare what the Twins and Pohlad would have captured from Dome revenues under the original Metrodome lease and what Pohlad netted from the lease under its various adjustments to him, he benefited, through 1998, to the tune of $22.3 million. That is, if there was no escape clause, and neither Griffith nor Pohlad had any leverage (like the Vikings have none), and if the original lease had stayed in place (as the Vikings' has), the commission would have collected $22.3 million more from Pohlad than it did between 1984 and 1998. What's more, Thatcher saw the 1988 lease battle as the first salvo in Pohlad's gradual process towards relocating the franchise.

Needless to say, the Vikings, who dominated the agenda when the Dome was built, were more than a bit miffed when Pohlad won all of his lease concessions in 1989. General manager Mike Lynn may have been enjoying his take of the luxury suites, but he didn't enjoy the fact that his team would be the sole means of visible economic support for the Dome. Of all the tenants in the Dome—including the brand-new expansion NBA Timberwolves, who would play their first season there—only the Vikings paid rent. And a hefty one, compared to other NFL teams, at that. The key reason: the Twins had the escape clause. The Vikings did not. Vikings management from that day forward would seek a renegotiated lease, hoping to get more money from the hot dogs and pop they sold and to reduce their 9.5 percent per ticket rental costs. Commission officials would firmly say, "Sorry, you've got a deal. A deal's a deal." That standoff caused continuous tension, almost a low-grade infection between the football team and the commission, and between the football team and baseball team. Between 1982, when the Dome opened, and 1994, when Twins attendance began to decline because of a lengthy Major League Baseball players' strike and owners' lockout, the Vikings paid $20 million more in rent to the commission than did the Twins.[21]

In 1994, when Pohlad began to act on his escape clause and seek public funding for a stadium, the Vikings had no choice but to begin throwing hand grenades at every turn. Such guerrilla warfare and unsettling relations between the teams was constant. The Vikings always sought parity in their Dome lease. But the Vikings never sought parity when the Dome was constructed. They seemed to want things both ways.

Character Assassination

As his team declined in the mid-1990s and he decided losing money hurt more than winning championships felt good, Pohlad became the brunt of the Twin Cities' news media's jokes and anger and of the public's mean-spirited bitterness. Civility knew no place in much of what was written about Pohlad. Some would argue that he deserved none, but the tenor of the bashing deteriorated as time wore on. For the man who seemed to have no exit strategy, there was no mercy.

Taking a beating in newspapers is the natural realm of the sports team owner. But Pohlad was targeted by some extreme critiques. He and his family still stew over a Christmas Day 1994 open "Christmas card" from *Star Tribune* Twins beat reporter Jim Souhan. In it, Souhan lambasted Pohlad for laying off sixteen employees during the extended players' strike. Accurately, Souhan noted Pohlad's wealth, then estimated at $710 million, versus the needs of the front-office workers, who had to buy holiday gifts with unemployment checks. But Pohlad's sons, Jim and Bob, who lived just across the street from their dad, literally hid the newspaper that Christmas morning so as not to ruin the theoretically joyous day for their father.

"The money is there. You just don't want to spend it on people you don't know, and have never wanted to know," Souhan wrote, adding

> [They are] people who had prompted national publications, as recently as the spring of '93, to proclaim the Twins baseball's model franchise. To round out this argument, I have done further painstaking calculations to arrive at another relevant statistic: You are 79.
>
> Enough said. Why don't you squander a few million now? Why not win another championship? Why not make a few loyal people happy—or at least allow them to struggle along at their former rate of pay? Why not spread a little cheer this holiday season, and bring those people back to work? Give them a present. Give them a break. And give us something to remember you by, besides gold trophies and a cardboard heart.[22]

Three years later, in a nastier vein, a radio personality named Cabe (pronounced Kah-bay) took center stage. On the highly rated and often off-color, racist, and sexist *Morning Show* on KQRS-FM, Cabe interviewed people on Minneapolis's Nicollet Mall about their attitude toward Pohlad. As Cabe held two cucumbers, one interviewee made an off-color suggestion as to what Pohlad could do with them. The next morning, Cabe went to Pohlad's home under the pretense of circulating a petition that said, "The Twins stay, the Pohlads go." Pohlad's wife, Eloise, answered the door and told Cabe that the eighty-two-year-old banker wasn't home, at which point Cabe said, "Is he out buying a cemetery plot?" Mrs. Pohlad slammed the door on him. Soon afterward, the Twins severed all marketing ties with KQRS.

That sort of stuff accompanied the relentless hammering on Pohlad. Entertaining to readers, perhaps, but nonstop nonetheless. *Star Tribune* columnist Patrick Reusse referred to Pohlad as Mr. Cheap twenty-three times between 1988 and 1998.

Laughably, Reusse, who drummed up most of the early antagonism around Pohlad—and deservedly so—for his inability to finance a winning team, wrote an article in *Twin Cities Business Monthly* in October 1998. There, Reusse tried to make up with Pohlad—without apologizing—by noting that much of the public sentiment that grew around a new 1990s stadium was based on the consistently mean-spirited characterizations of Pohlad in the media; of course, much of that meanness came from the computer terminal of Reusse himself. Quoting an unnamed Twin Cities businessman, who had apparently telephoned Reusse in response to an earlier column, Reusse wrote: "You can't ridicule a guy in the newspaper and on radio talk shows for 10 to 12 years, then turn around and act surprised that the public is against him ... that the politicians won't stand up and support a stadium for him. . . . And a big reason the public is against him is because of the things that were written and said in the media about Pohlad long before the stadium debate started."[23]

It's true. Although Pohlad may have deserved plenty of criticism for the way he shepherded the Twins through baseball's self-imposed economic minefield, the local sports columnists and talk show hosts continuously mocked and insulted Pohlad. This love-hate, willy-nilly, mean-spirited brand of sports journalism—if it can be called that—didn't cause Pohlad's downfall. Nor did it mean the demise of the stadium effort. It alone didn't cause Pohlad's problems. But along with the nastiness of sports talk radio, it created an atmosphere of virtual hate around the issue.

It triggered the sort of hard feelings that would cause Pohlad's sons to come to the office daily madder than the day before at the way their father was being treated.

"I'm tired of all of it, that's the understatement of all time," Carl Pohlad said, his powder blue shirt and dark blue tie neatly hanging on his thin torso. "I'm only human. I care about what other people think about me like you care what people think about you. I've been portrayed through the years as any number of things." He paused to chuckle. "It's not pleasant, not right, not nice. But I can't turn it off."

What's so maddening is that the columnists are the thinnest-skinned members of any newsroom and, it seems sometimes, don't even truly believe what they're writing. They are entertainers and goaders, not reporters or educators. Reusse, who was supporting a stadium at just about any cost, would often converse with metro columnist Doug Grow, who seemed to be opposed to a stadium no matter what. They would yuck it up about their recent zingers. Reusse would brag that he was "going to rip somebody today," and Grow would wander around the newsroom in search of a story to latch onto, just to criticize, just to paint the world as if it is only white or black, good or bad, hero or jerk. They were the Frick and Frack of the *Star Tribune* stadium one-two punch and never seemed to advance anything other than vitriolic opinions. In Reusse's case, there was also a tone of intermittent melancholy; someone was going to take his game away real soon, and life would never be good again. His concern for the team's departure wasn't based on any solid evidence, just his fear that his favorite sport would abandon him.

Even in columns or articles that had nothing to do with the stadium, commentators piled on because it was easy. As late as December 1998, when Pohlad paused his ballpark quest, columnist Tom Powers of the *Pioneer Press*, an inveterate grump, wrote about the inequities in the economics of baseball, about how players like California's Mo Vaughn and Arizona's Randy Johnson would make more money during the 1999 season than the entire Twins roster and front office, "and the fellow in charge of slicing a banana into Carl Pohlad's morning Cream of Wheat.... You can even add in the cash stipend Pohlad pays his mom for shoveling the driveway after blizzards."[24]

Exactly why that sort of insult was necessary was unclear. Anyway, put yourself in Pohlad's shiny shoes. Even if you have far less money in your retirement fund than he has in his wallet, for an instant it's possible to feel sorry for him. "I'm only human," Pohlad said of the slings and arrows that came his way. And on that afternoon, as he stood against the windows and the shadows fell on his stooping shoulders, he seemed human. He was, in some ways, if not a tragic figure, then a good reminder that money doesn't bring one happiness. There he stood, neatly dressed, showing me the carved full-length wooden cowboy with the "CRP" on his belt, a gift for a recent birthday. "I like Western art," he said. He showed me the replicas of jet airliners in his office, and the autographed *Field of Dreams* souvenir from actor Kevin Costner. He looked incredibly powerless, this multibillionaire. Some say it couldn't have happened to a nicer guy.

But as I left the office, Pohlad softly asked me again, as if I were someone who had found an answer, "What would you do?" It was, I think, a question he wanted answered, a question from a man who felt trapped. I said that the first thing I'd do is to invigorate the team, to make it a product worth seeing again. We were standing now in his office, with the wooden cowboy and the toy airplanes and the view of the Dome over his shoulder. Then, I said, I'd pay for most of the damn stadium myself. What's $250 million to a billionaire?

He was too shocked to smile. "Do you know how much that would cost?" he asked, first about pumping up the franchise with new and talented players. "That would be $40, $50 million a year, and I'd never get that back. I don't know how I'd feel losing $30 million. Maybe I'd love it, if I were your age," he said, and there was no twinkle in his eye, just a tone of sarcasm. "I don't mean to ridicule you, Jay, but that idea is laughable."

As for writing the check for a ballpark, Pohlad said, "I can't afford $250 million. The newspaper says you've got a billion dollars, but you don't have it in cash. Geez, Jay, I don't have $250 million in my checking account. I'd have to sell something and pay income tax. I don't have anywhere close to $250 million in my checking account. Geez, Jay."

He had more to say: "Because I'm in an impossible situation, because of the economic facts of the game, because I don't want to lose millions of dollars a year, I'm a son of a bitch."

It wasn't the answer he wanted. I tried to make some small talk. I told him he had a great view, which triggered a story from Carl Pohlad. He volunteered how he got discounted rent for ten years in this Dain Rauscher (previously Dain Bosworth) Plaza building because he was able to provide the developers with a nearby sliver of land that was adjacent to the Farmers and Mechanics Bank building that he owned. "Otherwise, I'd still be in that old Rand Building," he said of a more antiquated city office building. He was obviously proud that he'd saved some dough. We said good-bye. I wondered what was in Pohlad's future. The words of Mackay, the longtime Pohlad associate, stuck with me.

"There are three things that Carl does in negotiations," Mackay said. "Number one, wait. Number two, wait. Number three, wait. He gets more deals that way than any guy in the country. He's won everything all his life. Now he's going to lose? He's found that waiting has always produced everything. On this one, he's continuing to wait."

By Christmas 1998, Pohlad and his sons decided that they needed to slash the Twins' payroll and, essentially, surrender to the economics of the industry. Perhaps they wanted to show the Minnesota public that if it didn't build them a stadium, then the Pohlads were going to punish them with a rotten team. Perhaps "the boys" were sending a signal to other owners that Major League Baseball had become so unmanageable that teams in smaller markets without spanking-new publicly subsidized stadiums couldn't survive. Perhaps they came to understand that the Twins couldn't flourish even in a new ballpark, what with the widening gap between rich and poor teams. Still, no matter what they did, Carl Pohlad was at the center of the Twin Cities' enmity.

When *City Pages*, the Twin Cities alternative and entertainment weekly, published its annual "Best of the Twin Cities" issue in 1999, Pohlad received the honor of being named "Best Villain." "Obviously, the guy was lobbying for this honor," the newspaper's editors wrote. "The least we can do is give it to him."[25] The vaunted recognition came eighteen months after the last serious Twins stadium bill was defeated. Still, Pohlad was demonized. Owners' reputations die hard. Owners symbolize a team. Owners generate the feelings toward a team. For a man who viewed deal making and wealth enhancement as "keeping score," the end result for Pohlad looked more and more like defeat.

Despite their proliferation on twenty-four-hour cable television outlets, their discussion on twenty-four-hour radio talk shows, and their rehashing in voluminous newspaper sports sections and rumor-filled World Wide Web sites, pro sports were growing distant from their fans and from the general public that had once embraced them as a cultural amenity worth rooting for.

Early in 1998, soon after he suffered a legislative defeat that meant his dream for a new stadium would be delayed, Pohlad—and all pro sports boosters in Minnesota—read of a survey conducted by *Twin Cities Business Monthly* magazine. Polling the region's top four hundred executives, the survey showed that the corporate movers and shakers were as sick of Pohlad and the business of sports as the average Joe Sixpacks. In the survey,[26] conducted by nationally renowned pollsters Bill McInturff and Peter Hart, one a Republican, the other a Democrat, the business leaders said:

- The Twins were a "professional business endeavor that exists in the marketplace" (59 percent) rather than a "cultural and community enhancement that has special significance to the city" (37 percent).
- To only 19 percent, the Twins were "very important"; 31 percent said the team was "not at all important."
- Seventeen percent said if the Twins left the Twin Cities, Carl Pohlad was to blame; 53 percent said baseball's "runaway salaries" were to blame; 17 percent said political leaders were to blame; 1 percent said the business community was to blame.
- Fifty-one percent said if the Twins left town, it wouldn't have much effect at all.

It was, all in all, a breathtaking survey. It showed how far, and how low, the Twin Cities' attitudes had come and dropped since those remarkable years when meetings at the Minneapolis Club slapped stadium deals together as if they were auto purchases at the local Chevy dealership.

This disillusionment was the result of not just Pohlad's tango with the public but also more than six years of Minnesota pro sports owners demanding, seeking, whining. And of athletes getting more and more while appearing more distant and less like us.

Even before Pohlad campaigned, the owners of Minnesota's professional hockey and basketball teams came to stand for greed and threats, for financial ruin and reckless abandonment. Pohlad, incredible as it may seem, was still a relatively popular chap when Minnesota North Stars hockey owner Norm Green and Minnesota Timberwolves basketball owners Marv Wolfenson and Harvey Ratner took the brunt of the public's, politicians', and media's criticisms from 1993 to 1995. Pohlad's tussles with the Sports Facilities Commission were small potatoes compared to what Green and Wolfenson and Ratner had in store for the public.

The stadium games played by the North Stars and Timberwolves laid the groundwork for Pohlad's demise. On their shoulders stood the loneliness and humiliation that Pohlad felt in his conference room on that gray day in the winter of 1998. What Green, Wolfenson, and Ratner did was educate the Minnesota public to the cruel hoaxes of professional sports and their owners. Pohlad's demise—his journey over fourteen years from hero to villain—came in their wake.

Let's return now to our chronology; let's rewind to that transitional period soon after Pohlad bought the Twins in 1984. There was an orgy of success and a ramping up of the corporatization of sports in the Twin Cities. After that first World Series victory, the lease was improved, and the escape clause was loosened. Still, Pohlad was in place for ten years. The Vikings appeared trapped in the Dome well into the twenty-first century. The sun would shine. The birds would tweet in Minnesota's professional sports garden. Right.

That, of course, was too simple a request. In Minnesota's neverending struggle with its sports edifice complex, the real battles were still to come. They would be not about stadiums but about arenas. They would lay the foundation for a new relationship that was sweeping the nation: (1) no longer was the public going to help finance arenas and stadiums, it was also going to be asked to help subsidize owners so that they could buy expensive players; and (2) the public was going to move from lending money at a tax-free interest rate to build sports facilities to literally paying for them, writing the checks to pay the bills.

These were cosmic shifts in the public policy, although none of this—in Minnesota, anyway—was determined by policy, but rather by responding to one crisis after another and responding to one stumbling owner after another. In 1988, as the Metrodome's future seemed set for the next decade, the fate of the Minnesota North Stars hockey team was soon to be at stake, and another franchise, the NBA's Minnesota Timberwolves, was about to burst onto the sports scene, bringing with it modern marketing techniques and an admirable contribution: the totally privately financed arena. Marv Wolfenson and Harvey Ratner, the health club magnates and real estate owners who had tried in 1984 to buy the Twins, had landed an NBA expansion franchise in 1987. Their fortunes would quickly fizzle. Even as the state was on the verge of being called the nation's "sports capital" for hosting a plethora of mega-events in the early 1990s, Minnesota's off-and-on love affair with pro sports was about to turn very sour. The continued profiling of the sports facility as political football and the characterization of the team owner as nice-suited welfare recipient were the primary reasons.

CHAPTER 5

Off Target

Norm's Stars Go South along with Harv and Marv's Fortunes

As the economics of the Metrodome became problematic for the Twins and Vikings, money matters for the other Twin Cities major-league teams turned dicey, too. The fates of major-league hockey and major-league basketball were intertwined. Together they tangoed for ten years—from 1988 to 1998—with teams departing and arriving like so many 737s at the airport. By the end of the period, a new era arrived: for the first time since Johnson, McGrew, and Moore decided to make the Twin Cities major league, the legislature approved annual subsidies to arenas to help preserve pro sports franchises in city-owned facilities. No longer were major-league arenas funded only by users. Now, if you followed the money trail, the citizen was footing some of the bill.

This decade in which hockey and basketball owned their own mini-saga altered Minnesota's pro sports consciousness. The North Stars hockey team left town. the Timberwolves basketball team, a relatively new addition to the marketplace's offerings, nearly left town. No fewer than three NHL teams acted as if they might move to the Twin Cities. The nonstop debacles of Bloomington's Met Center arena being abandoned and then imploded, of downtown Minneapolis's brand-new Target Center being built and then facing bankruptcy, rendered the eventual ballpark push by Carl Pohlad and the Twins helpless. Minnesota grew tired of it all. Football players were accused of domestic abuse. Coaches and a team owner were accused of sexual harassment. Players tried to carry guns onto airplanes, assaulted fans who sought autographs, entered chemical dependency treatment, and all the while kept getting richer.

Some like to say that the NBA and NHL—younger and arena based—are tiny civic rabbits to the dominating elephants of the NFL and Major League Baseball, the traditional major-league stadium sports. Baseball has its eighty-one home dates, twice as many as hockey and basketball teams. Football has its $70 million a year in national network television dollars being imported into the state, more than the other three sports combined. But these Minnesota "rabbits" munched away and degraded the relationship of all the state's teams to the rooting public. When Pohlad and the Twins made their effort to get a stadium, first in 1996 and then full bore in 1997, the slippery slope toward defeat had already been well oiled. North Stars owner Norm Green, a mercurial sort with bad intentions, and Timberwolves owners Marv Wolfenson and Harvey Ratner, two fellows with a dream that turned into a nightmare, dug the hole. Pohlad stumbled into it.

Land Grab

As the 1980s became the 1990s, the North Stars, a long-standing state institution, complained that Met Center, their Bloomington home, needed improvements. Owned by the spectacularly wealthy brothers George and Gordon Gund, heirs to a massive Ohio family fortune, the North Stars saw Met Center as an outdated arena, too small, increasingly isolated, with no luxury suites. As with stadiums, arenas were getting bigger and economically bolder, focusing on corporate entertainment, not simply sports watching. Condominium-type suites were the revenue generators du jour. Met Center was owned by the Metropolitan Sports Facilities Commission; it was public and free of property taxes. But all of its revenues, including parking and nonhockey events, flowed directly to the Gunds. As part of their purchase of the North Stars in 1978—via a merger with their dying Cleveland Barons franchise—the Gunds acquired the Met Center mortgage from the team's founders. They had the best lease arrangement in town, but the Gunds felt lonely. And no wonder.

When Met Center was opened in 1967, it was at the heart of the

Twin Cities sports complex, just north of Met Stadium. It was a testament to the strength of the expanded National Hockey League, which doubled its size with new franchises in six U.S. cities hungry for major-league ice hockey. By all accounts, Met Center, with its unique green-and-gold seats, was the best rink in North America to watch a game. But by 1982, with the opening of the Metrodome, Met Center was a stand-alone facility in a Minnesota sports world that had turned distinctly urban.

This downtowning of Twin Cities sports reached its crescendo on April 3, 1987. That's when another gem—soon to turn burden—landed in the middle of the sports scene: an NBA expansion team. Brought to the Twin Cities by health club owners Wolfenson and Ratner, the failed bidders for the Twins in 1984, the new Timberwolves turned the Twin Cities market into the most cluttered in the United States. When the Wolves began play in 1989, Minneapolis–St. Paul became the smallest metropolitan area in the nation with four major-league sports teams—not to mention a Division 1 college sports program that fielded football, men's basketball, and men's ice hockey programs that sought to turn a profit. The options for sports fans were more varied than the community could handle. The discretionary dollar was at a premium. With stadiums and arenas as the economic generators for teams, the edifices became central to a franchise's health and wealth. They had to support rising salaries and rising franchise costs. Wolfenson and Ratner paid a whopping $32.5 million for their team. Even accounting for inflation, that amount in 1987 dollars was $30 million more than Max Winter paid for the NFL Vikings in 1961. Pro teams seemed less and less like public trusts and more and more like the fiefdoms of the superrich seeking to get richer.

Arena Required

As Wolfenson and Ratner sought the franchise, NBA commissioner David Stern made no demand on them to build their own arena. Wolfenson claimed in a 1999 interview that he hoped the Wolves could play at Met Center, a building that had once housed a series of failed efforts in the defunct American Basketball Association. But as the other expansion cities joining the NBA—Miami, Orlando, and Charlotte—opted to construct publicly funded facilities for their NBA properties, Stern altered his course. A new Minneapolis arena was required. By the time they won the franchise in the spring of 1987, Wolfenson and Ratner were telling local government officials that the NBA "requires that the team play in downtown Minneapolis in an arena designed and built for basketball."[1]

It is maddening and absurd that leagues continually force—but rarely help—team owners and communities to build facilities. The leagues—with the exception of the NFL—don't contribute the prospect of one dime to any construction costs. In the Wolves' case, Minnesota's public watchdogs even urged, if somewhat meekly, public officials to reexamine the need for the new arena that would go on to be called Target Center. A Metropolitan Council report in June 1987 noted that the metro area already had Met Center, just twenty years old, and the St. Paul Civic Center, barely fourteen years old. The Met Council report said there may be "sufficient capacity" available in the existing arenas for an NBA team. But it somehow concluded, based on a consultant's study, that Target Center would thrive financially and that "the most likely outcome is that the new arena will not result in the loss of any events at existing facilities." That was virtually impossible. But in the end, the Met Council staff report encouraged the city of Minneapolis "to reconsider construction of a new arena" and suggested that the Wolves' owners negotiate with the University of Minnesota about a new arena on campus.[2] Of course, no reins were placed on the arena plans. No public official stepped in to mediate. There was no statewide or metrowide pro sports facilities public policy. There was only a certain anarchy.

The facility went up, and not long after, Bloomington mayor Neil Peterson saw the handwriting on the wall. Noting that Minneapolis city officials didn't really care about the fate of Met Center or the St. Paul Civic Center, Peterson predicted even before Target Center opened that "they [will] close the Met Center, that eliminates the competition. It'll be bulldozed."[3] Like Met Stadium before it, Met Center became the first of the 1960s arenas in the United States to be demolished. Minnesota had a bad habit: it was eating its sports facilities young.

Wolfenson and Ratner sought very little from government bodies as they put their project together. They tried to get Minneapolis mayor

Don Fraser interested in aiding the arena construction. That went no-where. They fired up no loud or even circumspect public campaign to seek taxpayer dollars for the new edifice. Wolfenson and Ratner, up-from-bootstrap Jewish guys from North Minneapolis—out of the Max Winter profile—were too proud to make a big stink out of needing gov-ernment aid. They wanted to go it alone. They thought it would work

For others looking in, the failure of Wolfenson and Ratner's new arena was inevitable. High debt and high taxes are marks of privately funded arenas. Among those who expected there to be a major calamity was Gordon Gund, the North Stars' owner. As early as 1986, when Wolfenson was first planning his own arena, he approached Gund's chief operating officer, Lou Nanne, with an offer: the Stars could leave their aging Bloomington home and share in the planned sixty-eight suites, the in-arena advertising, the glamour of being in downtown Minneapolis, and the corporate dollars that were sure to follow. At that point, the pro-jected price of the arena was about $50 million.

Nanne was looking for ways to make more money for his bosses. He immediately urged Gund to get out of his Met Center lease. The oppor-tunities downtown were too good to be true. "Gordon, we've got to do this," Nanne excitedly told Gund. To compete with other NHL teams in larger and expansion markets with newer and plusher arenas, Nanne wanted to move downtown. To stay even with the new NBA, he thought the move was imperative. "No, Looie, we can't," Gund replied. "They'll never build that arena. It makes no economic sense." Nanne ran some numbers of his own. He agreed with Gund. Somehow, with two teams there, even with the splitting of the suite sales, the debt on a private arena was going to be too heavy. Nanne told Wolfenson that things didn't seem to add up. "Looie, I've made $200 million in my life," Wolfenson told Nanne. "If I lose it now, I don't care. I'll have my building."

Nanne returned to Gund, told him the story, and urged him again to move the Stars downtown. If ever there was a chance to get into a new building and reap its early rewards, it was now. Gund again refused. "This makes no rational sense," Gund told Nanne.

"Gordon, I'm going to answer that with one statement: do you know anyone in sports who's done something that makes any rational sense?" Nanne replied. "We should go in with them now and get it done, or we're both going to suffer." Gund delayed. Wolfenson built, not for $50 million but for more than $100 million. And, said Nanne, "In the end, we both suffered."

Wolfenson and Ratner, confident that their arena and an attached health club would succeed, broke ground on their arena construction program in July 1988. The site was very tight for an arena. The land off of First Avenue North was very hard and difficult to dig. Those were headaches for the contractors. But something awful happened soon after that construction problem. In early 1989, Midwest Federal Savings and Loan, Wolfenson and Ratner's longtime lender, was seized by federal authorities, one collapse in a national savings and loan meltdown. The bank was insolvent. The Timberwolves' owners were pouring concrete for their $100 million edifice. Now they had no construction cash to pay the contractors. They literally had to write out checks of their own before they secured new financing. Losing their operating cash was one thing. They'd also been robbed by Midwest chairman Hal Greenwood. In 1987, in what they thought was a safe investment, Wolfenson and Ratner purchased $15 million in so-called "subordinated debentures." In essence, they had lent money to the bank, which the bank lent to others. Wolfenson and Ratner hoped to earn 11.25 percent on their investment in Midwest Federal. They lost it all. It was considered a personal cushion for them as they embarked on their risky NBA mission. Soon Timberwolves president Bob Stein was on the phone, calling all around the world. Wolfenson and Ratner needed money to complete their arena's construction.

"Credit Agricole in France, Deutsche Bank, Bank of Tokyo, First Interstate in California, Sumitomo Trust in New York . . ." Stein rattled off the banks he approached. Finally, Sumitomo and six Japanese leasing companies put together a package for Wolfenson and Ratner. It came as lending markets worldwide were shrinking. The interest rates approached 11 percent. "The red button went on about then," said Stein.

Still, Wolfenson and Ratner pushed on. While all around them blood was flowing, they saw a glass that was half full. Their team, the sports franchise they'd longed for, had begun to play in the Metrodome for its inaugural season. It was a joyride. It gave Marv and Harv, as they came to be known, every reason to believe that prosperity would return their way. As their arena was being built in Minneapolis's Warehouse District—in a spot not too far from where the original Vikings domed stadium was proposed in 1971—the Wolves broke the all-time NBA season attendance record in the cavernous stadium. The season total of 1,072,572 meant an average of 26,160 fans per game. It was an eye-popping success. Life seemed good even if their mortgage payments at their new arena were soon to be oppressive.

"Most failed business deals are 4 percent stupidity, 1 percent bad luck, and 95 percent testosterone," Sports Facilities Commission finance chairman Paul Thatcher said of the Target Center situation. Along with commission executive director Bill Lester, Thatcher urged Wolfenson to drag his feet on the arena construction, to somehow show the NBA that perhaps the Wolves could play one more year in the Dome. During that time, perhaps, Thatcher thought his commission could aid Wolfenson and Ratner in getting public financing for the arena, so that their interest rates would be lower and their property taxes nil. Thatcher said he would attempt to make the Sports Facilities Commission an "accommodating agent" for the Wolves' owners. A financial structure like the Dome's could work; public bonds paid down by ticket taxes and rent.

A barrel-chested, impeccably dressed elitist, Thatcher was a political protégé of Hubert Humphrey and a business protégé of agribusiness guru Dwayne Andreas of the Archer Daniels Midland Company. Thatcher had been appointed to the commission soon after the Dome opened. A man with broad business experience, owning a host of his own companies, Thatcher, a large contributor to national Democratic politics, brought knowledge and unbearable pomposity to every situation he encountered. He also believed fiercely in protecting the public and in living up to the intent of the statute that had created the Sports Facilities Commission. It talks about acquiring and bettering sports facilities.

"We could have saved them millions ... millions, sir," Thatcher, in his early sixties, said. "But they were absolutely contemptuous in their dismissal of my suggestion." In their hearts, Wolfenson and Ratner were not the kind of fellows who sought a handout, or, for that matter, a wise helping hand. They were intent on building a monument to themselves and providing a certain kind of gift to the city where they'd been born and raised and where they'd become fabulously wealthy through their health clubs and real estate holdings. They thought that owning a state-of-the-art arena, with one of their successful health clubs attached to it, could succeed, no matter what kind of early trouble they found themselves in with the banks. The NBA franchise, concerts, and family shows would keep the new building percolating. The vision was sweet. But the future was sour.

This wasn't just a private problem. The city of Minneapolis funded $22 million in land and infrastructural costs for the Timberwolves arena project. That city piece was represented by tax increment financing bonds that were to be paid off by the increased property taxes paid by the new arena and health club. But those $3 million of taxes, above the $8 million a year in interest payments for construction debt, were like lead weights. The team owners had to turn to usurious lenders. The Ogden Corporation, a New York–based arena management and concessions company, swooped in to help the struggling entrepreneurs. Ogden agreed to build the concession stands for Wolfenson and Ratner and to advance them money to finish up the construction. Ogden's financial return would come via its pop, popcorn, and hot dog profits and in producing non-sports events. Driven by quarterly earnings for their shareholders, Ogden preferred rates of return that approached 20 percent. Not only did Marv and Harv owe the Japanese bank, but they also owed Ogden. They owed the city of Minneapolis. They owed a lot.

Their arena opened as planned under the name Target Center. For the first time, a sports facility in the Twin Cities sold its name to a corporation, a discount store. It was a sign of the times. No longer were the stadiums and arenas named for fabled political figures or for the region. No longer were they putting "us" on the map. Now they were putting "corporate sponsors" on the national map. The Timberwolves' first regular season game was played on November 2, 1990. The game was a sellout. Ten weeks later, the Persian Gulf War, Operation Desert Storm, broke out in Iraq. In 1991 this triggered a decided decrease in touring family shows and concerts. A war was on cable TV every night. People didn't buy tickets. They stayed home. It was safe there. At Target Center, there was only danger.

The Hockey Chill

A two-ring sports facilities circus unfolded. As Wolfenson and Ratner planned their new, supermodern arena in 1987 and 1988, the Gunds, richer than Marv and Harv, threatened to move their team out of town unless the Sports Facilities Commission gave them $15 million to spiff up Met Center. Fifteen miles of sprawling freeway apart, here existed, arguably, the two best arenas in any market in the United States. Met Center was once the finest hockey arena in the nation, with the best sight lines and the most parking, with an owner holding the best NHL lease in the nation. The North Stars controlled 98 percent of every dollar that poured into Met Center, be it a hockey game, a concert, a cup of pop, or a bag of peanuts. They owned a team that played, presumably, in the heart of hockey country. The Gunds invested $8.5 million of their own to build luxury suites, but they were at the doorstep of a new and exciting neighbor—the grotesquely large Mall of America. The nation's largest retail center was set to open on land where Met Stadium had once provided marvelous baseball and football memories. As far back as 1981, the Gunds had tried to buy the Met Stadium land, tried to get it for a virtual song of about $10 million, and planned to build excessively, with four to six hotels, offices, retail space, and high-density housing.[4] Nanne believes to this day that the purchase would have kept the Gunds in Minnesota, and the North Stars, too. That scheme was shot down by the Sports Facilities Commission, which expected more cash for that valuable piece of land and eventually got it.

By 1990, the Gunds weren't in land speculation and development anymore. Now they simply wanted cash to fix up Met Center so that they could create new revenue streams to cover hemorrhaging operating losses and compete with the new Target Center and the Wolves. The

Met Council's report was already being borne out. The arenas were competing for events, and Target Center was winning. The Gunds' demands for $15 million of arena improvements, paid for by the Sports Facilities Commission, was—history should record—the first blatant call for a public handout in Minnesota's four-decade-long journey of building sports facilities. For the first time, too, the Sports Facilities Commission's treasury came under scrutiny. In reality, the commission was a sort of Mosquito Control District on steroids. A tiny agency with little offices in the dark hallways of the Metrodome, it managed the Dome and turned the key at Met Center for the North Stars. But by 1990 it held a ton of cash in its reserve funds. What with the sale of the old Met Stadium land in 1984 for $15 million and with the collection of concessions and ticket taxes from Vikings and Twins games over the years, the commission had nearly $30 million in cash reserves. These dollars were out of the wallets of Twins and Vikings fans. They bought tickets that were taxed at a 10 percent rate. They bought food and drink, much of which turned into revenues for the commission. There had also been the matter of rising property values in Bloomington. All the land on which Met Stadium and Met Center stood cost less than $500,000 in 1955. Every team in town had its eyes on that cash reserve. Certainly as Wolfenson and Ratner scrambled to make their payments, they looked with envy at the commission's money, wanting to get their paws on it. But the agreement with Dome bondholders required, demanded, that any Dome reserves be used to pay off the Dome's debt, and nothing else. The commission could not serve as a banker to distressed teams. It could, perhaps, go to the Met Council or legislature and seek bonding, as Thatcher suggested to Wolfenson in 1989. But the commission had no bonding authority of its own. Besides, the Twins and Vikings were hoping to see some improvements at the Dome. They viewed the reserves as *their* money.

It wasn't long before the Gunds, with their eyes on San Jose and its new state-of-the-art arena, left Minnesota to own an NHL expansion franchise in the developing Silicon Valley. They decided simply to sell the North Stars and get out of the contentious Twin Cities atmosphere. When all the wheeling and dealing was completed, a fellow named

Norman Green from Calgary, Alberta, Canada, wound up as the North Stars' owner in June 1990. A new day dawned in Minnesota's sports industry. By that day's dusk, NHL hockey would be gone.

Green was obsessed with owning an NHL team. Owner of a Rolls Royce, constant companion of exotic dogs, well coifed, Green loved the idea of being on the hockey league's board of governors. In Canada, that was as high profile as an otherwise unknown businessman could get. He'd served on the NHL board as a small shareholder of the Calgary Flames, and now, for $40 million, he owned all of the North Stars. His background was in real estate and shopping mall development. He'd made his money that way. There was little doubt that his purchase of the North Stars had something to do with hockey and much to do with that megamall going up a slap shot away from his arena's front door. He had ideas. The megamall and the hockey team looked like a nice fit.

But soon after he bought the North Stars, Green's own mall empire in western Canada began to suffer reversals. As strapped as Wolfenson and Ratner were, Green was in trouble, too. The real estate market was tumbling everywhere. Marv and Harv saw the value of some apartments they owned decline. By the time Green's first season with the North Stars had ended, he was dealing with major cash flow problems with his primary business. And he was seeking aid from the Sports Facilities Commission, hoping to buy development rights around Met Center, to link up the arena with the Mall of America, with retail stores, restaurants, and a skyway.

The commission had other ideas. It didn't want to cheaply sell or virtually give away rights to a Canadian developer. Indeed, depending on whose story you believe, Green was asking to borrow money to build, or seeking the land for such a low dollar amount that he was, essentially, seeking a gift from the Sports Facilities Commission. The agency could rearrange a lease and find ways to direct more arena revenues to a team, but the Stars already had the cheapest possible rent a team could have, about $250,000 a year. Besides, this was 1991. Pro sports' changing rules, in which cities gave owners everything they wanted, hadn't made their way to Minnesota yet.

"I thought there was nothing else the stadium commission could or should do beyond providing almost literally free of cost the best hockey facility in the nation to the team," said Thatcher, who headed the commission's finance committee at the time and always made sure he sculpted its agenda. "I was unwilling to give away the patrimony of the commission. I thought it would have been an illegal act. He wanted fifty fucking acres, sir, the largest parcel and most significant piece of raw land available in the United States of America. Let's give this some context." It was, to be sure, an attractive plot of land, not exactly the cornfield on which Minnesota's major-league history had been born thirty years earlier.

Bill Lester, the commission's executive director, remembers his erratic discussions with Green. Lester points to the implications of Green's desires. Green wanted to change ad hoc policy that Twin Cities sports agencies had exercised since 1961. He didn't just want the public to help finance his aspirations of Met Center improvements. He didn't simply want tax-exempt bonding and no property taxes. He believed it was the commission's role—the public's—to aid him in putting a competitive team on the ice by subsidizing his mall business, not his hockey business. Griffith and Winter wanted a better stadium in the seventies. Green wanted a better mall in the nineties. He wanted everything.

"I need that land, I've got to control it," Green told Lester over breakfast at the Holiday Inn Metrodome one day. When he was told that his control of the land would precipitate the charging of property taxes, Green simply wondered if he could get a waiver of some sort. Although the commission believed in the early 1990s that the land on which Met Center stood was probably worth about $16 million, Green insisted he would pay only $4 million.

Maybe it's only semantics. Maybe it's a matter of degree. But before Green, Minnesota team owners hadn't asked for direct handouts. Twins owner Carl Pohlad and the Vikings repeatedly sought lease adjustments. The Timberwolves built their own arena, gaining only some aid to prepare the land on which the facility was constructed. The Gunds had sought some capital improvements at Met Center from the Sports Facilities Commission. But in Lester's view, Green's assertion that the commission had to sell him valuable land at less than a market rate was the first time a team owner had come to the community and said: "'Give us money because we need it. We won't be able to pay the salaries of competitive teams without you, the public, giving us real cash.' As I was sitting there with him, I realized that he felt it was the commission's responsibility that the North Stars have three good centers and a couple of good wingers. It was a radical sea change. He was telling us, 'You need to subsidize the changing economics of our sport,'" Lester said.

That was a sobering, transitional moment. That is what Green's demands and his relocation of the North Stars represent. The public would be expected to aid owners in making money, not in simply financing the construction of stadiums and arenas. What was so politically difficult was tolerating the contradictions. Green whined about poor attendance, poor corporate support, few seats, and fewer suites. As he complained, he kept signing players to absurd contracts, like a four-year $6.75 million contract for his young star Mike Modano. It was the fifth highest salary in the NHL. As he complained, the North Stars made it to the 1991 Stanley Cup finals, consistently selling out after their otherwise worst ticket-selling season ever; average attendance in his first year as owner was a paltry 7,838 per game. So he needed a public sports agency to get him land cheap that he could develop. Times *were* changing. Downtown, the Wolves were altering the economics of the market, aggressively selling arena naming rights, high-priced suites, and million-dollar corporate sponsorships and controlling their own broadcast rights. Under a hyperenergetic marketing director named Tim Lieweke, the Wolves dragged Minnesota into the modern sports marketing era. Their arena was the vehicle for that, a blank check, as it were, for local companies to affiliate with an NBA franchise. Meanwhile in 1991 the Twins won their second World Series championship, and the 1992 Super Bowl and Final Four were soon to be held at the Dome. The U.S. Open golf tournament was on tap. The Twin Cities' capacity for sports spending was exhausted.

Green wanted so much because he needed so much. The Alberta banks were beginning to pressure him. In early 1992, less than two years

after buying the Stars, after claiming losses of $5 million on team opera-
tions in his first season—a season in which his team went to the Stanley
Cup finals—Green began exploring other markets for his team. "To me,
it was literally out of the blue," said Pat Forciea, Green's vice president in
charge of marketing and public relations. Forciea was Green's spokesman
as the North Stars ship sank. Forciea was known as a crafty spin doctor.
He helped lead an unknown college professor named Paul Wellstone to
victory in the 1990 U.S. Senate campaign. A former college hockey
goalie, Forciea's job was now to stabilize Green's image. That was difficult
with such an unstable man.

Of course, dealing with the National Hockey League of the early
1990s was like entering the Twilight Zone. On his own, Green began
negotiating to move the Stars to Anaheim, California, home of Disney-
land, and where a new publicly financed arena was under construction. It
was to be managed by the Ogden Corporation, the same Fortune 500
company that lent money and resources to Wolfenson and Ratner. For
months, Green negotiated, attempting to get the best possible deal. "The
real short version is, Norm kind of blew it," said Forciea. The Ogden
officials burned out on Green's needs in California but began to discuss a
possible North Stars move to the Target Center instead. Ogden's main
negotiator was corporate vice president Dana Warg, an expert on arena
rental deals, executive director of Target Center, and leader of all of
Ogden's Midwestern and Canadian operations.

While Green fiddled, the Walt Disney Company, with its smash hit
movie *Mighty Ducks* under its belt, fired up its interest in placing an
expansion team in the NHL. Disney was a far more attractive ownership
group in Southern California than the silver-haired Norm Green. Still,
Green believed that he and NHL president John Ziegler and Bruce
McNall, owner of the Los Angeles Kings, were all pals. Green thought
Anaheim could be his for the taking.

But McNall, who would later be jailed (in unrelated schemes) for
bilking banks and sentenced to five years in jail, had other plans. He got a
whiff of Disney's money, and a new deal was struck. Norm Green was left
out in the cold. Disney could own the Anaheim NHL region, Ziegler and

McNall decided. Because McNall was ceding some territorial rights, he convinced Ziegler that half of Disney's $50 million expansion fee to enter the NHL should be paid directly to the Kings. In a league with no leadership, Green's California dream died. But he did receive a token of a gift from Ziegler and McNall in exchange: he could move his Minnesota team wherever he wanted at any time, and the league would charge him no relocation fee. It was a free pass. By the spring of 1992, Green was going to go someplace. His Canadian banks were pressuring him. He had to raise the value of his franchise some way, somehow, to keep the banks off his back. Keeping the North Stars in Minnesota, even at Target Center, couldn't create the appreciated value for his franchise that a move to another larger market could. An increased book value of his NHL franchise could buy Green time with his Canadian lenders. "When wealthy people go broke," said Forciea, "it's a pretty frightening experience."

Green poked around in Atlanta, in Phoenix, and in Dallas, seeking to relocate his team. Atlanta needed a new arena. Phoenix's America West Arena hadn't been built with hockey in mind. Dallas's political and business community seemed eager to land a hockey team. But it wasn't just financial worries that motivated Green. It was his alleged pawing of women in the North Stars offices that expedited matters. At the end of 1992, Kari Dzeidzic, an administator at the North Stars offices, was planning to file a sexual harassment lawsuit against Green. The critical mass for his departure was in place. If the Sports Facilities Commission seemed to be unreasonably obstructionist on his land and development aspirations, it now had a good excuse to stay away from the infected Green. "I agree, there was a deal to be made, and maybe that would have changed history," Lester said of working out something with Green. "But the combination of our statutory limitations and his insistence that he had to get this land free, or for $4 million, plus the sexual harassment stuff—that made it very tough."

Wolfenson and Ratner didn't care about Green's gender woes. They wanted a chance to keep him. They wanted another tenant. So did Ogden, who felt that with an NHL team at Target Center, the building might survive Wolfenson and Ratner's debt burden. Green was barely rational, but Forciea was attempting to direct him to a deal in downtown Minneapolis that would keep NHL hockey in Minnesota. In December 1992, Green, in one final act of seeming to care about staying in Minnesota, asked Forciea to pursue the Target Center option.

"Norm said, 'Here's what I'll say yes to,'" Forciea remembered. "I said, 'Great,' and I drafted a letter to Dana Warg." In the letter, Green said he'd pay 4 percent of net ticket receipts as rent. He said he wanted new offices built for him at Target Center at Wolfenson and Ratner's expense. He wanted $85,000 per suite; that is, he virtually wanted to control the luxury-suite money for the Stars *and* the Wolves. He wanted to share all in-arena advertising with the Wolves. He wanted to jointly market nonsports events with the Wolves. He wanted an escape clause if attendance was low.

"A week or two later we got back from Marv and Harv exactly what Norm wanted," Forciea recalled. "In two seconds, Norm said, 'This isn't going to work.' I said, 'Norm, this is exactly what we wanted.' He said, 'It's not going to work.'" By then, reports had his wife, Kelly Green, laying down an ultimatum: Green either sold the team, moved it, or divorced her. By then, he was going through the motions of staying in the Twin Cities. His heart and mind were already in Dallas.

Wolfenson and Ratner's response to Green included a clause tucked somewhat quietly at the bottom of their letter.[5] It was, though, the crux of the matter. The clause was titled "Ownership of Target Center," and it read: "This offer is contingent on the Metropolitan Sports Facilities Commission, or some other public body, assuming ownership of Target Center on terms reasonably acceptable to the ownership of the Timberwolves. The acquisition cost of this facility would be for the current outstanding debt, which is approximately $76 million. Once the North Stars and Timberwolves have reached agreement, we would then work with the public entity to complete the acquisition." Among men who were hoping against hope that all their creditors would just go away, this clause was the most wishful of all thinking. In early 1993 there wasn't one chance in a billion that the city of Minneapolis or state of Minnesota was going to buy Target Center or bail out Wolfenson and Ratner.

"Bail out" soon became Minnesota's sports business term of art.

So Green was run out of town or, at least, allowed to sneak out of town. He took the Minnesota North Stars with him. His nickname became "Norm Greed." His rental deal at Dallas's Reunion Arena wasn't as good as his Met Center arrangement. But in two years, his exit strategy worked. He sold the Stars for $79 million, plus a ten-year "consulting agreement" worth a total of $5 million.[6] Green reportedly needed all that to pay off $70 million in team debt. But that still left him with a cool $14 million.

The deal left Minnesota, land of ten thousand ice rinks, without its NHL hockey team. A thread of the state's cultural fabric was yanked out of place. The state learned that teams aren't forever. Facilities make a team. Facilities keep a team. It's the building, stupid.

Knock-Down-Drag-Out Fight

One team was gone. An arena stood empty. Another brand-new arena was in deep financial doo-doo. So what was Minnesota to do? You guessed it: form a task force. Set up by the Sports Facilities Commission, a group of business and political leaders were called on to look into the future of the abandoned Met Center in Bloomington. There was no longer a team there in the distant suburbs. As much as hockey boosters embraced the facility as the finest hockey rink in the land, it was these very same hockey boosters who formed an odd coalition with the patriots of downtown Minneapolis. Both constituencies urged that the twenty-six-year-old arena be knocked down, dusted.

The history of the demise of Met Center is one of the great misinterpreted and already rewritten episodes in Minnesota's edifice complex history. To this day, hockey lovers wonder, "Why the hell did the cigar smokers in Minneapolis knock down Met Center?" To this day, when citizens and legislators ponder why St. Paul and state taxpayers had to pay $130 million to build a new arena for a new NHL team, hockey boosters wonder, "Why'd *they* knock it down?"

They buy in to the asinine notion that "the Minneapolis manipulators" tore Met Center down, as the *St. Paul Pioneer Press*'s sports columnist Tom Powers wrote a few years afterward.[7] They allow Forciea, a man very good at changing his mind to fit the moment, to say, "What were we doing? It's a good thing they didn't tell us to run off the IDS Tower. We would have."

They? On August 24, 1993, it was Forciea himself who led the chorus to destroy Met Center. He told the task force that "the economics of professional hockey have passed this building by, and even if significant improvements were made to the building under new ownership I just don't think that the level of revenue that would be needed to sustain an NHL team at today's costs can ultimately happen in this building."[8]

So, let's ask again: why was Met Center knocked down? Because Governor Arne Carlson's specially selected working group to bring the NHL back to the Twin Cities urged anyone who would listen to make Met Center toast, that's why. It was the obstreperous Thatcher, always characterized as anti-everything, who urged his commission and others not to knock the Bloomington facility down. He warned that eliminating the Met Center from the arena mix would play into Wolfenson and Ratner's hands. He predicted that the NHL would never play at Target Center because the arena's economics wouldn't allow it. Unfortunately, Thatcher—with the inordinate ability to constantly piss everyone off—was right.

Cut to September 8, 1993, at the Minneapolis Convention Center, in a large meeting room, with the twenty task force members in a horseshoelike configuration. Wheelock Whitney sat alone at a table at the open end. Whitney was the noble figure who helped bring major-league baseball to the Twin Cities via his Continental League effort with the legendary Branch Rickey. This time, Whitney appeared as the chairman of Governor Carlson's ad hoc NHL committee. Whitney was in the role of hockey booster, not hockey detractor. Whitney was as certain as a man can be. He'd had meetings with the new NHL commissioner Gary Bettman. He'd probed Bettman's inner desires relative to the return of the NHL to the Twin Cities. Here's what Whitney said about what the Sports Facilities Commission should do with Met Center, that hallowed temple for many Minnesota puckheads:

[Bettman] made it absolutely clear to us that the only possibility for NHL hockey in this area is at Target Center. Now, I don't like to hear that. I love the Met Center. I was part of the group that built it ... but reality is it's not a state-of-the-art building, it's not a modern facility, the Target Center is.... The continued presence of Met Center interferes with our goal of getting an NHL team here.... It muddies the waters.... I don't see any constructive purpose served by the Met Center as it is now.[9]

In Bettman's view, any lack of solidarity over which Twin Cities arena was the right one for a relocated team would hurt Minnesota's chances for a new NHL team. One major arena—and one alone—had to be the crown jewel of the region. Bettman wanted the community to identify the Target Center as that site, give a new NHL team a deal like the one Green pursued, and everyone would live happily ever after. A former top aide to National Basketball Association commissioner David Stern, Bettman made a policy decision early in his administration, which began soon after Green left for Dallas. That policy was this: no NHL team in any city where an NBA team played would have a worse lease agreement than the NBA team. Bettman refused to place his NHL franchises in a second-class-citizen position to any rival NBA team in the same market. Were a new Minnesota NHL franchise to play in Bloomington, it simply couldn't generate the sorts of revenues that the NBA Timberwolves were in their new 19,000-seat, sixty-eight-suite Target Center. Bettman insisted on competing with the NBA on a level playing field; and who could blame him?

Still, days before Whitney's testimony, press reports swirled about "mystery" potential owners who believed that NHL hockey could be revived, and at Met Center. Thatcher confronted Whitney about that tidbit. Thatcher wondered how a hockey lover such as Whitney could, without one ounce of doubt, declare that Met Center should be bulldozed. "Don't you have at some level some concern that if we got on that bulldozer today and tore down Met Center, a year from now or six months or three months from now, we might wonder why we'd done that?" Thatcher asked. He wondered why Whitney would eliminate an option for "some billionaire [who] has the crazy idea" that Met Center could be rehabilitated.

Whitney wanted nothing of preserving the Bloomington arena. "When it comes to getting an NHL hockey franchise here I'm going with Gary Bettman, the commissioner, and not with a mystery group or groups that say they might come and play at Met Center," Whitney replied impatiently.

Thatcher parried and thrusted. He said that he believed the economics of placing a new NHL team in the Target Center would require public subsidies of the arena, what with Wolfenson and Ratner's financial problems. Also, Wolfenson steadfastly refused to open his books to the Sports Facilities Commission. The real innards of the Target Center's and Timberwolves' finances weren't known. Making a decision about how viable an NHL team could be at Target Center was choosing blindly, Thatcher said. He goaded Whitney, a former mayor of Wayzata and a candidate for governor and U.S. Senate from time to time, into admitting that he was opposed to bailing out the Target Center and that most Minnesotans were, too. Thus the economics of the building—with excessive debt and high property taxes—might not even change if and when an NHL team arrived. If the public didn't fund the refinancing Marv and Harv sought, then what?

Here's where Thatcher, his voice booming, confidence oozing out of his ears, his diction affected, stared firmly at Whitney. He reported to Whitney, one of the nation's leading investment bankers, the former head of Dain Bosworth, that the Sports Facilities Commission had asked experts to examine how the North Stars would fit into Target Center. And, Thatcher said, almost seething: "Every principal investment banking firm in this state, one that you formerly were the CEO of and principal owner of, were involved in a process to try and find a way to shoehorn the North Stars into that [Target Center] under its present ownership. They found that there was absolutely no way whatsoever to make a deal with Norm Green that was equal to the deal Norm Green had [at Met Center]. It was impossible to put [the North Stars] in there without substantial public subsidy. Are you aware of that?"

Whitney said that he was aware of it, but he wanted to discuss the future of Met Center, not the future of Target Center. Thatcher countered that the fates of the two arenas were inextricably linked. He believed that the tearing down of Met Center sooner rather than later would force a public subsidy of Target Center. He said that if the Sports Facilities Commission knocked down the Bloomington arena without knowing whether hockey could actually succeed at Target Center, that would be a blunder of the highest order.

What irony. Hockey boosters today and forever will blame the "Minneapolis downtown interests" for knocking down Met Center. They will blame the Sports Facilities Commission for not vigilantly working to get prospective franchises, such as the Hartford Whalers, Edmonton Oilers, and Winnipeg Jets, into Target Center in 1994 and 1995. But it was the most ardent downtown booster of them all, Paul Rexford Thatcher III, resident of a Minneapolis condo and daily luncher at the Minneapolis Club, who was the lone voice in trying to keep Met Center open in the fall of 1993 while the governor's hockey advocates—all suburbanites—were simply singing Gary Bettman's tune: Target Center and nothing but Target Center. Met Center be damned.

The next Met Center task force meeting came a week later, on September 15, 1993. It was a doozy. The stage was, appropriately enough, a party room on the luxury suite level of the Target Center. The night was Kol Nidre, the holiest pregame show of the Jewish New Year, the night that Jews begin to fast before seeking atonement on Yom Kippur. The leading actor was Marv Wolfenson, the sometimes persnickety Wolves co-owner and Target Center codeveloper, holding off for an hour his observance of the most solemn day of his faith's calendar to tell a group of government-appointed Gentiles that he just might take his goddamn basketball team out of Minnesota because this arena he built—these very suites—these monuments to himself and his business partner, Ratner, were bleeding.

Bleeding badly. Yes, maybe, mistakes had been made. Yes, certainly, the savings and loan debacle unfairly did them in. Yes, it's true, his team's value had increased by 100 percent—at least—since he bought it six years earlier. No, he didn't really want to hold the city of his birth hostage. But on that evening, with the sun setting and the Day of Atonement around the corner, Marv Wolfenson wanted some things. Amid a discussion about the future of Met Center, Wolfenson dropped a bombshell as the task force munched on lovely deli sandwiches and pasta salads. Wolfenson, who was in a particularly cranky mood that night, also showed just how poorly sports team owners relate to the political system.

About ten minutes into some questions from task force chairman Bob Vanasek, the former Speaker of the Minnesota House of Representatives, Wolfenson allowed that it was his hope that the city of Minneapolis or the Sports Facilities Commission would take over his $76 million arena mortgage. It was a reiteration of his letter to Green nine months earlier. Somehow, he didn't see it as a bailout but saw it as a good deal for the city. This came from a man who went forward in the construction of the arena proud of its privatization and eager to stay admirably independent of public funds. But his tone was angry. His tone was frustrated. Neil Peterson, the mayor of Bloomington, picked up on Wolfenson's high level of dissatisfaction.

"Maybe you don't want to talk about this," Peterson said, "but what happens if a decision can't be made that you feel comfortable with? Do you have a threshold point where you just say enough is enough?"

Remember now, Target Center was three years old at that moment. The Timberwolves were about to begin only their fourth season in the league. The North Stars had moved to Dallas exactly six months earlier. And Wolfenson, at what otherwise would have been an uneventful meeting of a boring task force, said: "There comes a time when I have to make a decision.... I'm at an age where I'm not going to live forever. I'm sixty-seven. I have to get things in order. I can't die and have an arena here and have my family taxed for it.... We do have the ability to move the team. That's not our intent. We're not trying to do it. You brought up the question and I'm trying to answer it accurately. Yeah, I've got other avenues."

As Minnesota was still recovering from the Stars' departure, Wolfenson declared publicly for the first time, that he too might have to check out the possibility of other cities. Minnesota's sports fans, taxpayers, and politicians were clearly in the belly of the pro sports beast. The sports business environment was spinning out of control. Thoughtfully, even helpfully, one task force member, Chuck Brown, sensed that Wolfenson believed the threat to move and the demand that the city buy the Target Center were easy propositions for the public to swallow. Brown began to tell Wolfenson that any decision by any government body would require that Wolfenson better reveal the specifics of his economic problems. This full financial disclosure was something the Sports Facilities Commission had sought for a year.

What Wolfenson didn't know was that Brown, of tiny Appleton, Minnesota, was the powerful chairman of the Local Government and Metropolitan Affairs Committee of the Minnesota House of Representatives. Little did Wolfenson know that in exactly five months, Brown was going to chair the first hearing about whether the state of Minnesota should fund the public buyout—nay, bailout—of the Target Center. Brown was critical to Marv and Harv's financial survival. But Marv was treating Representative Brown like dirt. Marv didn't get it. He was going to have to beg before this was all over. But on that night, Wolfenson's position was this: before he showed any financial data to anybody, they would have to agree to buy his arena.

"I mean, that's just normal business procedure," Wolfenson told Brown. "You want to buy a house from me, I don't show you everything until you enter into a purchase agreement. Then you get to see it, and then you can say yes or no because that's a contingency." Wolfenson was condescending. He was gruff. He was dismissive. He was digging his own grave. The lesson learned that night at the Met Center task force was enduring: keep pro sports owners as far away from politicians as possible.

A week later, another lesson could be learned: be careful of fans in politician's clothing. Sensing that every team and sport was after the public's money anyway, the quirky Vanasek called a late-afternoon news conference before the regularly scheduled meeting of the Met Center study group. He had nothing to say of hockey or basketball, of tearing down old arenas or buying struggling new ones. On a lark, Vanasek wanted to talk about baseball.

In what could only be considered a nasty curveball to the Target Center buyout process, Vanasek said Met Center should be knocked down and sold, but that any proceeds should go not to buy Target Center—as Wolfenson and Ratner had hoped—but to build a new open-air Twins ballpark next to the Metrodome "The stars might be lining up for the right things to happen," said Vanasek. As with others, he hadn't studied, or didn't care about, the legalities of the Met Center land sale requirements; all the cash had to be used to pay down the Dome's outstanding debt, not for other sports facilities.

Whatever the legal details, the debate about the fate of Met Center showed how complex the sports facilities solution could get. The Twins and Vikings wanted a piece of the money that would come from any Met Center sale. The land had potential use for the nearby Minneapolis–St. Paul International Airport, so that any decisions about whom to sell the land to and its future use demanded careful scrutiny. Its adjacency to Mall of America had huge financial implications. The city of Minneapolis, which controlled the Sports Facilities Commission, was opposed to using the eventually closed Met Center land for some sort of suburban convention center. Minneapolis was attempting to make its new convention center into the region's major gathering place. Wolfenson and Ratner were getting to the end of their financial ropes and were impatient for a solution to their needs. Governor Carlson and his supporters wanted an NHL team back in town, and there was legitimate disagreement over whether the 14,000-seat, twenty-suite Met Center could still support a team into the future.

But Vanasek, turning the already layered discussion into chaos, had this dream. He said as he gathered information about Met Center's future, "people kept asking, 'When are they bringing open-air baseball back to Minnesota?'" Vanasek believed any Met Center solution should serve "sports fans, not just hockey fans." So he came up with a plan for a stadium akin to Baltimore's Camden Yards. He figured it could reside next to the Dome, that it might cost about $100 million, and that maybe someone with "deep pockets" would help the public build the stadium. His suggestion for a new Twins ballpark came a full year before the Twins would even suggest one themselves, but it came, coincidentally, as Twins officials were beginning to conclude privately that they wanted a brand-new stadium. His suggestion tickled them to no end. Vanasek saw the fate of Met Center as a moment for free-form visions. "When a butterfly flaps its wings in China," he said, "you may end up with a hurricane in South Carolina."

Translation: en route to knocking down a hockey arena in Bloomington, Vanasek figured Minnesota should at least wind up with a baseball stadium in Minneapolis. Even if all of his dots didn't connect, Vanasek previewed the complications of the next six years. If Minnesota hoped to solve its pro sports facilities problem, it would have to do it in a coordinated fashion. Solving each crisis one sport at a time was going to be tiresome. It was going to wear Minnesotans out. His call for outdoor baseball also revealed a basic desire from the hearts and minds of local sports fans. Vanasek, if nothing else, was a diehard outdoor baseball fan. Outdoor baseball was something folks wanted and appreciated, more than a new hockey team, more than a publicly rescued NBA team. Baseball was romantic and refreshing. It was a cause that fans and citizens might be able to get behind. Baseball was the most affordable and family-focused sport. This hockey arena/basketball arena financial stuff, that was for the eggheads and the corporate types, the "Minneapolis manipulators." It wasn't up Vanasek's alley. The discussion about whether to tear down a twenty-six-year-old hockey rink had no soul. Outdoor baseball, now that's spiritual. In the end, Vanasek's baseball idea had a shelf life of about, oh, three hours at that point in history. It broke the monotony. But it couldn't change the inexorable streamroller poised to demolish Met Center.

Thatcher had one more plea left in him, but no one listened. On October 6, he asserted that knocking Met Center down would give all the financial cards to Wolfenson and Ratner. If they were going to get the public to bail them out, the public needed its own leverage. If Wolfenson was already threatening to move the Wolves, why shouldn't the public threaten to keep Met Center open as a competitor to Target Center? He urged the task force to understand that Met Center should stand until Whitney landed another NHL team for the Twin Cities. "In the meantime, we mothball [Met Center]," Thatcher said, "until we got a word from Wheelock when he says, 'Hey guys, I'm giving you the high sign, I not only got a hockey franchise but we can fit it in downtown.'. . . As soon as we heard that, we'd say, 'Well God, we've got excess capacity around here,' and we'd hire ourselves a bulldozer and tear that building down and then find a propitious time to sell the land."

If they didn't wait to destroy the old Met Center, Thatcher posited, they'd be trapped. Whitney might lure a franchise to the Twin Cities, but the only place for the new owner to go would be Target Center. To fit the hockey team into Target Center—to free up some economic space by lowering the mortgage payments or property taxes—a public subsidy of some sort would surely be needed. At that point, with Target Center as the only possible venue, Thatcher predicted that Wolfenson and Ratner would say, "We tell you the price."

"By tearing down Met Center we have given a blackjack to the owners of Target Center to make us pay a price over and above the fair and reasonable price for their facility," Thatcher said. He stayed mad about something else, the same thing that Representative Brown was angry about. Wolfenson and Ratner continued to refuse to disclose any financial details of the Target Center's operations. "They want the public to own that facility. And I say to you the price of doing business with the public is doing its business in public," Thatcher said.[10]

Change of Heart

As much as Thatcher felt that Wolfenson and Ratner shouldn't be coddled, he also feared where all this was headed. Green's departure had been a major wake-up call. Thatcher feared that the basketball owners were on the brink of personal bankruptcy, a point beyond which the community would lose control. He wanted to solve the problem. So on October 26, 1993, he drove his spotless black Mercedes to the Dome and asked commission executive director Bill Lester to take a stroll around the stadium's concourse. Thatcher recalls a firm talk with Lester, filled with urgency. "The time had come to get off the dime," Thatcher said. The 1994 legislative session was approaching. The 1993 Minneapolis mayoral election was nigh. The commission, Thatcher felt, needed to take a look at acquiring Target Center. Based on Wolfenson's threats, his treatment of Brown, and his total lack of political savvy, Thatcher concluded, "Marv was the problem, the impediment. He needed not only to get out of the driver's seat, but to get in the back seat, or where you stow the luggage, if that space was available to him." Thatcher wanted his agency to step forward and not get squeezed as it had by Norm Green's fiasco.

When Thatcher and Lester returned from their indoor stroll, Thatcher surprised his six commission colleagues with the suggestion that the group invite investment bankers to advise it about how to take over Target Center. Yes, the Sports Facilities Commission, considered a moribund gaggle of hacks, would take the first giant step toward the public "bailout" that Thatcher had repeatedly railed against during the Met Center task force hearings. But he couldn't stand by and be characterized once more as "the goat" that let another team get away. His idea passed, four to three. Commission chairman Bill Hunter, an innocuous Arne Carlson appointee with a political IQ of minus three, voted nay. Hunter voted against Thatcher even though it was his governor and his hockey task force that wanted Met Center dead and Target Center stable. "To go out and hire investment bankers, well, you can read about sharks, but they just happen to call them by different names," said Hunter, who added that the commission was "jumping the gun." Hunter, who did virtually nothing during his three years as chairman but smoke cigarettes in the smoke-free Dome, revealed himself to be way out of his league. A high school and college football referee and a former Hormel operations executive from Austin, Minnesota, he had not been Carlson's first choice. His boss, Hormel's CEO Dick Knowlton, a former University of Colorado football player, was. Knowlton passed but recommended Hunter. And guess who Carlson originally delegated the Sports Facilities Commission chairmanship decision to? His pal Wheelock Whitney.

Needless to say, that "nay" vote on finding a way to save Target Center was Hunter's last. Within ten days, he was a retired Hormel executive once more. The commission needed a more aggressive and politically savvy chairman.

Not to forget, it should be noted that weeks later, on November 3, over Thatcher's objections, the Met Center task force voted to blow up the building. Now all eyes were on the Sports Facilities Commission. It had to save Target Center. It was the only place in town to play hockey.

The Country Lawyer Arrives

On Tuesday, November 9, 1993, at 3:47 P.M., Henry Savelkoul was standing next to the lectern in the governor's reception room at the state capitol. The North Dakota farm boy was in charge of the Target Center takeover effort, the quarterback of an urban crisis. He was the new chairman of the Metropolitan Sports Facilities Commission, Carlson's pro sports plenipotentiary. In this introductory news conference, Carlson and Savelkoul spoke of preferring a private acquisition of the arena. Carlson said bringing an NHL team back to the Twin Cities was another goal. Savelkoul listened and immediately revealed that he knew the going would be tough. "I'm not sure how wise I am in stepping into this challenge," he said. "It could be a no-win situation." This was a man with foresight.

Days earlier, on a crisp Saturday morning at about 7 A.M., the phone rang in Henry and Margaret Savelkoul's lakeside home in Albert Lea, Minnesota, about one hundred miles south and west of St. Paul. It was the governor. "Henry, there's a problem," Carlson said. The two hadn't spoken in years, but their fondness for each other dated back a decade and a half. Both were veterans of the Metrodome legislative debate; they'd both voted to issue bonds for the Dome. Both were veterans of a time when the Republican caucus in the Minnesota House of Representatives numbered 31 out of 134 members. They had worn buttons then that read, "31 Ain't Fun."

Carlson, a fiery type, remained in politics, becoming Minnesota's state auditor and then governor. He was a fanatical University of Minnesota basketball and football fan, a close personal friend of Gophers' basketball coach Clem Haskins, and an inveterate wearer of a gold-and-maroon Gophers' cardigan. Carlson, a native New Yorker, rude by nature, was a balls-out fan. On the other hand, Savelkoul was a diffident sort. He was the minority leader of the Minnesota House of Representatives in 1976 and 1977 and had visions once of being governor himself. But his exploratory campaign floundered, and his years of raising money for the Republican caucus and flying in small airplanes around the state soured him on the whole notion. "I really got burned out," Savelkoul said. "My tolerance level maxed out." "Henry Savelkoul would have made a good governor," Carlson said. "He's a problem solver."

For fifteen years, he solved legal problems for clients big and small from his spartan law office in downtown Albert Lea, the one with a photo of him and Governor Ronald Reagan of California on the wall and the plaque signifying Savelkoul as one of 1975's "Ten Outstanding Young Minnesotans." He'd become a fabulously prosperous lawyer aiding clients on tax issues, business acquisitions, and farm matters. He maintained tenuous political liaisons—he was long a member of the State Commission on Judicial Selection, for instance—but devoted his time to his family and Albert Lea's economic development. An outdoorsman, he traveled frequently to the Wind River Range of Wyoming to hike and camp. Henry Savelkoul was politely minding his own business when Carlson's call came.

Savelkoul had never been to the Metrodome to see a baseball game before his selection. He was barely a fan of anything, maybe hockey because his sons had played. "I'm not there emotionally for sports and I think that's good," Savelkoul said. "If you have someone involved in sports, he might back something no matter what the costs."

Of this Target Center mess, Savelkoul knew very little. He'd read some snippets in the Twin Cities newspapers, but that was all. If it was a matter of urban-core stability, Savelkoul believed strongly in that. But only because he believed a strong Minneapolis translated into a strong Minnesota, and not because his city life experience was extensive.

Born a farm kid in Lansford, North Dakota (pop. 249), Savelkoul played football and basketball, despite his five-feet-seven slightness, at St. Leo's High School in Minot, thirty miles away. During summers of his high school years, Savelkoul made money as a custom cutter, hiring himself out at harvest time. He and friends would haul large combines from North Dakota to places like Oklahoma and Texas to assist farmers and ranchers. "We'd work eighteen hour days of dust and dirt, but you'd receive great satisfaction knowing you accomplished something every day," Savelkoul remembered. (Coincidentally, Savelkoul would soon meet and like another man who, as a youngster, custom harvested. His name was Carl Pohlad.) Besides the dirt and dust, Savelkoul was fascinated by numbers and, later, government. He majored in accounting at the College of St. Thomas in St. Paul in hopes of returning to farming. He was offered a job as a tax consultant with a prominent national firm in the Twin Cities, but professors influenced him to go into law and to think about politics. "But I didn't want to stay in the big city," he said. After graduating from the University of Minnesota Law School, he joined the Albert Lea law firm of O. Russell Olson. He'd been there for thirty years—taking time off for his legislative duties and a Harvard fellowship—when Carlson called and placed Savelkoul in this odd and difficult spot.

The law that created the funding authority for the Metrodome and the creation of the Metropolitan Sports Facilities Commission required that the chairman of the agency be from outside the Twin Cities. That was to balance the six appointments made by the Minneapolis City Council. But that natural tension between outstate Minnesota's Republican politics and Minneapolis's strident DFL positioning was too disparate for close working relations. As much as Savelkoul repeated how important a healthy big city was to the welfare of the entire state, he bore a grudge against Minneapolis. For one, to him the city seemed to want a lot from the state, from stadiums to convention centers to mass transit. On a tour of Albert Lea, Savelkoul was quick to point out boarded-up and frayed buildings and note that they needed as much help as any inner-city development. He carried a chip on his shoulder about rural Minnesota that never went away, even as he engaged himself with the politicians and staffers of Minneapolis. He also was a fervent Republican. Democrats were the enemy. His commission was a virtual DFL convention.

Finance chairman Thatcher, who wielded great influence in the commission's boardrooms, had close ties to the moderate wing of the party, with close friendships to the Humphrey and Mondale families, and social friendships with Massachusetts senator Ted Kennedy and former Democratic National Party chairman Robert Strauss. Peggy Lucas, the downtown developer and chair of the commission's marketing committee, was a personal friend of Mayor Sharon Sayles Belton. Don Early, the longtime Minneapolis labor leader, always stood up for union principles. John Pacheco, a full-time lobbyist for Northern States Power, was also a DFL community activist. Savelkoul was surrounded, save for the lone Republican apppointed by the DFL city council, Loanne Thrane. Thrane, a former Minnesota Republican Party chairwoman, lived in St. Paul. She was a fan of Sayles Belton. Savelkoul and Thrane never hit it off.

Living in a certain past, Savelkoul's analysis was one-dimensional: if any sports-related legislation—such as a Target Center buyout—looked as if it was driven by the city of Minneapolis and its Democratic fanatics, it would probably die. In his mind, it would be tainted. "If any deal has the appearance that Minneapolis wins all the marbles, it's counterproductive," Savelkoul said. He thought that St. Paul, suburban, and outstate legislators would reject any sports legislation that favored Minneapolis. He was wrong.

In the Target Center matter, because of some of his leadership and because of some superb lobbying efforts, the arena buyout bill passed the legislature. It passed *because* of strong city backing and the aid of Savelkoul's commission. Down the road, when he sought a new Twins ballpark, it was the team—and not the city—that led the legislative charge. The city's political *absence* from deep participation hurt that effort. There was no Minneapolis legislative or city council–linked energy to a Twins ballpark campaign. That lack of involvement destroyed any chance for a ballpark. Carlson and Savelkoul didn't know how to reach out to Minneapolis. They had only disdain. In the end, despite all his work and much creativity, Savelkoul's win-loss record wasn't sterling. He didn't build any coalitions. His Target Center plan blew up, and he needed a last-second rescue from Minneapolis city officials. His efforts to get a replacement for the North Stars fell short, mostly because he misjudged the growing price of NHL franchises during the Target Center buyout. And his plan to get the Twins a new ballpark fell very hard on its face. None of these shortcomings can be blamed only on Savelkoul. Indeed, without his participation, it's likely they would have failed earlier or harder. But his central role in all of them revealed one common thread: he was never a details person, and that character trait haunted him and his deals; he was never a fully communicative person. He continually straight-armed his own agency and its board members, losing a base of support he could have used. His only constituent turned out to be Carlson.

Savelkoul regularly attributed his lack of communicating fully with others to a lack of time; he was in Albert Lea, they were in the Twin Cities, his commission chairman job was supposed to be part-time, and there were only so many hours in the day. But mostly, despite a generally cheerful disposition and an always polite demeanor, he turned out to be a secretive, noninclusive type. As time wore on, the commission staff had a running joke that if you were looking for Savelkoul, he was likely to be in his three-point stance, as if at a track meet's starting line, getting ready to race off to his car to return to Albert Lea. Having a full conversation with him, in which input was as critical as output, was difficult for many. "We can choose to do nothing," Savelkoul repeated and repeated during every one of his efforts. "Or we can try." We? Savelkoul sometimes tried, but he rarely let anyone in to help out. It was mostly "I" or "Arne said." Over time, this isolation harmed him immeasurably. But over time, Savelkoul didn't seem to care. "Fortunately, I don't have a political future," Savelkoul said once, with resignation, but no bitterness. "I don't want a political future." He didn't have anything to worry about.

Hysteria

The Target Center buyout bill went through eleven different committee examinations. With Wolfenson and Ratner staying as far away from the capitol as interested parties could, the lobbying effort, quarterbacked by Sports Facilities Commission consultant Larry Redmond, was considered one of the finest in state history. The message was simple: allowing the Sports Facilities Commission to buy Target Center would preserve a special asset in downtown Minneapolis that had helped to spur the rise and coalescence of the highly successful Warehouse District, a sector for entertainment enjoyed mostly by young people. On the final day of the 1994 legislative session, a Target Center buyout package passed by one vote in the House. It passed because its numbers were manageable, unintimidating, and punitive. Wolfenson and Ratner would receive a grand total of $42 million in publicly backed money for their $104 million arena; another $12 million was to be raised by downtown Minneapolis business interests. An additional $750,000 a year was pledged by the legislature to aid the city of Minneapolis in operating the arena. There was no specific stipulation in the bill, but it was understood that a new owner would take over the Timberwolves in exchange for the public buyout. It was clean. It gave Wolfenson and Ratner a painful financial haircut of about $50 million. It also angered them. It wasn't enough.

Three weeks after the legislature adjourned, Wolfenson and Ratner announced they had sold the Wolves to Houston-based investors who planned to move the team to New Orleans. A secret deadline unknown to NBA officials had passed; with no local buyer in place, the Wolves were ostensibly sold to a shady group with plans to link their new NBA team to a floating casino in Louisiana. Hours after a late-afternoon news conference at Target Center, NBA commissioner David Stern said, "Whoa."

The league announced that it wanted the team to stay. Legal proceedings ensued. The alleged New Orleans buyers, according to Stern, did not have their finances in order. At least one seemed to be in jail. A series of antitrust lawsuits followed. One of the prospective Wolves buyers in Houston, attempting to avoid being served with a subpoena relative to the Wolves case, dressed in women's clothing to dodge a process server. This all led Stern to tell Sports Facilities Commission director Bill Lester that the entire Timberwolves–Target Center fiasco was "a colossal pig fuck," a description that has never been topped.

Meanwhile, the most active potential local buyer for the Wolves, a Minnesota insurance magnate named Bill Sexton, kept getting ice-cold feet over buying the team. He never made a formal offer. Eventually he dropped out. By July 1994 the Wolves and Target Center status seemed in limbo. Even as the NBA admirably forced the team to stay in Minnesota, no local buyer seemed willing to pay the price for the team that Wolfenson and Ratner needed to get above water. Then, a thirty-something stockbroker from Bloomington named Ed Villaume, trying to form a group to buy the Wolves, contacted Mankato printing mogul Glen Taylor, a former leader of the Minnesota Senate. Taylor had once considered buying the North Stars. He was richer than anyone knew. Villaume had an idea: Marv and Harv could stay in as partners, reducing the price slightly. He also tipped off Wolfenson and Ratner that Taylor was interested in buying the team. In August, as Villaume watched and received no credit, the Wolves changed hands. Wolfenson and Ratner were paid $80 million for a team they had bought seven years earlier for $32.5 million. They retained 10 percent of the team.

The saga didn't end. Because of legitimate delays and illegitimate procrastination, the final Target Center buyout deal wasn't completed as December 31, 1994, approached. The bond lawyers, hired for the Sports Facilities Commission by the Met Council and working for Savelkoul, screwed up. A new IRS ruling that the bond lawyers should have been aware of landed on Savelkoul's desk as the year ended. It shot down a ticket tax provision that would have helped pay off the bonds on the $42 million bailout. There stood Savelkoul, back to square one.

As it did with Met Stadium and the Metrodome, the city of Minneapolis came to the rescue. An entirely new finance plan—backed completely by city entertainment, property tax, and parking proceeds—was put in place. In March 1995, the Target Center became the property of the city of Minneapolis. Under a new deal worked out with Taylor, Wolfenson, Ratner, and the Ogden Corporation, the city paid $57 million for the arena, plus it bought out its own $22 million tax increment finance bond, which helped to acquire and clear the original Target Center land. Today that debt is paid off by a 3 percent city entertainment tax, by the state's $750,000-a-year stipend, which remained in place, and by city parking revenues. Ogden, to which Wolfenson and Ratner still owed about $10 million, stayed in the deal to get its money back. If attendance should dip or a catastrophe should occur, the debt load of Target Center was placed on the general-obligation backs of the citizens of Minneapolis—and no one else.

What should not go unmentioned here is Taylor's role. As Wolfenson often said, "I am the founder. Glen Taylor was the savior." Taylor's entrance into the Target Center/Timberwolves morass changed the profile of the debate and the process. It took Wolfenson and Ratner out of the line of fire. It created a personality of someone who was trying to solve a problem, not create it. Conveniently and thankfully, Taylor had a political background and was not a Minneapolitan. He was a moderate Republican, a person with whom Savelkoul was comfortable. The transfer of Wolves ownership to Taylor allowed, for the first time, a Greater Minnesotan to own one of the state's major-league sports assets. For sure, changing the ownership as the facility was refinanced meant that the old owner—the evil, rotten, greedy, no-good-bastard old owner, as depicted in the media—wouldn't benefit. It looked like this—and it was true; Taylor was taking a risk, and for it he was being rewarded by the city of Minneapolis buying the arena. If Wolfenson and Ratner stayed in, the city's arena buyout looked only like the bailout it was accused of becoming. Now the deal looked more like a necessary evil to keep the team, support the year-round facility, and allow a new owner to succeed.

With the basketball situation stablized, a funny thing happened. Hockey teams started to sniff around Target Center. Maybe, thought the owners of the Edmonton Oilers and the Winnipeg Jets, they could move to Minneapolis now that the city owned the arena. When Savelkoul sold the original buyout bill to the legislature, he suggested that a public buyout of the arena could help to facilitate the return of the NHL to the Twin Cities. Minneapolis officials assumed the same eventuality. But as Thatcher had predicted eighteen months earlier, the economics of the arena got worse, not better, once the public bought the building and once Wolfenson and Ratner sold their team. Rather than having a $32.5 million NBA franchise living at Target Center, Taylor now had an $80 million NBA team playing in the arena. He needed all the cash he could get from every revenue stream in the building to support such a purchase. To bring in a hockey team now, owned by someone else, would be to take cash from the Wolves. When Twin Cities–based health care executive Richard Burke bought the Winnipeg Jets in 1995 and tried to move them to

Target Center, he found that the economics didn't work. Savelkoul had miscalculated. When he pieced together the Target Center buyout package, he anticipated that NHL teams would cost no more than $50 million. But Burke paid $65 million for the lowly Jets. An arena designed to support a $32.5 million NBA team and a $40 million NHL team couldn't be expected to generate enough cash to service debt on teams with a combined cost of $150 million. Burke moved the Jets to Phoenix instead. The ghost of Met Center was giggling.

That "oops" you heard was NHL commissioner Bettman wondering if he'd done the right thing. Met Center was a pile of rubble and now a cleared piece of suburban real estate. There was nowhere for a hockey team to play in one of the most avid hockey regions in the nation; the St. Paul Civic Center, in need of its own repairs, was never seriously considered an option. At a stadium financing conference in Milwaukee soon after Burke's run at Target Center, Bettman pulled me aside. "Did we make a mistake?" he asked. Of course, as history played out, Met Center was as obsolete to house a 1990s NHL team as the Metrodome is to host a 1990s major-league baseball team.

In hindsight, somehow, more public money, mostly from the state, should have been poured into Target Center. The political will, of course, didn't exist for that to happen. But if a larger investment had been made in 1995, the resources of the state could have been preserved. Because by 1998, $130 million was committed by the state and the city of St. Paul to build a new arena to house a new $80 million NHL franchise. Just as Wolfenson and Ratner handed the NBA and Stern the gift of Target Center in 1990, so St. Paul mayor Norm Coleman hand-delivered, fully wrapped, with a ribbon on top, a totally publicly funded arena to Bettman. Coleman positioned the new facility as a "civic center," replacing the one that had been built twenty-five years earlier for another hockey team, the World Hockey Association's Fighting Saints. He claimed that the new arena would be used by "the boys and girls, moms and dads," of the state, that the new arena would play host to high school tournaments and civic events, that it was necessary for the vitality of downtown St. Paul. But he rarely mentioned that like the North Stars before them, the new NHL Minnesota Wild franchise would collect every penny of revenue that flowed into the new arena, even nonhockey dollars. Built for the "moms and dads," the arena finance plan was designed to benefit the owners of the Wild, who needed it because their league receives small amounts of national TV dollars and has no salary cap. They needed it all to pay their players.

The mayor did understand one thing, and he reprised it in 1999 in his effort to lure the Twins to St. Paul. Sports facilities get support if they possess a social value over and above their simple links to sports. Coleman turned this new NHL arena into a cause, into another piece of his effort to revitalize downtown St. Paul. It was more than just a place for a team to play. It was a monument to St. Paul's viability. He got the support of Carlson, of the St. Paul city council and the St. Paul legislative caucus. Even though the economics of the National Hockey League were perhaps the most precarious of any major-league sport, the arena's finance plan relied on the new NHL team attracting seventeen thousand fans per night, forty-one games per season, at average ticket prices reaching $50 by the time the team began play in the year 2000. A state holds it breath to await the Wild's first cries that they need a reduction in their rent. That should come any year now.

With the 1995 purchase by the city of Minneapolis of Target Center for $79 million and the new St. Paul arena, city and state governments had committed a combined $209 million to preserve the NBA and reestablish the NHL by 1998. Minnesotans had pro sports whiplash. For a state in which less than 33 percent of the people were identifying themselves as real sports fans, the politics of pro sports were filling too much of the front page and too much of the politicians' time. A 1997 Minnesota Poll showed that 77 percent of those surveyed believed that too much value was placed on pro sports.[11] It all seemed out of whack. No longer were sports fun and games. They were money and politics. No longer was Bob Allison living in a Minneapolis neighborhood and opening a bank account at the local branch as he sought an off-season job. Alienation was deep. Cynicism was high. Talk radio—including an all-sports station— provided outlets for the disaffected. A bubbling-right wing antitax movement was in place. A critical class-warfare left wing was poised.

With Met Center and Target Center controversies fresh in the memories of citizens and with the sports atmosphere toxically polluted, Twins owner Carl Pohlad entered the fray. It was his time to ask for a new publicly funded stadium. It was time, too, for the Vikings to make sure the Twins didn't get a leg up on them. It was time for the mother of all stadium games to begin. As Carl Pohlad prepared for his assault, he didn't carry with him the sentiments that drove Wolfenson and Ratner. As much as those two men were transformed into villains, there was something genuinely touching about their commitment to Target Center and Minneapolis. Ask the lawyers for the city. As they waded through the hundreds of pages of lease and sale agreements, they were struck by one of the covenants that Wolfenson and Ratner insisted on when they sold the arena. It had to do with the engraving on the black marble in the entrance-way of Target Center. The contracts between Wolfenson, Ratner, and the city of Minneapolis declare that that marble may never be altered. The engraving reads simply:

> THE PRIMARY PURPOSE OF THIS ARENA IS FOR THE ENTERTAINMENT
> OF THE PEOPLE OF MINNESOTA
> HARVEY & BARBARA RATNER FAMILY
> MARVIN & ELAYNE WOLFENSON FAMILY

The building sits as a monument to them. It should also sit as a lesson to the citizens of Minnesota. It is better to become dogged and vigilant watchdogs of major-league sports team owners *before* their deeds are done, not after. It is better to attempt to wrest some control of the process at the start, to demand scrutiny, to require that books be opened, to kick and scream and make certain that leagues understand the conditions on the ground of one's community. It is wise to leave old buildings standing before we think that new edifices will solve the constant problems of sports economics. Otherwise the public merely becomes those fellows at the circus with the shovels, cleaning up after the elephants ... and the rabbits, too.

CHAPTER 6

I Gotta Get Me One of These
Carl's Edifice Complex

Amid the North Stars' flight and the Target Center Sturm und Drang, the Twins began to make their own stadium move. Pohlad, still generally liked in July 1994, went public saying something had to be done, barely two months after Wolfenson and Ratner had claimed they were going to move their team to New Orleans and even as the legal theatrics about the basketball team's future continued. It wasn't a pro sports roller coaster that Minnesota was on; it was more like one of those moving walkways at the airport. Every time the public thought one team had asked for too much or threatened its last threat, another team hopped on the long, black, constantly rotating pro sports treadmill and dragged the fans and taxpayers along with it. It was hard to keep up with all the needs of all the teams, of the literal comings and goings. There was the oozing of a pro sports goo that was running down the face of the Twin Cities. The Vikings were soon to be heard from, too. It was a pro sports grand slam of need, even greed.

In the fall of 1993, Twins president Jerry Bell and team finance director Kevin Mather began to scrutinize every single penny that went into and out of the Metrodome, and determine how the Twins could capture as much of that money as possible. Since winning their second World Series in 1991 and drawing nearly 2.5 million fans in 1992, the Twins began to feel the walls of the baseball industry closing in on them. Although the team had generated $3 to $5 million in operating profits in

1988 and 1992, Pohlad was still carrying a load of debt from the team purchase and from some losses. He also had to pay a whopping $10 million to cover baseball's collusion settlement of $280 million; that resulted from an arbitrator's ruling that the sport's owners, under commissioner Peter Ueberroth, had conspired to not sign free agents and thus keep down players' salaries.

The Twins were the poster child for a little-read but chillingly prescient report written in December 1992 by a panel of economists selected by baseball's owners and players' union. The scholars, including former Federal Reserve Board chairman Paul Volcker, warned of a coming implosion in the game's economics, a prediction that has since been borne out. This four-man panel of economists—selected jointly by the game's owners and the Major League Baseball Players Association—concluded that the industry was "filled ... with money, conflict and distrust.... Baseball must be reconceived by its participants, the owners and the players, as a genuine partnership which pursues competitive excellence, leads by moral and athletic example, resolves labor disputes through negotiation rather than by insulting the public with lockouts and strikes, and tempers financial greed with a sense of mutual cooperation and accountability to the public."[1]

The panel noted the beginning chasm between have and have-not franchises. While revenues rose at an average annual rate of 9 percent between 1985 and 1991, baseball faced a downturn in national television dollars—the bread and butter of a pro sports league's stability—as 1993 approached. National TV dollars tend to be the foundation of leveling the playing field among teams. The more shared dollars in a league, the more cash every team has to work with. In theory, it allows teams in such diverse cities as New York and Cincinnati to compete. But after national television, the next greatest revenue generators in baseball are from local radio and TV rights fees and from sales inside and around the ballpark, be it tickets, parking, concessions, scoreboard advertising, or luxury suites.

"The financially weakest clubs must not be led by low revenues to slash payrolls dramatically by selling off their star players in an effort to reduce costs and become profitable," the panel wrote in 1992—seven years before the Twins management finally did just that. "Such practices would produce what is essentially minor league baseball in which some teams make no meaningful attempt to produce winning teams, would break faith with the public in the affected cities and harm baseball as a whole. Increased revenue sharing, we believe, would reduce the likelihood of such unfortunate behavior."[2] The entire notion of "large-market" and "small-market" teams—that terminology in the vocabulary of baseball and, for that matter, all pro sports—grew from this study.

One chart—out of an onslaught of charts—stood out. It graphed the average winning percentages of teams from 1984 to 1990 against the average player salary on those teams. The Twins stood smack-dab in the middle on winning percentage, playing just about .500 baseball over that seven-year period after Pohlad bought the team. And they sat in the bottom third in terms of average player salary, even though they won a World Series in that span and captured a second World Series victory in 1991. The gap between the average Twins player's paycheck of $400,000 a year and the top-paid Yankees player of $600,000 was, on a percentage basis, wide but not canyonlike. By comparison, of course, the average Twins salary of $700,000 per player in 1999 paled to the $3 million per player average of the Yankees. During the years when the Twins were winning, their payroll was an average payroll because their revenues were average revenues. "Overall," the panel of economists wrote in 1992, "baseball generates more than enough revenue to thrive; only greed, rashness, or a lack of reasonable cooperation can preclude economic viability for both owners and players."[3]

Unlike the National Football League, which agreed to share most of its joint revenues—mainly national network dollars—back in 1960, baseball's owners shared very little of their collected money. The NFL's TV rights have always been virtually totally national in scope, getting money from networks to control the local broadcasting of games. Thus, when we watch a Vikings game on a Twin Cities television station, it is the parent network—and not the local station—that has paid a rights fee to the NFL to show the game and sell the advertising that supports the fee. In baseball, national television dollars were on the decline in the early

1990s as local television rights fees—through the emerging cable television systems—were generally rising. Those locally paid fees in baseball—like $55 million a year to the New York Yankees—are not shared with the Yankees' "partners," that is, the other baseball team owners. Thus, in baseball—as opposed to football—the so-called large-market teams were seeing their revenues grow with increasingly lucrative local cable deals while the small-market teams, such as the Twins, were getting their revenues the old-fashioned way, via national TV dollars and in-stadium sales.

Just as significant, baseball's stadium infrastructure was being renewed across the country as the 1980s turned into the 1990s. The Chicago White Sox had a new stadium in 1991. The Baltimore Orioles had a new stadium, Camden Yards, in 1992. The Cleveland Indians and Texas Rangers moved into new ballparks on opening day of 1994. Baseball expanded to Denver and Miami, with an influx of new dollars from super-rich owners, such as the Florida Marlins' Wayne Huizenga. Teams got fatter, but so did the players' salaries. An underlying supply of capital was beginning to come from local units of government and states via direct payments to construction projects. Baseball was being subsidized by the public in some cities, and those subsidies were being passed through to the players and owners. Through the use of entertainment taxes, sales taxes, or lottery proceeds, public dollars built stadiums almost as gifts to team owners and players. The stadiums were hardware, built generally with public dollars. The teams were the software, placed into the stadium like so many floppy disks into a computer's "A" drive. Teams were owned by an increasing number of media companies: the Chicago Tribune Company, with its powerful WGN cable superstation, bought the Cubs in 1981, six years after cable giant Turner Broadcasting bought the Braves. Their franchises truly were programming software. (More recently, the Walt Disney Co. bought the California Angels; Fox Entertainment bought the Los Angeles Dodgers. And media mogul Tom Hicks bought the Texas Rangers in a play to expand a regional sports network.) If the economics of baseball were driven by ticket sales in the seventies and broadcast rights in the eighties, it was the stadium boom that fed the insatiable monster of the nineties.

Within these stadiums were the operating systems for increased revenues for the teams and their players. For instance, luxury suites were becoming as posh as party rooms at fancy hotels. Naming rights to stadiums were beginning to cost companies more than $1 million a year, and integrated marketing programs pushed the naming rights values even higher. In-stadium advertising signs proliferated, again linked to commercial time on a team's radio and television broadcasts. Unlike Met Stadium or the Dome, it wasn't just the users of a stadium—the fans of the teams or tourists downtown—who paid the bulk of the facility's debt. It was the general public via sales taxes or lottery purchases. And the teams, the tenants, shared less and less with the stadium treasuries and kept more and more for themselves. Team values increased. The rate of team sales were intensified. Old owners captured high appreciations on their franchises and exited. New owners needed those new facilities to help them pay off their large debt on their recent franchise acquisitions. Team owners relied on other private dollars from sponsors to cover increasing expenses.

The baseball world—mirrored by economics in all the major leagues—went round and round, its circles growing. In the center was the fan, feeling farther and farther away. In Minnesota, with fans and taxpayers alike shaking their heads over the Stars' move and the Timberwolves' demands, the distance between the teams and the consumers widened. Emotional gaps aside, there was also an increasing sense that the games were being priced out of reach. While, generally speaking, Minnesota sports fans continued to pay below-market prices compared to other cities, fans still *felt* as if they were being gouged. In a 1993 Minnesota Poll, 40 percent of Minnesotans believed the North Stars ticket prices were too expensive; the team had the lowest average ticket prices in the NHL. Similarly, 52 percent of those surveyed thought the Vikings were charging too much for tickets, but the team had the twenty-first most expensive tickets in a league of twenty-eight teams.[4]

The proliferation of new highly subsidized stadiums created a recycled phenomenon of the 1960s and 1970s when many cities believed the multipurpose, round, tall stadiums would be Band-Aids on declining urban cores. Two decades later, other cities—and some of the same ones from the sixties—were pounding their chests and saying, "Look at us, we've got shiny, new stadiums. We're special. We're rebuilding our inner cities . . . again. We support our teams." And the national marketplace for teams heated up once more. Like the Twin Cities of the fifties, new cities emerged or pretended to emerge, seeking teams, seducing owners. The Nashvilles, Charlottes, and Jacksonvilles got onto the radar. So, too, for a while, did a relatively unknown region of North Carolina called "the Triad," home to Greensboro, Winston-Salem, and High Point. In 1997 the Triad would try to steal the Twins from Minnesota.

In baseball, no franchise had moved since 1972, when the second incarnation of the Washington Senators moved to Dallas–Fort Worth. Finally, Dallas, one of Branch Rickey's original Continental League loyalist cities, got its major-league team. Indiviual team owners in baseball were limited in their ability to move teams because of the antitrust exemption that the sport owns. Because it is exempt from the Sherman Antitrust Act, the game's owners can decide as a group to restrict a member of their group to move his or her team. But in the NFL and in the expanding NBA and NHL, especially, teams were moving to communities—or expanding into newly emerging "major-league cities"—that were subsidizing them more deeply than their scorned hometowns. Those other leagues couldn't easily halt movements. Thus the necessity of David Stern's strong-arming of Wolfenson and Ratner. Whether to regain teams lost in previous rounds of stadium construction or to attract pro sports for the first time, cities like Baltimore, St. Louis, Nashville, Denver, Charlotte, and Phoenix were glad to put together diverse public (and private) financing arrangements to attract pro leagues. And in most cases, there remained more teams than cities. Thus scarcity pitted city against city, state against state, for the few teams. In football, the Los Angeles Rams moved to St. Louis to capture a public windfall. The Cleveland Browns moved to Baltimore to profit immeasurably. In hockey, an exodus was flowing out of Canada, with the Winnipeg Jets journeying to Phoenix and the Quebec Nordiques scooting down to richer Denver. In baseball, Denver, Phoenix, and Tampa–St. Petersburg built new or refurbished old

Table 1. Major League Baseball Stadiums in the Nineties and Beyond

City / Stadium Name	Opened	Cost (Millions)	Public Funding %, How
St. Petersburg / Tropicana Field	1990	$208	100%, county tourist tax, state sales tax
Chicago / Comiskey Park	1991	$185	95%, hotel tax
Baltimore / Camden Yards	1992	$234	90%, lottery
Cleveland / Jacobs Field	1994	$230	70%, cigarette, alcohol tax
Dallas / Ballpark at Arlington	1994	$191	74%, sales tax
Denver / Coors Field	1995	$215	75%, sales tax
Atlanta / Turner Field	1997	$239	87%, Atlanta Olympics
Phoenix / Bank One Ballpark	1998	$349	68%, sales tax
Seattle / Safeco Field	1999	$517	89%, food, rental car taxes
Detroit / Comerica Park	2000	$260	52%, hotel, car rental taxes, Indian casino revenues
Houston / Enron Field	2000	$250	79%, hotel tax
San Francisco / Pacific Bell Park	2000	$266	10%, tax increment financing to acquire land
Milwaukee / Miller Park	2001	$295	84%, sales tax

Various sources include confidential documents provided by industry consultants.

to get into the baseball family. There was a swirl of construction activity boosting the economics of sports.

But in 1993 the Twins were standing still. They were playing in a stadium that was only eleven years old, but one in which they got to keep few of the critical amenities that other teams were pocketing, such as rentals from luxury suites, extensive ad signs in the stadium, and naming rights for the ballpark. Remember, the Vikings and Mike Lynn got the suite dollars, the Sports Facilities Commission got the in-stadium advertising to help pay its mortgage, and the Dome, thankfully, was named after Hubert H. Humphrey, the political warrior, not a corporate buyer.

In the face of that 1992 report, as baseball attempted to renew itself with ballparks, the "retro" stadium became a trend. Baseball was seeking its roots. Seeing itself getting overtaken by the energy of pro basketball and the violence of pro football, bucolic baseball was repositioning itself with the baby boom generation as a family-oriented, almost nostalgic experience. Its roots existed outside on grass in the sun, not inside under a Teflon sky on plastic blades of fake turf. Baseball needed to remain the affordable sport so that the mythic tradition of dads taking sons to games could continue. The panacea was theoretically the new ballpark.

As other teams were building or trying to build, Pohlad wanted to be a part of that trend. The Metrodome was the last of those so-called multipurpose stadiums of the sixties and seventies. After the Dome opened in 1982, no other major-league stadium was built to accommodate both a major-league baseball and NFL team. Fans didn't like them. Watchers of baseball games felt too far away from the action. The economics of both sports were increasingly beginning to argue against shared stadiums. Each team needed its own place to afford to pay its players and to maximize profits for owners. Amid this landscape and a horizon that indicated a building boom, the Twins wanted their own new ballpark, too.

In April 1993, Pohlad called Sports Facilities Commission chairman Bill Hunter and Dome executive director Bill Lester to lunch to make the first of his informational pleas. "Mr. Pohlad wanted to reiterate what he sees as the *dire straits of baseball* as an industry," Lester wrote in a memo to the commission in reporting the meeting. At that time, all that Pohlad requested was more seats behind home plate. The notion of "quality seats" was born; it's a term that swam through the next years. Good seats and high prices were needed.

Soon after that luncheon, the Twins weren't thinking about a few thousand extra seats. They were thinking about a new ballpark. Bell engaged the Twin Cities–based sports accountant Larry Greenberg to determine if the Twins could privately build an outdoor stadium adjacent to the Dome. The idea was to build toward the west, toward downtown Minneapolis, and, at first, to devise an underground system to move equipment and concessions back and forth between the Dome and the new ballpark, depending on the particular day's weather. A nice day meant outdoor baseball. A rotten day meant Domeball. A preliminary study showed a victim of the notion would be the *Star Tribune* newspaper, which has its main offices on the site that Bell and Greenberg were dreaming about, near Fifth Street and Portland Avenue South. After some consideration, Bell concluded that the good-weather, bad-weather option wouldn't work. Logistics would be tough. Figuring out comparable seating locations would be a challenge. That idea quickly died.

In January 1994, Bell and Mather finished their research on the Dome's economics and pondered another concept: privatizing the Dome and sucking every dollar out of it for the teams, rather than sharing revenues with the public agency that operated it, the Metropolitan Sports Facilities Commission. Under this plan, Bell, the commission's former chief executive, proposed that the Twins and Vikings operate the Dome without the commission. Using the money that would come from the sale of the Met Center land, the commission would pay off the Dome's remaining $40 million debt. Then the teams would take over the stadium, sell its naming rights, control its advertising, manage its concessions, and control its rental fees to other events. Politically, the idea had problems. The commission had long done an exemplary job of cheaply renting the Dome for community and high school events. Would the teams be as generous and community minded? Second, teams had a tendency to not maintain stadiums as well as the public. Would the Twins and Vikings run down the old stadium, knowing that degradation could increase discussion about the need for a new ballpark? One more matter: privatizing could mean property taxes.

Mather's and Bell's numbers showed that in a best-case scenario, the Twins could increase their take by about $4 million per year, and the Vikings by as much as $7 million per year. "In the end, it looked like I was working for the Vikings," Bell said. Later, Vikings president Roger Headrick suggested he could wring between $8 and $10 million more a year out of the Dome if the Sports Facilities Commission turned control over to the team.

In a January 1994 memo to Carl Pohlad and his sons, Bell and Mather wrote, "With your approval, we would like to proceed exploring the opportunity to establish a Joint Venture between the Vikings and Twins. . . . For the first time, we will have complete control over our entire product; i.e., broadcasting, signage, promotions, tickets, concessions, etc. These changes, along with the pending labor settlement and revenue sharing, give the Twins the opportunity to provide a reasonable return to ownership."[5]

When Bell enthusiastically took his memo and findings to Carl and his sons, they applauded Bell's diligent efforts. "That's great, Jerry," Bell remembers Pohlad telling him. But there was a problem, Pohlad said. "It's not enough." The direction was clear. A new ballpark was the only answer.

There was, however, another problem known as politics, public opinion, and timing. Seeking a new Twins stadium in 1994 was simply not in the cards. The lack of ripeness of the baseball stadium issue dogged the Pohlads' efforts. In 1994, while Pohlad was shaking his head about the future of the Dome, the legislature was beating up on Wolfenson and Ratner. Those guys were about to lose $50 million of an empire that wasn't much larger while billionaire Pohlad was beginning to lay the groundwork for a plan that would guarantee that he would lose not one dime of his investment in the Twins. Bell knew that Pohlad couldn't just join the Marv-and-Harv train that was making stops and starts at the capitol.

"We could see all that was going on over there for a grand total of $750,000 a year," said Bell of the 1994 legislative session and the effort to get state money to buy out Target Center. "For $750,000, I wouldn't even waste my time. We were looking at hundreds of millions. We decided then and there, we'd better not go to the legislature with a crisis. We'd better go with an explanation and a plan." They knew that their lease, with its ever-present escape clause, expired in 1998. They knew that in 1997 they could trigger that escape with a year's notice. They assumed, given the operating losses that were mounting with increased salaries and the lack of new revenue streams, that they would reach—or fall to—the thresholds needed to escape.

As the plan developed, a vision solidified. Camden Yards in Baltimore was the first successful new ballpark, merging the synergies of a downtown with the new fan services of elite suites and creature comforts, a carnival atmosphere in a background that felt like the good old days. On April 4, 1994, Cleveland's Jacobs Field was opened, named after Pohlad's pal Dick Jacobs, owner of the Indians, who paid $13.8 million of his own dough to place his name on the city-built stadium. Soon afterward, Pohlad visited what has become one of the jewels of the nation's ballparks, a facility that rejuvenated the sport in Cleveland. A former Twins employee remembers Pohlad coming back from that visit and telling some Twins staff members, "This is what we need." He was, said the high-ranking staff person, "Like a kid in a candy store after seeing Jacobs." Pohlad didn't know where it would go or who would pay for it, but he knew he wanted it soon. In July 1994 Pohlad officially began his effort, saying, "Me, too," in the chorus of sports facilities.

On the one hand, this was wise and fair. The legislature and Minneapolis City Council, while tired of addressing pro sports matters, certainly had to appreciate an attempt at a reasoned approach. Pohlad was making his needs and plans known earlier rather than later. In a sense, Pohlad was kicking off the conversation to allow many ideas to flow. That was good. On the other hand, it was as if the hits just kept on coming. As in a crowded delicatessen, the Twins' number was up, and there stood Pohlad waving his little deli ticket high so that the workers behind the counter—the elected officials—could serve up some public-finance lunch meat. The beginning of the Twins' campaign added oil to the North Stars and Target Center fire.

Just ten weeks after the legislature passed the ill-fated Target Center buyout plan, Pohlad, Bell, and financial adviser Bob Starkey of the Arthur Andersen accounting firm appeared before the Sports Facilities Commission and said that the Twins were facing dire financial straits. "Unfortunately, the current controversy regarding the North Stars and Timberwolves understandably leaves little sympathy for major-league sports in the state of Minnesota," Pohlad told the commission, which listened intently in its tiny, spartan conference room on the first concourse level of the Dome. "Our purpose in appearing before you today is to explore opportunities for the stadium commission and the Minnesota Twins without deadlines or media hyperbole and without threat of relocation."[6]

Whenever a banker suggests he wants to "explore opportunities," it's time to guard your wallet. Whenever a team owner desires a conversation "without threat of relocation," beware—the threat will arrive sometime soon. Let history note that the first veiled warning about a possible Twins move came on July 18, 1994. It has hung over the Twins stadium debate—and been its underlying foundation—ever since. It has poisoned the conversation and continually alienated fans and taxpayers.

Looking back, that was a particularly absurd time for Pohlad to begin seeking aid for a baseball team. Of course, no time is good. Besides the noxious Target Center cloud hanging over him, Pohlad was one of the most hawkish baseball owners backing efforts by acting commissioner Bud Selig to cap players salaries. A devastating strike was looming, twenty-five days away. Indeed, on the very day that Pohlad politely previewed his eventual call for a new $350 million ballpark—a call that wouldn't fully materialize for two and a half years—baseball's players union was rejecting the owners' salary cap proposal. No one, including Pohlad, who sat in that cramped Dome conference room could have envisioned the kick in the groin that the 1994 work stoppage was going to deliver to the game and to its relationship with fans, especially Twins fans. The World Series, the symbol of community coziness in Minnesota, was about to be canceled by Selig, a close, personal friend of Pohlad's, so close that Pohlad was known to help Selig select his wardrobe. Still, not knowing what was to come down the pike on August 12—when baseball shut down its season and then the World Series—Pohlad was received with respect and sincere attention. Seventy-nine years old, still seemingly fit, his speech firm and his financial power at its height, he performed ably and even creatively. It was a fine performance. Unfortunately, it was soon swept away by the baseball industry's inability to heed the warnings of that 1992 study.

Before Pohlad took center stage, Bell and Starkey claimed that baseball was trying to get "its house in order." They pointed out that in their view, the Twins were paying high stadium maintenance fees, but no rent, and getting none of the typical in-stadium revenue streams, such as suite rentals. Starkey claimed that none of Pohlad's $36 million purchase price of the team had been paid down and that, in fact, Pohlad had already paid $50 million of interest expense on that acquisition in those first ten years of owning the team. (Remember that $86 million figure because it will come back again and again.)

Then Pohlad took a seat facing the seven commissioners in their typical U formation. Pohlad took his place at a long table at the top of the U, closing it to make a rectangle. Pohlad didn't mince his words. In fact, he established some principles that he carried forward throughout the stadium debate. One was to announce that he would "open his books" to the Sports Facilities Commission's accountants, an act that Wolfenson and Ratner had refused to do and one that any sports team owner seeking the public's assistance must be required to do. More progressively, Pohlad offered the groundwork for a certain kind of broad-based community ownership of the team and raised the possibility of merging the baseball team with the new owners of the Timberwolves. (At that point, Glen Taylor hadn't purchased the team. That was three weeks away. At that point, Pohlad was nearly five years ahead of New York Yankees owner George Steinbrenner, who merged his baseball team with the NBA New Jersey Nets in March 1999.)[7]

Calling the captains of local industry "bell ringers," Pohlad challenged "twenty-five to thirty" of them to each kick in what he called a "modest" $5 million to pool their resources and buy both the Twins and Wolves. "It could be a damn good investment and a partial answer to our question," Pohlad said, adding, "Let's not have any acrimony." He pledged to gather the business community to spread his gospel, but it never happened.

Besides showing that he was open to new ideas, Pohlad revealed his inability to state honestly what he wanted. It was a frustrating side of the entire stadium debate and eventual fake sale to North Carolina businessman Don Beaver in 1997. Pohlad, a man who has made hundreds of deals involving billions of dollars, simply couldn't decide from one day to the next what the heck he really wanted to do with the Twins. Back in 1994, while he repeatedly gushed about Jacobs Field to the commission, he didn't ask for an outdoor stadium, and Bell and Starkey spoke mostly of how to get more cash out of the Dome. But they wanted a new, publicly financed stadium, period, end of sentence.

Still, Pohlad said, "I don't know what I want." After his formal presentation, he stood in the back of the room, surrounded by Minicams and inquisitive reporters. "We have to make up our minds in the Twin Cities what we want.... It's not a Pohlad problem. I've directly made a contribution to this community. I'm willing to go another mile." (Note the word "contribution" and keep your eye on that bouncing ball of a word.)

As Pohlad established his tone and some guidelines, so did Sports Facilities Commission chairman Henry Savelkoul. Eight months into his tenure as the top dog on the commission, Savelkoul had proven to be a tough guy with Wolfenson and Ratner, pushing down the amount of money he was willing to direct their way to get them out of their hole. (Savelkoul's hand was strengthened by NBA commissioner Stern, who made it clear he had no intention of allowing the Wolves to move. Stern was distinctly different from acting Major League Baseball commissioner Bud Selig, who, as Savelkoul put it, was happy to do "whatever Carl wanted.")

Still, even knowing that Selig was Pohlad's servant, Savelkoul acted like Jell-O when it came to Pohlad. While a handful of commissioners privately said after the meeting that they wondered why the public should subsidize a baseball team that was being hurt by lower national television revenues, Savelkoul ebulliently declared a "new relationship" was nigh and, "We can't expect this [Pohlad] family to make this sacrifice forever."

Savelkoul also tipped his hand for the future, as did Pohlad. During his presentation on that July Monday, Pohlad waved a copy of the *New York Times Magazine* from the day before. On its cover, a sixtyish looking grandmother, arms raised, is yelping for joy as playing cards and chips dot the table in front of her.

"Gambling. America's Real National Pastime," the bold orange type under the photo said, with smaller teaser type reading, "It's bigger than baseball. Governments are addicted to it, the interactive future is riding on it. This great, teeming, itchy-fingered nation spends more money on legalized gambling than on all other forms of entertainment combined."[8]

Aha! Not only did the Twins have an economic problem—some of it brought on by the inherent inequities of the baseball industry—but we all had a villain to point to: gambling. That, of course, could only mean Indian gaming, for that was all that Minnesota had, begun in a major way after the signing of compacts in 1991 between the state and Minnesota's tribes. Pohlad whined that "the enormous numbers" going into local gambling were being diverted from pro sports. And Savelkoul, showing his leanings toward gambling as an enemy—and eventual funding source—chimed in , "Baseball does a ton more for [Minnesota's] economy than a couple of gambling casinos, or all the casinos put together," he said. "In the long term, hopefully [Pohlad's presentation] can help us to get away from creating bad press for professional sports when they do a lot for the economy."

It was the first salvo in the Twins stadium war. It told us a lot. Pohlad was open to new ideas, wasn't open to losing any more money, and was eager to figure out a way to get back the money he'd lost. Savelkoul was in Pohlad's corner.

"It was just such an up-front, right thing to do," Loanne Thrane remembers of Pohlad's inaugural presentation. On the Sports Facilities Commission, for a decade a former chief of staff to Senator Rudy

Boschwitz, a former member of the University of Minnesota Board of Regents, a former state chair of the Republican Party, Thrane was a scholar of what makes political sense in Minnesota. "Carl just made such a good impression. Of course, it went downhill from there."

The strike came. Baseball's house wasn't getting in order; it was getting burned down. Savelkoul and the commission staff were distracted, anyway. Taylor, the former state senator from Mankato and a billionaire in his own right, stepped in and bought the Wolves from Wolfenson and Ratner. He began to negotiate a tough lease with Savelkoul. Then a new Target Center plan had to be devised after the bond lawyers assigned to the commission by the Metropolitan Council screwed up. In the end, the city of Minneapolis—surprise, surprise—had to come to the commission's rescue, as it had when Met Stadium was built and as it had when the Metrodome was built. Under the whip of city council president Jackie Cherryhomes and the nimble number crunching of city finance officer John Moir, the Target Center finance plan was redone. Savelkoul breathed a sigh of relief. Key officials in the Minneapolis city hall believe that Savelkoul's embarrassment at having to be rescued in the Target Center process galvanized him to be even more insular in the Twins stadium process.

There's a sentiment among some city officials and Sports Facilities Commission members that as soon as the Target Center deal finally closed in March of 1995, Savelkoul was determined to vindicate himself. At Minneapolis city hall, which was kept out of the Twins ballpark negotiating loop quite tightly, there was a belief that Savelkoul was going to get a Twins deal done by hook or by crook. He wanted to prove he could do it without the assistance of Moir, who patched the Target Center deal together after the bond lawyers royally screwed up. There were even suggestions, from Vikings officials and Thatcher, that Savelkoul believed that a successful Twins deal could catapult him from tiny Albert Lea to continental prominence as the public official who figured out how to get a stadium built in a socially responsible way. "Cash and ambition clouded his judgment," Thatcher charged. Savelkoul vehemently denied such ambition. But Thatcher, who came to disrespect Savelkoul, believed that "Henry was trying to create the 'Savelkoul paradigm' that was to be new, novel, compelling, and to result in a new and national sports-financing legal practice, filled with notoriety and cash for Henry. He was breathtakingly audacious, certainly presumptuous. Remember one of the rules for life: 'Never presume the absence of hubris.'"

Savelkoul did attend one national stadium financing seminar, admitted he received two telephone calls soon afterward for potential jobs elsewhere as the Twins plan unfolded, and steadfastly refused to hire experienced stadium negotiators or investment bankers in either the Target Center or Twins stadium campaigns. As cities across the nation built stadiums and lured teams, an industry of sports consultants—from architects to accountants, from investment bankers to deal makers—formed. Experts were available. Save for Twin Cities–based sports accountant David Welle, a nationally recognized expert on stadium financing, Savelkoul—new to the sports business—never sought any professional assistance in negotiating either the Target Center deal or the Twins stadium deal. In a sense, Savelkoul walked into a new world with some very savvy players. His big-picture skills were solid. His attention to detail was nonexistent. His political sensibilities—gone from the legislature for more than thirteen years—were flabby at best.

By 1995, the Major League Baseball players strike, followed by an owners' lockout, was over, but the carnage was everywhere. Baseball was in a shambles, and Minnesotans were so mad they weren't just kicking the corpse, they were letting it lie on the street to rot. Alienated by the hockey move and the basketball buyout, impatient with a pro football team that couldn't seem to return to its glory days of the 1970s, some fans turned joyously to a niche phenomenon known as the St. Paul Saints, a minor-league baseball team that started operations in 1993, playing in a 5,069-seat outdoor ballpark in the Midway section of St. Paul.[9] In its first season, the franchise, playing in the low-level, unaffiliated Northern League, drew twenty-five sellouts. Baseball was outdoors again. The atmosphere was fun. Massage therapists offered fans therapeutic relaxation. You could get a haircut at the game. The players made less money than the customers. And a pig was the team's mascot. Although Twins officials pooh-poohed the Saints as competition, comparing the Saints to a sort of neighborhood theater competing against the Guthrie, the Saints offered an accessible alternative for baseball fans and for families in search of inexpensive entertainment. In response, the Saints and the city of St. Paul expanded the tiny stadium to 6,311 seats and delivered twenty-nine sell-outs in forty-one home games. On September 6, 1995, with the stink from the Major League Baseball work stoppage still apparent, the Saints outdrew the Twins on a day when the teams went head-to-head. The Saints attracted 4,637 fans, and the Twins a paltry 2,729. Any affection that seemed so deep in 1991, when the Twins won their second World Series in four years, had dissipated. As much as the Twins had a jam-packed bandwagon in October 1991, they were living an empty existence by the end of the 1995 season. The Saints were hip. The Twins were becoming invisible.

Five days later, five days after the Saints showed they were a more attractive product than the Twins, Pohlad and Bell were back at it, stirring up stadium thoughts. It was September 1995, the end of another season, and the 1998 lease expiration was dangling out there. Savelkoul became increasingly convinced that Pohlad had wandering eyes. Other regions—such as Charlotte, the suburbs of Washington, D.C., Las Vegas, and Port-land, Oregon—were making noise that they wanted baseball. Pohlad had been attracted to an idea of expanding baseball to Mexico City. Without a new stadium, the Twins could move.

Of course, it wasn't true. None of the potential recipient communities was prepared to accept a team. No stadiums existed elsewhere to house the Twins. But there was the implied threat, and so yet another task force was formed. Pohlad and Bell, in a glitzier presentation than their staid 1994 chat with the commission, had another chance to state their case.

This Minnesota Advisory Task Force on Professional Sports was urged by Metropolitan Sports Facilities Commission members, especially Thrane, who believed that the public, the business community, and legislators needed to be engaged with, and informed about the status of all pro sports in the state. She had a mantra: "If the public isn't there at the takeoff, they won't be there at the landing." Savelkoul, who had worked in the legislature in the 1970s when much of everything was decided behind closed doors, resisted the idea of a study group. Its existence was mandated by the Target Center legislation of 1994, but typically, neither Savelkoul nor the Carlson administration ever got around to organizing the panel. Independent as he was, Savelkoul didn't feel a need to consult with more people on the Twins stadium process. But Dee Long, the former Speaker of the Minnesota House and a Minneapolis patriot, was eager to create a policy governing the state's relationship to pro sports before people started pouring cement for a new ballpark. Long had clout; as the chair of the House Local Government and Metropolitan Affairs Committee, hers would be the first committee to hear any stadium bill during the 1996 session. In a strongly worded letter also signed by Senate Metropolitan and Local Government Committee chair Jim Vickerman, Savelkoul was urged—although it read more like he was ordered—to put together the new task force, to study the landscape of Minnesota pro sports, and, as an ulterior motive, to gain a cadre of political and civic leaders who would be knowledgeable advocates for a stadium plan.[10]

Savelkoul, at the urging of Thatcher, Thrane, and others, acceded to Long's demand, and in the end, the task force developed some worthwhile data for decision makers, many of whom came into the process thinking that no stadium was needed but left convinced that a new ballpark could be justified. Savelkoul learned how political the Twins ballpark process was going to be even before the task force convened. In previous interviews and open meetings, Savelkoul had casually mentioned that one thing he wanted the task force to examine was the possibility of renaming the Hubert H. Humphrey Metrodome. It would be a way for the public to raise money through private channels. Teams and communities were selling the advertising rights to arenas and stadiums as part of a growing trend. Target Center, named after the Twin Cities–based discount store, was among the first wave of facilities that sold its name to corporate sponsors, starting at about $750,000 a year and moving above $1 million in cash, promotions, and advertising for the arena and Timberwolves basketball team. Similarly, the new $214 million stadium in Denver had been named Coors Field, after the Colorado-based brewery. Coors Brewing paid a total of $15 million to have its name on the new ballpark for fifteen years, a very cheap price by year 2000 standards.

Privately, as I covered the ramp up to the task force hearings, I was told that tinkering with the Humphrey name on the Dome would be like putting the Nicollet Mall's naming rights up for bids. Sort of like, "the Diet Coke Mall." It was going to be gauche and, in the case of Humphrey, almost sinful to rename the Dome something like "Leinenkugel Stadium." But Savelkoul, as was his responsibility, was seeking as many avenues to raise money for the Dome—and the Twins and Vikings—without going to the taxpayers. Given the struggle of getting a mere $750,000 a year for Target Center eighteen months earlier, it was a noble effort on Savelkoul's part, if politically misguided. In the story that advanced the task force's first meeting on August 15, 1995, I reported the possibility that the Dome's name might be sold. And as they say in the news biz, the story turned into a real "talker," with the radio call-in shows jabbering back and forth.[11]

Humphrey zealots said they were outraged. The union leader who helped get Humphrey's name on the stadium in 1977 called the naming rights concept a "sacrilege." And Humphrey's son, Attorney General Skip Humphrey, who at that time was eyeing a variety of higher offices, suggested such a name sale should be left to the public to decide, not an ad hoc task force. (Indeed, by law the legislature would have to approve such an alteration of the Dome's name.) But the younger Humphrey asked a question that should guide the naming of any sports facility today or into the future: "Does the public think it should go to the highest commercial bidder or should it reflect our values and what our heroes are all about?"

Looking back, I felt sorry for Savelkoul that day. Here he was, about to chair a highly political task force that he didn't really want to have in existence in the first place. As always, he was rushing from Albert Lea to legal work in the Twin Cities to his Metrodome office. On this warm day, he had to find a parking space in downtown St. Paul, with the first meeting held in the auditorium of the St. Paul Companies. And there was a pack of television Minicams chasing after him wondering how it felt to be the Antichrist—that is, the anti-Hubert. From that first day, it was clear that any marginally controversial action surrounding even an existing stadium was going to be screaming headline and breathless TV news.

While Savelkoul digested that first naming rights episode with his characteristic sense of humor and resignation, all the excitement around that task force—and the difficult decisions about what to recommend to the legislature—served to push him even farther away from any consensus building. He became even more insulated and less sharing, and in the end, he disserved himself and his client Governor Carlson. "Henry was such a lone ranger," said Loanne Thrane. "There was an unwillingness to be collegial," said Paul Thatcher.

So it was that a month after the task force first gathered and after the naming rights brouhaha—which went absolutely nowhere—Pohlad made his anticipated appearance before the panel. He and Twins officials, especially Bell, came as close to saying for the first time that they needed and wanted a new stadium as human beings can come without shouting, "Gimme, gimme." With the TV cameras rolling, the Twins were allowed to put on a high-level dog and pony show. On the floor of the Dome, with the panel seated before them and a podium set up as if Billy Graham were to preach, Bell and Pohlad made their presentations.

Although Bell tried to stop just short of saying the Dome was no longer a viable facility—thirteen years after he had personally helped build it for the public—he failed. It was clear that the Twins wanted a new ballpark, and now. He said that the Dome was "economically obsolete for major-league baseball purposes" and that the Twins needed an immediate "one- to five-year quick fix" to help the team stay competitive. He pushed the idea that the Twins and Vikings should take over the management of the Dome—even though he knew it was inadequate for the Pohlads—and he said the team needed seven thousand more "quality seats" behind home plate and between first and third bases to sell higher-priced tickets.

"There was nothing explicit about a new stadium," Representative Dee Long said acerbically in reviewing Bell's comments. "But if you want to read between the lines, a logical person might have heard a hint of a new stadium."

It was a tap dance of a declaration, for Bell had already been taking the temperature of the legislature and had been told to wait until after the 1996 session, which hadn't yet begun. "I don't know of one legislator in Minnesota who would author a new stadium bill in 1996," is how Senate minority leader Dean Johnson assessed the situation then. And Johnson was a stadium *supporter.* After all, 1996 was an election year, and the capitol was still rocking in the wake of the Target Center deal and the attempts by Savelkoul to squeeze the Winnipeg Jets hockey team into the downtown Minneapolis arena via some state subsidies. But in 1997? "I think all options are open," Johnson said, predicting what would become truth. The battle would take place in 1997.

From the stage, Bell sensitively told the task force members: "We know there are many important competing needs for financial resources. We are not saying that baseball is our most compelling social need. We are saying that baseball in Minnesota creates jobs, taxes, and economic and social benefits equal to or greater than the required investment.... You need to answer two questions: Can you make an investment in the future of baseball? Should you make the investment?"

When he finished, hoping to let his message sink in, Bell was publicly confronted by the always outspoken Thatcher. "It seems to me all your solutions cost cash," Thatcher said, bringing the conversation down from the loftiness of "social benefits" to the dirtiness of money. "It seems to me that if we're going to find a solution, then we need to solve the ownership problem, too. Should we not come up with a solution that includes the transfer of ownership simultaneous with the stadium solution?"

Bell really had no answer. But Thatcher's point was an essential one, and it ran through the next two intense years of Twins ballpark debate and lingers today in any sports facilities struggle. If an owner asks for, and succeeds in getting, public money to build a stadium, then the value of his franchise instantly increases. New revenues come in, and the team flourishes. Then, if that owner sells to a new owner, that new owner has to pay a far higher price for the team than the old owner did. The public just gave all of its revenue streams to the old owner so that he could pocket the appreciated value of his franchise, quickly exit, and unload the stadium on the new owner.

As Thatcher left the Dome field that day, Pohlad, who was watching Bell's presentation from the field, buttonholed Thatcher. Pohlad got Thatcher's point, even if Bell didn't. "You're exactly right," Pohlad told Thatcher. "That's why we need a new owner." Pohlad denies the exchange; Thatcher is certain it happened. Assuming Pohlad's memory is hazy—which it seems to be in many areas—and assuming Thatcher doesn't fabricate, as early as 1995, Pohlad understood that new ownership should be simultaneous with a new ballpark. This concept finally reached fruition four years later when Pohlad, in desperation, struck a flawed deal with St. Paul's ambitious mayor Norm Coleman.

It is a concept that should guide any facilities construction in Minnesota, or elsewhere, for that matter. The transition to a new publicly funded stadium and new ownership should go hand in hand. Politically, it makes things cleaner. The current owner is often weighted down with baggage because of the demands he's made to get a stadium. Pohlad is the perfect example of that. In the case of Target Center, for instance, there was an assumption that the public's purchase of the arena would trigger the sale of the team by Wolfenson and Ratner. Financially, the sale transaction at the time of the stadium's construction means the old owner can't get all of the windfall from a public subsidy; the public can mediate the sale by negotiating a lease agreement with the new owner that has an impact on the team's sale price. Besides, perception-wise, new owners are always saviors. Old owners are always hated. Better yet, maybe, just maybe, at that magic moment when a stadium is built and ownership changes, the public could benefit from the increase in stadium revenues. Maybe, just maybe, the public could get a piece of the ownership action. And just as significantly, if the current owner moves into a new stadium that is subsidized when he sells his team, the price to the new owner will be significantly higher than the old owner's originial price. The debt burden on the new owner can be onerous. He must then seek lease adjustments—that is, further subsidies—from the public. If a new ownership configuration can be in place at the time a new lease for a new stadium is being negotiated, the public is best served.

Whatever the form of the transition from old stadium to new in 1995, this much was certain for Minnesota baseball: something had to be done to make sure the Twins could outdraw the Saints.

Denver

On a lovely Rocky Mountain evening three weeks later, a subgroup of the task force visited Coors Field. The goal was to inhale the beauty and fun of a modern, retro ballpark. And Coors is terrific. The Rockies were in their playoff season. The place was packed. Nine members of the task force— including Senate majority leader Roger Moe and Senate minority leader Dean Johnson—received a VIP tour with visits to the field dugouts and then enjoyed seats in the cushy club level, with an indoor buffet-style food area or waiter service at their seats.

Earlier in the day, they met with Rockies owner Jerry McMorris, who grew up in St. Paul, and leaders of Denver's public effort to build the stadium. McMorris, who had become a pal of Pohlad within baseball circles, told the task force members that Minnesota was going to have to build the Twins a new stadium. Soon.

His matter-of-fact assessment belied the different contexts in which Denver and the Twin Cities found themselves. The Denver situation was similar to Minnesota's in the 1950s, only longer overdue. Denver wanted, finally, to be on the major-league map. Long a pro football hotbed, and also home to an NBA team, Denver still felt that it hadn't arrived in the late 1980s. It had no big-league baseball. Denver was one of the Continental League cities that got screwed by baseball's owners in 1959. Denver thought it was going to get one of the major-league expansion teams in 1960; Minneapolis–St. Paul and Houston were the only emerging metropolises to benefit from that first expansion, with Los Angeles and New York getting second teams. Denver had been waiting for more than thirty years before the National League awarded the Mile High City a team in 1991 to begin play in 1993.

The franchise wasn't awarded until after a six-county summertime primary election referendum on August 14, 1990. That referendum was worded with the same sort of self-esteem–oriented sentiment that got Minnesotans to buy $500 Met Stadium bonds in 1955. "Shall, in support of efforts to gain a major-league baseball team for Colorado, the Denver Metropolitan Major League Baseball Stadium District be authorized to levy and collect a uniform sales tax . . . provided that the tax will be levied and collected only upon the granting of a major league baseball franchise?"[12]

Denver metropolitan area voters were asked: do you want to impose a 0.1 percent sales tax—that's one penny for every ten dollars spent—on yourselves to bring a baseball team to Denver? Every suburban county voted yes. Denver County, which includes the city, voted no. But the cumulative vote total was 187,710 to 158,283. A similar 0.1 percent sales tax was already in place to support arts and scientific research organizations in the Denver metro area. And the arts groups supported the baseball referendum. So there was a consensus in the region that limited sales taxes were appropriate to fund amenities. Furthermore, the baseball tax would sunset once the stadium was paid off, which would be as quick as eight years. Coors Field, with its cappuccino bars, kiddie play areas, restrooms for seniors, all-outdoors, all-real grass, one-dollar tickets, and Disney-like customer service, was essentially a "pay as you go" operation, meaning that the public would be carrying limited debt for a limited amount of time.

McMorris understood the Minnesota issues. "I think sooner or later you're going to have to do something," he said. "The only question is when. You're in the unfortunate situation that on paper, the Metrodome is too new. But where you are is where you are."

And there they were, these task force members, with no constituency other than their imaginations, leaving the frank pep talk from McMorris and walking through the empty concourse of the ballpark hours before the game. Savelkoul, Moe, and Johnson began discussing the Denver sales tax and the referendum notion. They were immediately wowed, as if dizzied by the mile-high air. Johnson, the Lutheran pastor from Willmar who is almost too nice of a man to be a politician, gazed out at the Denver skyline beyond the walls of the glistening baseball field.

"If we had this discussion yesterday I would have said there's little chance of an outdoor stadium in five to ten years," Johnson said. "But today, with all the emotion here, this is enough to wake up a Norwegian. This task force needs to bring back all this information to the people of Minnesota and begin a public debate in the Minnesota legislature."

Typically, Johnson's colleague Moe, the ultimate but wide-awake Norwegian, was more cautious, noting that discussing taxes for a stadium while the state was "cutting budgets on the poorest of the poor" amid national welfare reform would be a tough sell. Still, the key members of the task force came back from Denver the next morning with visions of a slam dunk in their eyes. They'd seen the future, and it was Coors. In fact, anyone who saw Coors Field that night, with the young crowd, the yuppie crowd, the busy pre- and post game in Lo-Do, (or Lower Downtown, similar to Minneapolis's Warehouse District), and the sheer fun of outdoor baseball would have agreed to such a measly tax. Denver had a tremendous community asset. Why couldn't Minnesota? One good reason was raised by a fellow who would, four years later, become a big shot in the Minnesota sports scene. His name is Jac Sperling, and he was the lawyer for Denver's Baseball Authority who helped navigate the referendum to victory. (He had also been Richard Burke's lawyer when he tried to squeeze Minneapolis city officials to bring the Winnipeg Jets to Target Center.) Sperling noted that there was a cause in Denver to build Coors Field. The cause was bringing a team to town. Any vote in Minnesota would be to pay for a new $200 to $300 million stadium to replace one that was only thirteen years old. For most people, thirteen year olds are moving into the most vibrant and indestructible years of their lives. Thirteen-year-old cars can still drive. Thirteen-year-old houses are just getting broken in. "To vote to keep a team there, that's harder," said Sperling.

As fate would have it, Sperling was also involved in getting another facility for another city in 1998. Recruited to St. Paul by the energetic Mayor Coleman, Sperling became president of the new National Hockey League team to be based in the capital city. With the backing of Governor Carlson, Sperling and Coleman were able to grab $130 million from state and city coffers to build a new arena. Unlike Denver, there was no referendum in St. Paul. Indeed, there was little opposition. The Twins could take the credit for that. The hysteria around their proposed stadium in 1997 kept the St. Paul hockey arena under the public's radar. One other thing: the new NHL team had no familiar owner breeding contempt.

Trapping Themselves

As the advisory task force worked hard to reach conclusions to put together a plan for the 1996 legislative session, Governor Carlson chose to make conclusions of his own, completely undercutting the independence of the task force. On October 20, 1995, making typically offhand comments, the governor proposed a metropolitan-area-wide public referendum to build a new baseball stadium and urged a public subsidy to aid in trying once more to bring the Winnipeg Jets to Target Center. Carlson also raised, for the first time, his preference for some form of "public ownership" of the local sports teams. "The public is going to have to sit down and listen to the debate and decide: 'Do we want this variety of professional sports in town or do we not?'" he stated.[13]

Exactly why Carlson felt he had to pop off at that moment was unclear. It served to militate against the impact the task force could have. As task forces go it did some decent work and came to a handful of significant conclusions. But it also shirked some major responsibilities. Basically, after five months of meetings, this blue-ribbon panel concluded that if Minnesota were to fall in line with the rest of the nation, then both the Twins and Vikings would need their own single-purpose facilities. The task force also concluded that the Dome, in the modern environment of teams needing as much cash as possible, could only accommodate one team. The group determined that the city of Minneapolis couldn't be expected to finance any future sports facilities, as it had most of the region's other stadiums and arenas beforehand. Finally, the group also stated, as did the 1992 national study group on baseball, "It is in the best interests of the citizens of Minnesota that the professional sports industry settles its league-wide outstanding issues." That is, baseball, in particular had to get its economic house in order.

As for its shortcomings, Savelkoul refused to challenge new Timberwolves owner Glen Taylor on the status of his new lease at Target Center, a lease, of course, that Savelkoul had helped negotiate. Some members of the task force were interested in finding ways to sneak a new or relocated NHL team into Target Center. But Taylor, under Savelkoul's cover, always seemed to be unavailable to appear before the task force. Long and Minneapolis City Council president Jackie Cherryhomes repeatedly asked Savelkoul to bring in Taylor. But it never happened. Also Long and Cherryhomes wanted a full, public discussion about whether and how a new NHL team could be accommodated in Target Center. As for the issue of the NHL, the task force meekly took no position.

The courageous position would have been "We don't need hockey now! We can barely afford baseball, football, and basketball." But after the failure to fit the Winnipeg Jets into Target Center showed the inherent problems in the new buyout deal, no one wanted to politically alienate the hockey buffs in Minnesota any more than they'd already been alienated.

Fact was, by January 1996, any thoughtful person analyzing the landscape of Minnesota pro sports would have concluded that this was a town that could only support three professional teams. And especially if a new baseball stadium was on the horizon. That's because as pro sports moved closer to being high-priced entertainment than to being an opiate to the masses, the economic engines of luxury suites and expensive club seating were at the center of any stadium plan and any franchise beef-up plan. And each team needed its own facility. A new Twins stadium would add 60 luxury suites to the Twin Cities' sporting inventory. An improved Metrodome or new Vikings stadium would add 35 suites to the Dome's 115. With Target Center's 68 suites, the suite supply rose to 278. That's a lot of corporate dollars needed to prop up teams. A fourth team at, say, Target Center could perhaps be tolerated; no new suites need be sold, no new naming rights, no new debt service on a new arena. The need to sell 12,000 to 15,000 more season tickets would stretch the local sports economy. But the thought of a new arena in St. Paul with 60 *more* suites wasn't even on the task force's mind.

The best Twin Cities attendance came in 1991 and 1992, when the Twins, Vikings, Timberwolves, and North Stars sold 4.2 million tickets, with strong average attendance figures: the Wolves attracted 18,757 fans per game; the North Stars, 13,447 fans per game; the Twins, 30,647 fans per game; and the Vikings, 56,652 fans per game. Those attendance figures reflect a time when ticket prices were significantly lower than what they would be in, say, 1999. For instance, when the Stars departed Minnesota after the 1992 to 1993 season, their highest ticket price was $31.50. Even accounting for inflation, that 1993 ticket price would only cost $35.55 in 1999. The average ticket price for the new Minnesota Wild will be about $50, with some "club-level" seats costing $78 per game. The real cost of going to a hockey game went up. The real cost of the Twin Cities being able to support four teams soared off the charts.

As the task force chickened out on setting sensible public policy on pro sports, and as the governor campaigned for a fourth major-league team, thoughtful analysis showed that the Twin Cities couldn't and shouldn't absorb more sports options. G. Scott Thomas, research coordinator for the nationwide chain of business weeklies, American City Business Journals, conducted a weighted study of the nation's fifty-five largest metropolitan areas. Through various unbiased calculations—population, total personal income, and number of teams—Thomas determined that the Twin Cities didn't have the "capacity, that is enough financial room," for a fourth major-league franchise.[14]

Ironically, it was St. Paul Companies chairman Doug Leatherdale, one of the region's sharpest executives, who was alone on the task force in asking—on the first meeting of the group—"Can we, in fact, afford three sports teams here, or four sports teams here? I don't know if it makes sense." It's ironic because three years later, Leatherdale was one of mayor Norm Coleman's biggest boosters in getting a new arena to St. Paul for an NHL expansion team, thereby adding more suites and more club seats to the marketplace cluttered with big-time college sports, a vibrant arts community, and flourishing Indian-owned casino gaming. Only time will tell how foolish it was for the state of Minnesota and the St. Paul City Council to allocate $130 million in direct public subsidies for that facility for a team in pro sports' least-stable league.

Leatherdale's tough question is the kind that the task force didn't answer. It didn't establish the beginnings of a firm statewide public policy on pro sports. It didn't talk about or decide appropriate forms of funding. It didn't decide any new form of governance—besides the Sports Facilities Commission—that could be in place to protect the public. It didn't set guidelines about the responsibilities of teams toward their communities. It didn't ask why. It assumed that the questions should be in the "how" mode. At the same time, for citizens who read the newspapers or attended any of the sessions, the panel did serve to raise the key issues that one needed to be equipped to make reasonable conclusions about the state of pro sports in Minnesota. And any intellectually curious citizen could only have concluded that as 1995 turned to 1996, the health of Minnesota pro sports was in decline.

CHAPTER 7

Falling in Love with the Deal

The Governor's Men Go to Bat for Carl

During the fall of 1995, while the task force met above ground in conference rooms all over the Twin Cities, a small working group of professional political consultants gathered regularly and quietly to devise strategies and tactics on how to get a stadium built. Their job was to figure out how to explain to the general public what the task force had learned. If all Minnesotans understood the value of the teams to the state—to our "quality of life"—and if most citizens realized the Twins or Vikings might feel a need to move without some financial improvements, then maybe public and legislative consensus could be built.

To do what? That was uncertain. But anyone with an open mind who sat through the sometimes tedious task force meetings could only conclude that the Twins needed a new ballpark to compete in baseball's careening economic system. Whether the public should pay for it, whether it was completely ridiculous to build just fourteen years after the Dome opened, whether Pohlad was rich enough to pay for it all on his own—these were all legitimate concerns. But a realization sunk in among the above-ground dignitaries and the sub-rosa worker bees: Pohlad wasn't just tired of the wallpaper in the Dome. The banker didn't only want to have a toy just like his pals in Baltimore and Cleveland. For the Twins to compete on the field, the exploding economics of the industry simply demanded a new ballpark. Sounds like a fairy-tale, but among these lobbyists and political analysts who were working on the problem was a hope that an acceptable plan could be hatched. But not right then.

The working group consisted of the state's best and brightest, most sophisticated and experienced. There was the Sports Facilities Commission's chief lobbyist Larry Redmond, who had been instrumental in getting the Target Center legislation passed. The commission's lawyers, Bill McGrann, a veteran of Dome battles, and Kathleen Lamb, a writer of technical legislation with few equals. Both were well connected to the DFL and city of Minneapolis officials. John Himle, a former Republican member of the House of Representatives from Bloomington, sat in, as did D. J. Leary, the old Dome advocate, and commission member Thrane, a wise political analyst. David Welle, a nationally known sports accountant based in the Twin Cities and on contract to the commission, advised the group on finance options.

With every meeting of the public task force, the private advising group became increasingly convinced that it was important that the state's political leaders not get out in front of the public. No matter what the insiders now knew—that a stadium could help the Twins survive—they also knew that there was absolutely no public appetite to fund any sports facilities. The North Stars' departure and the Target Center buyout were too fresh in the state's collective mind-set. Thrane repeatedly worried about forcing legislators to take a stand. "Legislators just aren't going to be ninety miles ahead of the public," she said. "And they shouldn't be." Thrane regularly argued that pro-stadium supporters shouldn't be thinking yet about how to get a stadium bill passed, but rather going among people in the countryside, listening, and then retreating to devise plans for another day—after the 1996 election. In the fall of 1995, the stadium issue was simply not politically "ripe." The stadium matter should not and could not be a part of the 1996 legislative session and, most certainly, not a part of the 1996 elections, Thrane believed. Every House member and every Senator would be up for reelection. No one would want to have to take a pro-stadium stance. The 1996 session would end in May, and almost immediately thereafter, door knocking would begin for the November campaign. The last thing a legislator wanted to be asked about—or decide about—was a new Twins stadium.

This impending stadium war was the first of the truly modern era.

Although there was great opposition to the Dome, the late seventies were still a time when elected officials weren't expected to do much listening. "I think the elected officials [in the seventies] believed they were elected to lead, and once they were convinced by the suits downtown which way to lead, away they went," said Thrane. "The dynamic of how things are done on tough issues has changed dramatically. There is more power to the people. We also have a different type of person in the legislature. They don't do much else. It's almost a full-time job. They used to be so much more willing to take a risk on a vote."

Understanding all that, Thrane, Redmond, McGrann, Lamb, Himle, and Leary, determined that—no matter what the task force recommended, no matter how conclusive the case for a stadium—the timing was all wrong. Redmond had the task of going to Savelkoul and advising him to slow down the wagon train. What was best for the state, what was best for the issue, was to say, "Whoa!"

On at least three occasions, Redmond met with Savelkoul and told him the underground crew's conclusions: don't do anything in 1996, and please don't let the Twins drive the project. Thrane felt strongly about all that, too. A public body such as the Sports Facilities Commission had to be in the political lead. Why would the public give money to the tenant of a public building? The public should only provide money for a facility that seems to belong to the public, not to a billionaire with a tin cup. Taxes build bridges. Taxes don't buy trucks for truck drivers. If this ballpark was to be "public infrastructure," a public agency had to advocate for it.

One late-fall day in 1995, as directly as possible, Redmond told Savelkoul: "If you go forward now and if the Twins drive this discussion, it is fated for disaster." Savelkoul, with Pohlad and Carlson figuratively breathing down his neck, looked at Redmond and replied cooly: "We're going to do it now, and the Twins are going to take the lead."

"I don't know if we made a conscious decision for the Twins to drive the whole thing," Savelkoul remembered months later. "It was just a fact. They felt it was their business. We weren't in a position to say they couldn't."

Of course, Savelkoul and Carlson were. They were the chairman of the state sports agency and the governor. But they had no interest in reaching out and listening to broad constituencies. Simply put, the Twins were looking at their potential 1998 escape and wanted to push the process. Carlson and Savelkoul thought they could somehow will a plan through the legislature. They blundered. The first idea was to attempt to place a referendum on the seven-county Twin Cities metropolitan area ballot in the fall of 1996.

This tactic created platforms for three central figures in the Twins stadium debate to emerge. One was for Tom Borman, the Twins' chief lobbyist. Hired because he was a friend of Jim Pohlad's, Borman had no lobbying skills, and admittedly so. He was well connected in DFL circles, and a former state commissioner of commerce. But as one other lobbyist said, "I kept saying to myself, 'He has such little clue he doesn't know he doesn't have a clue.' Frankly, I'm always impressed he could find his way into the [capitol] building." Yes, the man who was to orchestrate the political symphony for a Twins ballpark that needed to be practically perfect could barely find his baton. His respect among the key political consultants at the capitol was very low.

Another platform established was for a senator named John Marty to make his stand. Marty, in a loose coalition with other stadium opponents and antitax activists, shook the state. Humiliated in the 1994 gubernatorial election, when he was trounced by Arne Carlson, Marty had reasons to try to stick it to Carlson. On the other hand, Marty truly believed the people of Minnesota were being wronged.

The final personality to emerge—once more—in a critical Minnesota political and sports matter was Pat Forciea. The spinmeister from Coleraine, Minnesota, in the rugged Iron Range, was hired by Jerry Bell at the beginning of 1996, after the team and Savelkoul decided it must move forward at the capitol. The plan was to push an advisory referendum to take the collective temperature of the state, or at least the seven-county metropolitan area, on how to fund a stadium. Forciea had successfully developed a sort of Teflon personality because of his involvement in the 1990 Wellstone victory. He had also helped run Michael Dukakis's 1988 presidential campaign in Minnesota. Known as hardworking and a master of detail, he could tell any story—or sell any product—in support of any issue as long as he was being paid. Once an investment banker, since the Wellstone upset he'd cashed in with his own marketing firm and then moved into sports. He'd been in place when the North Stars moved and played both sides of the street, aiding his boss Norm Green as he pushed for assistance from the Sports Facilities Commission and others—but then privately badmouthing Green to reporters as the North Stars' situation deteriorated into certain relocation. Forciea was to add some pizzazz to the Twins' lethargic marketing effort and to build support for stadium sentiment. With his pal Bill Hillsman, who was also involved in the Wellstone campaign (and later in Governor Jesse Ventura's), Forciea was viewed as some sort of media and marketing miracle worker.

He and Hillsman mapped out a strategy designed to win approval for a new stadium in the 1997 legislative session. In a four-page pitch to Bell and the Pohlads, they suggested evoking two "emotional hot buttons." In so doing, they wanted to confront head-on the increasing public backlash against the Wolves and Vikings. Off-field antics by athletes and the Wolves' flirtation with New Orleans had poisoned the atmosphere. The Twins were relatively good citizens. Forciea and Hillsman urged the team to point out the good-guy image of Kirby Puckett and Paul Molitor, for instance, "in stark contrast to the conduct of our professional sports competition in the Twin Cities." The second hot button was to emphasize the localness of the Twins, with native Twin Citians Dave Winfield, Kent Hrbek, Jack Morris, and Molitor.

Wanting to bring fans closer to the team, they proposed preseason and in-season marketing that "will greatly enhance our prospects in the 1997 legislature." They suggested three marketing themes to heighten the likelihood that fans might want to support a new stadium: outdoor baseball, the new state-of-the-art ballparks going up around the country, and public ownership of the team.

Their idea was to film players such as Hrbek at Camden Yards or Jacobs Field and then incorporate his experiences at these new stadiums into advertising and public relations videos. In March 1996, when Forciea and Hillsman wrote the memo, there had been virtually no attempts by the team or the Sports Facilities Commission to engage the public in any stadium discussion at all. The ballpark effort was a one-way street, and the Twins were traveling down it about to ask for something. The marketers gazed into the future and assumed that showing Minnesotans glimpses of the new stadiums via television ads would work on "a variety of levels.... One is 'keeping up with the Joneses'—if small market towns like Cleveland and Baltimore have ballparks like these, we should, too," their memo read. The ads could also show how pleasant it is to watch a game in these new lavish ballparks. "And finally, it helps to position the ballpark as a community resource, much in the way of a state or city park or playground, rather than as a palace for rich fans and owners." In the end, the most powerful idea that Forciea and Hillsman suggested was public ownership. If Pohlad was willing to become a "partner" with the public, it could place the Pohlad family "at the forefront of a new breed of owners, and perhaps secure their place in the history of Minnesota and baseball."[1]

Borman, Marty, and Forciea would play roles of differing magnitude. But on one matter, they would find common ground: what they said or did—or didn't do—led to a series of political and public relations train wrecks. In Marty's case, the acts were intentional and could only be viewed as obstructionist. In Borman's case, the acts were attributable to a man who was in over his head. In Forciea's case, his one most glaring act— to come a year later—must be blamed on his belief that the public and media were even stupider than we looked.

Meanwhile, Savelkoul was at work. Before the calendar turned to 1996, he was exploring with investment bankers in town a new concept: selling stock in the Twins à la the Green Bay Packers. Investors wouldn't necessarily be guaranteed any rate of return on their investment. But perhaps they'd get premium seating, and maybe they'd get voting rights to halt any move of the team. Savelkoul had an expression, one that began during the Target Center battle and continued into early 1995 when Richard Burke was trying to move the Winnipeg Jets into the downtown Minneapolis arena. "We're trying to take the wheels off of the team," Savelkoul said. He was sincerely seeking mechanisms to ensure that teams couldn't continue to stick up the state. He'd learned that escape clauses meant big trouble. He'd included in the Target Center lease provisions that required Taylor to pay off the remaining bonds on the building if and when he tried to leave Minnesota. Savelkoul was always trying to protect the public. Sometimes he failed.

First Defeat

The best way to understand how the 1996 session went for the Twins is to simply note that the first and easiest bill the Twins ever sought to get passed was defeated when the team's lobbyists miscounted their votes and lost control of a committee. It was an ignominious example of where things were headed. It was also as if the consultants who watched the task force in 1995 had crystal balls.

After the Denver visit convinced Savelkoul and Carlson that a referendum on a primary election ballot could pass, and after the Twins determined that a referendum campaign could serve as an educational forum for their economic needs, they decided to go forward. It was also at this point that the Twins made their first major strategic mistake: they essentially ceded all political decisions to the Carlson administration. While Senate majority leader Roger Moe, the state's most powerful Democrat, was also on board on the referendum concept, it was Carlson who gave the go-ahead to take the referendum route. As teams in other cities had done, the Twins believed they should follow the lead of the governor. Chris Clouser, the influential vice president at Northwest Airlines, was a close friend of the Pohlad sons and a member of the Twins board of directors. Clouser told them about how Carlson had aided the airline in gaining its $270 million loan in 1991. "We just turned this over to the governor's office," Clouser told the Pohlads. "We let them run the deal."

The Twins figured they'd follow instructions. "When the governor and the most respected legislator in the state say, 'Do the referendum,' we didn't exactly say, 'Come on, you guys, you don't know what you're talking about,'" Borman remembered.

Even devoted baseball fans were skeptical of the whole idea. No one in the public was well informed. Julian Empson Loscalzo, the Save the Met organizer, conducted his annual Hot Stove League banquet that winter at the Prom Catering Hall in downtown St. Paul. With about 350 fanatical fans on hand, Empson decided to take an informal survey. His group, now called Ballpark Tours, which operated summertime bus trips to outdoor baseball stadiums, typed up a ten-item questionnaire. They sought the opinions of their constituents on the issue of whether and when a referendum should be held, whether there should be a roof on any new ballpark, and how much these baseball purists would be willing to pay for a new facility. These folks, many of them aging Save the Met patriots, had been asking for fourteen years that the clock be turned back and the Twins return to the great outdoors.

While 86 percent of the banquet's respondents supported the idea of a new stadium—significantly higher than the population as a whole—only 22 percent of them believed that the public should pay for 50 percent of the stadium or more. Forty-eight percent of them said the public should spend zero dollars on a ballpark. Soon after, Empson Loscalzo bumped into Jerry Bell at the capitol. "I said to him, 'You guys are in trouble.'"

Technically and legally, the outcome of a referendum would have been meaningless. The vote would have been advisory in nature. It would have been limited to the metro area. And if it won, it wouldn't have mandated any legislation. If it lost, it wouldn't necessarily have meant the end to the debate. Although the people may have spoken, there were numerous examples—most notably in Milwaukee and Seattle in 1995—where the voters said no to public funding but their legislatures and governors overrode the public's sentiment. Thus, this first referendum could have been viewed as a mere test drive through the corridors of the capitol.

Savelkoul saw the referendum as a defensive tactic. He figured that if the team and the governor didn't suggest a referendum as the first step toward a stadium, someone else would somewhere down the line. He figured stadium proponents should push for it, take it where it went, and know that once it was approved or rejected, at least it was over and wouldn't be reincarnated.

The question that was proposed by bill authors Representative

Ann Rest, a diehard Twins fan from suburban New Hope, and Senator Jerry Janezich, a bar owner and ambitious politician from the Iron Range's Chisholm, was direct. "Shall the legislature provide by law for the construction of an open air retractable roof stadium in the metropolitan area to be financed by: (a) contributions from the team using the stadium; (b) private sources; and (c) taxes imposed on those who use or benefit from the stadium, and limited to hotel and motel lodging, liquor, and a surcharge on admissions to the stadium?"[2]

Even that question met with opposition. There was legitimate concern that the issue was being taken out of the decision-making hands of the elected representatives. Minnesota has long fought off initiative-and-referendum as a way to make laws. The theory is that citizens elect their representatives to make the tough decisions, not to duck them. But on the stadium issue, so sure to be a hot one, Savelkoul thought it would be wise to go to the voters. It wouldn't be wise to seek voter approval during a general election when the turnout is high. Instead, a nice, low-key primary would allow stadium supporters to get out their handpicked voters and tilt the referendum.

Senator Marty, the outspoken ideologue from Roseville, weighed in for the first time. He argued that the referendum language was sculpted to ensure passage and to obfuscate. He felt the referendum language should be more explicit that taxes, and not the Twins or private money, would be building this thing.

"The governor and other public officials proclaim a desire to 'let the people decide,' then they slant the question to get the answer they want," Marty wrote in an Op-Ed piece in the *Star Tribune*, his first public salvo against stadium funding. He then went on to detail his analysis of Metrodome funding and about how "the public" footed the bill for the downtown Dome. Of course, he was incorrect in his understanding of how the Dome was paid for; users of the Dome and land deals by the Sports Facilities Commission paid off most of the facility's debt. He suggested an alternative question, which with some reworking could have been a good one to ask the folks, too. "Shall the legislature construct a new stadium to be financed, in large part, by taxes?"

Marty, seemingly a man of the people, criticized stadium boosters for taking the issue to the people. "We don't need a referendum on this issue. At a time when property owners face rising property taxes and governments are struggling to balance budgets, most working people object to having their tax dollars used to subsidize major-league sports with its multimillionaire owners and players," he wrote, digging up the class warfare rallying cry. With that, he became the antistadium senator. It was a dirty job, but somebody had to do it.

By the time the referendum idea reached the House committee on General Legislation, Veterans Affairs and Elections, on February 23, the devilish details got the best of the referendum idea. The notion of taxes for a stadium and a referendum for the voters was punched around like so many volleyballs. The culprit in stripping the bill was crusty Representative Tom Osthoff of St. Paul, who seemed to have gotten out of bed on the wrong side on that rainy February Friday. Osthoff lashed out at the idea of a referendum at all.

"This is advisory at best," he said, glaring at the eighteen other committee members. "Advisory referendums are meaningless. We as a legislature should decide on our own what's worthy of economic development." There were nods all around. But, Osthoff allowed, if people wanted a referendum, that was swell. Only the option of taxing for the stadium should be eliminated. "I haven't seen anywhere how much the team is going to commit," Osthoff said. With that, a vote of ten to six, with three members not voting, amended the referendum bill and put all the funding on private and team sources, eliminating any public funding piece. The public was welcome to vote, Osthoff declared, but it wouldn't vote to tax itself. Soon afterward, an overwhelming voice vote yelled a loud "Nay!" to the referendum idea.

Worse than the defeat were the mathematics of Borman and his top professional lobbyist at the time, Maureen Shaver, a pro's pro at head counting. Going into the hearing, Borman believed he had the votes to get the referendum out of committee. So did Shaver. But as Osthoff kept talking and as others started making noises about extending the referendum statewide, the votes spun out of control. A simple little committee vote got slam-dunked.

It was Borman's first misstep. Among the professional lobbyists, as the stadium effort wore on, he was viewed as a blockhead, as someone who didn't understand the ins-and-outs of the snakepit that is the capitol and as someone who used poor judgment. To be fair, Borman was often left out of the loop by the Pohlads on the details of things. In spite of that, he was the liaison between the Pohlads and the hired lobbyists. So none of the lobbyists knew what was getting through Borman to Pohlad, and God only knew what was getting filtered from Pohlad to the lobbyists. By February 1996, the Twins had ten lobbyists registered to aid them. That number would remain the same throughout their campaign, but the names would change. Coordinating the effort should have been an exercise in full two-way communications. But the way it seemed to the political consultants was that Borman believed that lobbyists should just be parrots for Pohlad, simple influence peddlers. "Tom thought we should just go out and tell [legislators] this or that," said one. "But if he understood anything, he'd know that 80 percent of the time I spend lobbying, I'm lobbying my client, not the legislators. Tom isolated the Pohlads from us, he didn't bring us together." Because of that, Pohlad was isolated from the political realities.

Jim Pohlad had actually tried to hire Borman to be the Twins president in 1987. Jerry Bell got the job instead. The way that Borman remembers it, Carl Pohlad felt sorry for him, so after telling Borman that he didn't get the top job, he offered Borman a position as the team's lawyer. He was so unimpressive and unskilled in negotiating a spring training lease for the Twins in Fort Myers, Florida, that Bell had to replace him. Still, Governor Rudy Perpich appointed Borman to be state commerce commissioner in 1990, where he stayed for a year before returning to his father's law firm, Maslon, Edelman, Borman and Brand.

Borman is heir to one of the finest legal legacies in the Twin Cities, son to Marvin Borman, a powerful Democrat. The younger Borman, who is a noted Democratic fund-raiser in his own right, works in a thirty-third floor office in the Norwest Center that is a virtual museum to what and to whom he's rubbed up against. There is a miniature Twins World Series trophy. There are photos of Ted Kennedy and Walter Mondale. There's a photo of Borman testifying before a U.S. Senate committee.

Once seemingly a rising political star, he'd had his fits and starts with elected office exploratory efforts. But to the Pohlads, the ultimate outsiders, Borman was the insider they felt they needed.

The Pohlads were not a family that sought much outside counsel; when you're worth a couple billion, who needs advice? They were loyal to a small stable of local lawyers and accountants. They preferred to hire friends like Borman. In this case, he was to navigate them through the land mines of state politics with the aid of a stable of hired hands. Carl Pohlad, the banker, wasn't used to reaching out for help. He was used to others coming to him for help. He was used to being in charge. Now he was the one who needed help. He didn't know how to ask.

A handsome man of forty-seven, with jet black hair, Borman is best remembered by the lobbyists he tried to direct as an inveterate note taker. He took so many notes that the other lobbyists, most of them lawyers, grew worried of just what might happen to all those handwritten documents. "Tom, you know, one day we're all going to get sued over this stadium," one veteran lobbyist told Borman. "And the first thing they'll do is subpoena your notes." Borman blushed and afterwards limited his note taking somewhat. But once when Senator Steve Novak, an unabashed stadium advocate, walked into a large lobbyists' meeting and shouted in frustration, "Roger Moe is an asshole!" Borman dutifully wrote down the quote about the powerful Senate leader on his yellow legal pad. The lobbyist sitting next to Borman could hardly believe it.

One of his other massive blunders during the course of the Twins ballpark push was recommending that Jim and Bob Pohlad personally visit the capitol and personally meet legislators. Bringing "the boys" to the beautiful domed government temple was discouraged by the professional lobbyists. They understood the imagery: the sons of a billionaire coming to the state's headquarters for democracy with a platinum-plated tin cup in their hands seeking change for their daddy's stadium. But Borman told the Pohlad boys to go. As Bob Pohlad remembers, he was told that during the Target Center campaign, Wolfenson and Ratner were criticized for being absent.

"They outsourced it," Bob Pohlad said of the Timberwolves

approach. "We were told to go over there. 'You should be talking for you.' There was going to be great benefits to all of this. It was the right way to do it. That's what we were told. But it wasn't."

"I wanted [the Pohlads] to know firsthand what it was like dealing with those people over there," Borman said, with a certain disdain in his voice. "And I wanted the legislators to know that [the Pohlads] weren't above going over there and talking with them."

The effect was the complete opposite of what was intended. Many legislators were offended by the presence of the sons. This is why Redmond and others had recommended that the Pohlads be placed squarely in the backseat of the stadium car with a public entity, such as the Sports Facilities Commission or the city of Minneapolis or someone, anyone, behind the steering wheel. After the Target Center buyout, anything that looked like another pro sports handout was doomed.

If only everyone had simply looked eastward. If only Governor Carlson had just telephoned his pal in Wisconsin, Governor Tommy Thompson, he might have handled the situation differently. Thompson, in pushing for a new baseball stadium for the Milwaukee Brewers just months earlier, caused the entire political balance of power in the state to tilt away from him because of a giant miscalculation on how much he could control his state's legislature.

Looking to the East

Milwaukee's drive for a new stadium for the Brewers had it all. A referendum was defeated by Milwaukee-area voters. There were threats the team would move to North Carolina, which, of course, would eventually become the Twins' option of choice. There was persistence on the part of an owner and governor. After the voters said no, Thompson brought a regional sales tax proposal to the Wisconsin legislature in a special fall 1995 session—just as the Advisory Task Force on Professional Sports was considering a referendum to build a new Twins stadium. The idea was to build a 42,000-seat retractable-roof stadium with a total cost of $322 million, with—theoretically—$90 million being raised by owner Bud Selig and the Brewers. The stadium bill passed in Madison, but not without its costs, especially to George Petak. He became a sacrificial lamb whose ghost hovered over the shoulder of every Minnesota politician who might vote for a Twins ballpark. A youthful forty-seven years old, Petak was an up-and-coming Wisconsin state senator. Until he voted for the Brewers' stadium, that is. In June 1996, eight months after his decisive vote, he became the first legislator in Wisconsin history to be successfully recalled.

His sin? In the early morning hours of October 6, 1995, on the final day of the Brewers' stadium debate, Petak voted yes and gave Selig a ballpark. His vote passed a $160 million five-county 0.1 percent sales tax; that's was a mere one penny on every ten dollars spent. Petak had long been a stadium supporter and stuck with it even after citizens defeated the referendum calling for a sports lottery to fund the stadium. But throughout the stadium debate, he made himself clear: the citizens of his Racine County, south of Milwaukee, would never be included in any baseball taxing district. "Frankly, I supported a one-county tax," Petak said. "I thought Milwaukee County should bear the brunt of it." When the stadium bill was first introduced in the summer of 1995, only two counties were part of the district, Milwaukee and Waukesha, to the west. In September, however, some of Petak's Republican colleagues proposed enlarging the district to include all counties adjacent to Milwaukee. That occurred, much to Petak's chagrin.

He, though, was just one little cog in a bigger political game-within-the-game when the October 5, 1995, voting day arrived. It was Governor Thompson and his control of Wisconsin government that had become the overarching issue. Wisconsin's Senate was controlled by Republicans, by a one-vote majority. The Brewers issue, backed vociferously by Thompson, had turned violently partisan.

Twice, on the evening of October 5, the stadium bill was defeated; only three Democrats voted yes. Petak, sticking with his promise to the voters of Racine, voted no two times. Twice, the issue was brought back for reconsideration. It was approaching 5 A.M., October 6. "I was totally convinced that without a new stadium, the Brewers were going to move,"

Petak said. "I couldn't win the battle to remove Racine County. Because I couldn't, should I bring the whole Brewers' package down?"

Petak, unfortunately, hadn't done his homework. The Brewers were going nowhere. There was nowhere for them to play in North Carolina, as Pohlad would bluff and learn two years later. There had been no formal thresholds crossed within Major League Baseball circles. Any Brewers threat to move would have had months, even years, of legal maneuvering. Still, Petak changed his mind and voted yes. The bill and stadium plan passed sixteen to fifteen. The vote turned into more than a ballpark thing. It was a "who's going to run the state of Wisconsin?" thing.

Within days, Democrats in Racine organized a drive to recall Petak. Wisconsin's recall law is broad, a sort of "throw the bum out" provision. Petitions were signed to recall Petak for "violating the public trust." In June 1996, after a brutal campaign, Petak was defeated 51 to 47 percent in his home district. Because of his defeat, the Democrats went on to control the Senate. He became a symbol of what can happen to an elected official when he takes a stand for a stadium, when he flip-flops and says, "I won't do it," and then does.

Now, it should be noted that in the November 1996 election, the first full-blown election after the Brewers stadium vote, not one Wisconsin legislator lost his or her seat because of the way he or she voted on the stadium. All things do fade away. As the Twins drive developed, Governor Carlson and Twins backers repeated their view that if legislators took "the tough vote" and sided with a publicly funded ballpark, they wouldn't regret it. Indeed, on the flip side, if they voted against a stadium and the Twins moved, the public would take it out on them. That was the message that Carlson wanted to impress upon legislators.

Still, Carlson, Anderson, Savelkoul, and others ignored another lesson from the Wisconsin experience. When a team goes to the state for a subsidy, it should develop a relationship with the legislature, not with the governor. He can always be a target. Second, Carlson should have made sure that any stadium deal he announced wasn't a house of cards. That's what happened with Thompson and Selig. In the Wisconsin legislation, the Brewers were supposed to kick in $90 million for the ballpark. Selig didn't put in a dime. Miller Brewing Company bought the stadium's naming rights for $40 million. The other $50 million wound up coming via loans from the city of Milwaukee, the local chamber of commerce, and three foundations.

Unfortunately, the only ones carefully studying the Brewers case were Jerry Bell, Bob Starkey, and Carl Pohlad. Starkey even worked on some of the ballpark financing plan. He knew how little Selig contributed. Starkey knew Pohlad would have to come to the table with more, given his wealth. But politically, the Twins looked at the Milwaukee scenario and figured, in the end, it had worked. They figured casting their lot with the governor was the way to go.

Back in Minnesota

Carlson had a far worse working relationship with the Minnesota Legislature and even his own Republican colleagues in the House and Senate than Thompson did with his. Carlson was erratic and politically distant from the lawmakers. His major act in relation to the legislature was vetoing bills. "In the Carlson administration, the legislature was an entity to be tolerated, and not much more," said Senate majority leader Roger Moe. "Meeting with us was not his favorite thing. He tolerated us, that was the extent of it." The point is this: poor Mr. Pohlad relied on Carlson to get a ballpark through the legislature, and the governor didn't have that much clout. As Thrane put it, "When Arne led, no one followed. Except Henry."

After the death of the referendum, Savelkoul and Carlson turned to Plan B, which is what they had wanted to do all along: strike a deal to build a stadium, even if the public wasn't ready for it. As early as April 1996, Savelkoul and Welle presented to Bell a preliminary plan to gingerly force the Pohlads to sell the Twins to some sort of group—or public agency—that would seek a limited return on its investment.[3]

In mid-April, just weeks after the legislature shot down the 1996 version of a stadium package, Carlson's forces started working on the 1997 rendition. The stadium effort was like a Timex watch; it just kept on ticking. It was the deal that would never die. Virtually days after Osthoff's committee said "forget about it," Anderson announced that he wanted to have a Twins ballpark finance package negotiatated by him and Savelkoul with Bell by July 1996. This would place the debate smack-dab in the middle of the 1996 election campaign, a concept that was strongly objected to by the state's top political strategists just six months earlier. Anderson's goal was absurd and one that Thrane, a fellow Republican, had standing to lash out at.[4] She thought the timing was awful and that the selection of Savelkoul and Anderson as chief negotiators was a bad choice.

"I think we're going to have to have people from both parties if we want to give it the best chance of passage," said Thrane. "If, say, the Democrats were going to have the two positions, I, as a Republican, wouldn't quite trust it."

Thatcher wondered then—and forever thus—whether Savelkoul was "the right person with the right skills." Thatcher said the state should hire an outside investment banker "with no history and no barnacles, who is enormously experienced in these professional sports negotiating matters . . . who does this all day, every day."

At this point, too, Savelkoul was thinking very globally. In the early spring of 1996, Savelkoul believed he could resolve the Twins stadium issue and the Vikings lease situation at a renovated Metrodome in one gigantic package. Throw in a new hockey arena in St. Paul, and he'd have a sports facilities hat trick. Of course, he'd also be searching for at least $500 million in public money.

Whatever Governor Carlson's wishes, whatever Carl Pohlad's desires, and whatever Savelkoul's visions, the political reality was that striking a deal in the summer of 1996 was "a time bomb," said Thrane. "There could be a real problem that [the stadium] becomes the issue at every candidates' forum. People will say, 'If you vote for it, I won't vote for you.'"

Soon afterward Anderson backed off. He said he didn't expect any deal until after the elections. Thrane's thoughtful point of view sank in. But it was too late. John Marty saw the story in the *Star Tribune* of Anderson's retreat. He saw Thrane's comments. He agreed with her. The stadium issue could become the issue at every candidates' forum. Marty would make certain of that.

Even as they wavered about when to complete this "deal," the Carlson gang began to rally its forces. In late April, Carlson, the Twins, and Carlson's former campaign manager and gubernatorial aide Joe Weber decided that it was time to form a corporate-backed public relations and lobbying organization. They named it "Minnesota Wins." To head the effort, Carlson selected Robert Dayton, who had participated in the final fund-raising for the Target Center buyout and who, by his own admission, had time on his hands. Dayton, a charming patrician of a guy with always-shined and tassled loafers, may have an identifiable name, but he possessed very little real clout in the business community. Besides, that business community was totally defused and, as surveys showed, mostly opposed to the notion of public funding for a ballpark. Dayton had overseen a failed development in downtown Minneapolis called the Conservatory and spent most of his time working with charitable causes and helping to oversee his family's investments. He was not on the level of John Cowles Sr. or his father, Donald Dayton, back in the fifties when the Twin Cities sought teams, nor did he have the clout of John Cowles Jr. and his uncle, Kenneth Dayton, of the seventies. For sure, Robert Dayton didn't have the energy of Harvey Mackay, who almost single-handedly sold the idea of a downtown Dome to Minnesotans far and wide. Dayton was Carlson's second choice. Real estate magnate Ralph Burnet was asked first, but he'd had a bad business experience with Pohlad and declined.

No, Dayton was a sort of figurehead for Minnesota Wins that would go on to raise nearly $2 million and garner virtually no public support or any legislative votes. Exactly what Minnesota Wins did in the end remains one of the mysteries of the Twins stadium campaign of 1996 and 1997 and one of the clearest signs that the Twin Cities business community must coagulate into a new formation if it is to take on the major issues of the coming decades. Weber, who led the telephoning and networking effort, was paid $60,000 in 1996 and $75,000 in 1997. But he never really got out into the field, and much of Minnesota Wins's work was conducted via focus groups and surveys overseen by John Himle. Whatever happened to the nearly $2 million they raised, there was a decision made early on about who was to be influenced. And it wasn't going to be the general public, said Himle, because the general public's view was hard, then harder, then as hard as Stearns County stone. Minnesota Wins, for all the names and all the phone trees and all the databases that Weber developed from his tiny office on University Avenue in St. Paul's Midway District, was in business to influence and threaten legislators.

"We were not out trying to change public opinion," Himle said. "To go out and change public opinion assumes you can change it. I've got to tell you, I sat through all those focus groups, and I came to the conclusion that we did not have the opportunity to change public opinion sufficiently to somehow translate into votes in the legislature. Our goal, as it related to the public, was at least to take off the sharp edge of the opposition. A legislator could say, 'OK, the majority of the people in my district don't like it, don't support the stadium proposal, but am I going suffer political consequences in the next election?'"

That's what Minnesota Wins was trying to do through its surveys and polling: to get those 201 legislators to ask themselves if an anti-stadium vote could hurt them in the next election. "You got to play with the hand you're dealt," said Himle, who was dealt a very bad hand and wound up getting trumped by democracy.

Mel Duncan, the passionate leader of the Minnesota Alliance for Progressive Action, a coalition of progressive citizens' groups, said Minnesota Wins was "trying to manufacture consent." They couldn't do it. Not among the average folks, and not among the big hitters either, whoever they are in this day and age. With players making more money than most CEOs, why go to bat for the state's second richest man?

Dayton had his work cut out for him. As he did and as he began to speak to Rotary Clubs and chambers of commerce from hither and yon to boost the stadium idea, he had a strange goal. He wanted to keep the stadium stuff quiet. He would actually instruct audiences to keep the stadium effort to themselves so as not to arouse any opposition to any plan. He'd place his index finger to his lips as if he were initiating his listeners into the stadium underground. Sh-h-h-h. He knew that Savelkoul,

Anderson, and the Pohlads were negotiating, but Dayton wanted it top secret. It would be better that way, he figured. So did the Twins. So did Savelkoul and Anderson. So did the governor. It was a silly idea, and it backfired miserably. Because in a secret environment, every little leak turns into a gusher.

Falling in Love with the Deal

Quietly, secretly, with no public or legislative input to the direction that Savelkoul or Anderson should take, a cell of men began to meet regularly to discuss how to get a stadium built. Generally at Starkey's conference room no. 2861 at the Plaza VII office tower attached to the downtown Minneapolis Radisson Plaza hotel, they met beginning in May. Once, after a round of golf at a tournament sponsored by Senator Dean Johnson of Willmar, the group met at the Eagle Creek Golf Club. Aggressively, they set up a meeting every two weeks through June, July, and August. There was never any dispute that a stadium was needed, not with the way the Pohlads felt and the way Savelkoul had been convinced that the Dome was inadequate. On his flank, of course, were the Vikings, who also wanted at the very least significant changes in what was arguably the worst lease agreement in the NFL. But Savelkoul had developed a fondness for Pohlad and sympathy for the problems he faced. On the other hand, Savelkoul—guided by Carlson—had a deep and abiding dislike for Roger Headrick, the CEO of the Vikings ten-headed ownership monster, a structure that was hard to get one's arms around. One other big thing: the Vikings' rotten lease was, as Savelkoul and the Sports Facilities Commission's lawyers saw it, as ironclad and airtight as they were going to get. Unlike the Twins and their escape clause, the Vikings were chained to the Dome unless they wanted a nasty legal fight on their hands. Savelkoul knew this and repeatedly muttered, "A deal's a deal," to anyone who would listen. In relation to the Vikings, Savelkoul seemed to be truer to his job description than with the Twins. That is, his relationship with the Vikings was contentious and totally in line with protecting the public interest. Headrick's natural tendency was to come off as an arrogant elitist. Savelkoul fashioned himself as a folksy small-town lawyer, which, in reality, he was. His relationship with the Pohlads, especially Carl, seemed to be one of obsequiousness and even reverence. Carl was somewhat of an idol to Savelkoul. As for Headrick, he'd have to wait his turn.

Whatever his personal motivations or feelings, Savelkoul was working on a special and thoughtful concept: getting a piece of the team in exchange for public funding for a stadium. It had the possibility to be truly revolutionary. He sincerely believed in it. It was his major contribution to the stadium debate in Minnesota. It's an idea that shouldn't be allowed to die as Minnesota's stadium debate continues.

"I always believed if the public was going to build the stadium there had to be a vehicle for the public to get the benefit of it," Savelkoul said one night in a tiny downtown Albert Lea café. "I'd studied other deals. Every one of them had the public make huge investments. And the appraised values of the teams just went up and up. We had to figure out a way to stop the owner from getting a windfall." What a great idea. But it was a tough one to sell to the Pohlads. As the secret talks commenced, the Pohlads' major interest wasn't civic-mindedness. It was recouping the millions of dollars Carl Pohlad had invested in the Twins. The term of art was "made whole." Pohlad wanted back what he had paid for the team, what he'd lost on operations, and what he'd paid in interest expense since 1984. He didn't want to lose a dime on this deal. There weren't any outspoken threats to move the team, as other owners had made. These talks were still between this small group of men. Threats weren't necessary. But code words were used, words like "options." The Pohlads, as they told Savelkoul and Anderson, always had their options.

Despite disagreements and some breakdowns, the cell of men fell in love with the process. Like lovers do on a blanket in a park on a nice spring day, these men kept gazing into each others' eyes and virtually insulated themselves from all things around them. They were doing a deal, and by God, they would do it, no matter how complicated, how hard to explain, and how politically unacceptable it was going to be. For sure, Savelkoul was enamored with Pohlad and with the possibility of "doing a deal" with the billionaire. Savelkoul became subsumed with strengthening that relationship and with succeeding for Carlson. These turned out to be more problem-solving sessions than negotiations. They weren't at odds. They were partners. It was a configuration that wasn't good for the public, whom Savelkoul and Anderson were there to protect. It meant that when push came to shove, all of the participants could use obfuscation as a tool. There was no one in the room with them forcing them to clarify and to come to their senses. They didn't let anyone in.

Removing the Wheels

There were some key concepts that each side presented early on in the discussions. Savelkoul and Anderson wanted the Pohlad family to put in serious, big-time cash. This is what all of the political consultants to the team were urging, too. And Savelkoul and Anderson wanted "a partnership" that could mean some form of public ownership in the team. Savelkoul was adamant about his other point: he wanted to win for the state the appreciated value of the team if and when it was sold. "The public builds it, and then they just give it to the owner?" he asked rhetorically. "That's just not right."

Sport Economics 101 teaches us that pro sports team owners buy teams so that they can sell them at a profit years later. For all their whining about high salaries and bad leases, team owners have consistently cashed out of their sports investments with rates of return that mirror or exceed the stock market. And they get a lot more publicity and status owning a team than owning 100,000 shares of AT&T.

But Pohlad had a major goal. All the money he had invested in the team and all the money he would give to the stadium, he wanted it back. Guaranteed. With interest. The word from the Twins camp was that Pohlad had no desire to be "enriched" by any stadium financing scheme. But neither did he want to be, to coin a new phrase, de-riched. He was a banker who expected to get a set return on his dough. Just the thought of foregoing a significant profit on the potential sale of the team was enough to throw Carl and others around him into a paroxysm. After all, selling the team to an out-of-town interest could generate $150 to $175 million in sales proceeds, nicely wiping out Pohlad's $85 million after-tax investment in the team and delivering to him a pretax profit of at least $65 million on the Twins ... as if he needed it. His other goal was to get a publicly funded stadium built for him just like his pals in Cleveland, Dallas–Fort Worth, and Baltimore had gotten.

By July, the negotiators had a printout from the Minnesota Department of Revenue that showed all the options. The basis was a seven-county metropolitan area tax. Take your pick: hotel/motel, liquor in bars, liquor at stores, restaurant food, or a good, old-fashioned across-the-board sales tax. They could add up to real money real fast. A 1 percent metro-area sales tax would raise $257 million in one year, enough to pay for the stadium with one seemingly painless downstroke.

Curiously, hand printed at the bottom of one internal document was the word "CASINO" and next to it "$50M," as in 50 million. The gambling card was being considered, and it, too, would have been more than enough to quickly pay off a new, state-of-the-art facility. After all, $200 million of debt at 7 percent interest needed just $18.9 million a year to be paid off in twenty years. The possibilities seemed endless. That's what Twins officials thought. They were being told that the public funding piece would be handled adeptly by the Carlson administration. No problem. So Bell, Starkey, and the Pohlad sons let the public's means of paying be the worries of the guys on the other side of the table.

In July and August, both sides rolled up their sleeves to figure out how to satisfy the desires of the other. Their discussions were rudely and sadly interrupted when the Twins superstar Kirby Puckett, the most natural ambassador of goodwill for the team, abruptly ended his career because of the onset of glaucoma; it was an omen that the entire process was going to be blinded by a desire to get back Pohlad's cash. Broad issues such as the future of the baseball industry, the lack of revenue sharing in the game, and the principle of public funding for a sports venue were whisked under the table. Those were just givens. There was never talk of challenging the system by Savelkoul or Carlson, only of figuring out a way to navigate Minnesota through it. They didn't study the history of the Twins arrival, when Wheelock Whitney and Branch Rickey confronted the powers that be rather than kowtow to them. Savelkoul didn't reach back to his experiences with NBA Commissioner David Stern and try to isolate the team owners, as Stern did with Wolfenson and Ratner. The Carlson administration joined itself to Pohlad's surgically repaired hip.

Savelkoul, whose political sensibilities were out of shape, believed that a quid pro quo—a stake in the team via a real partnership in exchange for "making Pohlad whole"—was reasonable if the team could be guaranteed to stay in Minnesota for the next thirty years and a stadium could be built, to boot. There was always the unanswered question of how much money the public was going to have to throw into the pot and where the money was going to come from. That question was never answered and hasn't been to this day. But according to Twins officials, Savekoul and Anderson repeatedly told the Twins folks and Pohlad family to stay cool on the political actions. "They said they'd take care of it," is how one person intimately involved in the talks from the Twins side remembers the assurances from Savelkoul and Anderson. The Twins officials thought they could rely on Carlson the way the Brewers and Selig had relied on Governor Tommy Thompson.

With secrecy important to them, the negotiators tried to stay below the radar as the 1996 elections approached. They carried with them the knowledge of confidential Minnesota Wins surveys that showed that despite the players strike, despite the decline of the Twins on the field, and despite the Twins' increasing talk of needing a new stadium, Carl Pohlad was still a popular man. Fifty-six percent of Minnesotans surveyed said they "trusted" Pohlad.[5] "Any politician would have seen those numbers and said, 'Hey, those are fine with me,'" said John Himle, who oversaw the polling and focus groups.

As the summer wore on, the pace intensified. Meetings were set for every Monday at 2 P.M. at Starkey's conference room. They were still secret. There were no public revelations. Just like with the task force, a small group of lobbyists was meeting on a parallel track to the ballpark finance talks. Among the Twins lobbyists and crisis management experts along the way were such pros as Maureen Shaver; her partner, Andy Kozak, who helped lead the Target Center buyout; Ross Kramer, a

Northwest Airlines pilot and perhaps the state's most influential lobbyist; and Himle, considered among the state's top public pulse takers. Among this consulting group there was a growing concern that Minnesotans' opposition to stadium funding went deeper than politics. Himle, who had grown up in tiny Hayfield, Minnesota, was especially concerned that there might be an inherent, almost genetic opposition to a stadium effort in the fall of 1996. "Minnesotans, by and large, like consensus," Himle told his colleagues. "Where it doesn't exist, we become the 'Land of Ten Thousand Studies.' We don't like conflict. And this had conflict written all over it."

Besides, as Himle and others had warned a year earlier in the fall of 1995, there was no compelling case that could be made to the people of Minnesota for the need for a new stadium. If you wanted to study the ridiculous idiosyncrasies of baseball economics, you might come to the conclusion that the Twins "needed" a stadium to stay in sync with the changing paradigm of publicly subsidized stadiums from Atlanta to Seattle. But if you were just a good ol' boy or girl from, say, Hayfield, your basic point of view was the following: "What's wrong with the Dome? Didn't we just build it ten years ago? [It was fourteen years by then.] I come here once or twice a year and look at that sea of blue seats and green carpet and that massive roof, and it kind of takes my breath away. And now you're telling me we need a new one of these?" The notion of obsolescence doesn't play well in Minnesota. Structures are expected to endure.

Besides, this wasn't schools. This wasn't roads. This was frills. The supporters gave it the highfalutin term "amenities." But baseball had lost its luster just two years earlier with the strike, and the summer of 1994 had passed just fine. As Himle was telling his other lobbying friends his thoughts, they reached a frightening conclusion: Minnesotans had once felt it was worth it to find ways to fund the frills, to make life on the frozen tundra bearable. Mostly, it was with private money or user-type fees. Now the dollar amounts for a Twins ballpark—and maybe improvements for the Dome for the Vikings—were going to run into the $400 to $500 million range. There was no way user fees were going to cover all those costs. Besides, we didn't need all those frills anymore. We had arrived. Our lives were just fine with or without a new ballpark.

"It could be an element of our Scandinavian and German conservative roots," Himle said. "Frills have less appeal when we're all being asked to pay for them. When others step up and get it done, then we can support those frills."

With Met Stadium, with the Metrodome, people had stepped up. By the fall of 1996, no one had done what Charlie Johnson or Gunnar Rovick or John Cowles Jr. or Ken Dayton or Harvey Mackay had done. There wasn't the same kind of energy and spirit. There wasn't the same kind of corporate base that pushed the Dome down some throats and downtown. With this aversion to the stadium idea, and with this vacuum of leadership and financial commitment, the lobbyists decided that Pohlad was the one who had to pull this process out of the hat.

"Number one, you got to put in substantial money in this deal," one Twins lobbyist told Borman during a heated meeting in the fall of 1996. "Secondly, whatever the money is, it has to be the real deal. I'd rather go over there to defend Pohlad for being stingy than to try and pull a fast one." The message: no cash shell games could be sold.

But Borman's talk was sending signals that seemed incredible. Borman told his team of lobbyists that Pohlad didn't just want a stadium. He wanted to erase his financial losses, too. What Savelkoul and Anderson knew for a few months was now known to the frontline lobbyists. Pohlad wanted to be "made whole" for all of his investment and time in the Twins. After all, if he didn't get his cash back in Minnesota, he could sell the team to some other city and get back his investment, and then some. "Made whole" isn't a dollar-for-dollar exercise. "I want to get my principal back, and I want to get my interest back, yes, that's what I mean," Pohlad told me months later when I asked him to define "made whole."

The lobbyists were stunned. "We told Borman legislators weren't sent to St. Paul to protect Carl Pohlad's investment," one lobbyist remembers. Those same legislators, soon up for election, certainly weren't going to be open to making Pohlad richer, not after they had so successfully beat up on Wolfenson and Ratner, two men who were considerably less wealthy than Pohlad. The lobbyists with thousands of miles on their professional odometers just shook their heads.

"I can understand people at the legislature wanting to give us a chance, to make sure that the enterprise is at least going to break even. But are you telling me we're trying to recoup his losses?" one lobbyist asked Borman.

The answer came back: "Basically, yes."

"That was a defining moment," one of the state's top lobbyists said. "They wanted all their money back." Guaranteed.

The Boat Ride

Suddenly, it was September. The primary election was six days away. Bob Dayton's dream of hushing up the stadium talks was coming true. Everything was cool. Then, as he was wont to do, Governor Carlson opened his big, fat mouth. He wanted to. He couldn't help himself. He was rollin' on the river, and the spirit moved him.

The occasion came on Wednesday, September 4. Carlson and Minneapolis City Council president Jackie Cherryhomes had been in conversations over the previous weeks about Mississippi riverfront development. Carlson was intent on pushing the city to develop a marina, an "aquatic center," and an entertainment-destination harbor like Baltimore's and San Francisco's. (Later, city officials said the U.S. Army Corps of Engineers probably wouldn't allow such development.) Carlson didn't think that Minneapolis mayor Sharon Sayles Belton had the right vision, but he was wrong. In fact, redoing the riverfront was Sayles Belton's personal pet project. Talk to her about it, and she is as energetic and passionate as on any topic. Her love was Mill Ruins Park, an interpretive center near where she had personally decided a stadium could go, on the riverfront, just north of Washington Avenue, just east of Portland Avenue, near the well-known Liquor Depot store, near the Stone Arch Bridge. The mayor was thrilled about new housing along the river. She was fed up with Carlson trying to promote St. Paul's riverfront development—and Mayor Norm Coleman—while Minneapolis's plans were years ahead of the capital city's. Rebecca Yanisch, director of the Minneapolis Community Development Agency, wanted to show the governor all of their proposals along different parts of the riverfront.

But on this day, Carlson seemed to have a one-track mind. And he seemed to want to broadcast it to anyone on board the ship. "Where's the stadium going to be?" he asked. He was chilly, if not downright impolite to the mayor, regularly interrupting her. Once, while she tried to describe plans for a display about her city's history as a grain-milling center, Carlson cut in. "Watching water grind mills, that's a C. Let's get to the A," he said. When Yanisch wanted to detail city plans to take industrial sites off the riverfront, Carlson urged her to get to the "exciting part," that is, the stadium site. And once he got there, he stirred emotions by saying that if Minneapolis didn't hop on the stick, St. Paul might like the Twins over there.[6]

For reporters covering the boat ride, it was the first time that anyone in a responsible position had openly spoken about the stadium effort for months. Reliably aggressive Patrick Sweeney of the *St. Paul Pioneer Press* turned the day into an opportunity to flush out the potential sites under consideration for a ballpark. While typically boorish in nature, Carlson, in retrospect, said he accomplished his goal: to stir the stadium pot.

"Obviously, I purposely did that; it wasn't an act of lunacy," Carlson said more than two years later, speaking in his capitol office weeks before he vacated it for newly elected Jesse Ventura. "A lot of people had hopes that you could 'keep things under the radar screen,' but that's not the way that politics works. Politics is essentially an open business.... How in the world do you tell Joe Moe in Koochiching County he's not going to discuss the stadium issue? Of course, you should discuss it. Why should I listen to a bunch of nonelected people who are quietly advising people to whisper under the blankets? I think the big mistake would be later to be asked, 'Why did you go along with the secrecy movement?'"

As for his devotion to the stadium site and his impatience with other projects under way on the Minneapolis riverfront, Carlson said, "When you call up a hot tootsie for a date, you're not going to go to the water treatment plant. There is limited potential. People do not spend a Saturday afternoon going to post offices." He wanted pizzazz. He got reaction.

Carlson thus inadvertently pushed the ballpark opponents out of their slumber. Nine days later, his jaw jutted, his rhetoric primed, his sense of fair play offended, John Marty emerged—and never went away. The man who had been humiliated in the gubernatorial election of 1994 was back to snipe at his conqueror. In his opening salvo at a St. Paul news conference, Marty blasted what he viewed as a pro-stadium "conspiracy of silence." And he vowed to block any efforts by Minnesota Wins or its supporters to convince candidates in the November election to refrain from staking out stadium positions. Of course, there was no deal on the table. There were no detailed public principles announced by Savelkoul or the governor. There was nothing to be for or against. But Marty was against it anyway. And Marty was going to guard the people.

Something else secretly occurred in September. Minneapolis lawyer Clark Griffith, son of former owner Calvin, called on Carl Pohlad. Clark Griffith, still well connected in baseball circles but not rich enough to buy the Twins, told Pohlad that he'd formed a group of investors to buy the team. Griffith offered $95 million. The proposal came two years after Griffith first met with Pohlad to inquire about obtaining the franchise.

Pohlad, who was always dismissive of Griffith, rejected the offer, wary of the firmness of Griffith's financing. Pohlad also told Griffith that it was the wrong time to sell. "I don't want anything disrupting my stadium effort," Pohlad said. Little did he know what was in store.

The Senator

"Let's see now," John Marty said, opening a dictionary. He sat behind his desk in the Minnesota capitol, a state senator in search of the definition for the label so often attached to him by Twins stadium boosters. "Demagogue, d-e-m-a-g-o-g-u-e," he said.

He read with some interest, with a bit of self-gratification, and with a hint of guilt or defensiveness, maybe even remorse. The hardworking senator from Roseville, the inner-ring St. Paul suburb, took the Twins stadium issue and pushed and pulled it from every which way, first criticizing a referendum effort in 1996, then trashing negotiations later that year for their secrecy, and ultimately kicking all the proposals in 1997 because of their welfare for the wealthy. Wherever the stadium issue went, Marty was there to criticize, to poke, never to say die.

"A leader of the common people," Marty read the first definition in his dictionary. He nodded his head. He was OK with that concept.

"A leader who makes use of popular prejudices and false claims and promises in order to gain support," was the second definition. He didn't like that, nor was it true. Marty's antistadium effort may have been based on Minnesotans' general dislike for the wealthy and the state's alienation from pro sports, but his rallying against public funding was not founded on false claims or wild promises. While he was accused of being "Senator No," there were a few things to which he believed the public should say yes. He believed that Congress should investigate major-league baseball. He believed that the game's owners should restructure the economics of their industry. And he believed that a new Twins stadium should be built with private dollars, not public tax money.

"This wasn't about stadiums," Marty insisted. "It was about subsidies. People from the stadium booster groups kept condemning me, saying I was irresponsible to take a position to say no when I didn't even know what their plan was. But why was it OK for them to say yes to whatever the plan was going to be?"

Marty was exactly the political leader and troublemaker that Sports Facilities Commission lobbyist Larry Redmond warned about when he urged Henry Savelkoul not to make the Twins stadium effort a 1996 election issue. As if looking into a crystal ball, Redmond knew that someone would make the stadium issue the hottest topic of the fall election. Marty did. The Twins debate was never the same.

"John Marty is very blessed," Governor Arne Carlson said. "Most of us just don't have the access to God that he does. We don't. This puts great limits on us." More than derision, more than sarcasm, bitterness and intense dislike dripped from Carlson's words. Marty symbolized the opposition to any pro sports funding efforts. His squeaky-clean principles also drove Carlson and others nuts. The champion of ethics in the legislature, a man who believed that campaign funding was inherently dirty and that a meal paid for by a lobbyist was a virtual bribe, Marty, just forty years old in the fall of 1996, was perhaps the most isolated member of the Minnesota Senate. He was an outsider's outsider, a man who purposely kept a distance from his colleagues. In 1994 the left wing of the DFL Party made him the gubernatorial candidate against Carlson. In the most merciless election in the state's history, Marty was smashed by Carlson, losing 64 to 34 percent, a humiliating defeat. It appeared as if Marty was seeking revenge against Carlson on the Twins matter. After all, this stadium subsidy was Carlson's baby, and Marty wanted to throw it out, bath water and all.

"Almost all the people in politics who are supporting sports, it's like they didn't grow out of it when they were kids, it's almost like adolescent hero worship," Marty said. "When I was a little kid I wanted to be a hockey player. And if I couldn't be a hockey player, I wanted to be a football player. And if I couldn't be a football player, I wanted to be a window washer. That was fourth grade. I had a Martin Luther King autograph, but the ones that really mattered to me were Bobby Hull, Stan Mikita, and Mike Ditka. But people like Arne, with his Gophers letter sweater, they never quite outgrew it all. If they can sit on the bench that would be their number one goal in life."

Marty brought a different sense of values to the stadium debate than just about everyone else in the legislature. Or, at least, he articulated them. Perhaps it was his ambition. Or maybe it was his deeply held sense of justice. Some scoff at such a notion, that a politician has a sense of justice and that he can apply it to pro sports. But wasn't the stadium a justice issue in the end? For most Minnesotans, it seemed to be. With no reason to build the ballpark other than that banker Carl Pohlad wanted one, Marty capitalized on the glaring contradictions of the process: a billionaire was seeking a massive state subsidy for a sport that was in economic disarray.

Marty brought with him the values instilled in him by his world-famous father, Lutheran theologian Martin Marty, and his mother, Elsa

Marty, who was a suburban Chicago gym teacher. While many of his friends were playing Little League baseball one summer, John Marty went with his family to a gathering of ministers in Virginia. He was six when he met Martin Luther King. There is a picture of that event in his capitol office. As he grew older and understood the nation's problems more, he and his four brothers would commute from their comfortable suburban home to attend church in Chicago's inner city. His parents would impose a "poverty diet" on him, a regimen that prohibited him from buying ice cream at the school cafeteria in second grade because "we were living on the diet of poor people."

Those were his roots. And he was the zealot in the stadium battle. He called news conferences whenever the spirit moved him, always needing to point out the flaws of the stadium effort. He was the first legislator to challenge his cohorts to take a position on the Twins negotiations, and he was joined soon after by a pair of Republican House members whose politics were at the opposite end of the spectrum from his, Representative Phil Krinkie of Shoreview and Representative Kevin Knight of Bloomington. In the days after the boat ride and after Carlson blew the lid off the behind-the-scenes stadium talks, Marty did what he loves to do; he went into the files of what was then the Ethical Practices Board and uncovered all the campaign contributions that lobbyists attached to the Twins and Metropolitan Sports Facilities Commission had given to legislators.

He called one of his news conferences for the State Office Building, and the reporters flocked, some rolling their eyes because Marty, with his committed fist and his high standards, was so predictable. He pointed out that a host of lobbyists gave money to both parties "to buy influence at the capitol. It may be smart business for them, but it's a rip-off for the public. It's time to confront the stadium lobby head-on," he said, instantly pissing off every lobbyist in the state. But he didn't care. He felt outraged by Carlson's chumming up to Pohlad, and in his own isolated way, Marty knew in his gut that the stadium issue was ripe for dissent among Minnesotans.

Most of his colleagues urged him to shut up, to let the stadium

Minnesota's drive to become big league was a grassroots community effort led by Chamber of Commerce chief Jerry Moore and a group called the Minute Men. The Minute Men split into sales teams to pitch revenue bonds to citizens to build Met Stadium. Copyright 1999 *Star Tribune/Minneapolis–St. Paul.*

Met Stadium was located where the sprawling city bumped up against Minnesota's agricultural roots. In 1955 Bloomington was as much farmland as two-car garages. Photograph from *Minneapolis Star-Journal,* Minnesota Historical Society.

By 1956, a tiny 18,000-seat stadium for the minor-league Minneapolis Millers was a cute jewel on the prairie. It was designed to lure a big-league team, but it would take five years for that to happen. Copyright 1999 *Star Tribune/Minneapolis–St. Paul.*

Left, Wheelock Whitney; *right,* Branch Rickey. The two men challenged baseball's powers and forced the American League expansion that brought the Washington Senators to Minnesota. Here, Whitney and Rickey reveled in their accomplishment during the 1965 Twins-Dodgers World Series. Photograph courtesy of Wheelock Whitney.

Calvin Griffith pulled up his family's Washington, D.C., roots and became the owner of the Twins. Courtesy of AP/Wide World Photos.

North Minneapolis's own Max Winter persevered to bring the NFL to Minnesota. Copyright 1999 *Star Tribune/Minneapolis–St. Paul*.

"Save the Met!" they yelled, trying to keep baseball outside and, they believed, out of the hands of corporate interests. In 1979, demonstrators tried to block construction of what would become the Metrodome. Their efforts fell short. Copyright 1999 *Star Tribune/Minneapolis–St. Paul.*

On December 21, 1981, a bundled football crowd at Met Stadium said good-bye to the joys of freezing and to the muffled sounds of mittens applauding their beloved Vikings. Copyright 1999 *Star Tribune/Minneapolis–St. Paul.*

In with the new and out with the old: by the summer of 1984, after just two seasons in the Dome, Calvin Griffith bailed out of the baseball business. A relatively unknown Minneapolis banker named Carl Pohlad stepped in to become the Twins' savior. Copyright *Star Tribune/Minneapolis–St. Paul.*

Fastball or curveball? This toss, soon after he bought the Twins, was made when Pohlad was a popular man. A decade later, he made other kinds of pitches to the legislature that met with stiff public resistance. Copyright 1999 *Star Tribune/Minneapolis–St. Paul.*

The Twins won the 1987 World Series, Kirby Puckett became a folk hero, and the once-hated Metrodome was sanctified as the region's championship gathering place. Copyright 1999 *Star Tribune/Minneapolis–St. Paul.* Reprinted by permission of the Minnesota Twins Baseball Club.

The Super Bowl, the nation's premier sporting event, came to the Dome in 1992. As always, it proved an ideal football venue. Copyright *Star Tribune/Minneapolis–St. Paul.*

North Stars owner Norm Green ran over his fans en route to a quick escape to the hockey hotbed of Dallas. Reprinted with permission from *Star Tribune*, Minneapolis.

This cartoon angered Timberwolves owners Marv Wolfenson and Harvey Ratner, who viewed it as part of a subtle anti-Semitism that wove its way through the Target Center buyout controversy. Reprinted with permission from *Star Tribune*, Minneapolis.

Met Center was demolished in 1994 when some local sports officials believed the National Hockey League would return to Target Center. Oops—didn't happen. Copyright 1999 *Star Tribune/Minneapolis–St. Paul*.

Jacobs Field in Cleveland opened Carl Pohlad's eyes. Soon after he visited the new ballpark in 1994, he told Twins staff members, "This is what we need." Photograph courtesy of Cleveland Indians/Mort Tucker Photography.

Senator John Marty of Roseville fashioned himself as the people's champion against the demands of pro sports teams. He forced most of his colleagues to take positions on a Twins ballpark before any proposals were on the table. Copyright 1999 *Star Tribune/Minneapolis–St. Paul.*

In the fall of 1996, two key players in the Twins' efforts for a new stadium met and, probably, argued. Paul Thatcher, a member of the Metropolitan Sports Facilities Commission, and the Reverend Ricky Rask, a lightning rod for antiballpark sentiment, found themselves face-to-face before a commission meeting. Copyright 1999 *Star Tribune/Minneapolis–St. Paul.*

For a while during the fall of 1996, stadium proponents wanted legislators to avoid talking about a proposed Twins stadium—doing so might rile things up. Reprinted with permission from *Star Tribune*, Minneapolis.

Opposition to Carl Pohlad's push for a new ballpark turned very personal. Here, stadium critic Paul Moberg designed a satirical "aid package" advertisement for Carl Po' Lad. Reprinted with permission from Paul Moberg.

Why are these men smiling? This is the day they shot themselves—and the entire stadium effort—in the foot. *Left to right*: Carl Pohlad, Henry Savelkoul, and Jerry Bell chuckled (but only briefly) on January 8, 1997. Soon after, the truth caught up to them. Copyright 1999 *Star Tribune/Minneapolis–St. Paul.*

The quarterback of the government's pro-stadium offensive was Minnesota's number one sports fan, Governor Arne Carlson. Copyright 1999 *Star Tribune/Minneapolis–St. Paul.*

On January 31, 1997, Carl Pohlad's vision was unveiled: he wanted a retractable-roof stadium. The ceremony that revealed the ballpark model was held at a sentimental spot—the former location of Met Stadium, now the site of the Mall of America in Bloomington. Courtesy of Minnesota Twins.

An artist's rendition of the Twins' model retractable-roofed ballpark of 1997, set in its Mississippi riverfront environment. Courtesy of Minnesota Twins.

In April 1997, interim baseball commissioner Bud Selig tried to explain himself and the economics of baseball at the Minnesota capitol. Listening were former Twins greats Kent Hrbek and Kirby Puckett. Courtesy of AP/Wide World Photos.

Don Beaver was the man that Carl Pohlad and Arne Carlson needed to create the illusion that the Twins were about to leave Minnesota for North Carolina. Courtesy of AP/Wide World Photos.

The proposal to add slot machines to Canterbury Downs was enough to make a legislator gag. Or so it seemed to Senator Dean Johnson of Willmar, who was caught off guard by Associated Press photographer Jim Mone in one of the most memorable images of the 1997 stadium battle. Courtesy of AP/Wide World Photos.

Speaking of gambling, how about this suggestion by *Star Tribune* cartoonist Steve Sack? Reprinted with permission from *Star Tribune*, Minneapolis.

During a special legislative session about the stadium, demonstrators showed up dressed as ballot boxes, urging their elected officials to vote "No." Photograph by Tom Olmscheid/Minnesota House of Representatives.

All business, that's for sure. *Left to right*: Carl Pohlad and aides Bob Starkey and Jerry Bell entered a capitol hearing room before critical testimony during the special session. Copyright 1999 *Star Tribune/Minneapolis–St. Paul*.

No, Carl Pohlad was not giving money away. Rather, he was telling legislators about a check he had received from a generous fan who wanted to help build the Twins a new ballpark. Photograph by Tom Olmscheid/Minnesota House of Representatives.

Whether it was Roger Headrick or Red McCombs, at every turn, whenever the Twins wanted something, there stood the Vikings right behind them, with their figurative tin cup at work, too. Reprinted with permission from *Star Tribune*, Minneapolis.

matter pass until after the election. But as September became October, as Krinkie and Knight began to stir up opposition on their own with a detailed questionnaire for all legislators, a host of politicians were finding Marty and telling him he was on the right track. Their constituents didn't want to fund a stadium, either.

Because he is so judgmental about every other politician, he annoys them. Because he speaks in simple sentences and concepts, he is accused of being a demagogue. "This is an easy issue to demagogue," Twins president Jerry Bell said throughout the 1996 and 1997 period, turning a noun into a verb, and other Twins officials and Savelkoul sang the same tune. But according to that dictionary, Marty wasn't demagoging. He was expressing a basic Minnesota tenet: "I don't begrudge the fact that rich people have more. I bemoan that there are a lot of people doing without. My feeling has never been 'let's stick it to Carl Pohlad.' It's been 'let's be a little more concerned about people who are struggling.' People accused me of being out for class warfare. No, I'm out for helping the middle and lower end of things rather than trying to see how we can help the upper end," Marty said.

Is that Minnesotan, or what? And it really angered Carlson. "Have you ever seen John Marty smile?" the governor asked. "Do you think he goes through life having a good time? In his mind, wherever two people are getting together, they're propagating evil. What nonsense."

Marty wound up performing most of the rhetorical sound biting on the political front, even if Krinkie and Knight, two purposely mischievous House members, did much of the day-to-day dirty work. Their group, Citizens for Fiscal Responsibility (CFR), truly put legislators on the spot, asking them all to respond about whether they supported public funding for a stadium. Krinkie and Knight used CFR to gather the data and then distribute it to constituents and the media.

If Marty brought this progressive sense of fairness to the table, Knight and Krinkie brought a roguish contempt for a rich man's efforts to better his lot and for the governor, whom they both viewed as a lapsed conservative. They actually got their self-generated antistadium effort under way at the State Fair a few weeks before Marty went public. As they each spoke with fair-goers, they came to understand the deep opposition to public funding for a ballpark. "We decided we had to get this thing on the radar screen," Krinkie said. They were both strident opponents of the 1994 Target Center buyout and vowed never to be fooled again. As time wore on, they quietly convinced colleagues on key committees to vote against any stadium bills.

Knight said anytime they could gather antistadium votes in the House, "we considered it bonus points." And as they racked up those points, Marty got most of the publicity, but Krinkie and Knight seemed to enjoy most of the satisfaction. They sort of giggled at it all. "Marty took the full brunt," said Krinkie. "We did the heavy lifting, but Marty got the face time," said Knight.

Once, at a hearing, Jim Pohlad, Carl's most sociable and compromising son, privately asked Krinkie, "What would it take to get you to vote for a stadium?"

Krinkie replied: "I have to become a Pohlad."

"Dinner's at six," Pohlad answered.

But the conservative antistadium forces and the banker's family never broke bread. They simply smashed Governor Carlson's goal of getting a stadium built. "I don't think I've ever talked to Kevin Knight, what a despicable legislator and what a reprehensible version of the truth," Carlson said. "What's the other one's name? Krinkie? Another one of life's great losers. Marty, Krinkie, and Knight, they all communicate with God." Or at least a ton of voters.

Voters, politicians, teams, and leagues may have been approving and forcing through pro sports funding in other states and cities, but Marty, Knight, and Krinkie served to push the Minnesota debate toward private funding. Why did an opposed public have to pay for a stadium that only a few of us would use? Into this void came Ed Villaume, a thirty-one-year-old Bloomington stockbroker, who became another thorn in the side of the Twins ballpark campaign in the fall of 1996. Villaume, who had a minor role in the 1994 Timberwolves' sale, had a plan to build a stadium cheaply and with, mostly, private money. He unveiled a stunning model of an open-air stadium even before the Twins did, solidifying a vision of a downtown stadium, on Nicollet Mall, across from the Minneapolis Public Library's central branch. He garnered attention because he claimed he could pay for it all with a minimal amount of tax dollars.

In the end, Villaume's numbers never added up. He speculated that he could generate $90 million from concessionaires, soft drink contracts, and beer-pouring rights, a figure never achieved in the history of pro sports. He assumed the Twins would kick in $55 million with limited return. He wished that the citizens would contribute $25 million to buy commemorative bricks. He dreamed that the Twins would average 40,000 fans a game, every game, for the rest of all of our natural lives, with never a rain out to wash away a game.

Villaume's true intent was to somehow buy the team. At times, he seemed to be a fantasizing storyteller, boasting about connections he had that seemed tenuous. But he had a plan that captured the imagination of stadium observers. And the mere fact that he could put together a plan—however flawed—with limited public money was another conceptual cloudburst that dropped on the Twins' increasingly disrupted parade. Villaume put the notion into people's minds that this ballpark could be built with private money, as was the case in San Francisco, where the Giants' owners invested $250 million in private cash for a new ballpark. In reality, in the Twin Cities market, unless there was a completely philanthropic owner, which Pohlad was not, there was no way a private ballpark made any economic sense. The debt service would be too stiff. It wasn't "the market" that drove the construction of ballparks; it was the competing subsidies around the nation that did. As long as every other city and state—from Maryland to Colorado, from Ohio to Texas—was going to give its teams sizable hunks of cash to build stadiums, Pohlad wanted and needed a similar subsidy in Minnesota to keep up with his peers. For him to build it on his own would have been to finance more of his ballpark than any ownership group but the Giants' wealthy gaggle of owners. Pohlad wasn't going to do it. But Villaume's plan, warts and all, challenged Pohlad.

Fold that economic challenge into the Marty-Krinkie-Knight anti-tax, anti–corporate welfare challenge and wrap it neatly with a heartfelt "priorities" challenge raised by a minister named Ricky Rask, and a loose, but large, public coalition against the stadium effort was being formed without any need for specific organizing. It was grassroots to the hilt. Rask would add real soul to an opposition that, to this point, was political and distinctly male.

Priorities

> Fear not, for I have redeemed you;
> I have summoned you by name; you are mine.
> When you pass through the waters,
> I will be with you;
> And when you pass through the rivers,
> they will not sweep over you.
> When you walk through the fire,
> you will not be burned;
> The flames will not set you ablaze . . .
> [Because] you are precious and honored in my sight,
> and because I love you.[7]

That is the Reverend Ricky Rask's favorite Bible passage. She recited it aloud one day in her living room, the one with the twenty-four clocks tick-tocking wildly, with the black-and-white springer spaniel named Emily snoring and with Fluffy the cat meowing constantly as if trying to wake up Emily or drown out Rask's rapid-fire chatter. Rask's silver hair shone on that fall day, two full years after she emerged as the lightning rod to galvanize a segment of Minnesota's population against a stadium.

In October 1998, the United Church of Christ minister, age fifty-two, a grandmother, was tired, very tired. Her health had been tested. Her fight was over. Senator John Marty may have served to put all of his legislative colleagues on the spot politically. But Rask burst onto the stadium scene in the fall of 1996 and placed the entire citizenry—and certainly Pohlad and stadium boosters—on the spot morally. Rask was not exactly a political amateur, having interacted with the legislature in 1994 over the rights of noncustodial grandparents. But she was the breath of fresh air that the debate required. Sometimes wearing the clerical collar that she preferred not to wear, Rask, a tall, maverick woman in public, a pensive, needy woman in private, performed two tasks that stadium supporters could never undo: she placed the beginnings of the 1996 to 1997 ballpark debate into an understandable political and emotional context, and she served to identify and leverage a gender gap that had been overlooked.

Her issues were unmistakable and simple. Why use public dollars to fund a stadium for a billionaire owner and millionaire players while even a single child went to sleep hungry at night, even a single mother couldn't find adequate day care for her kids, or even a single teenager was adrift and unable to find good job training? There was never an answer to sway most people. On her own, with some limited assistance from Roger Grussing of St. Paul's Macalester Plymouth Church, Rask formed an organization—which never had more than twenty members—called "Fund Kids First: When Kids Win, Minnesota Wins." And she went guerrilla, more than anyone else. Her style was direct. Her persona was appealing: the outraged, uncompromising minister-grandmother is a tough act to beat.

On December 3, 1996, when the Sports Facilities Commission was reporting on the status of Savelkoul's negotiations with the Twins, Rask decided the time was ripe to insert herself loudly into the state's percolating ballpark conversation. The formation of her group, with her argument that "priorities" were out of whack, had hit the local newspapers and radio talk shows. We were in search of a human face to place on the polls that showed opposition to public funding for a ballpark. And hers was a passionate face. Her actions distinguished her, too. Outside the doors of the Dome, she had gathered poor black mothers who needed child care assistance. On a bone-chilling day, they handed out leaflets telling of their plight, along with disposable diapers, which many of them couldn't afford. The flyers noted that $300 million could pay for 840 teachers' salaries for ten years or six hundred new police officers for ten years. Rask, assisted by number-crunching Jon Commers, a recent Carlton College grad, quantified the stadium's size, its slice of the state's pie.

Later, inside, commission chairman Henry Savelkoul attempted merely to present data on the Twins' and Vikings' economic situations. He didn't want public discussion on that day. He said public input would be invited at another time. But Rask rose from her front-row chair and asked, "Why are you not listening to people in a public meeting? You are not making the public part of the process."

As she spoke, her voice shook, and she rattled the room of commissioners and Twins officials. "It's about priorities and values," she said. "There should not be one hungry child in this state, and they're talking about public money for a stadium." It was classic Rask, a performance she would renew repeatedly at legislative hearings in 1997. It was as if the women of the state were all standing up and trying to be counted in this overwhelmingly male debate in which, Rask would later say, she could see "the testosterone dripping from the walls" of hearing rooms. Only Representative Ann Rest was allowed some significant input in the early stages of the stadium debate. Soon she was pushed aside, too, by Twins and Carlson administration officials, a painful experience even for Rest, who was as committed to a ballpark as anyone.

Rask's role—to strike a chord for the populace and strike a nerve with the stadium pushers—was one that developed from a collection of her life experiences. She grew up at her grandfather's knee, listening to Detroit Tigers games on the radio. She grew up in the fifties, the oldest, responsible daughter in a divorced family, with a mother who was verbally abusive. Rask grew up lonely in Kalamazoo, Michigan, grew up "different. I was very aware from an early age of injustice. I don't know why. It's rather puzzling to me still." Maybe it was the divorce of her parents when she was two; the separation isolated her within the conservative Dutch Reform church. Maybe it was her sympathy for the lone black boy in her class, a youngster who seemed as alone as she. By her teen years, she'd turned into a civil rights activist at Western Michigan University. Soon after, she took on the anti–Vietnam War mantle when she and her husband moved to the Twin Cities. She worked as a telecommunications marketer and in a brokerage firm until life seemed odd, out of kilter.

She was in her late thirties. The little girl who had listened to her grandmother read the Bible on the porch and who had been told that any kid who didn't love Jesus would burn in hell, decided to join the ministry. No, she didn't want a pulpit and a Sunday throng to preach to. She wanted to be a chaplain in a hospital. She wanted to minister to the ill and to their families. She wanted to be a hands-on spiritualist. She became a United Church of Christ minister. "That's the Church of Fallen Everythings," Rask joked.

Soon her own life needed God's guidance. Her daughter, at age sixteen, had a child. Their daughter had lost her way. The newborn was now living in an environment of chemicals and violence. Rask and her husband wanted to be able to have custody of their grandchild. But the state laws said if the grandparents took the grandchild, it could be kidnapping. Grandparents had no rights. Rask, in her first legislative fight, led the charge to change the Minnesota law. She won. She knew the system was difficult, but she'd achieved a victory. As those hearings on grandparents' rights faded into history in 1994, the first talk of the need for a new Twins ballpark surfaced. Rask's ears pricked up.

A former fan of Al Kaline, a big Vikings backer during their Super Bowl years in the seventies, Rask had become disaffected from pro sports because of players' strikes and owners' greed. She also saw the plight of her own daughter and other young people who, for whatever reason, had strayed. She saw how they scraped for funding for social programs to get them out of their binds. Her personal struggle and her spiritual commitment pushed her toward politics, toward this stadium issue.

"My call to the ministry was prophetic," Rask said. "Prophets usually got burned out, and they always died young. Nobody listened to them. What prophets say is, 'Quit your pissing and moaning, quit praying to give us this and give us that. You've got all you need, kids, just use it wisely. You want to change the future, you change today. It's not gloom and doom, we've still got a shot to make this a better world.'" Translated: there are enough resources to go around. Why give so many to athletes and their owners?

Frankly, stadium supporters didn't know what to do with her. At that testy Sports Facilities Commission meeting, men like Paul Thatcher and Savelkoul, both used to making decisions with other men motivated by self-interest, scoffed at her, pooh-poohed her, said that hungry children wouldn't get food, homeless men wouldn't get houses, and drug addicts wouldn't be cured whether the Twins got a stadium or didn't. These men and other stadium backers always attempted to disconnect the new reality that Rask was building, a reality that said the campaign for a Twins ballpark couldn't be conducted or perceived in some sort of social vacuum. Rask single-handedly pointed out the primary contradiction in any stadium debate, one to which ballpark boosters never adequately responded: powerful interests prefer to subsidize sports teams and facilities more willingly than they do poor people and social needs for the underclasses.

I believe that the powerful interests do a rotten job of articulating how tax dollars for sports and community building through sports can aid all groups. They also do an awful job of explaining exactly how much money is already being spent on children and their needs. But in general, the details had already become insignificant by the late fall of 1996. The stadium was a symbol of where the state's priorities stood. Rask was the critic who raised the entire state's consciousness. There was that biting contradiction and juxtapositon that ran through the 1997 session. On any given day, a visitor to the capitol could see a score of Hmong women holding signs seeking to retain their food stamps. On another day, a visitor could see a bunch of suited white men entering a committee room to discuss the details of a stadium bill. Even the key participants didn't understand it all.

To his credit, Twins president Jerry Bell frequently acknowledged that "the Twins weren't the most important issue facing Minnesotans," but in that concession, neither he nor any stadium boosters ever attempted to sincerely reach out to Rask or satisfy her unformed demands that the social ills be solved before Pohlad's baseball ills. Indeed, a thoughtful attempt to engage Rask might have helped form another impressive contextual debate: the "priorities" issue was hollow. Even a stadium subsidy of $350 million over a payout period of twenty years is a pittance compared to the state's total biennial budget of $22 billion. Take a $20 million annual general tax bite to pay for a stadium, and it would amount to 0.1 percent of the state's two-year budget. Compare that to the $4 billion a year that public schools get, and Rask's "priorities" argument seems flimsy.

Rask's raw emotion and her commitment to children's issues led her to believe that any dollar for sports was a dollar being taken from a kid. She personified that notion of "an opportunity cost" to any sports subsidy. It started with her quavering voice that December and continued through the 1997 legislative session. Marty, Krinkie, and Knight were politically motivated. Young Commers seemed motivated by a certain scholarly and intellectual fascination with the numbers and their meanings. Rask was completely motivated by her outrage. This made her refreshing; she was so driven by her feelings that in the midst of fighting against the pro sports machine, she paused to get Kirby Puckett's autograph one day, unable to hide her affection for a man she thought was a great player and one of the last athletes to help build community in the Twin Cities. Her genuine nature, her doggedness, made her dangerous to the stadium boosters. But in the end, it sapped her of all her strength. When the stadium game resumed in the summer of 1999 with the push by Mayor Coleman, she simply decided that she didn't have the energy anymore to fight what she considered the good fight. By 1999 Rask had gotten a job at a local gardening center and was a bystander. Her asthma acted up during her antistadium months of battle, of dutifully sitting through just about every legislative hearing as she worked feverishly on her embroidery. She was fifty-three years old. She had a second granddaughter. She'd fought the good stadium fight. She'd made her contribution.

It should be noted that some of the most capable players in the Twins stadium debate of 1996 and 1997 were women: Rest, who worked tirelessly and risked her political career; Sports Facilities Commission lawyer Kathleen Lamb, one of the state's finest writers of legislation; Sports Facilities Commissioner Loanne Thrane, one of the state's wisest political scientists; Maureen Shaver, one of the state's most influential lobbyists; Minneapolis City Council president Jackie Cherryhomes, a deal maker's deal maker; Minneapolis mayor Sharon Sayles Belton, who got a bum rap for not being forceful enough when she was the only politician to come out for a metrowide sales tax to pay for the stadium.

Almost to a person, these women were marginalized or, in some cases, abused. Rest, for her part, was treated with disrespect by the Twins, as was Lamb, as the legislative process wore on. Twins officials regularly wanted to be involved in the actual writing of the legislation. While lobbyists often make suggestions, Rest said it's uncommon for them to be in the room composing with the lawmaker. Lamb was asked to perform Herculean tasks of composition as the men around her changed their minds and their deals at a moment's notice. Thrane was never listened to. Shaver, who is good with her words, was never allowed to get a good word in edgewise. Cherryhomes, admired as a "tough broad" by the guys, was kept outside the process because the city of Minneapolis was essentially kept at arm's length by Savelkoul. And Sayles Belton, the black woman mayor, was always privately criticized for being missing in action when she had a Convention Center to get funded, a governor who held her in low respect, and an electorate opposed to pro sports funding.

It can't go unnoticed that these gigantic stadium projects are almost exclusively to the benefit of men. This Twins ballpark was planned for men to play in and to increase their salaries while most of the customers were to be men. The realization that this ballpark debate was, from the start and until this moment, "a guy thing," was brought home to me by author and sports critic Mariah Burton Nelson, a Washington, D.C.–based analyst who has written a number of books, including the marvelously titled *The Stronger Women Get, the More Men Love Football.*

"What strikes me about stadiums is that the entire community supports them through taxes and only men benefit," said Burton Nelson. "Men get to play in a ballpark," she said. "They get to coach. Men mostly do the maintenance work. Men are mostly the vendors. I don't think it's a family game, the national pastime, or builds community. How can it? Women aren't allowed to play in it."

The Web of Criticism

Much like the Vietnam War was the first international conflict to be seen in our living rooms, the 1996 to 1997 Twins debate was the first full-fledged Internet and full-blown talk radio stadium debate in Minnesota. Among the angrier, but certainly most bitingly humorous, critics was Paul Moberg. A thoughtful pamphleteer from Minneapolis who began his own group called GAGME, or Grass-Roots [or Geniuses] against Government-Mandated Entertainment, Moberg also created an extensive Web site called www.resonator.com. "We are just regular citizens, full up to here. Hence GAGME," Moberg wrote in one of his leaflets.

His politics were all over the board, and he was a sort of antitax, anti–big business, outrageous satirist born of the 1960s Yippie tradition of Paul Krassner and Abbie Hoffman. Moberg was always hysterically funny. He produced a song that received some local radio play in 1997, a blues ditty titled "Who Will Help the Po' Lad?" Among its lyrics:

> In this town of glitter and gold there lived a poor boy.
> He barely had a place to call his home.
> Just some cables and cement, not much more than just a tent
> His pillow set beneath the starless dome.
> Then one night he had a dream about a brand-new home.
> It seemed to be a magic castle in the air.
> With a roof so high and boxes in the sky
> And the sound of advertising everywhere.
> Tell me, who will help the Po' Lad?
> Who will help him pay for his magic clubhouse where his pals can play?
> Who will help the Po' Lad get the home he never had?
> Tell me who will help, who will help, who, who, who will help the Po' lad?

At the song's conclusion, the lead singer, now taking on the Po' Lad's persona, as would any bluesman, appeals to his audience.

> "I've only got a few billion left
> Would you dig a little deeper?

I know you ain't got no money so you might as well give me what you got
Give me some of that McDonald's money.

Moberg was always a little bit offensive, and sometimes blatantly so. Once Moberg, a woodworker by profession, accused Minneapolis's women politicians—such as Sayles Belton and Cherryhomes—of driving the stadium push. In a nicely designed flyer he distributed in December of 1996 titled "Somebody Stop These Bimbos," Moberg defined "bimbo" as a "Female machine politician who does *exactly* what the good old boys *tell* her to do." He was an ardent free-marketeer, distributing various brochures about how sports were a relatively small component of the entertainment industry. His leaflets were diatribes, but they confronted all the contradictions inherent in the stadium debate. For instance, under the heading "Bimbo Logic," he wrote, "The entertainment sector is already mega-healthy, so let's subsidize it with tax dollars. . . . Real businesses around the globe are downsizing but let's make sure that pro sports remains artificially bloated. Roberto Alomar, Albert Belle and Steve Howe help 'build community' (just like J. R. Rider, Michael Irvin, O. J. Simpson). Poor baby Carl Pohlad can't compete in the world's most vibrant economy all by his selfy self. It was too cold in Minnesota so we built a dome. But now the climate has changed so we have to move back outdoors again."[8] (Baseball second baseman Alomar once spit on an umpire. Home run hitter Belle assaulted a photographer. Relief pitcher Howe was a repeat drug offender. Former Timberwolves star Rider had various run-ins with the law, as did Dallas Cowboy star Irvin. And famed football hero Simpson was acquitted of killing his wife.)

On Moberg's Web site was a detailed chronology of the stadium debate, often ripping the *Star Tribune* and me for being a shill for the stadium effort. But he was right about the overbearing sense of urgency the *Star Tribune* and I brought to the process. So many of our stories sounded as if the Yugoslavian army was about to invade Eden Prairie. Other than his song, his finest hour came in a pamphlet during the legislative session that characterized Pohlad as a starving, diaper-wearing waif, as in a Sally Struthers "Save the Children" commercial. "My name

is Carl. Please help. Please, won't you give to Billion-Aid? Tonight, somewhere in this cold marketplace, a little billionaire boy cries out for help,"
reads some of the text. It was the kind of thing that Pohlad and his troops
certainly never expected, but the sort of material that reflected the deep-
seated resentment of the populace in general.

Later in the debate, as a special session approached and played out
in late 1997, a collection of good-government types and antitax fanatics
teamed up to form "Yer Out!" which flooded the capitol with e-mails and
created a cyber-energy that added to the level of protest and noise around
the stadium. "Yer Out!" even registered as a political action committee to
raise money to defeat candidates who supported funding for any pro
sports facilities. Hundreds of e-mails were posted on local politically oriented Web sites in the Twin Cities during the fall of 1997, passing on
information, rumors, and encouragement to harpoon any ballpark efforts.
The issue was bigger than baseball. It turned into "giving money to rich
guys." This loosely assembled antistadium movement delivered messages
far more effectively than any stadium booster group and via the new channels of the Internet.

The Other Team

In Roger Headrick, the antistadium forces had a strange bedfellow. The
Vikings president couldn't help himself. Whenever the Twins' momentum seemed to pick up the tiniest bit of steam, Headrick would say
something that would put the matter into perspective: if you think the
public will pay for a Twins ballpark, you ain't seen nothing yet. The
Vikings are next in line, he'd suggest. And if the legislature and public
knew what was best for everyone, they'd swallow the Vikings stadium
with a Twins stadium and get this whole darn problem fixed at once.
Headrick's repeated pushing of his needs just made the problem bigger,
even if he was bluntly telling the honest truth about the global nature of
the stadium problem.

Ever since the Vikings and Twins both began entertaining fans at
Met Stadium in 1961, the two organizations disliked each other and never
got along. The Vikings believed that the Twins took advantage of them at

the Met, what with the Griffiths controlling all of the concessions revenues and access to the field. The Twins believed that the Dome was built with the Vikings in mind and with them as an afterthought. But as the years wore on and Griffith and Pohlad took advantage of the escape clause, the Vikings kept falling further and further behind on collecting stadium related revenues. The Vikings still paid a high rent of 9.5 percent per ticket and received only 10 percent of their own concessions sales. The Twins paid no rent and got up to 45 percent of their concessions sales. Now, as the Vikings fought to keep up with their brethren who were moving into their own new stadiums with a series of new revenue streams, Headrick wasn't going to stand for the Twins getting a new stadium while the Vikings were left behind. If Minnesota's twenty-first-century sports facilities train was about to leave the station, Headrick didn't want to be stranded in the 1970s-designed Dome. Besides, through ticket taxes and food and beverage purchases, Vikings fans paid in millions of dollars more than Twins fans to the Dome's mortgage.

As the Twins negotiations thickened, I went to visit with Headrick in his office at the Vikings' suburban Eden Prairie complex. Called Winter Park, after the late owner Max Winter, the Vikings offices set them apart from the Twins and the stadium commission. They were secure and wealthy enough to have their own headquarters. That distance was more than symbolic. As I spoke with Headrick and Vikings marketing director Stew Widdess, Headrick said he wanted to show me something. From one of the corners of his office he pulled out an aerial shot of downtown Minneapolis. I wasn't quite sure what he had in mind until he pointed his index finger over an edifice that looked like the Minneapolis Convention Center. "Maybe we ought to be looking at something here," he said. He meant a new *Vikings* stadium. Such an idea wasn't then being publicly discussed.

I think I muttered, "You've got to be kidding," but I don't know if Headrick heard me. Whatever his real intent, on that Monday afternoon, October 7, 1996, Headrick said for the first time that a refurbished Dome for the Vikings was simply not going to be good enough.[9] He said if a Twins ballpark could be built on the Mississippi riverfront, then maybe there could be some connections between the Dome, where the Vikings would stay, and the new Twins facility. But mostly he wanted a new stadium himself because fixing the Dome would be costly, time consuming, and perhaps impractical. The Vikings might have to move out of the Dome for a year or two while the fix up ensued. Where would he play? Iowa City?

Headrick's fear was this: the Twins would get a new ballpark, a new NHL expansion team would get a renovated St. Paul arena, the Timberwolves would play in their still relatively new Target Center, and the Vikings would be the odd team out, stuck in the Dome, burdened by a lease without an escape.

Then, with that aerial photo leaning against one of the lounge chairs in his purple office, Headrick uttered fighting words: "We want to make sure we're being treated fairly and make sure we're not the last one in the game," he said and then went on to explain the plight in which Cleveland Browns owner Art Modell found himself before moving his team to Baltimore in November 1995. For seven years, Headrick said, Modell had warned Cleveland city officials that he needed an improved stadium situation. As Modell complained, the Indians baseball team got a new stadium, and the NBA Cavaliers got a new arena.

"I don't want to be sitting here five years from now saying, 'I told you so, you didn't listen to me,'" Headrick said, and I couldn't tell if there was a smile across his lips or a smirk. "That's what Art Modell said. He pulled the plug, which was entirely wrong and inappropriate. But"—oh, I love those conditional "buts" during such a diatribe—"you get to a point where you say, 'How long do we have to make our case?'"

From a reporter's point of view, Headrick's comments were too good to be true. From a citizens' point of view, his words were completely inflammatory and filled with sabotage for any Twins efforts. I went back to the office and told stadium editor Dennis McGrath about Headrick's comments, and we decided to hold the story until the next Sunday, as Headrick had told me he would be away for the next few days and not talking to reporters from any other news organization. We also didn't want to fan any sensational flames by just running with the story that next day.

I did some reporting, interviewing Savelkoul and Dome executive director Bill Lester, who reiterated their stance that the Vikings had a lease in place until the year 2012. I also decided to make sure that Headrick meant what he said. Widdess, who understood the damage that Headrick's comments might cause, called me a day or so later and called Headrick's musings "pie in the sky." He suggested I might want to minimize Headrick's comments. So on Friday, when my Sunday story was being completed, I called Headrick back. I told him I would be writing about his stadium ideas and just wanted to give him a chance to clarify anything he had said. A new stadium near the Convention Center? His comparisons to Art Modell? Was he comfortable with that?

No problem, he said. "You have dreams that you'd like to have something that puts you in the forefront, in a state-of-the-art facility, not in a stadium like ours that's not up-to-date," he added, not backing down, making matters worse. For Governor Carlson, Headrick's dreams were political nightmares. "The Vikings pitched that stadium as a first-class facility, the ultimate dream," Carlson said of the Dome. "To add another $100 million on top of the Twins package, where's that going to come from? I suggest Roger Headrick tone it down." Headrick rarely took Carlson's advice. I wrote the story. This stadium game kept getting more complicated.

Forging Ahead

By October, the Pohlad-Savelkoul vision began to take shape in the secret negotiations: a Minneapolis riverfront stadium, in close proximity to the Metrodome, with a surrounding "entertainment district" that could be subject to special taxes to aid in paying off the stadium. There was a public ownership component of some sort and the first inkling that the team was open to sharing the appreciation of the franchise's value with the public. But let's make one thing clear: Carl Pohlad didn't want to part with much of his money, and in the end, he wanted it all back.

"My dad has been very successful, there's no doubt about that, "Bob Pohlad said. "But there's no nice way to say this: You don't get to be successful, to the extent my dad has, by making decisions that are bad business. It is bad business to try to privately fund this kind of endeavor." It was clear that it was going to be the public's bad business to fund the endeavor.

Still, Bob Pohlad, the feistiest of the Pohlad sons, said the family would toss some money in. Noting that the Milwaukee Brewers' so-called private investment was backed by a $90 million loan from the state of Wisconsin—and not a dime from owner Bud Selig—Bob Pohlad said in October of 1996, "When we come in with ours, it will not be fake." He vowed one other thing in the name of his family, particularly his brothers and him. They would not make any threats to move, as Wolfenson and Ratner did with the Wolves and as Norm Green did with the North Stars, to no avail. Why no threats? "For the very simple, maybe borderline corny, but very true reason: We live here," Bob Pohlad said, softly, reasonably. "We want to continue to live here."[10]

Cozy, Very Cozy

Had it been a true arm's-length negotiations process, the public negotiators would have bargained harder. Savelkoul and Anderson should have taken advantage of the knowledge that the Pohlad boys, as far back as 1996, had no intention of ever letting their dad move the team. Solid intelligence gathering would also have revealed that there was never really anywhere to move the team. Northern Virginia, in the Washington, D.C., suburbs, and Charlotte, North Carolina, were always mentioned as potential sites. But neither had a stadium. Carl Pohlad repeatedly muttered that Northern Virginia wasn't an attractive market, and Charlotte was just getting used to being the home of an NBA team and an NFL team. Savelkoul and Anderson never challenged the Pohlads. They sought only to "strike a business deal." At one of their earliest meetings, Savelkoul talked about wanting the public to get "a fair return on its investment," and the Pohlad boys smiled. "You're looking at this like a business," either Jim or Bob said. "You're not looking at it like government."[11] But this stadium effort wasn't a private matter.

Carl Pohlad had a history of backing some top Democrats in his life—folks like Hubert Humphrey and Walter Mondale—but this time round, his political giving was eyebrow raising. The Pohlad family gave $43,200 to political parties that fall, almost equally. With contributions of $12,500 to the Republican Party of Minnesota and another $10,000 to the Republican National State Election Committee, Carl Pohlad tipped the balance of the contributions to the Republican side. But his sons were equal-opportunity givers, with Jim contributing $5,100 to the DFL House Caucus and Bob giving $5,000 to the Republican Senate Election Fund. They each then crisscrossed contributions of $2,500 to the opposite caucuses.[12] While probably equal to the Pohlads' monthly dry cleaning bill, it was unusually large for the family compared to previous years. For the three previous years combined, the family had contributed a total of $900.

"They all come to you, and they want you to give them money," Bob Pohlad remembered, with disdain in his voice for even being affiliated with the grimy political world. "They came asking for the moon, so to speak. Our approach was, we did give, but we gave the same to all." In theory, the Pohlads wanted to avoid making the ballpark a partisan issue. But in feeding both sides, it appeared to the public that they were simply lining everyone's pocket, regardless of principles, politics, or preferences.

The contributions came on the advice of their chief lobbyist Tom Borman, whose limited professional skills around the capitol showed in this instance. When Borman was confronted with the facts of the contributions, his answer didn't help matters. No, he seemed to say, how dare you imply they're buying votes. But—cough, cough—we have to buy some votes.

"They haven't been before the Legislature with a request of this size before, and now they are," Borman said nervously. "People can look at it cynically and say there's a motive here. What [the Pohlads] want to say to those who are running, those in positions of leadership, those who are candidates, is: [the Pohlads] understand, and they want to participate."[13]

Locked In

As the political consultants predicted in 1995, the antistadium voices pushed everyone in the fall of 1996 into staking out a position even before there was any substance on which to decide. While Marty railed against the original "conspiracy of silence," he promoted his own one-man hush squad. By forcing every candidate to declare yea or nay on the general concept of funding for a stadium, he effectively shut down debate about any possible details. It did not serve the debate well. But it lined up all the candidates, who eventually became victors and legislators and who, now in office, couldn't go back to their preelection pledges against public funding, no matter the specifics of a deal. That was too bad. Interesting possibilities existed: the plan that would come down the pike from the Carlson administration would be flawed but would include some enlightening planks; also, the state would be blessed with billions of dollars of budget surpluses, but no one seriously argued that the extra dollars be used for sports.

With all the candidates running scared, the *Star Tribune* and *Pioneer Press*, the monthly journal called *Minnesota Law and Politics*, and the right-wing Citizens for Fiscal Responsibility each conducted preelection surveys, and all printed the results in voters's guides or on Web sites. Candidates were forced to say whether they agreed or disagreed with a half-dozen statements by the *Star Tribune*, and they included, presumably, the six highest-priority issues among the people: health care, the economy, poverty and welfare, crime, education, and the stadium. Of all the candidates surveyed, not one said he or she agreed that "the state should provide financial assistance to help the Minnesota Twins build a new baseball stadium."[14] Of all the candidates in sixty-seven Senatorial districts and 134 House districts, among a slew of no responses or undecided, only three said they would support public funding for the stadium. By the time voters went to the polls, thiry-eight of the sixty-seven elected senators had gone on record somewhere as being flatly opposed to stadium funding.

Proposals-R-Us

In mid-November, with the stadium issue still the hottest in the community save for welfare reform, both sides exchanged their first formal, albeit rough, proposals. Again, this was all in secret. There were no leaks about the details. There was no consultation with legislators. Savelkoul,

Anderson, and Welle faxed a six-page proposed contract to Bell and Starkey. The next day, Bell sent back the Twins' opening salvo on two pages. The concept of "partnership" was the single commonality between the two, and Savelkoul's view of sharing was significantly broader and deeper than the Twins'.

In these opening plans we see the seeds of the ultimate "deal." Savelkoul desired a true partnership to build the stadium. While there were no specific numbers in the first proposal from Savelkoul and Anderson, there was a proposal to share the revenues of the new stadium *and the Twins* [emphasis mine] in "a unique arrangement that will be both (a) socially responsible and (b) a structure that will ensure the long-term viability of the Twins in Minnesota."[15] What Savelkoul envisioned was a new public authority taking over the existing Sports Facilities Commission, and that authority would share the stadium and team profits with the Pohlads. The proposal also sought the public's right to buy up to 49 percent of the Twins' stock, for a maximum price of $37.5 million. In this initial proposal, Pohlad would have received his investment in the team and the stadium back through the ongoing operations of the facility. There was no guarantee that Pohlad would be "made whole" for what he called his $105 million investment in the team or any investment in the stadium.

But then there's the Twins' response the next day, and it's titled "Minnesota Twins Contribution to a New Ballpark." In it, the Pohlads offered to "contribute" a 17 percent ownership stake in the team to the public and guarantee its worth of at least $25 million. That assumed the team's value would be about $147 million once the stadium was built. The Twins also offered to share 17 percent of the team's profits at the new stadium, with a guarantee of at least $1 million a year for ten years, and 17 percent of the increased appreciation of the franchise when it was sold. The team also offered to "contribute" $20 million in up-front cash. In essence, the Pohlads were offering a total of a possible $55 million up front for a stadium—including $25 million of the spun-off franchise value—that they knew would cost more than $300 million. The Twins also wanted all the revenues from nonbaseball events and a publicly funded parking ramp built adjacent to the stadium that would guarantee them at least $3 million a year.

Savelkoul and Anderson wanted a 49 percent sharing arrangement and hadn't yet broached the subject of real cash from Pohlad, although the lobbyists were telling both sides that real money of between $50 and $100 million (from the banker) was the only way the deal was going to make it through the legislature, if it made it at all.

The negotiations, long a mating dance and lovefest, were now in an overdrive mode, with proposals filling the fax machines in offices from Minneapolis to Albert Lea, killing countless and defenseless trees in the process. The legislature was set to open on January 7, the holidays were coming, and there were only about six weeks to go. There was nothing presentable or agreeable on the table to speak of.

By November 22, Savelkoul and Anderson proposed that 26 percent of the stadium be built with private dollars, 33 percent from "project revenues"—presumably ticket taxes, naming rights, and suite sales—and 41 percent from the public. Thus, by late November, the public negotiators conceded that on a proposed $343 million project, only $78 million need come from the Pohlads or the local business community. The rest must be generated by public taxes or stadium revenues.

The deal, still secret, still unknown to legislative leaders, still untested, was developing into a bundle, a package, a tightly wrapped concept. To move one part here was to change another part over there. By November 22, the vocabulary and complexity had been established. The out-of-touch cocoon in which the Pohlads, Bell, Starkey, Savelkoul, and Anderson negotiated was apparent from the language of their secret drafts. Could they really have expected an anxious public to understand clauses such as the following: "The public sector will use its best effort to place below market debt backed by project revenues. This will significantly decrease up front funding (through avoiding the funding of debt service reserve and debt placement costs) and significantly increase annual cash flow through reduced interest costs"?[16] They were contortionists. They were setting themselves up to fail. These were not negotiations that were protecting the public.

Cynicism

As 1997 approached, the Pohlads attempted to put a human face on the emerging plan and themselves. Bob Pohlad, especially, began appearing on the Dark Star radio show on WCCO-AM, placing a younger voice on the otherwise stodgy Twins image. In late 1995, he decided he wanted to be the new face of the Pohlad family as it reflected the Twins. Previously, the sons had moved in and out of being interested in the team. They attended games irregularly. Their knowledge of baseball was lacking. One former Twins employee remembered sitting in on a decision to release a top player after the 1993 season. In the midst of a discussion about how the public might react, Jim Pohlad asked, quite seriously, "How come all the baseball players don't have the same swing like golfers?"

In late November, after I made a request through Pat Forciea, the Pohlad sons agreed to an interview, for the first time, to talk about their family. I aided in the human-face campaign. I wrote the story with a *People Magazine* sort of approach. These were three local figures who had never been profiled in the *Star Tribune* before. I used the story as a means to develop a relationship with the three sons. But I was also struck by how out of touch they seemed to be with the real world. I allowed them to talk about feeling victimized by the stadium process. It was a sympathetic piece, to be sure. But I also attempted to kindly reveal that they didn't understand how different they truly were from the main swath of Minnesotans. An excerpt:

> "They grew up in Edina, the sons of a little-known banker.
>
> Said Bill: "People perceive our childhood as living in this mansion, but we lived in a regular neighborhood, nicer than most, but a regular place."
>
> Their mother, Eloise, swept the garage every Thursday, and still does.
>
> Said Bob: "We had a cleaning lady, but my mom would clean the house so the cleaning lady never thought the house was dirty."[17]

In the end, I quoted Bob Pohlad as saying, "If you think baseball plays a role in this community, give us a chance."

At this point, there was no plan on the table, and the Pohlads had made no threats to move the team. I knew nothing of how the secret deal was evolving. My favorable portrait of the Pohlad boys caused a stir.

Let me digress here. I was the lead reporter for the *Star Tribune* throughout this stadium debate. In the fall of 1996, the signals that were being sent by Savelkoul and the Pohlad family were all upbeat and positive. There were no finance plans, no funding sources from the public, and no firm commitments from the Pohlads. But there was a sense that something special was going to emerge. It was a time of some hope, and, I admit, I got hopeful. To a certain extent, there was no reason not to be hopeful. I assumed that after Marty, Knight, and Krinkie stirred the pot and Rask began her work, that the Pohlads, Savelkoul, and Anderson must have understood they were under pressure to produce a deal that would disarm the broad mass of Minnesotans who were skeptical of any plan. But the story that I wrote about the Pohlad sons instructed me that even a hint of marginal kindness directed toward Pohlad was going to be seen as a sign of media weakness.

My story drew an immediate negative reaction within the *Star Tribune* newsroom. People walked by my desk and mumbled about a "puff piece." Newsrooms, which are hotbeds and incubators of cynicism and negativity, have little room for supporting a legitimate public effort. It's our job to question and challenge, but it seems there is little room for newspapers to guide a process or simply introduce people—even rich people—kindly to our readers.

The sons' story was viewed as "too soft," as if I had somehow let them "get away with" talking about their mother as a regular person. On the contrary, I wrote the story to simply tell our readers who these men were. And I wrote it, I thought, with a tone attempting to show that the Pohlad sons *thought* they were just like the rest of us—but just a billion dollars or so richer. Within the walls of the *Star Tribune*, I guess I failed on that day.

Although dumping on people is part of the job of newspaper columnists—why, I don't know—I saw the consistent wrath directed at Pohlad and his sons in the newsroom embodied in a column that Doug Grow, the *Star Tribune*'s metro page columnist, wrote soon after my lengthy feature about the boys appeared. As usual, Grow, as do many columnists, wrote something about someone and never talked with him or her, nor to me. Instead, he simply made fun of them, an easy tactic of newspapering and talk radio during this stadium debate and an ingredient that served to degrade the public conversation.

Grow began honestly enough, being critical of the Pohlad sons for seeking public money for a ballpark. But then the column deteriorated, as did many pieces of so-called journalism during the debate. And what was clear was that the debate would center on a certain kind of class warfare. That profiling of the stadium issue was at the guts of the opposition to a ballpark. Not only was Pohlad supposedly the second richest man in Minnesota, but his serfs, the players, were millionaires, too. The issue was ripe for the simplistic critic who might not have embraced the history of Met Stadium, when a community came together to help build a meaningful piece of cultural infrastructure.

"In the article," Grow wrote of my piece about the Pohlad sons, "the Regular Guys talked of how they didn't grow up much different from other kids. One of the things the Regular Kids enjoyed doing was going to work with their father. Sometimes that meant piling into the family plane and winging off to one of EveryDad's banks. The boys would play on typewriters while EveryDad did the sort of things all dads do, such as demand higher profit margins, buy more banks, fire employees and call in loans," wrote Grow, among the highest-paid members of the *Star Tribune* staff. "I don't know about you, but I was overcome by a ripple of nostalgia as I read about the Everyday Family. The Pohlad kids, I thought to myself, grew up just as I did. Reading about their outings, I was reminded of Sunday afternoons when my parents would pile the family into our two-toned (blue and white) Plymouth and go for drives past the nicest houses in town, including those of the bankers.... Oh, for the next few months it's going to be sweet and thick. Baseball, apple pie and regular families—like your family, my family, the Pohlad family."[18]

Grow's column marked the kickoff of what would be a periodic offensive by columnists at both the *Star Tribune* and *Pioneer Press*, of name-calling—aimed at Pohlad, Marty, Rask, and others— and an analysis of the stadium debate that was colored in just two ways, black or white, good or bad.

CHAPTER 8

Spilling the Beans
The Twins' Crime of Omission

Away from the klieg lights of public attention and personal attack, Savelkoul, Anderson, Welle, Bell, Starkey, and Bob and Jim Pohlad were nailing down a deal. Their deal. They were certainly keeping it away from the Metropolitan Sports Facilities Commission, which Savelkoul headed. No one in that agency was privy to the depth of the talks, even though by law that agency had responsibility for preserving pro sports facilities and, by extension, retaining major-league teams. No one at the capitol seemed to be thoroughly informed. Savelkoul and Anderson told Twins folks that they briefed some leaders, including the powerful Senate majority leader Roger Moe. "Roger told me he had all the confidence in the world in Morrie and myself," Savelkoul remembered. But House Speaker Irv Anderson, who Savelkoul felt could knock heads and get a stadium bill passed, was ousted by unhappy members of the DFL caucus as the stadium negotiations heated up. He was replaced by Representative Phil Carruthers of suburban Brooklyn Center, who needed the 1997 regular session and some of the special session to seem to take the ballpark issue seriously. Senator Moe remembers being barely informed about "broad issues, but nothing specific."

The city of Minneapolis wasn't in the loop, either. Savelkoul and Anderson had no real contacts there. Savelkoul alienated many of the leaders in city hall, Mayor Sharon Sayles Belton, and City Council president Jackie Cherryhomes, with his style during the Target Center buyout talks. He was often exclusionary and secretive and, finally, burned bridges when he made a reference that seemed sexist about the female-dominated city government. Talking in 1995, after the Target Center deal, about how difficult it was to direct the Sports Facilities Commission, Savelkoul noted that he had to report to a host of other agencies, including the city of Minneapolis.

"You can't get anything done," he said then, at a time when he wanted to literally disband the commission and privatize its functions. "It's like negotiating with your mother. We're always negotiating with the city mothers."[1] Those comments—in a city in which the mayor, the president of the city council, and the council member from the Dome's ward were all women—didn't sit well at city hall.

The Put

By early December, stadium deal discussions, still secretive, still unenlightened by any input from any legislators or citizens, moved to the Twins "contributing" 49 percent of the team to a charitable trust or to selling that share to a public agency. The Pohlads were agreeing to forgo some revenue streams that other teams retain. Concessionaire payments, around-the-stadium development rights, and proceeds from private seat licenses would go to pay for the stadium, rather than solely into the Twins' pockets. Private-seat licenses are onetime payments by fans to, essentially, own a seat at the new stadium forever. It's sort of like buying the seat as a condominium. Then a fan must continue to buy the annual season ticket to ensure his or her retention of the seat license. In most instances, the license can be sold on the open market whenever a fan wants to cash in; the assumption is that the value of the seat—like the value of a franchise—will increase. At this point, the Pohlads offered only $10 million in cash to help build the ballpark in exchange for a percentage of public ownership in the proposed stadium. As Welle noted in a handwritten marking on the Twins' December 1, 1996, proposal, the $10 million Pohlad investment could easily be covered by the fees a corporation might pay to get the stadium naming rights. In effect, the Pohlads would be using other people's money to cover their costs.

In mid-December, with nothing substantial on the table that satisfied anyone, tensions rose. The talks exploded during a meeting at the state capitol in a tiny conference room in the basement. The room, generally used by Anderson and his staff, was suffocating as the legislative session stood barely three weeks away. In what a handful of participants call the "defining moment" of their negotiations, the Pohlads said they simply weren't willing to give the kind of up-front cash that Savelkoul felt was necessary to sell the legislature and the public.

"You know, I don't need this if I can't move this along," a frustrated Savelkoul said to Jim Pohlad. "I'll just go back to practicing law in Albert Lea. Life is too short." Jim Pohlad, the quiet son, a banker and accountant with the softest heart of the Pohlads, looked at Savelkoul and snapped, "To be honest with you, we don't need this, either."

That jolted both sides awake. They realized how close they all were to giving up. They began to rethink ways to get what each side wanted: the state wanted cash, the Pohlads wanted their investment in the team back. The Pohlads claimed they would be "made whole" for their investment in the Twins with $85 million. Because of the interest Pohlad was paying on his $105 million debt, he had been able to write off more than $20 million in interest payments over time. Thus his "net after-tax" investment in the team was $85 million. He wanted it back.

The lobbyists had known months earlier that recouping Pohlad with public dollars wasn't going to fly politically. But Savelkoul needed to make his deal. Jim Pohlad brought forward a concept, and out of that tense impasse, the seeds of defeat from the public and for a ballpark in 1997 were planted.

On December 16, soon after that blunt exchange, Welle reduced Pohlad's concept to paper. He sent a memo to Savelkoul and Anderson suggesting a "possible 'put' concept for discussion." A "put" is a business term that means the owner of a contract or an asset has the right to sell it for a specified price to another party who guarantees he will buy it.[2] What the public's representatives were offering was this: whatever the Pohlads had invested in their team would be guaranteed to go back to them when they sold the team. Plus, whatever the Pohlads gave to stadium construction would also be guaranteed to be returned to the family. Pro sports in Minnesota had come to that: the team was lending money to the state, not the other way around. Pohlad had that much money, and the banker in him was that instinctive: when in doubt, lend—and seek a guaranteed rate of return.

History should record that at that moment, the toothpaste was out of the tube and could not be pushed back in. From that moment on, the Pohlads realized that they could get what they had long sought: all their money invested in the team back, plus anything they "contributed" to the stadium, plus—if they played their cards right—interest on the money they'd invested. In fact, the more they put in at the start of the deal, the more they were guaranteed at the back end.

Four days later, the Pohlads responded. And again, the word "contribution" is used liberally. It is used accurately because no longer are any of the Pohlads' money inputs true investments. Investments suggest risk and a hoped-for market rate of return. In this case, the Pohlads were merely "contributing" money to the project that they knew they'd be getting back at the end of the process. Everyone involved knew this. The team owner was in essence subsidizing, in the short-term, the state's effort to build a stadium. Things were being turned on their heads.

In reading and trying to decipher the various models and exhibits faxed back and forth from Starkey to Welle and on to Anderson and Savelkoul, even the untrained eye can tell that the more the Pohlads were asked to put in at the front end of the deal, the more they were assured of getting at the back end. That is, once this framework of a deal was fully explained to the public, the Pohlads were going to be guaranteed somewhere between $166 million and $251 million, depending on which financial model was used. Whether they actually invested that amount, whether they actually deserved it, whether all the numbers truly added up, the political reality should have been clear to anyone with, as Governor Carlson liked to say, "an IQ approaching room temperature." Why would the legislature agree to pay billionaire Pohlad a potential quarter of a billion dollars just to preserve baseball? What could they have been thinking?

The major benefit anticipated in this scheme was that the public—even as it was forced to buy the team and return the team's investment in the stadium—would get something of value. That value was the appreciation of the franchise. That was the gem of the public's victory in this deal.

Rapid-fire adjustments were under way. The 49 percent of the team that the Pohlads were offering to the public was now not to be sold but to be given as "a charitable gift"; there could be tax advantages for Pohlad in taking this course. Savelkoul and Anderson wanted sizable cash up front to show the public that Pohlad was kicking in big-time dough. They wanted $95 million, a number that the Pohlads never expected to provide. Although it was "real money," it was all a ruse, because Pohlad was assured of getting it back in the end anyway. It would look like real money. Bob Pohlad had promised months earlier that the money, unlike Bud Selig's in Milwaukee, wasn't going to be fake. But it was.

As noted in one memo from Welle to Anderson, the put option financing plan "accomplishes" the ability of the public sector to say, "The ballpark financing plan can arguably be described as 'the best in major-league baseball' from the public's viewpoint."

That is, once the team moved into the new stadium and its value increased to, say, $170 million, the public would capture half of that, with Pohlad getting the other half. This was a good thing, a great idea, and should be the wave of the future in all stadium construction. But in the meantime, the public had a series of obligations that were albatrosses around its neck, such as building the stadium and buying the team.

Carl Pohlad wasn't real pleased. The idea of finding $95 million more to invest in this baseball operation wasn't a laughing matter. Known for diversifying his holdings, a $95 million hit would bring his investment in the baseball team toward $200 million, a lot even to a billionaire. "I remember our first meeting with Carl on the amount of cash that he'd have to put in," Bell recalled. "'You mean I've got $105 million in this team, and you want another $95 million?' is what he said. It was kind of like, 'No way.'"

Suddenly and finally, it was 1997, the year the Twins said they had to have a stadium deal in place, and there was none to speak of. Then news leaks appeared in the *St. Paul Pioneer Press*. People within the Carlson administration believe that Forciea was the culprit. Known as someone who often faxed memos to the sports gossip columnists in town—Charley Walters of the *Pioneer Press* and Sid Hartman of the *Star Tribune*—Forciea attended many of the Friday morning meetings at the Pohlads' offices, meetings in which details of the negotiations were kicked around.[3]

On Sunday, January 5, the first leak appeared in Walters column:

> Within two weeks, look for Twins owner Carl Pohlad to make an outdoor stadium contribution offer of approximately $90 million, plus an offer unique to sports of 25 percent of the franchise to the state of Minnesota while guaranteeing against losses. The public would be expected to share in about 25 percent of the Twins' profits, which would seem a given for at least several seasons because of the novelty of a new open-air ballpark. Pohlad's offer also is expected to include a 30-year negotiated guarantee that the Twins will remain in Minnesota.[4]

The next day the two sides exchanged proposals, but there still was no number inserted in the section titled "Cash Contribution (Pohlad Ballpark Investment)." Two days later, Walters had more, under a headline, "Pohlad's Contribution Might Be $95 Million":

> This deal ought to work: Word surfaced Monday that the contribution Twins owner Carl Pohlad plans to make soon toward an outdoor stadium for the Twins could approach $95 million and include a donation to the state of Minnesota of more than one-third of the franchise while ensuring against losses and allowing the public to share in profits.[5]

That day was Tuesday, January 7. It was a big day in the death of the Twins stadium efforts.

The End

It was about 10 A.M., and Savelkoul made an unusual visit to the Pohlads' Minneapolis offices. At the same time, the *Pioneer Press*'s Patrick Sweeney was near to completing his explosive interview in St. Paul with Carlson and Anderson, the one who spilled the beans.

"It almost unraveled again," Savelkoul said of his progressing deal with Pohlad, not knowing that it was actually unraveling ten miles away in Carlson's office, where Anderson was providing the damaging scoop to Sweeney.

Savelkoul learned the Twins were willing to contribute $70 million cash. That just wasn't enough to get the stadium built or the politics pushed through, Savelkoul thought. He was still seeking $95 million in cash, more than all but two other teams—the San Francisco Giants and Detroit Tigers—had pledged in their stadium deals. The Giants deal was the lone totally private stadium finance plan in recent baseball history. The Tigers deal involved related real estate development options for owner Mike Ilitch.

Unable to reach that $95 million figure, Savelkoul returned to the Metrodome, where the Sports Facilities Commission was planning a meeting on the economics of Gophers' football. Typically, Savelkoul informed no one affiliated with his commission about the details of the deal for which the agency was going to take credit or blame. Why tell anyone? Unbeknownst to Savelkoul, Anderson had already let Sweeney know too much.

In talking, Anderson broke a trust with the Twins and triggered an avalanche that created a public relations disaster. The horrific public relations, however, were wrapped in the deception that would unfold over the next thirty-six hours and that would be exposed, again by Sweeney, by the next Sunday. Within five days, the Twins stadium plan, born with such optimism and creativity, was killed by a critical mass of outlandish arrogance, purposeful omissions, and wild misstatements. Within two weeks, controversy would swirl so violently around the announced stadium plan that it would never recover. What would follow for the next eleven months was mere theater. The ballpark effort would never be the same. The death of credibility is the death of any public deal. That deal keeled over when Anderson spoke. Not because of what he said, but because of how the Twins and Savelkoul eventually reacted to his revelations in the

Pioneer Press. Mostly, the death of credibility arrived because none of the key players in the developing deal told the whole truth. The deal was politically unacceptable. The deal was economically incomprehensible to the citizens and too economically clear to those in the business world who automatically understood the deal was inherently favorable to Pohlad. Sure, the deal had some unique benefits for the state. But it had rock solid guarantees to Pohlad. What's worse, the deal wasn't complete. No one knew where it would finally take the negotiators. When Anderson spoke, when Sweeney wrote, when Savelkoul and the Twins reacted, the hope for a stadium—already dogged by legitimate opposition—fizzled into the stratosphere like a kid's deflated balloon.

"It was a huge break in our favor," is how Phil Krinkie, the inveterate critic remembers the moment. It was the ultimate disaster for the stadium supporters.

What Anderson told Sweeney was that a deal had been taken to the Pohlads and that they had "agreed in principle" to it, that the Pohlads would make what Sweeney called "a significant investment—perhaps more than $95 million.... The deal also calls for the Twins to transfer a minority interest in the team to some sort of public-ownership plan."[6] Anderson also told Sweeney that the state would have the right to find new owners for the team if and when the Pohlads decided to sell. "The agreement would spell out a mechanism for setting the price," Sweeney wrote, without any mention of the word "put."

But, Sweeney wrote, "Anderson said the amount the Pohlads would invest up-front is linked to the amount they might expect to sell their [team] share for if they invoked the agreement's buyout clause. That is one of the key areas where the negotiations were continuing, according to Anderson.... Anderson said he was trying to write a buyout clause for the Twins that would protect the public's stadium investment even if the baseball franchise declined in value."

Already, the team and the stadium were getting mixed together and, to a certain extent, confused in Sweeney's story and in Anderson's mind. Because while Anderson told Sweeney that he was trying to devise protection for the public in the buyout of the franchise, he also told Sweeney, "We have asked [the Pohlads] to put a substantial amount of cash on the table that is not generated out of the revenue-stream money." That is, Anderson was saying that the Pohlads would give cash to the stadium construction project. What he failed to tell Sweeney then was that this "substantial amount of cash" would be returned as part of this still-developing buyout. What Anderson didn't say then and what no one in authority said on that crucial day or the next critical day was that whatever Pohlad had put into the Twins, he was guaranteed to get back. He wouldn't get the potential benefit of selling the team to an out-of-town owner and receive the windfall that a relocation could bring him. No, he wouldn't maximize his profits. But Carl Pohlad wasn't going to take any losses.

That concept—no losses for Carl—wasn't honestly revealed at a time when honesty should have been the only policy.

As soon as Sweeney got all this down from Anderson, he told his editors. *Pioneer Press* sports columnist Tom Powers contacted Jerry Bell while Sweeney ran over to the Metrodome to find Savelkoul. Neither Bell nor Savelkoul would confirm for Powers or Sweeney any of the details that Anderson had supplied Sweeney.

But Savelkoul, always keeping facts to himself, didn't tell Sweeney another thing. As soon as he was done avoiding Sweeney's questions, but with the deal simply too close not to reach an agreement, Savelkoul, in his spartan, windowless Dome office, telephoned Pohlad in his regal office overlooking downtown Minneapolis just ten city blocks away. Savelkoul wanted one more chance to get Pohlad's up-front stadium cash layout as close to $100 million as possible.

"Carl, it comes down to whether you get an additional $20 million loan or we get a loan," Savelkoul told Pohlad. He meant one side was going to have to borrow money to fill the gap. Savelkoul wanted $95 million from Pohlad. Pohlad was willing to put in $70 million. Even a billionaire has to borrow that sort of dough. Savelkoul preferred that Pohlad borrow the money to make it look as if the banker were taking more of risk. "We have to be careful not to let our egos get in the way," Savelkoul remembers telling Pohlad. Pohlad, who sincerely liked and even trusted Savelkoul, listened and invited Savelkoul back to his office, with the photos of his grandchildren and his wife, Eloise, and the Twins mementos and some model airplanes, souvenirs from his stints on various airline boards of directors.

It was now about 5 P.M. Night was falling outside the wide picture windows. Savelkoul remembers thinking, "At this point, with the size of the issue, it can't be a matter of who's going to win this struggle." Pohlad agreed. In an agreement that would eventually lead to nothing, the two men split the difference, with the $95 million and the $70 million becoming $82.5 million. That's how much Pohlad would give. It was approaching 6:30 P.M. "I think we just said, 'Let's do it,'" Savelkoul remembered.

The pieces were falling into place. Pohlad's cash was set. The put concept was agreed to, if not the key details. The "public ownership" plank was solid, if there was uncertainty about how the state was going to get its money out of the stock. They agreed that they needed a couple of days before making it all public.

"You had to understand the deal," Carl Pohlad said, in explaining why he wanted a few days to prepare for an announcement. "It was a deal that could be easily enough misconstrued. We wanted to make a joint press release with full disclosure of every detail. But, shit, before I got home that night, it seemed people knew about it."

Savelkoul had a terrible cold. He worried Pohlad would catch it, so they refrained from the traditional deal-making handshake. Joined by Jim and Bob Pohlad, they walked out to the elevator. Nothing was fully written down. No other members of the negotiating teams or public relations teams knew of the deal. There was much work to do ... they thought. On that, they were right. When the sun rose on Wednesday, all hell broke loose. Sweeney had done his job, and no one was prepared to explain it all. Even if it were fully explained, it didn't have a chance. The nation's most complicated stadium deal was dead before arrival.

"You Will Be Defined in the First Forty-Eight Hours"

Of course, there was no deal of any substance. There was only a very tentative agreement among a handful of men who had, unfortunately, insulated themselves from any sense of political or public relations reality. More important than their disconnect from what was going on around them was a simple fact: none of them had any votes in the legislature. Not a one. On January 8, 1997, with the legislative session one day old, the only power the Pohlads held was the power of goodwill and the power to self-destruct. They exercised the latter.

The deal *wasn't* done. Savelkoul was known notoriously to commission staff and consultants as a non–details guy. But he had to know it was more than details that hung in the balance. The deal was so complex that even those in love with it couldn't figure out how to make sense of it. It *was* a proposal, right? Pohlad understood that, right? The legislature still had to weigh in, right?

Well, sure, but Carl Pohlad saw his agreements with Savekoul as more or less final. "We had every indication from Henry and Morrie and the governor that this was the deal that gave some public ownership and had all the qualifications to get it approved," Pohlad said in a December 1998 interview. "It was their deal that they put together that they thought would pass. We made the deal right here in this room," he said, in his Minneapolis conference room. "They gave us every assurance it would pass."

Because of the mating dance they had performed, Carl Pohlad began to assume—quite mistakenly, as it would turn out—that once they'd struck an arrangement with Savelkoul and Anderson, the stadium would be all but built. The political process wasn't Pohlad's kind of process. He was an instinctive businessman but a relative babe in the woods when it came to legislative matters. He was not a salesman. The Twins folks believed they had assurances from Savelkoul and Carlson's office that the legislature would be favorably disposed to a creative stadium plan, that Carlson would take care of the blocking and tackling over at the capitol when it came to getting the necessary votes. "Let the governor handle it," the Pohlads had been told. And they followed directions. Pohlad thought he was dealing with the chief executive and chief operating officers of a potential merger partner, and that Savelkoul and Anderson just had to go back to their board of directors for approval. Wrong. This "board of directors" was 201 elected representatives and senators. Little did the Pohlads know that Carlson's effectiveness with the legislature was generally rotten. Little did the Pohlads know that, politically, they were being hung out to dry. Of course, the Pohlads' lobbying chief, Tom Borman, hadn't adequately prepared Pohlad for the political realities, either. Borman barely knew the realities himself. Pohlad simply wasn't prepared for what was to come.

January 8, 1997, was a day that will live in infamy in Minnesota pro sports history. "TWINS, CARLSON DEAL NEAR; STADIUM CASH OFFERED IN PART-OWNERSHIP PLAN," the *Pioneer Press* headline screamed. Most of the Pohlad family didn't even see the story before the phones started ringing all over town. Living in the western Minneapolis suburbs, they didn't receive the St. Paul–based newspaper. But John Himle, one of their consultants and Minnesota Wins polling chief, received an early-morning phone call that told him of the story. He immediately drove to his Bloomington office to rework a preliminary news release he had been composing for four days, having been forewarned that the two sides were getting closer. But this sort of unexpected panic wasn't what Himle hoped for. His news release was generic. Himle knew none of the final details as he printed out the release from his computer screen.

For nearly two weeks, Himle urged the Twins management to begin a sequential process of announcing their plans for the stadium. He suggested a series of positive press releases to fill the public consciousness with what Pohlad was prepared to give. Himle suggested that the Twins try to separate themselves from state funding issues and from Carlson so as not to give stadium opponents the opportunity to reject the ballpark plan as Carlson's. Himle also didn't want state funding questions—that is, taxes—to dominate the discussion of what Pohlad was kicking in. Himle had a vision of how to "roll out" the plan: in stages, capped by an unveiling of the model for the ballpark. For weeks, everyone around the Twins and the Carlson administration kept mumbling "rollout." They were thinking as much about the rollout as the proposal itself. Communicating this plan succinctly and wisely was critical to its success. Everyone understood that. Their vision didn't include having to react in a wham-bam way to a partially correct newspaper report.

As he left his office tower on the I-494 strip and headed toward the Pohlads' downtown Minneapolis skyscraper, Himle didn't know anything of "the put." So he held in his hands the seeds of a troublesome document. Written with the sensibilities of someone eager to spin a happy tune, Himle's first draft of a proposed press release began like this: "Minnesota Twins officials announced today that the team will contribute \$_____ million to the cost of a new baseball stadium, give the State of Minnesota a significant ownership stake in the team, sign a long-term lease to remain in Minnesota and make other commitments as part of a comprehensive package related to the construction of a new outdoor baseball stadium in Minnesota."

All it needed was for that blank to be filled in with a number that would impress legislators and the populace. It was a number that Himle didn't know yet. It contained a dirty rotten word: "contribute." The word never changed as the day wore on. Indeed, even after Himle handed the release off to spin engineer Pat Forciea and Twins public relations director Dave St. Peter, the release barely changed. That was a big problem. The boilerplate press release never fully morphed into the honest page of information that was required.

By 10 A.M., Himle, Starkey, Bell, Borman, Forciea, and Jim and Bob Pohlad were trying to make sense of all that happened. How did Sweeney find out, anyway? Even though Anderson was clearly quoted, there were some in the Twins organization who still didn't know until I told them the story in the fall of 1998. As they wondered who told what to whom and why, Starkey and Jim Pohlad began to develop a list of deal points to streamline the discussion. This straightforward accountant's version would go on to accompany the Himle-generated news release. But the two documents were never reconciled. They had different typefaces, different vocabularies, different understandings.

The talk quickly turned to how they should address the endless phone calls from news organizations. Some in the Pohlad clan wisely believed there was nothing to say because the negotiations weren't complete. While it sure felt like a crisis, it truly wasn't. Although Savelkoul and Carl Pohlad had seemed the night before to strike a deal on the exact amount of cash the family would kick in up front, there clearly was no final agreement on the details of the "put." The Pohlad sons, wary of public disclosure, especially felt they just weren't ready to make an announcement.

The Pohlads' instincts were noble. But Himle and Forciea, two experienced media relations professionals, urged the family and Bell to conduct a news conference quickly to gain control of the situation. "The story was out there, and it was not entirely correct," said Himle, who had handled poisoned food scares, environmental spills, and messy litigations in his time. "There were people who were of a view, 'Let's wait, the deal is not fully completed, let's have a deal in hand, and then let's go out and have a news conference.'" But Forciea chimed in, supporting Himle.

"My view," Himle said, "and I take ownership responsibility, was to say, 'Look, you can't wait. Major elements of this deal are out there. You will be defined in the first forty-eight hours of this story, and after that it is extraordinarily difficult to correct bad information and misperceptions.'" Never have truer words been spoken.

Meanwhile, in St. Paul

Even as the Pohlads and their aides struggled with the moment and their explanations, Governor Carlson, Anderson, and legislative leaders met at the governor's residence on Summit Avenue in St. Paul. It was a regularly scheduled breakfast to get the legislative session off on the right foot, with Senate majority leader Roger Moe, Senate minority leader Dean Johnson, Speaker of the House Phil Carruthers and House minority leader Steve Sviggum, and some of their aides. As the gathering began at 8:30 A.M. in the dining room, there was little talk of ballpark politics—welfare and education issues were going to be hot items in the 1997 session. Moe remembers the *Pioneer Press* story being discussed, that it sounded "all right, but we needed to know more." Intermittently, Anderson excused himself to talk with Bell, who was moving in and out of his frenetic meetings in Minneapolis.

Anderson didn't mince his words with Bell. There was no deal. There should be no news conference. Anderson wouldn't participate in the news conference and he would discourage Savelkoul from participating. They had to get back to the negotiating table and work out the unfinished issues, especially "the put" and its real implications. Anderson told Savelkoul, who was in Albert Lea at his law office, the same thing. As they spoke, Savelkoul informed Anderson that he and Pohlad had worked out some final dollar figures Tuesday night. Still, Anderson resisted, and he went a step further.

At about 11 A.M., when Bell told him that the decision had been made that the Twins would conduct a 3 P.M. news conference, Anderson asked the governor and legislative leaders to take a break from their breakfast table and move into the nearby library. There, Anderson told the truth, as he knew it, about the deal.

"I told them, 'You're going to hear an announcement from the Twins today and it's going to have an eighty-some million dollar figure, and I'm going to tell you that I don't think that's a fair assessment of what they're doing. I want you to understand that I have not signed off on behalf of the governor on that deal,'" Anderson said.

Bernie Omann, who was then the governor's chief lobbyist and soon to succeed Anderson as chief of staff, remembers the same library gathering, but a bit differently. Omann said that as Anderson began explaining the deal, Vic Moore, Moe's chief lieutenant, quickly started asking pointed questions about the deal. Senator Johnson remembers starting with Anderson talking about a $100 million investment from the Pohlads, and then, as Moore kept asking, the dollar amount kept melting. "We started picking it apart," Moore remembered. "And Morrie kept saying, 'Well, if you net this out and you net that out . . .'"

"Was this a loan? Was it to Pohlad? Was it to the state? Was this a contribution, like charity? What was this?" Senator Johnson remembers people asking. "No one had an answer."

The first knowledgeable focus group—the state's legislative leaders—was having problems with the deal. This wasn't a good sign. As the most sophisticated political citizens in the state "netted out" the deal verbally, using Anderson's understanding of it, they went darn close to zero on the exact amount that Pohlad was giving out of his own pocket. Omann remembers Anderson saying it was more like "thirty-some million" that Pohlad would put in. Whatever the possibilities, whatever the numbers, however Anderson calculated them, Moore said he and others had enough of an answer to understand the deal was "funny money. The immediate reaction of the leadership and of Governor Carlson was that 'this is not going to fly, and don't announce it,'" Moore said.

"The general consensus was they shouldn't be doing this, they shouldn't be going public with this," said Moe. "But how do we spin it for the media? What's going to be our response? We'd try to put a happy face on something that we didn't expect to happen. And we certainly didn't know anything about a loan."

Another member of the group remembers a visibly upset Carlson ordering Anderson, "Don't [announce] it unless you're absolutely sure!" But it was out of Anderson's hands. The Twins were moving forward with their announcement.

A disaster was in the works. Four hours before their news conference to explain to the state's taxpayers a proposal on which a new stadium would rest, their plan was already tainted in the minds of the leading legislators. Before the public heard the first syllable, the Twins' credibility was in doubt with the state's most important decision makers. Save for Moe, the leadership had all been left out in the cold during the months of negotiations, and Moe had been told very little anyway. Now, in essence, in their first full briefing on the stadium plan, they were told that the Twins were about to announce a sham.

No matter what Anderson's or Carlson's view, there was a rationale to holding the news conference. The Twins' point of view, mostly fashioned by Himle, was that they didn't want the government parts of a ballpark deal to overshadow the private planks. There was a feeling that a unified announcement that included the Pohlads' piece and the state's piece would tend toward a discussion—and news reports—of which tax would be used to fund the ballpark. In the ideal, the Twins would trot out their financial "contribution" first. If there would be a joint announcement, Carlson would be forced to declare how he was going to pay for the state's $250 million (or more) chunk. To delay an announcement on this first day would be to push the conversation to taxes and not to all the private "cash" that Pohlad was allegedly prepared to give.

Still, in the governor's residence there was bafflement. Why would the Twins move forward before a deal was done? It seemed, said Senator Dean Johnson, as if the Twins were simply "throwing mud on the wall to see what sticks." Nothing stuck except charges of dirty dealing.

Put Aside the Put

As the clock headed toward noon back in the Minneapolis skyscraper, the Twins officials' discussions turned to the nitty-gritty: "the put." It was complicated, it was incomplete, and the word didn't even sound good. "Even to put the word 'put' out there was going to be difficult," said one man in the room. "It wasn't just the word, you know, to put it to the public. There was a feeling that no one would have understood it."

The fact that no one was going to understand it should have been warning enough to Twins officials—especially lead lobbyist Borman—that it wasn't going to be received well at the capitol or among the electorate. A leading legislator, Representative Loren Jennings, who would go on to become one of the Twins biggest backers, said afterward, "If a fourth grader can't understand it, it won't pass over here." This Twins deal was not the stuff for fourth graders. It was the stuff for high-level financial experts. "If you're explainin'," said Sports Facilities Commission executive director Bill Lester, "you ain't gainin'."

Twins officials weren't confident that Anderson understood the arrangement enough to even explain it. Savelkoul got the concepts, but according to two people in the know, he never studied the specific numbers and potential costs to the state. Every Twins official was convinced that Borman, their chief representative to the legislature, didn't know how the put worked. Himle doesn't seem to have gotten it, either, even if others in that conference room on January 8 are adamant that everyone in there was told of the put.

Its meaning was clear. The Pohlads would give the state $82.5 million in cash to help fund stadium construction. After some still underdetermined period of time, if the Pohlads wanted to sell the team, the state would be *required* to pay back the $82.5 million of construction-directed cash *plus* the investment the family had in the team, which was, after all the tax benefits, another $85 million or so. So whenever the Pohlads wanted to "put" the team to the state, the state *had* to take it and, generally speaking, pay the Pohlads upward of $160 million.

In exchange for owning that put, the Pohlads would "give" the state a 49 percent interest in the team, along with its 49 percent of projected profits in the new ballpark and an undetermined percentage of the franchise's appreciated value if and when the team was sold. The Pohlads, of course, would hope to maximize their tax benefits from this "gift," but conceivably, that "contribution" of 49 percent of the franchise could be worth as much as $60 to $75 million to the state. That's because the value of the Twins franchise would increase from about $90 million in the Dome to about $150 million, or more, in a new ballpark. In essence, Savelkoul and Anderson believed that when the team was eventually sold to a new owner, the state could take its 49 percent, sell it to the new owner or others, and garner close to enough money to pay off the $82.5 million stadium cash that the Pohlads had kicked in. Assuming the valuations of baseball teams kept rising, as they had been, the portion of the put that guaranteed Pohlad his $85 million investment in the franchise could be covered by the new private owner's purchase price.

Still, there was one other little thing we have to mention: the state had to find a way to fund the rest of a $350 million stadium. This was the critical issue from the beginning of this process to its end. Under this deal, Pohlad's up-front $82.5 million would reduce the state's need to raise money, but somewhere, somehow, another $267.5 million had to be raised with public funds for a spanking new retractable-roof stadium. That's what Pohlad believed he had agreed to when the Sweeney story hit.

From Starkey to Savelkoul, from Anderson to Bell, they will still argue to this day it was good for the citizens and good for the Pohlads, that it was a win-win. For sure, they still all say, no matter how complex, it's a deal in which the team owner offered more than most team owners have ever given, save for the fully privately funded facilities.

On the other hand, Pohlad was getting his cake, eating it too, and not paying—in the end—a dime. In 1996 he said he was willing to sell the Twins for $85 million. That's an asset, by the way, for which he had paid $36 million twelve years earlier. That $85 million figure included much of his interest for borrowing money. Most businesspeople note that adding in his interest costs and operating losses doesn't equal the value or worth of a property. It may all add up to a hoped-for recovery price, but not real worth. Now, under this put arrangement, he was guaranteed getting all of his investments back. And if the stadium that the public was mostly paying for was successful, Pohlad could retain his 51 percent ownership of the team and see his share of the enterprise continue to grow in value. It was sweet. As one local business leader put it in the crudest of male images: "It was like Carl was getting his foreskin back."

The major way that the state won was by blocking the team from moving—assuming that Pohlad had the guts to move and a place to go— and by capturing the value of that 49 percent of the team on the local market, if and when Pohlad wanted to sell.

Bottom line: this deal required hours of explanation, with charts and graphs. Even if it were completely positive for the state's taxpayers, it would have been difficult to sell. What made matters worse was the inherent insular nature and code-word character of the Pohlads and their associates. They spoke in language that average people don't. This is one of the reasons Anderson and Savelkoul got along so well with them. "Time value of money," and "above the line or below the line" were terms tossed around by these men as frequently as most Minnesotans might say, "Pass the butter," or "Hot enough for you?"

Let's take, for instance, that notion of being "made whole." In Pohlad's world that doesn't mean "Here, I give you a dollar, you give me back a dollar." It means "I give you a dollar, and then, over the next three years, I take into account how I could have used that dollar, or how much

I've spent to borrow a substitute dollar, and I tell you I could have earned a 7 percent rate of return, compounded, because of the time value of money. Therefore, you owe me $1.50, depending on the tax implications of the transaction." That's what the Pohlads mean when they say "made whole." Their financial adviser Bob Starkey has called it "the economic equivalent of breakeven." But to most people, it means more than whole or breakeven. It's whole, with interest. It's even, with a rate of return. It's not how folks see the world or talk to each other.

So when on this hyper, angst-ridden day, people were asked about "cash" and "contribution," they answered it in their way. According to people who were in that thirty-eighth-floor conference room, Himle asked two pointed questions that would become the key questions for legislators and the public. After months of meetings with lobbyists and hours of sessions with focus groups, Himle asked the Pohlads and their aides: "Is this cash?" and "Is this a contribution?" Twice, he was told by Pohlad financial aides: "Yes."

If Himle didn't understand the put, he should have. As a former legislator and top public policy consultant, such a concept was not beyond his ken. It was a confusing day, and he and others were moving in and out of side meetings. But Himle assumed that the Pohlads were listening to Borman, who had been repeatedly told by the lobbyists under him: cash on the barrelhead was going to influence the legislature, nothing more or less. "Don't get too cute" was the message coming from the key capitol consultants.

Still, Himle left the Dain Tower believing that the Pohlad cash was "nonrecoverable," that it was a typical investment by a businessman who was hoping he'd get some rate of return on his investment, but certainly no guarantee that he'd see his entire investment come back, and promised so by the legislature. Others in the Twins meetings that morning claim that Himle was "fully informed." But Himle, whose credibility among legislators is very high, left the Pohlad bunker for another appointment he couldn't break, thinking that the $82.5 million piece was what other typical Minnesotans would think it was: money that Pohlad would invest in the stadium in hopes of getting it back the old-fashioned way; he'd earn it via stadium and team profits. Himle left behind the foundation of the news release he had written three days earlier in preparation for the hoped-for orchestrated announcement. He assumed detailed changes would be made to his release. He didn't meet up with the issue again until minutes before 3 P.M., when the news conference was set to begin in the basement of the Dome.

But there was another conversation that occurred at the Pohlad Companies that morning. Here's where Forciea's point of view took over. Once an investment banker, he understood the concept of the put. He had been aware that it was being discussed for a number of weeks as he sat in on regular Friday morning meetings on the stadium issue in that same conference room. As the men kicked around how complicated their deal was, Forciea came up with the comment that rings in the minds of a number of Twins officials, most of whom had limited public relations sense. It was Forciea's advice that sank the Twins' ship.

Forciea understood that Pohlad was essentially lending money to the state to help build the stadium. Others in the Twins organization object to the reference of the put as a loan. The two are different. A loan, they say, suggests there is a coupon book, and every month, as with a mortgage or car payment, the borrower sends a check to the lender. That's not what was being negotiated here. Only at the end of this process, when the Pohlads "put" the team to the state, would there be a required repayment.

To those in the room, the opportunity to believe that they didn't have to explain everything—or that they could at least obfuscate it—came from Forciea. Rightly seeing that the whole mess was far too highfalutin for any nonspecialist to comprehend, Forciea asked the men in the conference room: "How am I going to tell somebody on the Iron Range what a put is?" With those words, he specifically discouraged Bell, Starkey, and the Pohlads from even mentioning the concept at the upcoming news conference. Besides, if the put were raised at the news conference, the up-front "contribution" of $82.5 million would be exposed for what it was: the temporary lending of Pohlad money to the state for a guaranteed payback at the end of the deal. When there were questions from others in the Pohlad conference room about not being fully forthcoming, Forciea added, according to participants in the meeting, "Don't worry. The whole concept will be fully looked at when it gets to the [legislative] committees anyway." Little did anyone know the deal would never get that far.

Borman's view is more benign and practical. "You make a decision what you can fit into one page," he said, in defending their limited announcement. "Political campaigns and media consultants do that all the time. We were fighting a deadline. We were trying to get ready for a three o'clock press conference. We had been ambushed by Morrie Anderson. A judgment was made collectively by that group as to what needed to go in and to even what you could expect people to absorb in a press conference. If we had put down every detail of that plan, the release would have been fifteen pages long. And there was another problem. That is [the deal] wasn't done." Big problem. Major problem. There were still too many moving parts in a deal built on odd bits and difficult pieces.

As they talked about how to explain the put or how to dress it up, Starkey and others solidified language for an additional document that would accompany the press release that Himle wrote. It was more or less a derivative of the deal points that Starkey and Jim Pohlad worked on earlier in the day. They wound up making "the put" the final item on a one-page, five-part synopsis. And they wound up gingerly explaining it.

It read: "In the event the Pohlad family desires to sell their interest in the Twins and the ballpark, they will agree to sell their ownership to the Public." That was the benign recognition of the put. It didn't say the public would be forced to buy. It didn't say the price could soar toward $200 million. It didn't explain that the $82.5 million "in cash" that Pohlad was "contributing" would be coming back to him as part of this arrangement. It didn't call it "a put" to signal its existence to the more sophisticated business people in the community.

More important—and to their detriment—the news release didn't positively point out that the public could benefit from the arrangement by pocketing much of the net income from a sale of the franchise.

In hindsight, it looks like a plot. At the moment of its conception, Starkey, Bell, Borman, and Bob and Carl Pohlad say there was no intention to deceive. But at its birth, the way they—and Savelkoul—explained the deal was deceptive. It was a crime of omission. The consequence was deceitful. "The conspiracy theory would be romantic," said Forciea, "but that's not what it was. It makes no sense to not put out there the totality of the whole package." But that's what they did. They put out nonsense, or rather, they decided not to put out the whole truth. As U.S. Supreme Court Justice Clarence Thomas wrote in a famous Minnesota-bred insider trading case, "Non-disclosure where there is a pre-existing duty to disclose satisfies our definitions of fraud and deceit."[7] The jury of the citizenry—most decidedly not peers of the Pohlads—would find the team owner guilty. In a sense, Forciea the Spin Doctor committed malpractice.

The Next Mistake

Soon after noon, they all prepared to reconnoiter at the Dome. But Borman first traveled, through a falling snow, to St. Paul to meet with an army of lobbyists to discuss with them the details of the deal . . . as well as he understood them. In the offices of Twins lobbyist Ross Kramer, in the League of Cities building kitty-corner from the capitol, a meeting ensued. Matters turned worse. There is nothing so rotten as misinforming a lobbyist who is about to promote an idea to legislators when the idea might cost the taxpayers $300 million. Professional lobbyists don't have one client, but many. Ideally, for many years. On January 8, 1997, the Twins had some of the most respected lobbyists in the state on their payroll, including John Apitz, who has close ties to St. Paul Mayor Coleman; former Minneapolis mayor Al Hofstede; Tom Kelm, formerly Governor Wendell Anderson's chief of staff; John Knapp, former leader of the Minnesota Governmental Relations Council, the lobbyists' trade organization; Andy Kozak, a veteran lobbyist who was key to the successful Target Center buyout; airline pilot and Vietnam War veteran Kramer, considered the most powerful lobbyist in the state; Robert Renner, former top aide to Governor Al Quie; and Maureen Shaver, the noted Republican political consultant. For all the criticism that Borman received in and out of the Twins organization, he had assembled a stellar crew of lobbyists. Most never got a chance to talk directly to the Pohlads. Most thought Borman was a hindrance, not a help. But still, this was an impressive team seemingly poised to earn its money by lobbying for, they hoped, a salable deal.

So when Borman started explaining the proposal and the upcoming news conference, the lobbyists listened knowing that they would soon have to go on sales calls around the capitol and State Office Building to oil up the receptivity for the proposal. The original plan was to advise legislators before anything hit the newspaper. But Anderson's revelations to Sweeney had altered that neat dream. Now the lobbyists wanted to quickly hit some key lawmakers even before the upcoming news conference, to provide their view of how good a deal this was. Having been kept in the dark about the details, many expressed enthusiasm and surprise at how much money the Pohlads seemed to be throwing at the plan. Wow, they thought, Carl really moved on this. But the lobbyists, masters at understanding legislative language and in anticipating questions from legislators, began to press Borman, as Vic Moore had pressed Morrie Anderson hours earlier at the governor's residence. And according to two witnesses, Shaver, the rail-thin, dark-haired lone woman lobbyist in the bunch, pointed to the term sheet that Starkey had put together and said to Borman, "Tom, this money here, is this cash? Is this a contribution?" She asked virtually the same question that Himle had asked of the Pohlads earlier in the day. "Tom," Shaver asked in her forceful, no-nonsense style, "is this contribution coming out of the Carl and Eloise Pohlad checkbook? Is this coming out of their vault?"

Borman replied, "Yes."

Hmm, they all said. At which point, the army of lobbyists emptied out of Kramer's office and spread like fish in the legislative ocean, finding anyone to whom they could extol the virtues of the soon-to-be-announced deal and the $82.5 million in cash and the 49 percent of the team that Pohlad was "giving away." Everyone was in a good mood.

The News Conference

Even as the cameras were setting up and the radio people were plugging into the sound boxes at the back of the room, Twins public relations director Dave St. Peter was helping make final changes to the release and copying the documents in the team's offices down the long hallway from the news conference site.

Savelkoul was late. He was in Albert Lea and couldn't get up sooner. He didn't arrive at the Dome until moments before the scheduled three o'clock news conference. He wasn't prepared and, typically, didn't focus on the necessary details. And Anderson, his partner, had of course rejected the idea of even participating in the news conference, knowing that the deal wasn't done and that it had serious problems. Anderson drove the nine miles to the Dome, reiterated his opposition to the news conference to Bell and Savelkoul, then sat in the audience of reporters and supporters, biting his lip and his tongue as the show unfolded. Savelkoul admitted he never read the news release.

In retrospect, this news conference could have made a pretty decent *Saturday Night Live* skit. Knowing what we know now, if it hadn't been so botched, it would be comical. Watching it now, it's almost a parody of a breathless, oh-so-important televised news conference—a bombing in a foreign nation? a verdict on a celebrity killer?—complete with the square-jawed, blow-dried anchorman and the edge-of-the-seat expectation and hyperbole that accompanies such choreographed news events.

There on your TV screen beamed Mike Max, the ultimate sports fan–type announcer for Midwest Sports Channel, the Twin Cities regional cable station. Sitting in his downtown Minneapolis studio, just a mile from the Metrodome, soon after 3 P.M., Max stated: "Breaking news from the Minnesota Twins. No, they did not sign a standout left-handed pitcher. Today what they're going to talk about is the proposed new stadium.... How will they build a new stadium? Who will pay for it? Taxpayers have talked about this for some time. It's been a hot topic on radio shows across the dial.... People are not budging with their dollars, and they want to understand how will Carl Pohlad get this done with the least amount of impact to them financially.... Do we have a signal from the Metrodome yet?... OK, we're working on setting up that signal.... Let's join the press conference in progress."[8]

Max, in his blue blazer and silver-gray tie, swiveled on his chair to his right, and behind him there appeared the live shot from the Halsey

Hall Room of the Dome, a large conference room in the basement of the stadium. Live television being what it is, the MSC feed began with St. Peter timidly telling reporters, "We'll have our press kits here momentarily, bear with us. But in the interests of time, we'll turn it over to Henry." So when the speaking began, the documents supposedly summarizing the deal weren't even in the hands of the reporters.

There sat Savelkoul, fresh in from his ninety miles from Albert Lea and, according to some, not totally sure of the deal's details, at a long table in the front of the room, with Bill Pohlad, Bob Pohlad, and Carl Pohlad to his right and Jerry Bell, Jim Pohlad and Bob Starkey to his left. A large Twins logo, directly behind Savelkoul, dominated the room and the TV picture. Savelkoul, who is not the clearest or savviest public speaker, began, and what followed can only be described as a superficial ramble stuffed with a series of facts, some accurate, some absurd.

"This is not a done deal," he said, echoing the words of Anderson, looking here and there, appearing nervous, trying to look as if he were in charge. "This is a major step towards having a new ballpark in this state, but it's not over. It is a creative and innovative solution to a problem that is confronting many states in this country. We aren't ready with the complete package. We have the principles of the deal worked out. . . . We created, we believe, a model for the country. We have created an opportunity for the citizens of this state to benefit from the creativity and the willingness of the Pohlad family to make a major commitment to keep major-league baseball in the state of Minnesota and create for the citizens of this state a new ballpark that will generate revenues for future generations. It will help our schools. It will help the citizens of this state as they go forward with what, I believe, is the most creative and innovative solution to the problem that I have seen. . . . Jerry."

Exactly what Savelkoul meant by all that gibberish only the ages will know. Exactly how this plan was going to help the schools, only the future generations of educational historians will determine. But remember, this was a parody of a bad news conference. "No one's going to understand what we're talking about here," Forciea remembers telling himself as Savelkoul finished his amorphous statement. "You could tell fifteen minutes into it this was not going to point us in the right direction."

The microphone was turned over to Bell, who grayed during the stadium campaign the same way Bill Clinton did during his presidency. Bell began by saying that in all his talks with groups around the state, people supported "a partnership.... What has been negotiated with Mr. Savelkoul and Mr. Anderson is, indeed, a partnership." Yes, they were all in this foxhole together. Bell, a decent man, paused for effect before going on: "The Pohlad contribution will equal one hundred and fifty seven million, five hundred thousand dollars. And it's in three elements. Number one, the cash contribution. The Pohlads would contribute eighty-two million, five hundred thousand dollars in the new ballpark." Element number two came in the form of Pohlad's allegedly forgoing some revenue streams that other owners traditionally have kept, such as the naming rights to the ballpark. In this concept, he and the state would share such revenues. Bell's voice was shaking now, whether out of emotion, showing how much the team would be giving up, or out of the knowledge that he wasn't telling the whole story, we'll never know. "And number three and the most interesting, the Pohlads ... will contribute a 49 percent interest in the Minnesota Twins to the public. The value is in excess of $50 million.... Future franchise appreciation, by and large, is granted to the public under this proposal, under this partnership," he said, reading now from the news release that the reporters were just receiving.

In some ways, Bell buried the lead, a journalistic term denoting the most important fact was placed at the bottom of the news pyramid rather than the top. That is, if and when this team would be sold, the public would get the bulk of the increase in the team's value. It would come, of course, after Pohlad got back every nickel he'd invested in the team, but at least it would come. That is, the owners of the team wouldn't be the only ones benefiting from the public's subsidy of the ballpark. And, by the way, nowhere in the formal presentations by Savelkoul or Bell was there any mention of how much money the public was going to have to "contribute" to this project.

"I personally believe—and I hope I don't get in trouble for saying this—the Pohlads have made a substantial commitment, I think bold and I think unique. And I think Carl would like to say a few words," said Bell, not getting into any trouble at all, and quickly turning the process over to his boss.

On his right was Pohlad, and he spoke as he does with a bit of slur, and with a constant half smile, his gray eyebrows bushy and unruly, tapping the white table with his hands. Typically, Pohlad will break the ice with a joke or anecdote that is difficult to understand, but his stories are always met with politeness because he is an aging billionaire. In this case, Pohlad began to ramble about former Twins star Kirby Puckett being in the back of the room and how Pohlad gave Puckett black wing tips when he named him a vice president after his career-ending eye injury. Only Carl appreciated the relevance of all that as he went into a disorganized verbal meandering that, stealing from Savelkoul, called the plan "innovative. . . . I think this will be used as a model for other plans. I think it's a fair plan. As a matter of fact, I think that it's more than fair," said Pohlad, not defining for whom it was "more than fair."

As he spoke, Himle and Joe Weber of Minnesota Wins sat in the audience and beamed. It would be their job to conduct opinion polls that would move lawmakers. Knowing what they knew then, Himle and Weber were ecstatic. Pohlad was becoming a hero. Life was good. They thought the political process would be nicely greased by such a generous plan.

Anderson watched with unease. Bell, Savelkoul, and the rest waited for the questions from the shocked media, shocked because it sure sounded like Carl was going to part with more of his money than anyone had ever expected.

"Carl, what if the public doesn't buy it?" asked Charley Walters, the *St. Paul Pioneer Press* gossip columnist who had been privy to some of the facts before hand.

Pohlad, hinting that he believed this proposal was very close to looking like what a final piece of legislation would look like, said, "We have every confidence that it's a fair plan and will be accepted."

Eric Eskola, the knowledgeable and politics-wise reporter from WCCO-radio asked a better question: "Where would you like the other $200 million to come from? Will you let the legislature decide, or do you have suggestions?"

Savelkoul, uncertain how to answer, responded with a nonanswer, admitting, "We need to, first of all, understand the principles ourselves," and then promising that the public's part would come from "some voluntary tax source or discretionary tax where people have an opportunity to make a choice [to] keep major-league sports in this market."

Eskola followed up. "The reason I ask, Mr. Savelkoul, is, do you consider this a first offer from the Pohlad family, or is this as far as you plan to go?"

This was a marvelous question because it went to the heart of the flaws in the entire negotiating process. Pohlad and Savelkoul believed that they were striking a deal that was going to be so good it was going to survive virtually unscathed through the rigorous legislative process. Savelkoul admitted as much on January 8, the second day of the legislative session when almost no bill begins and ends looking the same. "I think that in principle, this is a deal. If this isn't acceptable, then I think we've given it our best shot," Savelkoul answered Eskola.

Incredible. Breathtaking. Six guys get together, come to an agreement, go to the public, ask the state for more than $200 million, and say that's as far as they're willing to go. These men had no power other than that granted to them by Governor Carlson. What made the news conference so valuable from a historical point of view is that it reveals a mind-set of victory and celebration on the part of the participants and blindness to the incomprehensibility of the deal. Furthermore, they seemed to declare this the final offer, and yet they didn't even explain what the offer truly was. Not only did they omit the most difficult aspect of the proposal—Pohlad gets all his money back—but Savelkoul misspoke about those "principles" they seemed to have agreed on.

One, in particular, was Pohlad's "gift" of a share in the team. Savelkoul said, "That's what's really unique about this. It's that the Pohlads have not only agreed to make what we call a charitable gift—and incidentally the IRS has already decided in a similar case that a gift, and by that I mean a gift to preserve a major-league team in a community, is, in fact, a charitable purpose. They've also given up the future income."

For anyone coming to this proposed deal for the first time, the continuing use of the word "contribution"—and its various contexts—could only have been construed to mean "gift." In this instance, as the details of the deal were presumably flowing out of Savelkoul's mouth, he seemed to be asserting that the entire deal's uniqueness was marked by the "charitable" nature of Pohlad's "contribution." In fact, the Internal Revenue Service had ruled in 1995 that the estate of Kansas City pharmaceutical mogul Ewing Kauffman could donate his Royals baseball team to a foundation and gain the tax benefits accrued to a standard charitable gift.[9] However, only the 49 percent part of the Twins was ever being considered "charitable" by the Pohlads. Plus there remained a question at this stage as to whether Pohlad's "gift" of the team was a quid pro quo for building the stadium. If it was, then there were some doubts as to whether the IRS would approve the scheme; it would be not an act of charity but an act of self-interest. Kauffman's estate received nothing in exchange for its Royals gift. Here, then, Savelkoul, even if he honestly misspoke, was suggesting that the *entire* Pohlad cash "contribution" was a gift. And no one on the dais corrected him.

Finally, in this news conference that was so misinformed, Bell was asked how he could expect any citizen to support any stadium plan using public funding in light of high salaries in baseball, with an average of more than $1 million per player.

"If you can't get past that, this thing is probably dead on arrival," Bell said, presciently analyzing the situation. He said it wouldn't be just the Pohlads or the players who benefit from a new stadium. He said, "You don't need to support the orchestra, you don't need to support the [Minneapolis city-funded] Orpheum Theater, you don't need to support science museums, you don't need to support the Minnesota Twins. We would agree with that. But if you don't do these things, pretty soon it's not the same community. People need to evaluate whether or not the contribution from the Pohlad family and the team is a fair contribution. Then they need to evaluate whether or not what the public is being asked to pay for is also a reasonable and fair contribution to continue the opportunity of having major-league baseball as a family-oriented recreation opportunity for them. If the answer for the question is yes, he'll vote for it. If the answer is no, he'll probably vote against it."

Save for a few more harmless questions and answers, the news conference was over. Sighs of relief were breathed. For a day anyway, the media and the public had been fooled. That may not have been anyone's intent—and in interviews with every key player, that's the heartfelt assertion. But, gosh, there were a whole lot of shenanigans going on at the session where the stadium deal was announced and where it began to die its very quick death.

So it was back to the studio, and there sat square-jawed Mike Max of Midwest Sports Channel. A cheerleader by nature and profession, even Max seemed staggered by the confusion of what he had just seen. "There's lots of creative financing in there," he said. "It's going to be an interesting couple of months." And then he returned his head-scratching viewers to their regularly scheduled programming.

Despite all the poor diction, rotten sentences, and mistruths, Minnesota Wins' Himle thought it had all gone well. He even called Wins figurehead Bob Dayton, who, as he often was during key moments of the stadium struggle, was vacationing in Hawaii. Himle telephoned Dayton five hours away and said, "Bob, we exceeded expectations."

But Bernie Omann knew better. Then Carlson's number two man, he was driving home from the capitol to his house in Sartell, Minnesota, near St. Cloud. Listening to his car radio, he heard the breaking news: "Twins to give $157.5 million." Omann had been in that meeting earlier in the morning when Anderson said the team's real cash investment was closer to $30 million. He nearly swerved off of the highway. "I heard the 100-some million and I said we got a problem here. That's not real."

On the next day, Friday, January 9, the sun came up, and the headlines were big and favorable. No one but a handful of men in Minnesota knew that a deception had been spun on the people of Minnesota. "After pleading with them that this plan should not come out, it got pretty good play," said Vic Moore, Senator Moe's aide. "I called Morrie and said, 'Hey, I was wrong.'"

Devilish details aside, this was no longer a private deal. The public was now fully engaged. The other shoe was soon to drop. It would fall as if from the top of Minneapolis's noted IDS Building skyscraper, directly onto the head of a passerby, knocking him for a loop. The other shoe revealed that the gaggle of deal lovers either covered up, horribly misspoke, or simply got carried away at the news conference.

"I really kick myself for that," Savelkoul said, nearly two years later, nervously fingering the tiny opening of his pop can in his modest Albert Lea office. "I don't know if I'd been out of the intense political life too long or what. I should have picked up on all that we were saying and how it was being perceived. I just mishandled that."

Nearly two years later, sitting in his Mariucci Arena office as assistant athletic director of the University of Minnesota, Forciea was decidedly nondefensive. His lack of defensiveness was disarming. But he didn't deny his role. As is part of his style, he second-guessed, the same way he had jumped ship in the final days of Norm Green's decline and departure.

"I don't know if there was a decision to not talk about [the put], but whatever it was that was going to be put out that day people needed to be able to understand what it is we wanted to do," Forciea said calmly. "And the general public doesn't understand words like 'puts and calls.' They don't for the most part understand investment banking terms. We need to use language where everybody clearly understands what we're talking about."

As for his "Iron Rangers won't get it" comment, Forciea said: "I don't know if it was a comment made to discourage the concept from being explained. I just wanted to make sure we were being open with what we were trying to accomplish here." Open? By suggesting at that critical news conference that Bell, Starkey, and the Pohlads avoid the complexities of the deal, that was being open?

Forciea bobbed and weaved. "That was a mistake to not quickly and easily articulate it," he said. "It's not a complicated concept.... There should have been no hesitation to openly lay out, 'Here's exactly what we're talking about.'" So why hesitate? "I don't remember any magical reason for not putting [the put explanation] in [the news release and news conference]. Regardless of how much information came out on day one, there was going to be a lot of scrutiny. If we learned at the end of day one, if the public isn't understanding this, we're going to have to get all of this out over the next day or or two or three." But why not do it right there and then, at the start? That was, after all, the moment of truth, the first presentation to the public for the most awaited publicly funded infrastructure plan in Minnesota in the past decade. "By not going into details we left ourselves vulnerable, and there was no need or no reason to not get it all out," Forciea said.

The only reason to not get it all out: to hoodwink the public. Yes? "I don't remember any decision that day that there's this one thing to try to keep this from the public," said Forciea, who *recommended* that one big thing not be communicated to the public.

Why?

Morrie Anderson sat in the audience with the gaggle of reporters and knew that something was wrong. But he didn't stand and shout, "You're not telling it all!" Bell and Savelkoul acknowledge they should have clarified their comments but didn't.

"After the press conference, we talked amongst ourselves," Bob Pohlad said. "Why didn't they ask us about this $82 million more? We instantly decided they either were confused by it or totally understood. We didn't really believe that it was going to be the latter. It all happened too fast."

Anderson, while listening to the confusing announcement, came to understand that the Pohlads expected all their money back, and with interest. That is, they wanted their $82.5 million back, and with a profit attached to it. Sitting there amongst the Minicams and the excitement from the media that a "deal was in place," Anderson was thinking to himself, "These folks don't understand that I'm not going to negotiate a number on the back side of this deal that represents a 6 or 7 or 8 percent return for Pohlad. The question in my mind was, 'What the hell are we going to do at the next negotiation session?' Their expectation of it is going to be way off the mark."

Anderson also flashed on the tone of the negotiations. They were, he said, "pretty gentlemanly." When the discussions about the put heated up, "Henry and I probably weren't as firm with them as we could have been or should have been," Anderson said. "We weren't saying, 'Oh shit, that number's no good, don't bring that to us.' It was more, 'We'll take that under advisement and we'll give you a reaction to that.'"

Anderson, the man closest then to Carlson, continues to second-guess himself: He thinks he should have insisted on a meeting with the Pohlads before the news conference to say, "This is bullshit, but I didn't have all the documentation. I wasn't totally sure what they were going to say. I did go into their conference room and talk with Jerry. I said to Henry, 'You have to make sure that the public understand that the back side of this deal is still floating. Until we get the back-end number, nobody can say that they're putting this much cash in or there's all this largesse out there by well-meaning people.'"

Bell denies it, but others think the Twins were pulling a fast one. Knowing that Anderson and Savelkoul might eventually reject the details of the put, the Twins decided to float out the deal, thinking that once it was in the open, the state couldn't pull it back. This theory goes that rushing the news conference was an effort get the best face on a deal that was, at best, half-cooked.

Others are harsher. Paul Thatcher, stadium commissioner and ex-perienced businessman, believes the entire deal and the announcement was "a fraud, sir. A fraud, one for which people should go to jail. They were laughing about that news conference afterwards, I can assure you." Thatcher, it should be noted, owned a prison door company at the time of the January 8 announcement and so had a conflict of interest on just how many criminals entered the nation's jails.

Not Done

When Anderson says the deal wasn't done, he was exercising a sort of understatement that can't even be described. It was miles from comple-tion. On January 13, five days after the ill-fated news conference, David

Welle, Savelkoul's financial consultant, faxed a seven-page letter to Savelkoul and Anderson titled "Discussion of Open Items concerning Current Discussions with the Pohlads."[10] Among the items still unresolved and fully open for discussion were income tax considerations for the Pohlads, the sharing of operating expenses once the new ballpark was built, the interest rates to be used to calculate the so-called put, the risks to the state of the put, how to get a parking ramp built to cover stadium debt service, how to raise the state portion of the stadium's estimated $345 million cost, how to sell the 49 percent the state was going to get, the future of the Metrodome, and whether there should finally be some market research conducted on whether the Twin Cities market would support so-called private seat licenses. So as they entered the legislative arena, the so-called deal was a moving target even among those who believed they had some basis for understanding. That January 8 announcement was, frankly, a joke, and it was getting worse.

As the reporters left the Halsey Hall Room, named after the late Minneapolis sportswriter and sportscaster, they held in their hands a press release for the ages, the one first crafted by Himle, then edited by Forciea, with a fact sheet attached that was written with the help of Jim Pohlad and Starkey. Unlike the spoken words at the news conference, which could be attributed to nervousness and Savlkoul's basic poor public-speaking skill, this written document is a remarkable effort in subterfuge and a monument to parsing.

Fundamentally, the press release didn't lie. Like the rest of the news conference, it simply didn't tell the whole truth or anything close to it. It is a frozen-in-time exhibit reflecting the shortcomings of the news conference. "The Pohlad family announced today that the Minnesota Twins will contribute $157.5 million to the cost of a new baseball ballpark, give the State of Minnesota a significant ownership stake in the team, sign a long-term lease to remain in Minnesota and make other commitments as part of a comprehensive package related to the construction of a new outdoor baseball ballpark in Minnesota," read the first paragraph.

Any typical Minnesotan would read that and assume that the Pohlads would be putting in $157.5 million in cash to help build the stadium and that, someday, when the team and stadium are successful again, the Pohlads would recoup their investment. Not true. As the Pohlads, Starkey, Welle, Savelkoul, and Anderson knew, that $157.5 million included $82.5 million that was guaranteed to come back to the Pohlads. It included $25 million that would be raised by such items as naming rights and concessionaire fees; this was $25 million that was not Pohlad money at all. And finally, the last estimated $50 million piece was the value ascribed to 49 percent of the team that Carl Pohlad would gift to the state and attempt to receive significant tax benefits.

On page 2 of the release, four bullet points are highlighted with the $157.5 million figure used once more and identified as "significantly greater than almost any other team contribution" in major-league stadium construction. (Of course, other teams, while assuming they would get their money back from the enhanced revenues of their new ballpark, weren't assured of getting it back by "putting" their franchise and stadium investment to the public.) At the bottom of the second page is a canned quote from Bell that would cause a fan and taxpayer to chuckle if it weren't so sad. "We view this proposal as the most innovative public-private partnership ever offered in the history of major-league sports and one which can help re-connect Minnesota fans to their team and the excitement of outdoor baseball." Instead, this deal stuck the fork in the relationship between Twins fans and the team.

Almost two years later, I read the release's first sentence to Bob Pohlad. He was sitting in his tidy office, looking toward the southern end of downtown Minneapolis. "The Pohlad family announced today that the Minnesota Twins will contribute $157.5 million to the cost of a new baseball ballpark . . ."

"That doesn't mean you're going to get your money back, does it?" I asked him. Bob Pohlad is the most combative of the boys. "Well, it doesn't mean you're *not*," he said. "That sentence doesn't mean that you are [getting the money back], and it doesn't mean you're not." He was trying to defend himself and his organization. "I can read those words now and know exactly what it's supposed to mean." Then he paused. He perused the release another time. He laughed. "How come President Clinton is coming to mind?" Bob Pohlad asked.

We were talking during December 1998, when Clinton had become the prince of parsing and the king of verbal contortions. In his case, he was confused about what "is" meant, not to mention "sex." In the Pohlads' case, "contribution" and "cash investment" meant something totally different for them than for the large majority of Minnesotans. Whatever the syllables, the truth was the Pohlads were guaranteed to get their Twins equity and debt back, plus interest. To most people, though, "contribute" and "invest" mean give away or take a risk, and not get back all you put in.

In a sense, the flawed announcement was a microcosm, a symbol of the inadequacies of the effort and the players involved. Savelkoul, fast and loose with details and generally detached from the innards of the operations of projects, failed to contribute to the day. Borman, theoretically leading the lobbying effort, seems to have been uninformed. Pohlad, unable to see the political fallout from the omissions, took bad advice from outside consultants. Forciea, who really did nothing of substance to aid the Twins when he was their marketing consultant, did nothing again, except to lead them down an alley of discredit. Starkey, the always competent accountant and baseball finance expert, simply used words that accountants might use for themselves, but with no vetting by a regular human being.

Once again, these men who were determining the future of pro sports in the Twin Cities and the possible payment of up to $300 million in public dollars did their work in isolation. And that's the way it was, and that's what killed the deal. "We were out of touch," said Bob Pohlad. "We were naive. But all through this thing one of the frustrations is that people have believed there is a grand design here, that there was a strategy in place to do everything that happened. And there wasn't. Looking at that from the other side, there should have been *more* of a strategy."

All the participants said that there was no intention to deceive. Carl Pohlad himself is the most vociferous when confronted about the matter, literally banging the long table in his personal conference room. "Why would we deceive anyone?" he asked, his bushy, white eyebrows furrowed in anger. "We knew someone would look through the deal. We'd be silly not to make a disclosure. You can't pull the wool over somebody's eyes." But didn't he try? "We did not. Nothing," he said softly, "is under my control."

Savelkoul, months later, sitting in his Dome office, protested that there was never any intention to pull the wool over anyone's eyes. "There was never any deceit. It was a loan, I always knew it was a loan." But he didn't admit it until pressed. And, apparently, he didn't have time to tell his boss, the governor. Carlson said in a 1998 interview that he either didn't comprehend the put or never knew about it when that first news conference with the "contribution" concept occurred. "It was our understanding that was a contribution," said Arne Carlson. "We somewhere read it was a gift." Like other Minnesotans, the number one citizen was surprised that Pohlad would get back what he was giving. Like the rest of us, the governor was fully confused.

If we can believe that it was all a matter of harmless omission and rushed communications, then we must attribute the botched announcement to monumental and collective incompetence. Clearly, it was an inability to reduce the deal to plain English, or a fear of doing so. One lobbyist who worked closely with the deal said, "At times like this, you need to ask, 'Were they knaves or were they fools?'"

The conclusion can only be that they were a little bit of both, which added up to a lot of self-destruction. Loanne Thrane, who had long ago urged Savelkoul to reach out and bounce ideas off of the public, said the news conference was the end of any chance to get any stadium bill passed. "It just set in people's mind that they can't believe what's coming forward about this. And I really don't believe anything anymore," she said.

The use of the word "contribution" was also practically sacrilegious. Just twenty years earlier, sixty-two companies literally contributed—understanding they'd get nothing in return—a total of $15.6 million to help acquire the land in downtown Minneapolis to build a new domed stadium. The Minneapolis Star and Tribune Company kicked in $5.1 million.[11]

"In this state, 'contribution' means 501-c-3," said John Cowles Jr. the *Star and Tribune*'s former chief executive who led the Metrodome project and watched the Pohlad debacle from afar.[12] Five-oh-one, C-three, is the tax code that applies to charitable gifts. That wasn't what Pohlad was doing. And once the public figured that out—and the business community, too—the Twins stadium effort, so filled with hope in the fall of 1996, was on life support by the end of January 1997.

CHAPTER 9

It Sure Looked Like a Loan
Carl's "Contribution" Hits the Fan

John Himle was wrong. He told Twins officials that perceptions would be internalized by the public within forty-eight hours. In this case, it took ninety-six hours for a year's worth of trouble and worry and creativity to meet its maker. Again at the core of the implosion was Sweeney, the *Pioneer Press* reporter.

On Friday, January 10, Sweeney had been tipped off by a source that there was real risk to the public in the deal. That day, Starkey, Bell, and Jim Pohlad visited the *Pioneer Press* to meet with its editorial board to gain support for the proposed stadium deal. But as Twins officials recall it, early on in the explanation, Sweeney began probing: "Is your contribution really a loan?" And he wouldn't let go of that notion. Starkey, especially, repeatedly stated that the transaction wouldn't include "a loan." Rather, Starkey said, it was "a put," and to call it a loan would be to "cherrypick," that is, to isolate the front end of the deal from the rest of its complexities. Starkey acknowledged that the $82.5 million was not "a traditional equity investment," but he persisted in adamantly denying that it was a loan. A loan, Starkey insisted, would mean that the state would regularly issue payments to the Pohlads. In this case, the payback would come only once the team was sold.

Sweeney and editorial writer D. J. Tice, who also probed, knew they were on to something. By Sunday, Sweeney pushed the deal farther off the table. He didn't use the word "loan" in his front-page story, but he totally kiboshed the notion that the Pohlads' money was "a contribution."

"The $82.5 million in cash that Twins owner Carl Pohlad offered to help build a stadium would not be a contribution, but a virtually risk-free investment Pohlad and his family eventually would get back with some—perhaps modest—interest earnings," Sweeney wrote.[1]

That paragraph—and the implications of its meaning—set off a firestorm. Lobbyists, who had begun to sell the Pohlad "contribution" as a well-meaning gift, were red faced and had to go back to their contacts and apologize. Himle and Weber, leading the Minnesota Wins effort, say they were shocked—as they began to ask more questions—that the "contribution" was going to be returned to Pohlad, with interest.

The next day, Himle angrily confronted a Twins official and asked about the Sweeney story. Himle reminded the official that he was told on Wednesday that it was "cash," that it was "a contribution." Himle was told coolly, "You asked the wrong question." The question, apparently, should have been: "Allowing that this is cash, are you guaranteed to get all of it back?" Himle, like Shaver, didn't ask the unthinkable because the answer would be a bombshell politically: yes, the Pohlads were assured of getting all their money back from a public that already felt it was being mugged by pro sports.

Smeltdown

The *Star Tribune* was about to catch up. To digress, I was on vacation during this period and didn't return to the office until Monday, January 13. I had been doing some reporting from my car as I traveled back from an East Coast vacation with my family. In a story I wrote for the Sunday paper, Anderson told me about "the put," and the *Star Tribune* was the first news organization to report its existence. But no one told me—and I wasn't smart enough to ask—that the payback on "the put" also included Pohlad's cash investment in the stadium. That Sunday, I saw Sweeney's story and immediately called Savelkoul.

"Is that true?" I asked. "Will the Pohlads be assured of getting back their whole investment?"

Savelkoul answered, "Well, yes. Did you think it was a charitable contribution?"

I replied: "Well, Henry, I just got back into town, but that's how everyone understands this thing."

And Savelkoul said: "That's not what it is."

Still, on Monday, no one from the Twins or the governor's office tried to clarify anything. No one called me to correct me on my limited reporting on "the put." No one said, "Jay, the public should know that Pohlad is expecting the state to pay for his team *and* his cash in the stadium." No one called a second news conference to say: "Hey, folks, let's reexplain this." But no one denied Sweeney's story, either. The two largest newspapers in the state, which had followed the matter as closely as possible, were getting out dribs and drabs of the story. The two reporters who'd been as close to the story as anyone, Sweeney and I, needed to piece this mosaic together. And neither of us totally understood it. No one was forthcoming. It didn't feel right.

At the *Star Tribune*, we began to scratch our heads. What was this deal anyway? Had we been lied to? We had to get to the truth. Frankly, I felt uncomfortable. I also felt defeated. Sweeney broke the story of the deal being in place. Then, with his "risk-free investment" story, he'd shown the first lie. I decided I should stay out of the *Star Tribune*'s response. At that point, internally, I remained suspect. Some people believed I had been too soft on Pohlad and not dogged enough. Now Sweeney had new information revealing treachery in the deal. I was asked politely by state editor Dennis McGrath if I wanted some help on the story to find out the details of the deal. I said that someone else, perhaps someone from the newspaper's Business Section, with no relationships with any of the key players, should dive into the deal and flesh it out.

At the same time, editors decided that a Minnesota Poll, the *Star Tribune*'s long-standing and respected statewide poll, should canvass Minnesotans about what we believed the deal was. Meanwhile, the chatter around the capitol and on talk radio was building. What was this deal all about? And why were we all so focused on it? Why did the Twins need a stadium anyway? And how could we turn a ballpark debate into a reasonable discussion at a time when the real statewide conversations should be about welfare reform and the future of our schools? Rask's elevation of "priorities" struck a deep chord.

By January 22, Bell had developed a good case of gallows humor. Appearing on the KSTP-AM radio talk show of the staunchly antitax and antistadium Jason Lewis, Bell asked, "Is this a town meeting or a public hanging?" The entire debate was beginning to turn into a little bit of both. And the coming week was going to get rougher. As early as January 23—just fifteen days after the Twins announced their plan—it became clear that the details of any stadium proposal really didn't matter to the average citizen. The *Star Tribune* and KTCA–Channel 2, the Twin Cities public television station, sponsored an exercise in civic journalism, bringing in a scientifically selected panel of citizens to be briefed about the stadium issue and to reach some conclusions. Bell, Marty, Starkey, Dome director Bill Lester, and Federal Reserve Board economist Art Rolnick, a critic of subsidies, spoke. Only four of the twenty-three citizen panelists came into the day believing that public funding should be used for a stadium. By day's end, the Twins case seemed so weak that one pro-stadium panelist actually changed her mind and decided against the stadium effort. "I grew up thinking of the Twins not as a business, but more as a public entity. But the team isn't," said Deb McNeill, a forty-one-year-old convenience store manager from Northfield. "They are a business. I'm not able to defend public funding. I have nothing to defend it with."[2]

Into that environment of skepticism fell Terry Fiedler's story. Earlier that week, *Star Tribune* business writer Fiedler got Savelkoul, Bell, and Starkey to sit down. On January 25, for the first time in print, the public was told that the Pohlad contribution was "more akin to a loan" than anything else.[3] Although Bell and Starkey objected again to that characterization, Savelkoul himself was quoted as calling it "akin to debt." That is, the state was relying on the Pohlads to front money that would be repaid.

Just as important as the use of the word "loan" for the first time was the reaction to it all from Senator Marty, who capitalized on the general populace's increasing wariness toward the deal. Fiedler quoted Marty as calling the whole arrangement "just plain dishonest. This is not cash at all." Then Marty blasted the Metropolitan Sports Facilities Commission because Savelkoul, its chairman, "the chief negotiator for the public, showed that he wasn't out to get the best deal for the public, but the most salable package. Who's negotiating? Two people on the same side."

Stadium commissioner Loanne Thrane read the Fiedler story, saw the Marty comments, and flipped out. Although she led the commission's intergovernmental relations subcommittee, the agency's liaison to the legislature, Savelkoul hadn't kept her informed at all about the progress of the talks with the Twins. With Carlson as his lone constituent, Savelkoul straight-armed the commission. But now Marty was blaming all its members for failing the public. Reading the newspaper in her immaculate Crocus Hill home near St. Paul's Grand Avenue, Thrane exploded.

"I knew no more about this plan than John Marty," she remembered. "I didn't even know there was a news conference scheduled. I heard it on the radio. No one gave me a heads-up. I'll be damned if I was going to take the blame if I was not part of it. I was just so furious." She quickly began to write a letter to the editor of the *Star Tribune*. As she wrote, she called commission mate Thatcher and commission attorney Kathleen Lamb. After consultations, Thrane attempted to get all of her colleagues to sign the letter. She also called Savelkoul that Sunday and told him of her intentions to expose his secrecy. He politely said that was fine with him. He could already see the walls crumbling anyway.

That morning he and the rest of the state had woken up to the first comprehensive polling of Minnesotans on the Twins deal.[4] The reaction was devastating. Sixty-nine percent of Minnesotans were opposed to the announced deal. Only 43 percent of people who identified themselves as Twins fans applauded the proposal. Eighty percent of those polled said pro sports teams shouldn't get any public dollars. Looming larger for the Twins and their desire for a new ballpark was this somewhat baffling finding: 57 percent ranked the Metrodome as a good or excellent place to watch a baseball game. Even 58 percent of Twins fans said the Dome was OK. And finally, given their druthers, Minnesotans would rather give tax money to the arts than to sports.

The one good sign: 85 percent of Minnesotans said it would be bad for the state if the Twins moved. That final result would be the fact that all Twins and ballpark supporters would continue to live on. If eight in ten Minnesotans felt close to the Twins, there had to be a solution to the stadium dilemma, boosters reasoned.

By the following Tuesday, all six commissioners had signed Thrane's letter, which firmly asserted that no one on the commission had been consulted or involved in any phase of the negotiations and that Savelkoul was working as Carlson's personal agent, not as the chairman of the commission.[5] The Sports Facilities Commission is the agency that, by law, should have been overseeing such a process. But Savelkoul didn't want it to be that way, and certainly the Twins didn't either.

The letter was just the tip of that day's and week's icebergs for this Titanic-like sinking. Alerted to its arrival, I began calling around to the commissioners. Thatcher, of course, had something to say. As offended as Thrane, Thatcher was far more competitive with Savelkoul than anyone else on the commission. Besides, Thrane was a Republican, not a fan of Carlson's, but certainly more likely to publicly tone down her critique of Savelkoul. But Thatcher was an ardent Democrat and felt no compunction in politely slapping Savelkoul or Carlson on their deal-making wrists. "I've asked to see it all and I have been given nothing, always put off. I believe it has become a pattern of conduct to avoid full disclosure to the commission and the public. Why? I can only speculate that [the deal] won't stand the test of the light of the day," Thatcher said.[6]

Thatcher made sure of that. Two days later, Thatcher and Representative Dee Long of Minneapolis, powerful chairperson of the House Tax Committee, both called on Savelkoul to resign. Amid these suggestions, Thatcher uttered undoubtedly the finest and most distinctive quote of the entire stadium debate. Noting all of the confusion around the Twins-Carlson deal and the concern at the capitol, Thatcher said, "The deal is dead as a smelt. All it needs is the benefit of clergy for proper interment." Long chimed in, "Clearly [Savelkoul] is functioning as the governor's representative. Someone needs to be representing the public."[7]

Thatcher seemed to take great joy in confronting Savelkoul. Much of it had to do with Savelkoul's dismissiveness of the commission and, particularly, of Thatcher, who so desperately wanted to be in the middle of the Twins solution, even if the Pohlads didn't want him there, either. There was something else going on, too. Thatcher and Governor Carlson had a long-standing dislike for each other. The governor denies it, and even asked me, straight-faced, in an interview, "Who's Paul Thatcher?" This enmity dated back to their days together at the University of Minnesota when Carlson was still a Democrat. Thatcher, whose presentation to the world can be intimidating and overbearing, apparently shunned the young Arne, treating him like an insignificant fleck, which Thatcher is wont to do. Carlson apparently never forgot that. Now Savelkoul and Carlson were back working together, as they did in the legislature in the late seventies, when Savelkoul was the minority leader and Carlson his assistant minority leader. They would have no time for Thatcher, and he would regularly call them "small-minded." Of course, no matter what the size of their minds, on this first Twins deal, Savelkoul and the governor had blown it royally.

I remember reaching Savelkoul on his car phone as he headed back to Albert Lea on the day Thatcher compared the future of the stadium package to a dead fish. Savelkoul sounded tired and beat up. He knew that Senate minority leader Dean Johnson was already recommending that a new proposal be worked on, that as Thatcher said, this three-week-old disaster was in deep trouble. Savelkoul said he would step aside if the Twins and the governor thought that would help. Carlson and Bell told him to hang in there. Savelkoul, the loyalist, agreed to. But he hadn't been under fire with so much ammunition since his days as the House minority leader. Given all the flak, given all the mistakes, given all the opponents, I wondered, "Henry, do you think you're a little bit rusty on this political stuff?"

"You know, it could be," Savelkoul said, sounding as if he had been thinking about the topic as he drove. This was a man who was used to bringing critical issues into conference committees in the seventies and making deals. He always wondered why the commission's lobbyists couldn't just make all that happen the old-fashioned way. His voice and the cell phone connection started to fade. "Have a good day," he said, as he always did when he completed his conversations, good and bad.

For all the hand-wringing about whether it was a contribution or an investment, by February 9, 1997, even a draft of the formal agreement was referring to the Pohlad's $82.5 million as "a loan." The semantic battle was over. This was being considered a loan, and it would be paid back with interest through the cash flow of the stadium or at the time the Pohlads decided to sell the team.

The Bright Side

There is another way to see the deal. It is a positive way. It is to view it as brilliant and as a starting point for any other stadium deal that should come down the pike in Minnesota or elsewhere. Strip away Pohlad's wealth and his desire to get all of his money back and the arrogance, really, of an individual lending money to the state to pay for a stadium that will serve to preserve his wealth. Shake that off. Try to feel sympathy for a billionaire who is doing something that won't get him as much money as he might be able to get using the money in a diffent transaction. Try to get misty-eyed for a guy who is losing some "opportunity cost" by building a baseball stadium rather than acquiring another bank.

Once you're over those speed bumps, understand the core principle of the deal, one that no community has been able to grab from its sports team owners: a significant portion of equity in a team from the windfall of a new stadium. Let's say this slowly: the team owner was prepared to give the community part ownership in the team in exchange for the community building the stadium. This is a marvelous idea.

In the pro sports debate, the most heinous crime is not that the public subsidizes stadiums with tax dollars. It's been done, and cities survive; citizens wake up the next morning, and life goes on. Sometimes, depending on the amount of the subsidy, it's even worth it—or at least the people in the community believe it's worth it, as in a place such as Nashville, where a completely subsidized arena attracted an NHL team and put the city on the national map, just like Met Stadium did with the Twin Cities.

No, subsidies per se aren't the ultimate crime. The crime is this: the public builds new stadiums for teams, and then the value of those teams increases meteorically. Then the owner for whom the stadium was built has an exit strategy of the highest order. Look at the case of the Texas Rangers baseball team. That franchise, nowhere near as successful as the Twins on the field in the 1980s and early 1990s, was sold in 1998 for $250 million. That amounted to a gain of $164 million for an ownership group that purchased the team in 1989 for $86 million. Among the former owners who enjoyed an unconscionable windfall was the former managing partner of the team, a man named George W. Bush, who went on to become the governor of Texas and a presidential candidate. Bush reportedly invested $600,000, and it grew to $10 million when the team was sold to Dallas investment mogul Tom Hicks.[8]

The reason the value of the team rose so meteorically was that in 1994 the city of Arlington, Texas, used a half-cent sales tax to finance a $191 million stadium. Attendance nearly doubled, ticket prices rose, luxury suites were sold, and the value of broadcasting contracts increased because of the boosted popularity of the team driven by the advent of the new ballpark. Suddenly, at virtually no cost to the owners, they were given a far nicer store from which to conduct their business. Whether you're selling milk, men's clothing, or appliances, a virtually cost-free, state-of-the-art outlet will increase the value of your business and enhance its relationship with your customers. So, too, with selling baseball games and the goodwill attached to franchises.

One thing: while the sales tax payers of Arlington can drive by the new stadium and smile with pride that it's theirs, they have no stake at all in the operating profits of the team, nor did they capture any of the appreciated value of the team when Bush and his pals sold out for a 200 percent profit.

This is why this first Twins deal—negotiated in secrecy, announced mistakenly and arrogantly, but intended to be innovative—should not be tossed into the compost pile of sports history, left to disintegrate into dust. Throughout these talks, Savelkoul's heart was in the right place. And that's why this germ of an idea—for the public to get back a share of the team in exchange for helping to build the team a new facility—must be further explored, particularly by those who are advocates of public or community ownership of teams. The deal, while too complicated, was a brilliant attempt to get everything done that the players in the deal—Savelkoul, the Pohlads, and their consultants—believed was desired by the public.

Indeed, in the fall of 1999, the Vikings renewed their cries for a new stadium. McCombs, the new owner, stated publicly that he was willing to commit 25 percent of the construction costs. Assuming that the stadium, which he hoped would have a retractable roof, would cost $400 million, McCombs committed about $100 million. But that's chicken feed. Why? First of all, the public would have to find $300 million lying around somewhere to make up the difference. And more important, given the astronomical rate of inflation of NFL team values, any new state-of-the-art football stadium could increase the value of his team to $400 to $500 million, twice what he paid for it in 1998. Why should public dollars inflate the value of his franchise without the public getting some of that appreciation back? That's the question that Savelkoul asked and sought to resolve in this original Twins deal. It should be a principle of any public deal in any community: if we, the public, invest in the asset that is the franchise by paying for the building in which the team does business, then we must get a rate of return higher than alleged "economic impact." We must share in the upside of the appreciating franchise if we carry the burden of funding the depreciating asset, the stadium.

All new stadiums instantly increase the value of the franchise that plays in them. In most cases, the team owners alone capture that increased value and either take it to the bank to use as collateral or, eventually, sell the team for its increased value. What Savelkoul was trying to do was strip away Pohlad's so-called "upside" rewards. In exchange, of course, Pohlad wanted no "downside" risk.

Capitol Punishment

It was over but for months of shouting, voting, public opposition, character assassination, the guerrilla warfare by Vikings president Roger Headrick, a referendum in Minneapolis, demonstrations on the capitol steps, and the always changing "deals." Roof on, roof off. Tobacco tax, user fees. Taxes on players' salaries. Taxes on T-shirts. Taxes on Twins broadcasters. Pohlad gifting the whole team. This target wasn't just constantly moving. It had the jitters. "It was like trying to put a picture frame around a bowl of Jell-O," said Representative Dan McElroy—and he was a supporter of the effort.

The irony, of course, was that Pohlad was a businessman known for changing deals at the last minute. As he trudged into the legislative quagmire, he got a dose of his own medicine.

A perfect example was the funding source of choice selected by Carlson and Anderson: a tobacco tax. Given the antitobacco climate in Minnesota and the United States at the time, given that Minnesota was only the eleventh highest tobacco tax state in the nation, and given that it looked like a tax on folks who should otherwise want to kick the habit, it seemed to make a bunch of sense.

"I thought it would be a slam dunk," Anderson said. He and others knew that Carlson was alleged to have had close relationships with the tobacco industry. But Anderson added, "I thought the time was right to hammer the tobacco people. It was a no-brainer for most people."

Besides, legislators and Carlson had already boxed themselves in. Sales taxes, property taxes, a growing state budget surplus, and any general-fund dollars were ruled out-of-bounds even before the legislative session began. In a virulent antitax climate, Republicans didn't want to use *any* tax to fund a ballpark. Democrats wondered why people who weren't using the stadium or benefiting from it should be taxed. Everyone wondered why if a tax was going to be raised, its windfall should go to sports. Besides, it was viewed as a regressive tax, as studies showed that lower-income people were more likely to smoke than any other class of people. The other problem with the tobacco direction was that most of the Twins key, experienced lobbyists had business with the tobacco industry, including lobbyist quarterback Borman, whose law firm represented the pro-smoking Tobacco Institute. Somehow, the man who would be leading the legislative charge for the baseball team didn't have a clue that the governor was going to try to use tobacco to fund the ballpark. So just as the effort to get some kind of funding for the project was about to kick off,

Borman lost four of his heavy-hitting lobbyists who opted to keep their longtime business with the tobacco companies rather than stick with this one-shot clearly nosediving Twins effort. Maureen Shaver, Andy Kozak, Al Hofstede, and Tom Kelm jumped ship. Borman sought, and was granted, permission by both of his conflicting clients to carry on.

Worse than the inconvenience was Borman's inability to envision the tobacco tax coming down the pike. For months, Borman had been advised to try to limit the taxing district to the metropolitan area. Any statewide tax would shake up the troops in the hinterlands, he was told. But Carlson and Anderson never included Borman or Bell in the tax decision. As usual, they did things on their own. And this tobacco tax choice served to undercut the Twins' efforts to have a good relationship with the legislature, and gained nothing. Indeed, use of a tobacco tax lived as a stadium funding option for about as long as "the put" survived. Not very long. That tobacco episode was the start of a never-ending scrum that resulted in nothing but dirtied suits.

"Getting that stadium bill passed was like birthing a porcupine," said McElroy. Sad to say, it was worse than that. The porcupine was still-born. The porcupine was roadkill. Never again could the Carl Pohlad–owned Twins expect to get a publicly built ballpark. Even if the botched announcement and subsequent revelations didn't prove that their intention was to be deceitful, the result was that legislators and the public *believed* they had been deceived. It was Carl Pohlad again, trying to swing a deal that was only in his best interest.

When the matter got to the legislature for the 1997 session, there were innumerable incarnations and stark contradictions. Pohlad's $82.5 million became $15 million and $50 million. The "put" was here and there. McElroy, as smart as any legislator, worked out a thoughtful package of user fees that seemed to generate enough money to pay off a downsized stadium, or at least reduce the cost to the public. He first thought of taxing players' salaries at an increased rate, a method that has since been employed in other communities. Representative Ann Rest, a calm woman but a crazy Twins and baseball fan, looked under every possible rock for ways to pay for a stadium, trying sports memorabilia and souvenirs to tax. Rest sacrificed herself for the cause. Senator Jerry Janezich, a bar owner from the Iron Range, kept trying to get Pohlad to up his cash in the project. The Twins wanted the more biting Senator Steve Novak, of New Hope, to be the lead sponsor, but they lived with Janezich, who didn't seem to have the clout to rally the troops. As much as lobbyists and the governor kept pushing, the stadium matter just wasn't ripe in the spring of 1997. And the juxtaposition of the session's most significant issue, welfare reform, with the session's most notorious issue, the Twins stadium, was enough to make even the most dedicated Republicans—even Savelkoul—shake his head.

One day in March, after a Sports Facilities Commission meeting, he joked about how the mood of the state seemed to be changing. "I think we're making progress. Some of my best friends are for it now," he said, ruefully. We got to talking about the signs and the noise at the capitol around the stadium hearings. Some protesters had burned plastic diapers to express their disgust with "corporate welfare" while poor people still needed more support for child care centers. Citizens of Southeast Asian origins were often in the capitol hallways with protest signs. Some of them were being taken off food stamp rolls. I mentioned all this to Savelkoul and said that the contrasts were inescapable.

What he said surprised me. "You know, it makes me sick," he said. "All these years we've been talking about getting people off of welfare. And now here I am in this position." He meant getting what was being called "corporate welfare" for Pohlad. If Savelkoul saw the problem, then most of Minnesota must have, because there was no way for the stadium supporters to garner any votes. As Anderson, Savelkoul, Bell, Starkey, Rest, and Janezich scrambled to put together a plan that was "salable," they kept running into roadblocks that could be seen miles away. No, make that months away. Thanks to Krinkie, Knight, and Marty, legislators had locked themselves in before the 1996 election. No taxes. No public funding. By March 24, a Senate committee finally "passed" a bill that was a skeleton and a joke. It barely passed, and without any recommendation—a form of pushing something along that has no legs. The bill excluded all funding, with members rejecting even user fees such as player salary taxes, ticket taxes, and special sales taxes on sports memorabilia. That was considered a success.

In the House, a week later, Knight and Krinkie organized their forces for a showdown that was as much symbolic as substantial. Rest, the godmother of stadium backers, chaired the Local Government and Metropolitan Affairs Committee. If a stadium bill couldn't get out of her committee, then it wasn't going to live anywhere. Like the Senate version, it was mostly tied to user fees. It didn't all add up, and the Pohlads' input was set at $50 million, but it became a forum for antitax forces to draw the line. Krinkie called the whole concept "a huge financial risk." Before the session, he and Knight literally took at least one other legislator and stayed with her for four hours so that she wouldn't get lobbied intensely by pro-stadium forces. Carlson personally made phone calls to committee members. The stadium bill, on its first vote in the House, was defeated ten to nine. Krinkie and Knight were joyous. Rest was furious. Anderson, Savelkoul, and Omann, who was twisting arms all day, walked directly up to Krinkie and Knight and threatened: "You're never going to get anything from the governor again."

To which Krinkie wondered: "When did we get it the first time?"

Such a confrontation from the governor's chief lieutenant thrilled these two. But they weren't worth much. Soon after the stadium bill lost on the strength of Knight's and Krinkie's hard labor, the bill was revived and passed as two legislators changed their votes under pressure from the Carlson administration.

McElroy was still hard at work. Not wanting to give up, and convinced that the Twins might leave the state, the Burnsville representative and business consultant had the numerical and fiscal brilliance to come up with a user fee plan that seemed to have merit and seemed even to pique the Twins' curiosity. To understand user fees is to understand the bane of the existence of team owners and the taxes of choice of politicians.

User fees are taxes paid by the people and institutions that use and benefit from a public facility or activity. Hunting licenses are user fees. If you hunt, you pay them. If you're opposed to killing deer, you don't have to pay them. Obviously, some of everyone's taxes goes to keep our wilderness healthy so that deer can run around and get shot, but in theory, our taxes aren't covering the cost of monitoring the hunters or harvesting the deer stock. The user fees pay for most of that.

When it comes to teams, they view user fees as coming out of their bottom line. For instance, if a ticket is to cost $10, but a $2 ticket tax makes the price $12, the Twins want all $12. It's their belief that if the market can bear $12, then the team should pocket all $12. At some point, the user fees may push ticket prices too high, but even if they did, teams, on principle, want to capture all the dollars that fans pay in.

Similarly, under an idea hatched by McElroy, there would have been a surcharge on the income taxes of players. After all, any new stadium would increase the Twins' revenues, and for sure, those revenues would pass through to the players. The concept: tap some of those increased player paychecks with a 3 or 4 percent surcharge over and above what they'd pay in state income taxes. Again, the team and the Major League Baseball Players Association opposed the idea. Why? Bell said it was because it would put the Twins at a disadvantage; free-agent players would decline to play with the Twins because of the higher taxes, or just as critical, the Twins would likely have to pay players 4 percent more to compensate them for the uniquely high taxes.

Still, McElroy, reading the legislative tea leaves and wanting to save the Twins, put together the best piece of work of the 1997 legislative session. He insisted on selling it to the Pohlads. His presentation came "in one of the more remarkable meetings I've ever been to," McElroy said. He made it sitting at Carl and Eloise Pohlad's kitchen table on Sunday, April 13, as the snow was finally melting outside their window on the golf course of Edina's Interlachen Country Club. It was the first time McElroy met Pohlad, and he explained to Bob, Jim, Eloise, and Carl that if they couldn't stomach a user-fee-based finance plan, he was simply going to stop supporting a stadium bill. The Pohlads were in search of friends. They listened.

As he explained his plan, Mrs. Pohlad brought the assembled cookies and cans of pop (no glasses). What McElroy proposed was a series of fees on tickets, player salaries, and Twins-related souvenirs; a special sales tax in the stadium; a Twins-related Minnesota Lottery game; a sur-charge on cars parked around the stadium; and a tax on luxury-suite rentals. McElroy calculated that a typical fan would pay $1.66 more because of the user fees than he or she would have paid otherwise. It was a breakthrough because it fed into a popular need: find a way to fund this darn thing without general taxes. At the very least, it won McElroy a place at any table at which a solution was being discussed.

April Fools'

Spring had sprung. But the stadium effort was headed for the compost pile. Hearings continued. Deals kept getting reworked. But it was all meaningless. Despite attempts at creativity, a stadium bill was heading nowhere fast. It was now popular to be against anything that Carl Pohlad was for, even if he was beginning to be for more reasonable solutions.

In to save the day—theoretically—came Bud Selig, owner of the Milwaukee Brewers and the long-time acting commissioner of baseball, the man who had led the sport into its darkest days of 1994, who canceled the World Series, who didn't demand revenue sharing from his fellow owners, and who behaved in ways completely different from major-league sports' other leaders, such as the NBA's David Stern, the NFL's Paul Tagliabue, and even, for that matter, the NHL's Gary Bettman. Generally, if only for the sake of image, commissioners should side with the fans, the customers. No doubt, we all know that a league commissioner is actually the owners' commissioner. But some, particularly Stern and Tagliabue, develop such personal credibility and grandeur that when they enter a situation and roll up their sleeves there is a sense that they want what is best for the fans in any given market. Stern did that during the Timber-wolves crisis of 1994. In being forceful, he aided the public. As Governor Carlson put it, the state and Sports Facilities Commission didn't have to exercise much patience with Timberwolves owners Marv Wolfenson and Harvey Ratner because "David Stern had none for them either." And Tagliabue—his hands tied by previous and expensive antitrust rulings against the NFL—had to watch as Art Modell coolly moved the NFL Browns from Cleveland, but then sprang into action to get Cleveland a new team. Tagliabue also wisely watched the New England Patriots go through the ridiculous motions of moving to Hartford in 1999, only to come in at the final moments and preserve the team for Boston.

Bud Selig, though—he's another kind of commissioner. Until after the Twins stadium debate fizzled, he was also the president of the Brewers, thus in a position of clear conflict in any matter involving any other team. Second, his level of political sophistication was based not on problem solving but on declaring the obvious and whining. His entire involvement in mediating any successful conclusion in Minnesota was talking constantly on the phone to Pohlad and, sometimes, to a few Minnesota businessmen who were trying to inform Selig that Pohlad was not nearly as popular in the Twin Cities as he was among his fellow owners. Selig was in Pohlad's pocket, which was too bad. Because someone who Pohlad respected had to be constantly infusing him with a sense of reality. Someone had to be pushing Pohlad toward selling his team to a Minnesotan and letting that new Minnesota owner—or owners—take a new approach to rebuilding the Twins en route to building a new ballpark. That someone wasn't Selig, whose visit to the capitol on April 30 was the opening salvo in what Attorney General Hubert Humphrey III would soon determine was a conspiracy to push the Twins out of Minnesota, a conspiracy led by no less than Mr. Selig, the onetime car salesman and inveterate hot dog eater. In essence, Selig would attempt to replicate his own stadium experience: threaten, whine, push, make up stories, and in the end, by one vote after the state had been held captive, gain a victory. Meanwhile, make sure the team doesn't have to put too much real money into the pot.

Selig's role in the Twins stadium matter was deeply suspect. For one, NationsBank, the Charlotte, North Carolina–based megabank that merged with Bank of America in 1998, has always been a shadowy player in this Twins scheme. For two, according to published reports, the Brewers under Selig built a $63 million debt, much of it to—guess who?—NationsBank.[9] For three, the Brewers have one of the most contained television markets in the big-leagues, hemmed in by the Chicago franchises to the south and by the Twins to the north and west. As a man who was playing owner and commissioner at the same time, Selig was seemingly forcing the Twins out of the Twin Cities in a move that could only have benefited him and his franchise. Not coincidentally, in 1997 Midwest Sports Channel, which is the Twins' cable outlet, signed a six-year deal with the Brewers. While all involved said that wasn't a safety valve in case the Twins left town, the Brewers were creeping westward in their TV coverage. For his part, Selig protested when I asked him about all of his apparent conflicts. There he was, the owner of the team next door, pushing his business competition out of the region and on toward the area where his banker could control the departed team's destiny. Meanwhile, when the major leagues realigned, Selig further weakened the Twins by shifting his Brewers to the National League. Gone was the natural Twins-Brewers rivalry. Pretty fishy stuff.

"First of all, Jay, NationsBank is a part of a consortium of banks," he said of his debt. We were talking on the phone, and Selig was irritated. "They've never put pressure on me. That's just sheer nonsense. It's been a very mature and professional relationship. But I don't understand what that has to do with Minnesota's problem. All you're doing is raising all the sideshow or gossipy issues. That team can't make it without a stadium, and the people there need to know that."

But as Thatcher, the Sports Facilities Commission member, said, "That bank has Mr. Selig's nuts in their top right drawer. You think he might do what they want him to?" The bank is also one of the larger lenders to sports teams nationally, including Major League Baseball teams.

And as Senator Roger Moe said months later after meeting with Selig, "I would guess that he has a difficult time looking at this issue without some bias." On the one hand, Selig told Moe, "As a sport, we've paid a price for not moving a team for the last twenty-five years." "That certainly is the statement from an owner," Moe said. Then Selig told Moe: "I can't leave a team in an area where they can't make it." Which led Moe to observe, "That would be a quote from the commissioner."

Selig's April 30 visit was just the start of his unhelpful role in the stadium process. If only David Stern were baseball commissioner … ahh, what a thought. Selig's contribution in this tense period was to put his hand on the volume and crank it up. Pohlad, for his part, had been a virtual gentleman when it came to threats. He refrained from them. There was always a presumption that, at some time, he was going to make his Wolfensonian threat to move, but Pohlad was cautious there. Selig flew in to perform the dirty work.

Capitol room 15, a classic hearing room in which you expect someone to say, "I am not now, nor have I ever been, a Communist," was packed. A joint House-Senate tax committee was to convene. A line of eager spectators snaked along outside the circular room in hopes of grabbing a premium seat. It was late afternoon, and it was as if people were seeking entrance to a new *Star Wars* movie that was about to open, not to Selig's theatrics. Lobbyists filled the room. Minneapolis City Council president Jackie Cherryhomes made an appearance. The Pohlad sons were there, as were former Twins stars Kirby Puckett and Kent Hrbek, who also testified. All were trying to stay awake.

"Welcome to act 2," a capitol page at the door said. Selig's arrival followed a fiery morning hearing on gambling and the stadium. Selig, looking disheveled as always, delivered what would become a series of standard mantras about how teams in financial trouble can't be consigned to economic failure, about how other cities and states have built stadiums and now it's Minnesota's turn, and about how baseball hadn't moved a team since 1972, when the reincarnated Washington Senators became the Texas Rangers; but "if there isn't anything on the horizon to change the economics [of the Twins], baseball will allow that club to move. We'll have no alternative.... Unless somebody else has a different idea, a new stadium is the only option [to keep the Twins] economically viable."

He had platitudes, not solutions. He didn't even take off his jacket, let alone roll up his sleeves. He offered to meet with no legislators, promised no help from other owners or to alleviate the burdens on teams in smaller markets who needed massive revenue sharing from their media-rich larger-market brethren as much as ballparks. He also had no candidate cities that could catch the potentially relocating Twins. He tried to disarm everyone with his stories about how he was crushed when the Milwaukee Braves moved to Atlanta in 1965, and about how that changed his life. He spoke, too, of a 1970 American League owners meeting, a year after he had bought the Seattle Pilots out of bankruptcy and moved them to Milwaukee as the Brewers.

"I wish you could have been there," Selig told the fifty legislators. "We came close to moving the Cleveland Indians at least four times. Who would have believed that Jacobs Field would produce the results it did for Cleveland?"

Who would have thought that soon afterward the Indians would decide to become a publicly traded company and sell stock to fans and nonfans alike? Who would have thought that in their filings with the Securities and Exchange Commission, they would acknowledge that their ability to grow their revenues was small and that, with the new stadium and all, they might already have maxed out as a growing enterprise? A new stadium alone was not going to save the Twins.

What marked Selig's appearance the most, however, was a series of frank exchanges between him and committee members about the health of baseball and its future. He claimed that baseball was "in the early stages of a very powerful renaissance." With new ballparks built or on the drawing boards, he said the new century would belong to baseball.

Yet amid the ballpark debate, though there had been apprehension about the economics of the game, there was little statewide acknowledgment that baseball might just be a dying sport. Certainly, young people were playing less of it, what with the rise of soccer during the summer months. Statistically, minority youngsters were shying away from the game, moving instead toward basketball and football. Clearly, attendance was down at the Dome to watch the Twins as Minnesotans' attention was drawn to outdoor activities, to casinos, to gardening. Team management had let a once-great scouting system deteriorate. Top baseball minds such as Andy MacPhail, Bob Gebhard, and Kevin Malone, all once player personnel masters in the Twins hierarchy, moved on to bigger and better jobs with the Chicago Cubs, Colorado Rockies, and Los Angeles Dodgers. Local media contracts lost their value, and negotiations with local media outlets were botched. Once, when the Twins could have extended their radio deal with WCCO, they didn't; by the time they revisited the issue, the team's value on the air had plummeted.

Baseball was withering away in Minnesota, but the game's commissioner wasn't addressing the reasons why or how to fix it. He was flying in, fronting for the team owner, saying the only solution was a new publicly financed stadium, and heading back home to follow the construction of his very own publicly financed stadium. Indeed, even two years later, in April 1999, on another visit to the Twin Cities, Selig said the same thing. There had been no movement on his part about how to solve the revenue discrepancies between big-market and small-market teams. (As 2000 dawned, a "blue ribbon" committee, formed to improve revenue sharing, was poised to issue recommendations.) Such disparities had turned the game into a laughingstock. As local television revenues, subsidized stadiums, and corporate ownership propped up the richest teams, it was becoming obvious that new ballparks in middle-size markets wouldn't cure their economic ills. Until Selig could get his richest cronies—like the Yankees, Red Sox, and Braves—to share their revenues with the have-nots, competitive balance would be impossible. Still, all he could say, in his typically exasperated way, was that Minnesota had to build a stadium. "Do it and quit playing the blame game," he said. "Let me worry about revenue sharing. Everyone else is building a stadium. . . . Without a new stadium you don't have a chance."[10] But with a new stadium, what kind of chance do we have?

Back in April 1997, Representative Tom Bakk, a burly DFL House member from the Iron Range, didn't want to spoil Selig's tired monologue but felt compelled to express an honest Minnesota feeling. "I'm not as optimistic as you are that baseball is going to have a great resurgence," Bakk said. "I'm not as optimistic that baseball is going to be the grand old game again."

That sentiment was the heart of the matter in this debate. It went too unspoken. Baseball was no longer *the* sport that seemed to make a city "major league." Perhaps Minnesota could live without a big-league squad. Our children weren't playing it as they once did. And men like Selig and Pohlad hadn't been able to keep their industry economically sane without cities and states paying for its survival. "They're asking," Selig said of the Pohlads, "merely to have done here what every other city is doing. Everybody has come to the same conclusions. It's good for their cities." It's also helpful for the owners. The sport was not "market driven." It was subsidy driven. But support for subsidies was drying up.

In late April 1997, the *Star Tribune* published another Minnesota Poll. It showed that support for gambling was growing. Sixty-two percent of Minnesotans favored gambling proceeds, at least slightly, to fund a ballpark. And as with earlier polls, nearly 80 percent of those surveyed thought that the Twins' moving out of the state would be a loss. But there was a more troubling statistic for the people with the real votes at the capitol. It was Petak's ghost, a ghost created by none other than Selig during his Brewers stadium drive: 74 percent of those polled said that if their legislator changed his or her mind and voted for a Twins stadium after promising before the election not to, they'd be more likely to vote that official out of office. An equal number said Pohlad should give at least $100 million to the project, a dollar amount he hadn't come close to reaching—at least not without a guarantee of getting it all back.

There was one other troubling poll question. *Star Tribune* veteran capitol reporter Robert Whereatt, in his North Dakota–bred deadpan, informed Savelkoul: "Henry, we asked people if you were a bastard or a son of bitch. It says here they were fifty-fifty."

CHAPTER 10

Holding Up the Indians

Arne Plays the Race Card

An incendiary device had to be thrown into the fray. Senator Dick Day was a soldier of fortune who had the weapon to stir things up: state-backed casino gambling at Canterbury Park racetrack.

Polls consistently showed that many Minnesotans were on his side, that using gambling proceeds of some sort was an acceptable form of ballpark funding. With his index finger to the wind and his middle finger to the state's seventy thousand Indians, Day became the most destructive vector to enter the stadium debate. The caffeine-charged senator from Owatonna chose to take the state down a path of latent racism. The burly Baby Huey–like real estate salesman with the Newt Gingrich hair seemed to revel in skillfully harnessing centuries of irrational hatred for Indians and a decade's worth of resentment over tribes' control of the estimated $4 billion casino gambling industry in the state; that's more than half of all wagering in Minnesota, with charitable gambling, the state lottery, horse race betting, and illegal wagering accounting for another estimated $3 million.[1]

If John Marty could be accused of demagoguery on the class warfare front, Day trumped him on the racial front. Rather than celebrate the fact that some of the nation's and state's most downtrodden citizens had found a little bit of a windfall, Day wanted a piece of their action. No, he didn't want to talk to and listen to the Indians and gather their feelings and attitudes. (Neither, for that matter, did Governor Carlson.) Day simply wanted to get the state into the gambling business so that it would take away from the Indians' one major avenue of self-sufficient revenue production. Day, who allowed that his Catholic roots were steeped in church basement bingo, frequently chastised the members of the Shakopee Mdewakanton Sioux Community, who were lucky enough to own the Mystic Lake Casino, the closest Indian gaming facility to the Twin Cities metro area. "The two hundred millionaires at Mystic Lake is who he's listening to," Day said repeatedly of Senator Roger Moe, a stoic Norwegian from northwestern Minnesota, who was the Indians' best friend at the capitol.

For Day, it was as if most of the other legislators weren't listening to other kinds of millionaires in their decision making. Day seemed perturbed that individual members of the Shakopee tribe were pocketing as much as $600,000 a year and not sharing more of their gaming profits with off-reservation Indians. And yet there stood Day, seeking to fund a stadium in which the average player's salary was higher still than any Indian's. There stood Day, like many of his colleagues, poised to reduce welfare benefits for the state's poorest citizens. It all didn't add up.

In attacking the Indians' monopoly over casino gambling, Day also pointed to the large campaign contributions from the various tribes and their lobbyists to Moe's DFL Party. Day, who had political aspirations of his own, wanted to use the Indians to show that the DFL was unprincipled. Day claimed that Moe and his cohorts were "bought and paid for" by the Indian tribes to protect their gambling riches. For Day, somehow, only wealthy white businesspeople were allowed to influence the political process. And apparently Day wasn't concerned that increased gambling at Canterbury Park could increase the profits of, say, Curt Sampson, an honorable man, who owned the race track.

Day's idea: institute slot machines—and maybe even blackjack tables—at Canterbury, sponsored and supervised by the Minnesota Lottery. Use the proceeds to build a Twins ballpark, to improve the Dome for the Vikings, to help build a hockey arena in St. Paul, and to increase horse racing purses, and ship 40 percent of the net proceeds to the state's Environmental Trust Fund, as mandated by lottery laws. He also set aside gambling proceeds for urban Indians. Day estimated annual gross revenues of up to $150 million, using a similar slots operation in Iowa as his guide. He repeatedly denied that he was motivated to "get the Injuns," but his late session push was, sadly, accompanied by bigoted unsigned leaflets that began appearing around the capitol. There was no evidence such hate mongering was connected to Day. But he stirred up an atmosphere that gave cover to such shenanigans. The stadium's link to gambling joined some hunters' and anglers' resentment of Indian fishing rights.

"Please vote YES to allow slot machines at Canterbury Downs!" screamed one simple typewritten flyer found in a capitol hearing room. This wasn't written by the Twins to get a ballpark. It was written by fringe extremists to get the Indians. "Slot machines at Canterbury Downs would be a first step in restoring equal rights before tribal governments take over most of the state," one handbill said. "It is hard to believe that the country you understood to protect your rights of equality is now telling you the rules have changed. We are now granting more rights to one race of citizen by the reducing the rights of the 'non chosen race' of citizen.... Why are we so afraid of the self-proclaimed power and special rights for the Native Americans? The tribal governments seem to own the press and more and more the politicians. This summer I will have to tell my children that they will not be able to keep their fish on Mille Lacs because their skin is the wrong color. This precious resource will be netted out from under the citizens of Minnesota. Without having to spell it out, do you see a continuing trend that is wrong and will become a social toxin now and in the future? PLEASE VOTE YES ON SENATOR DICK DAY'S SLOT MACHINE BILL."[2]

With that kind of repugnant literature swirling around Day's bill, a bad, old-time Western movie scene played itself out at the capitol. Imagine the player piano tinkling in the background. Envision a barroom brawl breaking out. At first, the fight was over the stadium, taxes, subsidies, and priorities. As volatile as the stadium debate had been, at least it was focused. But with the boisterous introduction of gambling into the fracas, a second chair-over-the-head skirmish broke out in the balcony. Now not only was the state engaged in a debate about ballparks and pro sports. Now we were talking about expanding gambling, about competing with the Indians, and about state-tribal relations. A one-dimensional statewide conversation was transformed into a very touchy three-dimensional shouting match. Christian conservatives weighed in against gambling. Progressive activists supportive of the Indians' sovereignty showed up. Various anti-Indian opinions floated in, seeking to use the state's power to leverage the stadium issue to gain Indian concessions on sacred hunting and fishing rights, which were then in dispute. With all the brawls under way, before long, as in any black-and-white Western, the fights merged, with people swinging fists at whoever got in the way, and the once distinct scuffles turned into a full-fledged, out-of-control rumble.

As Day jabbered on about the Indians monopolizing the gaming industry, lobbyists for the Indian gaming interests and the tribes began to assert that any effort to link the ballpark with expanded gambling could only be construed as racism and as an effort to take back from the Indians what had been fairly negotiated in the "Tribal-State Compacts" in 1991. The language of that hysterical leaflet was all the proof the Indians' advocates needed. Nowhere did these Minnesota compacts prohibit the state from starting its own gaming industry. But the fundamental idea of the Indian Gaming Regulatory Act (IGRA), passed by Congress in 1988, was to provide a unique economic development tool for the nation's poorest group of peoples and to strengthen tribal governments and promote self-sufficiency. For better or for worse, casino gambling was the vehicle for this economic development. Some tribes, such as the Mille Lacs band of Ojibwe, under the leadership of Marge Anderson, had taken much of their gambling proceeds to improve the social and physical infrastructure on their reservation. For the state of Minnesota to promote a brazen attempt to compete with the Indians was to challenge their singlemost successful business venture.

"We're just starting," the leading Indian lobbyist Larry Kitto said of the various tribes' still-new casino businesses. "And they want to pull the legs out from under that."[3] Governor Carlson, late in the 1997 session, completely changed his position on gambling—just to get a stadium built. He suggested that adding fifteen hundred slot machines at Canterbury

Park, just three miles from Mystic Lake, would be "an extension" of gambling and not "an expansion." It was a marvelous parsing but not elegant enough for Kitto, who provided the most poignant comment of the entire stadium debate. "There's never been anybody standing in line to share our poverty," Kitto said. "Now everybody's in line to take away our money."[4]

It should be noted that tribal relations with the Carlson administration were already soundly on the rocks. By all accounts, and an examination of government records, Carlson, in his eight years in office, had two gatherings with the eleven tribal leaders in the state. One was a pleasant lunch at the governor's residence that warmed feelings. But the other was a total disaster and, literally, ended any direct face-to-face contact between the tribal leaders and the governor for the last three and a half years of his administration. The awful meeting, held on June 13, 1995, came to be referred to as "the bad hair day meeting" by Carlson staffers. Ostensibly, it was set up to discuss some issues about the state policing the casinos on tribal lands. The Minnesota Department of Public Safety had plans to increase enforcement in and around the casinos, something the tribes opposed. But it wasn't just the topic. It was the tone. And it was nasty.

The session got off to a bad start. The chairs in the governor's reception room were set up as if for a news conference or lecture, not for a meeting among equals. Unfortunately, under such a seating arrangement, the Indian executives, sitting like high school kids in rows, were confronted by a large painting on the east wall of the ornate room. The painting, pretty enough, is by Douglas Volk and is titled *Father Hennepin Discovering the Falls of St. Anthony*. In it, explorer Hennepin, with a crucifix in his hand, is gazing over the falls as a group of Indian scouts, including some bare-breasted women, lounge around him unmoved, obviously used to the scenery and a bit bored. He is "discovering" the falls around which the Indians have lived for hundreds of years. Although the painting is clearly historic, it is as if the Indians are thinking to themselves, "There goes the neighborhood."

Carlson, according to two participants, wandered into the meeting wearing his usual University of Minnesota Gophers cardigan, mumbling to a staff member, "Why am I here? What the hell is this all about?" He then proceeded to lecture the chiefs about various topics, but mostly about the tribes' responsibility to monitor the integrity of their gaming operations. At some point, two of the Indian leaders, Gary Donald of the Bois Forte band and Bobby Whitefeather, tribal chairman of the Red Lake Chippewa, whispered something to each other. Carlson snapped at them like a fourth-grade teacher. "I'd like everyone's attention while I'm talking," witnesses recall Carlson saying.

"He lectured them and belittled them," Kitto remembered. "They sat politely, but when he was done telling them about their responsibilities, they all stood up, walked out, and never came back again." Never. All communications from that day forth were at the staff level, but the governor of Minnesota and the chief executives of the eleven tribes didn't gather again. That was the tone of interaction that tribal leaders had come to expect from the Carlson administration. Nothing was going to surprise them. They were in no mood to help this man out.

As the 1997 session wore on, a message was being sent by elected officials from Governor Carlson to a broad swath of legislators. Pro sports facilities are important to the quality of life of the Twin Cities and the state, but not important enough to tax *ourselves* to pay for them. So, then, let's make like baseball owners and use other people's money. Let's make the sports facilities important enough to tax the *Indians* to pay for them. The stadium had to be built, and because no one had the guts to approve a tax, then it was time to barge in on the Indians' gaming monopoly and threaten them; "If you don't share your casino dollars, we'll start our own casinos."

As always with government relations with the Indians, it was an attempt to rewrite history. Few remember that legalized statewide gambling had begun in 1945 when bingo was approved for charitable organizations.[5] That broke an eighty-eight-year ban on gambling, which was first included in the state's 1857 constitution. In 1988 a statewide constitutional referendum passed authorizing a state-run lottery. The Minnesota Lottery would soon take hold as a daily phenomenon on television, with its numbers printed in prominent places in the newspapers. The same year, Indian gaming received its national approval when the Congress passed the IGRA. By 1991, Minnesota's eleven sovereign tribes negotiated compacts with the state. The agreements allowed the tribes to sponsor slot machines and blackjack on their lands. The deals were good for the Indians. The Minnesota compacts, the first in the nation to be negotiated, contained no end dates and allowed the Indians to retain virtually all of the revenues they collect. The compacts became known as the treaties that the Indians finally won after hundreds of years of deceit on the part of the white man. In the Minnesota compacts, unlike other states, there was no sharing arrangement negotiated by the state. In Connecticut, for instance, as much as 25 percent of the net revenues generated by one casino send about $250 million a year into the state's general fund. Not in Minnesota.

Some of Minnesota's tribes have flourished. Others in the more remote parts of the state barely get by. However prosperous or floundering, Indians controlled gambling in the state, state officials had no jurisdiction over any of the activity, and some people, such as Senator Day, didn't like it. Sovereignty just got in the darn way.

Day wasn't the first politician to latch onto gambling as a way to fund the stadium, and a bunch of other projects, too. On May 8, 1995, Speaker of the House Irv Anderson, the autocratic DFL leader from International Falls, backed a bill that would have allowed so-called "video lottery" machines in bars and restaurants with liquor licenses across the state. Looking like slot machines, these devices would function as electronic pull tab machines, with the cost ranging from twenty-five cents to two dollars per try. The purported goal was to aid in bringing the then-peripatetic NHL Winnipeg Jets to the Twin Cities. The promise was that slots peppered around the state could generate an eye-popping $250 million a year. Under Anderson's plan, the money would be used to subsidize the Jets move, help build more ice rinks for youth hockey, increase funding for girls sports, bolster school budgets, relieve the property tax burden, and set aside 1 percent for the state's Compulsive Gambling Account. It's tiring just thinking of all the causes that would have benefited from this newfound money, which, in reality, is a tax on poor people.

The historic significance of the Anderson bill went beyond its linkage of sports and gambling. It seems to be the first public mention of the term "level playing field." That has come to mean that somehow the Indians have a leg up on the state in their control of gambling. This, of course, is after hundreds of years of being beaten down on every other economic front. But because the Indians have been granted certain rights under the IGRA, and because of other elements of tribal sovereignty, they own certain rights—including hunting and fishing—that are different from those of non-Indian Minnesotans. It's the law. The U.S. courts have upheld these rights. Besides, as Ann Glumac, formerly Governor Carlson's liaison to the tribes, notes, there is a certain "dishonesty" to blaming the Indians for compacts that the state negotiated in good faith, at arm's length, with eyes open. "If the legislature wanted to expand state gambling, they could," Glumac said. "But why they need to beat up on the tribes in the process, I've never understood."

Kitto, a Mdewakanton Santee, whose ancestors were moved out of Minnesota to Nebraska in 1862, chuckled ruefully at the term "level playing field." "We'd love to be on a level playing field," he said. "The two things that irritate me most is when [Minnesota] public officials say, 'We need to be on a level playing field with the Indians' or 'We need to break that Indian monopoly.' The only monopoly we have had has been on poverty. In terms of a level playing field, it takes longer than ten years or even a generation to make up for three hundred years of being at the bottom of the barrel."

As much as there might be support for expanded gambling sponsored by the state, there is also long-standing animosity toward Indians in the state. Merging the two sentiments allowed for an insidious process to begin. The underlying prejudice is often reflected in the news media and in the language of gambling proponents. The most consistently public voice for raiding the Indians' monopoly was the *Star Tribune's* Patrick Reusse, who grew up in Fulda, Minnesota, a German American living on land that, like all of Minnesota, was once owned by Native Americans.

Even before Anderson officially announced his video lottery concept, Reusse touted the idea, dismissing any potential tribal opposition as "complaining" and calling their concerns "illegitimate." Using a point of view that can only be called comically absurd, Reusse suggested that with so many gambling opportunities already in the state, "Why not take advantage of the suckers' money"[6] to pay for a Twins stadium, the possibility of an NHL team coming to town, and the advancement of women's sports? Of course, save for big-league baseball, Reusse has consistently bashed hockey and, certainly, women's sports. His dismissive attitude toward Indian gaming was but the start of a steady campaign to take on the Indians in his column and on his KSTP radio shows.

Five months later, as the Advisory Task Force on Professional Sports considered how to attract an NHL team, Reusse took it upon himself to issue a threat to the tribes. In a convoluted argument used by Twins and Vikings management during this period, Reusse noted that the reason the pro teams in Minnesota may be financially in trouble and the reason this state may not be able to afford four major-league teams is because of the wide array of casino gambling operations competing for the entertainment dollar. His solution, of course, was to *add* state-run casinos. Exactly how many *more* casinos would create new discretionary dollars for the teams is uncertain. Presumably more dollars would go to gambling, not pro sports tickets. Throughout their efforts to gain a new ballpark, both Twins and Vikings officials have argued that gamblers were drawn away from sports to spend their discretionary dollars. During the 1994 Major League Baseball players strike, the Twins lost much of their group sales business as senior-citizens groups and small-town social clubs merely redirected their chartered buses to the gambling casinos. Exactly how to reconcile this with funding for a stadium via casinos was unclear. More casinos could only mean more potential ticket buyers using their disposable income at yet another competitive environment. Maybe the stadium would be built with gambling money, but who would still have money to go to the games?

Under proposals to open new casinos or gambling locations either at Canterbury or near the Mall of America, or in either downtown St. Paul or Minneapolis, the gambling dollars would leave the Indian casinos—punishing the Indians' economic development hopes—and arrive in white-guy casinos. At the very least, the threat of more casinos could be used to frighten those Indians to "pay taxes on your profits," despite a state-negotiated compact that doesn't require such payments.

With such fundamental issues as tribal sovereignty and Indian welfare at stake, Reusse was concerned only with his ability to watch baseball games:

> Major league sports are more important to this area than gambling. The Twins—the most important team of all—will leave before the casinos. So, what the public and politicians must do to guarantee the Twin Cities' major-league status is to get a share of the gambling take. Gov. Arne Carlson and the legislative leaders must make it clear to the casino operators: Pay taxes on your profits from the casino monopoly the state has granted to you, or face the competition of video gambling in hundreds of bars and restaurants. Either way, there would be a new source of public funds available to make Target Center work for two teams, to build a ballpark for the Twins and to turn the Metrodome into an improved football stadium for the Vikings.[7]

This was just the start of the threats, provocative language, and illogical thinking. It was the start of pushing gambling to pay for pro sports rather than explaining to the public that if pro sports is a worthy community-building amenity, the citizen taxpayers, team owners, and fans of the state of Minnesota should pay for it, not the Indian tribes.

What's wrong with using gambling to fund stadiums? Under the scenarios generally promoted at the legislature, it would be a tax that's not at all related to sports. It's not a user fee at all. It's a simple way to tax poor people. It is regressive. In Baltimore, the Orioles' Camden Yards baseball stadium and the new Ravens' football stadium were funded by a statewide lottery. At least buyers of lottery tickets there knew that their purchase would help build a stadium.

By August 1996, Sports Facilities Commission chairman Henry Savelkoul was deep in gambling thoughts, too. Some of his casino analysis was linked to the pending sale of the Met Center land in Bloomington.

As negotiations with the Twins were heating up, Savelkoul traveled to Owatonna, but not to see Senator Day. Instead, he met with a man named Don Laughlin, a self-made gaming zillionaire who has his own town, Laughlin, Nevada, in the middle of the desert. Laughlin had grown up in Owatonna and was visiting family there. In their meeting, Laughlin envisioned building a $200 million casino, with three thousand slot machines, one hundred table games, and six restaurants. Laughlin projected that such an operation, properly located, could generate $185 million a year. And he proposed giving the state half of those profits. Laughlin would privately build the facility—at Met Center attached to the Mall of America, or in downtown Minneapolis—and expected to pocket more than $40 million a year after its second year of operation.[8] But politically, Savelkoul understood that any private casino plan wouldn't fly. Certainly the Metropolitan Sports Facilities Commission, which was controlled by appointees of the Minneapolis City Council, wasn't going to allow such an attraction to be built in Bloomington. Besides, Bloomington officials didn't want a casino there.

At the same time that Savelkoul was getting ideas from private casino developers, Mike Lynn, the man who turned the Metrodome into his own personal retirement fund plan, was also on the move. Lynn, as usual, had selfish motives. His goal was to take control of the Vikings, whose ten-member ownership group was engaged in internecine boardroom warfare. The ownership group had developed into a real problem for the NFL's central office. Commissioner Paul Tagliabue wanted one owner to control at least 30 percent of the team's stock. Mike Lynn thought he could manage that. But such a re-takeover of the team he'd left in 1991 meant funding a new Vikings stadium, or at least a refurbished Dome. Of course, as long as the Vikings were in the Dome, Lynn would pocket 10 percent of the suite revenues. He sure didn't want to see that dear old Dome torn down. So Lynn, working as a wild card and free agent, came up with an idea that he labeled, in Orwellian fashion, "The Community Protection Act." It actually was "The Mike Lynn Resurrection Act."

Flying to Las Vegas and meeting with officials of three of the largest casino firms in the nation, Lynn in 1996 secretly began developing a plan to buy back the Vikings. It was based on a gambling-linked plan to raise $750 million to fund a new Twins stadium, a refurbished Metrodome, and the new Minnesota Wild hockey arena in St. Paul; pay down the Target Center's debt; increase purses at Canterbury Park racetrack; and further stock the rivers and lakes of Minnesota to aid the state's fishing climate. Under Lynn's fantasy, a private company would win the right to operate a full-blown casino, either at the Mall of America, downtown Minneapolis, or Canterbury. (Gambling industry executives preferred the Mall or a downtown site over the Shakopee location.) Under Lynn's projections, there could be pretax profits of up to $90 million a year, and he would skim up to 90 percent of those to fund all the sports facilities. He would have promoted a referendum to approve the idea. Sitting in his lovely screen porch on the banks of Lake Minnetonka, his mental wheels spinning, Lynn concluded that the business and political community that helped build the Metrodome twenty years earlier was powerless and the only way to preserve the region's pro sports teams was via gambling. Similarly, he feared that teams would eventually move, thereby increasing the bill for the community. Once teams left other cities, such as St. Louis, communities spent more money to lure them back than they would have paid to keep them in the first place. Not surprisingly, under his dream plan, the Dome's renovation would include the addition of 115 luxury suites, with a total of 230 suites, all costing $100,000. Just think how much his 10 percent clause on Dome revenues could mean for him then. Lynn was so committed to his idea that he even made a presentation about it to the Canterbury Park board of directors.

Eventually, Lynn exploited Reusse and another Twin Cities columnist and former sportswriter, the *St. Paul Pioneer Press*'s Joe Soucheray, to promote his politically undoable idea. According to Reusse, on Halloween Day 1997, as the stadium special session was facing deadlock, Lynn summoned him and Soucheray to posh Lynn's Orono compound. There, with both reporters apparently googly-eyed at being in Lynn's presence, the former Vikings president described his plan. On that Halloween Day, I remember Reusse trying to write a long story about the concept, arguing to the *Star Tribune*'s sports editor that it was a possible solution for stadium quagmire. As a courtesy to Reusse, I inserted four paragraphs of his notes into a main stadium story but then quoted Savelkoul as saying there was no chance such an idea would fly.[9] It was all self-centered, and Lynn fed it to two guys who he knew wouldn't get the other side of the story; there wasn't a chance in a billion that one private company would be allowed to control casino revenues in the state of Minnesota.

Soucheray wound up writing a column two days later that praised Lynn's plan and urged readers not to "take it lightly.... It was Mike Lynn who as much as anybody saw to it that this state got the Metrodome."[10] (Truth is, Lynn tried all he could to sabotage the Dome's existence until Max Winter paid him off with suite-related hush money.)

All that the Lynn interlude shows is that this particular stadium process had spun completely out of control. Guys with their own personal economic interests—and with no direct connection to the political dynamic—were willy-nilly coming up with all sorts of cockamamie ideas. And the newspapers were printing them!

Threats

Soon after the 1997 legislative session began in January, a couple of things became clear. Taxes of any kind to fund the stadium were going to have a hard time passing the legislature. In a sense, the antitax and antistadium voices, such as Marty, Krinkie, Knight, and others, had pushed the process away from state-backed taxation to, horribly, state-backed gambling as an option. That fed right into the hands of pro-gambling and anti-Indian forces who were motivated to stop at nothing to get a foothold in the lucrative casino gaming business. Moe and his friend Senate minority leader Dean Johnson met with tribal leaders. They had statewide poll figures at their fingertips. Minnesota Wins had private polls showing that gambling was the best chance for public funding. A *Pioneer Press* poll months earlier showed 59 percent of respondents statewide supported using the Minnesota Lottery to fund the stadium.[11] Moe and Johnson knew that the legislature would move in the gambling direction. The gathering at the Kelly Inn, the ugly slab of a hotel that sits three blocks south of the capitol, was as warm as the January air.

"Roger point-blank asked them to a consider a contribution to a new stadium in exchange for no expansion of gambling," Johnson remembers. "The general consensus was, 'We cannot contribute. We use it for our own infrastructure.'"

Stanley Crooks, head of the Mdewakanton Sioux, became especially peeved at the notion that the state was going to try to dip into the Indians' treasury to pay for a project that Minnesota's politicians were too chicken to fund with state money. He was among a group of tribal leaders who told Moe: "We have other pressing needs, our schools, our health care, our housing. Are you telling me that because your constituents don't want to pay for a stadium, mine should?"

Moe and Johnson had long cultivated respectful relations with the tribes. And their reaction to the Twins stadium question was shiveringly chilly. Moe and Johnson knew as early as the first weeks of the session that the Indians would rather sit out the stadium debate than become engaged in new negotiations to alter their casino monopoly.

Showing that he believed that brinksmanship was more productive than humane negotiations and listening, Governor Carlson decided to push the Indians into a corner. By mid-April, the governor and all stadium backers were desperate.

On April 17, with a month to go in the legislative session, Carlson sent letters to the eleven tribal chiefs and chairpeople, telling them they'd better watch out. Their wallets were his goal.

"I have spent considerable time of late assessing the $3.5 billion tribal gaming industry in Minnesota," Carlson wrote. "Clearly, Minnesota's 11 tribal governments seized an opportunity to better the lives of their members with the revenues derived from gaming operations. However, today the State of Minnesota is facing a challenge: The state is under tremendous pressure to weigh the gaming monopoly tribal governments have against the benefits that could be derived from non-tribal gaming, particularly if those benefits were directed toward public projects that create economic development. I believe tribal governments are facing a challenge as well, because the choice the state makes likely would affect Indian gaming significantly.... Warmest regards, Arne H. Carlson."[12]

The screws were being tightened. Senator Day began to whip the Republican Senate caucus into a pro-gambling frenzy. The *Star Tribune* was poised to release a new Minnesota Poll with results suggesting that the state's general populace was softening even more on gambling. Ann Glumac, Carlson's liaison for tribal relations, consulted with Maureen Shaver, the former Twins lobbyist who now represented the Minnesota Indian Gaming Association, the tribes' umbrella organization. Shaver advised Glumac that the tribes would want a quid pro quo if there was any chance they'd share their gambling money.

According to an e-mail and handwritten notes in Glumac's files, the tribes would be expected to contribute as much as $100 million a year, or a number similar to what a state-backed competing casino could propose.[13] But the tribes would be allowed to expand the sorts of games they conducted at their casinos, such as keno or craps. In exchange for the Indians' money, the Carlson administration would support a "moratorium" on any expanded state-backed gambling for at least the life of any bonds on a Twins stadium, which would be fifteen to thirty years. Under this dream scenario, with the kind of cash the tribes would be pouring into the state coffers, a stadium or stadiums could literally be paid off in two to five years. There were major questions to be answered, such as one Glumac had in her notes, "How will we enforce a moratorium—i.e. bind future Legislatures?" That is, if Dick Day ever became governor, how could the Indians be guaranteed he wouldn't ignore any deal struck by the 1997 legislature?

Devilish details aside, however, the parameters of a proposal were in hand on the afternoon of Thursday, April 24, when Carlson dispatched chief of staff Morrie Anderson, chief counsel Tonja Kozicky, and Glumac to confront the Indians.

The governor's reception room, the mostly public area just outside the governor's office, again was the setting as it had been for the meeting with the tribal chiefs nearly two years earlier. It is a lovely space, with oak and mahogany, bought or designed by capitol architect Cass Gilbert in 1905, filling a visitor's senses. A collection of stunning paintings covers the walls. They depict heroic scenes of Minnesota units defending the

Union in the Civil War. They also depict bits and pieces of the history of Minnesota's Indians and the invading white men.

Not for a lecture this time but for a business meeting ostensibly among equals, the lawyers and lobbyists congregated around the twelve-foot-long oak table in the east corner of the room. Anderson sat at the head of the table, on the north side of the room, right in front of the oak door that led to his office. Those who sat to Anderson's right looked up to see that goddamn Father Hennepin gazing at the newfound St. Anthony Falls once more. Those sitting to Anderson's left had the pleasure of staring across the forty-foot expanse of the reception room to another telltale piece of artwork, *Signing of the Treaty of Traverse des Sioux*. The official description of that painting, as distributed by the governor's office, reads as follows: "In 1851, the Dakota Indians were in rough shape. Their people were starving, [but] the traders said they would not give them any more credit. Government officials threatened to hold back horses and food that had been promised. So the Dakotas signed two treaties that sold most of Southern Minnesota for 12½ cents an acre and a small reservation along the Minnesota River. This is a painting of the two treaties signed by the Dakota Indians giving up land to the United States." And there stands Minnesota Territorial Governor Alexander Ramsey, with General Henry Sibley and Little Crow seated nearby, conducting the shameful business.

"The meaning of the artwork was not lost on the participants of that meeting," one lobbyist remembered. Amid the tension, there was a certain sense of confidence among the tribal representatives. They had been diligently counting votes all session. They knew that there weren't enough in either the House or the Senate to pass any stadium-linked gambling bill. For some reason, Anderson and Omann believed they could garner enough pro-gambling votes to make a plan fly. They miscounted and they miscalculated. Earlier in the week, Shaver had told Glumac that the timing was impossible and the topic had to be shielded.

"Do not talk about tribes having to save the Twins," Shaver told Glumac, according to Glumac's notes. "This money will have to go to the state.... Only reason that state has brought them to the table is to solve the problem and bail out Carl Pohlad. Hate it as much as everybody else up here. Has to be clear that it's not directly to the bonds, etc. Certainly not a matter of saying Indians have to bail out the Twins." But that, of course, is exactly what it was all about.

Moreover, Shaver told Glumac that the idea that some kind of deal with the tribes could be worked out by May 19, the end of the legislative session, less than a month away, was "scary and pisses [the Indians] off." With eleven different political structures—some that require tribal referenda—the chance of a deal being struck in twenty-five days was beyond remote.

Knowing all this—knowing that votes weren't there, that support for helping Pohlad didn't exist on any reservation, and that the timing was impossible—Kitto, the most outspoken Indian political consultant, was surprised at Anderson's tact. He thought Anderson would be more aggressive, more confrontational, more global in his presentation.

"I thought they put the wrong stuff on the table," Kitto recalled. With cries from some legislators to open the compacts, with cries to push the Indians on hunting and fishing rights, Kitto was expecting Anderson to link Indian funding for a stadium with other, extraneous issues. But Anderson didn't. Instead, he simply threatened that if the tribes would not find a way to help the governor fund nameless state "economic development"—a code word for the stadium—then the Indian gaming monopoly would be attacked.

"Anderson had, in effect, said that Indians had better help come up with a solution to the stadium funding crisis—or else a solution would be forced upon us," is how Mille Lacs band of Chippewa Indians chief executive Marge Anderson remembers the meeting, which was described to her by her representatives.

Kitto and Henry Buffalo, another leading Indian lobbyist, challenged Anderson in what others called a "tense and threatening" session. "The state entered into [the compacts] in good faith, and now it wanted to alter the deal, that's how I approached it," Kitto said. "More importantly, the state wanted tribes to do something that would not be politically acceptable to tribal constituents back home. Tribes were not then and are not now interested in the stadium issue. The reasons are not as complex as people make them out to be. There are social and economic problems that need our attention."

Morrie Anderson went on to become the chancellor of the Minnesota State College and University System. In his downtown St. Paul office, he had a traditional peace pipe and a dream catcher on his office wall, given to him by friends at the governor's office for his alleged peacemaking abilities. But on that day in 1997, peace was not in the air. Anderson took some of Kitto's and Buffalo's responses as "bluster," but the situation was crystal clear: unlike Little Crow, who had to give in 146 years earlier, the current leaders of the state's tribes weren't going to sell out for pro sports. They knew they had Roger Moe on their side. They had their vote counts, and they were retaking them every day.

Still, the next day, despite the obviously strained relations between the governor's office and the tribes, Marge Anderson, whose Mille Lacs tribe owns the prosperous Grand Casino Hinckley and Grand Casino Mille Lacs, wrote what appeared to be a conciliatory letter to Carlson. It was a letter that was leaked to the *Star Tribune* and *Pioneer Press* by sources affiliated with the Indian community.

Marge Anderson (who is surely no relation to Morrie Anderson) wrote: "Now, as always, we are very interested in pursuing win-win initiatives with the state of Minnesota.... We are interested in pursuing such a win-win course with the State of Minnesota."

The reaction from both newspapers was somewhat buoyant, displayed on both front pages, and I was part of it. There was no way to interpret Marge Anderson's letter any other way but to suggest that she had "opened the door" for possibly working with the state on the ballpark, and I wrote the story that way.[14] Pat Sweeney pushed his inferences even farther, stating, "Leaders of Minnesota's Indian tribes are willing to talk with Governor Arne Carlson about their casino proceeds with the state ... to help build a new baseball stadium."[15] Marge Anderson was unavailable that day for comment to help explain her correspondence, and Carlson's spokesman Brian Dietz took a tough stance, suggesting that it was just a matter of time before there was some sort of agreement. "What is it worth to them to protect that monopoly?" he asked.

In reality, as it turned out, Anderson's letter, one of a series that came from other elected officials of the other tribes, was nothing more than a polite way of saying, "I've heard the message, and thanks for thinking of us. We'll get back to you . . . someday." But whoever advised her on its language and demeanor did her a disservice. The letter sure looked, sounded, and smelled like a goodwill gesture and a signal that she was ready to roll up her sleeves with the state to find a stadium solution.

Months later, in a letter to me about the stadium situation, Anderson wrote: "I did not feel we could simply ignore" Morrie Anderson's overtures, even though "our financial people were skeptical of whether such a scheme would work." Other Indian leaders have asserted that the news media misread the letter and that it wasn't as forceful and engaging as we made it out to be. Whatever its intent, the letter served to drive the gambling-as-solution bandwagon.

Little did I or other reporters know then that other tribal leaders were soon to write other letters following up on Anderson's missive. Many of those letters were quite different from hers. They said, instead, "Hell, no!"

The lingering effects from the June 1995 lecture from Carlson were trickling through the relationship. Marge Anderson told me in a letter— she declined an interview—that when the stadium debate first began, "Indian tribal leaders considered then-Governor Arne Carlson to be a friend." But as Minnesotans showed their opposition to using tax dollars for a stadium, "it quickly became clear that [Carlson's] desire for a stadium outweighed any loyalty or concern he had for us."[16]

That was obvious. Even as Morrie Anderson was meeting with the tribal reps to persuade them, Dietz was talking to reporters: Carlson was prepared to sign a Canterbury slots package to fund a ballpark, Dietz said. The Indians better watch out.

Whatever It Takes

Somewhat lost in the shuffle were the owners of Canterbury Park, Curt Sampson and his son, Randy. While the public seemed to be outraged that billionaire Pohlad might be on the receiving end of a subsidy, the millionaire Sampsons and their fellow stockholders at Canterbury certainly would benefit from any gambling expansion at their racetrack.

The Sampsons wrapped their desire to add slots at Canterbury to a deeper, broader cause. They argued, as did Day, that increased dollars from casino gaming would improve the purses paid to horse owners. This would in turn improve the quality of horses that would race at Canterbury. An improved Canterbury would mean an improved horse-racing industry in the state, which could be a nice slice of Minnesota's agricultural economy. As the legislative session staggered toward its May 19 end date, the Sampsons picked up their efforts to link stadium funding with an improved farm economy. To their credit, they specifically shunned scapegoating the Indians, even if Day couldn't avoid it. As far back as 1994, when Canterbury had tried to get a state constitutional amendment passed to allow off-track betting on horse racing, the Sampsons had been encouraged to make the Indians the issue. In the end, they knew that the vote was going to be close. "There were voices who said that the race card ought to be played, that that would put us over the top," said John Himle, who advised the Sampsons before his Minnesota Wins days. "If I looked at it purely as a political consultant, I could have argued that you could have delivered that race message very discreetly at the end and it could have had some impact on behalf of that issue. I never recommended that, nor would I. But, number two, it was rejected by the Sampsons. That [racist message] could have put that issue over the top. But that strategy was never pursued. They said, 'We're not going to be part of that.'"

The Sampsons showed similar restraint as the stadium vote approached. They placed full-page advertisements in both the *Star Tribune* and the *Pioneer Press* on April 27 with the headline: "If Horse Racing, the Lottery, and the Legislature Play Ball, We Can Build a Stadium." It was a reasoned ad that informed as well as promoted. It was not provocative. And it finished with an appeal that read, "Whatever your opinion, we encourage you to express yourself by contacting the representative or senator from your district. They want to hear from you. Now."

The next day, Day rallied his Republican caucus even as more tribal leaders contacted Carlson, advising him not to get his hopes up. The pressure was building from Shakopee to St. Paul. So was the rhetoric. Stanley Crooks, chairman of the wealthy Shakopee Mdewakanton Sioux Community, owners of the lucrative Mystic Lake Casino, sent a terse letter to Carlson that ended, "Even though I find little merit in your proposal to expand gaming, we look forward to continued meetings with your office to explore other win-win projects not related to the expansion of gaming." It was a buzz-off-governor letter.[17]

A similar missive came from Dallas Ross, tribal chairman of the Upper Sioux Community, which operates the small Firefly Creek Casino in Granite Falls. Ross wrote: "While we are sympathetic to the dilemma faced by you and the State of Minnesota in your efforts to fund construction of a new stadium, we are justifiably concerned about what this off-reservation gambling expansion would do to our ongoing efforts to continue to march the citizens of the Upper Sioux Community out of poverty."[18]

Meanwhile, Eugene McArthur Jr., chairman of the White Earth Reservation Tribal Council, took his concerns not to Carlson but to Ann Rest, the stadium bill's chief author in the House of Representatives. "There's a misperception out there that all tribes are afloat in a sea of money," he wrote. "It's fueled by the fact that gaming has brought unlimited bounty to a few tribes across the country. Unfortunately, that is definitely not the case for most tribes, and especially not for us at White Earth.... This tribe needs to invest in its own infrastructure and people, not in a speculative baseball stadium 220 miles away."[19]

Even as those chiefs were making it clear where they stood, Day was making his power play. In the capitol's room 125, emotions rode high as Day told his colleagues that the Indians were contributing too much to the DFL and it was time to take a stand. In an unusual roll call vote within the caucus—so that everyone knew where everyone stood—eighteen of the twenty-four Republican Caucus members sided with Day. Caucus leader Johnson, the Lutheran pastor from Willmar, wasn't one of them. But as minority leader, Johnson remembered, "They all turned to me and said, 'You have to be the salesman.'" It was a test, the way the Mob or an urban gang requires a suspect member to display his courage by committing a crime. Day was angling for Johnson's job, and Johnson had to show solidarity with the turning pro-gambling tide.

The next day, a windy Tuesday, politics being what they are, Johnson dutifully led his troops to the south steps of the capitol and demonstratively declared, in a seemingly enthusiastic voice: "This is the only sensible solution to building an outdoor baseball stadium without using general tax revenues. Minnesota taxpayers will not allow their dollars to be used for stadium construction but have said they will allow proceeds from gambling to be used for this purpose."

Johnson, the husband of a public school teacher, a Republican who had supported gay rights, a National Guard chaplain, felt a breeze across his shoulders as he spoke. It was more than a late-spring chill. "I turned from the steps and saw Arne looking out his window," Johnson said of the governor, whose view from the southwest corner of the capitol was clear. "Everyone was watching us."

On the strength of that show of force, Carlson turned up the heat on the Indians three days later. He received political cover that morning with a double whammy of commentary in the *Star Tribune*. Minnesotans woke up to two inflammatory opinion columns prominently displayed adjacent to each other on the front cover of the sports section of the state's largest newspaper. Reusse was joined that day by outdoors columnist Dennis Anderson, a more reasoned, thoughtful commentator on state issues. They delivered a tandem ambush on the Indian tribes at a time when there was no political momentum for any stadium package. All that Reusse and Anderson served to do was pile on and exacerbate a situation that was a deep, open, ongoing wound.

Aggressively and typically, Reusse resorted to name-calling of Moe and Shakopee community leader Crooks, charging that Crooks was taking cover behind Moe. "Senate Majority Leader Roger Moe has been forced to move at a brisk pace while making his rounds at the Capitol in recent days," Reusse wrote. "If Moe were to slow down, the odds would be strong that Stanley Crooks, the diminutive chairman of the Minnesota Indian Gaming Association, would ram his head into the upper portion of Roger's spine, creating the potential for serious damage."[20]

Reusse asserted that the tribal members were taking their casino profits "tax free," which wasn't true, of course, with all members paying the same federal income taxes as any United States–based worker. It's true that those who live and work on the reservation land are exempt from Minnesota state income taxes, but then there's a tendency to forget that tribal members are subject to another local taxing unit: their tribal council. He stated, "A Canterbury casino would do no damage to the Minnesota Indians still trying to climb from poverty," knowing full well that a gambling parlor at the racetrack would be just the start of slot machines in every bar in Minnesota.

Inaccuracies aside, the consequence of Patrick Reusse's column, at such a sensitive time in the stadium debate, was simply to turn the desperation of sports fans who believed that a stadium was worth building at all costs into animosity directed at Indians. The tone of Reusse's column did nothing but point to the Indians and say, "It's their fault, folks. And it's the fault of the politicians who support them." But if baseball was worth saving, why weren't more non-Indian citizens willing to share their own money?

Anderson's opinion was more pointed, and to a certain extent more dangerous because of its thoughtfulness.[21] He laid on the table what Kitto had expected Morrie Anderson to place there in the meeting with tribal lobbyists eight days earlier. If the Indians were going to make any deals with the state on a stadium, then "those wishing to cut a ballpark deal with the Chippewa must stand in line to negotiate with the Indians behind a few hundred thousand hunters and anglers," Anderson wrote.

As Anderson wrote that, the Chippewa tribes and the state were engaged in a lengthy legal battle over the Indians' fishing rights. The U.S. Supreme Court upheld the Indians' rights in 1999, but only after the legislature refused a compromise plan supported by the tribes. Now Anderson was mixing the stadium issue with another scorchingly hot topic that would bring Minnesota's politically powerful hunters and fishers into the rumble. Anderson was suggesting that if and when the state and tribes moved closer together on a ballpark package, then the more sensitive natural resource access issue should be linked. His suggestion was that if the Indians wanted to maintain their monopoly of gambling, they'd have to trade off their traditional ways and lands.

"The Indians have signaled what it is they might want just as badly as those fish—more money through expanded gambling. But the state should not play handmaiden to those ambitions unless it gains considerable off-reservation hunting and fishing concessions. Stadium or no stadium, such an approach recognizes the Chippewa treaty-rights battle for the game it is: hard ball," he wrote.

Fact is, the tribes didn't want more money through expanded gambling. They wanted to be left alone. It was the Carlson administration that was attempting to extort the fruits of that expanded gambling from the tribes.

Emboldened by the cowboylike support from Reusse and Anderson, Carlson wrote some strong words of his own on that same Friday. In a letter to the eleven tribal chairs, Carlson stated flatly, "I believe it would be in our mutual interest to reach a consensus agreement sooner rather than later" on the ballpark matter.[22] In the letter, Carlson, using words that can only be described as blackmail, wrote: "I sincerely recognize the impact that widespread [state-sponsored] expansion of gaming could have on tribal governments and tribal members statewide." He went on to say that by agreeing to share casino proceeds with the state, the "risk to casino revenues would be diminished greatly."

As the stadium debate headed toward the final day of legislative session, on May 19, Carlson was setting up the Indians to be the scapegoats for any failure. New proposals from Senator Doug Johnson and Representative Bob Milbert envisioned inner-city or Met Center–based full-blown state-run casinos, more ammunition to frighten and push the tribes. Milbert even had Harrah's—the giant gambling firm—conduct a projection on the sort of revenues full-blown casinos could produce. Thomas M. Morgan, Harrah's vice president of gaming development, predicted that a downtown Minneapolis casino would generate $529 million a year.

Around the capitol, reporters and legislators fell prey to whiplash as charges and countercharges erupted, all ignited by the Carlson administration's and Dick Day's nonstop drive to break the Indians' casino lock.

Hours before Carlson's letter to tribal leaders was released, and hours after Reusse and Anderson weighed in, John McCarthy, executive director of the Minnesota Indian Gaming Association, said that the atmosphere was "gun-to-the-head, a hostage situation.... The Twins are going to leave, and it's our fault." He said that Indian kids were being harassed in school because the tribes wouldn't chip in for a Twins stadium. "Nobody wants the Twins to leave Minnesota, but the tribes don't have control over the Pohlad family," McCarthy said.

Day was shocked, just shocked, by accusations that his efforts were racist. "I can hardly believe because someone proposes a bill to build a stadium or help horse racing that someone is a racist. I think we should be above all that," he said. As disingenuous as that was, Day and Carlson achieved one goal: they changed the subject. Instead of wondering why Pohlad wasn't paying for the ballpark himself, the state's attention seemed to be turning to why the Indians wouldn't pay for it.

In a sense, Carlson, Day, and other backers of casino gambling as a funding source for a stadium were reverting to the approach that Charles Johnson took in the 1950s and Harvey Mackay took in the 1970s. Rather than focusing merely on a ballpark, they sought "a cause" that was wider than just baseball. In the fifties, it was "put Minnesota on the national map." Such a cause motivated bond sales for Met Stadium. In the seventies, it was "preserve the viability of downtown and keep these cities big-league." The proposed stadiums stood for something, symbolized some social value beyond their reality as sports facilities. Pohlad's forces could never articulate a real cause, other than "Carl wants a stadium." Now the "social value" and cause to sell seemed to be "tax the Indians, not us, for a stadium. Use the stadium issue as a tool against the Indians' growing—but still tiny—influence." Reusse, in a 1999 interview, said that he remains committed to a notion that "professional sports are more important than the Indian's gambling monopoly." But why? "That's just my opinion," he said.

Can state-backed gambling to fund sports really be more important than the racial tension that's sure to attach itself to a stadium package? To say it's worth taking on the Indians to preserve pro sports is to admit it's worth attacking the Indians on the one economic development tool that's been ceded to them by the federal government. Working *with* the Indians might have been a more novel and humane approach. Why must the state expand its sponsorship of gambling at the expense of the Indian tribes? Minnesota Indian Gaming Association officials said at one point that they may have been open to working with the Twins had someone approached them respectfully. Preserving pro sports *isn't* as important as good relations with the Indians. Besides, we need to justify public funding for sports beyond gambling. If pro sports are only supported by the public so that the state can compete with Indian gaming, then the value of pro sports to the community has been diminished.

The gambling gambit disserved Pohlad and the Twins effort. It wasn't just a sports subsidy debate anymore. The Minnesota Christian Coalition issued a statement opposing gambling. The Minnesota Licensed Beverage Association and the Minnesota Association of Innkeepers issued their statements, urging a lifting of the Indians' gaming monopoly. The bars and hotels wanted to take gamblers' money, too.

The first weekend of May came, and the capitol forces took a deep breath, with just two weeks left in the session. But Senator Dean Johnson used the time to rethink his position. Only he knew his inner turmoil. Johnson wasn't happy with how the slot machine effort was unfolding. He went off for his required National Guard duty that weekend, serving in his chaplain's role. Then he visited his father, Erlyn, in Lanesboro and told him of his confusion over the gambling issue. Johnson was troubled by it and felt pressured by it. Curt Sampson, the owner of Canterbury Park and a prominent businessman in rural Hector, Minnesota, was a constituent of Johnson's and had even nominated Johnson at the local Republican convention in 1996. But Johnson's father simply said to him: "Do what you think is right."

Monday morning, May 5, Johnson arrived at the capitol early and bumped into WCCO radio's capitol reporter Eric Eskola, who was in search of an early-morning guest. Eskola casually asked Johnson his thoughts about the Canterbury matter, which was soon to face a full hearing, and Johnson said, "I'm opposed to it." Just like that, he'd changed his mind after soul searching. His conscience wouldn't let him bash the Indians. It was the end of Johnson's reign as minority leader, pushed aside by Senator Day. It was a pin in the crisis-creating balloon at which Carlson was so adept. There's nothing like creating a crisis to get things done, was one of his philosophies. He'd try it again months later. But as time speeded up, as Moe solidified his forces, as the Indian lobbyists got the ears of their friendly legislators, it all became clear. The vote count that pro-tribal lobbyists had on April 24 when Morrie Anderson made his first threat still held.

After a week of posturing, a host of committees met in the House and Senate. Nothing passed. Day's bill to put slots at Canterbury lost in the Senate tax committee twelve to eleven. Two Republicans sided with the solid DFLers as Vic Moore, Moe's chief lieutenant, carefully watched. May 19 arrived. There was no stadium. There was talk of a special session. The pressure subsided. The Indians didn't give an inch. Maybe—a big maybe—Senator Moe would be open to seeing the rural Indian tribes, like those in his district, being able to pocket some substantial casino money at some point. Maybe a downtown St. Paul or downtown Minneapolis casino that redirected its money to urban Indians and poor reservation Indians could generate some support from Moe. Maybe other tribes would enjoy barging in on Mystic Lake's metro-area casino prosperity. But that was likely the only way anyone could ever be expected to move Roger Moe on the gambling issue.

Meanwhile I wrote a story that pissed off a lot of Twins officials and stadium boosters. It was one of the more instructive and helpful stories I wrote throughout the debate. It appeared in the May 12 *Star Tribune*, just a week before the session ended. It had a high degree of impact on the legislators who read it. The story basically said one critical thing: the Twins had nowhere to move.[23] Governor Carlson warned that without a new stadium, the team would soon be the "Charlotte Twins." And Jim Pohlad offhandedly told a fellow guest on a talk show that Mexico City was a real option. But it was all flimsy nonsense.

For sure, the Twins had an escape clause, and the public and the legislature needed to find a way to keep the team in the Dome. But just because they could escape didn't mean they had anywhere to go. Charlotte, North Carolina, which had been mentioned as the most likely relocation site, had no suitable stadium, no ownership group actively seeking a team, and an already cluttered sports marketplace. Another region in North Carolina known as the Piedmont Triad had big eyes about getting a major-league baseball team but a population of only 1.3 million people, no stadium, and not even a sizable downtown to speak of among its three anchor cities, Greensboro, Winston-Salem, and High Point. Mexico City as a major-league city was at least a decade away. And the suburbs of northern Virginia, just outside Washington, D.C., seemed to be reserved for a National League team so as not to compete too directly with the American League Baltimore Orioles. Pohlad had once expressed to me a real disdain for that northern Virginia market.

Besides, baseball hadn't moved a team in twenty-five years, and did it really want to plug up potential expansion sites by relocating an existing team? Every league needs a couple of lucrative markets to be available so that its existing owners have places to point to if and when they want to hold up their communities for certain concessions. As Stephen Ross, a University of Illinois law professor and baseball antitrust expert, put it: "If you're an owner and thinking, 'What are my options?' you don't want [Pohlad] to move to Charlotte because then you can't threaten to move there."

Such geographic and market material realities weren't going to stop Arne Carlson. The governor wasn't done. The next—the biggest—contrived crisis was still to come. The real government conspiracy was soon to commence. This was a classic conspiracy, "a planning and acting together secretly for a harmful purpose, a plot."[24] Carl Pohlad would join, but only because he would once more follow some bad advice.

CHAPTER 11

Leaving It to Beaver
The Special Session Fake Out

As the summer of 1997 approached, different forces went to work. The major power remained Carlson's office. Morrie Anderson was replaced by Bernie Omann, whose skill was alleged to be in working with—or over—the legislature. A more regular, accessible fellow than Anderson, more a vote getter than a deal maker, Omann, age thirty-three, was once a legislator himself and, better yet, a right-handed pitcher for Brainerd Community College. He had it all.

In the final days of the regular session, Dean Johnson, the man who wanted a Twins stadium but didn't want gambling, suggested that a rarely used special Legislative Commission on Planning and Fiscal Policy be activated to once again study the stadium situation. The same commission had forged the state aid package for a Northwest Airlines buyout six years before. Moe and House Speaker Phil Carruthers named a panel of high-ranking legislators to take another stab at the ballpark issue. They appointed two skilled compromisers to head the recycled effort. From the House, it was barrel-chested Loren Jennings, who owned a successful trash-hauling business in Harris, Minnesota, about ninety minutes north of the Twin Cities. From the Senate, Moe selected a taciturn farmer named Keith Langseth, who never seemed to want to be a part of the charade. For the fix was in. This panel wasn't to decide *if* there should be a new plan. This task force was set up to determine *how* to build it. Why they were formed—despite no public opinion shift—had to do with the timing of it all. The Carlson administration wanted this soap opera to end in 1997; 1998 was going to be Carlson's last in office, and he didn't want the stadium to dominate the 1998 legislative session. There were *other* things to do. None of the legislature's leaders wanted the stadium to be a 1998 election issue, either; the House was up for reelection, and more important, it was a gubernatorial year. If anyone had learned anything from 1996, it was to keep stadium politics out of the election cycle.

As for the Twins, they had that beloved escape clause. By October, they had to declare their intention to trigger it. By the end of the 1998 season, they could theoretically leave the Dome ... assuming they had a place to go. The end of the season, then, was a certain witching hour. Their lease was up. Their stadium effort would be in its last-ditch phase. Their leverage was at its strongest.

Even though a careful examination of the potential of the Triad would have led anyone to think otherwise, Omann, Savelkoul, and Carlson adopted a strategy that was based on a myth. No one from the Twins organization had yet visited Greensboro–Winston-Salem. Everyone assumed Charlotte was the proper North Carolina market to shift a team. But even Charlotteans acknowledged they weren't ready. Still, the Carlson strategy was to make everyone believe that the Twins were on the verge of moving out of town. That underlying current had been flowing beneath the Twins ballpark debate since Pohlad made his first presentation to the Sports Facilities Commission in 1994. But Pohlad and his sons had been relatively restrained in their threats. There were the buzz phrases of "It's up to the people of Minnesota," or "There is hemispheric competition for teams," or "It costs so much more to get a team back than it does to keep a team here." They had been spouted by stadium backers for years. But Carl Pohlad had never once held a news conference, thumped a table, and said, "If I don't get a stadium, I'm out of here." It was implied. It was surmised. But the overt threat was never employed.

Carlson, Omann, Savelkoul, and Jennings believed that the time had come. And Omann had a name for it: "Creating a crisis." It was a tactic that seemed to be near and dear to the Carlson regime. They had deployed the concept in other major tussles with the legislature. If there's a crisis, then there is brinksmanship. If there is brinksmanship, then power can be exercised. Problem solving was too hard. Power politics and perceptions were the way to get things done.

So, in agreement with Savelkoul and legislative leaders who wanted to keep the stadium matter from spilling into the 1998 session, Omann, the top aide to the governor of Minnesota, told Twins officials to pursue a sales deal out of the Twin Cities to prove that they were serious. "We were fairly firm," Omann said of his communications with, mostly, Jerry Bell. "We wanted some type of—I shouldn't say ultimatum—but something that we could say, 'Look, you've told us you have to move. You've said this is going to happen. We need you to do that.' And they did." The governor's office instructed the Twins' owners to sell the team to force a stadium vote.

As Omann related this eighteen months after the fact, I was struck by his matter-of-factness, that this is the way the government was doing business. To get legislators to feel vulnerable, the governor's office recommended that a private citizen make a deal—real or fake—so as to crank up the public pressure. "I remember being fairly frank with them, saying, 'Look, if people don't think you're going to move, and we've got one year to go in this, then we're going to have roll the dice,'" Omann said.

Asked if he had personally recommended to Pohlad or Bell that a contrived deadline be established, Carlson, in an interview, at first said, "That's entirely possible.... There was a lot of pressure. There was general agreement across the board that we did need the date." But, I wondered, is it proper for elected officials to urge a private businessman to set a deadline that triggers a special legislative session that paralyzes the state? Isn't that wrong? "No," Carlson said. "You're into at this point a protracted and very difficult political debate. You need to do everything you possibly can to put yourself in an advantageous position to win it. No, this isn't any form of collusion." It just looked, and smelled that way.

So it all began. The Twins ratcheted up their threats to leave. They held a news conference and said they would take their case to baseball's owners and begin to "explore their options" to sell the team. Soon after, in Philadelphia, Bell, Starkey, and Pohlad presented a document to Major League Baseball's Executive Council, of which Pohlad was a member. That report essentially started to create a record within baseball circles that the Twin Cities were a floundering market and couldn't support a team any longer. It asserted that there was no viable local owner in sight. It trashed the Dome as a facility. It bemoaned the team's lease terms. It highlighted the oppressive presence of casino gambling in the market as an onerous competitor for the entertainment dollar. "The Twins are requesting permission from the Executive Council to pursue relocation options beginning immediately," the report to their fellow owners concluded on June 10, 1997.[1]

In the hallways of the elegant Four Seasons Hotel in Philadelphia, friends of Pohlad, such as Colorado's Jerry McMorris, who two years earlier had hosted that first advisory task force in a Coors Field conference room, made supportive noise about baseball being ready to move a team. Other owners who were seeking stadiums of their own enjoyed the Twins' presentation. A major-league team hadn't moved since Nixon was president. All the idle threats nationwide meant nothing unless one of their kind finally up and moved. Bill Giles, the Philadelphia Phillies president, wanted a new ballpark for his club. An Executive Council member, Giles seemed to revel in the Twins' request to "explore their options." Why? It provided leverage for him with Pennsylvania's politicians. The Phillies could, maybe, move to New Jersey? "Yes, you got it," Giles said, with a mischievous smile.

That day, Clark Griffith returned from a trip to New York to meet with potential financiers. He was still planning an effort to buy the Twins. It was a thirteen-year-long dream, ever since his father sold the club to Pohlad. Griffith continually told reporters and others who would listen that he was "putting together an ownership group" to buy the Twins. But over the months and years, he never successfully did that. He, too, believed that the only way to make the economics of owning a baseball team work in Minnesota was with a new stadium, a rejuvenated scouting system, and a jump-started marketing effort. Former chairman of Major League Baseball Properties, the marketing arm of the big leagues, Griffith practiced law in Minneapolis, kept in touch with old baseball friends, and desperately wanted to reclaim the franchise that was in his family's bloodline. Pohlad had disdain for Griffith—the way he had disdain for Clark's father. Griffith never could assemble the cash. Moreover, Pohlad then didn't want to sell to someone who might, in the future, get the public to build a stadium. Pohlad wanted that public aid himself.

Whatever Griffith's aspirations then and into the future, a quieter and more attractive prospect for Pohlad entered the scene that June 12 afternoon. He was a baseball man with a less fabled name than Griffith. He was a small-town baseball owner with big-time ideas. His name was Don Beaver. He owned about 10 percent of the Pittsburgh Pirates with two North Carolina friends. For this year, he had a seat on the Pirates board and was attending the owners' meeting. He heard the Twins might be for sale. He sought out Bell. He gave Bell his business card. If the Twins were looking for a buyer, Beaver said, he was their man. He had partners. They were trying to get a stadium built in an area of North Carolina called the Triad. No, not the better-known Research Triangle of Raleigh-Durham–Chapel Hill, which sits seventy-five miles east of the Triad. This other three-angled community contained a troika of towns, Greensboro, Winston-Salem, and High Point. It was the poorest large commercial region in North Carolina. It was trying to get a place on the national map. It had Charlotte envy, what with that gleaming city ninety-five miles to the south of the Triad already home to an NBA team and an NFL team. The Triad wanted to play, too. Beaver was the guy. Barely a month after Omann decided that a crisis was the only way to get a ballpark passed through the Minnesota legislature, that crisis had what it needed: a buyer, a foil.

The Beav

Don Beaver was a good ol' boy with bucks. He'd made his fortune, upward of $250 million, and he wanted to have fun with it. He also wanted to do something good for his home state of North Carolina, even though after he'd cashed in on his business acumen in the nursing home industry, he'd moved to Florida. Taxes are lower in Florida than in North Carolina. It seems to be a sports owner's response to higher taxes. Robert Naegele

Jr., the owner of the new Minnesota Wild hockey team, left high-tax Minnesota after he made his fortune, too.

Perhaps Beaver knew what he was getting himself into when he handed that business card to Jerry Bell, but question marks are attached. Such an analysis was deeply flawed. The Greensboro–Winston-Salem–High Point region had a total population of 1.3 million and was ranked as the nation's forty-seventh largest television market. It was a relatively poor area, with disposable household income of $31,643 or 20 percent lower than the Twin Cities ($40,696). There was three times as much spending power in the Twin Cities as in the Triad. And households with buying income of $150,000 or more—an indicator of how many folks might be able to afford season tickets—amounted to one-third of the number in the Twin Cities. There were 17,800 households in the Twin Cities with buying income of $150,000 or more; the Triad had a mere 5,300 of such prosperous households. It simply was too small and too devoid of corporate dollars to support a big-league baseball team. Maybe Beaver always had Charlotte up his short sleeves. But then, Charlotte wasn't ready to integrate a baseball team into its crowded sports market-place in 1997 either, what with a still-new NFL franchise sucking millions of dollars out of the discretionary spending of the town and an NBA team that was already seeking a new arena ten years after arriving on the scene. Business and political support for a new stadium was uncertain.

Triad civic boosters spun all sorts of marketing numbers. Their favorite was that there were 6.4 million people within one hundred miles of the little-known pocket of North Carolina. But baseball relies on density, not on distance. Baseball needs fans within thirty miles, not one hundred miles, for those Tuesday night games. Besides, that circle of 6.4 millon people that Triad boosters spoke of included Charlotte and Raleigh-Durham, two separate and distinct marketplaces with separate distinct identities. The Triad couldn't seriously consider the residents of the Charlotte metropolitan area as potential regular customers for a new big-league team. Such talk was just silly. It was as if the Twins could rely on the bulk of their fans driving in from Duluth every night. Besides, you could take all of the $150,000-income families in Raleigh, Charlotte, and Greensboro and combine them, and there'd still be fewer of them than in the Twin Cities. You could also add all of the entertainment spending in those three markets, and they'd barely edge out the Twin Cities, which is the twelfth-ranked metro area in the United States when it comes to spending on sports, theater, movies, video games, and recreational vehicles.[2]

Still, Beaver hitched his wagon to the Triad after being approached by Tim Newman, an investment banker in Winston-Salem. Newman had once worked in New York and helped put together the finance package for the Dallas–Fort Worth area's Ballpark at Arlington. At least Greensboro–Winston-Salem–High Point didn't have the major-league competition that was beginning to worry Charlotteans. Hugh McColl, the powerful chief executive office of the megabank then called NationsBank, wanted a baseball team in his town, too, in clear view of his skyscraping office. McColl, with an ego the size of the North Carolina mountains, wanted that ballpark right near the new, mostly privately built football stadium for the new NFL Carolina Panthers; that's the stadium that truly put Charlotte on the map. But McColl had his hands full with real business—like buying banks from coast to coast. Plus, whenever he tried to get the Charlotte business community to pull together to help fund a new arena for the NBA Hornets, he met with opposition. As in Minnesota, in North Carolina there was growing reluctance to support more pro sports in Charlotte. Charlotte needed to grow some more to take on that third team, most felt. So, for Beaver, the Triad was more virgin, more eager territory.

The fact that a middle-level millionaire from a backwater metro area was Pohlad's best chance of moving the Twins suggested that baseball had experienced a serious tumble. The game had run out of cities to move to. Baseball stadiums are unique, one-purpose facilities that communities don't just build for the heck of it. Football—in places such as Nashville or Jacksonville—could expand without new stadiums in place, but with new stadiums in mind. Most middle-size communities had a large enough college football stadium that a moving team could rent before their own new palace was constructed. The NFL shares billions of TV dollars, boosting all franchise revenues. But a baseball team didn't have such a luxury. A major-league team needs a major-league ballpark to play in. And what city is going to build a $350 million edifice on spec?

Beaver had an idea. It wasn't a good idea, but it was an idea. As he engaged Pohlad, he also was buying the Class AAA Charlotte Knights. George Shinn, owner of the NBA Hornets and the Knights, sold the team to Beaver after Shinn concluded that Charlotte wasn't ready for big-league baseball. With the deal, Beaver also acquired the Knights' ten-thousand-seat stadium south of Charlotte in Fort Mill, South Carolina. It wasn't a great location—about two hours from the Triad—and a half hour from downtown Charlotte. It also happened to be in dreaded South Carolina, sort of like Iowa to Minnesotans. It wasn't a great stadium—a bigger Midway Stadium, home of the St. Paul Saints. Egress and ingress into Knights Castle was as favorable as threading a salami through a needle hole; there was one winding road that took fans off the interstate from Charlotte into the stadium's snug parking lot. There were plans to improve the access and increase seating, but it was all going to cost money, somewhere between $7 and $15 million. Beaver's idea was this: he could buy the Twins, move them temporarily to Knights Castle, expand the Castle to maybe 24,000 seats, and after a stadium was built in the Triad, move the team to Greensboro.

Putting all those hurdles aside, Beaver also faced a political component. As he and Bell began to chat, the North Carolina Assembly authorized a referendum in the Triad. It was set for May 5, 1998. If the public agreed to fund $140 million worth of a $210 million ballpark, Beaver and his partners said they'd fill the remaining $70 million construction gap themselves. That meant that if, say, Beaver bought the Twins for between $125 and $140 million, he'd be on the hook for about $200 million before he sold one ticket or paid one player. Given baseball's unsharing economics and the size of the Triad market, that looked like an absurd financial stretch. But with the possibility of a referendum that *could* approve a major-league ballpark in the Triad come May, Beaver's vision of a major-league team in the Triad was gaining legs, however wobbly.

As part of the referendum legislation, any victorious vote by the citizens of Guilford and Forsythe Counties would trigger a 1 percent "prepared-food" tax, which mostly affected restaurant patrons and owners. The other key element of the plan: any Triad ballpark had to be midway between Greensboro and Winston-Salem, which are thirty miles apart. That meant the stadium would be in the middle of absolutely nowhere, near a burg called Kernersville, which is barely a sleepy village. Such a location would have gone against the trend of every new and successful ballpark in baseball's 1990s construction renaissance. This ballpark was not going to be in the heart of a major metropolis. It wasn't even going to be in a reasonable suburb. Apparently, it was going to be the first rural ballpark. When Twins president Jerry Bell finally saw where the new ballpark was proposed to be built, he could hardly believe his eyes. Nor could Bell, who had been around ballpark planning for more than twenty years, imagine the use of Knights Castle as a temporary home.

Beaver's projections for his major-league team were way off the mark. In documents he filed with the North Carolina secretary of state's office, Beaver and the Triad boosters assumed that they would succeed in the year 2000 with a payroll of $30.4 million and an attendance of 2 million fans. That payroll would place them in the lower third among teams in 1999, and that level of interest would have placed the North Carolina Twins in the bottom third of American League attendance in 1998. For a team to win in the nineties and into the next century, payrolls of $50 million and above were imperative. A payroll of $30 million would have put Beaver's team in twenty-second place among franchises for the 1998 season. And attendance of more than 2.5 million was the only way to support such labor costs.

Beaver was an optimist. No silver-spooned elitist, he wanted to "do something good for North Carolina." It was time for him to give back to a state that had helped lift him from his father's working-class mixture of small-town general store operator, farmer, and textile mill employee.[3] Like Pohlad, Beaver was from a small town, called Troutman, population 1,500, with many of the townsfolk laboring in the surrounding furniture factories. It was a baseball-crazy area when baseball was king, and Beaver even pitched in the 1952 Little League World Series for nearby Mooresville. He lost 2–1 and cried, but he met pitching immortal Cy Young, who was in a wheelchair, as a consolation prize. Beaver went on to star in high school en route to a baseball scholarship at Appalachian State University in Boone, North Carolina His baseball career ended there, even as a new path was laid: after earning a bachelor's degree and an MBA, he went to work as a hospital administrator. In 1969, when he was twenty-nine years old, Beaver realized that people were living longer, that there was a shortage of nursing homes, and that the federal government (through Medicare and Medicaid) would pay for nursing home care. In other words, the cash flow of the nursing home business beckoned.

In 1972 Beaver saw an opening when an Arizona company went into bankruptcy after starting and failing to complete construction of a nursing home in Hickory. Beaver bought the home and finished it. It made a profit. So he bought another one, just up the highway in Statesville, a few miles from his hometown. He named his growing company Brian Center Corporation, after an infant son who died of a heart ailment in 1973.

With the ever-growing stream of Medicare and Medicaid revenues making long-term care more popular, Brian Centers began to spring up across the Southeast. By the mid 1990s, Beaver owned 49 nursing homes and retirement complexes in five states: 32 in North Carolina, 8 in Georgia, 5 in Virginia, and 2 each in South Carolina and Florida.

The growth of Brian Centers allowed Beaver to launch ancillary businesses that helped to supply his nursing homes as well as other health care clients. His development firm, for example, built nursing homes. His Medipack pharmacies and MedCare supply companies sold them drugs and equipment. His MedTherapy rehabilitation service helped patients to regain their motor skills. His Brian Center Management Corporation helped provide managers, nurses, and dietary consultants for the industry.

Beaver's big payday came in 1995. Houston-based Living Centers of America, with more than two hundred nursing homes in Texas, Colorado, and eight other states, was looking to expand in the Southeast. It paid a reported $282 million for Beaver's Brian Center Corporation, creating the nation's third-largest nursing home firm with annual revenues exceeding $800 million. Beaver, in the process, became the new company's vice chairman and largest stockholder, controlling 31.8 percent of its stock. Brian Center Corporation became, essentially, Living Center's southeastern division, still headquartered in Hickory.

As Beaver's wealth grew, he poured his dollars into minor-league baseball. In 1992 he bought the Class A Hickory Crawdads. In 1994 he added the Class A Winston-Salem Warthogs, the Class AA Knoxville Smokies, and the Class AAA New Orleans Zephyrs. He also agreed to purchase the Class AAA Charlotte Knights and to consider expanding their ballpark as his big league fantasy flourished.

In addition, Beaver and partner Frank Brenner, a metal recycler from Kernersville, North Carolina, bought 10 percent of the Pittsburgh Pirates in 1996 and occupied a seat on the team's board of directors. When he made his first contact with Bell, Beaver had already been approved by the major leagues as an owner. Thus, if and when his deal with Pohlad occurred, the blessing from the other owners would be a simple one. He was already a member of the club.

In some ways, his interest in the Twins—or any major-league team—during this summer of 1997 was both interrupted and heightened as he sought to bury his sorrows. Two weeks after the Philadelphia owners' meetings, Beaver's seventeen-year-old son Patrick was killed in a boating accident on Lake Hickory, North Carolina. After more than two months of mourning, Don Beaver decided to turn his attention to his biggest deal ever. It was therapy. He had to shake the grief.

Meanwhile, secretly, Pohlad and Bell traveled to Charlotte. It was August. There they met Hugh McColl, the high-profile, big-ego chief of NationsBank. As he'd done for others, he pointed to Ericsson Stadium, home of the NFL Panthers. He told Pohlad and Bell he wanted a baseball stadium right next to it. They talked about Pohlad staying in as the Twins owner if the team moved.

Bombshell

Governor Carlson said too much on at least two critical occasions during this saga, first when he frantically sought to have that Mississippi riverboat find the potential stadium site and then when he opened the door for Morrie Anderson to tell Pat Sweeney too much. Now another task force was meeting in this summer of 1997, and it seemed to be building some momentum toward consensus. Led by deal-making legislators Jennings and Langseth, the group of elected officials was very cautiously inching toward a stadium deal. Jennings liked a gambling solution all along. There was talk of a plethora of user fees. The mood was considerably laid-back compared to that of the legislative session. Critics wondered why the legislature was taking one more whack at the ballpark. Minnesotans were weary of the ballpark issue. So there was an uneasy calm before what would become a political hurricane. Carlson wanted a special legislative session to focus on the stadium, to get the "up or down vote" to, he thought, expose legislators who were voting to "let the Twins move."

Then, the bombshell. The pro sports goo, so thick, so omnipresent, got worse on August 12, 1997. The governor, mercurial as ever, couldn't control his emotions and opinions once more. This time, he spoke for all Minnesotans. This time, it wasn't the Vikings who were directly or indirectly sabotaging the Twins stadium effort. This time it appeared to be Glen Taylor, the NBA Timberwolves' sophisticated owner. Unless you knew better, you would have thought that Taylor—who was already seeking property tax reductions on his Target Center lease—was throwing this monkey wrench into the Twins machine so as not to let Carl Pohlad get all the legislature's goodies.

Taylor offered his star player Kevin Garnett $103 million that week, and Garnett, twenty-one years old, a South Carolina kid who had skipped college to turn pro, rejected the bid. It was the kind of baffling news event that caused fan and nonfan alike to recognize that professional sports were out of control. But the governor, more of a Gophers fan than a pro sports fan, was as upset by the University of Minnesota's increasingly expensive admission prices as he was by Garnett's absurd contract numbers.

At a news conference to announce judicial appointments, Carlson made judgments of his own about the nature of sports in society. They were right on. His words were applaudable. But they sure didn't help

Jennings and Langseth do their jobs of putting together a package for a special session that Carlson had called himself.

"This endless drive for money has to be curbed," Carlson said angrily. He worried aloud about the average citizen's access to sports in light of such rising salaries and the scarcity of tickets for popular teams like the Gophers men's basketball team, his favorite. He railed at $250 to $750 premium fees being required by the Gophers to insure the best seats in Williams Arena. He wagged his finger at the "the fur-coat corporate crowd" that was bound to dominate the top seats. "Once we start to deny access in our desperate search for endless money, then you've lost me."

Of Garnett, though, Carlson said: "I personally think that [$103.5 million] is an enormous amount of money. . . . The truth is professional sports, in time, will be market driven. It's inevitable, it has to happen. This escalation cannot continue."

It was a breathtaking statement from a man who, if he got his wish, was personally going to participate in the never-ending cycle of increasing players' salaries via a giant state subsidy to a stadium. The "market-driven" realities of the late 1990s were that cities and states were competing for teams. And in that competition, they were creating a new market: the national market for these scarce assets. Carlson was trapped, like any governor. What was he to do? Just wave good-bye to the Twins? Carlson tried once to assemble a coalition of states to sign a peace pact that would prohibit raiding of each other's teams. Of course, governors from potential recipient states such as North Carolina, Tennessee, and Nevada weren't about to "disarm." So like any good, sports-loving governor, Carlson couldn't help but be an enabler of the system he was bashing. He didn't resist. He collaborated.

Just as they thought they were making some baby steps toward some kind of acceptable stadium arrangement, the Garnett idiocy hit the fan. And as Bernie Omann put it, "We kept giving ammo to John Marty."

By then, too, Pohlad himself came to grips with the political reality. He began telling Bell, "They're not going to do anything for me." But the words came in a plaintive, oddly wistful tone. Pohlad was really asking, "They're not going to do anything for me, are they?"

Laughing Suits

In early September, the *Star Tribune*'s Patrick Reusse literally snuck a blockbuster of a story into the newspaper late one Saturday night.[4] A longtime beat reporter covering the team and for a decade the *Star Tribune*'s lead essay columnist, Reusse had great latitude to dictate what was printed in the newspaper. On that night, minutes before a deadline, with more than 600,000 newspapers set to hit the street, he used one unnamed source and contacted no one for confirmation or refutation. He put the story—a stop-the-presses sort, if true—as the lead item of his baseball notebook, a feature that is usually reserved for such major news briefs as players' ingrown toenails and DWIs.

He wrote in a story that appeared on page 15C: "Twins owner Carl Pohlad has a standing offer from NationsBank that would move the team to Charlotte, N.C., after the 1998 season. NationsBank is one of the country's largest banking firms and is headquartered in Charlotte. A team official said Saturday: 'NationsBank has told Carl: "Tell us what you want to do. If you want to move and still own the team, we'll build you a stadium. If you want to sell, we have buyers to put the team in Charlotte." Carl has had the deal on his desk for several months.'"

In an interview, Reusse declined to say who his source was or why he snuck the story in that way. But the story went on to say that "the Twins and their political allies have developed the following time line for the stadium debate: The special legislative task force on the stadium approves a bill, funded with either a state-run casino or with state-wide keno, by late September. Then, Carlson calls a special session in mid-October to vote the bill up or down."

At worst, the story was pure fantasy and the wishful thinking of a worried fan and gambling advocate. At best, it was horrendous journalism, relying on one source to reveal facts that required a series of inquiries and explanations. As it turned out, not a single fact in this story was correct. Pohlad denied it, noting accurately that no bank could use its own money to buy a team or build a stadium. NationsBank issued a nondenial denial, but nothing ever came of it. The notion that someone would just up and build a ballpark for Pohlad was as preposterous in Charlotte as it was in Minnesota. Reusse's relentless promotion of gambling as a funding source would soon be totally shot down when the Jennings-Langseth task force was told by Moe and House Speaker Carruthers that any gaming proposal had zero chance of getting to either of the chambers.

All the story did was create smoke and no fire and put a nick in the *Star Tribune*'s already shaky credibility among readers. Since the fall of 1996, when my coverage might have been considered "soft," and since January, when Sweeney had the *Star Tribune* for lunch with his breaking stories on the original stadium deal, capitol reporter Robert Whereatt and I had done a believable, evenhanded job. We broke as many stories as Sweeney and his *Pioneer Press* colleagues. We tried our best to be fair to all concerned. We had taken our lumps from the critics in the alternative press—such as the *Reader* and *City Pages*, the Twin Cities' competing entertainment tabloids. But that was to be expected; the *Star Tribune* was always the Big Media Monster Target. The *Star Tribune*'s editorial page was shamelessly pro-stadium, and that hurt the news pages' ability to seem fair. But we tried.

Now here came Reusse, joining the senior *Star Tribune* columnist Sid Hartman in promoting the stadium effort rather than reporting it fairly. It was also the first time a stadium-related story had appeared in the sports section for nearly a year. In the fall of 1996, an executive decision moved most of the stadium coverage into the Metro, or "B," section, reasoning that anything that affects taxpayers should be given a wider audience than the cloistered and often frivolous sports section. Whether the Metro section or the newspaper's front page were the only appropriate places for stadium stories, I don't know. But, for sure, such a provocative story as Reusse's deserved more reporting and better display than one source and page 15C. I view that story as one of the newspaper's darkest in its stadium coverage. An out-of-touch cheerleader shouldn't cover sports business news.

By September 16, the powerful Minnesota Business Partnership held its annual banquet at the Minneapolis Hilton. This is a group that's bigger and more impressive than just a Chamber of Commerce. It includes only the CEOs of the 104 largest companies in the state. The Business

Partnership is the crème de la crème. At this affair, they laughed uncontrollably at the whole stadium debate. With five hundred of the most influential political leaders, lobbyists, and business chiefs in attendance, the partnership's staff annually produces a humorous video. This time, with Pohlad and Carlson as the butts of all the jokes, it was so hysterically funny that people laughed so hard they missed most of the punch lines.

Here's what the stadium debate had been reduced to. It was a spoof on the 1959 movie *Ben-Hur* starring Charlton Heston. The twenty-minute gag used real clips from the movie but—à la *Mystery Science Theater*—dubbed in the supposed words of key stadium actors, such as Carlson and Pohlad. Partnership executive director Duane Benson, a former legislator and pro football player, took on the Heston role as he repeatedly muttered "No new taxes." In the end, Pohlad—played by the aging Sam Jaffe—came up with an idea. Benson/Heston should compete in a chariot race against a character supposed to be Mel Duncan, head of Minnesota Alliance for Progressive Action, the strident antistadium group and longtime advocate for community organizations that serve working-class and poor people. In a suspenseful race, in which Benson and Duncan whipped each other, Benson finally won. A stadium was to be built. Pure myth, of course.

The tape brought the house down. Men in pinstriped suits were holding their napkins to their mouths and wiping away tears. The chairman of one Minnesota company, on whose board Carl Pohlad sat, asked the Partnership's staff for a copy of the video and sent it as a gift to Pohlad, thinking that the Twins owner needed a good laugh.

But not everyone thought it was funny. Minnesota Wins' Bob Dayton stormed out of the banquet. He couldn't stand it. The world was against him. He later called Benson to denounce him for the satire. Love it or hate it, the stadium issue had become a joke, even among the men and women who were supposed to be its base of support, the same sorts of folks who, literally, had made the construction of the Metrodome a social cause in the 1970s. There was no Harvey Mackay taking a year off to sell the stadium idea, no D. J. Leary traveling around the state gathering intelligence, no John Cowles Jr. sticking his neck—and his wallet—out to push through what he believed was a necessary piece of cultural infrastructure. To the contrary, there were business executives who thought spending time and money on pro sports was a waste.

Between the time of the failed regular session and the soon-to-be assembled special session, Richard W. Schoenke, president and CEO of Firstar Bank of Minnesota, wrote a stinging article in "Executive Summary," a publication of the Minnesota Center for Corporate Responsibility. Titled "Hockey and Baseball—or Education?" it was mostly directed at the effort to get a new arena built for an NHL expansion team in St. Paul. But it was a pointed rejection from a leading corporate citizen that sports were worthy of his peers' support.

"There is no doubt that professional sports have a tremendous impact on our youth," Schoenke wrote. "From the athletic shoes and Starter jackets they wear to the multi-million dollar athletes they try to emulate, we have all done a great job of selling this message: Professional sports are important. Professional sports are 'cool.' They are worth our time, our effort, our devotion, even our love. The Twin Cities business community supports this message. We rally . . . we meet . . . we push . . . we call . . . we pledge. We get the deal done. We buy the rights to our hockey tickets now because we need to ensure our future—we don't want to miss that first face-off. But what sort of a message have we sent to our kids about education? What if we used the same tactics, resources and energy to sell them on the importance of staying in school? What kind of an economic impact might that make?"

This wasn't some wild-eyed antisports socialist talking. This was the head of a leading bank. Sports now, to the executives, are industries that are out of control and owned by people who are richer than they. If baseball or football can't figure out their own economic relationships, why should other businessmen plug the holes for them? What's more, the status of baseball has changed. The game is now the third most popular among Americans, after football and basketball. Baseball is no longer the national pastime. Baseball, indeed, might be past its time, and the executives who are now operating companies are of a generation that has seen the game fall from its grace.

For Pohlad and Carlson, the chuckling, snorting, and socially responsible editorials had to stop. Even as the Business Partnership crowd was yukking it up, Pohlad, Bell, and Starkey received their marching orders. It was time to force the issue. Before heading to regularly scheduled Major League Baseball meetings in Atlanta, Omann spoke with Bell. "Don't come back without a deal," he said. Pohlad added: "We were led to believe that we would never get anything done unless we had a fairly firm deal to move the team, and that would be the lever, so to speak."

So off they went to Atlanta, to get themselves a deal that would, in theory, force the legislature to build them a stadium. Experienced businessmen that they were, the Pohlads and their aides talked through all the possible scenarios. Nervously, they wondered: "What do we do if we *get* a deal?"

Hotlanta

When sports team owners meet, they don't fool around. I have stood in the lobbies of some of the nation's great hotels and resorts seeking—and often failing to obtain—innocuous quotations from captains of the sports industry while wondering why hotel rooms anywhere cost $300 and whether the *Star Tribune*'s accounts payable people would turn pale at my expense statements.

The furniture in the Arizona Biltmore in Phoenix is mission style and precious. The rugs at the Breakers resort in West Palm Beach must each cost more than my house. New York's St. Regis Hotel, where the NBA decided the fate of the Timberwolves, had crystal chandeliers to die for. That Four Seasons' lobby in Philadelphia, on that fateful day in June when Beaver gave his card to Bell, had terrific couches.

Sadly, for my most important lobby spying of this Twins saga, I was stuck in a relatively small space. The reception floor of the Ritz Carlton in Atlanta is designed to make a guest feel he or she is in a quaint hotel. During an inexplicably busy period for the Ritz Carlton, with security guys always trying to keep us ink-stained wretches away from the owner class, I was in search of Don Beaver. Before I went to the meetings, Bell told me Beaver was going to be there and that Beaver and Pohlad were likely to meet. My nose and eyes were peeled for a scent or a glimpse of Beaver. As it turned out, no other Minnesota media organizations had traveled to Atlanta. I was going to be the lone foil for what I know now was to become a charade.

I, of course, didn't know then the intensity with which Pohlad, Bell, and Starkey were going to pursue this transaction with Beaver. I assumed they would chat with the cigar-puffing nursing home mogul. But striking a deal in two days in a hotel in Atlanta just didn't sound like Carl Pohlad's deliberate style. In retrospect, I now recognize how Pohlad, with Beaver's cooperation, particularly exploited me in this instance as a messenger to the legislature and Minnesota's taxpayers.

Pohlad was recovering from serious back surgery in June. A tough cookie, he was getting around the hotel with a shiny aluminum walker, guided by a chaperone, looking a bit frail. In the late afternoon of Wednesday, September 17, Pohlad emerged from a meeting with other American League owners. The main topic was baseball's realignment and which team or teams should move to the National League from the American League. The Twins had been marginally mentioned. So when the Minicams saw slow-moving Carl Pohlad pushing himself towards the elevator, they swarmed all over him. Pohlad motioned me as he pushed himself onto the elevator. "Call me tonight," he said. "I might have something for you." He looked his eighty-two years. His tie was coming a bit undone.

Why this man who had accumulated so much was still driving himself so fiercely was a mystery to me. But at owners' meetings, Pohlad was in a certain kind of heaven. He was a respected elder, a man who had paid his dues and was becoming the last of a dying breed: the single owner with his own money in the project. As mega-corporations, media conglomerates, and diverse partnerships began to dominate the ownerships of baseball teams, Pohlad was standing alone as the old fellow with that Minnesota team. He loved the environment. He loved this element where big decisions about the nation's onetime pastime were made by gaggles of rich guys and their well-heeled hired help. It was more fun than banking. Unlike the business circles of the Twin Cities, Pohlad carried no baggage.

He was a beloved character. That was part of a disconnect between base-ball's view of the Twins situation and Minnesota's view of it. Baseball's other owners couldn't figure out how a man they generally embraced could be so disliked in his own town.

Beginning at about seven o'clock, I began calling Pohlad and Beaver in their rooms, to no avail. It appeared as if there would be little to write for the next day's newspaper. But late that evening, after ten or so, Atlanta time, the phone rang, and it was Pohlad. He and other owners had attended a Braves game at the new Turner Field, and the game had gone late.

"We're just talking, but we're in the serious talking stage," Pohlad said. He, Bell, Starkey, and Beaver had been meeting for more than two hours that day, gathering in Pohlad's room and beginning to hammer out a deal. Starkey and Pohlad were actually drafting preliminary documents. As for specifics, Pohlad was vague. He said they'd be meeting again the next day.

And they did. But not before the *Star Tribune* led its Thursday newspaper with a banner headline: "Pohlad Begins 'Serious Talks' with Carolina Businessman." When I saw Starkey and Bell that morning in the now-empty lobby, they asked me to retrieve for them a copy of my story. The office faxed it down. They showed it to Beaver. They must have all rubbed their hands with glee. The process of cranking up the pressure back home was under way.

On Thursday morning Pohlad shunned the formal sessions. In-stead, he was back with Beaver, and things were heating up. They were moving along. Beaver wanted the team. He was committed to that own-ership group in the Triad. But if baseball didn't want a team there—who knows?—maybe Charlotte would be the right place. Some specifics of getting out of any sale deal were discussed. So, too, was the pricing. Both sides were heading toward a letter of intent. Carlson, Savelkoul, Lang-seth, and Jennings had told Pohlad any deal had to be "real." It had to be written down. It had to be something they all could show to legislators. The vote was going to be positioned like this: "Do you, Mr. or Ms. Legis-lator, want to be knocking doors campaigning for the November 1998 election as the Twins are leaving Minnesota? Do you want that on your record?"

Bell assured me that Beaver and Pohlad would talk to me after their meetings that day. Sure enough, around lunchtime, here they came. First there was the relaxed Don Beaver, with big glasses on his wide face, a full head of hair, and a certain self-effacing aw-shucks demeanor. He was fifty-seven but looked younger. Exactly what he and Pohlad had to say to each other, only God knew. Baseball was the common denominator, presumably. Ego, too. There are only so many of these Major League Baseball franchises. Pohlad had one. Beaver wanted it.

No, Beaver said, he had no relationship to NationsBank, although Pohlad said the Charlotte bank recommended Beaver. Yes, Beaver allowed, he was interested in moving a team to "North Carolina," not solely the Triad. Sure, he said, he understood that Pohlad was trying to get a stadium in Minnesota, and that should be everyone's hope. But if the team was available, he and his partners were ready, thank you.

Suddenly, as if their appearances were choreographed, which they were, Pohlad wheeled his way from the elevator to me. He was heading for the airport, had to go, but he wanted to chat. Yes, he said, he and Beaver were inching toward an agreement. In his flat, raspy voice, he looked me right in the eye and said: "This is a real deal."

Right, sure, you betcha, Carl. It's all a ploy, right? You're just trying to squeeze those legislators, right? That was my response. I felt like egging him on. He didn't smile. He grew stern. He leaned his arms on the walker. He glared at me. "Nothing could be further from the truth. Why would I go through this charade of doing all this, if it's a phony deal, of spending hours and hours on this? I don't give a shit whether people believe me or not. I'm going about my business. [Legislators] have given us no alternative. What are we going to do? Sit there and lose our ass?"

He said he wanted to keep the team in Minnesota—that was always his desire. He was committed to making a "last-ditch effort" to get a stadium built. But, for sure, the team would exercise its Dome escape clause shortly. "And I want to do it with impact," he said. He wouldn't provide details, but the plan seemed apparent; link the escape with the Beaver sale announcement.

So, I wondered, where did the talks stand? Pohlad's aide was telling him they had to go. But Pohlad wanted to talk. He said he and Beaver were dickering on the price.

"How do you do that?" I wondered. "I've never been involved in such a big deal."

The master deal maker was happy to give advice. "With a deal this size, you don't throw out dollar amounts until you get all the facts, figures, and everything else put together," Pohlad said, and he sounded so wise and so confident. A smile cracked across his lined face. He leaned over his walker and got real close to me, as if to tell a secret.

"Jay," he said, with a crooked grin, "it's just arithmetic. You can think about $100, and just add a few zeroes." Just arithmetic. It was a chilling comment because it revealed to me that in the end, deals are just numbers to Pohlad.

In fact, we would learn later, the Twins were more than arithmetic to him. His heart was not missing in action. The Twins were too much a part of Carl Pohlad's personal history in Minnesota to be a mere calculation, a line on his life's balance sheet. But on this autumn day in Atlanta, Pohlad—oozing with the disease of loving money and transactions—was in his arithmetical glory. He was making a deal. He was frisky as Bob Dole on Viagra as he shuffled out of that Ritz Carlton lobby. As he said in 1985, in my first meeting with him, a deal is like a drug. And the octogenerian was high.

Now, this peskiness was a problem. When you get Carl Pohlad into a deal mode, he can't fake it. He gets the fever. He's like a dog with the mailman's pant leg. That was the case in Atlanta. On a certain level, this "sale" to Beaver was to be a mere symbol, a lever in Minnesota. Omann, Carlson, Savelkoul, and the others were drawing a very fine line for Pohlad. "Get a deal, Carl, but give us another chance after you get it," was Savelkoul's advice.

But when there was a real buyer on the hook, and when Pohlad began to realize he could recover that money he had long sought to recover, his love for cash got the better of him. He was buoyant. I thought to myself, as much as Pohlad wants a stadium for the Twins, he wants more to simply make a deal with someone. The legislature, Carlson, and Savelkoul had let him down. Dammit, Pohlad just wanted a deal. Those words of twelve years ago about him and Harold Geneen welled up inside my head. "It isn't money. It's a way of life. It's a disease," he said then. It was chronic.

As soon as Bell and Pohlad returned to Minnesota, the governor, according to a Twins insider, called Bell. Impatiently, he said, "Get that deal done." Publicly, Carlson said he wanted something settled quickly. The special session was approaching. There had to be a hammer. And so it was. On October 3, Beaver, his lawyer, George Little, and his top financial aide Tim Newman flew to the Twin Cities, zoomed back up to the thirty-eighth floor of the Dain Tower and signed a letter of intent to sell the Twins and, presumably, get the wheels in motion to move them to somewhere in North Carolina. Their arrival followed by days the latest *Forbes* magazine estimate of Pohlad's wealth. The publication reported that Pohlad's holdings had grown $300 million in the past year—just enough to pay for a stadium.

Neither Pohlad nor Beaver stopped at all. For six hours, they met in Pohlad's office and his conference room, hammering out details and language, setting dates and putative deadlines. If the Minnesota legislature didn't approve a stadium by November 30, the sale to Beaver would move forward, no ifs, ands, buts, or whereases. Meanwhile, state representatives such as Omann, Savelkoul, Jennings, and Langseth came by to watch the proceedings in Pohlad's office. There was an air of anticipation. There was an aura of sadness. Pohlad was coming to the brink, and he was understanding the magnitude of it.

"He was shook, he was very shook about doing this," said Omann, who was the orchestrator of this entire process. "He basically came to us and said, you know, he would participate in doing everything he can, but we've got a responsibility now to get this [stadium] thing through."

As I walked to my car parked near his Dain Tower office, my cell phone rang. It was Carl Pohlad. He was hoarse. He was tired. It was six o'clock, and he was still at work, returning phone calls. I asked him how he was feeling on this drastic day. "I'm sorry so far we didn't have a more favorable alternative," he said. "It's been an emotional thing for me, on my personal side."

I told him that many people believed he was taking this dramatic step to stick it to the legislature and the people of Minnesota. "It's not fair at all," he said. "You know how hard I've worked on this. You know what a beating I've taken in the press. My feeling is I want to keep it here. It's up to the legislature to decide."

But his son Bob had a feeling that day. He had deep and abiding knowledge. As much as his dad loved options, as much as his dad loved deals, as much as his dad was sick of the politics, Bob Pohlad knew on that day when Minnesota's news media suggested the Twins were sold and moving to North Carolina that, in fact, they weren't. They weren't going anywhere.

"It didn't happen—and you won't believe the answer—but my dad wasn't willing to pull the trigger, simple as that," Bob Pohlad said. "He could have." When did Bob Pohlad know of his father's inability or lack of desire to sell the team? "The day I was born," Bob Pohlad said, smiling lovingly. "I know my dad."

So the bluff quotient was very high. Everyone was calling everyone else's bluff. Carlson wanted Pohlad to create the illusion that the team would really move, even though Carlson couldn't bear the concept of another major-league team leaving on his watch. Pohlad was creating the illusion that the Beaver deal was real, although Pohlad didn't want to part with the team and truly wanted a new ballpark in Minneapolis. Beaver was creating the illusion that the Triad could support a team and would build a stadium, although any cursory examination of the facts would suggest that was all bluster and wishful thinking.

But Beaver was closer to what he wanted than was Pohlad. Beaver, Newman, and Little knew the letter of intent was just the first step. But it was the closest first step that any potential new city had taken since 1972 when Arlington, Texas, got the second go-round of the Washington Senators. They knew that Pohlad could get out of it if a stadium was approved. Indeed, he could get out of it at any moment. Letters of intent are just that, initial agreements to work toward a final agreeeement. At that point, they hadn't heard of Pohlad's business ways, of changing deals at the last minute, of suing when he became disillusioned with a deal. Now, on October 3, Beaver was where he wanted to be. And Newman, the investment banker, was giddy. When Justin Catanoso, the reporter from the *Greensboro News and Record*, was allowed into the Pohlad offices to interview Beaver, Newman didn't just say hello, he offered Catanoso an ecstatic high five. The Triad was to the Twins what the Twin Cities had been to the Senators forty years earlier. The Triad was a thrilled virgin entering pro sport's whorehouse. Newman claimed he knew "we didn't have it in the bag," but he carried a look on his face like the canary that had swallowed the cat; David was on the verge of taking over the Twins franchise from Goliath.

The North Carolinians knew their role. "If we were leverage or the straw man, if that was the case, fine," said Newman, who oversees all of Beaver's minor-league operations. "There was the benefit to us that was worth being leveraged. But for Mr. Pohlad, as it played out, I don't know that there was as much leverage as he thought."

Nicely stately, politely stately. Unfortunately for Pohlad, this act of apparently selling the franchise out of town created the biggest backlash of all from the Minnesota public. The disingenuous January 8 announcement stomped on Pohlad's and Savelkoul's credibility. But the October 3 letter of intent insulted people's intelligence and made them feel more than ever like hostages. It did for Pohlad exactly what he didn't need. It evoked the cheapness of Wolfenson and Ratner's theatrical fake move to New Orleans. If Omann wanted a crisis, he had it on his hands. Except this crisis was one of total and complete opposition to any funding for a stadium that was linked to manipulation of the political process. From afar, Newman and Beaver watched and realized that Pohlad had received bad political advice. "He was told if you strike a deal, it will get you a deal," Newman said. "That was very, very miscalculated and dead wrong. Instead of landing with a boom, it landed with a thud."

Still, the theater couldn't stop. Three days later, in a trip devised and arranged by Omann, Carlson and a group of legislative leaders traveled to Milwaukee to meet with Selig to hear him say that if no Twins stadium was built, the votes within owners' circles existed for the Twins to move. Exactly why the state spent $9,000 to find out what it already knew was a mystery.

"It's not a question of what I wanted to hear, it's a question of what all of us ought to hear," the governor said after meeting privately with Selig. "It's a reality of life. We have to confine ourselves to the realities, whether we like them or not. There are only two options: to build a stadium or not to build a stadium. If you choose the latter, there's no doubt in my mind the Twins will leave."

Selig played the role of chief threatener one more time. "I know there's always the feeling that baseball will not allow a move," Selig said, talking to reporters in the otherwise abandoned media dining room of Milwaukee County Stadium. "That is simply not true. That is wrong.... It is so clear that for the Minnesota Twins to remain in Minnesota, they need a new stadium. We need to move this process along.... Baseball has to say, we have to protect our own franchises, too. We hope this works out positively. But, if it doesn't, we will do what we haven't done in twenty-six years, and that's move a team."

As to where the Twins would move, Selig wouldn't say, merely broadly praising North Carolina. When I asked him how a team could move there without a stadium, Selig said, "May I remind you that in the most famous franchise move of all, Walter Francis O'Malley took the Dodgers to Los Angeles without a stadium deal." That was 1957, and O'Malley was moving his Brooklyn team to a temporary site, knowing a new ballpark was to be built in fertile southern California.

But minutes later, as the acting commissioner left the emptying room, I said to him, "Can a team really make it in Greensboro? Isn't Charlotte a better place?"

Selig smiled. As he rushed out of the room, he said, "I know where I'd go."

He meant Charlotte, never Winston-Salem, never Greensboro, never High Point. Even at baseball's highest level, the Triad was a stalking horse. That community was going to be a pawn for seven months until its ballpark referendum. It never had a chance. Selig knew it. Selig never helped them.

One other thing: with the 1998 season now over, the Twins completed their sixth consecutive season under .500. Everybody was fighting over a very bad team.

Fighting Back

It got too fishy. Senator Roger Moe felt uncomfortable about Selig's conflicted role in the whole affair, part owner, part commissioner. House Speaker Phil Carruthers, who sleepwalked through most of the stadium debate, woke up as the special session approached. When he awoke, he made the kind of contribution that Pohlad, Carlson, and Savelkoul didn't want, but that was rooted in Minnesota's most noble stadium history. Like Wheelock Whitney's forty years earlier, Carruthers's message was "Fight back." Carruthers believed it was time to legally challenge baseball and to investigate the game's tactics in relation to a threatened Twins move. Carruthers, in a State Office Building hallway, between hearings, uttered the "A" word: antitrust. Those are three syllables that give Selig and his henchmen the heebie-jeebies.

To understand the implications of the actions of Pohlad, Governor Carlson and his staff, Savelkoul, and Selig over the previous months, we have to return to a critical moment in baseball history: 1922. Long before major-league sports blessed the Twin Cities, the U.S. Supreme Court found that baseball is exempt from the nation's antitrust laws. It gives baseball a legal shield different from all other sports. It gives to the game's owners more blanket monopoly power than any of the other major-league sports. The owners of teams in other leagues—NFL, NBA, and NHL—have been allowed, through congressional action, to operate as partners rather than competitors on matters such as national television contracts and labor issues. That is, the Vikings and Packers, seeming business competitors, are actually business partners on a wide array of matters, from the college draft to sharing merchandising revenues to splitting money from lucrative national television contracts.

But because of the Supreme Court decision nearly eighty years ago, baseball's major-league owners not only control such matters as player movement from team to team and the minor leagues but also have ironclad control over franchise location. An individual baseball owner cannot simply up and move his team; he must get the approval by a set number of owners in his respective league and in the other league as well. For instance, if Carl Pohlad wanted to move the Twins, he'd have to get a three-quarters approval from his fellow American League owners and a majority OK from National League owners. This is in comparison to the NFL, for instance, in which courts have ruled that fellow owners can't join together to stop one of their brethren from moving. Recently, internal NFL rules have made it more difficult for owners to exercise their own form of free agency—moving their teams. But the league's history is filled with Baltimore to Indianapolis, St. Louis to Phoenix, Houston to Nashville, Oakland to Los Angeles, and Cleveland to Baltimore relocations. Specifically in regard to franchise movement, baseball's brotherhood can limit any one of its members. That's why, it's been argued, baseball has had so few relocations, and none since 1972.

But Carruthers, no dummy, saw something that troubled him. Selig, Pohlad, Carlson, Savelkoul, and others seemed to be turning the game's antitrust exemption and monopolistic tendencies on their heads. What Carruthers saw was baseball's acting commissioner twice saying—at the legislative hearing in April and in his meeting with Carlson and others in Milwaukee—that Minnesota must build a stadium or else the Twins would leave town. Now, it seemed, with Selig as the figurehead, baseball was using the exemption to force a team *from* a city rather than to keep a team *in* a city. "This is Major League Baseball using the exemption to move a team," Carruthers said. "It turns the exemption from a shield into a sword." What it looked like to Carruthers was that the owners were banding together to force the Minnesota legislature and the state's taxpayers to build a stadium ... or else. Yes, baseball had a fine record for keeping teams in place. But times were changing. Other owners didn't want to see weak links in their industry's chain. The more weak links, the worse off baseball was. The wealthy owners—such as the Yankees, Dodgers, and Braves—didn't want to share their revenues with smaller-market teams. They wanted *taxpayers* to share *their* revenues with smaller-market teams in the forms of public subsidies to build new stadiums. Carruthers was in search of a legal theory that could seek baseball's accountability for holding the Twin Cities hostage over the Twins matter.

Carruthers, a lawyer, suggested that Attorney General Hubert H. Humphrey III, who was preparing a run for governor in 1998, examine baseball's behavior and its antitrust exemption. In the halls of Major League Baseball, anyone challenging the game's antitrust exemption is viewed as a crazed terrorist.

Quickly, University of Illinois law professor Stephen Ross, a maverick expert on sports and antitrust, advised Humphrey's staff. There was a theory there that could stand, Ross believed. It had been used once before, and successfully. In Florida in 1994, that state's supreme court ruled that baseball's antitrust exemption didn't apply to franchise movement; that is, the game couldn't do whatever it wanted when it came to teams wanting to move. The Florida Supreme Court narrowly interpreted the series of U.S. Supreme Court cases that have upheld the 1922 "Federal Baseball" decision. In declaring that baseball's owners couldn't stand behind the antitrust exemption, the Florida court opened the door for Florida's attorney general to begin an antitrust investigation of Major League Baseball. The Florida court said it was OK for the state's lawyers to begin examining just how baseball makes its decisions.

The triggering event was the aborted move by the San Francisco Giants to Tampa Bay. The Florida theory was that baseball's owners had conspired to *halt* the Giants' move, even though the offer by Floridians to buy and move the team was financially more attractive than an offer to keep the Giants in California. When the Florida Supreme Court ruled that its attorney general could ask baseball officials questions about their actions and internal decisions in the Giants' case, baseball flatly refused to cooperate. Baseball said it didn't have to explain a darn thing; it was exempt, no matter what any state court said. But in the end, baseball settled with the Florida interests, not wanting to reveal its inner machinations. What did it settle for? Within months, an expansion team had been awarded to the Tampa–St. Petersburg region.

Jerome Hoffman, a former Florida assistant attorney general who was involved in that Giants case, said that one of the issues was whether baseball follows a consistent set of rules when it addresses franchise movements. In the Giants case, he said, baseball made up its rules as it went along. In the Twins case, there was also some question as to what the rules were. Selig insisted they were being followed. But Hoffman said, "If I were the attorney general in Minnesota, I'd be passing some subpoenas out and gathering some information, and once I reviewed the written documentary evidence, I'd take sworn statements. You can't wait. If the rules are being jury-rigged along the way so this team can move, you can't unscramble the egg."

Hoffman's big question that would suggest that a conspiracy was in play was this: "If baseball wants to set up a condition that they're not going to allow the owners of the Twins to entertain any local buyers unless there's a construction of a new stadium, is that a reasonable condition?"

What was the most galling was that the state's leaders—especially Governor Carlson, his chief of staff Omann, and his sports ambassador Savelkoul—were coconspirators. They created the atmosphere to force the legislature to vote for a stadium. They played into the hands of baseball's owners and their ignoble threats.

As it turned out, because of the baffling economics of baseball and the industry's refusal to share revenues among itself, even a new stadium in Minnesota might not be enough to allow a team to prosper. As it turned out, baseball's threats might have been meaningless: there was no place for the Twins to play other than the Twin Cities. But the more moral and political question was this: can baseball's owners force a city or state to build a facility? And if the community won't, can baseball punish that town by moving a team and never allowing another to return? Come to think of it, what about North Carolina? If Minnesota didn't build a ballpark for the Twins, would Selig let a team move to North Carolina even if citizens *there* didn't approve a new stadium? What's a commissioner to do when the whole nation is saying, "Hell, no!"

Theories and legalities aside, the Carruthers-Humphrey antitrust challenge would serve a more practical purpose. Months later, it would take the Pohlad-Beaver letter of intent and put it on ice. It would freeze baseball where it stood.

CHAPTER 12

"Baseball Lives If You Push Green"

The Public Calls Carl's Bluff

Other than some moral struggle with the lords of baseball, there was nothing to hope for as the special session approached. There wasn't a chance in hell that a stadium bill would pass. Pohlad's political stock was at zero. Many in-the-know legislators believed that if anything could happen, it would have to be without Pohlad. So it wasn't surprising that Glen Taylor's name kept being raised. His shining armor had saved the day for the Timberwolves three years earlier. Why couldn't he pull another sporting rabbit out of his hat? Even Pohlad understood that. Besides, ever since Taylor had bought the Wolves, he and Pohlad had spoken occasionally and publicly about a kind of merger of their franchises, with the combined company selling stock to the public. They were just two billionaires in search of another deal.

Taylor and Carl and Bob Pohlad began to meet, and theoretically, arrangements were quietly made for Taylor to begin making inquiries with legislative leaders. However, on the eve of such meetings on October 16, just a week before the special session was to begin, *Star Tribune* veteran reporter Robert Whereatt got a tip from one of his many capitol spies: Taylor was on the prowl for the Twins. Whereatt called me at about 9 P.M. with the information, and I called Taylor at home, not expecting to get much out of him. He answered. And he talked. Yes, he said, he wanted to buy into the Twins, but only if a stadium would be funded by the legislature. Yes, new ownership blood could change the political dynamic. "Sometimes you have to change something in order to get some-thing to move," Taylor said. But he said something stronger, and he said it for a reason. Glen Taylor always says things on the record with a purpose. It was as if he was sending a sharp message to Pohlad himself. Taylor said that if he was to get involved, then Pohlad would have to give up operating control of the team. "I have to be in a position to have the authority if I would be doing the negotiations [for a new ballpark]," Taylor said.

I called Pohlad. It was getting late. Surprised that Taylor had spoken about their meetings, Pohlad gruffly said, "If that's what Glen told you, then write it." Taylor had been bold. He was brash. At a time when the stadium deal appeared comatose, he had pumped fresh air into it. The headline the next day in the *Star Tribune* read, "TAYLOR TAKES LEAD IN TWINS DEBATE."

Sometime around 11 A.M. the telephone rang at my *Star Tribune* desk. It was Bob and Carl Pohlad on their speakerphone.

"What the fuck was that headline all about?" Carl Pohlad said, surprising me with his anger and language. Headline? I didn't remember wincing at all when I saw it.

"What headline?" I said.

"You know what I'm talking about," Carl Pohlad said.

"C'mon, Jay," Bob Pohlad said. "What's with this 'new pitcher' idea?"

I wasn't playing dumb; I just didn't understand. I asked them to hold on, and I grabbed a newspaper. I live in St. Paul, and the newspaper's St. Paul edition had the "Taylor Takes Lead" headline. But there in the Minneapolis office was the Minneapolis edition, which was distributed to the west side of the metropolitan area.

"NEW PITCHER: TAYLOR REPLACES POHLAD" was how the Minneapolis edition headline read. Carl Pohlad didn't like it one bit. He told me that his discussions with Taylor were preliminary. He implied he wasn't going to take a backseat to anyone in this bumpy ride. It was another of those defining moments because it revealed something that continued to drive and dog Pohlad: he simply didn't want to part with his Twins.

As it turned out, the Taylor-Pohlad concept then went nowhere. The Pohlad sons believed that Taylor got way out ahead of himself. They thought he was showboating. But really, Taylor was testing, and Carl Pohlad failed the test. One team wasn't big enough for both of these guys. Perhaps Pohlad wanted control, wanted his toy, more than he wanted a ballpark solution. For sure he wanted the windfall of a new stadium.

Special Session

No, that's not fair. Pohlad did want a solution. He began to prove that during the special session, a raucous festival of competing protest signs, jammed phone lines, and screaming e-mails. The 1997 stadium special session may have been the finest exercise in participatory democracy in the state's history. The crisis that Omann and Carlson wanted had arrived. But it was pushing them; it wasn't pushing the public and obstinate anti-stadium legislators. If there would be consequences, they would be for legislators who voted yes, not no.

Usually, special sessions are conducted with a deal in place between the legislature and the governor. This was a rare case. There was no deal in place. There was no consensus. There wasn't a single plan. The day before the governor ordered the lawmakers back to the capitol, the high-level Legislative Commission on Planning and Fiscal Policy couldn't reach an agreement on a single benchmark bill. There was only theater. It began with Pohlad writing "An Open Letter to Minnesotans" via ads in the two Twin Cities newspapers on October 23.[1] Railing against the "endless barrage of charges and assertions over a new ballpark," Pohlad said, "This is a debate that must come to a close." He went on to say he wouldn't build the stadium on his own. But he also urged Minnesotans not to take their anger toward all pro sports out on him. "Please don't throw the baby out with the bath water," Pohlad wrote. But he turned showman. He said he was ready to submit a figure that would be his "contribution"—there's that darn word again—to a stadium project. He endorsed the Canterbury slots idea as one that Minnesotans seemed to be embracing. He said that if a stadium wasn't approved, he would sell to the Beaver group. And he said that if he had to sell to Beaver, he would give all his profit "above my investment" to local charities. "Sincerely, Carl."

By that time, no one believed Pohlad. It was sad. The guy was trying as hard as he could, and he was virtually dismissed. It led to October 24, which had to be the most cynical day of them all. After his ad appeared, Carruthers and House majority leader Ted Winter, a stadium funding opponent, invited—or challenged—Pohlad to testify before a special House committee. Pohlad accepted and, first thing in the morning, visited Carlson at his Summit Avenue residence for a meeting of top legislative leaders. They urged Pohlad to put in at least $100 million. Maybe that would push some legislators over to the "yes" side. But Republican leader Steve Sviggum was totally honest: "This is very generous," Sviggum told Pohlad, "but we don't have the votes."

On that day, Pohlad, looking old and battered, sat through two hours of questioning. He joked about getting a $100 million check from a fan to break the ice, but he couldn't break the political logjam. In a hushed committee room, Pohlad said that he would put in $111 million up front to the stadium construction. His accountant Bob Starkey clearly explained the breakdown with no omissions this time. Pohlad would write a check for $111 million, but he would hope to recover his investment over the next twenty years via every revenue stream of any kind: naming rights, in-stadium advertising, any concession company's investments in the ballpark. It would include free rent for ten years and lease concessions at the Dome while the new stadium was being built. The $111 million offer was better than any other offer by a baseball owner but San Francisco's and Detroit's.

Amid that cash offer, Pohlad made another suggestion: instead of paying for the stadium, he'd give the franchise to a nonprofit foundation. That foundation could then sell the team and fulfill Pohlad's desire to "be made whole." He'd also get the tax benefits of the transaction. Any overage on the sale—any profit—could be used for charitable causes. He was saying: "Take the thing. Yes, I want my money back. I always have. I always will. I'm not going to make a dime or lose a dime. But I'm out of it now. I'm not the issue anymore. If you want to build a stadium, build it, but it's not for me."

Of course, he didn't articulate it that bluntly, and no one helped him to. But now the state's options were far less complicated than "the put" of ten months earlier. He was questioned gruffly by some, most notably Marty, but despite not hearing everything and not making much sense on other answers, the eighty-two year old held his own. When it was over and he shuffled out of room 5 with his cane, he was surrounded by microphones, Minicams, bright lights, and hangers-on. Bell and Starkey and others walked by his side like bodyguards. I sidled up beside him and said, "Carl, why'd do you it? Why'd you come up to $111 million? That's a lot for you?"

He kept walking and looking straight ahead, sweat beading on his forehead, and said, "Goddamn right it is. I don't know why. I want baseball to stay here."

As he finished his last sentence, he stumbled over a television cable on the floor, and a bunch of us had to catch him before he fell. It was a heart-stopping moment, a horrendous scene as the capitol police and cameras and the push of onlookers swept Pohlad into Omann's basement office, behind closed doors. For all he'd done—good and bad—in this ballpark brouhaha, it seemed he deserved a bit more dignity than a mobster or Monica Lewinsky.

His offers raised nary an eyebrow. As soon as the $111 million came out of his mouth, people questioned its veracity and value. No matter what the man said, it was disbelieved and undervalued. Besides, the $111 million cash offer meant that Pohlad would still keep the team and gain all the benefits from any new ballpark being built, and the state would still need to find $250 million to finish construction. There remained that thorny issue: no one wanted to vote for taxes for a ballpark, and Pohlad had just laid claim to all the revenue streams. There wasn't anything left for the state to grab. There still wasn't a plan that was workable. That Jell-O still couldn't be framed. That porcupine still wasn't born. The public was dug in. House leaders were ten minutes away from calling it quits, but Omann asked both Carruthers and Sviggum for even more time. "Come on, give me two more weeks," Omann pleaded. They did, extending the statewide agony for three more weeks. The session was pushed back, now until mid-November. It was headed for a dead end, but not without some speed bumps in the middle.

For sure, the governor was getting fed up and on edge. He was a man already difficult to get along with, and the stress was pushing him toward fits of dramatic anger. On November 3, 1997, with the final Twins vote ten days away, meetings were held constantly in that ornate reception room with the painting of the bare-breasted Indian women and the Cass Gilbert furniture. The state's finest minds sought financing and political solutions to the crisis that Carlson had stoked. David Welle, the slight, soft-spoken financial consultant to the Sports Facilities Commission and personal calculator for Savelkoul, was there. Welle was the unfortunate one who became the object of Carlson's wrath.

"We've got to get the right numbers!" Carlson screamed, and he was really perturbed, really cranky, as Welle, Bernie Omann, and the governor marched into Carlson's private office. Beads of sweat formed on Welle's upper lip. This was not his idea of a good time. As if to make matters worse, Omann suddenly announced he had to take an important phone call in his office down the hall from the governor's. There sat poor, defenseless accountant David Welle, looking for an exit, with the gubernatorially pissed-off Arne Carlson staring at him, nostrils flared. Carlson was in his Gophers cardigan, pacing, dissatisfied with the course of stadium events. It resembled that famous scene from *All the President's Men*. Welle feared that Carlson was so distraught that, like President Nixon did with Secretary of State Henry Kissinger, they'd both have to drop to their knees and pray. As Welle's life flashed before his eyes, the telephone rang. It was as if the governor had called with a reprieve. But that was impossible, because it was the governor who answered the phone.

It was good news, great news. On the other end was University of Minnesota basketball coach Clem Haskins, one of Carlson's best friends. Haskins wanted to let the governor know that Joel Przybilla, the highly sought-after seven-foot center from Monticello High School, had just committed to the Gophers. And, boy, did they need a big man.

"We got him," Carlson whispered to Welle, who didn't know

who "him" was but did know that the governor was suddenly all smiles. No new stadium solution had been devised in those moments in Carlson's office, but the governor happily left his private meeting with Welle to return to the group in the reception room. We got the big man we needed.

It was good that Welle didn't find himself in Carlson's office the next day. That's when the voters of Minneapolis sent a loud "Forget about it." In a referendum instigated by a left-wing group known as Progressive Minnesota, city voters placed a $10 million cap on any municipal costs for pro sports. In direct response to the 1973 referendum that was circumvented by city fathers, this one was all-encompassing. No longer was it limited only to the Board of Taxation and Estimate. Now any city department doing any work on any piece of any pro sports facility would have to go to the voters in a general election referendum if it planned to spend $10 million or more on an athletic edifice. It virtually meant no new Twins stadium could be placed in Minneapolis without a citywide vote. The ordinance sits there still like a giant paperweight on any plans to put a ballpark in the state's largest city. Exactly how city officials and business leaders will circumvent that amendment to the city charter will be a fascinating thing to watch.

That wasn't all of it. The Vikings' Roger Headrick had driven another car bomb into the crowded stadium marketplace. In this tense interim period between Pohlad's rejected offer and another last-ditch finance plan and vote, Headrick just happened to want the world to know that, by the way, even if the Twins got their new stadium, a refurbished Dome wouldn't satisfy the football team. A new stadium for the Vikings was also a necessity. Even as an army of legislators and consultants struggled to redesign a Twins finance plan, Headrick tossed oil onto the fire.

"Every time we made a step forward, what's-his-name would have a page one-er, asking, 'What about us?'" said Bernie Omann, Carlson's chief of staff. It constantly appeared as if the Vikings' strategy was to force the Twins out of town so that the football team would have the stadium war all to itself. Headrick denied that, asserting he was looking out for the Vikings' interests, not napalming the Twins. Still, Carlson would have none of Headrick's antics, not at this point in the battle, not with the Vikings playing with a lease that didn't expire until 2011.

On the day before the special session was to reconvene, Carlson summoned Headrick to his capitol office and, basically, let him have it. Sitting at his desk, wagging his finger and raising his voice, with key staffers there to watch the dressing-down, Carlson essentially told Headrick to keep his mouth shut. Headrick, not one to back down, tried to explain that he had free-agent football players to sign and that his stadium revenue situation militated against that.

"Well, I've got a baseball stadium bill to pass," Carlson countered angrily. "You guys don't know how this place works. You guys don't know how to run your own team. You've got a lease, and we'll go to the Supreme Court to enforce it. You can't solve your problem by talking to the media. You should be meeting with me."

Headrick countered that he'd requested a meeting between the NFL commissioner Paul Tagliabue and Carlson, but that the governor's office had rejected it. Headrick said his team needed some attention, too, or the Vikings would head into a "downward cycle."

Carlson said: "The problem with football isn't revenues, it's salaries. You should be smart enough to convince the other owners to keep the salaries down. There's not one person in this room here making $75,000," the governor said, looking at his staff. "And you want them to go help you pay your players $3 million a year?"

"What about baseball?" Headrick replied.

As voices got louder, Omann had to intervene. "Bernie saved the meeting," said one witness. "It was not a love-in," said Omann. "The old purple pride didn't really exist that day." Carlson told Headrick, in no uncertain terms, that he didn't want to see him again until the Vikings got their complex ownership situation resolved. In fact, the men didn't meet again. Nine months later, Headrick was out on the street when Red McCombs bought the team and instantly began campaigning for a new stadium.

Amid this occurred the most embarrassing public relations gaffe of all: the Twins placing an ad on television attempting to tug at people's hearts and seemingly exploiting a dying child. As part of a series of fifteen-second TV spots, all created under the heading "If the Twins Leave Minnesota," one commercial aired just twice, for a total of thirty seconds. It was produced by Bill Pohlad, the youngest and least involved of the Pohlad sons. He fashions himself as a film producer. With that half minute of display, the ad created days of bad publicity. And it aired just one week before the legislature was to vote on final stadium bills.

In the commercial, the words "8 year old" appeared against a black background in lowercase letters. As the viewer saw the words, a man's voice flatly said: "If the Twins leave Minnesota, an eight year old from Willmar undergoing chemotherapy will never get a visit from Marty Cordova." As those words were heard, a grainy, homelike video of the Twins left fielder popped onto the screen. There, Cordova was handing a short, bald, obviously ill boy, with his back to the camera, a baseball and, it seemed, a T-shirt. "Marty brought you something," a woman's voice—presumably a nurse or the boy's mother—was heard saying. The setting was clearly a hospital room. The implication was simple: if there's no major-league baseball, a dying boy won't get his last wish.

Now, the truth is that sports stars can provide some special moments for youngsters, no matter what the status of their health. The time-honored visit to the hospital by athletes evokes the fabled visit by Babe Ruth to the sick kid, complete with a promise to hit a home run for the hospitalized youngster. But the problems with this ad were plentiful: the boy had died two months earlier; he wasn't from Willmar; though his parents had signed a release to show the footage for charitable purposes, they didn't know it would be used to boost the stadium effort. Besides that, no one in the Twins organization checked any of the facts in the ad.

"A lot of things slipped through the cracks," said Twins marketing vice president Dave St. Peter, still saddened by the event nearly two years later. Bill Pohlad's company never cleared the facts, but neither did Pat Forciea, who was then the Twins' top stadium and marketing consultant. Forciea said it wasn't his responsibility; after all, Bill Pohlad's River Road Productions controlled it. But two Twins employees said that

Forciea popped the ad in a Dome VCR soon before it aired, and that he too should share some of the blame for the fastness and looseness of the presentation.

As with all these gaffes, the dying boy ad was seized upon even though its shelf life was that of an insect. On Tuesday, November 4, the ad aired once on WCCO-TV, Channel 4, and once on KARE-TV, Channel 11. The next morning, the raunchy men on Tom Barnard's KQRS-FM drive-time radio show talked about it. As the day wore on, St. Peter consulted with the Pohlads about the commercial and apologized profusely to officials at the Ronald McDonald House, the cancer center with which the Twins have had a long and warm relationship. "We thought the thing was put to bed," St. Peter said of the matter, as the team decided to stop running the ad. But Channel 4's Pat Kessler reported the problem on the 6 P.M. news that Wednesday night, and both the *Star Tribune* and *Pioneer Press* reported the facts and prolonged the controversy into the next day, and beyond.

Still, lawmakers such as Representatives Loren Jennings and Ann Rest, who miraculously saw the glass as half full, kept meeting. They believed—as they should have—that Pohlad's deal with Beaver would take on a new life after November 30. If there were no stadium, Pohlad would sell. The Twins would be gone. That was the presumption. That was what Carlson and Omann wanted the state to believe. But everyone was running in place. Harvey Mackay, of Metrodome fame, tried to pull together the business community with a show of force. Even Twins officials called it "a mirage." There were "pledges" of ticket buying and suite buying, but they were halfhearted. Rest and Jennings revived a user fee package, with a public ownership component. They were in the business of getting votes, not of creating a stadium plan that made any sense. No longer would the ballpark have a retractable roof. The legislature wouldn't decide where the facility was to be located; the Sports Facilities Commission would. A lottery specifically for the stadium would begin. And a host of sports-related taxes would be used to pay for it all under the theory that "but for" sports, the state wouldn't be collecting the taxes; players' income taxes and in-stadium sales taxes would be redirected from the state general fund to a stadium fund. Meanwhile, Day and Representative Bob Milbert of South St. Paul kept pushing for gambling to pay for it all. Pohlad would pass the team onto a foundation. He'd get his investment in the team back after the foundation sold it. The profits on the sale would help pay for the stadium. It was like some bazaar with politicians of various stripes attempting to sell their wares at a cacophonous marketplace. Except nobody was buying. And by November 12, the day before what was being called the final day, Minnesota was at a political standstill. The phone lines at the capitol hit gridlock. Citizens expressed themselves, an estimated 150,000 of them. As many callers as could get through were being listened to. One told Representative Dee Long, "If you don't make the Twins leave town, I'll never vote for you again." Long scratched her head, not seeing language in any bill that proposed kicking Pohlad out of the state—although *that* may have gotten enough votes for passage. It was the kind of sentiment that caused all but one of Minneapolis's eleven-member delegation to vote against any stadium bill. Only Representative Richard Jefferson, the lone African American in the Minnesota House, supported a stadium package, believing it was important to keep the team and stadium in Minneapolis. But other House members, like Long, saw it as a no-win. Their constituents were adamantly against it. Some—such as Governor Carlson—believed that a unified pro-stadium Minneapolis delegation could have signaled deep and broad city support for a ballpark. That signal could have garnered enough votes from other parts of the state to at least get a bill out of the House. But it wasn't to be. The people spoke, even poetically.

Souvenir knockoffs of the fabled World Series "Homer Hankies" were for sale. In 1987, these spiritual handkerchiefs were in the hands of every Twins fan, waved like flags to honor their team, our team, our beloved franchise. Now up-to-date hankies were distributed at the capitol; a couple drove in from Rush City to give "Hell No" hankies to the legislators. "Just say hell no to taxpayer funded pro sports," the cloth square read. By Thursday, November 13, it was clear the final day had arrived. A mobile billboard sat at the corner of Marion Street and I-94, where many legislators exit to get to the capitol. It read: "Publicity Fades.

Debates End. Baseball Is Forever." Burly union members were finally activated by an otherwise tentative AFL-CIO. They gathered around the entrance to the House chamber, all with bright red "Save the Twins" stickers attached to their shiny sheet-metal-worker jackets. They were countered by other demonstrators with handmade signs that read: "JUST SAY NO TO BALL 'PORK.'" Outside, the first real snow of winter fell. Inside, someone had to take a stand. House minority leader Steve Sviggum tried. All year long he'd opposed taxes for a stadium. He had the idea of selling the Dome to the teams for $1 and letting the Vikings and Twins figure it out. Otherwise, as an ardent antitax Republican farmer, Sviggum wasn't engaged in any solutions. Mackay had personally gone to Sviggum's Kenyon farm and appealed to him a week earlier. Impressed, yes, but not swayed. Finally, as this alleged sudden-death clock ticked, Sviggum called his Republican caucus together and told them the time had come to back a last-ditch user-fee stadium finance plan.

"Folks," Sviggum said as he paced inside room 118 with his colleagues at attention, "I'm struggling in my mind right now. I've preached to my wife that we've always got to be flexible. And now's the time."

Sviggum, a fit man who referees high school basketball games in his spare time, walked up and down the beautiful flowered rug in the historic conference room, with his caucus members gathered around a long conference table and others in rows of chairs on each end of the room.

Knight and Krinkie, still hand grenade throwers, looked at each other and rolled their eyes. "As soon as he started talking about his wife, I knew we were in trouble," Knight remembered. Sviggum proceeded to explain that he believed that a total user fee package would be passed, and that if it did "the Republicans have won, we've won," because "citizen-taxpayers' dollars are not going to be used."

Krinkie interrupted. He wondered why Sviggum and the caucus should support a user fee plan now. The Twins themselves had always been reluctant to rely on those fees, he said. The Twins believed all the fees came out of their bottom line. But Sviggum said it was important for their caucus to show that they were trying. And all stadium supporters really wanted was for something, anything, to emerge from the

House on that day. For sure, Senator Moe would be able to get some semblance of a stadium bill through the Senate. Then they'd all limp into a conference committee, where the two chambers would come to some sort of compromise. There, a smaller group of legislators could work out a deal.

But others spoke up. The user fee plan was based on the Twins drawing 2.5 million fans a season. If they didn't, the finance plan would tumble. It was based on the team being able to sell 20,000 season tickets for the next ten years. With only 8,800 in place in 1997, that seemed optimistic.

"I feel like I'm on the *Monty Hall Show*," said Sherry Broeker, a representative from suburban Vadnais Heights. "Door one, door two, door three. This is all a shell game."

Mike Osskopp, a bear of a man who is also a radio talk show host in Hastings was his typical frustrated self. "You can put in Barc-o-Loungers and have Domino's deliver, but if your team is 60 and 102, people aren't going to show up," he said of the projected high attendance.

But Sviggum was in a cheerleading mode. He believed that the Republicans could take credit. "I can imagine the headlines," he said. "REPUBLICANS HOLD FIRM. SAVE THE TAXPAYERS AND SAVE THE TWINS." His colleagues weren't biting. They began exchanging opinions on baseball's lack of revenue sharing, on the future popularity of the sport, on whether this was just a ploy to drag this thing into a fixed conference committee, on why "the shills," like the *Star Tribune*'s Sid Hartman and WCCO's Dark Star, were backing the package.

"If they don't have the Twins, they'd have nothing to talk about from the Super Bowl to the start of Timberwolves training camp," said Osskopp, sounding just like a radio talk show host.

As much as Sviggum tried, he couldn't get the group to agree on anything. As much as he wanted to be a last-minute hero, it wasn't in the cards. Soon afterward, the caucus dispersed to return to the House floor. The leader had done his job. But he hadn't changed many minds.

By 1 P.M., with no decisions made, Senator Dean Johnson was walking swiftly down the steps from the Senate chamber. He said he was in a hurry. "This is bed-wetting time," he said. "They've sent me down to Wal-Mart to get some Depends."

But there were no bodily movements or political movements of any kind. Omann says the "untold story" is how close he got to collecting enough votes to push the ballpark bill into a conference committee. The story was untold because it wasn't true. Jennings kept running down to Omann's basement conference room to make changes in the bill to get votes, but his efforts were all for naught. Tensions ran high. Expectations were sinking. Borman, derisively nicknamed "The Field General" by other more experienced lobbyists, fought with lawyers for the Sports Facilities Commission, calling the agency "the enemy" as amendments were proposed to abolish the commission. Some rural votes might be won if the Minneapolis-linked agency died. Kathleen Lamb, the commission's hardworking lawyer, who had put up with a tornado of guff throughout the stadium process, simply walked out of the room. The coalition was crumbling. Starkey and Bell made calls to legislators on the floor, not able to find Borman. Borman was upstairs, searching for Carlson, hoping he could twist arms. Not able to find Carlson, Borman tried to summon legislators from floor seats to talk via cell phone with Carl Pohlad. No one would come out of the chamber to meet with Borman.

Still, Borman thought he was getting close, within perhaps a half dozen votes. Other experts waiting outside the House chamber knew better. Bill McGrann, one of the lobbyists for the Sports Facilities Commission and a veteran of the Metrodome legislative sessions, had a glum, knowing look on his face. He just shook his head as the debate wore on. He knew the votes weren't there.

Why would legislators vote for a deal that didn't add up, a deal that the Twins would never have agreed to anyway? The numbers were not in the team's favor. Politically, the goal was to get to that safe haven of a conference committee, where the House and Senate deal makers could glue together a stadium package. But the discussions would have been a sham. The Senate never got around to passing its own bill, although there was support for an interest-free loan to build the ballpark. The Senate was waiting for the House to do its work first. The House package was at least $2 million a year short of raising enough money to pay for the ball-park. Even those calculations relied on some assumptions that still dog the Twins today; because of the distorted economics of major-league baseball, a new stadium might not be enough to help a team in a market the size of the Twin Cities survive. The finance plan associated with the last proposal was deeply dependent on attendance figures that the Twins had achieved only once in their thirty-seven-season history. If attendance hadn't averaged about 3 million fans per season over the life of the thirty-year bonding period of the ballpark, then the finance plan—reliant on user fees—would have faced troubles. And 3 million fans had passed through Twins turnstiles just once, in 1988, the year after their first World Series victory.

The plan simply didn't add up to the amount needed to fund $233 million worth of state-issued bonds that would have helped construct the open-air stadium. According to the Revenue Department, to repay those bonds would have required revenues of about $18.7 million annually, if the bonds were taxable and carried an interest rate of 7 percent. But the bill that the legislators rejected raised only about $16.9 million per year. Plus, two of the revenue sources—a surcharge on players' salaries and a surcharge on media companies that broadcast and telecast Twins games—were challenged by the Twins, the Major League Baseball Players Associ-ation, and the Minnesota Broadcasters Association. Of that $16.9 million total, $4.1 million was dependent on a 4 percent player income-tax surcharge ($1.7 million) and a new surcharge tax on the rights-holding broadcasters ($2.4 million). Donald Fehr, executive director of the base-ball players union, an organization that should contribute to stadium construction as should owners, trashed the proposed surcharge because it embodied "all kinds of problems, legal and otherwise. It also has a prac-tical effect: No player would want to play in Minnesota." He wondered if doctors would be taxed to build hospitals—which, come to think of it, isn't such a bad idea.

The Cleveland Indians, since moving into Jacobs Field, averaged more than 3 million people per season. Cleveland consistently drew far fewer fans in its old, windy Municipal Stadium than the Twins did. The

Baltimore Orioles averaged more than 3.5 million fans per season since moving into Camden Yards in 1992. But those teams had their stadiums built with more substantial direct public subsidies—such as a lottery or sales taxes—and not with a user fee package, as the House plan called for. User fees come out of a team's bottom line; subsidies come out of the public's bottom line.

And if the Twins drew only 2.5 million fans a year, which was actually above the 1997 American League average of 2.23 million per team, the finance plan would have teetered. That reduction by 400,000 fans could reasonably have been expected to reduce the finance plan by at least $1.4 million a year. Only once since 1961 had the Twins drawn more than 2.5 million fans. Still, the defeated plan included provisions for community ownership of the Twins after Pohlad's donation of the team to a nonprofit foundation. It also called for guarantees of at least $32.5 million a year in business support of the team through commitments for season tickets, suites and luxury seats, and personal seat licenses. Would business have supported that? The bill called for at least 10 percent of Twins tickets to sell for no more than $5, and 75 percent of the team eventually to be owned by small investors.

All in all, it was a decent compromise and included socially responsible provisions that forced the business community to ante up and provided family-priced entertainment. But it required hundreds of millions of dollars of public bonding. There was no site selected and no guarantee on how to pay for infrastructural costs. And there was no enthusiasm for anything. The debate had not brought people together, had not forged consensus. It polarized.

"It's exactly what most of the people in the state want," said Sviggum of the final user fee–based bill. "Vote yes."

But Representative Phyllis Kahn, a huge baseball fan and the backer of a public ownership bill, voted no. She claimed she did so because the proposal was "a house of cards." It was flimsy, to be sure, but with some more negotiating in the conference committee, perhaps something workable would have emerged. Wasn't Kahn concerned the Twins might move? "I don't think anybody cares anymore," she shot back.

As for the Senate, it was waiting for the House to pass something, anything. It never happened. Dick Day, of course, was in the wings hoping to pass a Canterbury slots authorization bill, but he didn't get his chance.

Jennings, the deal maker and chief Twins bill sponsor, dramatically declared, "On November 13th, professional baseball died in Minnesota." Just before the 8:30 P.M. vote, Jennings told legislators: "There will be no tomorrow. Baseball lives if you push green [a yes vote]. Baseball dies if you push red [a no vote]. . . . This is a vote you're not going to forget for the rest of your life." The House defeated the bill in a 47 to 84 vote, with more Republicans (26) saying aye than DFLers (21).

The board went red, and soon afterward few of the legislators seemed to have had any sense of history. They packed up and got out of town. For sure, the electorate didn't punish those who voted no.

Pohlad expressed shock, and over the phone from his home, his voice sounded stunned. Earlier in the day, Bell had informed him there was a chance. Later that night, on his ride home to North St. Paul, Bell telephoned Pohlad from his car and commiserated. But Pohlad, a bit dazed and confused, told me minutes later, "Don't put this in the newspaper. But I might just build the damn thing myself. Call me tomorrow."

No such announcement of a privately built stadium was forthcoming. It was never even seriously discussed by the Pohlad family. "If I ever even suggested that to my dad, he would know quickly that I hadn't learned very much about anything," Bob Pohlad said of a totally private stadium finance plan. "He would quickly ask me to maybe go to work at the Boys and Girls Clubs. For us to have, what, $400 million invested in baseball? Forget it."

Two weeks remained until that November 30 deadline. Diehards continued to scramble, even as Pohlad and Selig increased the pressure at yet another owners' meeting in Phoenix. Formally, the American League gave Pohlad "permission" to sell the team. AL president Gene Budig, a very nice but totally ineffectual administrator, made the official announcement: "The American League has no choice but to direct the Twins to move forward with the sale of the club."

Pohlad said $111 million, and they didn't even raise their eyebrows. He said they could have the team and do what they wanted with it; just build a stadium. "They raised the bar so high that when he agreed to it they figured, 'We'll have to vote no anyway,'" said Bell of the legislators. All the surveys, all the election guides, all the news of Kevin Garnett's salary and Pohlad's wealth, the North Stars' move, the Target Center buyout, the players' strike, all added up. Now things looked bleak.

Bill Lester, the man who ran the Dome, which looked as if it might lose its prime tenant, was poetic. "I still think there's a pulse," he said of the ballpark effort after the special session defeat. "If you put a mirror under its nose, though, you might not get anything." Still, as much as Pohlad might have wanted to stick it to the Minnesota political system that had made his life miserable over the past eleven months, he was trapped. There was really nowhere to go.

Oh, there was this referendum that was planned for May 5 of 1998 in this place called "the Triad," with three cities called Greensboro, Winston-Salem, and High Point, a community that said it was ready to steal a baseball team, just like another unknown area, "the Twin Cities," had forty years earlier. But no one—no one—in baseball wanted a major-league team to relocate to Greensboro, including Pohlad, the banker turned bluffer.

In the end, the special session cost the taxpayers about $82,000, according to state records, $24,000 in the Senate and $58,000 in the House, what with legislative per diems and other ancillary costs. The public's position, so dug in for so long, was now dipped in deeper cynicism.

For Himle and Redmond, it took all of one day to discover that even they may have been misled. Two of the state's most respected political consultants went back to the thirty-eighth floor of the Dain Tower and instructed the Pohlads that they now had to deliver a strong message that the team was, in fact, going to move. You know, a terse release that said, "Allied Van Lines was hired by Carl Pohlad to move every last jockstrap out of the Metrodome yesterday. Pohlad declined comment other than to say to all Minnesotans, 'Screw you.'" Something like that. Carl Pohlad couldn't do it. He issued instead a melancholy sort of statement: "The Minnesota Twins have been an important part of my life, and that of my family, for fourteen years. My dream was that they remain competitive and in Minnesota forever. It appears that may not be possible."

Pohlad was in denial. But Pohlad wasn't ready to move this team. He was recovering from being snookered. Omann, Jennings, and Savelkoul said a deadline would push the legislature. It did the opposite. It pulled the state apart. The threat didn't scare anyone.

What had begun on January 8, 1997, with battered credibility was ending even worse: no credibility at all. Various deadlines passed. November 30, 1997, that magic date beyond which there would be no point of return, faded into nothingness. A referendum awaited the citizens of the Triad, a pleasant-enough zone of sprawl that could never support a major-league baseball team, what with Greensboro a big Duluth and Winston-Salem a big Rochester. And baseball's owners watched from afar and worried that the North Carolina referendum might pass and that they'd have to figure out how to undo a favorable referendum—a new twist on the referendum game in which many governments have had to override unsuccessful votes, such as those in Cleveland, Milwaukee, and Seattle.

Former Major League Baseball commissioner Fay Vincent once said, "A new stadium makes the whole country sit up and take notice."[2] Such was the case in Minnesota. The nation was watching. Fans and citizens from near and far were cheering. Other owners were shaking their heads.

Cultural Phenomenon

That the Twins stadium debate had become embedded in the consciousness of Minnesotans was revealed by a curious advertising campaign pushed by a group called Prolife Minnesota. That campaign was hatched by Prolife Minnesota's director Mary Ann Kuharski with her husband, John, at the Main Event sports bar in Fridley, an inner-ring Minneapolis suburb. Mary Ann Kuharski says that her interest in sports is close to zero, that in fact, when the sports segment comes on the TV news, "I go and take a shower." But on a November day soon after the special session, she was seeking a new campaign to promote her belief that abortions should be stopped and that children should be adopted.

Prolife Minnesota doesn't organize demonstrations, endorse candidates, or debate pro-choicers. Its mission is to educate and advertise. What it does is leverage common themes to catch the public's attention and support a so-called pro-life stance. It's not easy to grab the eye of a motorist going sixty miles per hour when the theme is abortion and not cigarettes or the upcoming lottery jackpot.

In the past, Kuharski had created a billboard and newspaper campaign that focused on the term "Minnesota nice," but with a depiction of a fetus attached to the words. She'd placed a billboard near a casino with the "24 of hearts" playing card on display; the 24 of hearts meant that twenty-four days from conception, a fetus has a heartbeat.

As it turns out, eight days after the special session closed, Kuharski read an article in the *Wall Street Journal* about so-called pregnancy reduction. This is the process by which prospective mothers with multiple births in the offing could abort one of the fetuses. Thus a set of triplets could become merely twins, and a set of twins could become one baby.

"At the same time I'm hearing and reading all this hype about the Twins, I'm reading this story in the *Wall Street Journal* about people who don't want two babies because they only want to pay for one college tuition," Kuharski said, her tiny St. Anthony Village office filled with photos of billboards past.

A brainstorm arrived. Link the baseball Twins with in utero twins.

"Wasn't that fun?" Kuharski asked, her eyes gleaming, her energy super high. "I use anything to get people's attention."

She took the Twins blue-and-red colors. She placed an illustration of twin fetuses on the left side of the billboard and the smiling faces of the twin babies on the right side. Smack-dab in the middle were the words "SAVE THE TWINS!"

How could it be? Two of the state's most controversial topics were reduced to the art of the billboard. Indeed, there were about 230 of them statewide at a cost of about $110,000. One even stood a block away from the Metrodome in one of the Twins' parking lots.

"Those ads got us more hate calls than any ad I ever had," Kuharski said of the whole campaign.

But the hate wasn't from pro-choicers blasting Prolife Minnesota for its poor taste. The twenty or so calls came from antistadium fanatics who thought that Kuharski's organization was supporting a publicly funded stadium.

"Right here on the phone we were accused of being a front for the people who wanted a new stadium," she said. "They'd yell and scream and threaten things. I'd tell them we have 4,400 babies a day who die and 4,400 women needing help. Those billboards save babies' lives, and all these people wanted to scream about was the stadium."

Fact is, she said, her calls from men increased as the billboard caught their eye more than any previous Prolife Minnesota billboards. And for a woman who is in the firing lines of one of the nation's most contested issues, the bitterness she heard was palpable. "I didn't realize the vindictive feelings towards the Twins and the owner," she said.

Antitrust

Something else occurred in the interim. Attorney General Skip Humphrey threw a monkey wrench into the works. Following from House Speaker Carruthers's comments months earlier, wanting to protect the Sports Facilities Commission from the Twins' attempt to escape their Dome lease, Humphrey's staff went on the offensive.

On December 17, 1997, Assistant Attorney General Peter Hofrenning sent a brief letter and an eighteen-page fishing-expedition-like request to Pohlad, Selig, American League president Gene Budig, and Don Beaver. Called an "investigate demand," it asked Pohlad to answer and or produce hundreds of answers to forty-eight distinct requests. It was part of, Hofrenning wrote to all of the desired respondents, "an investigation of possible violations of the antitrust laws" of Minnesota. In the request to Pohlad, the demands included the following:

- Provide all documents relating or referring to proposals to sell
  and/or relocate the Twins, and/or to build a new stadium in Minnesota or North Carolina.
- Provide all documents relating or referring to revenues generated
  by other teams (including the Baltimore Orioles, Cleveland Indians, Chicago White Sox, and San Francisco Giants) after a new stadium was built and the revenues generated by the same team before
  the stadium was built.
- Provide all documents relating or referring to the relocation of the
  Washington Senators to Minnesota.
- Describe in detail the substance and dates of any communications
  you have had with Allan H. Selig regarding: (1) the relocation of the
  Twins; (2) the building of a new stadium in Minnesota; (3) whether
  Major League Baseball would approve a transfer of Twins' ownership without a new stadium being built in Minnesota; (4) whether
  MLB would approve a transfer of Twins' ownership without a new
  stadium being built in North Carolina; and (5) whether an expansion team would be located in Minnesota if a new stadium was not
  built in Minnesota.

You get the idea. From 1958 to 1998, Hofrenning wanted to know every
type of cereal Pohlad, Selig, Beaver, and their stockbrokers had for breakfast every morning. The attorney general's office wanted simply to get to
the point of being allowed to ask those questions. Once the Minnesota
courts allowed him the right to ask those questions, he had won. Baseball would refuse and, as it had done in Florida, likely settle. For what? A
long-term Dome lease? A new owner? Who knew?

Baseball took Humphrey's challenge seriously, sending in their top
antitrust expert from New York to challenge the state. The Twins employed Roger Magnuson, a glib and brilliant litigator with the Dorsey &
Whitney law firm. At first, a Ramsey County district court judge in St.
Paul sided with the state. Judge Margaret Marrinan said the attorney
general's office could ask some of the volumes of questions it sought to.
Baseball's lawyers said the state couldn't ask any of the questions because

baseball is exempt from antitrust laws. If it's exempt from the laws, then it must be exempt from investigations of violations of the laws. How, baseball's lawyers wondered, can baseball violate laws that don't apply to it?

The case, plus another brought by the Sports Facilities Commission challenging the Twins' exercise of the escape clause, froze Pohlad and Beaver in their tracks. Even if their business deal was going nowhere, the legal roadblocks forced a pause. Unfortunately, in April 1999, the Minnesota Supreme Court sided with baseball, saying its exemption protected it from an antitrust investigation and that any changes were to be left to Congress. In late 1999 the state appealed to the U.S. Supreme Court, but the high court refused to hear the case. Also, unfortunately, Humphrey's staff missed the real target. Sure, Selig and Pohlad joined forces to leverage a stadium. But the real conspiracy to stick up Minnesota's voters was not hatched in a banker's tower in downtown Minneapolis or in Selig's cluttered office in aging County Stadium—the first publicly built facility, which allowed the Boston Braves to move to Milwaukee. No, it was born in the hallowed offices of the governor of the state of Minnesota.

Reality Sets In

With the arrival of 1998, reality set in. In mid-January in Phoenix at the posh Arizona Biltmore, home to an exquisite collection of mission-style furniture, baseball's owners met once more to discuss a wide variety of pressing matters, none of them involving the Twins. Pohlad and Bell had their typical and cursory meeting with top officials explaining how they had lost again at the Minnesota legislature. In Minnesota, there was a decreasing amount of angst because the November 30 deadline had passed and not a thing had happened. In fact, according to North Carolina sources, as soon as the legislature did its deed, Pohlad stopped talking directly with Beaver.

Still, reporters waited outside yet another chandeliered hotel meeting room to hear Selig issue yet another threat about how the people of Minnesota had to understand that an owner couldn't be consigned to bankruptcy and how, if we could only understand it all, a new stadium was the best solution to our community's sense of malaise … something like that.

But this time, Selig didn't come out swinging. He came mysteriously meekly, with sober Pohlad at his side virtually speechless after a four-hour meeting. Selig suggested that the Twins weren't going to move at all. It looked as if Humphrey's lawsuit, which Twins officials had dismissed as a political ploy, had an effect.

Two months after Loren Jennings had said that baseball was dead in Minnesota, Selig and Pohlad were cautiously saying that wasn't the case. Were they establishing a record for the courts to show that the conspiracy was backtracking?

Pohlad, incredibly, said that "the ball" was in the Minnesota legislature's court. "We haven't offered anything. But if they want to come back with something, fine, we'll listen." It was an odd proposal, given that it was Pohlad who had been trounced, not the other way around. Losers are the ones who traditionally ask for a second chance, not winners. Be that as it may, Selig joined Pohlad in seeking another round with the legislature, and as he had at County Stadium the October before, he distanced himself from the Triad, just as the campaign in Greensboro and Winston-Salem was beginning to become a daily issue in those cities. With Justin Catanoso of the *Greensboro News and Record* covering these meetings, Selig sent a strong message to Triad voters. It was, basically, "We don't want this team going down there."

"I don't know that Minnesota has said no," Selig said, leaving open the modern question of "Which part of 'no' don't you understand?" He went on to demonstrate how out of touch he was with the political situation in Minnesota. "In the state of Washington, people said no in a referendum, and the legislature a couple weeks later came back and did what they had to do," Selig said of the way in which the Seattle Mariners got their publicly financed stadium. "I'm not saying that'll happen [in Minnesota]. I'm just saying, in our attempt to try to keep teams where they are, Mr. Pohlad and his family have every right to pursue all options."

Twice during that first day of the owners' meetings, Selig chatted with reporters about the Minnesota situation and twice separated North

Carolina's baseball future from the Twins' ongoing crisis. Typically, Selig was confusing and contradictory, stating that "the North Carolina situation is independent" of the Twins' need for a new ballpark in Minnesota, then later observing, "The fact of the matter is we've got to know that his team will be viable in Minnesota. If someone thinks there are not attractive alternatives [in North Carolina] . . . they're not dealing with the real problem in the Twin Cities. . . . There's no question that the North Carolina area is a great area, and it will be an extraordinarily attractive area someday for a big-league baseball team."

To me, that word "someday" was the first major backing off of Selig's repeated and baseless threats. "Someday" is what sports marketers and critics of the potential move of the Twins had been saying about North Carolina's chances for months. With all the owners gathered, there was behind-closed-doors chatter that a move from the fifteenth-largest market in the nation to the forty-seventh largest didn't make sense. And Charlotte, well, where was its stadium?

"If there's not a park in place and not a vote, how do you move the team?" asked Vince Naimoli, managing general partner of the expansion Tampa Bay Devil Rays of the American League. As for placing the Twins in a refurbished minor-league stadium temporarily, Naimoli noted that baseball delayed its expansion so that Tampa Bay and Phoenix, the new National League team, would be in new stadiums, not temporary, renovated parks. The bluff was formally collapsing. It was as if Pohlad and Selig were saying, "Uh-oh, we've gone a little too far down this road and now we need to put on the emergency brakes."

The poor Triad was being insulted. Never in the history of pro sports has a community wanted to build a stadium, wanted to tax itself, wanted to throw all of its might behind the luring of a pro sports team, and been rejected like a homely wallflower seeking a prom date.

Within baseball circles, the dynamics had shifted. Yes, Pohlad was having trouble pulling that trigger. He just couldn't allow himself to move a team, an act that would jeopardize his family's reputation for the next fifty years. For someone who had once been a decisive businessman, the Twins dead end stymied Pohlad, whose wavering was part emotion, part aging, part no-way-out. "There's 5.8 billion people in the world, and he's the only one who knows what he's going to do," said his friend Harvey Mackay. "And guess what, he doesn't even know. He can't quite pull the trigger on this."

Now that the Twins situation had been examined fully by the other owners, the potential for a franchise relocation became a frightening thought to them all. Baseball had other matters to address, such as the purchase of the Los Angeles Dodgers by Australian media magnate Rupert Murdoch, and what his spending could mean for other owners. Indeed, as Pohlad met with his other owners, outgoing Dodgers owner Peter O'Malley sat in a plush, elegantly upholstered chair outside the room. He had seen the economic handwriting, and he was bailing out of the industry. The future of one of baseball's crown jewels was far more disconcerting to the other owners than the matter of the lowly Minnesota Twins. In Minnesota it may have been big news. At these owners' meetings, the Twins' situation seemed more a bother than a crisis.

That night, a well-connected, high-ranking baseball official with intimate knowledge of the Twins deal, in a semidrunken interview, laughed at the idea that the Twins might move to the Triad. He laughed at the idea that Don Beaver was ready to own a major-league team. "Beaver doesn't know what he's doing," the man said, sitting in the cool desert air. "He's a nice guy, but he doesn't know what he's getting into. The other new owners are all corporate media types, Murdoch, Disney, Hicks."

As for the Triad referendum, the baseball man, cigar in one hand, scotch in the other, said, "If it passes, that's the owners' worst nightmare."

But, this official said, the idea that the Twins and Pohlad would somehow move to Knights Castle in the interim was a joke. Something else came out, though, that was an eyepopper. Team relocations aside, the owners and leaders of the game were talking about something more significant and, perhaps, practical. Rather than riding the wave of sports expansion—which had put the Twin Cities on the map nearly forty years earlier—owners were privately beginning to discuss "contracting" rather than expanding.

Maybe, he said, such a move would shake the game to its senses.

He laughed about a memory of Paul Beeston, who had just been named Selig's number two operating officer. Beeston, once president of the Toronto Blue Jays, had taken him on a tour of SkyDome, the Jays' retractable-roof stadium, soon after it opened in 1989. "This is financially irresponsible, but I love it," Beeston said.

So, with the Montreal Expos facing the same kinds of economic pressures as the Twins, some owners thought those teams should simply be shut down. The players would be dispersed, the free-agent market would be somewhat glutted, and salaries, in theory, would be dragged down. (In the summer of 1999, this notion of consolidation received widespread media attention when it was revealed by Colorado Rockies owner Jerry McMorris.)

"If I were God, baseball would suspend play in Montreal and Minnesota," my interviewee said. By January there wasn't a chance in hell that a team was going to go to the Triad. Or at least baseball had its fingers crossed that it wouldn't have to ever deal with that silly eventuality.

A month later, Selig visited Charlotte to speak at a $150-a-plate dinner for the Charlotte Regional Sports Commission. There, five hundred enthusiastic business leaders showed up to prove how important they thought baseball could be to that city. Remember now, a vote was three months away in the Triad, and Selig was pressing the flesh and talking up North Carolina as a future Major League Baseball market in Charlotte.

Catanoso wrote: "Despite all appearances to the contrary, Charlotte is not vying for a major-league franchise. At least not officially, not yet. The Triad is.... But that was hard to tell Wednesday night in Charlotte. During a reception prior to Selig's speech, waiters and waitresses wore Milwaukee Brewers baseball shirts and chatter turned on just where exactly a ballpark would be located in downtown Charlotte."[3]

When Selig was pressed by Catanoso about whether he was sending a sour message to Triad voters, the acting commissioner dodged the question. But he didn't more than two months later when I asked him about it all. The Triad vote was approaching. On April 27, 1998, just eight days before the vote, I called Selig to gather his analysis of the referendum's chances. I asked if baseball would move the Twins if the Triad referendum passed.

"Even if the referendum passes there," Selig said, "it won't necessarily be built there."

There it was. Finally. The Twins would never move to the Triad. I immediately called Catanoso to tell him of Selig's comments. We were stunned together. Selig had just told the voters of Greensboro, Winston-Salem, and High Point that their votes didn't matter. The referendum was a charade. The crisis was created for no reason whatsoever. For all that happened, nothing changed.

CHAPTER 13

Resuscitating the Deal

Norm and Sharon Wrestle for Riverfront Baseball

History was being made. A major-league sports commissioner was attempting to *defeat* a referendum. Selig knew that the Triad couldn't support baseball. He knew that Charlotte was a better fit. But did he know that the only real hope for baseball in Minnesota was for Carl Pohlad to sell his team?

Such sentiment had been whispered for nearly two years. Henry Savelkoul, Minnesota's de facto minister of sports, had pondered the ownership change option before he'd begun negotiations with Pohlad in the spring of 1996. Legislators mentioned Pohlad's removal as a prerequisite to any stadium funding. But when Pohlad *tried* to take himself out of the picture with his final give-the-team-away ballpark plan, no one moved a finger.

Now it was February 1998, and there was silence. Dead silence. Pohlad's communications with Beaver fizzled. All parties feared the outcome—win or lose—of the Greensboro–Winston-Salem–High Point vote. Pohlad was resigned to losing more money at the Metrodome. The prospect of the 1998 legislature addressing the Twins stadium matter was dead ... and frustrating. As the baseball owner stewed in his downtown Minneapolis office, totally rejected, a new hockey team owner named Robert Naegele was on the brink of getting a $130 million public gift. As part of the state's 1998 massive bonding bill, the city of St. Paul was granted $65 million to help build a new arena for the NHL expansion

Minnesota Wild. The city council, whipped into a frenzy by Mayor Norm Coleman, approved another $65 million appropriation of city funds. As Coleman became the politician of choice for sports team owners, his mentor, Governor Arne Carlson, admitted that the contradiction challenged all reason. A line was drawn in the sand for the ballpark: "No state general fund money." For the hockey arena, anything went. On the widely watched *Almanac* television show on KTCA-TV, Carlson said, "It doesn't make a lot of sense, but I think that's the way it's going to happen."[1] It was a true, but damning, analysis by the man who allegedly was in charge but couldn't influence a single vote for the Twins. Without a policy, without a thoughtful strategy, senseless things happen. Coleman was able to deftly convince even liberal Democratic lawmakers that the new arena was necessary for the state high school hockey tournament and other civic events, in addition to the NHL. It was a snow job. This arena, with its luxury suites, club seats, and corporate naming rights, was built to house a pro sports team. Newness won the day. Naegele, widely unknown, didn't adversely affect the politics; Pohlad was a drag on any ballpark plan.

As Coleman celebrated and won praise for his "leadership," the mayor of Minneapolis tried not to get defensive. Sharon Sayles Belton had been misunderstood when it came to stadium politics. The straight-and-narrow white-guy politicians generally dismissed her. They felt she wasn't "out front" enough in rallying the public to a stadium. A black woman with roots in the city's neighborhoods and not its business community, Sayles Belton wasn't your typical stadium booster. But the record showed that she had a favorite site, near the Mississippi riverfront; a favored tax, a regional sales tax; and a plan in place to get the city's major banks to help assemble the land. Her deep affection for redeveloping the riverfront led her to believe a ballpark site just east of the Hyatt Whitney Hotel could be an urban jewel.

Understated in public, not the vacuous salesperson that Coleman was, Sayles Belton was nonetheless a forceful and energetic advocate for a stadium in the privacy of her office. She walked a very tight rope. The citizens of Minneapolis were clear. They'd already capped the amount of money any sports franchise could expect at $10 million. When the anti-stadium referendum was held the previous November, Sayles Belton didn't even attempt to oppose it. She was up for reelection, and staying away from the stadium was a very good idea.

But November turned into winter, and it was quiet, too quiet. Sayles Belton, who had cultivated a working relationship with Pohlad, felt uneasy. Now that she was in office for another four years, the Twins' future was in her hands, for sure. Over the past year, Sayles Belton had received a few stadium pep talks from other African American mayors with whom she was close. San Francisco Mayor Willie Brown firmly backed new stadiums for the baseball Giants and football 49ers. Cleveland mayor Michael White took on the NFL after the Browns football team left his city on the spur of the moment. After White threatened the NFL with an antitrust challenge in Congress, the league expanded back into Cleveland. Detroit's Dennis Archer worked hard to get two new stadiums for the baseball Tigers and football Lions. The mayors spoke about the importance of such edifices in their downtowns. Mayor Sayles Belton could taste and smell a Camden Yards–like structure in the shadow of the mills of the riverfront. She needed to talk with Pohlad.

In late January, the mayor and Minnesota Wins lobbyist Larry Redmond happened to be in Washington, D.C., together. She was attending a U.S. Conference of Mayors gathering. Redmond, a longtime lobbyist for Minnesota arts organizations, had traveled to the nation's capital to see Governor Carlson honored. In 1997, so as not to be accused of thinking only of sports, Carlson increased arts funding in the state by a whopping $12 million. Americans for the Arts, a national group, thought that the contribution was worthy of an award. Redmond and Sayles Belton attended the ceremony. Afterward the mayor asked Redmond to meet with her. There she asked him just where the Twins situation stood. It was in limbo, Redmond said. He wasn't sure of Pohlad's mind-set.

Upon her return to city hall, Sayles Belton set up a meeting with Pohlad. She was accompanied by Redmond, who Pohlad got to like during the 1997 special session, and by Pohlad's friend Harvey Mackay. The Pohlad sons sat in on the meeting, as did Twins president Jerry Bell. The meeting, in that very active conference room near Carl Pohlad's thirty-eighth-floor office, was about keeping the Twins in Minnesota more than about how to get a stadium built. The mayor simply wanted an update. The mayor simply wanted to send a message.

Midway through the hour-long meeting, as blunt as she could get, Sayles Belton told Carl Pohlad what he'd heard a bit, but not as frankly as she stated it. "Carl," she said, her face impassive, her voice authoritative, "you've got to sell the team. The people of Minnesota won't ever build you a stadium. As long as you're the owner, the Twins won't get a new ballpark."

She wasn't mean-spirited. She didn't say, "You no-good, rotten slimeball, get out of my town." She was, Sayles Belton felt, doing her job. "Blunt is maybe one word," Sayles Belton said ten months later, carefully recalling her session with Pohlad. "What I really believed I was doing was presenting Carl Pohlad and his sons with what I saw the facts to be. Other people were thinking these things and saying these things, but nobody was sharing them with Carl. I want to say I like Carl Pohlad and have a lot of respect for him. But my view is if he wanted the Minnesota Twins to stay here, it would be in his best interest to sell the team to a bunch of investors who would keep the team here. He had become the issue. I didn't think it was fair. I didn't think it was right. But it was the fact."

Carl Pohlad, at age eighty-three, was becoming immune to all the jabs to his head and his heart. He didn't like what he heard from the mayor of the city where his team played. But he got over it even as he heard it. "I don't get mad at people anymore," Pohlad said. "It doesn't pay to get mad." But his sons were offended. Jim Pohlad, in particular, told the mayor he got the message. It wasn't what the mayor said but how often she said the same thing during the course of the conversation. And to the Pohlad sons, Sayles Belton had been completely ineffectual during the prime of the stadium campaign. There was Coleman over in St. Paul making like the Music Man for a hockey arena that the Twin Cities barely needed. And Sayles Belton could deliver just one vote from the Minneapolis legislative caucus. Her priority was the expansion of the

Minneapolis Convention Center. The Twins were left behind. And now she was telling Carl he should sell his most prized and most painful possession.

What she didn't know was that Pohlad was trying constantly to sell the team. During the special session, he was on the phone repeatedly with business leaders in town trying to get CEOs to buy into the franchise. "This is ridiculous," Pohlad told one visitor. "If I was Calvin Griffith, I could get this team sold."

But he wasn't lowly Calvin Griffith. He was filthy rich Carl Pohlad. For all he'd done, it was time to get out of the picture. He couldn't. He wouldn't. Sayles Belton returned to her office four blocks away knowing she'd done what a mayor is supposed to do. The next month, Sayles Belton and Pohlad lunched together. For them, it was just business. But it was getting old, this wondering about the future of the Twins.

Defeated in Two States

On May 5, with nary a contest, the voters of the two North Carolina counties that could have tried to lure the Twins to their rural backyard said, "Thanks, but no thanks." They overwhelmingly defeated the stadium plan. Charlotte said it was now poised, but that was just smoke. Instantly, the Twins and the Sports Facilities Commission began to negotiate a lease extension. There were also discussions about settling Humphrey's antitrust suit, but the commission had no power over that complex litigation. With nowhere to go and no options, the Twins extended their lease for two more seasons. But Carlson and Savelkoul again missed an opportunity to secure baseball in the Twin Cities for more than two years. First seeking a longer-term arrangement, then simply giving in, Savelkoul merely extended the Twins lease through the end of the year 2000 baseball season. Why the Sports Facilities Commission didn't demand a four- or five-year arrangement was mind numbing. The claim was that Pohlad simply wouldn't sign on. Savelkoul explained that "politically it would have been impossible" to press for more years in the new lease. But why? Where could the Twins play? And even though others on the commission pressed for it, there was no requirement in the new lease that Pohlad sell the team sometime soon, either. There was an agreement that Pohlad would seek qualified buyers, but that lease extension should have been the moment to force Pohlad to sell, as Mayor Sayles Belton had hinted months earlier. Savelkoul backed down. "This isn't Cuba; we don't get to tell people what to do with their property unless we own it," Savelkoul said, in shooting down the possibility that the commission could force Pohlad to set a reasonable sale price for the team as part of the lease extension. Commissioner Paul Thatcher was pressing for such a price-setting clause in the extension. "I know Thatcher is after it [this part of the agreement], but there isn't anything I can do about it," Savelkoul said. It was an odd comment for Savelkoul to make. After all, a year earlier, he had been in deep and private discussions with Pohlad about doing exactly that: setting a price for the team that Pohlad was *guaranteed* to get back. Setting the sale price was the key element to the failed January 1997 deal. Why not set it when Pohlad had no leverage? Governor Carlson and Savelkoul wanted to see their terms end without any more sports catastrophes. With the stroke of a few pens, the Twins problem was temporarily settled.

As those loose ends were tied up, a postmortem ensued. First Borman, the unsuccessful quarterback of the Twins' lobbyists, offered one more stunning performance. It came eleven months after the conclusion of the most flawed lobbying effort in the history of Minnesota. In a tiny meeting room of a Bloomington motel, with a small group of sports lawyers, Borman publicly explained what happened. Since we all wanted to know, there was an air of anticipation. Bottom line: It was everybody else's fault.

In theory, Borman meant well in his speech at a "continuing legal education" session for twenty lawyers to get professional brownie points to maintain their licenses. Borman gave a presentation that reeked of characteristics heretofore unmentioned. The October 1998 speech was dipped in arrogance and denial, a reflection of the entire Twins stadium campaign, from the team's side and the government's side. Borman revealed a point of view that could only be shared by men who blew it, who knew it, and who needed to lash out at someone, anyone. He blamed

Minnesota Wins for being more "telephonic" in its alleged organizing of support for the ballpark than directly one-on-one. He ripped Senator Marty for his alleged demagoguery. He, of course, blamed "the media.... The stadium effort suffered seriously from the intense media scrutiny that was paid to every step of the process.... There are examples of cities where the media showed much greater restraint than they did in Minnesota.... I read the paper each morning and learned things about the process that my group didn't know." He ripped the Sports Facilities Commission for its lack of support, but neither he nor Savelkoul had ever genuinely sought the cooperation of the agency's members or staff. He praised Mayor Coleman for finagling a hockey arena—"quietly and not in the newspapers"—and criticized Mayor Sayles Belton for not taking the "political heat" off of Pohlad. Borman chastised chairpeople of legislative committees because "they wanted more, they wanted more." But it was the team asking for $300 million that put the lawmakers on their heels.[2]

I shook my head and muttered as I listened to Borman. Here was a man who was the chief legislative liaison for the Pohlads, and he didn't have a clue. The best and most reasonable argument Jerry Bell, the team's chief spokesman, made during the process was that any new ballpark would be the community's asset, not Carl Pohlad's. I actually believe that, depending on how the financing and use of the ballpark are structured. But Borman seemed to think that a stadium deal could and should be negotiated in private. There was no self-criticism for a reluctance or inability to reach out to a diversity of people within the community. Clearly he and his clients saw a stadium initiative as "deal making" and not "a community decision-making process." A private deal is exactly what his clients struck, and it is exactly why no one trusted them after January 8, 1997.

Countering Borman on that same day was a relaxed, blunt Savelkoul. If there was a hint of bitterness, it was overshadowed by a blanket of painful experience. His term as the chairman of a commission he had learned to disdain was winding down, and Savelkoul made the most cogent public presentation of his six-year appointment, and the most chilling for anyone who cares about sports in Minnesota. In a speech titled "The Viability of Four Major Sports Teams in Minnesota," Savel-koul outlined his conclusions. It was a sort of exit interview. No longer was Savelkoul promoting any idea or course. No longer was he acting as a virtual agent for Pohlad. The dust had settled, and he was gazing into an uncertain future and was harsh about the troubled past. He said that all players unions and team owners were merely negotiating over "us [the public] picking up the tab." He said that he thought one solution to the Twins' and Vikings' frustrations with the Dome was simply "writing them a check," that is, a direct cash subsidy, which might be cheaper than build-ing a stadium. "We were told it was politically unacceptable." He said he didn't see any statewide solution to the pro sports puzzle, and that Hen-nepin County might have to fund facilities in the future. He reiterated his belief that the Sports Facilities Commission had to be abolished and broadened beyond Minneapolis representation.

But mostly he warned of "that light you see at the end of the tun-nel," and he said it's "the Empire Builder coming your way. One of the big train wrecks is coming." He meant the Vikings. Riding the headlight of the roaring train was McCombs, the new Vikings owner, who swept into the Twin Cities from San Antonio with a great spirit and an awesome misconception. McCombs, coming from Texas, where football is king and football stadiums are cathedrals, assumed that Minnesota was ready to help build his newly acquired team a new stadium. He didn't get that most Minnesotans thought the Metrodome was just fine for football. The Vikings were winning. The Vikings were selling out the stadium. The Vikings seemed to have a home-field advantage at the noisy, enclosed Dome. McCombs was just another rich fellow at the end of the endless line of Twin Cities pro sports team owners who were seeking a handout— or that's how it looked.

It was the kind of stuff that made Jesse Ventura mad. The former professional wrestler, bad movie actor, and radio talk show host ran as the Reform Party candidate for governor of Minnesota. Against all odds, three weeks after Borman and Savelkoul made their presentations, Ventura—a rabid sports fan opposed to public funding for stadiums— shocked the world by defeating St. Paul mayor Norm Coleman and

Minnesota attorney general Hubert H. "Skip" Humphrey III. Soon after his upset victory, Ventura told students at the University of Minnesota: "Win if you can, lose if you must, but always cheat."

Somehow, it was a proper conclusion to the stadium process, which seemed to be headed for a certain kind of closure and a much-needed hiatus at the end of 1998. Ventura's victory reflected a "plague on both houses" attitude that grew out of the stadium political fervor. There wasn't a formal statewide stadium referendum—as the Twins and Carlson administration had sought in 1996—but there was an organic statewide debate that found its way to the capitol loudly and clearly. That critical mass of antistadium sentiment could be felt in St. Paul. The same folks who were saying no to a stadium without even knowing the details of a plan were saying yes to Ventura: he was different; he challenged the power structure; he was a regular guy; he didn't want a damn thing from anyone, and he didn't promise a damn thing to anyone. He was no banker or government official cozying up to the banker. He was no zillionaire pampered ballplayer. He was a professional wrestler—that is, a bulked-up circus entertainer—from South Minneapolis. He was the kind of guy who could be expected to oppose a publicly funded stadium—against the deal makers—although he was a season ticket holder to Timberwolves games in the publicly rescued Target Center and a huge Vikings fan. He reflected his political base: citizens fed up with the power establishment.

During the campaign, the spotlight still shone on the stadium issue. It remained a litmus test for candidates. The *Star Tribune*'s "Voter's Guide" before the September 13, 1998, primary asked all of the gubernatorial candidates for their positions on what were presumably the state's most pressing issues. Taxes, education, poverty and welfare, crime, and sports facilities. Abortion wasn't among them. The Carlson administration had done such an awful job in articulating a professional sports policy position that when voters went to the polls in November, eight out of ten said they were opposed to public funding for pro sports. That despite—or probably because of—three full years of efforts to get a stadium built and millions of dollars of lobbying and advertising costs. Twins president Jerry Bell figured the team spent $4 million, but that might be on the low side. State records showed that in 1996 and 1997, the Twins spent $1.6 million on lobbying expenses, not counting fees to the lobbyists. The largest expenses were direct mailing and advertising costs. Twins money accounted for about 17 percent of *all* lobbying costs in the state during those two years. Minnesota Wins spent another $460,000 in 1997 and 1998. Jon Commers and Ricky Rask, the stadium gadflies, spent a total of $296, according to state records. "Not Carl Pohlad's most effective investment," said Senator Marty, who couldn't help but giggle at Goliath's hard tumble.[3]

Ventura, for his part, said the Twins should "build the damn thing" on their own. Early on in the campaign, he allowed that slot machines at Canterbury Park were a way to fund sports. Indeed, his astonishing victory celebration was held at the racetrack, which has for a decade tried to get off-track betting or slots to boost its revenues. But as election day grew closer, Ventura's antitax position vis-à-vis stadiums hardened, even as Coleman, his top opponent, was the candidate of choice among sports figures.

Among sports money that flowed to Coleman—the lone candidate to leave some room that he would support a Twins stadium—were contributions from Carl Pohlad ($1,000); his wife, Eloise ($500); Carl's three sons, Jim ($2,000), Bob ($1,750), and Bill ($500); Bob's wife, Becky ($1,750); and Jim's wife, Mary ($2,000). Together, their contributions added up to more money than any other single Coleman donor.

But the Twins owner wasn't alone in backing Coleman. So did Gophers football coach Glen Mason ($1,000) and University of Minnesota athletic director Mark Dienhart ($125), who was always seeking lease concessions from the Metropolitan Sports Facilities Commission. Other Coleman contributors were Robert Naegele ($2,000), owner of the new Minnesota Wild hockey team, and Peter Karmanos ($2,000), owner of the Carolina Hurricanes hockey team; that team once played in Hartford, Connecticut, and Karmanos, who lives in West Bloomfield, Michigan, once considered moving his Hartford Whalers to St. Paul. Also, Wild president Jac Sperling ($250) gave to Coleman. Timberwolves owner Glen Taylor ($1,000), a former Republican senator, also contributed to Coleman. Not to be outdone, WCCO sports radio talk show host Dark

Star, who championed public funding for sports facilities and who is legally known as George Chapple, contributed $500 to Coleman.[4]

Curiously, though, Ventura supporters were not blanketly opposed to public funding for pro sports. While only 15 percent of a statewide sample said in November election exit polls that they supported public funding for sports, 33 percent of those pro-stadium folks voted for Ventura. Forty percent were Coleman voters, and 27 percent of the pro-stadium vote went to Humphrey. In other words, if the statewide sample interviewed a total of 1,000 residents, 150 people (15 percent) said they supported the use of taxes for a stadium. Of those 150 stalwarts, 40 voted for Humphrey, 50 for Ventura, and 60 for Coleman. Of course, 850 people of that 1,000 sample said, "Hell, no."

Three days after his victory, Ventura said that he would even oppose the state's backing bonds for a stadium. And on the first Sunday after his win, at halftime of the Vikings game when owner McCombs attempted to suck up to Ventura, the governor-elect told a national TV audience that the Dome was only sixteen years old and that "we don't build new schools after sixteen years ... There's nothing wrong with this stadium."[5]

That same night, on Mark Rosen's sports talk TV show, the Channel 4 sportscaster, who is often a shill for the Vikings, pressed Ventura and wondered if there wasn't some way to find a solution to the Twins and Vikings problems. It was as if Rosen were pleading with Ventura to save his beloved teams.

Ventura, wearing his Vikings jersey, didn't back down. He reiterated that the Dome was too new to be replaced. He cited Champlin Park High School, where he worked as an assistant football coach, and noted that it surely won't be rebuilt when it's sixteen. But, Rosen said, there just aren't enough revenues in the stadium for the teams. "The Twins need to put a winning team on the field first," Ventura said. "They weren't asking for a new stadium in 1987." He meant, when the team did well, it attracted fans and created its own civic excitement.

It was clear that Ventura understood where the public still stood. Perhaps he even saw other election results besides his own. Representatives Ann Rest and Loren Jennings, the two most out-front legislative backers of a stadium, got serious runs for their money, winning two of the closest legislative races in the state. Both were seemingly secure, running for their eighth terms; Rest won her election by a grand total of 340 votes out of more than 14,000 cast, and Jennings won his by 535 votes out of 19,000. Rest's opponent used her stadium efforts against her. "Twins owner Carl Pohlad is so pleased Ann Rest went to bat for him to get millions for a new sports stadium . . . MAYBE HE'LL EVEN RETIRE HER JERSEY," said a campaign flyer of Lynne Osterman, Rest's Republican challenger. On the literature was a football-like jersey with the words "REST $300 MILLION" emblazoned on it. Rest, one of the House's most diligent and intelligent members, was castigated for, seemingly, devoting all of her time to a ballpark. Shades of George Petak, the Wisconsin stadium martyr. For her part, Rest said she would no longer support a publicly funded ballpark. It just wasn't worth it to her.

As 1998 came to a close, with the Minnesota House controlled by an increasingly conservative Republican Party and the Senate still controlled by Senator Roger Moe, whose loyalty to the Indian tribes is deep, there was no way that a stadium plan was going to emerge from those ornate chambers. Ventura's comment that the state shouldn't even back bonds meant that a city—or a county, such as Hennepin—would have to put its financial neck on the line, perhaps the Metropolitan Council as in the Metrodome's case. The $10 million cap on any city of Minneapolis investment in pro sports continued to isolate Sayles Belton's ability to jump-start a stadium effort there.

But Ventura's position seemed precarious, even contradictory. He had been swept into office by a political base that seemed to be more in touch with Fantasy Football statistics than state tax codes. His base was a working-class grouping of white men who wanted one of their kind in the governor's residence. Would they allow teams—even the shunned Twins—to leave the state on Ventura's watch? Were they as stuck in cement on the issue as the governor repeatedly indicated? Ventura administration officials, in private meetings with stadium boosters, implied they were not, and that when push came to shove he would become engaged. Still, Ventura wasn't in the lead as 1998 turned into 1999. It was the man who was backed by the sports money who decided to take another stab at it. Coleman was the new general to watch in yet another battle. He began to talk about building a new open-air ballpark for the Twins in downtown St. Paul.

But Nooo

The stadium saga, as has been the case since major-league sports found their way to the Twin Cities, couldn't take a break. Why ruin the fun? The Vikings began to make their noises, even visiting key legislators during the 1999 session. They downplayed their desires, saying they merely wanted to explain their problems to the lawmakers. But it was clear from the beginning. McCombs paid $250 million for a team that couldn't get enough cash flow out of the Dome to support such an investment. McCombs knew it coming in. He knew the minute he bought the team that he needed a new stadium. He wasn't known as the kind of fellow who likes to make the safe 6 to 8 percent return on his investment. He liked 20 percent. Swiftly, he hired Tim Connolly, who had extensive stadium marketing experience, both with the Kansas City Chiefs football team and a related sports marketing firm controlled by the Chiefs' zillionaire owner Lamar Hunt. McCombs, Mr. Personality, and Connolly, Mr. Bulldog, came in like gangbusters. They were poised to lead the charge and set the tone for Minnesota's own Y2K problem, the next stadium fight. McCombs and Connolly arrived claiming patience. That lasted about two weeks for the foreigners. They drove around the Twin Cities, saw the arts facilities and the gleaming downtowns, and couldn't believe that there wasn't similar public support for a shiny new football stadium. At the same time, McCombs never shot down suspicions that he could move the team anytime he wanted. Houston, in his own San Antonio backyard, desperately wanted another NFL team after the Oilers left town for Nashville. But the NFL, under the patient and skillful leadership of Paul Tagliabue, knew how to put a lid on any relocations. Because of antitrust laws that applied to football, but not baseball, it was illegal for the NFL commissioner or fellow owners to block a franchise move. But the move of the old Cleveland Browns to Baltimore in 1995 simply cost the league too much in dollars and public relations. Tagliabue delicately and ingeniously halted the threatened move of the New England Patriots from suburban Boston to Hartford, Connecticut, in the spring of 1999. And similar intervention could be expected in the Twin Cities if McCombs totally lost his sense of reality and tried to move the Vikings somewhere, anywhere. For all his investment, McCombs didn't perform adequate political due diligence. He didn't understand the depth of feelings and informed sophistication of Minnesota's citizens and fans.

As McCombs readied himself for an assault on the public and the legislature, Pohlad licked his wounds. The effects of his and baseball's reluctance to make a drastic decision had come home to roost. Son Jim Pohlad took over the decision making on the business side of the team. To satisfy his father's desire not to lose any more money, the team announced it would reduce its player payroll to skeletal proportions.

Typically, critics dredged up the "Mr. Cheap" moniker for Pohlad. In essence, with no stadium on the horizon and no way out of Minnesota until after the 2000 season, Carl Pohlad threw in the competitive towel. His sons agreed to take the heat for the decision. A group of men with more of a sense of humor and spirit could have positioned their cost cutting in a more radical way. Jim Pohlad's real feelings were expressed in an interview when, speaking of baseball's other owners, he asked: "When are those guys going to learn?" He meant: When will baseball's owners share more of their revenues so that struggling teams could put competitive teams on the field? In a sense, the younger generation of Pohlads could be viewed as taking a subversive stance, of standing up to baseball's powers by exposing the industry's inequities. If it was subversive, it was futile. The team continued to lose horribly on the field with a roster filled with Class AA and AAA players. The local fans' attitudes toward the Pohlads were set. Marketing of the team was nonexistent, save for an advertising campaign that featured a "Joe Fan" character trying to get "closer to the game" who happened to be—guess what?—a pudgy, middle-aged white man. The team was destined for last place again.

Meanwhile, Senator Dick Day didn't give up. For someone who said his penchant for promoting gambling wasn't based on any anti-Indian sentiments, he seemed focused on thrashing the tribes in March

1999. That's when the U.S. Supreme Court ruled that eight Chippewa tribes could retain the fishing rights granted them as part of an 1837 treaty with the state of Minnesota. In immediate reaction to that, Day said it was time to pursue Canterbury gambling again. The message: the Indians can't have "everything." Exactly what fishing rights had to do with gaming remained unclear. The only connection was that Senator Day and his ilk had a one-note song, and it was to challenge the Indians at every turn.

In April 1999 St. Paul mayor Norm Coleman declared in his State of the City address that he wanted to figure out a way to bring the Twins to St. Paul. That statement, along with some secret planning he'd conducted, immediately put the mayor in the hot seat. It sounded like 1996 all over again. He didn't really have a finance plan. He didn't really have a viable site. He didn't have answers to infrastructural matters, such as how anyone can get 40,000 people at once in and out of downtown St. Paul. Still, the same sort of parochial small-mindedness that had often intervened in stadium debates past quickly crept into Coleman's effort. He was known as a politician who virtually stood for nothing other than himself and who pandered to the right wing during his gubernatorial campaign. With public subsidies to the new NHL arena, to a computer software company, and to parking ramp operators, he appeared to be putting St. Paul taxpayers into a risky public debt quagmire.

But, so what? This was St. Paul trying to take an asset from Minneapolis, in much the same way Minneapolis had taken pro sports from Bloomington twenty years earlier. The mayor was creating "a cause," and that's what the stadium effort had long lacked. At least Coleman had guts enough to stick his neck out for a ballpark. At least he didn't let the matter lie there like that dead smelt of 1997. No one was trying to revive the Twins in 1999, not even the Pohlads. Coleman showed some leadership, even if there was limited substance to all the style and razzmatazz.

As much as the mayor and his minions mouthed the belief that the resuscitated ballpark plan was "grassroots," it was truly a creation of Coleman and his chief image maker, Erich Mische. The effort was backed by the St. Paul Chamber of Commerce and some Coleman-linked downtown business organizations. Coleman's first overtures weren't to the public but to Twins owner Carl Pohlad. Coleman didn't canvass the public; he called baseball commissioner Bud Selig and won him over. As much as Coleman and Mische wanted to put a smiley face on the stadium effort, the tough issues wouldn't go away.

Mische left the Coleman administration before the 1998 gubernatorial campaign and went into, theoretically, higher-paying public relations work. In his private business, Mische helped bring a touring show of Titanic memorabilia to the Union Depot in the Lowertown section of St. Paul, near the river, near the railroad tracks in an area reminiscent of the LoDo area of Denver. The Titanic show, which took advantage of popular interest in the sunken ship because of the Academy Award–winning movie, attracted 400,000 people to the Lowertown area. It showed one thing—you can move people in and out of that area—and they can find it. It was in the back of Mische's mind that this was a test of the area for a new baseball stadium. Mische figured he could help solve the Minnesota baseball problem and, more important, jump-start Coleman's political profile, battered by his defeat at the hands of Governor Ventura. It could also serve to end Coleman's boredom. Defeat and the realization he'd be the mayor of St. Paul, and nothing else, for another three years was stifling Coleman. Thus the Twins gambit.

By early May—a month before their campaign went public—Mische walked to a closet in his barren city hall office and produced a rendering of a stadium, right next to Union Depot, the redeveloped train station near the river. Just weeks after Coleman mentioned his interest in a Twins ballpark in St. Paul, Mische had already commissioned drawings of a stadium. It was a flashback to Roger Headrick's yanking out an aerial shot of downtown Minneapolis, pointing to the Convention Center, and noting that's where he wanted his new stadium. But Mische's plan was seemingly better thought out. This guy had a semblance of a plan. And that cause: revive Norm's political fortunes, at any cost, by linking the ballpark to St. Paul's downtown revival, by trying to take something from Minneapolis.

At the base of their plan was a city-wide referendum. No matter what they did, no matter what plan they devised, Mische figured their out was a vote of the citizenry. "At least the people will decide," Mische said. And there didn't seem to be any downside for Coleman. If he was able to pull off the miracle and get voters to approve a plan for an increased city sales tax, he would look like a true leader. If he failed, well, gosh, at least he tried, and he still appeared like the heroic public figure taking on the unpopular but worthy cause.

As the mayor began to drum up support for the St. Paul ballpark idea and show that he was a can-do guy, he appeared on a WCCO radio talk show. He was his typical glib self, passionate for what he believed in. He envisioned related housing attached to an outdoor, unroofed ballpark. He jabbered about the alleged economic impact. He was quick to gloss over the facts of baseball's horrid economics and the realities that even a new ballpark might not make the Twins competitive in the long term. After some unchallenged minutes on the air, a listener called and wondered what a new stadium would fix if the ownership of the team wasn't willing to invest in good players who could win games and make the stadium a worthwhile place to visit. Coleman acknowledged the validity of the caller's concern and promised that "if [commitment from ownership] isn't there, then you don't do the deal."

It was a comment that made me realize that the mayor—and perhaps the Twins—hadn't learned a thing about the stadium process in Minnesota. It's not "a deal." It's a public decision-making process. It's not an arrangement between a handful of men, who—presto!—come up with an idea and try to "sell" it to the public. Savelkoul and Anderson did that. They were enamored with striking a deal with Carl Pohlad. So, it seemed, was Coleman. His first contact was with the owners of the team, not with the public. His first ideas of how a ballpark should look and what it should do were based on the tired ideas of other cities' stadiums and the desires of the Twins. He wanted to emulate Camden Yards or Coors Field. There was nothing new. Coleman wanted to be a copycat. Eventually, Coleman did strike a deal with Pohlad.

In the deal, Pohlad felt no pain. The deal required the banker to sell the team to new owners, and Pohlad could set the sale price. The term sheet didn't require any up-front cash from the Twins and their new owners, just a relatively high rent of $8 million. What the Coleman-Pohlad deal did require was about $100 million in state funds, and it called for the state to bond all $325 million of a proposed downtown St. Paul open-air ballpark. Why anyone thought the state would buy into such a plan, after citizens from Ada to Zumbrota had loudly and repeatedly said no to public funding, was unclear. But Coleman, fast and loose with his facts, was a lone ranger, and he was thinking only of St. Paul. Their complex but tentative deal, which had all the substance of the Pohlad-Beaver charade two years earlier, seemed to have little support, except among Coleman boosters.

Whatever Coleman's style, the effect was instant: Minneapolis mayor Sayles Belton popped back onto the scene, too, reviving an earlier plan for a regional sales tax to support stadiums and other regional infrastructure. This time she was aligned with Hennepin County officials, who tried to block Coleman and keep the major-league teams on the west side of the metropolitan area. The entire county board, however, couldn't agree on anything about sports, nor could the Minneapolis City Council. The Twins, who preferred Minneapolis—or, for that matter, Blooming-ton—were forced to turn their lonely eyes to St. Paul and Coleman. He was the only game in town. It was déjà vu all over again; just like the Minneapolis–St. Paul baseball park face-off of the 1950s and the hockey arena competition of the late sixties and seventies. The two river cities competed; it was good only for the teams, not the public.

Meanwhile, the Metropolitan Sports Facilities Commission attempted in mid-1999 to extend the useful life of its asset, the Metrodome, by suggesting a massive overhaul of the facility. The idea was to recycle the Dome for either the Twins or Vikings and get a new stadium for the other. It would soon transform the stadium war into a reasonable conversation: it wasn't just a baseball debate or just a city competition thing. This phase of Minnesota's fifty-year-long stadium saga required a comprehensive reevaluation of what the Twin Cities could afford and an understanding that the dollar amounts were fundamentally eye-popping. It was now "B word" time; any solution required at least a half *billion* dollars in funding from somewhere. As always, complicating Coleman's idea and Pohlad's hope was the Vikings' reality.

The proposal to fix the Dome for either baseball or football was, without a doubt, the most ambitious public-policy effort ever put forth by the agency. It was also arguably the first time since suggesting the buyout of Target Center that the commission—and not its lone-wolf chairman—attempted to set public policy. The message was clear: Minnesota shouldn't build two new stadiums, no matter what the Twins or Vikings want. The commission suggested that the Dome could be redone for $160 million for the Vikings or for $200 million for the Twins. The presentation was thorough and thoughtful. The natural inclination for any listener was to say that the Twins should get a new outdoor ballpark and that the Vikings should be happy in the Dome; after all, their lease tied them there until the year 2011.

But both teams pretty instantly rejected the renovation concepts, actions that endeared them to no one. This particularly applied to the Vikings. After all, history shows that the Dome was built for them. If there was a salable reason to move the Twins outdoors, it was as much aesthetics and ecology—baseball in the elements—as it was economics. Fans wanted baseball under the sun. As for the economics, well, that was the owners' problem. But for the Vikings, the idea of a new stadium was beyond just about everyone's comprehension. The Dome seemed perfect for football, save for a shortage of women's bathrooms and crowded concession stands. McCombs's front man Tim Connolly said the Vikings couldn't continue to succeed in the Dome because it was too small and didn't have the revenue-generating amenities of newer stadiums. With charts and graphs and the pitch of an IBM computer salesman (which he once was), Connolly made a compelling case. Studying the changing economics of the NFL, Connolly was right: the big new stadiums around the league would soon subsume the Dome and constrain the Vikings' chances of signing expensive free-agent players.

But, new to town, Connolly and the other McCombs aides were horribly out of touch. They actually thought that a rational discussion about the economics of the NFL would somehow move Minnesota legislators and citizens to help McCombs build a $400 million football stadium. Within weeks after telling the Sports Facilities Commission that the renovation idea wasn't good enough, Connolly was already frustrated by the lack of activity around his efforts to get a new stadium. I told him the Dome took eleven years. He didn't smile. Whatever his demeanor, or McCombs's true intentions, Minnesota wasn't about to move on a Texan's time schedule. Connolly repeatedly said that McCombs had no plans to move the Vikings out of town and out of the Dome, but the words seemed hollow. Connolly seemed to be the manager of a branch office; exactly what was being discussed at corporate headquarters in San Antonio may not have been fully known to him.

The cacophony of stadium noise didn't affect Governor Ventura. He held strong to his stance of no public funding and even tweaked his nose at the teams and the process. For sure, he was anti-Coleman; the mayor had been dismissive of Ventura during their gubernatorial race, calling a vote for Ventura a wasted vote. Ventura didn't forget. The governor also felt that private dollars should pour in before the public was asked to pay. He announced the formation of a stadium fund administered by the Sports Facilities Commission. As part of a massive state tax rebate he delivered, Ventura suggested that pro-stadium citizens send their tax checks to the commission to help build the Twins and Vikings stadiums. He sent $1,000 of his own, but the total amount topped only $80,000 before contributions petered out. Five hundred people took the time to write checks, but $80,000 is enough to pay Wolves star Kevin Garnett for about one half of a game.

While Ventura was having fun with the issue and Coleman was trying to sell the Twins ballpark idea, McCombs was picking up his intensity. In an interview in Mankato, Minnesota, as the Vikings' 1999 training camp began, wearing a "Purple Pride" straw hat, McCombs told me, "My take on professional sports forty years ago is still the same today. I think the communities that, for whatever reason, want to have professional sports should provide the facilities. The owners should provide the teams and market them. Hey, that's my take."

As to why the public should subsidize his football business, but not his mega auto sales business, McCombs was to the point: other cities, counties, and states subsidize, so Minnesota had to. "I'm not expecting the public to do anything that's not part of the industry I'm competing in," he said. "This whole [new stadium] issue is about what we have to do to meet competition."

To his credit, McCombs didn't mince words. And some of those words seemed to come back and bite him on August 31. That dear old stadium-maker, the *Star Tribune*, would play a role once more. McCombs spoke that Tuesday morning at the Dunkers Club at the Minneapolis Athletic Club. Columnist Sid Hartman, the lone media member of the somewhat secret society, introduced McCombs to the assembled upper-level business group. Traditionally, these gatherings are considered "off the record." No reporter but Hartman has ever been allowed to join the club. He is in a special class, to be sure.

On that day, McCombs issued, by all accounts, a straightforward, passionate plea for the construction of a new Vikings stadium. He said that the NFL's economics were changing, that the Dome was outmoded, and that the power elite of the Twin Cities, with which his audience was filled, had to pull together and get the job done. Hartman listened and was struck by the ferocity of McCombs's comments. Hartman didn't tape the speech, but he interviewed the owner afterward. Now, Hartman figured, the speech could be *on* the record. Minutes later, he walked quickly into the *Star Tribune* newsroom and claimed that McCombs had threatened to move the Vikings out of town if a new stadium wasn't built. Hartman had a scoop. A scoop to him was like a deal to Pohlad. It was a drug.

If true, this was the first time that McCombs had crossed the line from suggestion to threat. But again, there was no tape, only a scrawled note by Hartman that said, "We need a stadium right now or the Vikings won't be here five years from now."

Those inflammatory words, unfortunately, weren't directly heard by anyone else. And Hartman, in his story, seemed to add that smoking-gun quote to others that were more innocuous and that McCombs had uttered in the postspeech interview. McCombs's sentiment was clear.

Surely he had sent a firm message. But did he say he'd move the team in so many words? According to a handful of leading business and civic leaders who attended the speech, the answer was no. Hartman had either pieced different sentences together or misunderstood McCombs or made it up.

"McCombs Demands Stadium," the *Star Tribune* headline roared the next morning, further mucking up the entire debate, dropping a bomb on Coleman's St. Paul effort, and steaming Vikings officials who swore that McCombs never said what Hartman said he said. Historically speaking, it was a perverse kind of poetic justice. Remember, more than forty years earlier, Hartman sat on a story about how Met Stadium might be financed, fearful that citizens would rebel. During the seventies, he was an unabashed cheerleader for the construction of the Dome. Now he was stoking the flames for another stadium. He believed he was keeping the community "major league." Really, he was carrying water for an owner. And as in the past, the *Star Tribune*'s management applied no restraint.

Indeed, the newspaper stood by Hartman. (I helped write follow-up stories that attempted to support him, although most in attendance couldn't remember McCombs saying those specific words.) At a time when sports writing, public policy, and taxation were intersecting, the *Star Tribune* management continued to allow Hartman to voice irresponsible positions or report questionable facts.

Like a table tennis match, Coleman's campaign was launched even as the McCombs aftershocks were still being felt. It became increasingly difficult to discern exactly what Coleman and his aides were pursuing: Was it a rejuvenation of the mayor's political career? Was it a rallying of St. Paul chauvinism? Was it the affection of Carl Pohlad, his sons, and Bud Selig? Or was it a legitimate attempt to solve the state's pro sports dilemma?

A group called Yes! St. Paul was the campaign committee. Its literature pushed the theme of putting St. Paul back on the map, à la the Met Stadium effort of forty-three years earlier that wanted to put the entire Twin Cities on the national marketing radar. Did they try to keep the price of the stadium down? No. Did they work with legislators, the governor, and the St. Paul City Council? No. Did they seek opposing points of view? No. Their literature trashed the publicly funded Dome, which was a completely irresponsible action to take if the idea was to preserve pro sports in Minnesota. "Vibrant Urban Village vs. Domed Wasteland," read one of their ads. Even though Coleman promised he would, he didn't challenge the continuing sad state of baseball's economic affairs. As he carelessly attempted to put a stadium in St. Paul, the game continued to bleed.

The new Safeco Field in Seattle came in at $517 million, $100 million more than planned. The team threatened to trade all its top players unless the public picked up the tab on the cost overruns. Pittsburgh Pirates owner Kevin McClatchy acknowledged that his team's new stadium wasn't the answer to its economic woes or its ability to compete with large-market teams in the long term. He noted that the Los Angeles Dodgers, for instance, could continue to pay gigantic salaries because they are bankrolled by the media empire of Rupert Murdoch. In 1999, the Dodgers had a payroll of $80 million. McClatchy was hoping to afford $50 million in player salaries by 2001, when his new stadium was due to open. "Just because we're getting a new ballpark doesn't mean everything is fixed," he said.[6]

And now even Selig, the man who tried to convince us that the Twins were bound for North Carolina in 1997, acknowledged that his industry was only bluffing about franchise relocation. With a handful of teams in financial trouble, there was public talk by some owners in the fall of 1999 of possibly eliminating some weak franchises. It was a rationalization to not restructure the game's economics. "Moving franchises was a solution in the forties, fifties, and sixties," Selig told reporters at an owners meeting. "Today it merely switches problems from one area to another." The threat of a team moving somewhere was undercut by the man who was once the chief threatener.

On November 2, 1999, the people of St. Paul got their chance to vote. It was a 58–42 percent landslide against raising the city sales tax one half-cent to help fund a Twins ballpark. It may have been Coleman's idea to rejuvenate the stadium issue, but his referendum served to injure it further. Now, for the first time, antistadium legislators and other political leaders could point to the resounding St. Paul defeat as positive proof that there was no support for publicly funded facilities. Now, there was no part of "no" that could be misunderstood. Sure, Coleman and his operative Mische got their voters out in record numbers. But it truly was a stadium game. While the well-heeled boosters spent $640,000—or nearly $20 a vote—the truly grassroots opposition organically coalesced and made democracy work on a total of $20,000. Pohlad alone kicked in $200,000 to the pro-stadium effort. Even McCombs, who had no dog in that fight, contributed $50,000 to support pro-ballpark activities. Coleman, desperate because his internal polls showed a whopping defeat, played to the electorate's basest instincts. He tried to reframe the stadium debate by making it a do-it-for–St. Paul–stick-it-to-Minneapolis thing. In the end, the ballpark referendum was all about lifting Coleman's profile around the state. St. Paul's voters didn't bite. Coleman's political career faltered further.

In the process, Pohlad's credibility also took another hit. At Coleman's urging, Pohlad "sold" the Twins to Naegele, the new NHL owner, and Glen Taylor, the Timberwolves owner. It was intended to somehow change voters' minds. If Pohlad were out of the picture, the theory went, voters might be more inclined to support public funding for a ballpark. It was a reasonable assumption; Sports Facilities Commission chairman Henry Savelkoul felt the same way three years earlier. But, by the fall of 1999, Santa Claus could have owned the Twins and that wouldn't have changed the political dynamic of pro sports public subsidies. Besides, the so-called sale of the Twins was a theatrical production of the highest order, with late-night news conferences orchestrated by Mische to manipulate the local news media.

Soon after a staged news conference to announce that Naegele and Taylor would "own the Twins" if the ballpark referendum passed, Pohlad offered a touching and tearful "farewell" at the Metrodome. No doubt, he thought it was genuine. He was sad at the prospect of being out of the limelight. And the Pohlad news conference at the Dome was a stark illustration of just how personally important the franchise was to him. Owning the Twins, for better or for worse, had become Carl Pohlad's major source of self-esteem. But that "sale" and that "good-bye" was all helium. There was no sale; just another "letter of intent," the kind of paper transaction that Pohlad engaged in with Don Beaver two years earlier. And as soon as the votes were counted, as soon as the St. Paul ballpark idea—a longshot to begin with—faded, Pohlad retained ownership of his baseball team. So much for sobbing farewells.

As 1999 turned to 2000, the debate about a new Twins and a new Vikings stadium could only turn toward maximizing private dollars into any project. In Minneapolis, some city council members were meeting quietly with at least one developer who was trying to piece together a totally private baseball stadium plan. A scaled-down ballpark plan was being considered. As the value of National Football League franchises continued to soar beyond $600 million, the likelihood that McCombs was going to get a lot of Minnesota public money for his football team—which cost him a bargain basement $250 million—dimmed. McCombs couldn't figure Minnesota out. He was frustrated. He wanted to make a deal. He believed in a certain kind of NFL cookie-cutter: the owner would give 25 percent and the city or state would come up with the remaining 75 percent. Presto—a new stadium would be baked. But there was no dough, no yeast, and no political will in Minnesota. There was no compelling reason for any public officials to come to the table. The NFL expanded to Houston, taking away an option city that McCombs could threaten to move to. Los Angeles remained an open market, but citizens there refused to fund a stadium. McCombs's hometown of San Antonio stood as a remote possibility, but its Alamodome would require some renovation for it to be up to NFL standards. Besides, the NFL's recently tightened relocation rules—written in large part by the U.S. Conference of Mayors, including Minneapolis's Sayles Belton—required the naturally impatient McCombs to be patient. Besides, there was that Dome lease that tied the Vikings to the great Teflon temple until the year 2011.

Jim Pohlad, Carl's oldest son, didn't chant "Purple Pride" like McCombs and endear himself to fans. Jim Pohlad was a bit more downbeat after the St. Paul vote and the prospect of another losing season faced him. He was also more realistic than McCombs. At a gathering of the

Minnesota Chamber of Commerce, Pohlad told some of the state's most influential business leaders that public funding for pro sports was like "taking your kids to the dentist." Under this political theory, Pohlad allowed that no children really want to go to the dentist for root canal work, but when they're mature adults, they'll thank their parents for the character-building experience.

His analogy shocked lobbyists and governmental affairs consultants at the chamber luncheon in Bloomington and led the respected *Politics in Minnesota* newsletter to rip Pohlad. "With an attitude like that toward the public, you have to wonder if the Twins will ever sell this puppy," the insiders' newsletter opined. The Pohlads felt that they were at a dead end as 2000 approached. McCombs kept on selling.

During a visit to his Metrodome luxury suite, McCombs continued to explain to Governor Ventura that the seventeen-year-old stadium just wasn't up to NFL standards. That meant the Dome didn't generate as much money as McCombs wanted. Ventura privately told McCombs that he didn't want to see the Vikings move during his watch as the state's chief executive. Ventura seemed increasingly more open to listening to McCombs. At least that's what Vikings officials had themselves believing.

Unanswered to most of the public still following the issue was why McCombs bought the team in 1998 if he knew he'd have a stadium battle on his hands. Apparently, McCombs thought it would be a slam dunk to get a new stadium in Minneapolis. He had done very little political intelligence work. He was a risk taker, not a planner. By the end of 1999, it was easier to get a ham sandwich with mayonnaise in Tel Aviv than a politician to support a stadium finance plan in Minnesota. "Excuse me while I laugh," said Minneapolis city council president Jackie Cherryhomes to McCombs's naivete. A deal maker who could be at the vortex of any stadium solution, Cherryhomes vowed as 1999 ended to be "on a mission to shift the paradigm." How and to where remained a mystery.

An election of all the state's representatives and senators was on tap for the fall of 2000. An election for Minneapolis's city council and mayor was set for the year 2001. And then, because of statewide redistricting, the entire legislature is to be up for election again in 2002. Assuming public opposition to pro sports funding remains hard, no elected official who wants to be reelected is likely to carry the torch for stadium plans any time soon. That means that each team is hoping the other team moves or stumbles first. Whoever remains in town could then grab the benefit of a scorned and desperate community concerned about the prospect of losing two of its big-league teams.

Of course, the Twin's lease at the Metrodome was set to expire after the 2000 baseball season. An extension beyond that seems probable. The Vikings' Dome agreement runs for eleven more seasons, but McCombs did not become a car-selling billionaire by having a long attention span. People who know him predict McCombs will simply sell the team in Minnesota before doing anything catastrophic; then the new owner would have to play the stadium game. So, in the real world of sports and business in the twenty-first century, it looks as if Minnesotans will be the nation's singular freeloaders. As the millenium begins, we are the last American community to give in to owners', players', and leagues' demands. To borrow from Jim Pohlad, we just won't go to the dentist.

Fact is, the Twin Cities remain a solid major-league sports market. Teams and leagues will always want to be here. That is the leverage this community owns. That's why it's time to hatch a new kind of plan, one that's cheap and simple and that challenges the owners and leagues rather than rewards them. No major-league sports stadium should be built because it's what a mayor, governor, team owner, or league commissioner wants. It has to be about what *we* want, on our terms. To build a stadium for others is to face failure. It has to reflect our community. The solution—the prescription—must be about this place, our place, and not a carbon copy of someone else's stadium. The stadium has to stand for something. It has to have values attached to it, not just corporate naming rights, fancy scoreboards, gambling casinos, and lucrative exit strategies for wealthy owners. It has to be cheaper than the $400 to $500 million monsters that other cities are putting up in hopes of putting their finger in baseball's dike and in honor of football owners who are laughing all the way to their bank with unconscionable appreciation on the value of their franchises. A stadium has to have some soul; it has to be a part of the public realm; it has to serve us, not just them, or all the debates, all the finance plans, all the consultants' hours, all the elections, all the conspiracies—they're just not worth it. All has not been fair in Minnesota's stadium games. That's got to change.

CHAPTER 14

Building a Public Trust
Striking a Fair Deal with Pro Sports

In the year 2000, the typical Minnesotan's opinion of pro sports is so low that it's easy to throw in the towel rather than creatively attempt to solve our unique major-league quagmire. As the debate over stadiums and arenas continuously divided us, it became increasingly difficult to defend pro sports as a community building tool. The knee-jerk antitax political machine that took over the halls of government and the airwaves of talk radio further complicated a reasonable approach to preserving the state's pro sports assets. A deep-seated Minnesota suspicion of the rich and powerful militates against working out a humane accommodation with even well-intentioned team owners. The bond between team and fan, between game and fan—sometimes so precious, other times so fragile—was damaged, even severed, by a deep and broad loss of faith. The economics of major-league professional sports are so out of kilter and so disconnected to the everyday lives of most Minnesotans that bridging the gap seems impossible, even irrelevant. Players are paid too much. Owners' franchise values are too high. Tickets are unaffordable. Athletes rarely stay in one place anymore. The examples of other stadiums being built in other cities are, frankly, obscene: domed monstrosities that reach to the sky, that cost $500 million, that detract from—rather than add to—the games they are intended to showcase.

Recognizing that, where do we go from here? How do we set an example for the rest of the nation, for other cities that are now and will in the future struggle with the same issues? We can change the direction and tone of the pro sports facilities debate. We can preserve major-league sports in Minnesota in a socially responsible way. We must because, in the end, most Minnesotans want to be able to cheer for and celebrate their teams. We must to keep the region symbolically and spiritually competitive with other like-sized regions in the United States. We should because all great cities and states must strive for differentiation. Major-league sports make a community distinctive. Ignoring them, punishing them, or—in the worst case—losing a baseball or football team would be a civic defeat that we can avoid.

But as we continue to play the stadium game, we need to change the rules. We must maintain pro sports on our terms, on our scale. For the first time, we must get ahead of the curve. We can't do as we did in 1956 and 1982. We opened shiny new stadiums that were, practically speaking, obsolete from day one. We must create a Minnesota model that fits us, and that others nationally can borrow from. We must listen to the "experts," learn what we can from them, and then kick them out of town. We must reject pro-stadium "consultants" who make their money putting together deals and who know what's best for us because it's best for a team owner, his league, the architect, and the investment bankers who have never seen a stadium deal they didn't like. We must also dismiss anti-stadium "scholars" who claim that pro sports do nothing positive for a community and that somehow the gathering of 35,000 baseball fans under a summer's sky, eighty-one times a year, carries no social benefit. That just doesn't make sense. We must thank them for their opinions and then make our own decisions.

That also goes for personalities such as baseball commissioner Bud Selig, who has simply never gotten Minnesotans' deep resentment for the 1994 baseball players' strike, for the horrendous—even deceitful—way the Twins and the Carlson administration tried to get a stadium bill passed, and for the arrogance of demanding a stadium even as baseball failed to solve its own internal problems. Selig's mantra and point of view are what we must fight against. "They've built a stadium in Baltimore, in Cleveland, in Denver," Selig said. "When you look at all the communities that have looked at this and raised the same issues, the same arguments, and with the same social problems ... they all built stadiums and all are thrilled with [them]. What's different about you?"

Everything, Mr. Selig—but mostly the relentlessness of our victimization by teams, owners, and leagues. In December 1997 *Sports Illustrated* labeled Minnesota the "microcosm" for the entire nation's tango with publicly funded sports facilities.[1] But we're more than, and different from, the quintessential model of the worst of the sports world. We're an oddity. The true microcosms have rolled over and built stadiums that the owners and the leagues wanted. Target Center and the new St. Paul arena are our examples of that; in those cases, we failed to ask the tough questions and make the tough choices. With Target Center, we quickly paid for our mistake by having to buy the arena from its crumbling owners. With the new NHL arena in St. Paul, it's just a matter of time before we have to come to its rescue; Governor Carlson's political support for St. Paul Mayor Norm Coleman and a lack of statewide pro sports policy created the arena we didn't need and will undoubtedly have to bail out within five years. This region simply can't support two major-league arenas.

As for baseball and football—those elephants to the NBA's and NHL's rabbits—we're the last ones to say no. We've put ourselves in an ideal position to develop new solutions and to establish core principles.

For the past seven years, we've come to understand what we *don't* want. It's time, finally, to develop a Minnesota Pro Sports Manifesto that represents what we *do* want. Clearly, our solution on baseball must be different from that in cities with similar populations and similar attitudes. Milwaukee, Seattle, San Diego, Cincinnati, and Pittsburgh recently completed or are still in the process of constructing ballparks, and absent significant changes in the way baseball's owners share their revenues, those ballparks are doomed to fail in achieving their goal of making their tenants competitive, and their citizens happy about their teams. They surely aren't going to be kind to their taxpayers, who are virtually handing over the ballparks but getting nothing in return—certainly, to use Selig's words, nothing of "social value."

A general principle should be that the public's subsidy of pro sports shouldn't create a windfall for any team owner. In baseball, a new ballpark would increase the Twins' value by at least 50 percent.[2] As for football, a new publicly built stadium could double the value of the Vikings franchise overnight. Because of the flush economics of his league, because of its labor peace, and because of its special status as the best game that television can buy, NFL owners like Red McCombs are sitting on gold mines. Moving those gold mines into luxurious new stadium environments benefits only the owners while using our dollars. Enabling the meteoric rise of franchise values without exacting some public value in exchange is unconscionable. Either team ownerships must legally change at the moment new stadiums open or existing owners must share the increased value of their team with the public. This can either create a de facto public ownership partnership or the owners must pledge that the increased value of their franchise will help pay for the new stadium. This is essential to any Minnesota solution.

There are those who argue that we in Minnesota can't "change the world" of sports or "unilaterally disarm" from the realities of the industry's economics, that we should go along to get along, build like every other community and pay what it costs. I disagree. First of all, there is no political will in Minnesota to copy what other cities have done. None, even from stadium boosters. The Norm Green–Target Center–Pohlad contribution–McCombs arrival run-on sentence has reeled in even the sports fanatics. In a market our size, even devoted sports fans know that stadiums won't solve all the problems of large-market and corporate-owned teams dominating the standings. We can be a leader in altering the landscape of major-league sports with a comprehensive public policy that stands for

- reducing the public's share of construction costs and, generally, lowering the costs of sports construction;
- instituting a continuous, affordable sports and recreation endowment that is regularly distributed on a matching-grant basis;
- elevating management of the sports facilities and the development of sports policy making to a statewide board with a full-time,

powerful chairperson who works closely with Minnesota's congressional delegation and with sports policy makers in other states;

- ensuring some form of public ownership of all local teams that play in publicly funded buildings;
- demanding that our sports facilities be *more* public, not less;
- confidently recognizing the major leagues need us more than we need them.

The Twin Cities stand as the nation's fifteenth-largest television and commercial market. We have corporate headquarters and dollars. We have wealthy potential ticket buyers. We have a competitive media market that promotes and covers pro sports extensively. The leagues and television networks want our television sets and our consumption. We shouldn't minimize our size or strength. We may not be New York, but neither are we Jacksonville, Nashville, or Milwaukee. We're bigger and richer. The leagues, which are running out of cities to move and expand to, want markets of our size. Witness the return of the NHL. Witness the NBA's intervention in the Timberwolves crisis. Witness baseball's inability to find a market more attractive than the Twin Cities. The options for the leagues are narrowing.

From our driver's seat, we must superimpose Minnesota values. We must confront arrogant and independent team owners, not blindly partner with them. We must challenge our elected officials to be honest with us. "I believe in the market," St. Paul mayor Norm Coleman said one day on a sports talk show, discussing his vision for a new Twins stadium.[3] But major-league professional sports is not based on true market forces. It's based on subsidized forces. If our community must subsidize our teams so that they can compete—and we can compete—with the subsidized teams of other cities, then we must force owners to compensate us. Unlike the Carlson administration and Coleman, who hopped into bed with the Twins, we must be at arm's length from, and with fists prepared for, the owners, like Wheelock Whitney and Branch Rickey in 1960.

At minimum, team owners must fulfill the public trust they've been given along with their antitrust exceptions by the U.S. Supreme Court and Congress. They were granted the privilege to operate their businesses outside the realm of the free market. That privilege allows them great power over cities and states. We must rein in the effects of the privilege and remind players and owners that absent the privilege, their franchises wouldn't be worth as much and their salaries wouldn't be as high. We must limit their ability to move their teams; even threats to move must trigger penalties in their lease agreement. If they take our tax dollars, then they need to supply us with some public good, over and above games. Building stadiums so that owners can flourish must be a minor consideration. An overarching consideration must be rethinking how our stadiums and arenas are used, and by whom and how the revenues are gathered and distributed. Owners can't take all the stadium money. The underlying concept must be this: The stadiums and arenas should be ours, not theirs.

At the same time, we must maintain a sense of proportion. In these days of superhype, of twenty-four-hour news channels, of governors who are celebrities rather than statesmen, it's difficult to win the battle for the proper scale of anything. Sports thrives on promoting bigness. It's a male-dominated institution. In other cities, counties, and states, this drive to construct large, overly expensive show-off facilities has won the day. Testosterone has pumped up sports facilities. A mere look at the oversized, overpriced stadiums, such as Phoenix's $400 million Bank One Ballpark or Seattle's $500 million Safeco Field, is all the evidence one needs. The only scale into which these facilities fit is a *Star Wars* set.

The new $300 million Miller Park in Milwaukee is a sad example. A fan saying good-bye to County Stadium, the Met Stadium prototype, was haunted by this vision: as we watched a game in a perfectly comfortable 1950s baseball park, we saw behind center field the emergence of an architectural catastrophe. There, beyond the County Stadium fences, rose a retractable-roofed stadium built on the political career of George Petak. Its size was so imposing, its girth so uninviting. County Stadium, may it rest in peace, stood and functioned on a proper scale. Miller Park makes baseball more important than it really is. The working-class fans of Milwaukee—the joyous beer guzzlers in the shiny union jackets who so warmly populated the concourses of County Stadium—will undoubtedly feel out of place in luxury-suite-filled Miller Park when it opens in 2001.

Let us remember that Americans spend nearly three times as much money on flowers, seeds, and potted plants as they do on spectator sports. Don't forget that Americans spend seven times as much on participation sports—such as bowling, skating, golfing, and swimming—than they do on spectator sports.[4] In 1998 more than 900,000 people visited Minneapolis's Walker Art Center and Sculpture Garden, about the same number as saw the Twins. Still, sports media seem to be inflating the importance of every game even more today than in years past. In a 1997 *Star Tribune* Minnesota Poll, 66 percent of those who called themselves "real sports fans" said Americans' love for sports is out of whack.[5] When asked how they would spend their tax dollars out of a $1,000 budget, Minnesotans ranked sports dead last after education, crime prevention, mass transit, and the arts. Still, mass spectator sports, with their time frames, their structure, and their clear outcomes—victory or defeat—grab us and capture our imaginations. For those who lead lives of quiet desperation, simple humdrum or gated isolation, sports provide a theater of emotions to fantasize about and to casually share. Ballparks—and water coolers—become "neutral ground" for people who otherwise have little in common when it comes to sports talk. That same Minnesota Poll found that 61 percent of Minnesotans said pro sports give them something to talk about with others.

When we debate the value of major-league sports and the costs, we must make our arguments with our eyes wide open. We mustn't accede to the cynicism that contends there is no relationship between housing the homeless and feeding the poor and a discussion of a $400 million ballpark. If a sports team such as the Twins leaves town, that view goes, crime won't evaporate, and schools won't improve. So fund the stadium and enjoy the civic pride the Twins or Vikings bring the community. There is an attractiveness in that perspective, one in which we take no responsibility for the community's problems and embrace fun and games. But it misses the point. No one articulated just how much it misses the point better than Susan Kimberly, Mayor Coleman's deputy mayor and chief of staff. But when we talked three years ago, Kimberly was the executive director of the St. Paul Coalition for Community Development, a nonprofit group that promotes small businesses and housing in neighborhoods.

Stadiums won't halt or harm the homeless, she noted. But just as ballparks symbolize the vitality of a city, just as they are signs of an urban area that wants to be recognized, they also represent the stark juxtaposition between a community's haves and have-nots. When we spoke in 1996, we were discussing the side-by-side legislation that, in one case, was aimed at getting a stadium referendum and, in the other case, was aimed at forcing some poor and working people off of welfare.

"In the last year, we have changed the public attitude about using public money for bread," Kimberly said of mid-1990s welfare reform. "So we probably need to look again at what it means to use public money for circuses," which was her description of professional sports. Thus, while we continue to figure out a way to build and pay for ballparks and arenas, we struggle with a contradiction. "If we have come to believe that helping the poor makes them dependent, what does it mean to consider public money to pay for amusement?" Kimberly asked. Perhaps the answer is that sports team owners, athletes, and fans have become dependent, too. And so, she said then, it will come down to this: "What values do we honor? What balances do we strike?"

Such serious matters must hover above us when we take to the table to decide how to keep major-league sports in Minnesota. We are, I am certain, the most sophisticated citizenry in the nation on the issue of pro sports. We have lived in the belly of the beast. Owners and politicians can't hoodwink us. We can preserve pro sports and still maintain our self-respect. But we have to be careful as we go. We need to reinvent the whole concept of our relationship to pro sports. Team owners must change the way they treat us. We need to redesign all the models.

A Sense of Place

We have here in Minnesota a special kinship to the notion of place, and this cultural attribute should be harnessed within the stadium debate. I bow here to a speech and article by writer Paul Gruchow titled "Discovering the Universe of Home."[6] In this deep and heartfelt ode to the specialness of "home," Gruchow touched some nerves that relate to the pro sports debate. I know he didn't mean to, but for someone who is seeking solutions to the muck that is now major-league sports, Gruchow provided insight and food for thought. In his essay, Gruchow discusses the importance of "home" as a "crossroads between history and heaven." If we can stipulate that pro sports have brought us indelible experiences and have provided—if only for a series of brief episodes—a certain communal paste, then we can build on Gruchow's personal observations and apply them to this stadium debate. For so much of what lies beneath the struggle over funding, the resentment of rich men, and the legitimate concerns about other priorities is a recognition that the Twins or Vikings or North Stars or, more recently, the Timberwolves have provided each of us and all of us with exquisite memories that attach us to our grandparents, our parents, our neighbors, our siblings, our children. What has been so disappointing is that the stadium debate has tended to minimize those memories, to degrade them, to taint them, to make them seem less special because the memories are now affiliated with greed, not sharing, with demands, not embraces.

If, for instance, your first child was born on the day that the Twins won their first World Series—as mine was—then there is a forever connection that links me, and my friends and family, to a moment that arguably was the most communally giddy for Minnesotans in the past twenty-five years. It was also personally giddy. Randy Moss jerseys became the rage during the Vikings 1998 playoff drive, honoring the exciting wide receiver, no matter what inner-city neighborhood or suburban strip mall you visited. Tailgating at Met Stadium and Met Center was a regional campfire. Grandfathers took granddaughters to Twins opening days. For a while every kid who scored a goal imitated the "Goldy shuffle," pumping his arms like the North Stars great Bill Goldsworthy.

Gruchow writes about how, in the throes of his mother's death, he and his siblings sat around the family living room gazing at photos and retold stories while asking questions. "Do you remember the morning we floated a pound of butter in Mother's hot laundry starch? ... Do you remember? Do you remember?" Sports are not the memories of family. But pro sports in a metropolitan area the size of the Twin Cities can especially become the collective memory of a diverse citizenry constantly seeking common ground. Bill Lester, the Metrodome executive director, talked of that 1987 World Series period. He and his family were serving meals at the Dorothy Day Center for homeless and hungry people in downtown St. Paul. Men walking through the food lines wore Twins hats and jabbered about the fate of the team. Across the street at the towering headquarters of the St. Paul Companies, the insurance conglomerate, men and women in three-piece suits donned Twins hats and jabbered about the fate of the team. The region had something in common, and that can only be good.

"All history," Gruchow writes, "is ultimately local and personal. To tell what we remember and keep on telling it is to keep the past alive in the present. Should we not do so, we could not know, in the deepest sense, how to inhabit a place.... We own places not because we possess the deeds to them, but because they have entered the continuum of our lives. What is strange to us—unfamiliar—can never be home."

Such comments evoke a certain warmth and fuzziness that may be out of style. Free-agent players and peripatetic owners grind such sentiments down. We have become, for sure, a cynical culture, compartmentalized and untrusting. If there is any institution in the United States and Minnesota that has lost its glow, pro sports rank right up there with politics and journalism. But Gruchow eloquently concedes such disaffection and then directs us to take a deep breath and look forward. We can feel a certain nostalgia or a hazy fantasy for what pro sports used to be like—with Harmon Killebrew hitting home runs in his baggy pants or Fran Tarkenton scrambling like no one else before or after. But we must blend that with the economic and political realities of the day. We can't dismiss our memories as being the dead "good old days," nor can we accept the realities and mutter, "Nothing can change, nothing will change, nothing should change." We need to harness our memories to change the future.

By extrapolating from what Gruchow writes, we can recognize that the events that pro sports have given to this community can't be minimized. Yes, the drunken-driving episodes of Vikings, the abandonment of the Twin Cities by Norm Green, the irresponsibility of athletes such as former Timberwolves star J. R. Rider, and the stadium chicanery of Pohlad and Governor Carlson are beginning to outweigh some of the marvelous memories on the teetering sports seesaw. But, on balance, I'd say, the glorious moments in Minnesota sports history still glow over the stains.

"I'd say that the past is vital because it is primarily through the agency of thinking about history that we come to a sense of the ideal," Gruchow writes. "In remembering what has gone before, we are inevitably reminded of what we have especially hated or cherished, and this information equips us to imagine a world better than the one we currently inhabit. History gives us the imagination, in other words, to plan for the future."

The "stadium problem" is just one on the pallet of a spectrum of challenges any place faces. But to solve the matter we need to take it seriously, and we need to use our imaginations to plan for the future. We need to do it in a Minnesota way, too, in a way that reflects honestly who we are and what we want to be.

Gruchow wrote: "One might say about country places, about midwestern places, about Minnesota places, what is said all the time with such assurance and authority that even the people who live in them often accept them as true: that such places are mediocre, that they are sleepy, that they are places in which ambition is either absent or irrelevant—there is not, for example, in Lake Woebegon a single person with a shred of ambition—that they are simple, whatever that means.... Such perceptions, believed, have a way of becoming self-fulfilling."

And that is true. We become meek because we are bombarded daily with notions that the solutions for all problems are developed on Madison Avenue or in Hollywood or, for that matter, in Silicon Valley or Tokyo. But we can develop our own solutions that apply first to us and that, hopefully, can be borrowed by others to aid them in addressing their particular problem in their particular place. To have the events that generate the history, we need the facilities to host those events. We need those facilities to be ours, to be constructed and used the way we want, to be located where it makes sense, and to cost only what can be justified. The facility need not be like the one in Milwaukee or Cleveland or Pittsburgh. Those places own different family snapshots. The solutions don't have to come from consultants. They don't have to come from politicians trying to keep up with the Joneses. They can come from us.

The Process

After you finish reading Gruchow's essay, I have some more reading for you. For after we come to recognize that our solution can only be based on the specifics of our experiences and our location, we then need to figure out how to get from here to there. The stadium battles are so polarized and positions so locked in that to seek communal flexibility might be to ask the impossible. Daniel Kemmis, the former mayor of Missoula, Montana, in his book *Community and the Politics of Place* offers some insight.[7]

He tells a story about a controversy in Missoula between urban residents and rural residents relative to development and sprawl. The specifics aren't important. The process was. A public hearing was called, and out of courtesy, the city dwellers allowed the country folks to testify first before the special commission studying the matter. The rural participants had miles to drive, and the urban dwellers thought it fair that the rancher types got home before it was too dark.

But that caused two things to happen: when the urban advocates got their chance to testify, the rural proponents were in their pickup trucks heading back home; and when the rural proponents testified early in the evening, the city folks "greeted the testimony of the rural residents with disdain and contempt. . . . In fact," Kemmis writes, "out of everything that happens at a public hearing—the speaking, the emoting, the efforts to persuade the decision maker, the presentation of facts—the one element that is almost totally lacking is anything that might be characterized as 'public hearing.' A visitor from another planet might reasonably expect that at a public hearing there would be a public, not only speaking to itself but also hearing itself. Public hearing, in this sense, would be part of an honest conversation which the public holds with itself. But that almost never happens."

During the 1996 and 1997 legislative sessions, I sat through innumerable public hearings, and I can't remember one in which much real sharing and exchanging of ideas occurred. It was always dueling statements. People assumed they wouldn't agree. Kemmis, like Gruchow, argues that if we commit to making our community a better place, if we are true to our shared traditions, memories, and hopes, we can begin to hear each other. One of the reasons the Twins ballpark issue died, and one of the reasons future stadium discussions could be unsatisfactory, is because stadium proponents—Governor Carlson, Henry Savelkoul, Carl Pohlad, Tom Borman, Roger Headrick, Mayor Coleman—failed to listen. They had their points of view, and they ran with them. Sports Facilities Commissioner Loanne Thrane pleaded with political leaders to travel the state and find out people's opinions. But the ballpark juggernaut thought it could push ahead, using 1970s tactics on a 1990s problem.

The old ways of getting the "business community" and the unions to coalesce with the Minneapolis City Council and legislative caucus are no longer operative. Ownership and government threats don't frighten the electorate anymore. The news media no longer blindly editorialize for the value of pro sports. We're past that, in case no one noticed. On this issue, we need to share new ideas and hear each other out. Kemmis, quoting poet and philosopher Gary Snyder, writes: "Doing things right means living as though your grandchildren would also be alive, in this land, carrying on the work we're doing right now, with deepening delight." Now that's a high standard to reach in our pro sports debate.

Rethinking the Ballpark

We must rethink what our ballpark will look like and do. For my guidance, I turn to Chicago architect Philip Bess, whose pamphlet "City Baseball Magic" must be the bible for any thoughtful stadium advocate.[8] Although the Metrodome was built in downtown Minneapolis, it was far from an urban ballpark. It was, in fact, a suburban structure dropped unceremoniously on a few city blocks relating to absolutely nothing but a freeway on-ramp and a distant central business district.

Bess celebrates the asymmetrical ballparks of the early twentieth century, such as Wrigley Field, Fenway Park, and Yankee Stadium. These ballparks took on the shapes and idiosyncrasies of the city blocks on which they were built. In short, they fit into the character of a neighborhood or district. Unlike the Metrodome, they didn't just land there. There was a reason and a relationship. They were also exclusively baseball stadiums, not multipurpose, not built so that thousands of cars could park around them, not copycats of the last one built. Speaking of the multipurpose stadiums of the sixties, seventies, and eighties, Bess quotes former Pirates star Richie Heber as saying, "I stand at the plate in Philadelphia and I don't honestly know whether I'm in Pittsburgh, Cincinnati, St. Louis or Philly. They all look alike."

The same thing is happening today. After the success of Baltimore's Camden Yards, a "retro" ballpark movement began, with architects attempting to evoke the spirit of the early-twentieth-century ballparks while including the revenue-producing amenities—such as luxury suites—that the owners demanded. Camden Yards wrought Jacobs Field in Cleveland, Coors Field in Denver, the Ballpark in Arlington (which is somewhat suburban), and a series of new ballparks in Milwaukee, San Francisco, Detroit, Houston, and Seattle that are supposed to feel old-fashioned, even if some have roofs and are monstrous. Like Camden Yards and Coors, there is an effort to "mall" these ballparks, to have them build on the "synergies" of a downtown, linking them to a district of restaurants and bars, of retail and entertainment. The stadium is all about revenues, not aesthetics. It is, to borrow a phrase from architectural critic Michelle Thompson-Fawcett, "regressive nostalgia."[9] We should instead seek a certain kind of progressive traditionalism.

Bess had a plan in 1986 to develop what became the new Comiskey Park in Chicago, arguably the only ballpark of the modern era to be an abject failure. His plan, called Armour Field, would have been a success, I'm convinced. With Comiskey located in one of Chicago's poorest neighborhoods, Bess proposed that the new ballpark be part of a newly designed, compact urban village, with housing, retail, and office space across the street from the intimate ballpark. A public park, a public build-ing for meetings and other civic functions, and a community gym were also part of Bess's design. It was rejected. HOK, the Kansas City architec-tural firm that takes credit for Camden Yards but wants people to forget its awful work on Comiskey, got the job instead.

What is so intriguing about Bess's ideas is that they run counter to the typical "economic development" notion of making a stadium part of an entertainment district. Target Center happens to be part of an enter-tainment district. It has enhanced the Minneapolis Warehouse District, but the arena didn't create the district. It moved into an already existing successful zone. Mayor Coleman read Bess's material, but St. Paul's plans in advance of the November 1999 referendum still were on the bombastic side, with envisioned hotels and restaurants blooming around the anchor stadium. They were driven not by the social needs of a neighborhood but by the more typical "revenue-producing" consciousness of sports archi-tects and urban designers. When considering how to finance sports facil-ities, public officials, including Minnesota's, regularly attempt to justify construction with economic impact theories that suggest the surrounding "entertainment zone" can help "increase" tax revenues and somehow pay for the new stadium. Or they try to develop "synergies." Just about every economist will tell you that there is no substance to that argument, that the "entertainment dollar" being spent in the new zone would have been spent in another zone if the new zone didn't exist. Dollars from out of state won't increase dramatically because of a new stadium.

Stanford University economist Roger Noll likes to tell a story that frames the "economic impact" debate. When he was fourteen and grow-ing up in Salt Lake City, his parents decided to spend their summer vaca-tion visiting relatives in Minnesota and Chicago. Along the way, they drove through Milwaukee, and Noll attended his first major-league base-ball game, between the Braves and the Pirates. "So the puzzle," Noll says. "Does the money my parents spent on dinner and a hotel in Milwaukee get attributed to my relatives in Minnesota, my mother's cousin in

Chicago, the Pabst brewery that my parents visited, or the Braves?" The point is that the economic impact is hard to isolate and can't be attributed solely to one destination or attraction. Similarly, local money is simply being transferred from one site to the next—from a movie theater to a Twins game—and the state is going to get its taxes one way or the other.[10]

The heart and soul of Bess's Armour Field concept is not some forced pie-in-the-sky notion of economic impact but rather legitimate community development through its interface with a neighborhood. This is why baseball ballparks, with eighty-one games a year allotted to them, are better suited to relating to a neighborhood than are football stadiums, with their limited number of games per year.

I believe that any new Twins ballpark design should seek to emulate Bess's concept of a reasonably priced mixed-use project. Housing, office space, and community buildings—more than retail or entertainment venues—should relate to Minnesota's new stadium. We have enough malls. Coleman's St. Paul plan would have had ballpark interacting with the Lowertown area, which already has attractive loft living, warehouse offices, and some open space. But it never offered any ideas about integrating the neighborhood's needs with the ballpark.

A Mississippi riverfront site in Minneapolis, long favored by Mayor Sharon Sayles Belton, could possibly lend itself to a ballpark that fits into a neighborhood setting. But the riverfront is not the ideal spot for a Minneapolis ballpark; it must be closer to the center of downtown or closer to a neighborhood that needs a real face-lift. I think any new ballpark should be more of a civic building than a commercial "entertainment district" building. It must be more a part of the public realm than of the private sector. Public funding can be justified more easily if the ballpark is truly part of urban redevelopment, not gentrification.

Recently, I met with a Twin Cities architect who told me of the lack of public meeting spaces in south Minneapolis. There were so few rooms and spaces for community groups to meet that when an ad hoc committee tried to get together to discuss plans to develop more meeting spaces, they couldn't find an available room in which to meet! Communities in both

Minneapolis and St. Paul have other needs and limited spaces or resources. I believe we need to begin to merge a neighborhood's needs with a ball-park. That neighborhood could be the downtown of either city, what with the increasing population in both core cities. Or it could be a neigh-borhood near downtown that needs rejuvenation. We must think of the residents' needs twenty-four hours a day, twelve months a year, not just a few hours a week to eat or drink. That's why any downtown stadium must be in the heart of downtown, not on the periphery. And that's why any downtown stadium need not be required to generate significant sums of related entertainment dollars for the interlopers who come to games eighty-one times a year. It should be required to create services for those who live and work downtown or in a central city neighborhood all the time.

Imagine a stadium in which sports are just one element of its pur-poses. Remember this: even the most active single-purpose ballpark hosts only eighty-one events a year ... that's a major-league ballpark. When it comes to a football stadium, that's a place for ten NFL games a year. It's difficult enough to justify the expenditure of $300 to $500 million of public money for the baseball stadium. But how can you justify a $300 million investment for fewer than twenty football games a year? How can we use our facilities for the other 350 days a year? Bess's basic concept can be extended.

I believe we should place new kinds of things *within* the stadium. It might mean expanding the so-called footprint of the structure or might just mean changing the character of it. It might mean better using the empty innards of a stadium under bleachers or in concourses. It could mean turning the often useless facade into street-level storefronts for community use. Why can't a ballpark have a series of year-round services within its building? Remember, we are rethinking this ballpark to create a Minnesota model. Coleman's plan during the summer of 1999 margin-ally addressed my concerns. The mayor's urban design consultant, Ken Greenberg of Toronto, talked of the notion of "living walls" that would somehow buffer stadium noise and the facility itself from its neighbors. A drawback to such an idea, Greenberg and other St. Paul development officials said, was the need to "attract substantial private investment before the ballpark is built."[11] Of course, garnering private investment is a great idea and should enhance the political support and economic viability of a ballpark. What was troublesome about Greenberg's ideas, or lack of them, was how tied they were to retail and the continued "malling" of stadiums. Why don't we rethink the goals of ballparks?

What do neighborhoods need? Or what does a downtown with increasing numbers of residents need? An elementary school? A charter school? A police station? An urgent-care health clinic? (The new San Francisco Giants stadium will have one.) A day care center? Art galleries? A community organization's headquarters? A YMCA? A hairdresser or barber? A sandwich shop that is open during games but then opens onto the street level the rest of the year? Could the University of Minnesota or a local technical college place one or more departments (perhaps one that teaches students about stadium management or hotel-motel administration or sports medicine) within the stadium? How about a multiplex cinema? All of these are institutions whose work could relate to the events in a ballpark—the police, the clinic, the barber, the sandwich shop. Or whose work and hours run at times almost completely complementary to the games—a school, a day care center—and can attract private investment or can help better justify public funding. Consider a stadium in Monaco: it includes public swimming pools, a 5,000-seat gym, physical education facilities for kids, offices for public agencies, a pizza restaurant, a gas station, and underground parking.[12]

During the site location debate of 1996 in Minneapolis, there was an area in the north end of the Warehouse District, near the new Federal Reserve Bank and the Theatre de la Jeune Lune. That stadium proposal was rejected because it might have had to eliminate the theater. There was an assumption that this part of town wasn't big enough for both a theater and a stadium. But why? Do stadium plans have to destroy? What a jewel a new ballpark would be if it could incorporate existing institutions into its design rather than relocate existing institutions. Would we not be totally rethinking the modern ballpark if we tried to place a theater *within* the ballpark structure? Wouldn't our new urban ballpark benefit from reaching out to other constituencies? The St. Paul idea of integrating its farmers' market with its proposed ballpark was on the mark.

From April to September, for about twelve nights or days per month over just seven months, a baseball stadium is used for baseball. The rest of the metro area would be invited into a neighborhood, or a downtown. For the remainder of the days and nights of a year, the ballpark structure must meet some of the community's full-time, long-term needs. Rather than the malling of stadiums, I propose the socializing of the ballpark. You could have a few restaurants or a movie theater within the ballpark that might continue to attract customers once the sports season is over. But otherwise the facilities would belong to the residents or neighborhood users around the ballpark. For sure, it could change the debate about a stadium; it wouldn't be just for rich athletes and owners. It would be a community center, a local institution, not a monument to rich-guy sports. There would be "a public purpose" and a "public good." It would bring a community's priorities together with its subsidized entertainment. There would be balance.

Rethinking stadiums as public gathering places and as neighborhood centers would respond to the legitimate concerns of those who oppose "corporate welfare" for team owners and others who might profit from ballparks. Enhancing economic diversity and stabilizing the community were among some of the principles established by Minnesota's Corporate Subsidy Reform Commission as it determined what sorts of activities warrant state subsidies.[13]

Now, what neighborhoods am I speaking of? Where exactly should these facilities go? Do they work best in a downtown? Is the Midway District of St. Paul a possibility? Or the East Side of St. Paul? St. Paul identified a site on the West Side, on the opposite side of the Mississippi River from downtown; what a marvelous opportunity that could be, near downtown, but truly in and among a neighborhood. Would North Minneapolis or the Phillips neighborhood of Minneapolis view such a structure as intrusive or useful? Is there some land in the near south side of Minneapolis—at Nicollet and Lake, near the site of the Minneapolis Millers' old stadium, or Chicago and Lake? I don't know the answers for sure.

I do know that selecting *where* a community places its sports facilities is just about the most important decision to be made. In 1977, when Governor Rudy Perpich came up with his stadium legislation, it was "site neutral," so as not to create a collection of opponents whose communities didn't get the stadium. Similarly, in 1997, there was no site specified in any legislation, although it was generally assumed it would be in downtown Minneapolis. We need, as a state, to first decide where the new ballpark should be and how it can be used before we determine how it will be funded. Even in the summer of 1999, when the ballpark debate was renewed in St. Paul, funding became the first matter to address, not where the stadium would be built, how it would be used, and who would use it other than the team. A Minnesota stadium process can never again be "a deal." It must be "a decision." To avoid site selection until after funding is to decide to build a facility before we know that it will be located and used in as responsible a manner as possible.

As for the notion that a ballpark must also be an active community center, or must be a 365-day-a-year operation that serves the citizenry, not just consumers, it's possible that such an idea works better in a New York or a Boston, where the urban needs and traditions are greater than in the Twin Cities. It's always difficult to know, too, whose backyard might be trampled and whose might flourish. These are all difficult political problems.

But I know that experts such as Kemmis have strategies to make good decisions. I also know that we can continue to build stadiums that benefit owners and that are virtually one-dimensional, or we can begin to devise ballparks that truly benefit the people who live and work around them. I think the next cycle of stadiums should be gifts to a city's residents, not to a city's teams. Ballparks that are isolated structures, that are designed only with parking lots and the team's revenues in mind, are not socially responsible. Minnesota must kick off a new cycle of stadium construction. By the time we get around to it, the Camden/Coors/Jacobs model will be at its useful end. The rest of the nation will thank us and hurry to catch up to us, rather than the other way around.

The Governance

No matter what we build or where we build it, a new statewide public agency must oversee it. Teams want to control their own facilities these days. The model in place for the new St. Paul hockey arena is typical; the public builds it, and the team runs it, controls all the cash and all the events, and pays rent.

In the case of the Minnesota Wild hockey team, it signed an agreement with the Minnesota Amateur Sports Commission (MASC), the state agency that supports and promotes Olympic-affiliated sports in the state. In the agreement, *the team granted the agency* the right to use the building for six skating events, ten days of amateur sports use, and six days when MASC can bring in national or international events. Of course, MASC pays all the costs, and the team collects all the concessions revenues.[14] It is similar to an agreement MASC struck with Target Center and the city of Minneapolis after legislation to use public dollars to buy out the downtown Minneapolis arena. That deal, too, limits the revenues and the number of days that MASC can actually use the arena. In both cases, the St. Paul arena and Target Center are compensated by the state for their "generosity." The Target Center gets $750,000 a year for fifteen years; the Wild arena will receive a $17 million reduction on its $65 million loan from the state by virtue of its MASC deal.

As long as the public is investing in a pro sports facility's construction costs and ongoing capital improvements, it is the public agency that should be granting rights to teams, rather than vice versa. These buildings should be ours to own and manage, not the teams'. Assuming that any public dollars that are used for any new ballpark will be state based, a new Minnesota Sports Agency should be established. It should merge the current Metropolitan Sports Facilities Commission with the Minnesota Amateur Sports Commission and perhaps even the Minnesota State High School League. The new agency's responsibilities and jurisdiction should go beyond the current responsibilities of both of the existing agencies.

Right now, the Sports Facilities Commission, which has been given wide-ranging statutory responsibility for the construction of sports facilities, is mostly the manager of the Metrodome. It should today be called the Metrodome Management Agency, not the Metropolitan Sports Facilities Commission. It once oversaw the Met Center arena, but that is now ancient history. It tried to buy Target Center, but it failed. It was virtually ignored during the 1996–97 Twins stadium debate, with the team negotiating with the governor's office. Tied to Minneapolis, because the city stuck its neck out to back the Dome's bonds, the state's most powerful sports agency needs representation beyond the city.

The Minnesota Amateur Sports Commission is one of the state's great success stories, and one of its most prolific producers of pork—that is, local funding for pet projects. While the state's legislators and taxpayers stood aghast at how much money pro sports teams have sought for facilities enhancement, MASC has quietly spent $49 million in state tax dollars to build or help build and refurbish soccer fields, ice rinks, ski trails, kayak runs, and volleyball training centers. MASC's state money has triggered the investment of more than $122 million in local and private funding in ice rinks alone; the Mighty Ducks ice rink program was begun in response to the pressure on local communities because of the rise of girls' and women's ice hockey participation. With Mighty Ducks grants being awarded to 146 different communities, MASC's impact has been felt statewide and, generally, felt beneficially.

Upon its creation in 1987, with the vision of former Governor Rudy Perpich to bring an Olympics to Minnesota, MASC first got its funding from a tax; it was a tax assessed to country clubs and health clubs around the state. At one point, that tax generated far more revenues—about $10 million a year—than MASC needed to fund the debt service on its facilities in Blaine, Biwabik, St. Cloud, and other communities. Soon, though, the legislature determined that "dedicated taxes" (that is, taxes that flow directly to a specific project) should be discontinued and that all tax revenues should flow only into the state's general fund. But that sports and health club tax still generates considerable sums of money. The MASC concept was a marvelous one: promote health, fitness, community sports facilities, some events, and tourism and pay for it with a health-and-fitness tax. While $49 million is a lot of money, it pales in comparison to what the major-league teams have pleaded for; and all things considered, that MASC money has gone a longer way.

A new sports governance structure in Minnesota would incorporate the state's commitment to local amateur sports and to the pros. It could be funded by the return to a dedicated tax from the users of health clubs and country clubs, plus those taxes generated by the users of major-league stadiums. Ideally, it could be supplemented by a short-term statewide sales tax that would generate an endowment that we could use for all sports facilities. According to the most recent Department of Revenue figures, a 1 percent statewide sales tax increase for one year could raise about $500 million. If that money could then be set aside as a Minnesota Sports Endowment, providing funds for pro sports construction and amateur sports grants, the endless debate about how to fund pro sports in this state would end in one twelve-month period.

The new agency would control that endowment. It would be charged with all that MASC and the MSFC currently do, and more. Because it would control the facilities in the state, it would be in the agency's interest to attract a variety of high-profile sporting events to the state, just as the Dome and Target Center currently do. More significant, the new Minnesota Sports Agency would regulate and monitor local teams and the national leagues of which the teams are part. Just as the Pollution Control Agency, the Public Utilities Commission, and the Attorney General's Consumer Protection Office oversee the public's interest, so too should the new Minnesota Sports Agency look out for cities and fans.

As much as it may have wanted to, the Sports Facilities Commission never has set policy per se. It has had authority to address the "acquisition and betterment" of sports facilities, but no authority to challenge, engage, or partner with teams or leagues. Its chairman has traditionally negotiated lease and business arrangements with the commission's tenants, but there was never any attempt to turn the commission chairman into a Minnesota-based national spokesperson for small-market major-league teams. The time is ripe for that. I envision a sort of Jim Hightower–type model (Hightower is the former Texas agriculture commissioner who became an outspoken national figure on the topic of farming and now has his own populist talk radio show). We need the new chairperson of the Minnesota Sports Agency to work as much out of the state as in it, building alliances with officials in other states. He or she needs to lobby Congress, annoy leagues, and push teams. This is a concept that other small-market states and cities must consider. Every state, it seems, has a commissioner who is working with corporations on matters of pollution, workplace safety, affirmative action, and zoning. Why not begin to take sports as seriously, what with all the taxpayer dollars involved? To this date, all the state and its agency have done is to be a landlord to the teams. We're past that now. Governor Jesse Ventura is the perfect leader for such a campaign. Building and refurbishing facilities for the local sports teams must only be part of the Minnesota model: simultaneously fighting the leagues and fixing their structures at every turn, in every forum, must be the other part.

In merging the two existing sports agencies, the state could also begin to link the social responsibility that is inherent in community-based and youth sports, with the otherwise callous and for-profit motives of the major-league teams that are tenants. For as much as pro sports teams brag about their charitable contributions and public service, they are generally scofflaws on this front. For instance, if you add up all the money donated to charity in 1997 by the Twins ($140,721), Vikings ($320,180), and Timberwolves ($234,442) foundations, it amounted to $695,343, or about half of what local businesses contributed to Minnesota Wins, the pro-stadium group that failed miserably to garner support for a new Twins stadium that same year. Where's the community commitment? And who audits it? No one. Where are the links between community-based sports and mass-entertainment pro sports? The Wild and Timberwolves have those weak agreements with the Minnesota Amateur Sports Commission that grant the power to the teams over the public agency. Such agreements must be strengthened, and the public agency must act as an official public watchdog on what the teams do for the community if the teams receive massive subsidies from the public sector.

Another role of the new agency—of any governmental body over-seeing pro sports—must be the honest assessment of the sports market in which the teams play. In the case of Minnesota, the new Minnesota Sports Agency must determine whether this state and market can and should attempt to support four major-league teams. Why build and refurbish if the facilities and their teams are doomed to fail? Too often, as with the state law that created the Sports Facilities Commission, the sport-related agency is expected to be a constant proponent for pro sports. Is it not the duty of government to regulate and make tough choices about our scarce resources?

Triage

In the end, I believe we in Minnesota can't truly afford four major-league teams. Former Metropolitan Sports Facilities Commission chairman Henry Savelkoul frequently stated his skepticism about the idea that four teams can flourish. He always pointed to one critical measure to show how the local sports market would be stretched beyond repair: luxury suites. The Vikings have long struggled to sell their suites; Timberwolves officials have long been concerned about the arrival of the Wild, which begins play in the year 2000. And remember, during the Twins ballpark battle, the corporate community more or less stood on the sidelines. For better or for worse, the new Wild franchise and the Wolves are here for the long haul. Both play in publicly financed arenas. Both are committed well into the new century. As irresponsible as the construction of the St. Paul arena was—what with state-of-the-art Target Center standing just eleven miles away—we're stuck with it. But the Minnesota sports marketplace—if the teams get their wishes—is faced with the prospect of having to sell more than three hundred luxury suites, each averaging at least $80,000. That's $24 million a year in luxury suite sales in a metropolitan area that is regularly losing its headquarters companies. Can we do that? I doubt it. So what of the Twins and the Vikings? Can a market the size of the Twin Cities afford them both while supporting NHL and NBA teams?

Imagine an accident with two victims. One is bleeding and screaming, but merely in shock. The other is close to death. Whom do you rescue? "The person with the most life-threatening injury is the top priority," Captain Mark Beckman of the Minneapolis–St. Paul International Airport rescue unit told me. "But a decision you have to make in your mind is, 'Is this person going to make it?' If he's not going to make it, you have to make that tough call, and go to the next person."

The concept is known as triage, the sorting of the injured so that the most serious cases are treated first. It is also a decision-making process for identifying priorities in an environment of scarce resources. Which team should be given all of the resources it needs to survive? And if those resources aren't available, shouldn't policy makers and the public make "the tough call" and let a team go? "I think that's the public's attitude," former Vikings president Roger Headrick said. "They're not willing to do what is being done in Seattle or Cincinnati and Detroit, where stadiums are being built for both the baseball and football teams. We operated under that assumption pretty much all along, that it would be choosing between the Twins and us."

Although the Twins have long been in the most serious financial condition, it's mostly been because they play in a stadium built for football and in an industry that hasn't been able to control its costs or maximize its revenues, what with relatively low broadcasting-rights fees. The Twins ownership has also been loath to invest in the team over the past five years, precipitating poor teams, poor attendance, and a bad relationship with its fans. Furthermore, baseball participation among youngsters is down compared to basketball, football, and soccer. Overall baseball participation among anyone six years old or older is down a full 12 percent since 1987, when the Twins won their first World Series.[15]

Amid this decline in baseball's popularity and the fading affection for it from a jaded fan base, the Vikings have been able to produce great excitement with well-paid teams that perform well and bring the state together every Sunday, mostly through the glue that is the television. They play in a league that is healthy. On the business side, much like the Twins, the Vikings' revenues seriously trail those of competitors in their league. Washington's privately built stadium generates more than $5 million per game in revenues, whereas the Dome can produce only about $1.8 million per game for the Vikings. Over ten home games, that's a disparity of about $30 million. But the Vikings benefit from an NFL network contract that provides an average of $70 million a year in national television and merchandising dollars. The Vikings are virtually assured of breaking even under the NFL's economics. They might not be able to win and break even, but they can surely be competitive and break even.

Beyond what teams need for themselves, we should also analyze what economic offerings they bring to the community when determining which team should be rescued and which should be left for dead. The best recent figures are a bit dated, but still illustrative. Based on attendance and sales from 1995, local sports business consultant David Welle concluded that the Twins generated more tax benefits than the Vikings for the state and the city of Minneapolis, about $6.1 million a year. The Vikings produced $5.6 million in public dollars. But as Twins attendance has decreased and Vikings attendance and TV revenues have increased, the Vikings have crossed over to bring more tax dollars to the state coffers.

But if a new Twins stadium is built, attendance, concession sales, and players' salaries could be expected to more than double; a study during the stadium debate of 1997 suggested that the team would generate $13.5 million annually in tax revenues. (That's substantially less than what the public was being asked to contribute to subsidize a new ballpark annually, of course.) A new Vikings' stadium could be expected to increase the teams' tax contributions as well. (By the way, the Timberwolves, using 1995 figures, generated the most tax dollars at that time, about $7.5 million, but only because they were the lone team to pay property taxes, a novel concept.) Of course, most of these "increased" taxes are merely transfered from other entertainment spending, but they still indicate the value of the teams.

One tax item to note: because the Twins play so many more games, visiting baseball players pay considerably more in state income tax dollars than do players in other sports. According to the most recent figures available from the Minnesota Department of Revenue, the Twins' opponents paid $774,000 in income taxes in 1995; the Vikings' opponents chipped in only $97,000. Tax collections aside, sports economists—including those who believe there is fundamentally limited economic impact from pro sports facilities versus the cost to the public—point to baseball as the sport with the highest economic impact on a community. Why? If the Twins attract the average American League attendance, that means 2.4 million visits to the ballpark every year. Even a sold-out Dome for the Vikings generates only about 650,000 annual visits. On the other hand, baseball needs lots of bodies moving through the turnstiles for a team to succeed. If the Twins sold 2.4 million tickets, team president Jerry Bell figures that about 300,000 individuals would need to buy them. The Vikings could sell about 60,000 season tickets and not need any other customers. That's why cities such as Jacksonville, Florida, and Nashville can attract and support NFL teams, but not baseball. Baseball requires population density. Baseball creates the most constant flow of downtown activity.

Baseball is the most affordable of all four major-league sports. In 1999 the Twins had ticket packages as low as $25 for a family of four, including tickets, hot dogs, and pop, as well as a program and parking. They even sold season tickets for $99. The cheapest single Vikings ticket was $23. Projections for a new stadium had a Twins average ticket price at $17 in the year 2001. By then, Wolves and Wild tickets could be expected to average $50. "Baseball is a more democratic sport, with cheap seats for lower-income families and kids," said Noll. "Football in most cities has become a yuppie sport because the ticket prices are so high and because you have to buy season tickets to get a reasonable seat." That leads to another question, if triage is the mode: which sport best reflects the community? Baseball is agricultural and bucolic. Football is, at its essence, violent. Baseball markets itself toward families. Football is more corporate. Baseball is a throwback to a slower time. The NFL's marketing vice president used to work for MTV. The choice may come. Which sport deserves our support more? Which sport is a better investment for the community? The new Minnesota Sports Agency must decide. All cities and states should ponder just how many teams they can afford.

For sure, preserving the Metrodome must be a priority in keeping public costs down for professional sports. It is a facility that is less than twenty years old. It was built for football and should be rehabilitated for football, as the Sports Facilities Commission has argued. Abandoning it for a new football stadium would be socially and fiscally irresponsible. The Vikings' lease runs through the year 2011. No responsible public official can argue for a new football stadium when the football team is committed for another decade to the current facility. Fixing the Dome would limit public costs and fend off our need to triage a franchise ... maybe.

Public Ownership and Stopping the Windfall

In Minnesota there is no doubt that some form of public ownership of the sports teams is the only way in which a stadium finance package can be accepted. The windfall for owners must stop here. Even Savelkoul, who became too close of a "partner" with Pohlad while he should have been better representing the state's citizens, was the major proponent of public ownership; Governor Carlson, too. There are various forms in which such an ownership structure can exist.

The state or host city could consider buying the teams from the current owners; this is an option exercised by some smaller cities in taking control of minor-league baseball teams. The teams could issue stock, and individual fans or investors could invest; this is the so-called Green Bay Packers model. The Packers, however, attempted to raise money in 1997 by issuing new shares of stock, but their offering, even after a Super Bowl victory, was a bust. The team raised only $24 million, about one-third of its goal. Or the owners can take their private asset, make it public, and list it on a stock exchange, as have the owners of the Boston Celtics, Florida Panthers, and Cleveland Indians. That tends to benefit the owners more than the citizens of the city where the team is located.

In the end, the easiest way for the public to get a piece of the team is to build on the creativity of the Savelkoul-Carlson-Pohlad deal of January 1997. The fact is, in Minnesota and in other cities, the way for teams to succeed over time is to play in viable facilities that help generate competitive amounts of revenues for the teams. If communities are going to aid in providing those facilities, the communities must also share in ownership. Periodic appraisals of franchise values must be part of any lease agreement that teams make with communities. The increased value of the franchise must be capitalized somehow and shared with the public. As long as owners tout the need for a "public-private partnership," they must share franchise appreciation as the public shares its facility.

The Cost

Wheelock Whitney wagged his finger at me. You remember Whitney. He was the young whippersnapper who created much of the leverage to get Minnesota the Twins back in 1960. He was the young stock salesman who teamed with Branch Rickey to form a new league that actually was a threatened hammer to compete with the long-standing American and National Leagues. Later he helped bring the North Stars to Minnesota by being an investor in the team and Met Center. Later still, he owned 10 percent of the Vikings. He was also the man who urged the Met Center task force to knock down the building he helped put up. Whitney has great standing to analyze the costs of major-league sports in this community over time.

He sat in his Foshay Tower office and wagged that right index finger at me, ordering me, in his gruff but affectionate voice, to engage in an exercise. "Goddammit, tell me how much these pro sports have actually cost us. I don't know. There are all these critics saying we've spent millions of dollars on pro sports, but I know we haven't. We don't fund sports around here. We finance them. And there's a helluva big difference."

Whitney had a point. Up until the 1995 buyout of Target Center, the state of Minnesota had literally never given a dime to pro sports in the Twin Cities. The city of Minneapolis and the Metropolitan Council had acted as banks, lending money via publicly backed revenue bonds. From 1952, when Met Stadium was a dream, until 1995, when the Twins and Vikings had been in the Dome for fourteen years, very limited direct subsidies were given to a pro sports team or facility in this state. Understanding this can help us to figure out how much "the public" has truly paid for pro sports facilities since 1961 when the Twins and Vikings first arrived. It also helps to expose some "experts" whose calculations are based on fantasies. I particularly refer to James Quirk, a retired Cal Tech sports economist, who wrote a thoughtful but completely flawed article about the alleged "subsidies" to Minnesota's pro sports teams through the years.[16]

Take Metropolitan Stadium. With original construction and some later expansion, the total cost to build the stadium that housed the Vikings and Twins for twenty-one years was less than $9 million in its day. The costs for building were paid for by revenue bonds issued by the city of Minneapolis. Those bonds were paid off by the customers of the stadium. That is, via ticket taxes, team rent, and parking revenues, the old Metropolitan Area Sports Commission was able to pay off the annual debt service of about $400,000. No money from any citizens other than those who attended events at Met Stadium paid off that facility's debt.

For more than two decades, Minnesotans bathed in the glory of a World Series and of numerous NFL playoff games, of Rod Carew's hitting and Chuck Foreman's running. Arguably, if you never attended a game, never watched one on television, and didn't know a Viking from a Packer, it didn't cost you anything. Quirk contends that because no property taxes were paid over time and because the city of Minneapolis got no rate of return for issuing the bonds, the city suffered a net loss. But if you examine the photographs of what the land in Bloomington looked like in 1955, the likelihood of property-tax-generating structures being built in that area was slim, at least for a number of years. Besides, that was Bloomington property, not Minneapolis land. Using the principle of present valuing money, Quirk contends that Minneapolis even lost out when it netted $12.4 million from the sale of the Met Stadium land in 1984. He said the sale fell short of covering the city's original investment.

But I disagree. Remember, the entire parcel of land in 1955 for 164 acres cost about $480,000, or in 1999 dollars the equivalent of $29.8 million. The Met Stadium land accounted for only about 100 acres of that, with the Met Center land eventually covering 50 acres. In 1998 the commission sold the remaining Met Center land for $25.7 million. In those land sale transactions, the Sports Facilities Commission netted more than $38 million, or $9 million more than the original cost, brought to its present value, of the land. Those land sales freed the city of

Minneapolis from its obligation to bondholders and eventually helped to pay off the Metrodome's debt.

Let's move now to the Metrodome, which was by all standards built cheaply, at $55 million, while other stadiums around the country were costing far more. Again, the construction costs were initially funded by $55 million in revenue bonds issued by the Metropolitan Council. Over time, to support those bonds, the commission paid out $82 million in interest to bondholders, for a total of $137 million. But "the public"— that is, the nonfan, nonuser of the Dome—paid only about $32.3 million from 1977 until today. The Dome is fully paid off now.

First, $23.8 million was raised via a metrowide liquor tax that became a Minneapolis-only bar tax in 1984. The entire metro area paid in $8 million, and those who drank in Minneapolis—many of whom were not Minneapolis residents—contributed $15.8 million in direct payments to the Metrodome. The city of Minneapolis subsidized the Dome with about $4.5 million in parking revenues. This was to make up for parking dollars lost when the commission operated in Bloomington. And finally, the city spent $4 million to reroute sewer, water lines, and streets when the Dome was built. Thus a total of $32.3 million in nonuser taxpayer money was used to help build the Dome.[17] The rest was paid off by *users* of the facility.

Again, amortized over eighteen years, through two World Series, an All-Star Game, a Super Bowl, a Timberwolves season, a Final Four, hundreds of high school and college football games, Billy Graham revivals, Rolling Stones concerts, and monster truck extravaganzas, nonusers kicked in $1.7 million annually. Most of that nonuser contribution actually ended in 1984. That's because with the sale of the Met Stadium land, the Sports Facilities Commission had enough cash reserves on hand to pay down the bonds without going to the alcohol drinkers in Minneapolis.

Has the Dome been worth $1.7 million a year to the community? I think so. If someone said today that we could have the Twins and Vikings secure in the Twin Cities for a total cost of $1.7 million a year, would that be an acceptable "subsidy"? I think so. It would be a very cheap date. Seeking that little amount per year would be a referendum I believe even Minnesotans would pass.

(For sure, the Sports Facilities Commission, a public agency, has helped the Twins significantly since the Dome opened in 1982. Via the reduction of rent and the increase in the team's take on concessions, the Twins through 1998 pocketed $28.5 million more than they would have under their original Dome lease. But again, that money came from the normal Dome operations and not from any outside revenue sources.)

Quirk, too, makes an absurd assertion about the subsidies the Dome has provided to the teams via property taxes. In a complex calculation, he tries to show how much property taxes would be generated by the Dome if it were operating on a for-profit basis. That is, if there was, say, a skyscraper or other commercial building on that site, how much would it generate for the city's tax rolls versus what the Dome does not? In attempting to rebut Quirk's notion that the Dome would be paying more than $3 million in property taxes each year, I contacted a number of local experts, including Minneapolis city assessor Scott Renne and Minneapolis city finance officer John Moir. Both could only laugh at the notion that there'd be some tax-generating property on the Dome's land. It is precisely because of its out-of-the-way location that John Cowles Jr. and Charles Krusell selected the land for the stadium site. One wonders how much property tax the city would be forbearing if the Atlantic Ocean fronted up against the Dome rather than Interstate 35W. And even if one reasonably assumed that some building or buildings would produce some property taxes were they situated at Fifth and Chicago, it wouldn't approach Quirk's $3.6 million calculation, Renne said.

While it is true that private tenants are benefiting from the tax-free status of the Dome, it is recognized that having a stadium and those teams in the state has a legitimate public purpose. I believe at that rate of subsidy—less than $1 million per year per team—there *is* a reasonable public purpose.

Still, the best justification for some public dollars going to a ballpark was made by Twins financial adviser Bob Starkey. In testimony before a legislative committee in 1997, Starkey said: "No one can tell me that it's not better to have three million people a year coming to downtown Minneapolis to watch baseball than having none." I agree with that assessment. It's difficult to quantify "civic energy." But it has to be worth

$1 million a year. I believe it is reasonable to state that in the case of Met Stadium and the Dome—and thus in the cases of Major League Baseball and the NFL—since 1961 to 1999, general citizen–taxpayers–nonusers of the stadium have paid less than $1 million per year to fund the facilities. That is a cheap date.

As for the other sports:

- Met Center cost the taxpayers zippo, save for the waived property taxes. Private business people built it and turned it over to the Sports Facilities Commission to preserve its tax-exempt status. When the Gund brothers bought the team in 1978, they assumed its mortgage. There were no tax dollars of any sort involved in that facility. Indeed, the commission was criticized by some for *not* lending or giving the Gunds and subsequent owner Norm Green public dollars.
- Target Center, built privately, was the first major-league facility that was moved into the modern era when the city bought it in 1995. For the first time, a direct state general fund taxpayer subsidy was put in place. In 1999, under its current finance plan, $750,000 a year comes out of the general state tax coffers. The rest of the debt service is paid by a Minneapolis 3 percent entertainment tax, the property taxes that Wolves owner Glen Taylor pays, and some downtown parking revenues. If the finance plan collapses, it would be backed up by the property taxes of the city of Minneapolis.
- The new St. Paul arena, to be opened in the fall of 2000 for the new NHL hockey team, also involved real public dollars. A full $130 million in state and city bonding has been issued to pay for the construction. Most of the revenue bonds will be paid back via the team's "rent," but $17 million of the state's $65 million interest-free "loan" is scheduled to be forgiven in a program that assumes the team will open the building to community programs. Thus $17 million in state money is a direct payout to the team, or $680,000 per year over twenty-five years, somewhat similar to the Target Center state subsidy. The city of St. Paul's $65 million portion will be paid

off via game-day parking revenues and other arena revenues, but about 10 percent will come from a half-cent city sales tax. The Wild has a lease similar to the one the North Stars had at Met Center; the team controls all of the events.

As we continue the stadium debate in Minnesota, we should keep these numbers in mind. We can reduce the emotionalism by showing that all things considered, to this date, pro sports hasn't sucked the treasuries dry. There has been very few nonuser taxpayer dollars spent on pro sports. That's not to say we shouldn't proceed with caution. In both Minneapolis and St. Paul, the arenas pushed the cities to their bonding limits. But we should note one other fact: 85 percent of all pro sports–related dollars wind up in the state's coffers and not the cities'. Because most taxes—sales and income—are collected, generally, by the state of Minnesota, it bene-fits more than do the cities. In analyzing how to pay and who should pay for any new facilities, the state must weigh what benefits it believes it derives from the teams, economically and spiritually.

In the current environment, the notion of taxes to support profes-sional sports seems to be anathema. But if the stadiums and arenas were owned and operated by a public agency, and if the teams did not control all the revenues, then some tax dollars could be justified. Look at the Metrodome; in 1979, $55 million in revenue bonds were issued by the Met Council to build the facility. That would amount to $123 million today, or still a cheap stadium. The difference between the Dome and the modern baseball or football stadium is that the Dome is used constantly and is completely accessible to the public. In 1998, managed by a public agency, it was used for 64 high school baseball games, 68 college base-ball games, 107 days of indoor rollerblading, the Hmong American New Year Festival, 8 days of a religious revival, 23 days of high school football, and 4 motor sport events that attracted more than 180,000 fans. Now, that's a public building worthy of support and with unquantifiable public equity invested.

The Dome is a model for what our other arenas and stadiums should be, now and into the future. Can an NFL football–only stadium,

with all the revenues from its use going to the team, be as socially responsible as the Dome? Can we justify tax dollars going to a facility that is used
only ten to twenty times a year? Can we justify abandoning a facility like
the Dome that can be improved for pro sports but that is already a temple
for a diversity of events?

Have major-league sports in Minnesota since 1961 cost the taxpayer
an exorbitant amount of money? No.

Funding

If a new baseball ballpark or a refurbished football stadium can have true
public benefit, then some of it can and should be paid for with public
dollars. Some of the facility should be paid for with user fees. Some of
the stadium should be paid for by the owner. Some of the facility should
be paid for by the business community. And some of the facility should be
paid for by the league in which the team participates. Sharing the pain is
the way to go.

In 1999 the NFL was the only league that had established a system
to help its owners build new stadiums. Under the NFL's plan, the league
lends money to its owner during the construction phase. The owner
repays it from the revenues derived from luxury seating. This is a wonderful model that makes perfect sense: all teams need each other to play
against. No team is an island. The leagues, in all cases, forced Minnesota
to build facilities. The NFL wanted the Vikings in a bigger place; hence
the Dome. David Stern wanted his expansion teams in new arenas; hence
Target Center. Gary Bettman said Met Center and Target Center weren't
good enough; hence the machinations that led to the new St. Paul arena.
Leagues have to pay their fair share.

Local businesses have to pull their weight. Their entertaining of
clients and customers benefits them. If the stadium boosters are correct,
some corporations believe they recruit employees because of the presence
of major-league sports. Frankly, I believe that the expectations the Twins
placed on the business community during the 1997 legislative session
were overly aggressive. Under the language of the proposed legislation,
22,000 season ticket pledges, commitments for forty suites and 4,000

club seats, and the purchase of exotic personal seat licenses were required before public funding kicked in. I understand that we shouldn't subsidize a ballpark that's not going to be a success, but we also have to be realistic about the health of the marketplace.

Again, this is where the power of the new state agency comes in. Rather than allow the teams to evaluate the marketplace, the new Minnesota Sports Agency must be the traffic cop for the sports business environment. To a certain extent, we are stuck with four teams now. Depending on the future of the Twins or Vikings, that may change. But honest assessments of the ability of this market to support four major-league teams must enter into any decision to supply public dollars to facilities. If there won't be support for a team and a sport, why build, why subsidize?

"User fees" are dirty words to teams. Teams consider them diverted revenues. That is, if a ticket tax skims 10 percent off the ticket price, that's 10 percent that would otherwise have gone into the team's pocket. Still, users should pay for the stadium that brings them pleasure. Those of us who don't use the stadium shouldn't pay for it all. Those of us who use the stadium just twice a year shouldn't pay for it all, either. During the Twins campaign, a laundry list of user fees was suggested. We should revisit these, especially surcharges on player salaries.

In 1997 the idea was to capture *all* of the user fees to help finance the stadium. Critics said that was dipping into the general fund because the user fees—such as athletes' income taxes, in-stadium sales taxes, and memorabilia sales taxes—were already pouring into the general fund. But we should take the view that a new ballpark or renovated football stadium must increase revenues for the teams, not merely sustain them. Only the *increased* collections of user fees or *new* user fees should be used to help pay for a new ballpark. This is a concept that was first attempted by hockey supporters in 1995 when the Winnipeg Jets tried to move to Target Center. The theory is that but for the teams there would be no tax revenues. It is a type of tax increment financing, based not on property taxes but on the income and sales taxes brought in by the new or improved facility. Pennsylvania is using this concept for its pro stadiums. It's an idea that Coleman attempted to sell in 1999 for a Twins ballpark.

So, only the surcharge on athletes' salaries—not their baseline income tax—should help pay for the ballpark. Only a higher sales tax on in-stadium items—not the flat 6.5 percent state sales tax—should help pay for the stadium. Only the ticket taxes over and above what were regularly collected at the Dome should go toward a new Twins ballpark. If, in fact, this new ballpark is designed to increase the Twins revenues, then the public should share in some of those increases. By capturing some of the increases, we can help pay for the stadium. Some prices will rise, but we can protect families by requiring that at least 15 percent of all tickets sold in the stadium be no more expensive than the average price of a Twin Cities–area movie ticket.

An owner should be expected to pay the costs of the amenities of a ballpark. If a new sports facility is truly a community center, the portion that is devoted mostly to the public should be paid for by the public. I believe even the basic seating within a stadium should be borne by the public. But the luxury suites, the club seats, the exclusive restaurants, the high-tech scoreboards, any roofs or domes—they should be the responsibility of the teams. It is these items that enhance the revenues to the team. If they want the enhanced revenues, they must invest in the vehicles that drive those revenues or get private businesses to help pay for them.

Other creative methods must be explored. In Minneapolis, for instance, the city has constantly been asked to fund certain public facilities that other cities in the state have not. The Convention Center is a good example. Now carrying nearly $300 million in debt, it stands alone among such centers in other cities, which otherwise have been financed by state bonding. Today the Convention Center is paid for with the same tax that once paid down the Dome's debt. If the state took Minneapolis off the hook for the Convention Center, would the city's voters allow a citywide entertainment tax to pay for sports facilities instead? There'd be no new taxes, just a new cause—the stadium—for the alcohol and hotel-motel tax.

Or, in keeping with the Minnesota Wild model, would the state be willing to lend money interest free to either St. Paul or Minneapolis to help build a new ballpark?

Frankly, the most logical—but politically most difficult—way to go is via a permanent Minnesota Sports Endowment. This endowment would be funded by a short-term statewide sales tax. It would help to fund the ongoing programs of what was the Minnesota Amateur Sports Commission, and it would serve as a capital improvement fund for all of the major sports facilities in the state. A statewide half-cent sales tax could produce nearly $250 million in one year. Perhaps we should blink this tax on for a span of two years. That pot of $500 million would be set aside and allowed to grow safely. Every year, the new Sports Agency would assess the needs of the state relative to sports. It would combine the traditions of the old Amateur Sports Commission with the new pro sports public policy planks: Are there enough hockey rinks to accommodate all the girls who want to play? Is there a shortage of soccer fields? What county needs bike trails? Which major arena needs its seats replaced or its women's rest rooms refurbished? What sorts of facilities are needed for disabled athletes?

In each of those cases, all requests would be considered as matching grants. That is, there would be no 100 percent grant from the Minnesota Sports Endowment. Teams, leagues, counties, cities, and local recreation programs would have to raise at least half of their money on their own. There would be no free lunch. There would merely be a partnership. As the public sector made grants to build and refurbish pro sports facilities, it would share in the increased value of the franchises, too.

Whatever our method of funding, it has to be understood by the citizens. The "put" of 1997 was inexplicable. Even the governor of the state didn't get it. To reiterate, "If you're explainin' you ain't gainin'." And there has to be honesty: to keep major-league sports vital in Minnesota, it will cost the public money. The goal is to limit the costs and to be able to justify it with a redefined stadium that does more than just provide revenues to increase players' salaries and owners' franchise values.

Naming Rights

One popular source of modern funding is corporate naming rights of facilities. Companies of various sorts are committing $3 to $5 million a year now, getting their names on arenas and stadiums and winning contracts affiliated with their deals; power companies in a deregulated era win the electricity rights to a facility, for instance. It is clearly a way to fund facilities. But most times, the naming-rights fees pass through to the team, not to the unit of government that's funding the building. For instance, in the case of the Minnesota Wild, whereas all of the money to build their new facility is coming from public sources, the naming-rights fees will go to the team to—guess what?—help them to pay their rent.

Until the Wild's new arena, no publicly affiliated sports facility in Minnesota was allowed to carry a corporate name. Target Center, of course, was built privately. Private owners of buildings can do what they want with the naming rights. But by way of policy, we should use caution in placing corporate names on public buildings. If we do, then the public should get its proportionate share of the naming rights to reduce our subsidy of the building. Teams can't control all of the naming-rights dollars.

Second, we should weigh the civic cost of having a public building named after a corporation. The airport doesn't have a corporate name. Parks don't have corporate names. Bridges don't have corporate names. If, as political leaders and sports boosters claim, stadiums and arenas are components of our social and cultural infrastructure, then why not honor public heroes and heroines by naming our sports venues after them?

Diving headlong into historic documents at the Minnesota History Center, I came across literally thousands of documents about the construction of Met Stadium and the Metrodome. None was as touching as the short note dated December 23, 1977, sent to Sports Facilities Commission chairman Dan Brutger.

Dear Dan,

Thank you for your letter officially informing me of the action by the Metropolitan Sports Facilities Commission in naming the proposed stadium the Hubert H. Humphrey Sports Center.

I am indeed honored and at a loss for words by this great honor that you and the commission have bestowed upon me.

You can't imagine how this action has touched my heart and brought a warmth all over me. I just don't know what to say.

Thank you, thank you.

Sincerely,

Hubert H. Humphrey

That's how important the public's retention of naming rights is. Twenty-one days later, the greatest political leader in Minnesota history died . . . happy. We celebrate his memory every time we gather for a major sporting event. His name attached to our building preserves and promotes our sense of place.

Recognizing Our Strength, Accepting Our Size

There is little doubt that major-league sports have run out of cities to go to. The NHL has resorted to towns such as Columbus, Ohio, and Raleigh, North Carolina, as it has sought emerging markets with no other major-league competition. But baseball, for all its noisemaking about the downfall of the Twins and the Montreal Expos, hasn't been able to encourage any cities to build new ballparks on spec; thus moving a team is difficult. Football, because of its reliance on television revenues and ratings, can't continue to award franchises to low-order markets, such as Jacksonville, Florida. Yes, a city of less than one million can support a football team; but the forty-sixth largest metropolitan area in the nation is not attractive to television advertisers. Unless leagues begin to look outside of U.S. and Canadian cities, the sports owners have lost their leverage to threaten cities; their teams can't go anywhere.

Still, economics could organically change the organizational structure of major-league sports. It's something that smaller markets need to contemplate when addressing future stadium dilemmas. Geographer John Borchert believes that the twenty-first century will bring the rise of the international superleagues in which only the largest North American cities can compete. Borchert envisions a mega–baseball league with, say, teams in Los Angeles, New York, Chicago, San Francisco, Mexico City, Osaka, Tokyo, and Toronto. Those markets could support the best, highest-paid athletes and generate the sorts of corporate dollars and television interest necessary. Meanwhile he sees smaller metropolitan areas playing in their own leagues.

"I see a Mid-Continent League," Borchert said, gazing into an imaginary crystal ball. He mentions cities such as Minneapolis–St. Paul, Calgary, Denver, Kansas City, St. Louis, San Antonio, and El Paso–Juarez joining together in the next twenty years to form major leagues that are a step below the global circuits that only the megacities can afford. As much as cities the size of the Twin Cities long to compete with the larger markets, it just might be that second-tier metro areas will need to form alliances. With that in mind, the size and investment in stadiums and arenas must be tempered. A cozy 35,000 to 40,000-seat open-air ballpark for baseball will service the Twin Cities whether the local team plays in the new "Mid-Continent League" or tries to play up with the big-boy cities. Indeed, even in the unlikely event that the Twins move, it would be in the community's interest to have that 35,000-seat open-air ballpark in place.

(This is an appropriate place to put an end to any discussion of another domed or retractable-roofed ballpark. Even Twins internal data show that at the most, eight games a year would have been lost to weather since the Dome opened in 1982; the average of potential rainouts per year was five. Doing the math, with a roof costing anywhere between $80 and $100 million, it would take at least ten years of full schedules to earn back the value of a roof. But why fool with the aesthetics? Minnesotans want outdoor baseball. And if Phoenix, Seattle, and Milwaukee are examples of what retractable-roofed ballparks must look like, then there is no justification for such monstrous eyesores. Besides, some marketing creativity could assist those fans who traveled far and wide to come to the game only to be rained out; why not place them cheaply in a local hotel or offer coupons to downtown restaurants, museums, and retail outlets?)

If Bud Selig didn't like our cozy ballpark, a Class AAA team would enter the Twin Cities market in a nanosecond. There is no doubt that a Triple-A team, playing in an outdoor downtown ballpark could attract 18,000 to 25,000 fans a night under the summer stars. A better-case scenario is that another big-league team—Montreal, Oakland, Tampa Bay, Miami—would consider moving to the Twin Cities to play; this is a better market than the rest of them. No middle-size market wants to be in a position where a prospective team owner has the leverage to seek a new stadium, and to promise that he will move his team into the marketplace if only the public will build him a new facility. An outdoor ballpark is a reasonable component of any metropolitan area's cultural infrastructure. Whether the Twins stay or go, whether the Twin Cities is a Class AAA market by the year 2010 or playing against the Tokyo Giants, we should have an enjoyable outdoor ballpark that our home team can play in. To build it is to ensure that we'll have pleasurable days outdoors, gathering together, having fun. It will be our baseball park. To not build it is to rob the community of a reasonable amenity and to invite disaster.

If we build the ballpark that we want, making the desires of the Twins secondary, we will win. Major League Baseball will be hard-pressed to abandon a metro area that proposes to build the most modern and thoughtful of facilities. Would big-league owners be so arrogant as to punish a city for building a stadium that serves the people first and the team second? If so, we'd enjoy our Triple-A team—until baseball's arrogance was superseded by its desire to have a big-league team in this fifteenth-largest television market, or until Congress and the courts stepped in.

Humanizing the Facility, Compelling the Teams
The terms and requirements of a lease agreement between the teams and the public are critical to the ongoing economic, political, and spiritual relationship between the "tenants" and "the building." No funding for any facility should ever be approved by any legislative body until teams have first agreed to certain basic principles about their relationship and their commitment to the public. No sports stadium or arena should be funded at any level by the public without full consideration of a series of needs for the surrounding community and without first deciding what a stadium will look like, where it will be, and how it will function.

Funding should be the last piece in a stadium "deal." A community must know what it's getting before it takes out its checkbook. A stadium lease is an agreement filled with exchanges: the team gets to keep all the money from hot dog sales, but the team must agree to pay an admissions tax to maintain stadium upkeep; the team gets to use a publicly financed facility, and the team agrees to play all of its games there, bringing in the best pro sports entertainment that money can (or can't afford to) buy. A lease is a give-and-take between landlord and tenant.

I believe that under any stadium lease, teams must agree legally to provide social contributions to the community in the way the public legally provides cash to the teams. Those team contributions can come in the form of money, or in-kind contributions, or athletes' monitored hours in community service. As the Twins and Vikings seek new or improved stadiums and new or improved leases, the new Minnesota Sports Agency should make social responsibility as much a priority as rent payments. And we should get those commitments *before* going to the legislature, county boards, city councils, or citizens for funding.

Some of the "give" is now voluntary on the part of the teams. During the 1997 stadium debate, Twins management showed a willingness to be open to some community contributions. (Indeed, the franchise— and the potential profits from the team's sale—were proposed "donations" to a foundation in exchange for the elimination of the team's debt.) In 1999 the new Women's NBA pro team, the Lynx, donated $1 per ticket to local breast cancer efforts; that raised $164,000. The Vikings have long supported a children's health fund. Sometimes players perform instructional clinics for kids. Sometimes teams make cheap tickets available for school groups. Sometimes teams fund youth sports leagues or fields. But within the context of the lease, teams' social responsibilities must be specified and enforceable.

The 1977 legislation that brought the Metrodome into being provided some guidance. In that law, no bonds could be issued for the Dome without the release of all relevant corporate and financial data by the teams. We must know the full financial health of teams. Access to public transportation had to be considered when a site was selected; this is important to minimize pollution, to maximize accessibility to inner-city fans, and to encourage the synergies of mass transit with a new publicly funded facility. Under the Dome legislation, the Metropolitan Sports Facilities Commission had to learn, and make available to the public, the total cost of the stadium to all government agencies and the total cost of lost property tax revenues because of the stadium's construction. The needs of the University of Minnesota's sports programs also had to be taken into consideration.

I believe that those planks are good beginnings. I also believe that when the public pays for a large chunk of a facility and/or provides the land free and/or waives property taxes, it should also demand, among other things, from teams the following:

- All workers in the stadium during games must make livable wages.
- The teams must abide by a thoughtful jobs program that the new Minnesota Sports Agency devises. The plan should attempt to create a sports facilities workforce that is employed in all the local major-league arenas and stadiums, thus making many of the part-time workers full-time.
- A percentage of the increased revenues generated by the new stadium must be set aside by the teams for local junior high and high school after-school programs, including sports.
- Teams must implement and reveal annually their records on front-office affirmative action programs so that the agency can compare local teams to other teams around the nation. Incentives can be devised so that achieving higher-than-league averages could mean a reduction in team rent.
- Teams must guarantee that their players will meet with students in the local public schools and after-school programs a total of 365 times a year. With four teams and more than one-hundred major-league athletes in the Twin Cities, that would mean, at most, four visits per player per year.
- Teams must return to the public coffers a percentage of their revenues if attendance exceeds 3 million fans for the Twins or 600,000 for the Vikings.
- Teams must guarantee that 15 percent of their tickets cost the same price as a movie ticket.
- Teams must guarantee that local artists are commissioned to enhance the ballpark's concourses, rest rooms, and public spaces.

Each community can and must determine what it wants in exchange from its teams for providing state-of-the-art facilities. But no community should miss the opportunity to leverage what it needs at the time that it is essentially acting as a banker for the teams.

The Twin Cities, and markets of this size, must retain major-league sports to preserve their "brand identity" as big-league cities. But that preservation must come with integrity. We must remain major league in our terms, and in our values. Mel Duncan, the former executive director of the Minnesota Alliance for Progressive Action, said that one way to heighten our "brand" as a community is to continually say "No!" to publicly funded stadiums.

"It could spark momentum in other communities. It could provide impetus for congressional action. It would say, 'We're independent. We're tough. We look after our own people. We've got our priorities straight. We don't buckle under to billionaires.' It would be great for Minnesota's image," Duncan said. But what, in the worst-case scenario, if pro sports finally abandoned the Twin Cities? "We'd be a warm Winnipeg," Duncan said. "As a community, we could all go to the park for a swim."

Is that truly who we want to be? As former Sports Facilities Commission and Minnesota Wins lobbyist Larry Redmond so succinctly put it, "Minneapolis was a great place to live before we had indoor plumbing, too. But I don't think we want to go back to those days." Redmond saw the defeat of the stadium efforts in 1997 as "a systemic community breakdown," the culmination of our inability to have a civil discourse, to bring together the business and political communities and to find common ground with a sophisticated citizenry. And he warns: "We're at an important juncture here. I do not want to be part of the generation of Minnesotans that loses all of these wonderful institutions that other generations before us brought to this state."

One supposes there would be nothing drastically wrong with being a cold Omaha or a warm Winnipeg. But I believe the Twin Cities would be a better place to live if we remember our major-league roots and find a way to remain competitive—psychologically and as a distinguishable region—with the Milwaukees, Kansas Citys, St. Louises, and Denvers. A happier, more satisfying ending than a shivering Omaha or a sweaty Winnipeg would be a self-respecting Twin Cities, with major-league sports to entertain us and bring us together a couple hundred times a year. We could be a new model community, with stadiums and arenas that belong to us, with teams that are beholden to us and that feel like ours. We could be a metropolitan area that built and refurbished facilities that were affordable and that used sports for the public good, not solely for the private owners' (and players') benefit. We could try to take sports back, not concede defeat. We could challenge pro sports, not merely accept them for what they've become. The happy ending could be a stadium game that the public, finally, wins.

Notes

Introduction

1. Charley Walters, "Stadium Offer: $90 Mil, plus Percentage of Team," *St. Paul Pioneer Press*, 5 January 1997, 2C; Walters, "Pohlad's Offer Might Be $95 Million," St. Paul Pioneer Press, 7 January 1997, 2C.

2. Gerald W. Scully, *The Business of Major League Baseball* (Chicago: University of Chicago Press, 1989), 152.

1. If You Build It

1. Metropolitan Sports Area Stadium souvenir booklet, 1956.

2. John R. Borchert, *America's Northern Heartland* (Minneapolis: University of Minnesota Press, 1987), 7.

3. U.S. Census Bureau, 1950, "Rank of Standard Metropolitan Areas in Continental United States."

4. Charles O. Johnson, *History of the Metropolitan Stadium and Sports Center*, 1971. Published by Midwest Federal Bank, this twenty-eight-page brochure is a treasure of historical details, some tainted by Johnson's point of view.

5. John Helyar, *Lords of the Realm* (New York: Ballantine Books, 1994), 52.

6. Richard Hartshorne, "The Twin City District: A Unique Form of Urban Landscape," *Geographical Review* 22 (1932): 431–42.

7. John S. Adams and Barbara J. VanDrasek, *Minneapolis–St.Paul:*

People, Place, and Public Life (Minneapolis: University of Minnesota Press, 1993), 93.

8. John Borchert, interview by author, Scandia, Minn., 21 October 1998.

9. *Minneapolis Tribune*, 24 January 1954, sports section.

10. George Brophy, interview by author, Minneapolis, 12 November 1998.

11. *A Prospectus of a Metropolitan Sports Area for the Twin Cities*, November 1954, Minnesota Historical Society archives.

12. Tim Brown, interview by author, Minneapolis, 17 November 1998.

13. "Barber's Memorandum as to Legal Aspects of Negotiations," 19 August 1957, Metropolitan Sports Facilities Commission files, Minnesota Historical Society.

14. *New York Times*, 20 August 1957.

15. Gunnar Rovick, interview by author, Edina, Minn., 5 October 1998.

16. Metropolitan Sports Area Stadium souvenir booklet, 1956.

17. St. Paul Midway Stadium prospectus, 10 August 1955, Minnesota Historical Society.

18. *Minneapolis Tribune*, 20 May 1956.

19. Robert Dayton, interview by author, Minneapolis, 26 October 1998.

20. Neil J. Sullivan, *The Dodgers Move West* (New York: Oxford University Press, 1987), 117.

21. Helyar, *Lords of the Realm*, 56.

22. *Washington Post*, 15 January 1957.

23. Metropolitan Sports Area Commission minutes, 6 June 1957.

24. Sullivan, *The Dodgers Move West*, 118.

25. *Minneapolis Star*, 27 May 1957.

26. *Minneapolis Star*, 28 May 1957.

27. *Minneapolis Tribune*, 29 May 1957.

28. *Minneapolis Tribune*, 29 May 1957.

29. *Minneapolis Star*, 20 August 1957.

30. *Minneapolis Star*, 21 August 1957.

31. Sid Hartman with Patrick Reusse, *Sid!* (Stillwater, Minn.: Voyageur Press, 1997), 84.

32. *Minneapolis Tribune*, 10 July 1958.

33. *Minneapolis Star*, 21 July 1958.

2. Something to Cheer For

1. *Minneapolis Tribune*, 30 August 1958.

2. *Minneapolis Tribune*, 28 August 1958.

3. *Minneapolis Tribune*, 8 September 1958.

4. *Minneapolis Star*, 9 September 1958.

5. "People's Column," *Minneapolis Star*, 6 September 1958.

6. Helyar, *Lords of the Realm*, 49.

7. Wheelock Whitney, interviews by author, Minneapolis, 12 October 1998 and July 1995.

8. *St. Paul Dispatch*, 2 July 1959.

9. Undated article from Wheelock Whitney's personal scrapbook.

10. Murray Polner, *Branch Rickey: A Biography* (New York: Atheneum, 1982), 260.

11. Undated clipping from Wheelock Whitney's personal scrapbook.

12. Peter Dorsey, letter to O. L. Bluege, 12 September 1959, Minnesota Historical Society archives.

13. *St. Paul Pioneer Press*, 23 October 1959.

14. Gordon Ritz, letter to Wheelock Whitney, 17 November 1959, from Whitney's personal files.

15. *Minneapolis Star*, 8 January 1960.

16. Ibid.

17. Daniel Okrent and Steve Wulf, *Baseball Anecdotes* (New York: HarperPerennial, 1989), 204.

18. Helyar, *Lords of the Realm*, 50.

19. Branch Rickey, letter to Wheelock Whitney, 2 August 1960, from Whitney's personal files.

20. *Washington Post*, 19 October 1960.

21. Polner, *Branch Rickey*, 261.

22. "Baseball Playing Agreement," 18 January 1961, Minnesota Historical Society archives.

23. Calvin Griffith, interview by author, Edina, Minn., 28 July 1998.

24. *Toolson v. New York Yankees*, U.S. Supreme Court decision, 9 November 1953.

25. Griffith interview.

26. Wheelock Whitney, letter to investors, 15 November 1962, from Whitney's personal files.

27. David Q. Voigt, *American Baseball*, vol.3 (University Park: Penn State University Press, 1983), xxvi.

3. Where the Sun Don't Shine

1. Philip J. Lowry, *Green Cathedrals* (Reading, Mass.: Addison-Wesley, 1992).

2. Metropolitan Sports Area Commission Study Report, 22 April 1970.

3. Borchert, *America's Northern Heartland*, 158.

4. "The Public Purpose," Web site of urban affairs consultant Wendell Cox; U.S. Census Bureau data.

5. Amy Klobuchar, *Uncovering the Dome* (Minneapolis: Bolger Publications, 1982).

6. "Downtown Woos Vikings with Promise of Home," *Minneapolis Tribune*, 3 October 1971.

7. "Stadium Wars Minneapolis, 1971–81," is an undated, uncredited, seventy-nine-page chronology of the entire Dome debate. It is part of Charles Krusell's complete files of 1970s stadium history, which he graciously shared with me.

8. For the lurid details, please consult Klobuchar's book, which provides the sort of details that I prefer not to report here.

9. *What Business Thinks 1997* (Vadnais Heights, Minn.: What Business Thinks Project, 1997).

10. Metropolitan Council staff report, March 1978, in Minnesota Historical Society files.

11. "State's Sentiment on a New Stadium: 42% No, 38% Yes," *Minneapolis Tribune*, 26 November 1978.

12. "Bigwigs Don't Care Enough about Teams," *Star Tribune*, 9 November 1993.

13. From chronology in Charles Krusell's personal files.

14. "Documents Hint at Why Griffith May Have Been Ready to Sell," *Minneapolis Star* and *Tribune*, 29 August 1984.

15. "Minnesota Major League Baseball Task Force Marketing Study," Febuary 1984.

16. Peter Richmond, *Ballpark* (New York: Simon and Schuster, 1993), 114.

4. "I'm Only Human"

1. "Q & A with Carl Pohlad," *Minneapolis Star and Tribune*, 14 April 1985.

2. "Dealing with Carl Pohlad," *Minneapolis Star Tribune*, 20 April 1997. The most complete and comprehensive account of Pohlad's financial dealings appeared in this article, written by reporters Paul McEnroe and Chris Ison. Other biographical details were gleaned from the yellowing but invaluable clipping files of the *Minneapolis Star* and the *Minneapolis Tribune*.

3. "A Flamboyant Player and His Mentor," *Minneapolis Star Tribune*, 13 October 1985.

4. "Marquette Bank Names New President," *Minneapolis Tribune*, 10 August 1955.

5. *Minneapolis Tribune*, 17 April 1960.

6. *Minneapolis Star*, 26 December 1960.

7. "Pohlad's Game Plan for the Twins May Have a Historical Precedent," *St. Paul Pioneer Press*, 31 August 1998.

8. "Suite against MEI Back in Court," *Minneapolis Star Tribune*, 21 October 1996.

9. "Donors," *Showcase*, program of Minnesota Orchestra, October 1974.

10. Stadium Site Task Force, "Report on Investments and Contributions," 1 February 1982, files of Charles Krusell.

11. "Carl and Eloise Pohlad Family Countation," press relase, 25 November 1998.

12. "Q & A with Carl Pohlad," *Minneapolis Star and Tribune*, 14 April 1985.

13. "Quiet, Modest—and Influential," *Minneapolis Star and Tribune*, 30 May 1982.

14. "City Banker, Eagles Discuss Team's Sale," *Minneapolis Star and Tribune*, 21 April 1983.

15. "Twins Dome Escape Clause Hot Item Again," *Minneapolis Star and Tribune*, 12 July 1984.

16. "4-Year-Lease Being Considered for Twins," *Minneapolis Star and Tribune*, 11 July 1984.

17. Metropolitan Sports Facilities Commission analysis, 31 December 1998.

18. "Twins See Red Ink, but Maybe Not," *Minneapolis Star Tribune*, 1 September 1987.

19. "Metrodome Officials, Twins Disagree on Profits, Losses," *Minneapolis Star Tribune*, 1 May 1988.

20. "Twins Win 10-Year Rent-Free Lease," *Minneapolis Star Tribune*, 18 May 1999.

21. "Minnesota Vikings Presentation to the Advisory Task Force on Professional Sports," 25 September 1995.

22. "Fine Time for Giving," *Minneapolis Star Tribune*, 25 December 1994.

23. "Image, Perception, and Reality," *Twin Cities Business Monthly*, October 1998.

24. "Rich Teams Putting Squeeze on Twins," *St. Paul Pioneer Press*, 2 December 1998, 1E.

25. "Best of the Twin Cities," *City Pages*, 5 May 1999.

26. "What Business Thinks 1998," *Twin Cities Business Monthly*, January 1998.

5. Off Target

1. "Metropolitan Significance Review Report, Proposed Arena of

the NBA Franchise for Minneapolis," 12 June 1987, Metropolitan Council staff.

2. Ibid.

3. *Minneapolis Star Tribune*, 16 February 1990.

4. Minnesota North Stars news release, 9 June 1981, Minnesota Historical Society files.

5. "Dear Norman," letter from Wolfenson and Ratner to Green, 15 January 1993, Pat Forciea files.

6. "Local Buyer Strikes Deal for Stars," *Dallas Morning News*, 11 December 1995.

7. "They Fast-Talked Us Out of Met Center," *St. Paul Pioneer Press*, 10 November 1995.

8. "Advisory Task Force on Met Center," 24 August 1993, official transcript, 9.

9. "Advisory Task Force on Met Center," transcript of meeting, 8 September 1993.

10. "Advisory Task Force on Met Center," transcript of meeting, 6 October 1993.

11. 9 January 1997 Minnesota Poll, internal documentation, *Minneapolis Star Tribune*.

6. I Gotta Get Me One of These

1. "Report of Independent Members of the Economic Study Committee on Baseball," 3 December 1992, 1.

2. Ibid., 12.

3. Ibid., 5.

4. "If Ticket Price Too High, Area Fans Won't Buy," *Minneapolis Star Tribune*, 11 April 1993.

5. "Metrodome Operations Proposal," January 1994, Minnesota Twins private files.

6. Minnesota Twins MSFC Presentation, 18 July 1994, formal document submitted.

7. "Pohlad Paints Dire Picture in Seeking Better Metrodome," *Minneapolis Star Tribune*, 19 July 1994.

8. *New York Times Magazine*, 17 July 1994, cover.

9. "St. Paul Saints History," posted on the Saints World Wide Web page, www.spsaints.com, 1999.

10. Representative Dee Long, letter to Sports Facilities Commission chairman Henry Savelkoul, 2 June 1995.

11. "The Name Game: Task Force Might Put Dome's 'HHH' Up for Sale," *Minneapolis Star Tribune*, 15 August 1995.

12. Ballot question, from the files of the Denver Metropolitan Major League Baseball Stadium District.

13. "Carlson Talks Big-Picture Sports," *Minneapolis Star Tribune*, 21 October 1995.

14. "ACBJ Study Identifies Best Sports Expansion Sites," ACBJ Research Report, Buffalo, N.Y., 19 May 1997.

7. Falling in Love with the Deal

1. "Twins Marketing Strategy," 4 March 1996, internal memo.

2. House File 4586, introduced on 18 January 1996.

3. "Minnesota Twins Acquisition Plan," 29 March 1996, files of Metropolitan Sports Facilities Commission.

4. "Twins Stadium Initiative Resurrected by Carlson," *Minneapolis Star Tribune*, 15 April 1996.

5. Results of Minnesota Wins polls, October 1996.

6. "Carlson Goes Fishing for Stadium on Riverfront," *St. Paul Pioneer Press*, 5 September 1996.

7. Excerpted from *Compton's Interactive Bible New International Version*. Copyright 1994, 1995, 1996 SoftKey Multimedia Inc. All Rights Reserved

8. "Somebody Stop These Bimbos," leaflet procuced by GAGME, December 1996.

9. "As Twins Ballpark Talk Swirls, Vikings Pipe Up about a New Stadium," *Minneapolis Star Tribune*, 13 October 1996.

10. "Twins , Carlson's Staff Swap Stadium Ideas," *Minneapolis Star Tribune*, 10 October 1996.

11. "How the Deal Came About without Even a Handshake," *Minneapolis Star Tribune*, 12 January 1997.

12. Minnesota Campaign Finance Office records.

13. "Pohlads Spread Their Political Aid Around," *Minneapolis Star Tribune*, 30 October 1996.

14. *Star Tribune* "Voter's Guide," 1 November 1996, V16–V17.

15. "Preliminary Draft," 14 November 1996, Metropolitan Sports Facilities Commission files.

16. "Preliminary Draft," 22 November 1996, Metropolitan Sports Facilities Commission files.

17. "Pohlad Boys Poised to Deliver Their Sales Pitch to the Populace," *Minneapolis Star Tribune*, 29 November 1997.

18. Doug Grow, "'Regular' Family Has Big Slice of American Pie," *Minneapolis Star Tribune*, 4 December 1997.

8. Spilling the Beans

1. *Minneapolis Star Tribune*, 18 October 1995.

2. CNN Financial Network Reference Desk of Business Terms, 1999, CNNfn Web site; Wall Street Directory, 1999, www.cnnfn.com/resources/referencedesk.

3. On Monday, January 6, 1997, Forciea left a voice mail message for me at the *Star Tribune* office, advising me that the Pohlads may have an announcement by the end of the week. Out of town, I retrieved that message on Wednesday, January 8. Clearly, Forciea was in an informing mode.

4. "Stadium Offer: $90 Million plus Percentage of Team," *St. Paul Pioneer Press*, 5 January 1997, Charley Walters column.

5. Charley Walters column, *St. Paul Pioneer Press*, 7 January 1997.

6. "Twins, Carlson Deal Near," *St. Paul Pioneer Press*, 8 January 1997.

7. *U.S. v. O'Hagan*, U.S. Supreme Court ruling, 25 June 1997, 117 S.Ct. 2199.

8. Videotape of 8 January 1997 news conference, Midwest Sports Channel.

9. Internal Revenue Service Letter Rulings Reports, letter 9530024, 1 May 1995

10. Document included in Metropolitan Sports Facilities Commission files.

11. Stadium Site Task Force documents, 1 February 1982.

12. John Cowles Jr., interview by author, Minneapolis, 3 November 1998.

9. It Sure Looked Like a Loan

1. "Risk or Reward in Twins Deal?" *St. Paul Pioneer Press*, 12 January 1997.

2. "Panel: Just Say Know to Public Funding," *Minneapolis Star Tribune*, 23 January 1997.

3. "A Closer Look Alters View of Pohlad Deal," *Minneapolis Star Tribune*, 25 January 1997.

4. "Public Unmoved by Twins Proposal," *Minneapolis Star Tribune*, 26 January 1997.

5. "Facilities Commission Has Public Interest at Heart in Stadium Debate," *Minneapolis Star Tribune*, 28 January 1997.

6. "New Snags for Stadium," *Minneapolis Star Tribune*, 29 January 1997.

7. "Stadium Deal Is Unraveling," *Minneapolis Star Tribune*, 31 January 1997.

8. Richard Alm, "Rangers Owners Cash In," *Dallas Morning News*, 8 January 1998.

9. "Troubled Waters," *Milwaukee Magazine*, November 1996.

10. Baseball notes, *St. Paul Pioneer Press*, 30 April 1999.

10. Holding Up the Indians

1. "Legislative Briefing," 28 April 1997, presented by Senator Dick Day.

2. Unsigned, untitled flyer, 7 May 1997.

3. "Republican Senators Back Slot Machines for Ballpark," *Minneapolis Star Tribune*, 30 April 1997.

4. "Ballpark Effort Drives Gambling Policy Changes," *Minneapolis Star Tribune*, 4 May 1997.

5. "Minnesota Policy Blueprint, Gambling, Center of the American Experiment," 19 November 1998.

6. "Video Gambling Would Solve Money Crunch," *Minneapolis Star Tribune*, 2 May 1995.

7. "We'd Be Idiots to Pass Up Chance at NHL Team," *Minneapolis Star Tribune*, 12 October 1995.

8. "Minnesota Casino Financial Proforma," Laughlin Gaming Enterprises, 17 October 1997.

9. "Vikings Stadium Request Not Popular," *Minneapolis Star Tribune*, 1 November 1997.

10. "Immodest Mike Lynn Makes Modest Proposal," *St. Paul Pioneer Press*, 2 November 1997.

11. "Affection for Twins Stops at Tax," *St. Paul Pioneer Press*, 11 October 1996.

12. Arne Carlson, letter to Stanley Crooks, chairman of Minnesota Indian Gaming Association, 17 April 1997.

13. Minnesota Historical Society, Ann Glumac's files, State-Tribal relations, box 3.

14. "Tribe Says It Could Help Pay for Ballpark," *Minneapolis Star Tribune*, 26 April 1997.

15. "Tribes, State Talk about Using Casino Profits for New Stadium," *St. Paul Pioneer Press*, 26 April 1997.

16. Marge Anderson, letter to author, 25 January 1999.

17. Stanley Crooks, letter to Arne Carlson, 28 April 1997.

18. Dallas Ross, letter to Arne Carlson, 28 April 1997.

19. Eugene McArthur Jr., letter to Ann Rest, 29 April 1997.

20. "Stadium Funding Proposal No Gamble," *Minneapolis Star Tribune*, 2 May 1997.

21. "Legislators Should Play Hard Ball with Indians," *Minneapolis Star Tribune*, 2 May 1997.

22. Arne Carlson, letter to Robert Peacock, 2 May 1997.

23. "Few Cities either Ready or Willing to Adopt Twins," *Minneapolis Star Tribune*, 12 May 1997.

24. *Webster's New World College Dictionary*, 1996

11. Leaving It to Beaver

1. "Twins report to Major League Baseball's Executive Council, Executive Summary," 10 June 1997.

2. "Sales and Marketing Management Guidebook," 1997.

3. "Leave It to Beaver," *Business North Carolina*, March 1998.

4. "Twins Have Offer from Charlotte," *Minneapolis Star Tribune*, 7 September 1997.

12. "Baseball Lives If You Push Green"

1. "An Open Letter to Minnesotans," *Minneapolis Star Tribune*, 23 October 1997.

2. Richmond, *Ballpark*, 16.

3. "Selig Dodges Question of Triad Ball," *Greensboro News and Record*, 19 February 1998.

13. Resuscitating the Deal

1. *Almanac*, KTCA-TV, 19 December 1997.

2. Tom Borman, "The Public Process for Financing a New Stadium," Minnesota Institute of Legal Education, 14 October 1998.

3. Campaign Finance and Public Disclosure Board, September 1998; "Twins Top State Lobbying Expenditure List," *Minneapolis Star Tribune*, 15 September 1998.

4. Minnesota Campaign Finance and Disclosure Board, October 1998.

5. Fox television, during Vikings game, 7 November 1998.

6. "New Ballparks Create Revenue, Debt," *Street and Smith's Sports Business Journal*, 12 July 1999.

14. Building a Public Trust

1. "Curtains?" *Sports Illustrated*, 22 December 1997.

2. American Appraisal Associates, letter to Metropolitan Sports Facilities Commission, 4 March 1997.

3. Mayor Norm Coleman on KFAN radio, 27 May 1999.

4. *Standard and Poor's Industry Reports*, 1996.

5. "Sports Worship," *Minneapolis Star Tribune*, 26 January 1997.

6. Paul Gruchow, "Discovering the Universe of Home," *Minnesota History*, spring 1998.

7. Daniel Kemmis, *Community and the Politics of Place* (Norman: University of Oklahoma Press, 1990).

8. Philip Bess, "City Baseball Magic" (Madison, Wis.: Minneapolis Review of Baseball, 1989).

9. "A Remedy for the Rootlessness of Modern Suburban Life?" *New York Times*, 1 August 1998.

10. See, especially, the work of Mark Rosentraub and Robert Baade to understand that all spending is finite and that "new dollars" generated by a stadium were once "old dollars" in some other part of the state.

11. "Planners Studying Stadium 'Buffers.'" *St. Paul Pioneer Press*, 22 July 1999.

12. "Be Sure New Stadium Reflects City Values." *St. Paul Pioneer Press*, 25 October 1999.

13. 1997 Corporate Subsidy Reform Commission Report, 6 February 1998.

14. "Arena and Contribution Agreement," between MASC and Minnesota Wild, 29 December 1998.

15. "State of the Industry Report," National Sporting Goods Association, February 1999.

16. James Quirk, "Stadiums and Major League Sports: The Twin Cities," in *Sports, Jobs, and Taxes*, ed. Roger Noll and Andrew Zimbalist, (Washington D.C.: Brookings Institution Press, 1997).

17. "Metrodome Backgrounder," presented to Advisory Task Force on Professional Sports, November 1995.

Jay Weiner is a sports reporter for the *Minneapolis Star Tribune*. For the past decade, his work has focused on the business and political aspects of pro sports in the Twin Cities, the quintessential "small market" within the major leagues. Weiner's reporting and analysis have appeared in the *New York Times* and *Business Week*, and he has also been a frequent commentator for Minnesota Public Radio.